CONTRACTS AND COMMERCIAL TRANSACTIONS

ASPEN CASEBOOK SERIES

CONTRACTS AND COMMERCIAL TRANSACTIONS

DAVID ZARFES
Associate Dean and Schwartz Lecturer in Law
The University of Chicago Law School

MICHAEL L. BLOOM
Lecturer in Law
The University of Chicago Law School

Wolters Kluwer
Law & Business

Published by Wolters Kluwer Law & Business in New York.

Wolters Kluwer Law & Business serves customers worldwide with CCH, Aspen Publishers, and Kluwer Law International products. (www.wolterskluwerlb.com)

To contact Customer Service, e-mail customer.service@wolterskluwer.com, call 1-800-234-1660, fax 1-800-901-9075, or mail correspondence to:

> Wolters Kluwer Law & Business
> Attn: Order Department
> PO Box 990
> Frederick, MD 21705

Printed in the United States of America.

1 2 3 4 5 6 7 8 9 0

ISBN 978-0-7355-9819-5

Library of Congress Cataloging-in-Publication Data
Zarfes, David.
    Contracts and commercial transactions/David Zarfes, MichaeL L. Bloom.
        p. cm.—(Aspen casebook series)
    Includes index.
    ISBN 978-0-7355-9819-5
    1.   Contracts—United States. 2.   Business enterprises—Law and
legislation—United States. 3.   Casebooks I. Bloom, Michael L. II. Title.
    KF889.85.Z37 2011
    346.7302—dc22
                                                2011006745

About Wolters Kluwer Law & Business

Wolters Kluwer Law & Business is a leading global provider of intelligent information and digital solutions for legal and business professionals in key specialty areas, and respected educational resources for professors and law students. Wolters Kluwer Law & Business connects legal and business professionals as well as those in the education market with timely, specialized authoritative content and information-enabled solutions to support success through productivity, accuracy and mobility.

Serving customers worldwide, Wolters Kluwer Law & Business products include those under the Aspen Publishers, CCH, Kluwer Law International, Loislaw, Best Case, ftwilliam.com and MediRegs family of products.

CCH products have been a trusted resource since 1913, and are highly regarded resources for legal, securities, antitrust and trade regulation, government contracting, banking, pension, payroll, employment and labor, and healthcare reimbursement and compliance professionals.

Aspen Publishers products provide essential information to attorneys, business professionals and law students. Written by preeminent authorities, the product line offers analytical and practical information in a range of specialty practice areas from securities law and intellectual property to mergers and acquisitions and pension/benefits. Aspen's trusted legal education resources provide professors and students with high-quality, up-to-date and effective resources for successful instruction and study in all areas of the law.

Kluwer Law International products provide the global business community with reliable international legal information in English. Legal practitioners, corporate counsel and business executives around the world rely on Kluwer Law journals, looseleafs, books, and electronic products for comprehensive information in many areas of international legal practice.

Loislaw is a comprehensive online legal research product providing legal content to law firm practitioners of various specializations. Loislaw provides attorneys with the ability to quickly and efficiently find the necessary legal information they need, when and where they need it, by facilitating access to primary law as well as state-specific law, records, forms and treatises.

Best Case Solutions is the leading bankruptcy software product to the bankruptcy industry. It provides software and workflow tools to flawlessly streamline petition preparation and the electronic filing process, while timely incorporating ever-changing court requirements.

ftwilliam.com offers employee benefits professionals the highest quality plan documents (retirement, welfare and non-qualified) and government forms (5500/PBGC, 1099 and IRS) software at highly competitive prices.

MediRegs products provide integrated health care compliance content and software solutions for professionals in healthcare, higher education and life sciences, including professionals in accounting, law and consulting.

Wolters Kluwer Law & Business, a division of Wolters Kluwer, is headquartered in New York. Wolters Kluwer is a market-leading global information services company focused on professionals.

To my father with gratitude. To my mother in loving memory. To Alan for his guidance and so much more. To Michael with thanks.

—D.Z.

To my parents for never asking—but always expecting—much of me.

—M.L.B.

. SUMMARY OF CONTENTS .

. CONTENTS .

Contents

· CONTRIBUTIONS ·

Contributions

· ACKNOWLEDGMENTS ·

We owe a tremendous debt to the numerous friends, colleagues, and benevolent strangers (whom we hope we may now count among our friends and colleagues) who made this book possible. We are eternally grateful to the many people who took time out of their very busy schedules to contribute their observations, knowledge, and expertise. Their invaluable contributions make this book more rich and useful than it would have been otherwise. All errors and omissions are ours alone. (Contributor names are listed in the order in which their pieces appear in the book.)

For their comments on the state of legal education and the profession, we thank: Thomas A. Cole, Martin Lipton, Stephen L. Ritchie, Robert A. Helman, Keith C. Wetmore, and Evan R. Chesler.

For their thoughts and comments on legal education and their law firm experiences thus far, we thank: Bradley P. Humphreys, Cadence A. Mertz, Jaime E. Ramirez, Ian N. Bushner, Garrett Ordower, and Sean Z. Kramer.

For providing "A Practitioner Perspective" on various complicated issues, we thank: William L. Horton, Jr., Neal Stern, John Levi, Michael Delikat, Nancy Laben, Michel Gahard, Alan A. D'Ambrosio, Steven Barnett, Jack Bierig, Paul Roy, Julia Hickey, Mark Chandler, Tony Bangs, Stephen P. Anthony, Peter L. Flanagan, Jeffrey S. Rothstein, Timothy M. Swan, Gary "Skip" Stern, Martin D. Jacobson, Allison J. Satyr, Lee C. Buchheit, Teresa Harmon, Bianca A. Russo, Anne M. Wildhaber, Preston Torbert, William A. Von Hoene, Jr., Bruce G. Wilson, Natalia Delgado, Holli A. Simone, Beatriz M. Olivera, Mark H. Berlind, Brian Hoffmann, and Philip A. Gelston. We are also grateful to Michael Delikat, Neal Stern, Martin D. Jacobson, Allison J. Satyr, Teresa Harmon, and Scott Davis for providing us with their thoughts, ideas, suggestions, and critiques of various sections of the book.

We thank Professor Richard A. Epstein, Professor Douglas Baird, Justice Jack B. Jacobs, and Professor M. Todd Henderson for sharing their esteemed wisdom in their respective commentary pieces.

We are grateful to the many students who provided us with their indefatigable assistance. For providing research assistance, we thank: Joseph Mueller, Jeffery Lula, Jeanette Stecker, Alex Roitman, Michael Eber, and Salen

Churi. For assisting with the development of materials for the teacher's manual and/or otherwise helping with the final production of this book, we thank Alex Roitman, Salen Churi, Azi Lowenthal, and Daniel Render. For providing "focus group" feedback, we thank Oren Lund, Kathryn Hines, and Sean Z. Kramer. For source and citation assistance, we owe a great debt to the following students, all of whom found time between their school work and Law Review obligations to help with this project: Molly Grovak, Daniel Rosengard, and Kevin Swartz, and those who helped them, including Diana Watral, Chris Hagale, Kristen Mann, David Didion, and Charles Woodworth.

Finally, we would like to extend a special "thank you" to The University of Chicago Law School and to Sidley Austin LLP for their support throughout this project.

· PREFACE ·

Background

Before one can hope to draft a contract with any deftness or comfort, one must understand how to read a contract; one must understand the "language of contracts"—their provisions, their conventions, and their structure. We hope that, through this book, the reader will gain a certain facility and familiarity with contracts as found in the "real world."

We stumbled upon the idea for this book while teaching an introductory transactions course at The University of Chicago Law School. David taught contractual documents, drawing upon his fifteen years' worth of experience as a general counsel at a major corporation. Michael taught contractual provisions, as treated by U.S. courts, drawing upon his research. We decided to expand this formula in published form—to teach contracts from the married perspectives of experience and judicial treatment and to reach out to a field of expert practitioners and esteemed academics to provide additional insight and expertise. This book is one attempt to fill some of the space between traditional law school education (with its classically heavy orientation toward litigation) and transactional practice, whether in a solo-shop, corporate-legal-department, or law-firm setting.

We were encouraged by the great enthusiasm and support we discovered for the teaching of transactional matters in law school, in general, and for our idea, in particular. For one, there are the widely cited institutional positions strongly in favor of the teaching of practical courses in law school, such as the Carnegie Report's call for an emphasis on practical legal education[1] and the Association of American Law Schools' requirement that law schools offer professional skills courses.[2] In addition, throughout the process of distilling and executing the

---

1. WILLIAM M. SULLIVAN ET AL., EDUCATING LAWYERS: PREPARATION FOR THE PROFESSION OF LAW (2007).

2. Bylaws AALS—The Association of American Law Schools, at § 6-7(c), *available at* http://www.aals.org/about_handbook_bylaws.php. The 2009-10 ABA Standards and Rules of Procedure for Approval of Law Schools also require that law school curriculum include substantial instruction in "professional skills generally regarded as necessary for effective and responsible participation in the legal profession." AMERICAN BAR ASSOCIATION, PROGRAM OF LEGAL EDUCATION std. 302 (2009), *available at* http://www.abanet.org/legaled/standards/2009-2010%20StandardsWebContent/Chapter3.pdf.

idea for this book, we asked a few distinguished practitioners who sit atop the legal profession to share their thoughts with us on the topic. We also asked a few former students (of David's and/or Michael's) to share their experiences in law firms, having had benefited from some version of the instruction encapsulated in this book. Their responses follow in the order in which they were received.

Comments from Distinguished Lawyers in Practice

Whether a student will ultimately become a transactions lawyer, a regulatory lawyer or a litigator, a good grounding in all forms of corporate transactions provides a critical window into the business milieu within which he or she will practice. A study of transactions and the agreements by which they are documented also illustrates to the student how different elements of substantive law, together with accounting and tax considerations, meld together in the real world. An earlier appreciation of these considerations is something that clients, and thus law firms, are demanding of the young lawyers who serve them. While many firms provide excellent in-house training, that often comes several months after a new associate has arrived on the scene. Thus, the young lawyer who has received a grounding while still in law school may be able to hit the ground running—even in a summer program—and create the positive first impression that can be so important at the start of a career.

Thomas A. Cole, Partner
Sidley Austin LLP

Mr. Cole serves as Chair of the Firm's Executive Committee.

A casebook on transactional law has long been desired. Transactional law is a hybrid—part contracts, part securities, part antitrust, part tax, part litigation and part other areas too numerous to name. To properly advise on a transaction, it is necessary to bring all the relevant aspects into focus and craft a transaction designed to combine all into an organized transaction that accomplishes the parties' objectives.

The ability to combine multiple disciplines is critical to a transaction lawyer. Having a law school course with a well organized casebook will be greatly appreciated by students who intend to become transaction lawyers. And I'm sure will be a factor in placement with business law firms.

Martin Lipton
Founding Partner
Wachtell, Lipton, Rosen & Katz

One of the most common complaints we receive from new corporate associates is that law school has not adequately prepared them for transactional practice in a law firm and, in particular, for what that practice requires of them in their first few years. This is not a new development; I experienced similar challenges when I was a new associate a little more than 20 years ago. Although law schools have certainly made some strides in this area since that time, introducing courses that bring more real-world situations into the classroom, a discrepancy remains between what even the finest law schools teach and what the transactional practice requires. As a result, we devote substantial resources to training our new lawyers for the tasks that they will perform as associates in the transactional practice, including drafting contracts. Our training focuses not on issues highlighted in traditional casebooks but instead on how contracts are actually drafted, how certain provisions can be varied to favor one party over another, how various provisions work together (or may be at odds with one another), and how mistakes can be made if one is not careful in drafting a contract. One can only appreciate these issues by working with—reading, analyzing and drafting—actual contracts.

As a result, law schools would perform a valuable service if they offered "hands-on" courses that focused on the contracts themselves rather than on cases involving those contracts. Of course, case study will always be important in teaching law students key legal principles and, more importantly, how to "think like a lawyer." However, I am confident that law firms would be pleased to welcome new associates who were better prepared for the demands of corporate practice and better able to make a more immediate contribution upon their arrival at the firm.

Stephen L. Ritchie, Partner
Kirkland & Ellis LLP

Mr. Ritchie serves on the Firm's global Management Committee, is Chairman of the Firm's Nonshare Partner and Associate Compensation Committee, and serves on the Firm's Administrative Committee.

I've been asked, as someone who has had a general corporate law practice for 54 years, and chaired Mayer Brown LLP from 1984-98, whether it is important for a law school graduate to have a basic knowledge of how the legal, business and public policy aspects of common and somewhat complex business transactions are reduced to writing, and the related question of whether it is important for the leading law schools to provide the education that leads to that knowledge. My answer to both questions is an unequivocal "yes!" There are some obvious but limited exceptions: if a student "knows" that he or she will have a specialized practice totally unrelated to business, e.g., criminal law of the non-white collar variety or public international law, a transactional law knowledge base would be ornamental but not essential. (However, no one can foresee the future with certainty.) For the rest, whether pointing toward a law firm, a law department, a legal aid program, the government or a career in business, this book meets an important and unmet need.

It is my belief in this practical aspect of legal education that led me to encourage Dean David Zarfes and Professor Michael Bloom's plan to undertake the preparation of this book.

My experience as a lecturer at the University of Chicago Law School has sharpened my ideas about legal education at the leading law schools, which justifiably think of themselves institutionally as being involved primarily in providing an intellectual foundation in the U.S. legal system for their students. Often, but not always, this leads to a certain disdain for problem-solving and clinical courses—"we are not a trade school" is the refrain. I believe that attitude is mistaken: an intellectual foundation is not valuable, except for certain scholars, unless the law school experience connects it to the solving of problems—that is what lawyers are called upon to do. And this book, born of lawyers' experience, with its suggested forms and commentary, will help students (and I daresay many practioners) learn to do just that. Intellectual understanding and its application to the world of law practice are not, and should not be, mutually exclusive.

(A relevant personal experience: My first-year contracts class at Northwestern was taught by Dean Harold Havighurst, a stimulating teacher and a scholar. I enjoyed it immensely and learned a lot, but we were all surprised and dismayed when, after a full year course, the principal final exam topic described a "real world" business transaction and told us to draft and annotate, as appropriate, an agreement to reflect the apparent meeting of the minds. Except for extracts from contracts in the judicial opinions in Dean Havighurst's casebook, I had never read, let alone drafted, a business contract. Well, under the pressure of an unanticipated exam question, I learned; but I also learned the importance of connecting an understanding of doctrine to practice. This book makes that connection, and that is why it is important.)

Robert A. Helman, Partner
Mayer Brown LLP

Mr. Helman was Chairman of the Firm's Management Committee from 1984 to 1998.

Sophisticated contractual drafting reflects a mathematical elegance. All possible events in a commercial relationship—default in payment on a loan, failure of performance by an employee, impossibility of delivery of goods, decline in stock value, increase in stock value, no change in stock value—are usually intended to be addressed within the agreement, with specified consequences for all events. The darkest hours in a transactional lawyer's life are those spent looking through last year's documents for the provisions that address this year's circumstance that no one anticipated.

Sophisticated contractual drafting requires careful, sometimes artful, use of words. Real world outcomes vary, and dollars change hands, based upon the drafter's use of "or" versus "and" or "before" versus "before and during."

Sophisticated contractual drafting follows custom and practice. Counsel for multinational corporations expect banking documents to follow the format and terminology used by banks globally. Sales warranties resemble each other, except to the extent the parties choose quite noticeably to vary them. That consistency simplifies commerce and allows high confidence in the meaning of many words and clauses, through repeated judicial interpretation and broad commercial understanding.

These hallmarks of sophisticated contractual drafting cannot be learned from reviewing cases, which usually address one flawed phrase in a contract. They are learned by reading the contracts themselves, and writing them yourself, and having your contracts edited by more experienced lawyers, and negotiating those contracts with opposing counsel, and disagreeing with opposing counsel a year later on the meaning of your own words. Nothing in law school can provide all of that—that's what careers are made of—but this course book is a great start.

Keith C. Wetmore, Chair
Morrison & Foerster LLP

There are few skills that are more important for a young lawyer to possess than a familiarity with the law, logic and sense of contracts and the transactions they represent.

So much of what lawyers do centers around the relationships in which their clients are involved. Those relationships, and the transactions that arise from them, typically involve contracts. A level of comfort and facility with contracts is, therefore, critical to a solid foundation as a practicing lawyer.

Evan R. Chesler
Presiding Partner
Cravath, Swaine & Moore LLP

Comments from Former Students

Law school courses, especially those taught in the first year, are unquestionably geared toward litigation. But for those considering a career in transactional law, there are few opportunities to understand what might lie ahead. As one of Dean Zarfes's former students, I benefited tremendously from a hands-on learning experience, and gained confidence critiquing and improving upon real-world corporate contracts. It's an experience I would recommend for all students with an open mind as to where their careers will take them.

This book offers some of the same concrete examples, along with many others, which will prepare students to hit the ground running when they graduate. Just as first-year classes teach students to grapple with the foreign language of legal vocabulary and the peculiarities of judicial opinions, these materials will introduce those students interested in transactional law to a similarly eye-opening experience.

Bradley P. Humphreys
The University of Chicago, J.D. 2009

Dry as desert sand and every bit as apparently identical as one grain from the other. That is, until the contract lands on your desk and you have to either get out of it or make it stick. All of a sudden every italicization, word, comma, semi-colon outside the quotation mark or inside the quotation mark is going to mean the difference between indemnity or not, liability or not, insurance coverage or not. You simply cannot appreciate this until you've held that contract in your hands, heard the counter-argument and applied the words on the page in front of you in the service of your client's position.

Cases are helpful. Has the Eleventh Circuit already decided that an insurance clause identically worded to the one now in front of you means what your opponent wants it to mean? Has the Supreme Court defined the term of art you're now staring cross-eyed at? These are benchmarks; you cannot ignore them. But re-read your contract. There's a comma in your paragraph A.4(d) that isn't in the contract they interpreted. In a separate provision, your contract defines a word left undefined in the contract on which those cases were decided. Every contract is different. You learn this from considering each one individually. And, it takes practice to spot those differences. More, to know which ones really matter, which ones you can exploit. A contracts textbook that confines you to the learning of case law ignores this principle. It will teach you the basics, but it won't make you fluent. To get there you need to handle the documents, read them, defend them, enforce them, argue them. Having the real documents to consider from the first day of your first contracts class will ensure you get there well before your opponent.

Cadence A. Mertz, Associate
Williams & Connolly LLP
The University of Chicago, J.D. 2008

For those law students hoping to enter the world of corporate law, it's sometimes difficult to imagine how traditional law school classes fit into a future role as an advocate in a negotiation. It's only following graduation and well into your practice as a new lawyer that you begin to fully - comprehend how the law contributes to and in many instances shapes commercial decisions in a contract negotiation.

Professor Zarfes' teaching method has always combined the Socratic method and traditional law school techniques with a refreshing and helpful combination of real-world negotiating exercises. Consistent with this method, this new textbook will undoubtedly serve to bridge the divide between theory and practice for an aspiring corporate attorney. Furthermore, this textbook will provide a much needed supplement to the traditional legal curriculum and a helpful introduction into the art of negotiating commercial agreements.

Jaime E. Ramirez, Associate
Sullivan & Cromwell LLP
The University of Chicago, J.D. 2007

Based upon my study of transactional law with attorneys (they are as much lawyers as professors) David Zarfes and Michael Bloom at The University of Chicago Law School, I can assure you that their combination of real world experience and academic depth is unparalleled in most of legal academia. Their students not only learn about the law, but more importantly they learn how to be lawyers. I benefited greatly from their method, and so will you.

Like most law students, I entered law school with little idea about what lawyers really do. At best, many of us had sentimental notions drawn from courtroom dramas, novels extolling the honest attorney, and history books describing landmark litigation. While the traditional law school curriculum, through civil procedure and intensive case law analysis, does give lawyers to-be some exposure to a litigator's tools, most students remain ignorant about transactional practice. As a result, many young transactional lawyers face a steep learning curve and, relative to their peers in litigation, have far more catching up to do before they can be effective. Long overdue, this book will serve to remedy these shortfalls and minimize the lag time before young lawyers can deliver real value to their clients.

Many law students graduate without ever having analyzed, much less drafted, complex contracts. Even in most contracts classes, students only read cases about contracts and do not review the agreements themselves. This is a mistake. Every young transactional lawyer has seen or heard the same story: he or she is pulled into a partner's office, given a basic overview of the deal, handed a document to use "as precedent" (often a contract between parties not involved in the current deal), and told to turn a draft of some agreement they have never heard of. The terror felt by these lawyers, and the ensuing frustration of the partners, is real, and so too is the bill footed by the client.

However, if during law school a student can get exposure to a range of transactional matters, gain familiarity with a variety of agreements, practice drafting in a deal context, and start developing their negotiating skills, the situation is reversed. A young lawyer with this legal education is ready to hit the ground running. He or she can understand a partner's instructions and ask appropriate, insightful questions regarding the assignment. The partner is freed to focus on strategy and client-specific concerns while skipping rudimentary instruction. Perhaps the clients receive the greatest benefit, for they no longer must subsidize on-the-clock basic transactional education.

Additionally, the transactional perspective presented in this book emphasizes client needs. Law is a service industry, and no lawyer can survive without the appropriate attention to client service. Unfortunately, reading cases, while necessary, will not itself expose students to the client side of practice. Working with contracts, on the other hand, forces students to ask several important questions. What is a client's specific objective in this transaction? How does this relate to its broader business plan? What is the relationship between the client and the counterparty? What is the industry standard? Over time, students who have studied from a transactional perspective can develop an intuition regarding client concerns. Young lawyers who develop this client-centered attitude will be far ahead of their peers who continue analyzing legal problems in the theoretical, Socratic vacuum they encountered in the law school classroom.

In the end, transactional lawyers must eventually learn these skills somewhere. They might as well learn them in law school where students can make mistakes in an environment which, relative to actual practice, is low pressure and consequence free. What's more, transactional lawyers will be learning the basics on their own dime, instead of the client's. After studying this book and putting forth required effort to develop their transactional skills in law school, young lawyers will be ahead of their peers and will enter the practice of law ready to benefit themselves, their firms, and their clients. Everybody wins.

Ian N. Bushner, Associate
Jenner & Block LLP
The University of Chicago, J.D. 2009

The moment any law student enters the real world, they will quickly realize that their 1L "Contracts" class was a bit of a misnomer—rarely, if ever, will they have actually examined a real contract or learned how a contract affects the parties to a transaction—this book aims to fill that gap.

Dean Zarfes is the rare law school professor who knows both the classroom and the boardroom, and in this book, as in his classes, he bridges the significant divide between the two using interesting, understandable, and, most importantly, relevant examples that illustrate the transactional practice students will be facing before they know it.

Zarfes and Bloom's students—both those who learn from this book or have either of them in class—will be uniquely prepared to handle real-world work the minute they walk in the door of a law firm or business, and these lessons will stay with them throughout their careers. Today, more than ever, that type of preparation is an asset that could mean the difference between success and failure.

Garrett Ordower, Editor-in-Chief
The University of Chicago Law Review
The University of Chicago, J.D. 2010

Simply put, there is much more to the practice of law, and, thus, to legal education, than litigation and the traditional case method of law school. Not only does the historical method—when used exclusively—fail young litigators, but it leaves the myriad law students who go into transactional fields completely unprepared.

Although I enjoyed most every aspect of law school and reveled in extrapolating complicated legal principles from seminal case law, I was surprised to finish the first year and select transactional-based classes, only to find that such courses were taught in the same way as the core classes: by analyzing fact-specific litigations.

I was always left wanting to combine the intellectual pursuit of the case method with the practical means of examining and drafting actual contracts; it seemed obvious that applying the legal principles—gleaned from the cases—to actual contracts, would more fully concrete one's knowledge of the concepts.

It was not until David Zarfes and Michael Bloom's courses on contract interpretation and negotiation and complex business transactions that I found the practical (yet still academic) teaching style that I had been looking for. After taking these courses and reading early versions of this book, the advantage that I had over my (highly qualified) colleagues in my summer associate program was obvious, and, throughout the summer, I received strong praise from partners for my understanding of the interplay between complicated contractual terms.

Zarfes and Bloom's book—and their teaching methodology—should be mandatory for any law student going into a transactional area of the law. The casebook makes complex concepts easy to understand and will leave students asking themselves something that law professors and practitioners take for granted due to their years of experience: How can students learn the language of contracts necessary to understand business relationships in the real world?

The answer lies in this book.

Sean Z. Kramer, Associate
Kirkland & Ellis LLP
The University of Chicago, J.D. 2010

What This Book Is, What It Is Not, and How to Use It

We took great stock of the above comments, as they came from people well positioned to speak to what many in the legal profession value in young lawyers as well as to what young lawyers have found to be valuable in their legal careers. We also realized we cannot be all things to all people and that, while the comments above call for a plethora of fantastic things, we had to pick a focus for this book. This book's mission is simple: to familiarize the reader with the basic "language of contracts," with some of the basic and common provisions found in "real-world" contracts, and with how those provisions act and interact to serve a party's position and interest. We will consider it no minor victory if the readers of this book no longer view contracts as strange, foreign creatures written in a strange, foreign language.

Accordingly, this book is intended to be "of this world," which means, for instance, that the contracts used in this book were contracts used by real-life parties in real-life transactions. These contracts are drawn from the Security and Exchange Commission's Electronic Data Gathering, Analysis, and Retrieval ("EDGAR") system, which is a database of documents that public companies have filed with the SEC. This also means that these agreements have their flaws. We do not hold this book's agreements out as model documents. On the contrary, we see these documents as teaching tools and as exemplars of the type and quality of documents a lawyer is likely to encounter in practice—as a precedent document used to draft a contract for a new transaction, as a document first drafted by opposing counsel, as a document reviewed at the behest of a client, etc. We consciously decided not to break up the agreements in this book because we think a great part of our mission is to "force" the reader to read whole contracts—much as other courses instill in students the skillful habit of reading cases and statutes.

We also note that, in this book, we do not consciously adhere to or adopt any particular style or school of drafting; for instance, the "plain language" school of drafting may have its admirable tenets, but we do not hold this book or (certainly) its agreements out to be in compliance with the "plain language" school's scriptures. Indeed, this book is not a "contract drafting" manual or guide, at all. We see this book as serving a very different purpose. To reiterate, the focus of this book is to introduce the reader to contractual documents and their parts, in the context of actual contracts and transactions. Along the way, we offer some drafting notes here and there, but this book is not intended to be a comprehensive guide to contract drafting, grammar, style, or clarity.

This book is also not a practitioner's guide, and it is not a fifty-state survey. That is, in the United States, most of contract law is state law, and states may vary in their treatment of certain provisions or issues that arise in contracts. Of course, this book cannot comprehensively survey how every state addresses every issue. Necessarily, we have to speak at a certain level of generality, in terms of "majority" and "minority" rules, and, where we have not been able to discern a particular trend, we can only say that certain courts have taken a certain approach and others, another. This operates to flag some of the issues for the reader, but, of course, one cannot practice directly from this book, and one must research the law that will govern a particular contract. In addition, this book takes as its core focus U.S. domestic law but also attempts to include global perspectives to enrich this focus and broaden the scope of discussion.

A thematic lesson running throughout this book is the importance of understanding the intended purpose and the likely effect of a contract. One must understand and appreciate a contract's target audience—there may be several—in understanding the purpose of a contract. Inasmuch as a contract is intended to be enforceable in court (or arbitration), one should draft with an appreciation for how a future court (or arbitrator) might read and enforce the contract. Cases provide a source of information for how courts have treated contracts and some evidence for how they might treat them going forward.

This can be highly instructive for the contract drafter or reviewer, but the inquiry should not end there. Contracts may be enforced in ways that do not involve formal dispute resolution, including by the threat or in the shadow of litigation (the so-called "in terrorem" effect of contracts) and through a concern for business reputation. What is the dynamic between the contracting parties? Is this a "once-off" contract or is this a "repeat-game" scenario where the parties expect or hope to do business together going forward? Process may also be important; as an illustration, in a particular negotiation, a party may wish to keep contentiousness to a minimum and to draft accordingly, perhaps avoiding harsh-sounding language or picking and choosing which changes to suggest to the other party's offered draft. Contractual parties may understand a contract as a code of conduct or as a manual that documents their expected behavior throughout the course of a relationship or undertaking. These parties may conform their behavior to their written bargain without a consideration for overt enforcement mechanisms (again, perhaps with a concern for business reputation and perhaps even due to a more basic normative instinct to behave as promised). The reader is encouraged to reconsider these concerns on a consistent basis throughout this book. As you read, ask yourself: What is the drafter trying to accomplish here, and is the drafter going about this in the best way?

This book operates as follows. The first four chapters explore basic commercial agreements—non-disclosure agreements, employment agreements, services agreements, and sale-of-goods agreements—with the overarching objective of teaching provisions and concepts common to most all contracts. These basic commercial agreements serve as vehicles for teaching more generalizable lessons, while also familiarizing the reader with several types of "real-life" agreements and transactions. Chapters 5 and 6, then, ask the reader to apply the lessons learned in those earlier chapters to the more complex agreements found in these later chapters. In Chapters 5 and 6, we present lending and mergers-and-acquisitions ("M&A") agreements that are relatively simple and straightforward (at least as compared to those generally found in lending and M&A practice) and offer practitioner pieces to highlight and explain the more nuanced aspects of these types of agreements and practice areas. As we do in the earlier chapters, we walk through the agreements in these later chapters and explore their provisions and their interaction. It is our hope that, by these chapters, the reader will find many of the devices and provisions used in these more complex agreements to be familiar.

The premise of this book is that the reader will acquire a meaningful set of skills and a certain level of facility through reading contracts, through slogging through their seemingly foreign text, and through wrestling with their meaning, purpose, and effect. Before (or at least in addition to) learning how to write contracts through acquiring finely tuned grammatical and stylistic tools for drafting an unambiguous sentence, students should learn how to understand whole agreements, to understand their basic provisions and their interaction, to understand what parties might want to accomplish through contracts, and to understand how contracts can (and cannot) go about accomplishing these objectives.

David Zarfes
Michael L. Boom

Chicago, IL
April 2011

CONTRACTS AND COMMERCIAL TRANSACTIONS

· CHAPTER ONE ·

NON-DISCLOSURE AND CONFIDENTIALITY AGREEMENTS

Williams, who was employed by the Coca-Cola Company as an executive assistant to a high level Coca-Cola employee, approached co-defendant Edmund Duhaney in November 2005 at a family Thanksgiving dinner and told him that they needed to discuss a private matter. Afterward, Williams began calling and sending text messages to Duhaney about the matter. In late December 2005, Duhaney met with Williams at her apartment in Norcross, Georgia. Williams told Duhaney that she had copies of confidential Coca-Cola documents that were worth money to some competitors.

Specifically, Williams told Duhaney that she had memory sticks containing information, and she showed him confidential Coca-Cola marketing documents and a product sample. Although Williams was angry with Coca-Cola because she felt she was not "treated right," she told Duhaney that she had signed a nondisclosure confidentiality agreement with Coca-Cola and was therefore unable to do anything with the confidential materials. She wanted Duhaney to determine if someone could use the confidential information to obtain money from another company.

About one week later, Williams contacted Duhaney to ask about his progress with the Coca-Cola documents. . . . In February [2006], Duhaney contacted a friend of his, Dimson, who was interested in the documents because he realized they were worth money. Dimson agreed to travel to Georgia to review the documents. . . .

While Williams explained the documents to Dimson, Duhaney listened and then began thumbing through a magazine. During the meeting, Williams stated that this happens all the time in corporate America and Pepsi would be interested in this type of information. Dimson and Duhaney then decided to travel to a nearby Wal-Mart store to purchase a black roller bag and plastic folders for the documents.

United States v. Williams, 526 F.3d 1312, 1316 (11th Cir. 2008).

Unfortunately, situations of this sort occur often in corporate America.[1] Given this reality, how do corporations protect sensitive and confidential information from disclosure? This chapter addresses this question through examination of non-disclosure agreements.

Non-disclosure agreements, often referred to as NDAs, frequently arise in commercial and employment contexts and operate to prevent the wrongful disclosure (whether negligent or intentional) of confidential information. These agreements may impose confidentiality obligations on one or both (or several) parties. The basic purpose of an NDA is to obtain a legally binding promise from someone (natural person or company) before giving that someone access to information one wishes to keep secret. As we will observe in many instances throughout this book, obligations of confidentiality often arise in provisions within larger, more complex contracts.

At what point in a commercial transaction does it become advisable to issue or exchange NDAs? In the employment context, employers will require those employees who are likely to have access to sensitive company information to execute[2] NDAs protecting this information prior to, and as a condition of, the start of employment. Indeed, as we will discuss further, courts sometimes treat the promise of new, future employment as the consideration that supports these contracts. In some cases, employers may include confidentiality obligations as part of a comprehensive employment agreement, outlining the complete terms of the relationship. In the commercial context, parties will typically seek to protect the disclosure of confidential information at an early stage, prior to entering into sales or other commercial discussions and certainly well before they put pen to paper on a contract containing the full terms of their relationship. The NDA is used to protect the information one or both parties will need to evaluate the proposed relationship.[3] To amplify this discussion, we asked a seasoned practitioner to discuss the use and importance of NDAs in the "real world."

---

1. Joya Williams was found guilty of conspiracy to steal trade secrets and received a sentence of eight years. *United States v. Williams*, 526 F.3d 1312, 1316 (11th Cir. 2008).

2. Throughout this book, unless otherwise specified, we use "to execute" and the "execution" of a contract interchangeably with "to sign" and the "signing" of a contract, respectively. Note that there is some confusion as to whether execution refers to the *signing* or the *performance* of a contract. *See, e.g., Missouri-Indiana Inv. Grp. v. Shaw*, 699 F.2d 952, 954 (8th Cir. 1983) (Missouri law) ("Although the Supreme Court of Missouri has defined an 'executed contract' as one where nothing remains to be done, it did so in distinguishing an executed from an executory contract. In other contexts the Missouri court has equated execution of a contract with signing and delivery. Whatever the range of definitions of the verb 'to execute,' Missouri cases recognize that in popular speech, 'execute' is often used to refer merely to the act of signing a written contract.") (internal citations omitted).

3. For example, in the context of a sales transaction, one may wish to keep confidential the price and scope of the deal along with the underlying products to be delivered or services to be performed; or, in the mergers and acquisition context, one may wish to keep confidential information such as employee lists, intellectual property portfolios, and corporate assets.

A Practitioner Perspective: The Use and Purpose of NDAs

Non-disclosure agreements, also called "NDAs" or confidentiality agreements, play a very important role in modern commercial relationships. In order to develop complex technical products, provide broad-based client services and engage in activities that cross industry lines, companies and individuals frequently are required to work closely with and share proprietary, competitive information with unaffiliated third parties. NDAs provide the contractual basis on which this information is exchanged and give the participants the comfort they require in order to share their business strategies, financial information and competitive data with others outside their organizations.

NDAs serve myriad purposes in a corporate context. They are used by entrepreneurs who are seeking early-stage financing from angel investors in order to maintain the confidentiality of a new business idea. When a company sells itself or one of its businesses, prospective purchasers will not be permitted to see any of the company's financial or operating information prior to signing an NDA. Commercial agreements frequently include confidentiality requirements, sometimes limiting the disclosure of the existence of the commercial arrangement itself. In the employment context, a company may ask employees who are assigned to work on a particularly sensitive matter to execute NDAs related to that matter as a supplement to their general confidentiality obligations contained in the company's broad-based employment policies.

This last example of an employee signing a supplemental NDA highlights some of the essential features of all NDAs. One is that the NDA defines the information or topics that are considered confidential or proprietary and highlights the fact that those items are to remain confidential. The second feature is that such an NDA is a formal, written agreement to keep information confidential that the employee personally signs. This characteristic of NDAs is important because it relates to the incentives parties have to comply with their obligations under the agreements. People seem to give greater weight to, and may be less inclined to violate, an agreement they have signed than an oral agreement. In addition, individuals frequently see a general benefit in being perceived as someone whose word can be trusted. Similarly, in the corporate context, companies who are repeat players in a field, such as providing merger advisory services, typically believe it is important to the success of their businesses to be trusted by others with confidential information.

The seriousness with which a party takes an NDA is particularly important due to some of the inherent weaknesses of NDAs, which are different from other contracts. These weaknesses relate to enforceability of the contract itself—particularly the ability to prove a violation of the contract and to recover any damages. If two companies are parties to an NDA related to merger discussions and word of the discussions leaks to the press, it may be very difficult to prove that one or the other company (or any of their respective financial advisors, financing sources, attorneys or accountants) violated their obligations under the NDA, because the leaked information is known to so many people within each organization. The difficulty of proving a violation can also be seen in the context of a company that is trying to sell a business and permits a competitor who may be an interested purchaser to review the operating information for the business under an NDA. If the competitor does not purchase the business but in the future adopts operating strategies or solicits customers of that business, it may not be possible to demonstrate that the competitor is taking those actions in violation of the NDA as opposed to as a result of its own strategic thinking and business acumen.

The second weakness that can apply to NDAs relates to recovering damages. Even if a company can demonstrate that another breached its obligations under an NDA, in many cases the initial breach of the agreement is effectively irreparable. Once the market, or a competitor, hears the confidential information, the damage to the aggrieved party is done but the amount of damage to that company may be highly speculative and therefore very difficult to recover. As a result of these characteristics, depending on the circumstances surrounding the NDA, the parties may see little practical financial risk to breaching the agreement.

NDAs are essential to corporate and commercial relationships in our increasingly interdependent economy. However, for the reasons described above, when entering into a confidential relationship with a third party, a company needs to be mindful of the nature of the NDA relationship and its inherent limitations. In order to determine whether the company's confidential information is likely to be reasonably secure, it is important for practitioners to carefully assess all of the counterparty's incentives and motivations related to the relationship, not just the contractual obligation contained in the NDA.

> William L. Horton, Jr.
> Senior Vice President, Deputy General Counsel,
> and Corporate Secretary
> Verizon Communications Inc.

A. NON-DISCLOSURE AGREEMENT IN THE EMPLOYMENT CONTEXT

The following agreement sets forth the rights and obligations between an employer and its new employee.

Things to Consider . . .

As you read through the following agreement, please consider these items. You will want to return to the agreement, as you study the substantive discussion that follows.

> **Parties, Rights, and Obligations.** Who are (and who are not) the "parties" (i.e., the persons manifesting assent) to this Agreement? Consider who

has the obligation to do what and, on the flipside, who has the right to benefit, under this Agreement.

> **Prefatory Provisions.** Before it imposes obligations or rights on either party, the Agreement contains language ("In consideration of . . ."). The provisions prior to the substance of an Agreement are often called "recitals." Consider what purposes this language serves in this Agreement and what purposes the inclusion of introductory text may serve in contracts generally. Similarly, what purposes may provisions like those contained in § 2 ("Acknowledgement") in the Agreement serve in the context of an Agreement (whether they exist among an Agreement's recitals or substantive terms)?

> **"Confidential Information" and Definitions.** Consider how this Agreement defines "Confidential Information" and how the Agreement uses this definition throughout. Taking the perspective of both parties in turn, does this definition strike you as particularly broad or narrow, given the circumstances of this relationship (from what you can tell from the Agreement)?

AGREEMENT ON CONFIDENTIALITY, NON-COMPETITION AND NON-SOLICITATION[4]

In consideration of my continued employment by The Coca-Cola Company, a Delaware corporation, I agree with The Coca-Cola Company as follows:

1. Definitions. For the purposes of this Agreement, the following definitions apply:

(a) "Confidential Information" means any data or information, other than Trade Secrets, that is valuable to The Coca-Cola Company and/or its subsidiaries and affiliates (collectively "the Company") and not generally known to competitors of the Company or other outsiders, regardless of whether the information is in print, written, or electronic form, retained in my memory, or has been compiled or created by me, including, but not limited to, technical, financial, personnel, staffing, payroll, computer systems, marketing, advertising, merchandising, product, vendor, or customer data, or other information similar to the foregoing;

(b) "Trade Secret" means any information, including a formula, pattern, compilation, program, device, method, technique, or process, that (i) derives independent economic value, actual or potential, from

---

4. Coca-Cola Co., Agreement on Confidentiality, Non-Competition and Non-Solicitation (Form 10-K), at Exhibit 10.47 (Feb. 26, 2010), *available at* http://www.sec.gov/Archives/edgar/data/21344/000104746910001476/a2195739zex-10_47.htm.

not being generally known to, and not being readily ascertainable by proper means by, other persons who can derive economic value from its disclosure or use and (ii) is the subject of efforts that are reasonable under the circumstances to maintain its secrecy; and

(c) "Customer" means anyone who (i) is or was a customer of the Company during my employment with The Coca-Cola Company, or (ii) is a prospective customer of the Company to whom the Company has made a presentation (or similar offering of services) within the one-year period immediately preceding the termination of my employment with The Coca-Cola Company or, if my employment has not terminated, the one-year period immediately preceding any alleged violation of this Agreement.

2. Acknowledgement. My services for The Coca-Cola Company are of a special, unique, extraordinary, and intellectual character, and are performed on behalf of the Company throughout the world. My position as a high-level executive of The Coca-Cola Company places me in a position of confidence and trust with the Customers and employees of the Company. So long as I shall remain in the employ of The Coca-Cola Company, I shall devote my whole time and ability to the service of the Company in such capacity as The Coca-Cola Company shall from time to time direct, and I shall perform my duties faithfully and diligently.

I acknowledge that the rendering of services to the Company's Customers necessarily requires the disclosure of the Company's Confidential Information and Trade Secrets to me. In addition, in the course of my employment with The Coca-Cola Company, I will develop a personal acquaintanceship and relationship with certain of the Company's Customers, and a knowledge of those Customers' affairs and requirements, which may constitute a significant contact between the Company and such Customers. Finally, the Customers with whom I will have business dealings on behalf of the Company are located throughout the world.

I further acknowledge that the provisions in this Agreement, including, but not limited to, the restrictive covenants and the governing law and forum selection provisions, are fair and reasonable, that enforcement of the provisions of this Agreement will not cause me undue hardship, and that the provisions of this Agreement are necessary and commensurate with the need to protect the Company's established goodwill and proprietary information from irreparable harm. In the event that I breach, I threaten in any way to breach, or it is inevitable that I will breach any of the provisions of this Agreement, damages shall be an inadequate remedy and The Coca-Cola Company shall be entitled, without bond, to injunctive or other equitable relief. The Coca-Cola Company's rights in this respect are in addition to all rights otherwise available at law or in equity.

3. Non-Competition and Non-Solicitation. [Omitted]

4. Confidential Information and Trade Secrets.

(a) During my employment with The Coca-Cola Company, I will acquire and have access to the Company's Confidential Information. I agree that while I am in The Coca-Cola Company's employ and for two years after the termination of my employment with The Coca-Cola Company for any reason whatsoever, I shall hold in confidence all Confidential Information of the Company and will not disclose, publish, or make use of such Confidential Information, directly or indirectly, unless compelled by law and then only after providing written notice to The Coca-Cola Company. If I have any questions regarding what data or information would be considered by the Company to be Confidential Information, I agree to contact the appropriate person(s) at the Company for written clarification; and

(b) During my employment with The Coca-Cola Company, I will also acquire and have access to the Company's Trade Secrets. I acknowledge that the Company has made and will continue to make reasonable efforts under the circumstances to maintain the secrecy of its Trade Secrets. I agree to hold in confidence all Trade Secrets of the Company that come into my knowledge during my employment with The Coca-Cola Company and shall not directly or indirectly disclose, publish, or make use of at any time such Trade Secrets for so long as the information remains a Trade Secret. If I have any questions regarding what data or information constitutes a Trade Secret, I agree to contact the appropriate person(s) at the Company for written clarification. Nothing in this provision shall be interpreted to diminish the protections afforded trade secrets under applicable law.

5. Company Property. Upon leaving the employ of The Coca-Cola Company, I shall not take with me any written, printed, or electronically stored Trade Secrets, Confidential Information, or any other property of the Company obtained by me as a result of my employment, or any reproductions thereof. All such Company property and all copies thereof shall be surrendered by me to the Company on my termination or at any time upon request of the Company.

6. Inventions, Discoveries, and Authorship. [Omitted]

7. Governing Law. This Agreement shall be construed, interpreted, and applied in accordance with the laws of the State of Delaware, without giving effect to the choice-of-law provisions thereof.

8. Mandatory Forum Selection. The Company and I hereby irrevocably submit any dispute arising out of, in connection with, or relating to this Agreement, including with respect to my employment by The Coca-Cola Company or the termination of such employment, to the exclusive concurrent jurisdiction of the state and federal courts located in the State of Delaware. The Company and I also both irrevocably waive, to the fullest extent permitted by applicable law, any objection either may now or hereafter have to the laying of venue of any such dispute brought in such court or any defense of inconvenient forum for the maintenance of such dispute. Finally, I waive formal service of process and agree to accept service of process worldwide.

9. Severability. In the event that any provision of this Agreement is found to be invalid or unenforceable by a court of law or other appropriate authority, the invalidity or unenforceability of such provision shall not affect the other provisions of this Agreement, which shall remain in full force and effect, and that court or other appropriate authority shall modify the provisions found to be unenforceable or invalid so as to make them enforceable, taking into account the purposes of this Agreement and the nationwide and international scope of the Company's business.

10. Waiver. No waiver of any provision of this Agreement shall be effective unless pursuant to a writing signed by me and the Company, and such waiver shall be effective only in the specific instance and for the specific purpose stated in the writing.

11. [Omitted]

12. Assignment. This Agreement shall inure to the benefit of the Company, allied companies, successors and assigns, or nominees of the Company, and I specifically agree to execute any and all documents considered convenient or necessary to assign transfer, sustain and maintain inventions, discoveries, copyrightable material, applications, and patents, both in this and foreign countries, to and on behalf of the Company.

[Signature Page Omitted]

1. Recitals and Acknowledgments

The Agreement begins with a recital (sometimes called a "whereas clause," as oftentimes each clause will begin with "WHEREAS"), which is a clause that appears at the very beginning of a contract. While the recital in the above Agreement is very thin (just a basic recital of consideration), recitals may be several paragraphs, as you will see in the agreements throughout this book, typically depending on the complexity of the transaction and the relationship for which the recitals provide context.

A recital purports not to state substantive terms of the contract but rather to suggest the motivation or purpose of undertaking the relationship. As a general rule, a recital does not create legally binding contractual obligations,[5] and other evidence may controvert a fact stated in a recital, even if the recital is part of a completely integrated document.[6] Despite that the substantive terms of a contract control, courts may read recitals in order to discern the parties' intent and to inform the reading and construction of the contract.[7] You will notice that § 2 of the Agreement explains the underlying relationship between the parties and the motivation for entering the Agreement and contains the sort of language that sometimes may be found in a recitals section to frame and precede the main body of a non-disclosure agreement. For example, in an agreement similar to the one above, it would not be surprising to find the following at the top of the document:

> WHEREAS, my services for The Coca-Cola Company are of a special, unique, extraordinary, and intellectual character, and are performed on behalf of the Company throughout the world;
>
> WHEREAS, my position as a high-level executive of The Coca-Cola Company places me in a position of confidence and trust with the Customers and employees of the Company;
>
> WHEREAS, the rendering of services to the Company's Customers necessarily requires the disclosure of the Company's Confidential Information and Trade Secrets to me;

---

5. *See, e.g., Fab-Tech, Inc. v. E.I. DuPont De Nemours and Co.*, 311 F. App'x 443, 446 (2d Cir. 2009) (Vermont law) ("While introductory recitals in a contract may shed light on the motives behind forming the contract, they are not strictly a part of the contract. . . .") (internal citations and quotation marks omitted); *Pieper, Inc. v. Land O'Lakes Farmland Feed, LLC*, 390 F.3d 1062, 1065 (8th Cir. 2004) ("[U]nder Minnesota law, recitals do not create legal obligations."); *Atlantic Mut. Ins. Co. v. Metron Eng'g and Constr. Co.*, 83 F.3d 897, 899 (7th Cir. 1996) ("Under Illinois law introductory language or recitals are not binding obligations unless so referred to in the operative portion of the instrument as to show a design that they should form a part of it.") (internal citations and quotation marks omitted).

6. *See* RESTATEMENT (SECOND) OF CONTRACTS § 218(1) cmt. b (1981) ("A recital of fact in an integrated agreement is evidence of the fact, and its weight depends on the circumstances. Contrary facts may be proved. The result may be that the integrated agreement is not binding, or that it has a different effect from the effect if the recital had been true. In the absence of estoppel, the true facts have the same operation as if stated in the writing."); *see, e.g., Fulton v. L & N Consultants, Inc.*, 715 F.2d 1413, 1419 (10th Cir. 1982). Please see below for a discussion of "integration" and "integration clauses."

7. *See, e.g., Aramony v. United Way of Am.*, 254 F.3d 403, 413 (2d Cir. 2001) ("[A]lthough a statement in a 'whereas' clause may be useful in interpreting an ambiguous operative clause in a contract, it cannot create any right beyond those arising from the operative terms of the document.") (internal citations and quotation marks omitted); *Hagene v. Derek Polling Constr.*, 902 N.E.2d 1269, 1274 (Ill. App. Ct. 2009) ("The contract recitals create a context through which the operational portion of the contract can be better understood, because they indicate the relevant circumstances to its execution."); *Gwaltney v. Russell*, 984 So. 2d 1125, 1135 (Ala. 2007) ("If the recitals in a contract are clear and the operative part is ambiguous, the recitals govern the interpretation.") (internal citations and quotation marks omitted).

NOW, THEREFORE, in consideration of my continued employment by The Coca-Cola Company, a Delaware corporation, I agree with The Coca-Cola Company as follows: . . . .

In addition, a party to a contract may be estopped from denying the truth of a specific fact asserted by a recital, if the recital is relied upon in good faith and such reliance would prove unjustly detrimental should the truth of the recital be denied.[8] As an example, a party may be estopped from challenging a contract for lack of consideration, where the contract contains a recital that consideration was received (a recital of consideration is commonly found in contracts, including this Agreement).[9] Even if estoppel is not appropriate, recitals of consideration are sometimes given at least some weight in determining whether a contract is supported by consideration.[10] Estoppel may also be available where a party "acknowledges" a fact in an agreement—whether in the recitals or body of an agreement.[11] Estoppel premised on a recital or acknowledgement in a contract is generally only proper in an action founded on that contract; that is, with respect to a claim that does not arise from a contract, one will not be estopped from denying the truth of a recital made in that contract.[12]

As a matter of drafting prudence, a party should avoid agreeing to recitals that express the other party's desired outcomes of the contract (e.g., saving costs) or that make additional promises the party does not wish to be bound to perform, even if the recital states that these unperformed promises were already performed. This avoids the potentiality of the other party, desiring an outcome or performance, later arguing that the recitals warranted or promised such.

2. Consideration in "Unilateral" Non-Disclosure Agreements

As discussed later in this chapter,[13] the consideration in exchange for the obligations assumed by an employee in an NDA is sometimes found in

---

8. *See* John J. Dvorske et al., 31 C.J.S. Estoppel and Waiver § 73 (West 2009).

9. *See, e.g., Keller v. Bass Pro Shops, Inc.*, 15 F.3d 122, 124 (8th Cir. 1994) (holding that the plaintiff could not challenge the patent assignment for lack of consideration because consideration was recited in the contract); *Carroll Touch, Inc. v. Electro Mech. Sys., Inc.*, 15 F.3d 1573, 1581 (Fed. Cir. 1993) (noting that the party was estopped from claiming he did not receive consideration). *But see* Restatement (Second) of Contracts § 218 cmt. e (1981) ("An incorrect statement of a consideration does not prevent proof either that there was no consideration or that there was a consideration different from that stated. In some such cases the recital may imply a promise not explicitly stated.").

10. *See* Richard A. Lord, 3 Williston on Contracts § 7:23 (West 4th ed. 2009) ("[T]he solution of the law has been generally to entitle the recital to some weight, but to permit the introduction of contrary evidence except in a few narrowly defined areas.").

11. *See, e.g., Two Men and a Truck/Int'l Inc. v. Two Men and a Truck/Kalamazoo, Inc.*, 949 F. Supp. 500, 508 (W.D. Mich. 1996) ("Defendants entered into valid franchise agreements acknowledging the fact that plaintiff owned the 'Two Men and a Truck' name and mark; thus, defendants are estopped from claiming that the plaintiff's name and mark are invalid.").

12. *Bank of Am. v. Banks*, 101 U.S. 240 (1879); *see also* John J. Dvorske et al., 31 C.J.S. Estoppel and Waiver § 73 (West 2009) (citing *Popplewell v. Stevenson*, 176 F.2d 362 (10th Cir. 1949)).

13. See *infra* the discussion of consideration in the context of NDAs.

the promise or performance of future employment.[14] While an NDA itself may be "unilateral" in that it only imposes obligations on the employee,[15] an NDA in the employment context is ancillary to an employment agreement or relationship, ideally, with consideration flowing both ways. With this in mind, while this Agreement is designed to impose confidentiality obligations on only the employee, it may be supported by consideration found in the greater employment relationship—for example, in the employer's promise of continued employment.

3. Tortious Interference: Legally Reaching a Third Party

"Tortious interference with contract" refers to a third party's intentional and improper act that causes a party not to perform under a contract, where such nonperformance proximately results in actual damages or losses.[16] In the NDA context, tortious interference provides a legal theory for holding third parties—that is, persons not party to the NDA—liable for causing a party to the NDA to breach her contractual confidentiality obligations.[17] For example, suppose an employer requires an employee to sign an NDA, and the employee then leaves to work for another company. At the new company, the employee discloses the original employer's confidential information in contravention of the NDA. If the new company improperly acted with an intention of causing the employee to breach her NDA, the new company may be liable to the original employer for tortious interference with the NDA.[18]

On the issue of tortious interference in the context of non-disclosure agreements, we invited a seasoned practitioner to share some practical insight.

---

14. In addition, as previously discussed, a recital of consideration will help satisfy some courts not to invalidate a contract for lack of consideration.

15. Note that the distinction drawn between "unilateral" and "bilateral" NDAs, which focuses on whether the underlying non-disclosure obligations are unidirectional or reciprocal, is not intended to mirror the distinction between "unilateral" and "bilateral" contracts, which are terms of art with specific meanings.

16. See RESTATEMENT (SECOND) OF TORTS § 766 (1979) ("One who intentionally and improperly interferes with the performance of a contract (except a contract to marry) between another and a third person by inducing or otherwise causing the third person not to perform the contract, is subject to liability to the other for the pecuniary loss resulting to the other from the failure of the third person to perform the contract."); see also Nova Consulting Grp., Inc. v. Eng'g Consulting Servs., Ltd., 290 F. App'x. 727, 737 (5th Cir. 2008). For a list of factors important in determining whether an interference is improper, please see RESTATEMENT (SECOND) OF TORTS § 767 (1979).

17. See, e.g., Nova, 290 F. App'x at 738 (finding new employer—who required employee to disclose old employer's confidential information and who knew of non-disclosure agreement between employee and old employer—liable for tortious interference with that non-disclosure agreement).

18. As an illustration, in Nova, the court explained, "The evidence supports a reasonable jury's finding that ECS was aware of the agreements; yet, in contravention of them, and ignoring the warning from Nova lawyers that the agreements would be enforced through legal action if necessary, continued to require former Nova managers to load their client information into the ECS database." 290 F. App'x at 739.

A Practitioner Perspective: Tortious Interference and NDAs

In industries such as IT and finance, newly hired employees may arrive with vestiges from their previous employers in the form of nondisclosure agreements. How should the new employer address this possibility? In no event can the new employer turn a blind eye. The business risk is too great—an employee who violates an NDA may expose himself and his new employer to serious legal risks. Additionally, the employee may be enjoined from working for his new employer.

One approach is for the prospective new employer to require a candidate for employment to provide a copy of his NDA for the new employer's review. While this course gives the new employer the opportunity to assess fully the candidate's obligations to his former employer and to determine whether the candidate will be able to fulfill the requirements of the new position without violating the NDA, it also enhances the likelihood of a successful tortious interference claim by the former employer should the new employer hire the candidate regardless of the terms of the NDA. The new employer's review of the NDA would serve as compelling evidence that the new employer had knowledge of the contract and obligations owed to the former employer, critical elements of a tortious interference claim.

Another approach is to ask the candidate to make a written representation as to whether he is subject to any restrictions that would preclude him from working for and performing all of his contemplated duties with the prospective new employer. If the candidate answers no, then the new employer can take some comfort in the fact that it has no knowledge of any NDA (or non-compete) restrictions. Of course, absent review of all agreements between the candidate and the prior employer, the new employer will not have certainty. To manage this risk, the new employer may wish to seek an indemnification agreement by which the candidate would compensate the new employer for any losses it suffers because the candidate failed to disclose a nondisclosure obligation (although the value of such an agreement may be ephemeral if the candidate does not have deep pockets). If the candidate answers that he is subject to post-employment restrictions, the new employer would then request the relevant agreements for review.

Neal Stern
Assistant General Counsel
National Basketball Association

4. Employee's Duty of Confidentiality

Employees often have a duty of confidentiality to keep secret the confidential information of their employers. Indeed, as one commentator explains, "a relationship of confidence and trust inheres in most employment relationships," and "[an employment relationship] imposes a duty upon the employee not to use or disclose the employer's confidential information to the employer's detriment."[19] However, given that a court may characterize a relationship as not of the kind that imposes a duty of confidentiality, NDAs can be useful: They direct a court to find the relationship to be a confidential one, which avoids the vagaries of a court's fact-and-circumstances inquiry.[20] In light of this discussion, why else might NDAs be useful in the employment context?[21]

5. Trade Secrets

The Coca-Cola NDA above excludes "Trade Secrets" from the definition of Confidential Information and separately imposes obligations on the employee regarding Trade Secrets in § 4(b). What is a trade secret? Under the Uniform Trade Secrets Act ("UTSA") (and, not by coincidence, under the Agreement's definition, as well), a "trade secret" is information that:

> (i) derives independent economic value, actual or potential, from not being generally known to, and not being readily ascertainable by proper means by, other persons who obtain economic value from its disclosure or use, and
> (ii) is the subject of efforts that are reasonable under the circumstances to maintain its secrecy.[22]

Non-disclosure agreements are important in the context of trade secrets for at least two reasons. First, NDAs can help ensure one *has* a trade secret. As the UTSA provides, for information to be a trade secret, the "owner" of the information must make efforts to maintain its secrecy.[23] Requiring those who come into contact with the information to sign an NDA protecting that information is such an effort.[24] This matters when trying to recover from a party for misappropriation of a trade secret: If the would-be trade secret has been freely shared, it may fail to qualify as a trade secret in the first place. Note, however, that an NDA

---

19. MILGRIM ON TRADE SECRETS § 5.02(1) (2009); *see also Eaton Corp. v. Giere*, 971 F.2d 136, 141 (8th Cir. 1992) (Minnesota law) ("Even when there is no contractual duty, employees have a common law duty not to use trade secrets or confidential information obtained from their employer."); RESTATEMENT (THIRD) OF AGENCY § 8.05 (2006) ("An agent has a duty . . . not to use or communicate confidential information of the principal for the agent's own purposes or those of a third party.").

20. *See* MILGRIM ON TRADE SECRETS § 4.02(1)(b) (2009) ("For parties reluctant to rely upon prediction as to how a court will define a relationship, it is advisable to contractually define the relationship and to state whether it is a confidential one . . . .").

21. For a partial answer to this question, please see this chapter's discussion of trade secrets.

22. UNIFORM TRADE SECRETS ACT § 1(4) (1985).

23. *Id.* § 1(4)(ii).

24. *See, e.g., Veteran Med. Prods., Inc. v. Bionix Dev. Corp.*, No. 1:05-cv-655, 2008 WL 696546, at *8 (W.D. Mich. Mar. 13, 2008) (noting that under Michigan UTSA, "[t]he execution of the nondisclosure agreement and confidentiality notice on the e-mails constitute a reasonable effort . . . to maintain the secrecy of [the] information"); *Tom James Co. v. Hudgins*, 261 F. Supp. 2d 636, 641-42 (S.D. Miss. 2003) (noting that under Mississippi UTSA, execution of a non-disclosure agreement advising employee that certain information was a trade secret and confidential constituted a reasonable effort to maintain secrecy); *Liberty Am. Ins. Grp., Inc. v. WestPoint Underwriters, LLC*, 199 F. Supp. 2d 1271, 1286 (M.D. Fla. 2001) (noting that under Florida UTSA, restricting access to employees who executed confidentiality agreements and to third parties under a licensing agreement constituted a reasonable effort to maintain secrecy).

that expressly limits confidentiality obligations to a certain term has been held to place an express time limit on the trade-secret *status* of the underlying information.[25] Accordingly, an NDA may also work to *limit* trade-secrets rights that might exist absent the NDA.[26] How does the above NDA address this concern?

Second, NDAs can provide one with a claim under trade-secrets law. Trade-secrets law works to prohibit "misappropriation" of trade secrets.[27] The performance of various "improper means" may qualify as misappropriation of another's trade secret, and the disclosure or use of a trade secret in violation of a confidentiality agreement is one type of misappropriation actionable under the UTSA.[28] Moreover, trade-secrets law allows one to reach even persons who are not party to an NDA. Under the UTSA, a trade-secrets owner may recover for misappropriation against a third party who (1) acquires a trade secret by inducing a party to breach her NDA; or (2) uses or discloses a trade secret knowing (or with reason to know) that they (the third party) acquired the trade secret from a party to an NDA.[29] This gives a trade-secrets owner a cause of action—potentially in addition to tortious interference, which can be a difficult-to-prove claim—for reaching third parties.

However, an NDA is unlikely to make a trade secret out of otherwise non-trade-secret information. Often, in non-disclosure agreements (as is the case in §§ 2 and 4(b) of this Agreement), a recipient of information will "acknowledge" that the recipient has received information that qualifies as a trade secret. These acknowledgments are of limited effect.[30] Indeed, despite having acknowledged

---

25. *See* Callmann on Unfair Competition, Tr. & Mono. § 14:6 (West 4th ed. 2009); *see also infra* note 73 and accompanying text. *But see Wilson Mfg. Co. v. Fusco*, 258 S.W.3d 841, 847-48 (Mo. Ct. App. 2008) (explaining that misappropriation claim under Missouri UTSA could be brought after termination of NDA).

26. *See supra* note 25. Absent an NDA, a recipient of information may still be subject to a duty of confidentiality. On this, please see this chapter's discussion on an employee's duty of confidentiality for further discussion.

27. *See* Uniform Trade Secrets Act § 1(2) (1985) ("'Misappropriation' means the (i) acquisition of a trade secret of another by a person who knows or has reason to know that the trade secret was acquired by improper means; or (ii) disclosure or use of a trade secret of another without express or implied consent by a person who (A) used improper means to acquire knowledge of the trade secret; or (B) at the time of disclosure or use knew or had reason to know that his knowledge of the trade secret was (I) derived from or through a person who has utilized improper means to acquire it; (II) acquired under circumstances giving rise to a duty to maintain its secrecy or limit its use; or (III) derived from or through a person who owed a duty to the person seeking relief to maintain its secrecy or limit its use; or (C) before a material change of his position, knew or had reason to know that it was a trade secret and that knowledge of it had been acquired by accident or mistake.").

28. *Id.* § 1(2)(ii)(B)(II).

29. *Id.* §§ 1(2)(i), 1(2)(ii)(A), 1(2)(ii)(B)(III). Under the UTSA, "improper means" includes "breach or inducement of breach of a duty to maintain secrecy" in its definition. *Id.* §1(1).

30. *See, e.g., Vincit Enters., Inc. v. Zimmerman*, No. 1:06-CV-57, 2006 WL 1319515, at *6 (E.D. Tenn. Mar. 12, 2006) (explaining that a recital that trade secrets are "valuable" is insufficient to allege trade secrets had "independent economic value" under the Tennessee UTSA); *Iroquois Indus. Corp. v. Popik*, 415 N.E.2d 4, 6 (Ill. App. Ct. 1980) (explaining that a recital that certain information was confidential was insufficient to give rise to trade-secrets interest, where information was not actually confidential); *Follmer, Rudzewicz & Co., P.C. v. Kosco*, 362 N.W.2d 676, 683 n.16 (Mich. 1984) ("[T]he mere fact that the employer puts self-serving statements in the 'Whereas' clause of an employment contract to the effect that many trade secrets will be disclosed cannot itself determine the existence of such secrets in the absence of hard proof."); Milgrim on Trade Secrets § 15.01(1)(a)(v) (2009).

the trade-secret status of information, a party is unlikely to be estopped from arguing that such information is not a trade secret because, for an acknowledgment to give rise to estoppel, "the party to be estopped must know the true facts and intend that its conduct be acted upon by the party asserting the defense."[31] Accordingly, the recipient's mere contractual acknowledgment of the trade-secret status of the discloser's information likely neither makes the information a trade secret nor denies a recipient the right to argue that such information is not a trade secret.[32] Still, a contractual acknowledgment of trade-secret status is likely to give at least some weight and persuasive bite to the argument that the underlying information is a trade secret.[33]

Not only are NDAs important for the work they do in buttressing trade secrets, but also they may provide additional protection where trade-secrets law stops short. For instance, as discussed above, trade-secrets law generally only protects information that is valuable for being secret and which the putative owner takes steps to protect. However, an NDA may protect information that fails to qualify as a trade secret but that a party would still like to keep confidential.[34] On this point, consider the above Agreement's definition of "Confidential Information" and that it excludes "Trade Secrets." Section 4(a) of the Agreement imposes confidentiality obligations on the employee with respect to confidential, non-trade-secret information.

B. NON-DISCLOSURE AGREEMENT IN THE COMMERCIAL CONTEXT

The following agreement sets forth the obligations between two parties planning to enter into a commercial relationship.

---

31. *Computer Assocs. Int'l, Inc. v. Am. Fundware, Inc.*, 831 F. Supp. 1516, 1530 (D. Colo. 1993) (denying a motion to estop a party who signed a contract acknowledging trade secrets) (internal citations omitted).

32. However, subsequent behavior or "explicit and repeated recognition" that evidences a recipient's treatment of information as a trade secret may either estop the recipient from denying that such is a trade secret or weigh heavily in the court's decision to treat such as a trade secret. *See* Milgrim on Trade Secrets § 15.01(1)(a)(v) (2009).

33. *See, e.g.*, *Pre-Paid Legal Servs., Inc. v. Harrell*, No. CIV-06-019-JHP, 2008 WL 111319, at *11 (E.D. Okla. Jan. 8, 2008) (explaining that a contractual acknowledgment of trade-secret status provides evidence of efforts to maintain secrecy). Indeed, "[p]rotecting a trade secret 'calls for constant warnings to all persons to whom the trade secret has become known and obtaining from each an agreement, preferably in writing, acknowledging its secrecy and promising to respect it.'" *Incase Inc. v. Timex Corp.*, 488 F.3d 46, 53 (1st Cir. 2007) (Massachusetts law) (quoting *J.T. Healy & Son, Inc. v. James A. Murphy & Son, Inc.*, 357 Mass. 728, 738 (1970)).

34. *See, e.g.*, *AMP Inc. v. Fleischhacker*, 823 F.2d 1199, 1201 (7th Cir. 1987) ("While an enforceable restrictive covenant may protect material, such as confidential information revealed to an employee during the course of his employment, which does not constitute a trade secret, an employer's protection absent a restrictive covenant is narrower and extends only to trade secrets or near-permanent customer relationships."). For more on protecting non-trade-secret information, please see the discussion of the enforceability and reasonableness of NDAs below.

Things to Consider . . .

As you read through the following agreement, please consider these items. You will want to return to the agreement, as you study the substantive discussion that follows.

> **Parties and Third Parties.** Who are (and who are not) the parties to *this* Agreement? Consider who has the obligation to do what and, on the flipside, who has the right to benefit, under this Agreement. What is the right and power of a party to transfer its rights and its obligations under this Agreement to a nonparty?

> **"Confidential Information" and Definitions.** Consider how this Agreement defines "Confidential Information" and how the Agreement uses this definition throughout. Taking the perspective of each party in turn, does this definition strike you as particularly broad or narrow, given the circumstances of this relationship? Compare this to the previous agreement's definition and use of "Confidential Information."

> **Remedies and Redress.** Where may (and may not) a party bring suit for an action related to the Agreement? What types of remedies and relief may the party obtain? How deferential do you think a court will be to the Agreement's specification of these matters?

MICROSOFT CORPORATION NON-DISCLOSURE AGREEMENT (STANDARD RECIPROCAL)[35]

This Non-Disclosure Agreement (the "Agreement") is made and entered into as of the later of the two signature dates below by and between MICROSOFT CORPORATION, a Washington corporation ("Microsoft"), and Electronic Arts [Inc.], a Delaware corporation ("Company").

IN CONSIDERATION OF THE MUTUAL PROMISES AND COVENANTS CONTAINED IN THIS AGREEMENT AND THE MUTUAL DISCLOSURE OF CONFIDENTIAL INFORMATION, THE PARTIES HERETO AGREE AS FOLLOWS:

1. Definition of Confidential Information and Exclusions

(a) "Confidential Information" means nonpublic information that a party to this Agreement ("Disclosing Party") designates as being confidential to the party that receives such information ("Receiving Party") or which, under the circumstances surrounding disclosure

---

35. Electronic Arts Inc., Microsoft Corporation Non-Disclosure Agreement (Standard Reciprocal) (Form 10-Q), at Exhibit 10.6 (Nov. 10, 2009), *available at* http://www.sec.gov/Archives/edgar/data/712515/000119312509230789 /dex106.htm.

ought to be treated as confidential by the Receiving Party. "Confidential Information" includes, without limitation, information in tangible or intangible form relating to and/or including released or unreleased Disclosing Party software or hardware products, the marketing or promotion of any Disclosing Party product, Disclosing Party's business policies or practices, and information received from others that Disclosing Party is obligated to treat as confidential. Except as otherwise indicated in this Agreement, the term "Disclosing Party" also includes all Affiliates of the Disclosing Party and, except as otherwise indicated, the term "Receiving Party" also includes all Affiliates of the Receiving Party. An "Affiliate" means any person, partnership, joint venture, corporation or other form of enterprise, domestic or foreign, including but not limited to subsidiaries, that directly or indirectly, control, are controlled by, or are under common control with a party. Prior to the time that any Confidential Information is shared with an Affiliate who has not signed this Agreement, the Receiving Party that executed this Agreement below (the "Undersigned Receiving Party") shall have entered into an appropriate written agreement with that Affiliate sufficient to enable the Disclosing Party and/or the Undersigned Receiving Party to enforce all of the provisions of this Agreement against such Affiliate.

(b) Confidential Information shall not include any information, however designated, that: (i) is or subsequently becomes publicly available without Receiving Party's breach of any obligation owed Disclosing Party; (ii) became known to Receiving Party prior to Disclosing Party's disclosure of such information to Receiving Party pursuant to the terms of this Agreement; (iii) became known to Receiving Party from a source other than Disclosing Party other than by the breach of an obligation of confidentiality owed to Disclosing Party; (iv) is independently developed by Receiving Party; or (v) constitutes Feedback (as defined in Section 5 of this Agreement [Omitted]).

2. Obligations Regarding Confidential Information

(a) Receiving Party shall:

(i) Refrain from disclosing any Confidential Information of the Disclosing Party to third parties for five (5) years following the date that Disclosing Party first discloses such Confidential Information to Receiving Party, except as expressly provided in Sections 2(b) and 2(c) of this Agreement;

(ii) Take reasonable security precautions, at least as great as the precautions it takes to protect its own confidential information, but no less than reasonable care, to keep confidential the Confidential Information of the Disclosing Party;

(iii) Refrain from disclosing, reproducing, summarizing and/or distributing Confidential Information of the Disclosing Party except in pursuance of Receiving Party's business relationship with Disclosing Party, and only as otherwise provided hereunder; and

(iv) Refrain from reverse engineering, decompiling or disassembling any software code and/or pre-release hardware devices disclosed by Disclosing Party to Receiving Party under the terms of this Agreement, except as expressly permitted by applicable law.

(b) Receiving Party may disclose Confidential Information of Disclosing Party in accordance with a judicial or other governmental order, provided that Receiving Party either (i) gives the undersigned Disclosing Party reasonable notice prior to such disclosure to allow Disclosing Party a reasonable opportunity to seek a protective order or equivalent, or (ii) obtains written assurance from the applicable judicial or governmental entity that it will afford the Confidential Information the highest level of protection afforded under applicable law or regulation. Notwithstanding the foregoing, the Receiving Party shall not disclose any computer source code that contains Confidential Information of the Disclosing Party in accordance with a judicial or other governmental order unless it complies with the requirement set forth in subsection (i) of this Section 2(b).

(c) The undersigned Receiving Party may disclose Confidential Information only to Receiving Party's employees and consultants on a need-to-know basis. The Receiving Party will have executed or shall execute appropriate written agreements with its employees and consultants sufficient to enable Receiving Party to enforce all the provisions of this Agreement.

(d) Receiving Party shall notify the undersigned Disclosing Party immediately upon discovery of any unauthorized use or disclosure of Confidential Information or any other breach of this Agreement by Receiving Party and its employees and consultants, and will cooperate with Disclosing Party in every reasonable way to help Disclosing Party regain possession of the Confidential Information and prevent its further unauthorized use or disclosure.

(e) Receiving Party shall, at Disclosing Party's request, return all originals, copies, reproductions and summaries of Confidential Information and all other tangible materials and devices provided to the Receiving Party as Confidential Information, or at Disclosing Party's option, certify destruction of the same.

3. Remedies

The parties acknowledge that monetary damages may not be a sufficient remedy for unauthorized disclosure of Confidential Information and that Disclosing Party shall be entitled, without waiving any other rights or remedies, to such injunctive or equitable relief as may be deemed proper by a court of competent jurisdiction.

4. Miscellaneous

(a) All Confidential Information is and shall remain the property of Disclosing Party. By disclosing Confidential Information to Receiving Party, Disclosing Party does not grant any express or implied right to Receiving Party to or under any patents, copyrights, trademarks, or trade secret information except as otherwise provided herein. Disclosing Party reserves without prejudice the ability to protect its rights under any such patents, copyrights, trademarks, or trade secrets except as otherwise provided herein.

(b) In the event that the Disclosing Party provides any computer software and/or hardware to the Receiving Party as Confidential Information under the terms of this Agreement, such computer software and/or hardware may only be used by the Receiving Party for evaluation and providing Feedback (as defined in Section 5 of this Agreement) to the Disclosing Party. Unless otherwise agreed by the Disclosing Party and the Receiving Party, all such computer software and/or hardware is provided "AS IS" without warranty of any kind, and Receiving Party agrees that neither Disclosing Party nor its suppliers shall be liable for any damages whatsoever arising from or relating to Receiving Party's use of or inability to use such software and/or hardware.

(c) The parties agree to comply with all applicable international and national laws that apply to (i) any Confidential Information, or (ii) any product (or any part thereof), process or service that is the direct product of the Confidential Information, including the U.S. Export Administration Regulations, as well as end-user, end-use and destination restrictions issued by U.S. and other governments. For additional information on exporting Microsoft products, see http://www.microsoft.com/exporting/.

(d) The terms of confidentiality under this Agreement shall not be construed to limit either the Disclosing Party or the Receiving Party's right to independently develop or acquire products without use of the other party's Confidential Information. Further, the Receiving Party shall be free to use for any purpose the residuals resulting from access to or work with the Confidential Information of the Disclosing Party, provided that the Receiving Party shall not disclose the Confidential Information except as expressly permitted pursuant to the terms of this Agreement. The term "residuals" means information in intangible form, which is retained in memory by persons who have had access to the Confidential Information, including ideas, concepts, know-how or techniques contained therein. The Receiving Party shall not have any obligation to limit or restrict the assignment of such persons or to pay royalties for any work resulting from the use of residuals. However, this sub-paragraph shall not be deemed to grant to the Receiving Party a license under the Disclosing Party's copyrights or patents.

(e) This Agreement constitutes the entire agreement between the parties with respect to the subject matter hereof. It shall not be modified except by written agreement dated subsequent to the date of this Agreement and signed by both parties. None of the provisions of this Agreement shall be deemed to have been waived by any act or acquiescence on the part of Disclosing Party, the Receiving Party, their agents, or employees, but only by an instrument in writing signed by an authorized employee of Disclosing Party and the Receiving Party. No waiver of any provision of this Agreement shall constitute a waiver of any other provision(s) or of the same provision on another occasion.

(f) If either Disclosing Party or the Receiving Party employs attorneys to enforce any rights arising out of or relating to this Agreement, the prevailing party shall be entitled to recover reasonable attorneys' fees and costs. This Agreement shall be construed and controlled by the laws of the State of Washington, and the parties further consent to exclusive jurisdiction and venue in the federal courts sitting in King County, Washington, unless no federal subject matter jurisdiction exists, in which case the parties consent to the exclusive jurisdiction and venue in the Superior Court of King County, Washington. Company waives all defenses of lack of personal jurisdiction and forum non conveniens. Process may be served on either party in the manner authorized by applicable law or court rule.

(g) This Agreement shall be binding upon and inure to the benefit of each party's respective successors and lawful assigns; provided, however, that neither party may assign this Agreement (whether by operation of law, sale of securities or assets, merger or otherwise), in whole or in part, without the prior written approval of the other party. Any attempted assignment in violation of this Section shall be void.

(h) If any provision of this Agreement shall be held by a court of competent jurisdiction to be illegal, invalid or unenforceable, the remaining provisions shall remain in full force and effect.

(i) Either party may terminate this Agreement with or without cause upon ninety (90) days prior written notice to the other party. All sections of this Agreement [relating] to the right and obligations of the parties concerning Confidential Information disclosed during the term of the Agreement shall survive any such termination.

[Section 5 Omitted]

[Signature Line Omitted]

1. Integration and Merger Clauses

Under the parol evidence rule, an "integrated" contractual document prevents evidence of additional terms of agreement not found within the document from being admitted to *contradict* the document's terms.[36] A contractual document is considered integrated if it is the *final* expression of an agreement between the parties. In addition, an integrated document may be considered either "partially" or "completely" integrated. Where a contractual document is *partially* integrated, it represents the final agreement of the parties but contains only *some* of the agreement's terms,[37] and, under the parol evidence rule, extrinsic terms that are *consistent* with the contractual document may be part of the agreement.[38] In contrast, if a contractual document is *completely* integrated, it is both the final and the *complete* expression of the terms of the agreement,[39] and, under the parol evidence rule, only the completely integrated document contains the terms of the bargain struck between the parties as of contracting—consistent, outside terms are excluded.[40] Even if a contract is integrated (completely or partially), extrinsic evidence might still be admitted in order to resolve an ambiguity in the contract.[41] Also, notice that the parol evidence rule does not speak to whether the parties may vary (or have varied) an integrated agreement after contracting.[42]

A court will look to the intent of the contractual parties and to the face of the contractual document to determine if the document is the final (i.e., integrated) and complete expression of the agreement.[43] For this reason, subsection 4(e) of the above Microsoft Agreement provides that the Agreement "constitutes the

---

36. *See* RESTATEMENT (SECOND) OF CONTRACTS § 215 (1981). Notice this is different from the question of whether the parties later modified their agreement. The parol evidence rule bars the admission of extrinsic terms to show that the parties agreed to terms that differ from the terms in an integrated document as of the signing of the agreement—and does not speak to the question of whether the parties later varied their agreement. This latter question is one of "modification," which we take up in Chapter 2 in the context of "no-oral-modification" provisions.

37. *See id.* § 210(2) ("A partially integrated agreement is an integrated agreement other than a completely integrated agreement.").

38. *See id.* § 216(1).

39. *See id.* § 210(1) ("A completely integrated agreement is an integrated agreement adopted by the parties as a complete and exclusive statement of the terms of the agreement.").

40. *See id.* § 216(1).

41. *See, e.g., Kripp v. Kripp*, 849 A.2d 1159, 1161-62 (Pa. 2004) (finding a contractual term ambiguous and admitting extrinsic evidence to discern the parties' intended meaning). The Supreme Court of Pennsylvania in *Kripp* explained, "A contract is ambiguous if it is reasonably susceptible of different constructions and capable of being understood in more than one sense." *Id.* at 1163 (citation omitted).

42. Please see Chapter 2 for a discussion of "modification" and "no-oral-modification" provisions.

43. *See, e.g., Metoyer v. Chassman*, 504 F.3d 919, 935 (9th Cir. 2007) (under California law, "the central question in determining whether there has been an integration, and thus whether the parol evidence doctrine applies, is whether the parties intended their writing to serve as the exclusive embodiment of their agreement.") (citation and internal quotation marks omitted); *Naimie v. Cytozyme Labs., Inc.*, 174 F.3d 1104, 1112 (10th Cir. 1999) (under Utah law, "[t]he issue of whether a contract is integrated and thus supersedes prior agreements depends on the parties' intent."); *Ozerol v. Howard Univ.*, 545 A.2d 638, 641 (D.C. 1988) ("Whether an agreement is integrated ultimately depends upon the intent of the parties."); *see also* RESTATEMENT (SECOND) OF CONTRACTS § 210 cmt. c (1981) ("It is often clear from the face of a writing that it is incomplete and cannot be

entire agreement between the parties." Commonly called an "integration" or "merger" clause, this type of provision serves as a manifestation of party intent and operates as evidence to render a contract integrated (although query whether this Agreement's integration clause expressly evidences the *final* integration of the document). To determine whether a document is integrated, a court may also look to extrinsic evidence, as the parol evidence rule generally will not bar evidence as to whether a contract is actually integrated in the first place.[44] An integration clause, while evidence of integration, is not dispositive of the issue.[45]

In whose interest is it that the Agreement be considered integrated? Is this Agreement's integration clause well drafted? Would you draft the clause any differently to communicate to a court that the document is integrated (i.e., the final expression of the parties' agreement) and supersedes any prior negotiations or agreements between the parties? Does this integration clause suggest that the Agreement is *partially* or *completely* integrated?

2. Severability Clauses

Should a court decide not to enforce a particular provision in the Agreement, § 4(h) attempts to "sever" the unenforceable provision in order to save the rest of the Agreement. This type of provision is called a "severability" clause.[46] In deciding whether or not to sever an unenforceable term, courts will look to whether or not the parties intended this.[47] To this end, courts will generally

---

more than a partially integrated agreement. Incompleteness may also be shown by other writings, which may or may not become part of a completely or partially integrated agreement."); *id.* § 216(2). Note the distinction between "writing" and "agreement."

44. *See* RESTATEMENT (SECOND) OF CONTRACTS § 210(3) (1981) ("Whether an agreement is completely or partially integrated is to be determined by the court as a question preliminary to determination of a question of interpretation or to application of the parol evidence rule."); *see also id.* cmt. b & c.

45. *See, e.g., Jarvis v. K2 Inc.*, 486 F.3d 526, 536 (9th Cir. 2007) (Washington law) ("The integration clause is not dispositive but it certainly suggests that [the parties] intended the contracts to be fully integrated."); *LaHaye v. Goodneuz Grp. LLC*, 172 F. App'x 733, 735 (9th Cir. 2006) (California law) ("Although the contract states that the agreement is binding and that no other agreements exist, the parties' inclusion of an integration clause in the written contract is but one factor in this analysis.") (internal citation and quotation marks omitted); *see also* RESTATEMENT (SECOND) OF CONTRACTS § 210 cmt. b (1981) ("That a writing was or was not adopted as a completely integrated agreement may be proved by any relevant evidence. A document in the form of a written contract, signed by both parties and apparently complete on its face, may be decisive of the issue in the absence of credible contrary evidence. But a writing cannot of itself prove its own completeness, and wide latitude must be allowed for inquiry into circumstances bearing on the intention of the parties."); *id.* § 216 cmt. e.

46. This section discusses "severability" clauses and not "savings" clauses, inasmuch as the former instructs a court to sever whole provisions or language and the latter instructs a court to interpret or modify the language of a provision so as to maintain its enforceability. In practice, the terms "severability clause" and "savings clause" are often used interchangeably. For the willingness of courts to modify provisions so as to make them reasonable (and enforceable), please see the discussion of judicial tailoring in Chapter 2.

47. *See, e.g., Jackson v. Cintas Corp.*, 425 F.3d 1313, 1317 (11th Cir. 2005) (Georgia law) ("The intent of the parties determines whether a contract is severable."); *Booker v. Robert Half Int'l., Inc.*, 413 F.3d 77, 84 (D.C. Cir. 2005) ("A critical consideration in assessing severability is giving effect to the intent of the contracting parties.") (citing *Frankenmuth Mut. Ins. Co. v. Escambia Cnty.*, 289 F.3d 723, 728-29 (11th Cir. 2002); *Transamerica*

honor a severability clause—as evidencing party intent—and enforce the rest of the contract pursuant to the terms of the severability clause.[48] However, this is not without its limits. For instance, a severability clause will not save a contract from a finding of procedural unconscionability (where a contract is the product of unfair bargaining).[49] Likewise, where a contract would be incoherent or left without an essential part if devoid of an invalid provision, courts are unlikely to sever the invalid provision—severability clause or not.[50] Accordingly, in these situations, the entire contract fails. This is consistent with the general proposition that, while it is the province of the courts to give effect to party intent, it is not their role to rewrite contracts.[51]

3. Third-Party Rights and Duties: Assignment and Third-Party Beneficiaries

a. Assignment: Transferring Rights and Duties to a Third Party

"Assignment" refers to the transfer of a party's rights (and, as the term is often used, obligations) under a contract to another person or entity. The effect

---

Ins. Co. v. Avenell, 66 F.3d 715, 722 (5th Cir. 1995)); *Sosa v. Paulos*, 924 P.2d 357, 363 (Utah 1996) ("[C]ontract provisions are severable if the parties intended severance at the time they entered into the contract.").

48. *See, e.g., Anders v. Hometown Mortg. Servs., Inc.*, 346 F.3d 1024 (11th Cir. 2003) ("Alabama law favors severability, and it gives full force and effect to severability clauses."); *Pilato v. Edge Investors, L.P.*, 609 F. Supp. 2d 1301, 1309 (S.D. Fla. 2009) ("Severability clauses are recognized and enforceable under Florida law."); *Vegesina v. Allied Informatics, Inc.*, 572 S.E.2d 51, 53 (Ga. Ct. App. 2002) ("The parties' intent may be expressed directly, through a severability clause.") (quoting *Bulloch S., Inc. v. Gosai*, 550 S.E.2d 750 (Ga. Ct. App. 2001)); *Kraisinger v. Kraisinger*, 928 A.2d 333, 341 (Pa. Super. Ct. 2007) ("A court is bound by the clear language of a contract as to severability.") (quoting *Jacobs v. CNG Transmission Corp.*, 772 A.2d 445, 451 (Pa. 2001)).

49. *See Sosa*, 924 P.2d at 364-65.

50. *See, e.g., OCA, Inc. v. Hassel*, 389 B.R. 469, 480 (E.D. La. 2008) ("[T]here is no apparent way to excise the unlawful provisions and leave anything to govern a relationship between [the parties]."); *Hill v. Names & Addresses, Inc.*, 571 N.E.2d 1085, 1100 (Ill. App. Ct. 1991) ("[C]lear and unmistakable specific provisions, which plainly exalt the invalid provisions of the restrictive covenant as 'essential' to the agreement, necessarily overcome the general and all-encompassing severability clause. . . ."); *CS-Lakeview at Gwinnett, Inc. v. Simon Prop. Grp.*, 642 S.E.2d 393, 398 (Ga. Ct. App. 2007) ("A severability clause indicates the intent of the parties where the remainder of the contract can exist without the void portion.") (quoting *Capricorn Sys. v. Pednekar*, 546 S.E.2d 554 (Ga. Ct. App. 2001)); *John R. Ray & Sons, Inc. v. Stroman*, 923 S.W.2d 80, 87 (Tex. App. 1996) ("However, when the severed portion is integral to the entire contract, a severability clause, standing alone, cannot save the contract.") (citing *Budge v. Post*, 544 F. Supp. 370, 382 (N.D. Tex. 1982)). Note that the failure of a severability clause to save a contract from procedural unconscionablility can be understood as an example of this concept: If a contract suffers from procedural unconscionablility, then striking the parts of a contract infected with the procedural unconscionablility is likely to leave little left of the contract.

51. *See, e.g., Booker*, 413 F.3d at 84-85 ("If illegality pervades . . . such that only a disintegrated fragment would remain after hacking away the unenforceable parts, the judicial effort begins to look more like rewriting the contract than fulfilling the intent of the parties."); *Federated Mut. Ins. Co. v. Bennett*, 818 S.W.2d 596, 599 (Ark. Ct. App. 1991) ("In order to accomplish appellants' purpose, it would be necessary to rewrite the covenant not to compete, and this we will not do. It has long been the rule that . . . we will not make a new contract for the parties."); *Simpson v. MSA of Myrtle Beach, Inc.*, 644 S.E.2d 663, 674 (S.C. 2007) ("[W]e hold that the intent of the parties is best achieved by severing the arbitration clause in its entirety rather than 'rewriting' the contract by severing multiple unenforceable provisions."). Furthermore, a severability clause has been held not to undo the oppressive, unenforceable nature of a contract such that the clause did not obviate the wrongfulness of the termination of that employee for failure to sign such agreement. *See Latona v. Aetna U.S. Healthcare Inc.*, 82 F. Supp. 2d 1089, 1097-98 (C.D. Cal. 1999).

of an assignment is that the "assignee" (the party to whom the contract is assigned) steps into the shoes of the "assignor" (the party assigning the contract) and enjoys the rights that the assignor would have enjoyed under the contract going forward. Traditionally, assignment refers only to the transfer of contractual *rights*, whereas "delegation" refers to the transfer of contractual *duties*. When a third party agrees to take on the duties of a contract, she is bound to perform those duties, but this does not relieve the original party (i.e., the "delegating party") of her obligations under that contract.[52] Because parties often use terms of assignment to refer to the transfer of both rights and duties, courts are likely to presume that broad language of assignment conveys both the rights and the unperformed duties of a contract, absent contractual language or evidence to the contrary.[53]

Rights and obligations under a contract are generally transferable,[54] and, accordingly, contractual provisions allowing parties to assign their rights and to delegate their obligations under an NDA are generally enforceable.[55] However, § 4(g) of the NDA provides explicitly that neither party has the right to assign the Agreement, without the other party's prior written consent. Sometimes called an "anti-assignment clause," these provisions are also generally enforceable.[56]

However, note that, as a matter of construction, a court is likely to read a provision that *prohibits* assignment of "the contract" only to prohibit the delegation of *duties* and not the assignment of *rights*.[57] Still, as the Sixth Circuit explains, "These rules of interpretation do not override express statements of the will of the parties. If the contract shows an intent by the parties to limit both

---

52. Whereas an assignor loses those rights she assigns, a delegating party is *not* relieved "of the ultimate responsibility to see that the obligation is performed." *Contemporary Mission, Inc. v. Famous Music Corp.*, 557 F.2d 918, 925 (2d Cir. 1977).

53. *See Am. Flint Glass Workers Union v. Anchor Resolution Corp.*, 197 F.3d 76, 81 (3d Cir. 1999) ("[The] dominant consensus conforms to the clear meaning of the language involved: that an assignment of a contract as such involves a commitment by the assignee to perform all obligations under the contract, as well as to acquire all rights created by the contract."); Restatement (Second) of Contracts § 328 (1981) ("[A]n assignment in . . . general terms is an assignment of the assignor's rights and a delegation of his unperformed duties under the contract."); *see also* U.C.C. § 2-210(4) (2003).

54. *See Physical Distrib. Servs., Inc. v. R.R. Donnelley & Sons Co.*, 561 F.3d 792, 794-95 (8th Cir. 2009) ("Contract rights are generally assignable, except where the assignment is (1) prohibited by statute; (2) prohibited by contract; (3) or where the contract involves a matter of personal trust or confidence.") (quoting *Travertine Corp. v. Lexington-Silverwood*, 683 N.W.2d 267, 270 (Minn. 2004)); *Contemporary Mission*, 557 F.2d at 924 ("In fact, most obligations can be delegated as long as performance by the delegate will not vary materially from performance by the delegant."); *see also* Restatement (Second) of Contracts § 317 (1981). However, some rights are not generally transferrable; notably, licensed intellectual property rights (e.g., patent, copyright, trademark) are not transferable absent language in the license that expressly provides that the licensed rights are transferrable. *See Cincom Sys., Inc. v. Novelis Corp.*, 581 F.3d 431, 436 (6th Cir. 2009).

55. *See, e.g., Chemetall GmbH v. Zr Energy, Inc.*, No. 99 C 4334, 2000 WL 1808568, at *2-4 (N.D. Ill. Dec. 6, 2000) ("Illinois courts have recognized the assignability of confidentiality and non-compete agreements.") (citing *Hexacomb Corp. v. GTW Enters., Inc.*, 875 F. Supp. 457 (N.D. Ill. 1993)), *aff'd*, 320 F.3d 714 (7th Cir. 2003).

56. *See, e.g., Physical Distrib. Servs.*, 561 F.3d at 794-95 (finding that although anti-assignment clauses are enforceable, the rights under the clause in this case were waived); *Travertine*, 683 N.W.2d at 273; *Rumbin v. Utica Mut. Ins. Co.*, 757 A.2d 526 (Conn. 2000); *see also* Restatement (Second) of Contracts § 322 (1981).

57. *See* Restatement (Second) of Contracts § 322(1) (1981); *see also* U.C.C. § 2-210(4) (2003). *See, e.g., Cedar Point Apartments, Ltd. v. Cedar Point Inv. Corp.*, 693 F.2d 748, 753 (8th Cir. 1982); *Charles L. Bowman & Co. v. Erwin*, 468 F.2d 1293, 1297-98 (5th Cir. 1972).

delegations of duties and assignment of rights . . . , then the interpretive default rules are inapplicable."[58] Accordingly, an express prohibition of the assignment of *rights* under the contract would not implicate the interpretive rule and would express the parties' intent to prohibit the assignment of rights.

Here, the Microsoft Agreement prohibits assignment of "this Agreement" (without the other party's consent). How is a court likely to construe the clause? To effect a prohibition of the assignment of *rights* and, thereby, to avoid this rule of construction, how would you draft this provision? Do note that, "[g]iven the importance of free assignability, . . . antiassignment clauses are construed narrowly whenever possible,"[59] and that, despite a drafter's best efforts, a court may still decide not to enforce an anti-assignment clause in certain circumstances.[60]

Furthermore, subsection 4(g) specifies that assignment includes assignment "by operation of law, sale of securities or assets, merger or otherwise." Why do you suppose the parties included this language? A party may transfer her rights under a contract by means other than an ordinary "assignment," namely when another entity acquires the party or merges with the party (a topic we take up in much greater detail in Chapter 6). Accordingly, § 4(g) attempts to protect a party against the nonconsensual transfer of duties (and perhaps rights) no matter the name or form of the transaction that accomplishes the transfer (or something tantamount to a transfer).

Assuming an anti-assignment provision is effective to prohibit the assignment of rights, what remedies does a contracting party have if the other party breaches an anti-assignment provision and assigns her rights under an agreement? Most courts will distinguish between the *right* to assign and the *power* to assign.[61] Under this view, an enforceable anti-assignment provision that bars the assignment of contractual rights only withholds a party's *right* to assign her contractual rights.[62] Accordingly, if a party assigns her rights in contravention of the enforceable anti-assignment provision, the party *will* have breached the contract, but the non-breaching party will only be entitled to damages for the

---

58. *Riley v. Hewlett-Packard Co.*, 36 F. App'x 194, 196 (6th Cir. 2002) (Michigan law) (internal citations omitted).

59. *Rumbin*, 757 A.2d at 531.

60. *See, e.g., Seaboard Constr. Co. v. The Weitz Co.*, No. CV208-105, 2009 WL 3855185, at *5 (S.D. Ga. Nov. 17, 2009) ("[O]nce a party to a contract performs its obligations under a contract, its right to enforce the other party's liability for payment under the contract may be assigned without the other party's consent, even if the contract contains an anti-assignment clause."); Restatement (Second) of Contracts § 322 cmt. b (1981) (explaining that certain anti-assignment provisions will not be effective).

61. *See Rumbin*, 757 A.2d at 531 ("In interpreting antiassignment clauses, the majority of jurisdictions now distinguish between the assignor's 'right' to assign and the 'power' to assign. . . . ").

62. *See id.* at 528 ("[A]n antiassignment provision that does not limit the power to assign or expressly invalidate the assignment does not render the assignment of the annuity ineffective."); *Pravin Banker Assocs., Ltd. v. Banco Popular Del Peru*, 109 F.3d 850 (2d Cir. 1997); *Pro Cardiaco Pronto Socorro Cardiologica, S.A. v. Trussell*, 863 F. Supp. 135 (S.D.N.Y. 1994).

breach.[63] On the other hand, an anti-assignment provision that explicitly provides that an assignment is "void"—or that the putative assigning party otherwise has no power to assign her rights under the contract—will likely be found to have withheld a party's *power* (in addition to her right) to assign.[64] Such a provision, if enforced, renders the assignment itself void, as if the transfer to the third party never occurred at all.[65]

b. Binding Third Parties

Note that § 4(g) contains an extremely common provision that attempts to make the Agreement binding on successors and assigns—a successor, being the legal entity that exists after a party merges or is acquired, and an assign, being the party to whom a party transfers its rights under the Agreement.[66] It is a basic proposition of contract law that a party must manifest assent to (i.e., accept) a contract before she can be legally bound by that contract.[67] Accordingly, query the work done by § 4(g) itself and whether the Agreement may actually bind—that is *impose duties* on—third parties, not party to the Agreement. Likewise, § 1(a) defines "Affiliate" and imposes a duty on the Receiving Party, before sharing Confidential Information with an Affiliate, to have the Affiliate sign an agreement, binding her to the terms of this Agreement. Under this Agreement alone, could the Disclosing Party have a claim against an Affiliate for breach of the Agreement?

c. Benefitting Third Parties

Conversely, a contract between two parties may *give rights* to persons not party to that contract. Such persons are called "third-party beneficiaries." Whether a third party is a beneficiary of a contract generally turns on the intent of the parties to the contract.[68] Because this Agreement is silent about third-party beneficiaries, it is unlikely that a court would characterize a third party as having

---

63. *See Rumbin*, 757 A.2d at 534 ("An assignor who breaches a contractual provision limiting his or her right to assign will be liable for any damages that result from that assignment."); *Bel-Ray Co. v. Chemrite (Pty) Ltd.*, 181 F.3d 435, 442 (3d Cir. 1999).

64. *See Rumbin*, 757 A.2d at 531 ("[A]n antiassignment provision that limits the *right* to assign does not void an assignment between an assignor and assignee unless there is also an express provision limiting the *power* to assign or a provision voiding the assignment itself."); *Pravin Banker*, 109 F.3d at 856 ("To reveal the intent necessary to preclude the power to assign, or cause an assignment violative of contractual provisions to be wholly void, [a contractual] clause must contain express provisions that any assignment shall be void or invalid if not made in a certain specified way.") (internal citations and quotation marks omitted).

65. *See supra* note 64.

66. We separately discuss the issues of when a successor is liable for the obligations of a company it acquires in Chapter 6.

67. *See* Restatement (Second) of Contracts § 17 (1981).

68. *See, e.g., Robins Dry Dock & Repair Co. v. Flint*, 275 U.S. 303, 307 (1927) ("Before a stranger can avail himself of the exceptional privilege of suing for a breach of an agreement, to which he is not a party, he must, at least, show that it was intended for his direct benefit.") (internal quotation marks omitted); *Cooper Power Sys., Inc. v. Union Carbide Chems. & Plastics Co.*, 123 F.3d 675, 680 (7th Cir. 1997) (finding that there was no evidence

rights under the Agreement, absent evidence otherwise to suggest that the parties intended to benefit the third party.[69] To this end, agreements will often contain prophylactic provisions that expressly state that the parties did not intend to benefit any third parties whatsoever. These provisions are generally enforceable. However, when a separate provision specifically states an intention to benefit a third party, the specific provision granting third-party rights will be effective despite a blanket provision in the same agreement that disclaims any third-party benefit. For example, a contract, that included the following provision (section 10.5), was held still to create third-party beneficiaries:

> This Agreement, the exhibits and schedules hereto, the Surviving Intercompany Contracts and the Confidentiality Agreement . . . are not intended to confer upon any Person other than the parties hereto, the Company, the Company Subsidiaries, the Purchaser Indemnified Persons and the Seller Indemnified Persons any rights or remedies hereunder.[70]

This is because that same contract included, by amendment, the following provision (section 6 of the amendment):

> (a) Purchaser [GTG] agrees that neither Purchaser nor the Company [VeriFone] nor any Company Subsidiary will terminate any U.S. employees of the Company or its affiliates (the 'U.S. VeriFone Employees') during the first sixty (60) days after Closing.
>
> (b) Purchaser agrees that the Equivalent-Severance Policy (as defined below) for U.S. VeriFone Employees that it would otherwise apply in the first ninety (90) days of its ownership of the Company will instead apply in the ninety (90) days beginning sixty-one (61) days after the Closing. In other words, if Purchaser concludes that it will terminate any U.S. VeriFone Employees at any time through one hundred fifty (150) days after Closing, any U.S. VeriFone Employees who are notified within that time that they will lose their jobs will receive severance benefits from Purchaser or the Company or a Company Subsidiary that are approximately equivalent to the cash compensation element of the Seller's [Hewlett-Packard's] unassigned pool benefits for the Seller's U.S. employees which the parties agree shall be no less than six months base salary (the 'Equivalent Severance Policy').[71]

The California Court of Appeals explained:

---

of intent to benefit a third party, and as a merely incidental beneficiary, the party could not maintain its claims); *McCarthy v. Azure*, 22 F.3d 351, 362 (1st Cir. 1994) (noting that intent is the crux of the issue in third-party beneficiary contract interpretation cases).

69. *See, e.g., Bridas S.A.P.I.C. v. Gov't of Turkmenistan*, 345 F.3d 347, 355 (5th Cir. 2003); *Fleetwood Enters., Inc. v. Gaskamp*, 280 F.3d 1069, 1075-76 (5th Cir. 2002) (under Texas law, "the intent to make someone a third-party beneficiary must be clearly written or evidenced in the contract"); *Azure*, 22 F.3d at 362 ("[A] person aspiring to such status must show with special clarity that the contracting parties intended to confer a benefit on him.").

70. *Prouty v. Gores Tech. Grp.*, 18 Cal. Rptr. 3d 178, 180 n.1 (Cal. Ct. App. 2004).

71. *Id.* at 180 n.2.

Applying the law of third party beneficiaries to the language of the contract discloses GTG and Hewlett-Packard expressly intended to grant plaintiffs the promises contained in section 6 of the amendment. Indeed, section 6 is a classic third party provision. It is patently intended to preclude early termination of the affected employees and to provide those terminated soon after the closing with severance benefits similar to what they would have received had they been terminated when employed by Hewlett-Packard. The provision expressly benefits them, and only them. . . .

GTG disagrees with our conclusion, asserting section 10.5 precludes plaintiffs from becoming third party beneficiaries. . . . If GTG and Hewlett-Packard had not wanted to benefit plaintiffs, they would not have written section 6, nor would they have amended section 5.7 of the agreement to indemnify Hewlett-Packard from GTG's breach of section 6.

Section 6 of the amendment does conflict with section 10.5 of the stock purchase agreement, and as incorporated into the amendment by section 8(b) of the amendment. Under rules of contract construction, however, the mere existence of sections 10.5 and 8(b) does not end this matter. The latter two provisions cannot be harmonized with section 6. Sections 10.5 and 8(b) state generally no rights or remedies exist under the contract to third persons; section 6 expressly grants rights to specific third persons regarding their employment with GTG. In this circumstance, under well established principles of contract interpretation, when a general and a particular provision are inconsistent, the particular and specific provision is paramount to the general provision. Section 6 of the amendment thus is an exception to section 10.5 of the original contract and section 8(b) of the amendment, and the plaintiffs can enforce it.[72]

4. Termination and Survival

Notice that § 4(i) of the NDA provides that either party may terminate the Agreement with or without cause (that is, for any or no reason at all), after providing 90 days' notice. However, § 4(i) further provides that the parties' confidentiality obligations survive the termination of the Agreement. "Survival" works much as you might expect: The "termination" of an agreement means that the contract no longer imposes rights or obligations on any of the parties thereto; however, "survival" of some or all of an agreement's terms means that the rights and obligations imposed by those terms still apply with legally binding force, beyond termination. Is it clear to you from the NDA which provisions are to survive termination? Note that contracts will commonly list which specific provisions are to survive.

---

72. *Id.* at 184-86 (internal citations omitted).

In the context of NDAs, survival of confidentiality obligations is important, as neither trade-secrets law nor the common law is likely to step in to continue any obligations of non-disclosure.[73]

5. Choice of Law and Forum

Subsection 4(f) of the Microsoft NDA contains a "choice-of-law" provision, which specifies that the Agreement should be interpreted and enforced in accordance with the laws of the State of Washington. Choice-of-law provisions are very common in commercial agreements.

As seen in the Coca-Cola NDA at the beginning of this chapter, choice-of-law provisions will often provide that a certain state's law governs the contract *without regard for the state's choice-of-law principles*. The purpose of this language is to preempt the forum court (the court where the action is brought) from engaging in its own choice-of-law analysis. That is, this language instructs the court to disregard its own choice-of-law principles and to defer to the parties' specification of governing law. Courts are often unwilling to abide by such instructions and will still engage in their own choice-of-law analysis.[74]

Still, courts are likely to arrive at the same ends, as, in applying their own choice-of-law rules, courts generally give great deference to the parties' contractually specified choice of governing law.[75] Indeed, a court may even defer to a contractual designation of governing law with regard to a *tort* action between contractual parties (at least where the tort action is incidental to the contract), where the language of the contractual choice-of-law provision is sufficiently broad to apply to the relevant tort.[76] Generally, courts will defer to choice-of-law provisions so long as there is either some reasonable basis for the parties' choice of law or some substantial relationship between the parties (or their contract)

---

73. *See* CALLMANN ON UNFAIR COMPETITION, TR. & MONO. § 14:6 (West 4th ed. 2009) (citing *All West Pet Supply Co. v. Hill's Pet Prods. Div., Colgate-Palmolive Co.*, 840 F. Supp. 1433 (D. Kan. 1993)); *see also supra* note 25. That is, trade-secrets law only forbids misappropriation of trade secrets, and it may not be misappropriation to use what was another's trade secret, when such trade secret is acquired pursuant to a confidentiality agreement, after the confidentiality agreement expires by its own terms.

74. *See, e.g., Lynch Grp. v. Pohlman, Inc.*, No. 06-13501, 2007 WL 118937, at *3 (E.D. Mich. 2007) (noting that courts should consider a number of factors in choice-of-law analysis); *Airtel Wireless, LLC v. Montana Elecs. Co.*, 393 F. Supp. 2d 777, 783-84 (D. Minn. 2005) (noting that the parties' choice of forum will still be considered valuable evidence in the court's determination).

75. *See, e.g., Cook v. Little Caesar Enters., Inc.*, 210 F.3d 653, 656 (6th Cir. 2000) (noting that Michigan law allows parties to choose what law will govern their contract); *Herring Gas Co., Inc. v. Magee*, 22 F.3d 604, 605 (5th Cir. 1994) (recognizing that the law chosen by the parties will always be applied unless it would be "contrary to a fundamental policy of a state which has a materially greater interest than the chosen state in the determination of the particular issue").

76. *See, e.g., Hitachi Credit Am. Corp. v. Signet Bank*, 166 F.3d 614, 628 (4th Cir. 1999) (Virginia law) (citing *In re Allegheny Int'l, Inc.*, 954 F.2d 167, 178 (3d Cir. 1992); *Moses v. Bus. Card Express, Inc.*, 929 F.2d 1131, 1139 (6th Cir. 1991)).

and the state of the chosen law.[77] To illustrate, the official comment to the *Restatement (Second) of Conflict of Laws* explains:

> When the state of the chosen law has some substantial relationship to the parties or the contract, the parties will be held to have had a reasonable basis for their choice. This will be the case, for example, when this state is that where performance by one of the parties is to take place or where one of the parties is domiciled or has his principal place of business. The same will also be the case when this state is the place of contracting except, perhaps, in the unusual situation where this place is wholly fortuitous and bears no real relation either to the contract or to the parties. These situations are mentioned only for purposes of example. There are undoubtedly still other situations where the state of the chosen law will have a sufficiently close relationship to the parties and the contract to make the parties' choice reasonable.
>
> The parties to a multistate contract may have a reasonable basis for choosing a state with which the contract has no substantial relationship. For example, when contracting in countries whose legal systems are strange to them as well as relatively immature, the parties should be able to choose a law on the ground that they know it well and that it is sufficiently developed. For only in this way can they be sure of knowing accurately the extent of their rights and duties under the contract. So parties to a contract for the transportation of goods by sea between two countries with relatively undeveloped legal systems should be permitted to submit their contract to some well-known and highly elaborated commercial law.[78]

Note that New York and Delaware have passed statutes that provide that parties to certain contracts (in the case of New York, involving consideration of $250,000 or more; in the case of Delaware, involving $100,000 or more) may contractually select New York law or Delaware law, respectively, regardless of whether a reasonable relationship exists.[79]

On the other hand, a court may refuse to honor a choice-of-law provision where the application of the chosen law would contradict a fundamental public policy of the forum state.[80] For example, a court in California has refused to enforce a choice-of-law provision (selecting the law of a non-California state)

---

77. *See* Restatement (Second) of Conflict of Laws § 187(2) (1971); *see also, e.g., Tschira v. Willingham*, 135 F.3d 1077, 1083 (6th Cir. 1998) (Tennessee law).

78. *See* Restatement (Second) of Conflicts § 187 cmt. f (1971); *see also, e.g., McBride v. Mkt. St. Mortg.*, No. 07-804, 2010 WL 2180608, at *6 (10th Cir. 2010) (Wyoming law) ("Georgia has a reasonable relationship to the parties and transaction in this case. Market Street's parent corporation, NetBank Inc., is headquartered in Georgia and the Agreement was derived from a form created and used by NetBank."); *Armarine Brokerage, Inc. v. OneBeacon Ins. Co.*, 307 F. App'x 562, 564-65 (2d Cir. 2009) (New York law) ("[T]he parties had a 'reasonable basis' for selecting Pennsylvania law as it is where the relevant corporate predecessor of OneBeacon was incorporated and had its principal offices, and where the parties negotiated the Broker's Agreement.").

79. N.Y. Gen. Oblig. Law § 5-1401 (Consol. 1984); Del. Code. Ann. tit. 6, § 2708 (2005).

80. *See Dykes v. DePuy, Inc.*, 140 F.3d 31, 39 (1st Cir. 1998).

with respect to a non-competition covenant because non-competition covenants are unenforceable under, and contrary to a fundamental public policy of, California law.[81]

Subsection 4(f) of the Microsoft NDA further contains a "forum-selection" clause, which is a provision that specifies an exclusive (as in this case) or non-exclusive jurisdiction and venue for disputes to be adjudicated between the parties. Here, the clause provides that the parties may only bring an action in federal or state court in King County, Washington. While once viewed with disfavor by American courts, forum-selection provisions are now generally viewed as presumptively valid.[82] Absent a showing of some compelling reason (e.g., fraud, undue influence, unfair bargaining) *not* to enforce a forum-selection clause, they are likely to be honored.[83] Notice, then, that selecting, say, New York as an exclusive forum allows parties to take advantage of the New York statute that honors the selection of New York law, in certain contracts, even absent a reasonable relationship to New York. Also, of interest, a court in California has honored an exclusive forum-selection clause, even where doing so meant an action regarding a non-competition covenant would be heard in a forum willing to enforce non-competition covenants.[84]

Drafting Note: Forum-Selection Clauses; Exclusivity and Courts

In reading or writing a forum-selection clause, a couple of basic questions are whether the provision specifies a permissive (i.e., non-exclusive) or mandatory (i.e., exclusive) forum, as discussed above, and to which courts the provision refers.

For example, specifying that parties "may" bring suit in certain courts generally has a permissive and non-exclusive effect; this means that the non-moving party has consented to jurisdiction and venue in the specified courts. Alternatively, parties may specify that jurisdiction is mandatory and exclusive, by providing that the parties "may only" bring suit in certain courts or by stating plainly that the parties agree to "exclusive jurisdiction" in certain courts, as the parties did in Section 4(f) in the above Microsoft NDA. While this linguistic distinction

---

81. *See, e.g., In re Gault S. Bay Litig.*, No. C 07-04659 JW, 2008 WL 4065843, at *5 (N.D. Cal. Aug. 27, 2008). Please see Chapter 2 for more on non-competition covenants.

82. *See* RESTATEMENT (SECOND) OF CONFLICTS § 80 (1971) ("The parties' agreement as to the place of the action . . . will be given effect unless it is unfair or unreasonable."); *Nat'l Equip. Rental, Ltd. v. Szukhent*, 375 U.S. 311, 315-16 (1964) ("[I]t is settled . . . that parties to a contract may agree in advance to submit to the jurisdiction of a given court, to permit notice to be served by the opposing party, or even to waive notice altogether."); *see also M/S Bremen v. Zapata Off-Shore Co.*, 407 U.S. 1, 15 (1972) (noting that in federal courts, forum-selection clauses "should control absent a strong showing that it should be set aside"); *Hugel v. Corp. of Lloyd's*, 999 F.2d 206, 210 (7th Cir.1993) (noting that forum-selection clauses are "*prima facie* valid and should be enforced unless enforcement is shown by the resisting party to be unreasonable under the circumstances") (emphasis in original and internal citations omitted); RICHARD A. LORD, 7 WILLISTON ON CONTRACTS § 15:15 (West 4th ed. 2009).

83. *See supra* note 82.

84. *See, e.g., Whipple Indus., Inc. v. Opcon AB*, No. CV-F-05-0902 REC SMS, 2005 WL 2175871, at *9-10 (E.D. Cal. Sep. 7, 2005).

may appear basic, this very issue is a common feature of litigation, and a prudent party will be careful to specify precisely whether the parties agree to permissive or mandatory jurisdiction and venue.

Another issue involves the specification of the courts with regard to which the parties are consenting to jurisdiction. Unclear drafting has led to litigation over the meaning of "of"—namely, whether a federal court sitting in a state constitutes a court "of" that state.[85] Put simply, the answer is "no."[86] If a party wishes to include federal courts among those specified for jurisdiction, the party should refer to the courts "*in*" (and not "of") a desired state. Or, more to the point, a party wishing to select federal courts may wish to specify "federal" courts expressly by name. We see the parties did just this in Section 4(f) of the Microsoft NDA, selecting exclusive jurisdiction in the "federal courts sitting in King County, Washington," and providing that, should there be no federal subject matter jurisdiction, the parties agree to exclusive jurisdiction and venue in the state courts in that same location.

6. Stipulating Remedies by Contract

a. Stipulating Equitable Relief by Contract

Section 3 ("Remedies") of the Microsoft NDA attempts to bolster a party's ability to obtain injunctive or other equitable relief. In general, before issuing a preliminary or permanent injunction, courts typically require a showing that the moving party will suffer irreparable harm should an injunction not issue and that remedies at law (e.g., monetary damages) will not provide the plaintiff with an adequate remedy, such that a remedy in equity is necessary. In § 3, both parties acknowledge that there would be an inadequate remedy at law (i.e., "monetary damages may not be a sufficient remedy") in the event of a breach of the NDA and that each party is entitled to seek injunctive relief. Parties also commonly stipulate in a contract that a breach of the contract may or will cause irreparable harm. What is the actual effect of these provisions? Will courts follow contractual parties' designations or acknowledgments in awarding injunctive relief? Please consider the following case.

---

85. *See, e.g., Am. Soda, LLP v. Filter Wastewater Group, Inc.*, 428 F.3d 921, 926 (10th Cir. 2005) ("[T]he federal court located in Colorado is not a court *of* the *State* of Colorado but rather a court *of* the *United States of America*.") (emphasis in original); *Dixon v. TSE Int'l Inc.*, 330 F.3d 396, 398 (5th Cir. 2003) ("Federal district courts may be *in* Texas, but they are not *of* Texas.").

86. *See supra* note 85.

Dominion Video Satellite, Inc. v. EchoStar Satellite Corp.
United States Court of Appeals, Tenth Circuit, 2004.
356 F.3d 1256.

SEYMOUR, Circuit Judge.

[Dominion and EchoStar were operators of direct broadcast satellite systems. Dominion broadcast its network as SkyAngel, and EchoStar broadcast its network as the DISH Network. For purposes of complying with Federal Communications Commission ("FCC") regulations, EchoStar and Dominion entered into a contract (the "Agreement") for the lease and sublease of various transponders and accompanying FCC license rights held by Dominion. The parties included an exclusivity clause in the Agreement, giving Dominion "the exclusive right to transmit Christian programming from EchoStar's satellite" and allowing EchoStar to "broadcast everything except predominately Christian programming." EchoStar proceeded to broadcast two predominately Christian channels on the DISH Network, and Dominion sued for breach of the exclusivity provision and sought to enjoin EchoStar from broadcasting the two channels.]

. . . The Agreement . . . states that should either party breach the agreement, money damages would be insufficient, the harm from the breach would be irreparable, and the non-breaching party would have the right to obtain specific performance or injunctive relief.[5] The Agreement stipulated that "[a]t the election of either party, any matter not resolved amicably between the parties to the satisfaction of both parties, shall be subject to mandatory binding arbitration, and the other party shall submit to arbitration." . . .

It is well established that in order to obtain a preliminary injunction, the moving party must establish four factors: (1) it will suffer irreparable harm if the injunction is not granted, (2) its threatened injury outweighs the harm caused to the opposing party as a result of the injunction, (3) the injunction is not adverse to the public interest, and (4) it has a substantial likelihood of success on the

---

5. Article XII (Term, Termination and Other Remedies on Default), section 12.3.1 (Specific Performance) states:

> the rights and benefits of each of the parties pursuant to this Agreement are unique and that no adequate remedy exists at law if any of the parties shall fail to perform, or breaches, any of its obligations hereunder; that it would be difficult to determine the amount of damages resulting therefrom, and that such breach would cause irreparable injury to the nonbreaching parties. . . . Accordingly, each of the parties hereto hereby agrees that the nonbreaching parties shall, in addition to any other remedies that such nonbreaching parties may have hereunder, at law, in equity or otherwise, have the right to have any and all obligations, undertakings, agreements, and other provisions of this Agreement specifically performed by such nonbreaching parties and shall have the right to obtain an order or decree of such specific performance, or a preliminary or permanent injunction (without the necessity of posting or filing a bond or other security) against the breach or threatened breach of any term or in aid of the exercise of any power or right granted in this Agreement. . . . It is expressly agreed that monetary damages alone would not be adequate to fully and fairly compensate for a breach by the breaching party of any provision of this Agreement.

merits of the case. In examining these factors, courts have consistently noted that "[b]ecause a showing of probable irreparable harm is the single most important prerequisite for the issuance of a preliminary injunction, the moving party must first demonstrate that such injury is likely before the other requirements for the issuance of an injunction will be considered." Likewise, because "a preliminary injunction is an extraordinary remedy, the right to relief must be clear and unequivocal."

In granting Dominion's request for a preliminary injunction against Echo-Star, the district court found, in part, that Dominion had suffered irreparable harm as a result of EchoStar's alleged breach of the Agreement. The court based its determination on two intertwined grounds. First, it gave great weight to section 12.3.1 of the parties' Agreement, in which EchoStar and Dominion agreed that any violation of their contract would constitute irreparable injury and would therefore warrant injunctive relief. While the court declined to bind itself wholly to the parties' private determination regarding irreparable harm, it nonetheless concluded that "the understanding reflected in § 12.3.1 of the parties' Agreement in this case is a clear and unavoidable concession of [irreparable harm] and I will treat it as such."

In making its irreparable harm determination, however, the district court rejected all of Dominion's proffered arguments regarding how it suffered harm as a result of EchoStar's breach of the Agreement. Based on evidence presented by EchoStar, the court dismissed Dominion's assertion that its very existence was threatened by EchoStar's broadcast of Daystar and FamilyNet, noting Dominion had not shown it was "losing customers or [its] competitive position in the marketplace because of the violation of the exclusivity provisions. At most, Dominion simply states that such losses are an inevitable result. The statement is wholly conclusory and, standing alone, would not justify the issuance of a preliminary injunction." The court similarly rejected Dominion's contentions that it was close to business failure and that damage to its business could not be quantified:

> In fact, the opposite appears to be the case. EchoStar's expert witnesses persuasively demonstrated that a loss in the marketplace because of a particular reason would be readily determinable if proper methodology were used. There is simply no basis for finding that Dominion has suffered harm to its goodwill as a result of EchoStar's actions.

In the appeal before us, Dominion does not challenge any of these findings.

Despite the court's wholesale rejection of Dominion's specific arguments regarding irreparable harm, the court nonetheless found Dominion had satisfied the irreparable harm factor of the preliminary injunction test. In reaching its conclusion, the court focused on what it deemed to be the unique nature of the exclusivity provisions of the Agreement. The court found that by leasing eight transponders on EchoStar's satellite and then subleasing six of those transponders and their accompanying FCC license rights back to EchoStar,

Dominion limited its viewing market to customers who will either own or purchase DISH-brand equipment. Moreover, Dominion did so in exchange for the exclusive right to broadcast Christian programming to such customers, while granting EchoStar the exclusive right to broadcast all other types of programming. In examining EchoStar's alleged breach of the Agreement's exclusivity provisions, the district court found "it is the loss of programming exclusivity itself that creates the irreparable harm. Not only did Dominion and EchoStar say as much in § 12.3.1, but the very essence of the Agreement establishes it."

In making its irreparable harm finding, the district court thus essentially determined that Dominion's loss of exclusivity rights, in and of itself, constituted the requisite irreparable harm. It found such harm existed regardless of Dominion's inability to show any threat to its existence, damage to its goodwill, loss of customers, or loss of its competitive position in the market. Such harm existed, the district court held, irrespective of its conclusion that Dominion's potential marketplace losses could be quantified in damages. . . .

The district court's related justification for finding irreparable harm was the parties' stipulation to it in section 12.3.1 of the Agreement. While courts have given weight to parties' contractual statements regarding the nature of harm and attendant remedies that will arise as a result of a breach of a contract, they nonetheless characteristically hold that such statements alone are insufficient to support a finding of irreparable harm and an award of injunctive relief.

Although, EchoStar and Dominion agreed that any breach of the Agreement would constitute irreparable harm and would warrant an award of injunctive relief, that stipulation without more is insufficient to support an irreparable harm finding. Because the district court articulated no other ground to substantiate a finding of irreparable harm, the court erred in determining Dominion suffered irreparable harm by EchoStar's breach of the Agreement. On this record, it is apparent that should Dominion win in arbitration on the merits, any damage caused by EchoStar's breach of the exclusivity agreement can be quantified in damages. Consequently, we reverse the preliminary injunction entered in this case.[8] . . .

Comments

A court is only one of several potential audiences for a contract, and as touched upon in *EchoStar* and discussed further in Chapter 2, parties may find themselves before an arbitrator, attempting to enforce their contractual rights. An arbitrator may have the power to award injunctive or other equitable relief—and courts are likely to enforce such an arbitral decree—if the parties

---

8. Because we determine the district court erred in its irreparable harm finding, we need not address the other preliminary injunction factors. . . .

intended for the arbitrator to have these powers.[87] Accordingly, while a contractual provision that stipulates that injunctive relief is available may give some weight to a party's argument for injunctive relief for breach of contract,[88] this provision is also helpful for *empowering* an arbitrator to award injunctive relief.[89] However, this is not to suggest that a provision stipulating equitable relief will determine the matter of whether a court or arbitrator will award equitable relief.

b. Stipulating Monetary Damages by Contract: Liquidated Damages

As parties may attempt to provide by contract that equitable relief will be available upon breach, they may also attempt to establish an amount of monetary damages by contract. Given that damages for breach of contract are often difficult to prove or calculate, a party may wish to negotiate for a "liquidated damages" provision in her contract. A liquidated-damages provision sets by contract the amount of damages a party will be due in the event of a specified breach of the contract. Such clauses may specify damages as a fixed sum or with a formula or schedule that calculates damages based on certain inputs. What makes damages liquidated is not that they are a fixed sum but that their measurement is determined by contract.

(1) The "Reasonableness" of Liquidated-Damages Provisions

Courts respect the intent of contractual parties to agree upfront and freely to contract about what damages a party should recover in the event of a breach of the contract. However, it is a fundamental principle of contracts that contract law compensates and does not punish.[90] Accordingly, courts will only enforce a liquidated-damages provision that does not amount to a "penalty." So, the question is: What qualifies as an enforceable liquidated-damages provision and what qualifies as an unenforceable penalty?

While courts historically viewed liquidated damages with skepticism and favored a construction of the provisions as penalties, the law of liquidated damages is "chastened by an emerging presumption against interpreting

---

87. *See* Thomas H. Oehmke, 3 Commercial Arbitration § 119:1 (2010).

88. *See, e.g., Ticor Title Ins. Co. v. Cohen*, 173 F.3d 63, 69 (2d Cir. 1999) (New York law) ("In fact, the employment contract sought to be enforced concedes that in the event of Cohen's breach of the post-employment competition provision, Ticor shall be entitled to injunctive relief, because it would cause irreparable injury. Such, we think, might arguably be viewed as an admission by Cohen that plaintiff will suffer irreparable harm were he to breach the contract's non-compete provision.").

89. *See supra* note 87. Please see the discussion of arbitration in Chapter 2.

90. *See* Restatement (Second) of Contracts § 355 cmt. a (1981) ("The purposes of awarding contract damages is to compensate the injured party. . . . For this reason, courts in contract cases do not award damages to punish the party in breach or to serve as an example to others unless the conduct constituting the breach is also a tort for which punitive damages are recoverable.").

liquidated-damages clauses as penalty clauses."[91] The test for whether a liquidated-damages provision is enforceable varies from state to state. The basic formulation requires that the provision be "reasonable" and that actual damages be difficult to estimate.

In general, before enforcing a liquidated-damages provision, a court will require that the contractual determination of damages bear a reasonable relationship to the actual damages that would result from the breach. Under the *Restatement* approach, a provision may be "reasonable" if the contractually determined amount of damages either: (1) "approximates the actual loss that has resulted from the particular breach, even though it may not approximate the loss that might have been anticipated under other possible breaches"; or (2) "approximates the loss anticipated at the time of the making of the contract, even though it may not approximate the actual loss."[92] Accordingly, that actual damages *turn out* to be disproportionate vis-à-vis a liquidated amount is generally not enough to make a liquidated-damages provision a penalty.[93] However, courts vary in their approaches to liquidated damages; for example, some courts *will* invalidate a provision as a penalty if the liquidated-damages amount turns out to be disproportionate to the actual damages, at the time of breach, without considering whether the amount approximated the loss anticipated at the time of contracting.[94]

As an illustration, the Seventh Circuit found the following provision to include an unenforceable penalty:

> In consideration of the special equipment [i.e., the new bagging system] to be acquired and furnished by LAKE-RIVER for handling the product, CARBORUN-DUM shall, during the initial three-year term of this Agreement, ship to LAKE-RIVER for bagging a minimum quantity of [22,500 tons]. If, at the end of the three-year term, this minimum quantity shall not have been shipped, LAKE-RIVER shall invoice CARBORUNDUM at the then prevailing rates for the difference between the quantity bagged and the minimum guaranteed.[95]

---

91. *XCO Int'l Inc. v. Pac. Scientific Co.*, 369 F.3d 998, 1003 (7th Cir. 2004).

92. RESTATEMENT (SECOND) OF CONTRACTS § 356 cmt. b (1981).

93. *See, e.g., Choice Hotels Int'l, Inc. v. Chewl's Hospitality, Inc.*, 91 F. App'x 810, 817 (4th Cir. 2003) (Maryland law) ("The fact that actual damages turn out to be less than those stipulated in the liquidated damages provision does not characterize or stamp the stipulation as a penalty.") (internal citations and quotation marks omitted); *Yockey v. Horn*, 880 F.2d 945, 953 (7th Cir. 1989) ("As we have noted, the Restatement provides that the reasonableness of the amount set in a liquidated damages clause is to be looked at as of the time of contracting and at the time of actual breach. If at *either* time the estimate is reasonable, the clause will be enforced. Illinois law seems to conform to this model.") (internal citations omitted).

94. *See, e.g., In re Dow Corning Corp.*, 419 F.3d 543, 549-50 (6th Cir. 2005) (Texas law) ("In addition, . . . liquidated damages must not be disproportionate to actual damages, as measured at the time of the breach. Thus, if the liquidated damages are disproportionate to the actual damages, the clause will not be enforced and recovery will be limited to the actual damages proven.") (internal citations and quotation marks omitted).

95. *Lake River Corp. v. Carborundum Co.*, 769 F.2d 1284, 1286 (7th Cir. 1985).

This was because, as Judge Posner explained, the provision would liquidate damages at an amount greater than actual damages in all possible worlds.[96] The actual damages calculation would require reducing any damages award by the amount Lake River saved due to Carborundum's breach. However, the liquidated-damages provision in this case did not take into account expenses avoided due to breach. Instead, the clause required that Carborundum pay Lake River the same price it would have had Carborundum met its minimum quantity obligations. Accordingly, under the provision, Lake River would receive all of the benefit it would have received if Carborundum had fully performed the contract, with none of the additional costs.

In addition to requiring a reasonable estimation, courts also generally require that actual damages were speculative or difficult to estimate at the time of contracting.[97] Moreover, the more speculative and uncertain actual damages are, the more latitude parties may receive in determining what amounts to a reasonable estimate at the time of contracting.[98] For example, in contracts involving intellectual property (in particular, trade secrets), damages may be particularly difficult to calculate and a liquidated-damages provision may be appropriate.[99]

Furthermore, some states include additional requirements for the enforcement of liquidated-damages provisions. For example, in Illinois, courts at least sometimes have required that the parties agree to a liquidated-damages provision with the intent to settle in advance future damages under the contract.[100] In addition, many courts state as a separate requirement that the parties intend the provision "solely to compensate the nonbreaching party and not as a penalty for breach or as an incentive to perform."[101]

---

96. *Id.* at 1291.

97. *See, e.g., Ladco Props. XVII v. Jefferson-Pilot Life Ins. Co.*, 531 F.3d 718, 720 (8th Cir. 2008) ("Under North Carolina law, a liquidated damages provision is enforceable and will not be considered a penalty where (1) damages are speculative or difficult to ascertain, and (2) the amount stipulated is a reasonable estimate of probable damages or the amount stipulated is reasonably proportionate to the damages actually caused by the breach."); *Barrie Sch. v. Patch*, 933 A.2d 382 (Md. 2007) ("Maryland courts will uphold a liquidated damages clause as valid, and not a penalty, if it satisfies two primary requirements. First, the clause must provide a fair estimate of potential damages at the time the parties entered into the contract. Second, the damages must have been incapable of estimation, or very difficult to estimate, at the time of contracting.") (internal citations and quotation marks omitted).

98. *See* Restatement (Second) of Contracts § 356 cmt. b (1981) ("The greater the difficulty either of proving that loss has occurred or of establishing its amount with the requisite certainty . . . the easier it is to show that the amount fixed is reasonable. To the extent that there is uncertainty as to the harm, the estimate of the court or jury may not accord with the principle of compensation any more than does the advance estimate of the parties.").

99. *See, e.g., Midwest Oilseeds, Inc. v. Limagrain Genetics Corp.*, 387 F.3d 705, 717 (8th Cir. 2004) ("Because the breach involves the release of MO's intellectual property to its competitors, damages are extremely difficult to determine in this case.").

100. *Energy Plus Consulting, LLC v. Illinois Fuel Co.*, 371 F.3d 907, 909 n.2 (7th Cir. 2004).

101. *See, e.g., Renaudette v. Barrett Trucking Co., Inc.*, 712 A.2d 387, 388 (Vt. 1998) (internal citation omitted); *see also* Richard A. Lord, 24 Williston on Contracts § 65:3 (4th ed. 2009).

Drafting Note: Specifying Relevant Breaches in Liquidated-Damages Clauses

Contracts are often complex documents imposing all sorts of obligations on the parties thereto. Accordingly, not all failures to perform an obligation are equal, and, therefore, not all breaches of a contract will necessarily result in the same amount of damages. A liquidated-damages provision may be reasonable vis-à-vis certain breaches and wholly disproportionate vis-à-vis others. (Indeed, the Federal Circuit went so far as to find a liquidated-damages clause unenforceable under Missouri law because actual damages would have been easy to estimate for a hypothetical breach of just one of the contract's provisions![102]) For this reason, some courts will read liquidated-damages provisions—that do not provide otherwise—to apply only to material breaches of the contract and will evaluate their enforceability based on this presumption.[103] More importantly, for this reason, a prudent party should specify to which breaches of which contract provisions a liquidated-damages clause applies. Indeed, the Supreme Judicial Court of Massachusetts has counseled:

> Failing to provide any recognition for the type, or timing, of the default, while by no means determinative, tends to indicate that the provision's intended purpose was not to estimate the different types of damages that might arise from a future default, but to penalize for any failure, however immaterial.[104]

If a provision is found to operate as a penalty, then the provision will be ignored, and the court will award actual damages, as if the contract did not contain the liquidated-damages provision.[105] If a liquidated-damages provision is enforceable, then "the measure of damages for a breach will be the sum in the clause, no more, no less."[106]

---

(2) "Optional" Liquidated-Damages Provisions

A classic liquidated-damages clause provides the exclusive monetary remedy available to a contractual party for a specified breach of the contract. In this way, a liquidated-damages clause provides both an upper and lower bound—located at the same amount—on the liability available for breach of contract. In contrast, as we discuss in Chapter 3, a contract may include a limitation-of-liability provision, which imposes only an upper limit on liability.

---

102. *Monsanto Co. v. McFarling*, 363 F.3d 1336, 1348 (Fed. Cir. 2004) ("[A] liquidated damages clause is invalid if even one breach covered by the clause fails to qualify for enforceability as liquidated damages."). However, please note that the Federal Circuit did not evaluate whether this rule would apply when the damages amount called for by the liquidated-damages provision turns out to be reasonable vis-à-vis the actual damages resulting from the breach that actually occurred. *See id.*

103. *See, e.g., JMD Holding Corp. v. Cong. Fin. Corp.*, 828 N.E.2d 604, 612 (N.Y. 2005) (citing *United Air Lines, Inc. v. Austin Travel Corp.*, 867 F.2d 737, 741 (2d Cir. 1989)).

104. *TAL Fin. Corp. v. CSC Consulting, Inc.*, 844 N.E.2d 1085, 1093 (Mass. 2006).

105. *See JMD Holding Corp.*, 828 N.E.2d at 609 ("If the clause is rejected as being a penalty, the recovery is limited to actual damages proven.") (internal citations and quotation marks omitted).

106. *Id.*

A variation of the classic, an "optional" liquidated-damages provision speci-fies that, in the event of a breach, a non-breaching party may either obtain the contractually specified damages *or* sue for actual damages. Notice that a "ratio-nal" party will invoke this type of liquidated-damages provision only if actual damages (minus any additional costs associated with suing for actual damages) turn out to be less than those provided by the liquidated-damages provision and will opt not to invoke the provision if actual damages promise richer spoils. In effect, then, an optional liquidated-damages provision provides only a lower bound on liability.

Some jurisdictions refuse to enforce such optional liquidated-damages pro-visions. For example, in a jurisdiction requiring that liquidated-damages provi-sions reflect a "settlement" of prospective damages, a court has held that an optional provision, leaving open the potential for actual damages, does not evince an actual settlement of future actual damages.[107] However, some courts have been willing to enforce optional liquidated-damages provisions, especially as between sophisticated parties.[108]

(3) "Alternative-Performance" Contracts

Note that liquidated-damages provisions operate to stipulate a damages amount in the event that a party *breaches* a contract—that is, in the event that a party fails to perform in accordance with a contract. When a contract provides that a party may satisfy an obligation under the contract by one of several means, on its face at least, the contract states an "alternative-performance" provision—and not a liquidated-damages provision. Accordingly, a contract may provide that a party has a duty to perform by doing X or by paying Y dollars, where paying Y dollars is simply one of several performance alternatives avail-able to a party. Query the functional difference between an "alternative-performance" and a "liquidated-damages" arrangement. Is the difference in form alone? Is the payment of damages (actual or stipulated) not always an "alternative" performance?

Courts often state that whether a contract contains a liquidated-damages provision is a question of substance and not form.[109] Indeed, courts often give

---

107. *Grossinger Motorcorp, Inc. v. Am. Nat'l Bank and Trust Co.*, 607 N.E.2d 1337, 1346 (Ill. App. Ct. 1992) ("[T]he optional nature of the liquidated damages clause shows that the parties never intended to establish a specific sum to constitute damages in the event of a breach."); *see also, e.g., Jefferson Randolph Corp. v. Progressive Data Sys., Inc.*, 553 S.E.2d 304 (Ga. Ct. App. 2001), *rev'd on other grounds*, 568 S.E.2d 474 (Ga. 2002).

108. *See, e.g., Nw. Airlines, Inc. v. Flight Trails*, 3 F.3d 292, 294-95 (8th Cir. 1993); *Avery v. Hughes*, Civil No. 09-cv-265-JD, 2010 WL 338092, at *3-4 (D.N.H. Jan. 20, 2010) (finding optional liquidated-damages provision to be enforceable); *McMaster v. McIlroy Bank*, 654 S.W.2d 591 (Ark. Ct. App. 1983) (finding optional liquidated-damages provision to be enforceable); *Noble v. Ogborn*, 717 P.2d 285, 287 (Wash. Ct. App. 1986) ("A liquidated damages clause does not preclude a party from suing for actual damages if that right is preserved in the contract between the parties.") (internal citation omitted).

109. *See, e.g., JKC Holding Co. v. Washington Sports Ventures, Inc.*, 265 F.3d 459, 468 (4th Cir. 2001) (New York law) ("In interpreting a provision fixing damages, it is immaterial what the parties choose to call the provision."); *In re Graham Square, Inc.*, 126 F.3d 823, 829 (6th Cir. 1997) (Ohio law) ("Neither the parties' actual

short rhetorical shrift to whether the parties call a provision a "liquidated-damages" provision, in considering whether a provision is for liquidated damages or a penalty.[110] Still, in practice, some courts have given some weight to the language used by parties in their contract, for instance, where parties have labeled a provision "liquidated damages" or a "penalty."[111] Similarly, courts recite that determining whether a provision is for alternative performance or stipulated damages is a question of substance and not form. The *Restatement* advises:

> Sometimes parties attempt to disguise a provision for a penalty by using language that purports to make payment of the amount an alternative performance under the contract, that purports to offer a discount for prompt performance, or that purports to place a valuation on property to be delivered. Although the parties may in good faith contract for alternative performances and fix discounts or valuations, a court will look to the substance of the agreement to determine whether this is the case or whether the parties have attempted to disguise a provision for a penalty that is unenforceable under this Section. In determining whether a contract is one for alternative performances, the relative value of the alternatives may be decisive.[112]

Courts have frequently found a contract to involve an "alternative-performance" arrangement and not a liquidated-damages provision, sidestepping the law of liquidated damages and its penalty inquiries. For example, in the case of prepayment fees, courts have often found that a borrower that opts to prepay her loan in accordance with a prepayment provision in her contract is merely performing alternatively and that the prepayment provision does not operate as a stipulation of "damages," as there has been no breach.[113] In addition, courts have found "take-or-pay" gas contracts, where a buyer agrees either to purchase a certain quantity of gas or to pay a sum for such gas,[114] and "early termination fee" provisions, where a party agrees to continue to receive services

---

intention as to its validity nor their characterization of the term as one for liquidated damages or a penalty is significant in determining whether the term is valid.") (internal citations and quotation marks omitted).

110. *See supra* note 109.

111. *See, e.g., Kalenka v. Taylor*, 896 P.2d 222, 229 (Alaska 1995) (noting that the court was "inclined to disallow the 'penalties' sought by the Kalenkas based on their moniker alone"); *Equity Enters., Inc. v. Milosch*, 633 N.W.2d 662, 672 (Wis. Ct. App. 2001) ("In short, the label the parties apply to the clause, which might indicate their intent, does have some evidentiary value, but it is not conclusive.").

112. RESTATEMENT (SECOND) OF CONTRACTS § 356 cmt. c (1981).

113. *See, e.g., Great Plains Real Estate Dev., LLC v. Union Cent. Life Ins. Co.*, 536 F.3d 939, 945 (8th Cir. 2008) (Iowa law) ("Here, the Note gave GPR the choice of paying according to the Note's terms or prepaying the Note in full and paying the PPP. When GPR elected to prepay, GPR was not breaching the contract but was in fact acting in accordance with an express option provided under the contract."); *Carlyle Apartments Joint Venture v. AIG Life Ins. Co.*, 635 A.2d 366, 373 (Md. 1994) ("We have matched the contract against the facts and find no breach. Absent any breach by the borrower, there is no occasion to consider damages or to look for a liquidated damages clause in disguise. . . . ").

114. *See, e.g., Prenalta Corp. v. Colorado Interstate Gas Co.*, 944 F.2d 677, 689 (10th Cir. 1991) (Wyoming law) (noting that "a take-or-pay contract provides for performance in the alternative" and that "courts have distinguished the 'pay' provision from a liquidated damages provision").

under a contract or to pay a fee to terminate the contract,[115] to be alternative-performance contracts and not to involve liquidated damages.

In contrast, the Tenth Circuit found a provision that required a party to pay a sum "as liquidated damages" in the event the party failed to meet a minimum volume requirement to be a liquidated-damages provision and not an alternative-performance provision.[116] The court further explained, "PSO's commitment to ship 2,600,000 tons of coal annually via BN was not set forth in the Agreement as one of the two alternative performances to be given by PSO."[117] Accordingly, while the test for whether a provision operates as liquidated damages or an alternative performance turns on the substance of the arrangement, courts may still look to the language and structure of the contract to determine this substance. That is, courts will look to the contract to determine whether the parties intended to create a provision as a remedy for a breach or to provide one of several ways to satisfy a performance obligation. As Professor Corbin is oft-cited for explaining, "If, upon a proper interpretation of the contract, it is found that the parties have agreed that either one of the two alternative performances is to be given by the promisor and received by the promisee as the agreed exchange and equivalent for the return performance rendered by the promisee, the contract is a true alternative contract."[118] A party wishing to create a "true" alternative-performance contract, then, should be clear in structuring her agreement to specify several performances, each of which the promisor may elect in satisfaction of a contractual obligation.

C. THE ENFORCEABILITY AND LIMITS OF NON-DISCLOSURE AGREEMENTS

When will courts enforce or not enforce a non-disclosure agreement? Are there limits to what may be included or to how long the confidentiality obligations persist? Consider the following case.

Coady v. Harpo, Inc.
Appellate Court of Illinois, First District, Fifth Division, 1999.
719 N.E.2d 244.

Justice GREIMAN delivered the opinion of the court:

Plaintiff Elizabeth Coady appeals the dismissal of her cause of action seeking a declaratory judgment that a confidentiality policy established by defendant

---

115. *See, e.g., Hutchison v. AT & T Internet Servs., Inc.*, No. CV07-3674 SVW (JCx), 2009 WL 1726344 (C.D. Cal. May 5, 2009).
116. *Pub. Serv. Co. v. Burlington N. R.R.*, 53 F.3d 1090, 1099 (10th Cir. 1995) (Oklahoma law).
117. *Id.* (internal quotation marks omitted).
118. 11-58 CORBIN ON CONTRACTS § 58.18 (2010).

Harpo, Inc., was unenforceable against plaintiff, a former employee of defendant. . . .

In her complaint, plaintiff stated that from November 1993 to March 1998 she was employed by defendant in a number of positions, most recently as a "senior associate producer" for defendant's television series, "The Oprah Winfrey Show." Plaintiff alleged that for some time prior to March 26, 1998, defendant engaged in a course of conduct designed to force plaintiff from her employment and defendant's treatment of plaintiff became so intolerable as to amount to constructive termination. On March 26, 1998, plaintiff notified defendant by letter from her attorney that she resigned effectively immediately.

Paragraph 16 of plaintiff's complaint states that she, "a trained journalist, intends to write or otherwise report about her experiences as an employee of defendant, matters of legitimate public interest and concern." Plaintiff further alleged that her intention to exercise her rights of free speech and free press was not prohibited by a confidentiality policy, which was entitled "Business Ethics, Objectivity, and Confidentiality Policy" and contained in defendant's September 1996 employee manual. Plaintiff maintained that the purported restrictions of the confidentiality policy, as stated in the employee manual, were unenforceable for one or more of eight enumerated reasons.

In a letter dated April 24, 1998, and attached to plaintiff's complaint, defendant "reminded" plaintiff that she had signed a document entitled "Business Ethics, Objectivity and Confidentiality Policy" on March 12, 1995, and provided her a copy of the agreement in the letter. Defendant's letter further stated that in the March 12, 1995, agreement, plaintiff "agreed (among other things) to keep confidential, during her employment and thereafter, all information about the Company, Ms. Winfrey, her private life, and Harpo's business activities which she acquired during or by virtue of her employment with Harpo." Defendant further stated that it intended to enforce and ensure compliance with the confidentiality agreement. . . .

Both the independent document entitled "Business Ethics, Objectivity and Confidentiality Policy" (hereinafter the 1995 agreement) and the portion of the employee manual with the same title (hereinafter the 1996 employee manual) include a section entitled "Confidentiality Assurances," which provides in pertinent part as follows:

> 1. During your employment or business relationship with Harpo, and thereafter, to the fullest extent permitted by law, you are obligated to keep confidential and never disclose, use, misappropriate, or confirm or deny the veracity of, any statement or comment concerning Oprah Winfrey, Harpo (which, as used herein, included all entities related to Harpo, Inc., including Harpo Productions, Inc., Harpo Films, Inc.) or any of her/its Confidential Information. The phrase 'Confidential Information' as used in this policy, includes but is not limited to, any and all information which is not generally known to the public, related to or concerning: (a) Ms. Winfrey and/or her business or private life; (b) the business activities, dealings or interests of Harpo and/or its officers, directors, affiliates,

employees or contractors; and/or (c) Harpo's employment practices or policies applicable to its employees and/or contractors.

2. During your employment or business relationship with Harpo, and there-after, you are obligated to refrain from giving or participating in any interview(s) regarding or related to Ms. Winfrey, Harpo, your employment or business rela-tionship with Harpo and/or amy [*sic*] matter which concerns, relates to or involves any Confidential Information."

. . . The relevant documents also provide that commitment to the stated policies is required as a condition of employment: "Your commitment to the guidelines set forth in this policy is a condition of your employment or business relationship with Harpo."

In addition, defendant's motion to dismiss attached a copy of plaintiff's acknowledgment of the employee manual, which she signed upon the com-mencement of her employment at defendant in 1993. The acknowledgment signed by plaintiff states in relevant part:

> "I acknowledge and understand that I may not use any confidential or proprietary information of HARPO for my own purposes either during or after my employment with HARPO, and I understand that I am prohibited from removing, disclosing or otherwise misappropriating any of HARPO's confiden-tial or proprietary information for any reason."

. . . [P]laintiff asserts that the confidentiality policy is not enforceable, pri-marily arguing that it is overly broad and not reasonably necessary to protect defendant's legitimate business interests. Defendant, however, contends that the confidentiality agreement is enforceable because it does not violate any public policy, was supported by adequate consideration, was not an adhesion contract and properly protected defendant's legitimate business interests.

Until the filing of her appellate reply brief, plaintiff relied on the 1996 employee manual to support her cause of action, contending that the confiden-tiality policy contained therein was not enforceable because the 1996 employee manual included a contract disclaimer, *i.e.*, "[t]his manual is not a contract." Plaintiff relied on case law that addressed whether an employee handbook creates contractual rights.

In light of the facts in the present case, the employee-handbook analysis is unnecessary because defendant attached the 1995 agreement to . . . motion to dismiss as the affirmative matter refuting plaintiff's crucial conclusions of law based on the 1996 employee manual and the language in both documents is identical. As acknowledged by plaintiff in her appellate reply brief, "[t]he covenant in the manual contains precisely the same language and terms as the confidentiality agreement which plaintiff signed on March 12, 1995." Plaintiff further stated that her arguments as to the enforceability of the restric-tive covenant remain the same regardless of which version is considered.

Accordingly, we will not unnecessarily elongate this opinion by conducting a pointless exercise to determine whether the 1996 employee manual created a contract. Instead, we consider the identical language contained in the 1995 agreement to determine its validity.

"A postemployment restrictive covenant will be enforced if its terms are reasonable." To determine the reasonableness of a restrictive covenant, "it is necessary to consider whether enforcement of the covenant will injure the public, whether enforcement will cause undue hardship to the promisor and whether the restraint imposed by the covenant is greater than is necessary to protect the interests of the employer."

The reasonableness of some types of restrictive covenants, such as nonsolicitation agreements, also is evaluated by the time limitation and geographical scope stated in the covenant. However, a confidentiality agreement will not be deemed unenforceable for lack of durational or geographic limitations where trade secrets and confidential information are involved.

Postemployment restrictive covenants typically involve agreements by a past employee not to compete with the business of her former employer, not to solicit clients or customers of her former employer, and not to disseminate trade secrets of her former employer. The covenants in these typical cases are carefully scrutinized because Illinois courts abhor restraints on trade.

Although restraint of trade is a significant concern, "[a]n equally important public policy in Illinois is the freedom to contract." Furthermore, postemployment restrictive covenants "have a social utility in that they protect an employer from the unwarranted erosion of confidential information."

Unlike the traditional line of restrictive covenant cases, the confidentiality agreement at issue in the instant case does not impose any of the typical restrictions commonly adjudicated in restrictive covenant cases. Defendant does not seek to restrain plaintiff's future career. Plaintiff is free to choose her future occupation, the locale in which she may choose to work, and the time when she can commence her new career. Defendant does not object to plaintiff becoming a journalist, competing with defendant in the same venue and in any locale, including Chicago, and in beginning her new venture immediately. The confidentiality agreement does not restrict commerce and does not restrict plaintiff's ability to work in any chosen career field, at any time. Instead, the 1995 confidentiality agreement restricts plaintiff's ability to disseminate confidential information that she obtained or learned while in defendant's employ. Most certainly, plaintiff had no problem with keeping confidences as long as she was a senior associate producer and continued her work with defendant.

Moreover, we find unpersuasive plaintiff's argument that the confidentiality agreement is too broad because it remains effective for all time and with no geographical boundaries. Whether for better or for worse, interest in a celebrity figure and his or her attendant business and personal ventures somehow seems to continue endlessly, even long after death, and often, as in the present case, extends over an international domain.

Under the facts of this case and the terms of the restrictive covenant at issue, we find that the 1995 confidentiality agreement is reasonable and enforceable. Accordingly, we affirm the trial court's order dismissing plaintiff's cause of action as stated in count I of her complaint. . . .

Comments

The court in *Coady* explained that at least one reason that the confidentiality agreement at issue was neither overbroad nor unenforceable was that the underlying confidences pertained to celebrity Oprah Winfrey, and, accordingly, it was reasonable for such confidentiality obligations to extend indefinitely. In terms of the substantive law, as outlined in the opinion, and, as a matter of policy, what significance would you anticipate courts to attribute to the celebrity status of the subject of a confidentiality agreement?

Might the public's interest in public figures suggest a narrow construction of, or a different conception of "reasonableness" for, confidentiality obligations in matters surrounding public figures? In *Coady*, the plaintiff argued "that her intention to exercise her rights of free speech and free press was not prohibited by a confidentiality policy." Might a broad confidentiality agreement be more "reasonable" in the context of an unknown than a public figure? Does the court satisfyingly address this argument? Consider, for instance, that the First and Fourteenth Amendments have been found to make it generally more difficult for a public figure to prevail against an accused for intentional infliction of emotional distress[119] and for defamation.[120] Why not also make it more difficult for a public figure to prevail against an accused for disclosure?

1. The Limits of NDAs: Reasonableness, etc.

The central question concerning the enforceability of an NDA is whether or not the restrictive covenant is "reasonable."[121] Whether or not a non-disclosure covenant is reasonable turns on "if it (1) is no greater than required for the protection of the employer, (2) does not impose undue hardship on the

---

119. *Hustler Magazine v. Falwell*, 485 U.S. 46 (1988).

120. *New York Times Co. v. Sullivan*, 376 U.S. 254 (1964).

121. *See, e.g., 1st Am. Sys., Inc. v. Rezatto*, 311 N.W.2d 51, 57 (S.D. 1981) ("[Non-disclosure covenants are] enforced only to the extent reasonably necessary to protect the employer's interest in confidential information."); *see also Eden Hannon & Co. v. Sumitomo Trust & Bank Co.*, 914 F.2d 556, 560-61 (4th Cir. 1990) ("The Virginia courts have held repeatedly that employment agreements are enforceable if they pass a three-part reasonableness test.") (citing *Paramount Termite Control Co. v. Rector*, 380 S.E.2d 922, 924 (Va. 1989)).

employee and (3) is not injurious to the public."[122] In *Coady*, the court found the confidentiality agreement in question to be reasonable, explaining that the NDA in question need not contain time or geographic limitations to be enforceable. Courts are split as to whether an NDA must be limited by time and/or geography in order to be reasonable and enforceable.[123]

Generally, an NDA may impose confidentiality obligations pertaining to any information, whether or not such information constitutes a "trade secret."[124] However, some courts have been reluctant to enforce an NDA as to information that is not at least actually confidential.[125] Courts are not uniform on this matter, as some have explained that a confidentiality obligation is enforceable according to its bargained-for terms, irrespective of whether or not the underlying information is publicly known.[126]

---

122. *1st Am.*, 311 N.W.2d at 59. It would seem that a similar "reasonableness" test would generally inform the enforceability of NDAs in the commercial context; however, the case law on this issue is surprisingly lacking. Note that at least one court has explained that NDAs are presumptively valid and, accordingly, do not require a "reasonableness" inquiry to be enforced. *See Zep Mfg. Co. v. Harthcock*, 824 S.W.2d 654, 663 (Tex. Ct. App. 1992).

123. *Compare, e.g., Synergetics, Inc. v. Hurst*, 477 F.3d 949, 958-59 (8th Cir. 2007) (holding that under Missouri law, confidentiality agreements need not contain time or geographic restrictions), *Everett J. Prescott, Inc. v. Ross*, 390 F. Supp. 2d 44, 46 & n.3 (D. Me. 2005) (finding non-disclosure obligations unbounded by time or geography appropriate), *Wang Labs., Inc. v. CFR Assocs., Inc.*, 125 F.R.D. 10, 13 (D. Mass. 1989) (holding non-disclosure agreement, without time or geography restriction, enforceable), *Revere Transducers, Inc. v. Deere & Co.*, 595 N.W.2d 751, 762 (Iowa 1999) ("[A]bsence of restrictions concerning time or geographic location do not render a nondisclosure-confidentiality, agreement presumptively unenforceable."), *and Zep Mfg.*, 824 S.W.2d at 663 ("[N]ondisclosure covenants are [not] subject to reasonable time, geographical, and scope-of-activity requirements"), *with Nalco Chem. Co. v. Hydro Techs., Inc.*, 984 F.2d 801, 803 (7th Cir. 1993) (holding that under Wisconsin law, a non-disclosure clause without a time limit is void unless the underlying information is a trade secret, as statute provides that no time limit is required for trade-secret restrictions), *and Opteum Fin. Servs., LLC v. Spain*, 406 F. Supp. 2d 1378, 1381 (N.D. Ga. 2005) ("Although a nondisclosure clause with no time limit is unenforceable as to information that is not a trade secret, the GTSA carves out an exception for written agreements that do not contain a time limit for maintaining the trade secret.").

124. *See, e.g., Eaton Corp. v. Giere*, 971 F.2d 136, 141 (8th Cir. 1992) (Minnesota law); *Am. Software USA, Inc. v. Moore*, 448 S.E.2d 206, 209 (Ga. 1994) ("[N]on-disclosure restrictive covenant, which is strictly limited to appellant's 'trade secrets' and 'confidential business information,' is not unreasonable."); *Cincinnati Tool Steel Co. v. Breed*, 482 N.E.2d 170, 174 (Ill. App. Ct. 1985) ("[A]n enforceable restrictive covenant may protect material which does not constitute a trade secret."); *1st Am.*, 311 N.W.2d at 58 ("Even if the contract protects information which is technically not a trade secret, it clearly reveals the intent of the parties to create a confidential relationship. A breach of this relationship is actionable even if Rezatto could glean some of the information from public sources.") (internal citations omitted).

125. *See, e.g., Rivendell Forest Prods., Ltd. v. Georgia-Pacific Corp.*, 824 F. Supp. 961, 968 (D. Colo. 1993) ("[I]information already known to competitors or readily ascertainable elsewhere cannot be protected as confidential.") (internal citations omitted), *rev'd on other grounds*, 28 F.3d 1042, 1046 (10th Cir. 1994); *Durham v. Stand-By Labor of Georgia, Inc.*, 198 S.E.2d 145, 149-50 (Ga. 1973) (noting that the reasonableness of a non-disclosure obligation turns on "whether the employer is attempting to protect confidential information related to the business").

126. *See, e.g., Health Alliance Network, Inc. v. Cont'l Cas. Co.*, 354 F. Supp. 2d 411, 422 (S.D.N.Y. 2005) (holding, under Illinois law, that a breach of confidentiality claim does not turn on general definitions of "confidential" but rather on how the contract defines "confidential"); *Forest Labs., Inc. v. Lowey*, 218 U.S.P.Q. (BNA) 646, 658 (N.Y. Sup. Ct. 1982) (explaining NDAs are enforceable as to coverage of even public knowledge).

There is one—at least partial—solution that addresses the concern that a court may find an NDA unreasonable and, so, unenforceable: the "savings" clause.[127] A savings clause can work as a stopgap measure to float an otherwise overbroad and unenforceable agreement down to the level of reasonableness. That is, the clause instructs the court to ignore the unreasonable aspects of the NDA and to enforce the remaining enforceable parts. On this measure, courts may obey; however, a prudent party who wishes later to enforce an NDA will attempt to draft a provision no more restrictive than reasonable.[128] Of course, a savings clause does nothing to save, or to bolster the enforceability of, the "unreasonable" aspects of the confidentiality obligations.

2. Consideration and Employee Non-Disclosure Agreements

Given that the employee in this case began work for Harpo in 1993, was there consideration to support either of the 1995 Agreement or the 1996 Agreement? Courts take divergent views on this issue, with some treating "substantial continued employment" after the execution of an NDA as sufficient consideration and with others finding an NDA void for lack of consideration, where the NDA is executed after an employee begins the underlying employment.[129]

---

127. A "severability clause," which is discussed earlier in the chapter, is similar to a "savings clause." This book uses "severability clause" to refer to clauses that instruct a court to "sever" any unenforceable provisions in order to enforce the remaining portions of the contract and "savings clause" to refer to clauses that instruct a court to interpret or modify a provision in order to render the provision enforceable. However, please note that in practice the terms are often used interchangeably and that the distinction is a blurry one.

128. Please see the discussion of judicial tailoring in Chapter 2, which details the various approaches that states take to modifying overly restrictive covenants. Note that not all courts are willing to modify provisions. *See, e.g., Rollins Protective Servs. Co. v. Palermo*, 287 S.E.2d 546, 549 (Ga. 1982) (holding, in the employment context, that if any portion of a restrictive covenant is invalid, the entire covenant must fail). However, under Georgia law, "a severability clause will allow a court to excise the *entire* restrictive covenant so as to preserve the other covenants in the contract." *Johnstone v. Tom's Amusement Co., Inc.*, 491 S.E.2d 394, 397 (Ga. Ct. App. 1997) (emphasis in original).

129. *Compare Curtis 1000, Inc. v. Suess*, 24 F.3d 941, 945 (7th Cir. 1994), *Dixie Homecrafters, Inc. v. Homecrafters of Am., LLC*, No. 1:08-CV-0649-JOF, 2009 WL 596009, at *6 (N.D. Ga. Mar. 5, 2009) (noting that, under Georgia law, continued employment is sufficient consideration for non-disclosure agreement, where employment was otherwise at will), *and Woodfield Grp., Inc. v. DeLisle*, 693 N.E.2d 464, 469 (Ill. App. Ct. 1998) ("Illinois law provides that substantial continued employment may constitute sufficient consideration to support a restrictive covenant agreement."), *with Rivendell*, 824 F. Supp. at 968 (finding that an employee confidentiality agreement signed after the start of employment is void for lack of consideration), *rev'd on other grounds*, 28 F.3d 1042 (10th Cir. 1994), *and Jostens, Inc. v. Nat'l Computer Sys., Inc.*, 318 N.W.2d 691, 703 (Minn. 1982) (noting that continuation of employment is insufficient consideration to support a confidentiality agreement). *See also SFX USA, Inc. v. Bjerkness*, 636 F. Supp. 2d 696, 709-10 (N.D. Ill. 2009) (finding that a restrictive covenant was supported by consideration, where agreement recited adequate consideration and there may have been continued substantial employment had employee not voluntarily resigned); *Picker Int'l, Inc. v. Blanton*, 756 F. Supp. 971, 982 (N.D. Tex. 1990) ("Special training or knowledge acquired by an employee during employment may constitute independent valuable consideration."); *Mann Frankfort Stein & Lipp Advisors, Inc. v. Fielding*, 289 S.W.3d 844, 850-52 (Tex. 2009) (finding consideration for non-disclosure and non-compete agreement in employer's "implied promise" to disclose confidential information to employee). For a thoughtful discussion on the various approaches taken by courts to assess consideration in restrictive covenant agreements in the

3. The Distinction Between Non-Disclosure and Non-Compete Obligations

The distinction between non-disclosure and non-competition obligations is significant.[130] Non-disclosure obligations impose a duty to refrain from sharing confidential information, whereas non-competition obligations impose a duty not to work for competitors, as defined by the agreement. The distinction is important because courts are more suspicious of covenants not to compete, requiring that they meet a more stringent standard to be enforced.[131] Why? Covenants not to compete are considered "restraints of trade" (or, "restraints on trade"), which serve to impede the freedom of the marketplace by restricting labor and business activity.[132] Non-disclosure obligations are generally not considered restraints of trade and, accordingly, are unlikely to be subjected to the higher degree of scrutiny,[133] unless such provisions operate, in effect, as obligations not to compete.[134]

---

employment context, see *McGough v. Nalco Co.*, 496 F. Supp. 2d 729, 744-52 (N.D. W. Va. 2007) (finding continued employment to be valid consideration, under Alabama law, for a non-disclosure agreement entered into after employment began).

130. Courts sometimes mistakenly conflate an analysis of non-disclosure covenants with that of non-compete covenants. *See, e.g., Guy Carpenter & Co., Inc. v. Provenzale*, 334 F.3d 459, 465-66 (5th Cir. 2003) (Texas law) (concluding that the district court made faulty assumption that statute governing restraint of trade informed merits of non-disclosure claim); *Perman v. ArcVentures, Inc.*, 554 N.E.2d 982, 986 (Ill. App. Ct. 1990); *1st Am.*, 311 N.W.2d at 56 (noting that the "trial court erred because the contract was divisible and a nondisclosure agreement differs from a noncompetition agreement").

131. *See, e.g., Guy Carpenter*, 334 F.3d at 465 (noting that non-disclosure covenants are evaluated less strictly than non-competition and non-solicitation covenants); *Revere Transducers, Inc. v. Deere & Co.*, 595 N.W.2d 751, 761 (Iowa 1999) ("Nondisclosure-confidentiality agreements enjoy more favorable treatment in the law than do noncompete agreements.").

132. *See* Terry Morehead Dworkin & Elletta Sangrey Callahan, *Buying Silence*, 36 Am. Bus. L.J. 151, 156 (1998) ("Anti-competition covenants are legally disfavored because they restrain trade by inhibiting promisors' freedom of movement among employment opportunities. Accordingly, these agreements are limited or prohibited by statute in some states, and are closely examined in others. Confidentiality agreements, in contrast, are enforceable even in states in which anti-competition clauses are prohibited. Concerns regarding restraint of trade are much less directly implicated in this context; restrictions on access to information, rather than employee movement, are involved. Thus, the policy in favor of freedom of contract is given precedence.").

133. *See, e.g., Guy Carpenter*, 334 F.3d at 465 (Texas law); *Lear Siegler, Inc. v. Ark-Ell Springs, Inc.*, 569 F.2d 286, 289 (5th Cir. 1978) (Mississippi law) ("Furthermore, such an agreement not to disclose information, unlike the covenant not to compete, cannot be challenged as an unreasonable restraint of trade."); *Papa John's Int'l, Inc. v. Pizza Magia Int'l, LLC*, No. CIV.A. 3:00CV-548-H, 2001 WL 1789379, at *4 (W.D. Ky. May 10, 2001); *Revere*, 595 N.W.2d at 761 (noting that "noncompete agreements are viewed as restraints of trade . . . while nondisclosure agreements seek to restrict disclosure of information, not employment opportunities"). *But see Central Monitoring Serv. v. Zakinski*, 553 N.W.2d 513, 515-16 (S.D. 1996) (noting that non-disclosure agreements are restraints of trade).

134. *See, e.g., Quixote Transp. Safety, Inc. v. Cooper*, No. 03 C 1401, 2004 WL 528011 (N.D. Ill. Mar. 12, 2004) ("[I]f we accept that [one] can establish a violation of this particular non-disclosure agreement by showing [recipient] will inevitably use the confidential information if employed by a competitor, then the non-disclosure agreement as written effectively becomes a permanent non-compete agreement. The Illinois courts have long rejected the reasonableness of such restrictions; the agreement cannot be enforced if it does not place reasonable limitations on the duration of the restriction.").

· CHAPTER TWO ·

EMPLOYMENT AGREEMENTS

This action asserting breach of contract and related tort claims arises out of a September 8, 2004 broadcast that plaintiff Dan Rather narrated on the CBS 60 Minutes II television program about then President George W. Bush's service in the Texas Air National Guard. Rather alleges that CBS disavowed the broadcast after it was attacked by Bush supporters, and fraudulently induced him to apologize personally for the broadcast on national television as well as to remain silent as to his belief that the broadcast was true. Rather alleges that, following President Bush's re-election, CBS informed him that he would be removed as anchor of the CBS Evening News. Rather claims that although his employment agreement required that, in the event he was removed as anchor, CBS would make him a regular correspondent on 60 Minutes or immediately pay all amounts due under the agreement and release him to work elsewhere, CBS kept him on the payroll while denying him the opportunity to cover important news stories until May 2006 when it terminated his contract, effective June 2006. . . .

Contractually, CBS was under no obligation to "use [Rather's] services or to broadcast any program" so long as it continued to pay him the applicable compensation. This "pay or play" provision of the original 1979 employment agreement was specifically reaffirmed in the 2002 Amendment to the employment agreement.

Rather v. CBS Corp., 886 N.Y.S.2d 121, 123-24 (N.Y. App. Div. 2009).

As with most relationships, a prudent party enters an employment agreement with hopes for the best and plans for the worst. Here, a New York court found that CBS owed its anchor of four decades only that which the employment agreement between the two parties required.[1] Indeed, as the court explained, Rather "negotiated a contract that was extensively amended several

---

1. *Rather v. CBS Corp.*, 886 N.Y.S.2d 121, 125 (N.Y. App. Div. 2009) ("Rather claims that his 'four-decade history' with CBS constituted a 'special relationship that imposed fiduciary duties upon CBS toward [Rather].' The law in this Department, and indeed enunciated in every reported appellate-division-level case, is that employment relationships do not create fiduciary relationships.") (alterations in original).

times, that paid Rather a lucrative salary, and that detailed, in 50 pages, everything from his assignments and on-air work at CBS Evening News to requirements that he attend rehearsals and join the union."[2] Accordingly, CBS was able to terminate the services of its employee in accordance with the terms of its negotiated employment agreement, without being liable to its employee for anything more.

In this chapter, we discuss the rights and obligations of employers and employees as allocated by employment agreements.

Subject to limited exceptions,[3] in the absence of a written agreement providing for a fixed term of employment, employment is considered to be "at will." This means employment can be terminated by the employer or the employee for any reason or no reason absent unlawful discrimination. One of these aforementioned exceptions is where the employer has recognized a union and is party to a collective bargaining agreement. While labor law and collective bargains are outside the scope of this chapter, in order to provide context, we asked a seasoned practitioner with expertise in the area to explain the history and difference between labor and employment law.

> ### A Practitioner Perspective: The Emergence of Employment Law
>
> Forty-five years ago, a law firm department specializing in U.S. labor and employment law would have dealt almost exclusively with what we now refer to as traditional labor law. "Labor law" as we in the practice think of it, involves the relationship between employers and their unionized employees or their employees being unionized. The legal framework for this field of law is primarily set forth in the National Labor Relations Act (which includes the Taft-Hartley Act), although a number of other acts such as the Labor Management Reporting and Disclosure Act, the Davis-Bacon Act and the Railway Labor Act also impact the field. The relationship between an employer and a union representing its employees is usually set forth in a collective bargaining agreement (CBA), which establishes for a period of years the pay, benefits and other terms of employment to be provided to employees in the bargaining unit. In addition, a CBA typically contains a method for handling employee performance issues (i.e., progressive discipline) and provides for the ultimate resolution, through a final, binding arbitration process, of any dispute between the union and the employer. As a part of this dispute-resolution system, the CBA would also likely contain a no-strike, no-lockout provision for the duration of the agreement. Labor law, as a field, also involves the rights of individual union members to receive fair representation from their union.

---

2. *See id.* at 125-26.

3. The principal exceptions exist in public policy and implied contract, or where the employer has recognized a union and belongs to a collective bargain.

As a part of, and following, the Civil Rights movement of the 1960's, workers in non-union and unionized workplaces acquired numerous individual rights through federal and state law protections, primarily in the discrimination area, and with this legislation, the modern field of employment law emerged. Workers acquired these rights from a variety of sources including the Civil Rights Act of 1964, the Age Discrimination in Employment Act, the Employee Retirement Income Security Act, the Americans with Disabilities Act, the Consolidated Omnibus Budget Reconciliation Act, the Family Medical Leave Act, the Worker Adjustment and Retraining Notification Act, and the Occupational Safety and Health Act, as well as countless related state laws and local ordinances. These laws substantively govern the employer/employee relationship and give significant rights to non-unionized (as well as unionized) employees. Furthermore, state laws and local ordinances mirroring the federal laws gave rise to the creation of state and municipal departments overseeing employee rights, which in turn incentivized companies to institute significant internal departments of human resources to ensure compliance.

Employment law, as a field, has thus developed around these statutes and various common law rights affecting the workplace, including such matters as discrimination, wrongful termination, workplace safety, harassment, rights of whistleblowers, family leave, health care coverage, pay for overtime, etc. Because of the many issues that may arise in the workplace, employers frequently create employee manuals setting forth company policies and those polices are often the subject of legal review and scrutiny. Employment law also includes the law governing individual agreements between employers and employees establishing the significant terms of employment, or those agreements prepared in connection with an employee's separation from employment. These agreements, when involving executives, typically contain post-employment restrictive covenants involving non-solicitation of customers or employees and non-competition clauses. Over the past 45 years, the field of employment law has developed into one that affects most of the U.S. workforce and occupies a prominent place in many U.S. law firms.

John Levi
Partner
Sidley Austin LLP

The terms of employment contained in an employment agreement extend beyond just duration or term of employment. They typically include scope of employment and employment responsibilities, whether the work is full- or part-time, compensation and frequency of payment, employee position and reporting relationship, work location, benefits (including medical and dental coverage, sick leave, vacation days, and participation in an employer-sponsored retirement plan), restrictive covenants (most often limiting use of confidential materials and preventing work for competitors), severance rights, and dispute resolution procedures.

The employment agreement may also incorporate by reference the employer's code of conduct as well as specific policies and procedures pertaining to travel and expense reimbursement, pre- and post-employment background checks, drug testing, surveillance of employee communications, and other privacy rights. In some cases, an employee handbook or a code of conduct may add to the rights and obligations specifically contained in the employment agreement and provided by applicable law.[4] Consider, for example, a handbook that American Colloid Company distributed, entitled "For the New Employee of American Colloid Company," which provided, in part:

Probation

All new employees are automatically on a probationary period at the beginning of their employment. During this period, their abilities and work performance are closely evaluated by their supervisor. If for any reason, on or before the end of this period, it is determined that an employee is not suited for the job for which he was hired, his employment may be terminated. At the completion of the probationary period, you will become a permanent employee.[5]

As a result of this company policy, the Supreme Court of Wyoming found that a former American Colloid employee had an "enforceable right to be discharged only for cause" or, in other words, that the employee, after the probationary period, was no longer an at-will employee.[6]

Employment agreements for executives may or may not provide for a specific term of employment but are likely to distinguish between "for cause" and "for convenience" termination and address the payments the executive will receive in the event of termination on each of these grounds. They are also likely to contain

---

4. *See, e.g., Weiner v. McGraw-Hill, Inc.*, 457 N.Y.S.2d 193 (N.Y. 1982) (finding that the employee stated a cause of action where certain rights in the employee handbook were not respected when he was fired); *Leithead v. Am. Colloid Co.*, 721 P.2d 1059, 1062-63 (Wyo. 1986) (noting that terms included in the employee handbook were considered a binding part of the employment contracts); *Parker v. Mat-Su Council on Prevention of Alcoholism and Drug Abuse*, 813 P.2d 665, 666 (Alaska 1991) ("When the provisions of a personnel manual create the reasonable expectation that employees have been granted certain rights, the employer is bound by the representations contained in those provisions."); *Gagliardi v. Denny's Rests., Inc.*, 815 P.2d 1362, 1366 (Wash. 1991) ("This handbook formed a contract between defendant and plaintiff."). In addition, in cases where an employee manual is contractually binding, some courts find that an employer may make unilateral changes to the handbook and that these changes will be binding upon the employee who continues to work at the company, as long as the employee is given proper notice of the changes. In contrast, other courts require something more (e.g., a new benefit to the employee or a new detriment to the employer) to provide adequate consideration for the modification. *Compare Browning v. 24 Hour Fitness, Inc.*, No. C05-5732RBL, 2006 WL 151933, at *2 (W.D. Wash 2006) (consideration for modification found in continued work), *with Doyle v. Holy Cross Hosp.*, 708 N.E.2d 1140, 1144 (Ill. 1999) (holding that a unilateral modification of a contractually binding employee handbook failed for lack of consideration and that the employee's continued work did not constitute the requisite consideration).

5. *Leithead*, 721 P.2d at 1061.

6. *Id.* at 1063. *But see Stedillie v. Am. Colloid Co.*, 967 F.2d 274 (8th Cir. 1992) (holding that, under South Dakota law, employee of American Colloid given the same handbook was still an at-will employee subject to termination at any time).

elaborate provisions addressing payments to the executive in the event the corporate employer experiences a change in control or ownership.

A Practitioner Perspective: Negotiating the More Challenging Terms of Employment and Separation Agreements

Although the vast majority of American workers are employed "at-will" and the number of unionized workers covered by collective bargaining agreements has declined, an increasing number of employees, especially at the executive level, are entering into employment contracts covering the terms and conditions of their employment. And with many employees, including those who do not have a written employment agreement, the use of a separation and release agreement has become common when the employee leaves the employer and receives additional consideration above and beyond what they were otherwise entitled to receive. Employment lawyers play an increasingly important role in the drafting of these agreements and the interpretation and enforcement of them when disputes arise.

The most heavily negotiated and carefully drafted provisions of employment agreements generally involve compensation and benefits, grounds for termination, severance payments and post-employment restrictions. While the "base salary" terms are simply a matter of negotiation, the lure of many agreements will be the incentive or bonus compensation provisions. Whether bonuses are guaranteed, tied to the achievement of performance targets or completely discretionary, whether they are paid in cash, deferred compensation or equity, and whether or not such compensation can be forfeited or "clawed back" for competition or negative performance in the future are some of the most intensely negotiated provisions of these agreements. Another extremely important provision involves the definition of termination for cause by the employer and termination for "good reason" by the employee. Interpretation and application of these provisions are typically at the center of most disputes when the employment contract is terminated before its natural expiration date. Careful attention needs to be paid to the precise reasons for termination, whether any notice needs to be given and whether or not there are cure periods for reasons that could eventually justify a termination. Post-employment restrictions range from notice or garden leave provisions to full-blown covenants not to compete, with intermediate restrictions like customer non-solicitation and employee non-solicitation.

The most heavily negotiated terms of separation and release agreements typically involve consideration to be paid for the release of claims, the scope and breadth of the release, confidentiality with respect to the terms of the separation, non-disparagement, the type of reference the employer will give, whether the individual can apply for re-hire and the tax treatment of the consideration being paid. If claims under federal statutes like the Age Discrimination in Employment Act are being released, a bevy of additional requirements under the Older Workers Benefit Protection Act apply to the terms of the release including a requirement that the agreement be in plain English, that the employee be given up to 21 days to consider the proposed release and then 7 days to revoke any acceptance.

> In the event of layoffs where at least two individual employees are involved, additional requirements govern the enforceability of the release. It is critical that the employment lawyer carefully draft the release to ensure its ultimate enforceability.
>
> Michael Delikat
> Partner and Global Chair,
> Employment Practice Group
> Orrick, Herrington & Sutcliffe LLP

A. EXECUTIVE EMPLOYMENT AGREEMENT

The following agreement sets forth the rights and obligations of a corporate employer and a high-level executive.

Things to Consider . . .

As you read through the following agreement, please consider these items. You will want to return to the agreement, as you study the substantive discussion that follows.

> **Rights and Obligations.** What is the Executive getting, and what is the Executive giving under this Agreement? Specifically, what are the various forms of the Executive's compensation, and what are the Executive's responsibilities?
> **Termination.** What is the term of this Agreement? What allows each party to terminate the Agreement prior to its expiration? What are the consequences of the various types of termination under this Agreement? What provisions will continue to be in effect despite the expiration or termination of the Agreement?
> **Restrictive Covenants.** What purpose is served by the restrictive covenants (e.g., not to disclose, not to compete) found in this Agreement? Are these overbroad or reasonable given the relationship at issue? How does the Agreement attempt to ensure their enforceability?

EMPLOYMENT AGREEMENT[7]

EMPLOYMENT AGREEMENT, dated as of July 28, 2009 (this "Agreement"), between SIRIUS XM RADIO INC., a Delaware corporation (the "Company"), and SCOTT A. GREENSTEIN (the "Executive").

In consideration of the mutual covenants and conditions set forth herein, the Company and the Executive agree as follows:

---

7. Sirius XM Radio Inc., Employment Agreement (Form 8-K), at Exhibit 10.1 (July 29, 2009), *available at* http://www.sec.gov/Archives/edgar/data/908937/000093041309003897/c58358_ex10-1.htm.

1. Employment. Subject to the terms and conditions of this Agreement, the Company hereby employs the Executive, and the Executive hereby agrees to continue his employment with the Company.

2. Duties and Reporting Relationship. (a) The Executive shall be employed in the capacity of President and Chief Content Officer of the Company. In such capacity, the Executive shall be responsible for management of all aspects of the Company's programming and corporate brand marketing functions and all personnel working in such areas shall report to the Executive. During the Term (as defined below), the Executive shall, on a full-time basis and consistent with the needs of the Company, use his skills and render services to the best of his ability. The Executive shall perform such activities and duties consistent with his position as the Chief Executive Officer of the Company shall from time to time reasonably specify and direct. During the Term, the Executive shall not perform any consulting services for, or engage in any other business enterprises with, any third parties without the express written consent of the Chief Executive Officer of the Company or the General Counsel of the Company, other than passive investments.

(b) The Executive shall generally perform his duties and conduct his business at the principal offices of the Company in New York, New York.

(c) The Executive shall report solely to the Chief Executive Officer of the Company.

3. Term. The term of this Agreement shall commence on July 28, 2009 (the "Effective Date") and end on July 27, 2013, unless terminated earlier pursuant to the provisions of Section 6 (the "Term").

4. Compensation. (a) During the Term, the Executive shall be paid an annual base salary of $850,000; provided that on (i) January 1, 2010 such annual base salary shall be increased to no less than $925,000, (ii) January 1, 2011 such annual base salary shall be increased to no less than $1,000,000, (iii) January 1, 2012 such annual base salary shall be increased to no less than $1,100,000, (iv) January 1, 2013 such annual base salary shall be increased to no less than $1,250,000, and (v) thereafter may be subject to increase from time to time by recommendation of the Chief Executive Officer of the Company to, and approval by, the Board of Directors of the Company (the "Board") (such amount, as increased, the "Base Salary"). All amounts paid to the Executive under this Agreement shall be in U.S. dollars. The Base Salary shall be paid at least monthly and, at the option of the Company, may be paid more frequently.

(b) On the date hereof, the Company shall grant to the Executive an option to purchase 27,768,136 shares of the Company's common stock, par value $.001 per share (the "Common Stock"), at an exercise price of $0.43 per share, the closing price of the Common Stock on the Nasdaq Global Select Market on the date hereof. Such options shall be subject to the terms and conditions set forth in the Option Agreement attached to this Agreement as Exhibit A.

(c) All compensation paid to the Executive hereunder shall be subject to any payroll and withholding deductions required by applicable law, including, as and where applicable, federal, New York state and New York City income tax withholding, federal unemployment tax and social security (FICA).

5. Additional Compensation; Expenses and Benefits. (a) During the Term, the Company shall reimburse the Executive for all reasonable and necessary business expenses incurred and advanced by him in carrying out his duties under this Agreement. The Executive shall present to the Company an itemized account of all expenses in such form as may be required by the Company from time to time.

(b) During the Term, the Executive shall be entitled to participate fully in any other benefit plans, programs, policies and fringe benefits which may be made available to the executive officers of the Company generally, including, without limitation, disability, medical, dental and life insurance and benefits under the Company's 401(k) savings plan.

(c) During the Term, the Executive shall be entitled to participate in any bonus plans generally offered to executive officers of the Company. Bonuses may be subject to the Executive's individual performance and satisfaction of objectives established by the Board or the compensation committee thereof (the "Compensation Committee"). Bonuses may be paid in the form of cash, stock options, restricted stock, restricted stock units or other securities of the Company.

6. Termination. The date upon which the Executive's employment with the Company under this Agreement is deemed to be terminated in accordance with any of the provisions of this Section 6 is referred to herein as the "Termination Date." A termination of employment shall not be deemed to have occurred for purposes of any provision of this Agreement providing for the payment of any amounts or benefits upon or following a termination of employment unless such termination also constitutes a "separation from service" within the meaning of Section 409A ("Section 409A") of the Internal Revenue Code of 1986, as amended (the "Code"), and the regulations thereunder (a "Separation from Service"), and notwithstanding anything contained herein to the contrary, the date on which a Separation from Service takes place shall be the Termination Date.

(a) The Company has the right and may elect to terminate this Agreement for Cause at any time. For purposes of this Agreement, "Cause" means the occurrence or existence of any of the following:

(i) (A) a material breach by the Executive of the terms of this Agreement, (B) a material breach by the Executive of the Executive's duty not to engage in any transaction that represents, directly or indirectly, self-dealing with the Company or any of its affiliates (which, for purposes hereof, shall mean any individual, corporation, partnership, association, limited liability company, trust, estate, or other entity or organization directly or indirectly controlling, controlled by, or under direct or indirect common control with the Company) which has not been approved by a majority of the disinterested directors of the Board, or (C) the Executive's violation of the Company's Code of Ethics which is demonstrably and materially injurious to the Company, if any such material breach or violation described in clauses (A), (B) or (C), to the extent curable, remains uncured after 15 days have elapsed following the date on which the Company gives the Executive written notice of such material breach or violation;

(ii) the Executive's act of dishonesty, misappropriation, embezzlement, intentional fraud, or similar intentional misconduct by the Executive involving the Company or any of its affiliates;

(iii) the Executive's conviction or the plea of *nolo contendere* or the equivalent in respect of a felony;

(iv) any damage of a material nature to any property of the Company or any of its affiliates caused by the Executive's willful misconduct or gross negligence;

(v) the repeated nonprescription use of any controlled substance or the repeated use of alcohol or any other non-controlled substance that, in the reasonable good faith opinion of the Board, renders the Executive unfit to serve as an officer of the Company or its affiliates;

(vi) the Executive's failure to comply with the Chief Executive Officer's reasonable written instructions on a material matter within 5 days; or

(vii) conduct by the Executive that in the reasonable good faith written determination of the Board demonstrates unfitness to serve as an officer of the Company or its affiliates, including a finding by the Board or any judicial or regulatory authority that the Executive committed acts of unlawful harassment or violated any other state, federal or local law or ordinance prohibiting discrimination in employment.

Termination of the Executive for Cause pursuant to this Section 6(a) shall be communicated by a Notice of Termination for Cause. For purposes of this Agreement, a "Notice of Termination for Cause" shall mean delivery to the Executive of a copy of a resolution or resolutions duly adopted by the affirmative vote of not less than a majority of the directors (other than the Executive, if the Executive is then serving on the Board) present (in person or by teleconference) and voting at a meeting of the Board called and held for that purpose after 15 days' notice to the Executive (which notice the Company shall use reasonable efforts to confirm that Executive has actually received and which notice for purposes of this Section 6(a) may be delivered, in addition to the requirements set forth in Section 17, through the use of electronic mail) and a reasonable opportunity for the Executive, together with the Executive's counsel, to be heard before the Board prior to such vote, finding that in the good faith opinion of the Board, the Executive was guilty of conduct set forth in any of clauses (i) through (vii) of this Section 6(a) and specifying the particulars thereof in reasonable detail. For purposes of this Section 6(a), this Agreement shall terminate on the date specified by the Board in the Notice of Termination for Cause.

(b) (i) This Agreement and the Executive's employment shall terminate upon the death of the Executive.

(ii) If the Executive is unable to perform the essential duties and functions of his position because of a disability, even with a reasonable accommodation, for one hundred eighty days within any three hundred sixty-five day period ("Disability"), the Company shall have the right and may elect to terminate the services of the Executive by a Notice of Disability Termination. The Executive shall not be terminated following a Disability except pursuant to this Section 6(b)(ii). For purposes of this Agreement, a "Notice of Disability Termination" shall mean a written notice that sets forth in reasonable detail the facts and circumstances claimed to provide a basis for termination of the Executive's employment under this Section 6(b)(ii). For purposes of this Agreement, no such purported termination shall be effective without such Notice of Disability Termination. This Agreement shall terminate on the day such Notice of Disability Termination is received by the Executive.

(c) The Executive shall have the absolute right to terminate his employment at any time with or without Good Reason. Should the Executive wish to resign from his position with the Company during the Term, for other than Good Reason (as defined below), the Executive shall give at least fourteen days prior written notice to the Company. This Agreement shall terminate on the effective date of the resignation set forth in the notice of resignation, however, the Company may, at its sole discretion, instruct that the Executive perform no job responsibilities and cease his active employment immediately upon receipt of the notice from the Executive.

(d) The Company shall have the absolute right to terminate the Executive's employment without Cause at any time. This Agreement shall terminate one day following receipt of such notice by the Executive, however, the Company may, at its sole discretion, instruct that the Executive cease active employment and perform no more job duties immediately upon provision of such notice to the Executive.

(e) Should the Executive wish to resign from his position with the Company for Good Reason during the Term, the Executive shall give seven days prior written notice to the Company. This Agreement shall terminate on the date specified in such notice, however, the Company may, at its sole discretion, instruct that the Executive cease active employment and perform no more job duties immediately upon receipt of such notice from the Executive.

For purposes of this Agreement, "Good Reason" shall mean the continuance of any of the following events (without the Executive's prior written consent) for a period of thirty days after delivery to the Company by the Executive of a notice of the occurrence of such event:

(i) the assignment to the Executive by the Company of duties not reasonably consistent with the Executive's positions, duties, responsibilities, titles or offices at the commencement of the Term, any material reduction in the Executive's duties or responsibilities as described in Section 2 or any removal of the Executive from or any failure to re-elect the Executive to any of such positions or the Executive not being the most senior executive, other than the Company's Chief Executive Officer, who is responsible for all programming and corporate brand marketing activities and personnel (except in connection with the termination of the Executive's employment for Cause, Disability or as a result of the Executive's death or by the Executive other than for Good Reason); or

(ii) the Executive ceasing to report directly to the Chief Executive Officer of the Company; or

(iii) any requirement that the Executive report for work to a location more than 25 miles from the Company's current headquarters for more than 30 days in any calendar year, excluding any requirement that results from the damage or destruction of the Company's current headquarters as a result of natural disasters, terrorism, acts of war or acts of God; or

(iv) any reduction in the Base Salary; or

(v) the Company's failure to make a *bona fide* offer in writing to renew this Agreement, for an additional one-year term, on the terms and conditions set forth in this Agreement (including the Base Salary set forth in Section 4(a), but excluding any equity-based compensation set forth in Section 4(b)), at least 90 days prior to (x) the fourth anniversary of the Effective Date and (y) each subsequent anniversary of the Effective Date following the fourth anniversary of the Effective Date; provided that (for purposes of this clause (y) only) this Agreement has been renewed on the previous anniversary of the Effective Date; or

(vi) any material breach by the Company of this Agreement.

(f) (i) If the employment of the Executive is terminated by the Company for Cause, by the Executive other than for Good Reason or due to death or Disability, the Executive shall, in lieu of any future payments or benefits under this Agreement, be entitled to (A) any earned but unpaid Base Salary and any business expenses incurred but not reimbursed, in each case, prior to the Termination Date and (B) any other vested benefits under any other benefit plans or programs in accordance with the terms of such plans and programs (collectively, the "Accrued Payments and Benefits").

(ii) If the employment of the Executive is terminated without Cause or the Executive terminates his employment for Good Reason, then the Executive shall have an absolute and unconditional right to receive, and the Company shall pay to the Executive without setoff, counterclaim or other withholding, except as set forth in Section 4(c), (A) the Accrued Payments and Benefits, (B) a lump sum amount equal to the sum of (x) the Executive's annualized Base Salary then in effect and (y) an amount in cash equal to the bonus, whether denominated as an annual, performance, incentive, retention or other bonus, last paid (or due and payable) to the Executive in respect of the fiscal year immediately preceding the year in which the Termination Date occurs, and (C) the continuation, at the Company's expense (by direct payment, not reimbursement to the Executive) of (1) medical and dental benefits in a manner that will not be taxable to the Executive and (2) life insurance benefits, on the same terms as provided by the Company for active employees for one year following the Termination Date. The lump sum amount contemplated by clause (B) above shall be paid on the 60th day following the Termination Date.

(g) The Company's obligations under Section 6(f)(ii) shall be conditioned upon the Executive executing, delivering, and not revoking during the seven day revocation period a waiver and release of claims against the Company, substantially in the form attached as Exhibit B (the "Release") within 60 days following the Termination Date; provided that the Executive shall have no obligation to execute such Release in order to receive the payments and benefits under Section 6(f)(ii) in the event that a Release executed by the Company has not been delivered by the Company to the Executive within five days following the Termination Date.

(h) Notwithstanding any provisions of this Agreement to the contrary, if the Executive is a "specified employee" (within the meaning of Section 409A and determined pursuant to policies adopted by the Company) at the time of his Separation from Service and if any portion of the payments or benefits to be received by the Executive upon Separation from Service would be considered deferred compensation under Section 409A ("Nonqualified Deferred Compensation"), amounts that would otherwise be payable pursuant to this Agreement during the six-month period immediately following the Executive's Separation from Service that constitute Nonqualified Deferred Compensation and benefits that would otherwise be provided pursuant to this Agreement during the six-month period immediately following the Executive's Separation from Service that constitute Nonqualified Deferred Compensation will instead be paid or made available on the earlier of (x) the first business day of the seventh month following the date of the Executive's Separation from Service and (y) the Executive's death.

7. **Nondisclosure of Confidential Information.** (a) The Executive acknowledges that in the course of his employment he will occupy a position of trust and confidence. The Executive shall not, except in connection with the performance of his functions or as required by applicable law, disclose to others or use, directly or indirectly, any Confidential Information.

(b) "Confidential Information" shall mean information about the Company's business and operations that is not disclosed by the Company for financial reporting purposes and that was learned by the Executive in the course of his employment by the Company, including, without limitation, any business plans, product plans, strategy, budget information, proprietary knowledge, patents, trade secrets, data, formulae, sketches, notebooks, blueprints, information and client and customer lists and all papers and records (including computer records) of the documents containing such Confidential Information, other than information that is publicly disclosed by the Company in writing. The Executive acknowledges that such Confidential Information is specialized, unique in nature and of great value to the Company, and that such information gives the Company a competitive advantage. The Executive agrees to deliver or return to the Company, at the Company's request at any time or upon termination or expiration of his employment or as soon as possible thereafter, all documents, computer tapes and disks, records, lists, data, drawings, prints, notes and written information (and all copies thereof) furnished by or on behalf of the Company or prepared by the Executive in the course of his employment by the Company, provided that the Executive will be able to keep his cell phones, blackberries, personal computers, personal rolodex and the like so long as any Confidential Information is removed from such items.

(c) The provisions of this Section 7 shall survive indefinitely.

8. <u>Covenant Not to Compete</u>. During the Restricted Period (as defined below), the Executive shall not, directly or indirectly, enter into the employment of, render services to, or acquire any interest whatsoever in (whether for his own account as an individual proprietor, or as a partner, associate, stockholder, officer, director, consultant, trustee or otherwise), or otherwise assist, any person or entity engaged in any operations in North America involving the transmission of radio entertainment programming, the production of radio entertainment programming, the syndication of radio entertainment programming, the promotion of radio entertainment programming or the marketing of radio entertainment programming, in each case, in competition with the Company (each, a "<u>Competitive Activity</u>"); <u>provided</u> that nothing in this Agreement shall prevent the purchase or ownership by the Executive by way of investment of less than five percent of the shares or equity interest of any corporation or other entity. Without limiting the generality of the foregoing, the Executive agrees that during the Restricted Period, the Executive shall not call on or otherwise solicit business or assist others to solicit business from any of the customers of the Company as to any product or service described above that competes with any product or service provided or marketed by the Company on the date of the Executive's termination of employment with the Company during the Term (as such Term may be extended in accordance with Section 6(e)(5) of the Agreement) (the "<u>Milestone Date</u>"). The Executive agrees that during the Restricted Period he will not solicit or assist others to solicit the employment of or hire any employee of the Company without the prior written consent of the Company. For purposes of this Agreement, the "<u>Restricted Period</u>" shall mean the period of one year following the Milestone Date. For purposes of this Agreement, the term "radio" shall mean terrestrial radio, satellite radio, HD radio, internet radio and other audio delivered terrestrially, by satellite, HD or the internet (which audio is not coupled with moving visual elements, such as television, movies, or other moving visual images delivered via the internet or otherwise). Notwithstanding anything to the contrary in this Section 8, it shall not be a violation of this Section 8 for the Executive to join a division or business line of a commercial enterprise with multiple divisions or business lines if such division or business line is not engaged in a Competitive Activity; provided that the Executive performs services solely for such non-competitive division or business line.

9. <u>Change in Control Provisions</u>. If the Executive is, in the opinion of a nationally recognized accounting firm jointly selected by the Executive and the Company, required to pay an excise tax on "excess parachute payments" (as defined in Section 280G(b) of the Code) under Section 4999 of the Code as a result of an acceleration of the vesting of stock options or otherwise, the Company shall have an absolute and unconditional

obligation to pay the Executive in accordance with the terms of this Section 9 the amount of such taxes. In addition, the Company shall have an absolute and unconditional obligation to pay the Executive such additional amounts as are necessary to place the Executive in the exact same financial position that he would have been in if he had not incurred any tax liability under Section 4999 of the Code. The determination of the exact amount, if any, of any "excess parachute payments" and any tax liability under Section 4999 of the Code shall be made by a nationally-recognized independent accounting firm selected by the Executive and the Company. The fees and expenses of such accounting firm shall be paid by the Company. The determination of such accounting firm shall be final and binding on the parties. The Company irrevocably agrees to pay to the Executive, in immediately available funds to an account designated in writing by the Executive, any amounts to be paid under this Section 9 within two business days after receipt by the Company of written notice from the accounting firm which sets forth such accounting firm's determination. In addition, in the event that such payments are not sufficient to pay all excise taxes on "excess parachute payments" under Section 4999 of the Code as a result of an acceleration of the vesting of options or for any other reason and to place the Executive in the exact same financial position that he would have been in if he had not incurred any tax liability under Section 4999 of the Code, then the Company shall have an absolute and unconditional obligation to pay the Executive such additional amounts as may be necessary to pay such excise taxes and place the Executive in the exact same financial position that he would have been had he not incurred any tax liability as a result of a change in control under the Code. Notwithstanding the foregoing, in the event that a written ruling (whether public or private) of the Internal Revenue Service ("IRS") is obtained by or on behalf of the Company or the Executive, which ruling expressly provides that the Executive is not required to pay, or is entitled to a refund with respect to, all or any portion of such excise taxes or additional amounts, the Executive shall promptly reimburse the Company in an amount equal to all amounts paid to the Executive pursuant to this Section 9 less any excise taxes or additional amounts which remain payable by, or are not refunded to, the Executive after giving effect to such IRS ruling. Each of the Company and the Executive agrees to promptly notify the other party if it receives any such IRS ruling. The payments contemplated by this Section 9 shall in all events be paid no later than the end of the Executive's taxable year next following the Executive's taxable year in which the excise tax (and any income or other related tax or interest or penalties thereon) on a payment is remitted to IRS or any other applicable taxing authority; or, in the case of amounts relating to any claim by IRS or any other taxing authority that does not result in the remittance of any federal, state, local and foreign income, excise, social security and other taxes, the calendar year in which the claim is finally settled or otherwise resolved. Any amounts required to be repaid to the Company pursuant to this Section 9 will be repaid to the Company within five business days of the Executive's receipt of any refund with respect to any excise tax.

10. **Remedies**. The Executive and Company agree that damages for breach of any of the covenants under Sections 7 and 8 will be difficult to determine and inadequate to remedy the harm which may be caused thereby, and therefore consent that these covenants may be enforced by temporary or permanent injunction without the necessity of bond. The Executive believes, as of the date of this Agreement, that the provisions of this Agreement are reasonable and that the Executive is capable of gainful employment without breaching this Agreement. However, should any court or arbitrator decline to enforce any provision of Section 7 or 8 of this Agreement, this Agreement shall, to the extent applicable in the circumstances before such court or arbitrator, be deemed to be modified to restrict the Executive's competition with the Company to the maximum extent of time, scope and geography which the court or arbitrator shall find enforceable, and such provisions shall be so enforced.

11. **Indemnification**. The Company shall indemnify the Executive to the full extent provided in the Company's Amended and Restated Certificate of Incorporation and Amended and Restated Bylaws and the law of the State of Delaware in connection with his activities as an officer of the Company.

12. **Entire Agreement**. The provisions contained herein constitute the entire agreement between the parties with respect to the subject matter hereof and supersede any and all prior agreements, understandings and communications between the parties, oral or written, with respect to such subject matter, including the Employment Agreement between the Executive and the Company dated May 5, 2004, as amended, but excluding any equity award agreements between the Executive and the Company.

13. **Modification**. Any waiver, alteration, amendment or modification of any provisions of this Agreement shall not be valid unless in writing and signed by both the Executive and the Company.

14. **Severability**. If any provision of this Agreement shall be declared to be invalid or unenforceable, in whole or in part, such invalidity or unenforceability shall not affect the remaining provisions hereof, which shall remain in full force and effect.

15. **Assignment**. The Executive may not assign any of his rights or delegate any of his duties hereunder without the prior written consent of the Company. The Company may not assign any of its rights or delegate any of

its obligations hereunder without the prior written consent of the Executive, except that any successor to the Company by merger or purchase of all or substantially all of the Company's assets shall assume this Agreement.

16. <u>Binding Effect</u>. This Agreement shall be binding upon and inure to the benefit of the successors in interest of the Executive and the Company.

17. <u>Notices</u>. All notices and other communications required or permitted hereunder shall be made in writing and shall be deemed effective when delivered personally or transmitted by facsimile transmission, one business day after deposit with a nationally recognized overnight courier (with next day delivery specified) and five days after mailing by registered or certified mail:

if to the Company:

[Company Notice Information Omitted]

if to the Executive:

[Executive Notice Information Omitted]

with a copy to:

[Law Firm Notice Information Omitted]

or to such other person or address as either party shall furnish in writing to the other party from time to time.

18. <u>Governing Law</u>. This Agreement shall be governed by and construed in accordance with the laws of the State of New York applicable to contracts made and to be performed entirely within the State of New York.

19. <u>Non-Mitigation</u>. The Executive shall not be required to mitigate damages or seek other employment in order to receive compensation or benefits under Section 6 of this Agreement; nor shall the amount of any benefit or payment provided for under Section 6 of this Agreement be reduced by any compensation earned by the Executive as the result of employment by another employer.

20. <u>Arbitration</u>. (a) The Executive and the Company agree that if a dispute arises concerning or relating to the Executive's employment with the Company, or the termination of the Executive's employment, such dispute shall be submitted to binding arbitration under the rules of the American Arbitration Association regarding resolution of employment disputes in effect at the time such dispute arises. The arbitration shall take place in New York, New York, before a single experienced arbitrator licensed to practice law in New York and selected in accordance with the American Arbitration Association rules and procedures. Except as provided below,

the Executive and the Company agree that this arbitration procedure will be the exclusive means of redress for any disputes relating to or arising from the Executive's employment with the Company or his termination, including disputes over rights provided by federal, state, or local statutes, regulations, ordinances, and common law, including all laws that prohibit discrimination based on any protected classification. The parties expressly waive the right to a jury trial, and agree that the arbitrator's award shall be final and binding on both parties, and shall not be appealable. The arbitrator shall have discretion to award monetary and other damages, and any other relief that the arbitrator deems appropriate and is allowed by law. The arbitrator shall have the discretion to award the prevailing party reasonable costs and attorneys' fees incurred in bringing or defending an action, and shall award such costs and fees to the Executive in the event the Executive prevails on the merits of any action brought hereunder.

(b) The Company shall pay the cost of any arbitration proceedings under this Agreement if the Executive prevails in such arbitration on at least one substantive issue.

(c) The Company and the Executive agree that the sole dispute that is excepted from Section 20(a) is an action seeking injunctive relief from a court of competent jurisdiction regarding enforcement and application of Sections 7, 8 or 10 of this Agreement, which action may be brought in addition to, or in place of, an arbitration proceeding in accordance with Section 20(a).

21. <u>Compliance with Section 409A</u>. (a) To the extent applicable, it is intended that the compensation arrangements under this Agreement be in full compliance with Section 409A (it being understood that certain compensation arrangements under this Agreement are intended not to be subject to Section 409A). The Agreement shall be construed, to the maximum extent permitted, in a manner to give effect to such intention. Notwithstanding anything in this Agreement to the contrary, distributions upon termination of the Executive's employment may only be made upon a Separation from Service. Neither the Company nor any of its affiliates shall have any obligation to indemnify or otherwise hold the Executive harmless from any or all such taxes, interest or penalties, or liability for any damages related thereto. The Executive acknowledges that he has been advised to obtain independent legal, tax or other counsel in connection with Section 409A.

(b) With respect to any amount of expenses eligible for reimbursement under this Agreement, such expenses will be reimbursed by the Company within thirty (30) days following the date on which the Company receives the applicable invoice from the Executive in accordance with the Company's expense reimbursement policies, but in no event later than the last day of the Executive's taxable year following the taxable year in which the Executive incurs the related expenses. In no event will the reimbursements or in-kind benefits to be provided by the Company in one taxable year affect the amount of reimbursements or in-kind benefits to be provided in any other taxable year, nor will the Executive's right to reimbursement or in-kind benefits be subject to liquidation or exchange for another benefit.

(c) Each payment under this Agreement shall be regarded as a "separate payment" and not of a series of payments for purposes of Section 409A.

22. <u>Counterparts</u>. This Agreement may be executed in counterparts, all of which shall be considered one and the same agreement, and shall become effective when one or more counterparts have been signed by each of the parties and delivered to the other party.

23. <u>Executive's Representation</u>. The Executive hereby represents and warrants to Company that he is not now under any contractual or other obligation that is inconsistent with or in conflict with this Agreement or that would prevent, limit, or impair the Executive's performance of his obligations under this Agreement.

24. <u>Survivorship</u>. Upon the expiration or other termination of this Agreement or the Executive's employment with the Company, the respective rights and obligations of the parties hereto shall survive to the extent necessary to carry out the intentions of the parties under this Agreement.

[Signature Page Omitted]

[Exhibits Omitted]

---

1. Familiarity Breeds Fluency: A Review

Prior to this Agreement, you had not encountered an employment agreement in this book. Yet, hopefully you found much of the Agreement to be somewhat familiar.

- Section 7 of this Agreement imposes confidentiality obligations. Why do you suppose confidentiality obligations are important in the context of this relationship? Are these obligations mutual or unilateral? How does § 7(b) define "Confidential Information"? How does this definition compare to the definitions found in the two NDAs in Chapter 1? What is the effect of the Executive's acknowledgments in § 7(b)? (See Chapter 1.)

- Section 10 provides that both parties agree that equitable relief is appropriate and that damages would be an inadequate remedy. What effect is this provision likely to have in court? What are some reasons one or both parties may wish to include this type of provision? (See Chapter 1.)

- Section 12 contains an integration clause. What is the effect of integration clauses? Are they dispositive of the question of integration? Does this clause purport that the Agreement is *completely* or *partially* integrated? (See Chapter 1.)

- Section 14 contains a severability clause. What is the effect of severability clauses? (See Chapter 1.)

- Section 15 contains an anti-assignment provision. Does this provision prohibit the assignment of rights and duties, or is it likely that a court will read this provision only to prohibit the delegation of duties? Does this provision render a prohibited assignment void? (See Chapter 1.)

- What law likely governs this Agreement? How do you know? (See Chapter 1.)

- Section 6 provides the mechanisms by which the Agreement may be terminated, which we discuss at greater length below. Section 24 further provides a vague statement that the parties' rights and obligations shall survive "to the extent necessary to carry out the intentions of the parties under this Agreement." To make clear at least one of those intentions, note that § 7(c) provides that § 7 ("Nondisclosure of Confidential Information") shall survive termination indefinitely. (See Chapter 1.)

2. No-Oral-Modification Provisions

In Chapter 1, we discussed integration and the application of the parol evidence rule. There we saw that the parol evidence rule helps determine what actually were the terms of agreement at the time of contracting (i.e., whether a contractual document contains the final terms of agreement). However, integration and the parol evidence rule do not apply to prevent *future* terms from becoming part of a contract. That is, a contractual document may indeed be completely integrated and contain the universe of an agreement's final terms, but the parties may "modify" this agreement going forward. Given this, the parties may attempt to provide by contract how modification of that contract may or may not be effective.

Section 13 ("Modification") provides that modifying any aspect of the Agreement is only valid if certain conditions—that the modification is in writing and signed by both the Executive and the Company—are satisfied. Can a contract control how it may be modified? Provided that there is consideration sufficient to support a later contract,[8] can an earlier contract stop parties from entering into a later contract that effectively alters the parties' contractual relationship?

The general, common-law rule is that an earlier contract cannot bind a later contract, and that a contract purporting to limit the power of the parties to modify that contract has no effect.[9] Some states—notably New York and California—have attempted by statute to alter the common-law rule and to give bite to no-oral-modification provisions.[10] Still, courts (and the statutes themselves) have narrowed the effect of these statutory incursions on the right of parties to modify their contracts. For example, a New York court has held that a party may be equitably estopped from barring proof of oral modification, notwithstanding the New York statute, where such party "has induced another's significant and substantial reliance upon an oral modification," and where such "conduct relied upon to establish estoppel [is] not otherwise . . . compatible with the agreement as written."[11]

As with acknowledgments of trade-secret status (as discussed in Chapter 1) and of reasonableness (as discussed below), it may still make sense to include a no-oral-modification provision despite that a court might not give effect to it. Are contracts only as useful as courts will enforce them? Consider that business

---

8. Additional consideration is not necessary for the modification of contracts governed by Article 2 of the U.C.C. Please see Chapter 4 for further discussion of this.

9. *See, e.g., Quality Prods. & Concepts Co. v. Nagel Precision, Inc.*, 666 N.W.2d 251, 253 (Mich. 2003) ("We hold that parties to a contract are free to *mutually* waive or modify their contract notwithstanding a written modification or anti-waiver clause because of the freedom to contract.") (emphasis in original); *Cambridgeport Sav. Bank v. Boersner*, 597 N.E.2d 1017, 1022 (Mass. 1992) ("[A] provision that an agreement may not be amended orally but only by a written instrument does not necessarily bar oral modification of the contract."); *A.W. Wendell & Sons, Inc. v. Qazi*, 626 N.E.2d 280, 287 (Ill. App. Ct. 1993) ("However, under Illinois law, parties to a written contract may alter or modify its terms by a subsequent oral agreement, even though the terms of the contract preclude oral modification.").

10. N.Y. GEN. OBLIG. LAW § 15-301 (Consol. 2001); CAL. CIV. CODE § 1698 (West 1985); *see also* U.C.C. § 2-209(2) (2003).

11. *Rosa v. Spa Realty Assocs.*, 366 N.E.2d 1279, 1283 (N.Y. 1977) (further explaining that partial performance may avoid the requirements of section 15-301, "[b]ut only if the partial performance [is] unequivocally referable to the oral modification is the requirement of a writing under section 15-301 avoided"); *see also MacIsaac & Menke Co. v. Cardox Corp.*, 14 Cal. Rptr. 523, 528 (Cal. Ct. App. 1961); *Nutrisoya Foods, Inc. v. Sunrich LLC*, 626 F. Supp. 2d 985, 990 (D. Minn. 2009). Note that CAL. CIV. CODE § 1698(b) (West 2009) provides that to the extent executed (where "[a]n executed contract is one, the object of which is fully performed," CAL. CIV. CODE § 1661 (West 2009)), an oral modification is effective to amend a written modification, and § 1698(d) preserves "the application of rules of law concerning estoppel, oral novation and substitution of a new agreement, rescission of a written contract by an oral agreement, waiver of a provision of a written contract, or oral independent collateral contracts." Also, U.C.C. § 2-209(4) (2003) provides that parties may waive a contractual provision that requires an amendment to be in writing. (Note that Article 2 of the Uniform Commercial Code only applies to contracts for the sale of goods; for more on this topic, please see Chapter 4.)

Also, note that the statute of frauds may require a modification to be in writing in order to be an effective contract. The general rule is that the modification must be in writing if the resultant contract, given the modification, must be in writing under the statute of frauds. For example, CAL. CIV. CODE § 1698(c) (West 2009) provides, "The statute of frauds . . . is required to be satisfied if the contract as modified is within its provisions."

reputation may animate contractual compliance and that parties may understand their contract as a manual of conduct.

3. Implied Waiver and No-Waiver Provisions

Section 13 of the Agreement, in addition to speaking to modification, provides that any "waiver" of any provision of the Agreement must be in writing to be effective. Waiver refers to the voluntary, intentional surrendering of a known right.[12] One may voluntarily and intentionally waive a right either by words that expressly waive the right or by deeds (which may also be words) that impliedly waive the right.[13] What deeds may rise to the level of an implied waiver? "An implied waiver may arise where a person against whom the waiver is asserted has pursued such a course of conduct as to sufficiently evidence an intention to waive a right or where his conduct is inconsistent with any other intention than to waive it."[14] The burden of showing evidence sufficient to show an intention of waiver is high—indeed, finding an implied waiver requires inferring that a party has given up a right. The more valuable this right, the greater the evidence generally must be to ensure that waiver of the right was intended.[15] In general, to find a waiver of a right, the waiver must be evidenced by "a clear, unequivocal, and decisive act of the party showing such purpose."[16]

Jurisdictions vary in their treatment of so-called "no-waiver clauses." In some states, courts enforce these provisions by their terms to prevent certain acts (e.g., acceptance of less than full performance) or failures to act from constituting a waiver of a right to damages and/or a waiver of a right to demand full performance in the future.[17] Still, even these courts are unlikely to find that a

---

12. *Delta Consulting Grp., Inc. v. R. Randle Constr., Inc.*, 554 F.3d 1133, 1140 (7th Cir. 2009); *Bott v. J.F. Shea Co., Inc.*, 388 F.3d 530, 533 (5th Cir. 2004) ("Under Texas law waiver is an intentional relinquishment of a known right or intentional conduct inconsistent with claiming that right.") (internal quotations omitted).

13. *Delta Consulting*, 554 F.3d at 1140.

14. *Id.*; *see also S. Colorado MRI, Ltd. v. Med-Alliance, Inc.*, 166 F.3d 1094, 1100 (10th Cir. 1999) ("[A]n implied waiver of a contractual right must be free from ambiguity and clearly manifest the intention not to assert the benefit.") (internal quotation marks omitted); *Little Beaver Enters. v. Humphreys Ry., Inc.*, 719 F.2d 75, 79 (4th Cir. 1983) ("Generally, this implied waiver is most often recognized where the party's conduct is inconsistent with any other intention than the waiver of contract rights or where the party accepts alternative performance which provides roughly the same protections as strict performance would have provided.").

15. *See, e.g., Groves v. Prickett*, 420 F.2d 1119, 1126 (9th Cir. 1970) ("As minimum requirements to constitute an 'implied waiver' of substantial rights, the conduct relied upon must be clear, decisive and unequivocal of a purpose to waive the legal rights involved. Otherwise, there is no waiver."); *Bank of Boston v. Haufler*, 482 N.E.2d 542, 547 n.9 (Mass. App. Ct. 1985) ("Unless required by some rule of law, waiver of valuable rights should not be lightly inferred.").

16. *Barnes v. Bradley Cnty. Mem'l Hosp.*, 161 F. App'x 555, 559 (6th Cir. 2006) (Tennessee law) (citation and internal quotation marks omitted); *see also Bott*, 388 F.3d at 533 (5th Cir. 2004) (Texas law) ("Waiver is largely a matter of intent, and for implied waiver to be found through a party's actions, intent must be clearly demonstrated by the facts and circumstances.").

17. *See, e.g., Wis. Elec. Power Co. v. Union Pac. R.R.*, 557 F.3d 504, 508 (7th Cir. 2009) (under Wisconsin law, no-waiver provisions are enforceable); *Cornus Corp. v. GEAC Enter. Solutions, Inc.*, 356 F. App'x 993, 995 (9th Cir.

no-waiver provision operates to nullify an express waiver.[18] Some jurisdictions will regard no-waiver clauses as only one piece of evidence in discerning whether or not a party has intended to waive a right.[19] In addition, some courts will find that no-waiver clauses themselves may be waived.[20] Still, a waiver of a no-waiver clause requires proof "by clear and convincing evidence" (a high evidentiary threshold) and must be proven as any other waiver.[21]

Contracts sometimes will also include "no-continuing-waiver" language, which does not speak to whether a particular act or omission rises to the level of a waiver of a right under the contract, but, rather, takes up the situation once there *is* a waiver of a contractual right and specifies that a single waiver of a right does not waive this right for all time.[22] These provisions are likely to give at least some weight to a finding that a single waiver or omission did not waive that right for all time.[23]

4. Arbitration and Dispute Resolution

Section 20 ("Arbitration") in the Agreement provides for exclusive, non-appealable, and binding arbitration for any dispute relating to the Executive's

---

2009) ("Non-waiver provisions are enforceable under Oregon law, at least so long as a party is alleged to have waived a right by a failure to act rather than by an affirmative act."); *America's Collectibles Network, Inc. v. MIG Broad. Grp., Inc.*, 330 F. App'x 81, 88 (6th Cir. 2009) (Tennessee law) ("The Agreement's no-waiver clause also renders defendants' argument unavailing."); *MAFCO Elec. Contractors, Inc. v. Turner Constr. Co.*, 357 F. App'x 395, 398 (2d Cir. 2009) (Connecticut law) ("Because of the subcontract's non-waiver provision and its incorporation by reference in the change order form, MAFCO must offer written evidence that Turner expressly waived its contractual rights and not simply that it engaged in some alleged course of dealing."); *Long Island Sav. Bank, FSB v. United States*, 503 F.3d 1234, 1252-53 (Fed. Cir. 2007) (non-waiver clause sufficient to prove no implied waiver of right occurred). *But see Republic Ins. Co. v. PAICO Receivables, LLC*, 383 F.3d 341, 348-49 (5th Cir. 2004) (citing *Cos. of Kingston v. Latona Trucking Inc.*, 159 F.3d 80, 85 (2d Cir. 1998)) (no-waiver clause of no effect when a party otherwise waives its right to arbitration).

18. *See supra* note 17.

19. *See, e.g., A LoPresti & Sons, Inc. v. Gen. Car & Truck Leasing Sys., Inc.*, 79 F. App'x 764 (6th Cir. 2003) (Ohio law); *Bott*, 388 F.3d at 534 ("Texas courts consider a contract's non-waiver clause to be some evidence of non-waiver, but not a substantive bar to finding that a particular provision was indeed waived.") (citation and internal quotation marks omitted); *Perry Eng'g Co. v. AT & T Commc'ns. Inc.*, No. 92-2050, 998 F.2d 1010, at *5 (4th Cir. 1993) (Virginia law) ("Although the contract's 'no waiver' clause provides evidence of AT & T's intent, it does not necessarily control. Like all contractual rights, the rights under the 'no waiver' clause are themselves subject to waiver.").

20. *See, e.g., Wis. Elec. Power Co.*, 557 F.3d at 508-09 (7th Cir. 2009); *A. LoPresti & Sons, Inc.*, 79 F. App'x at 769 ("[N]on-waiver clauses notwithstanding, parties that have acted in contradiction of their contractual rights have been held to have waived them.").

21. *Wis. Elec. Power Co.*, 557 F.3d at 508-09; *PPM Fin., Inc. v. Norandal USA, Inc.*, 297 F. Supp. 2d 1072, 1087 (N.D. Ill. 2004) ("[No-waiver clauses] are strictly enforceable under Illinois law, though they may be waived by [the] words and deeds of the parties, so long as the waiver is proved by clear and convincing evidence.") (quotation marks omitted).

22. *See, e.g., Perry v. Wolaver*, 506 F.3d 48, 54 (1st Cir. 2007) ("Perry's reliance on the 'non-waiver' provision is misdirected. Under the Note, a forbearance by Perry regarding a default does not waive Perry's right to any remedy under the Note during any *continuing* or *subsequent* default. That, however, is beside the point. The real issue is whether Perry could choose to excuse a specific default and waive the penalty for that specific default.") (emphasis added).

23. *See, e.g., N. Helex Co. v. United States*, 455 F.2d 546, 554 (Fed. Cl. 1972) ("With this provision in the contract it is very hard to infer a continuing waiver."); *Chapman v. VLM Entm't Grp., Inc.*, No. 00 C 7791, 2002 WL 1610970, at *5 (N.D. Ill. July 22, 2002).

employment. Arbitration is classically understood as beneficial, vis-à-vis traditional adjudication, for its increased speed and efficiency and reduced costs of process.[24] In addition, arbitration decisions may be kept private, unlike court decisions. However, arbitration is not without its downsides and detractors, who contend that society loses out when cases move from public adjudication to private settlement.[25] Moreover, a common complaint is that arbitrators are more apt to deliver "split the baby" decisions that attempt to strike a middle ground than to rule "correctly."

Exclusive (or mandatory) arbitration means that the movant may only proceed with his action through the arbitral process—and not, say, in state or federal court. In contrast, arbitration may be permissive. However, despite a contract's mandatory arbitration clause, a party generally need not submit to arbitration those questions that go to the existence or enforceability of the arbitration agreement itself.[26] This makes good axiomatic sense, as before an arbitration agreement can be enforced, there must be an enforceable agreement to arbitrate. Furthermore, that the Agreement qualifies arbitration as *non-appealable* means that an arbitrator's rendering of the claim may not be appealed to state or federal court (or anywhere else for that matter). Similarly, the Agreement specifies that arbitration is *binding* so as to make clear that the resulting decision is not mere recommendation but is rather a binding, final resolution of the issue. Contractually providing for these arbitration features is commonplace, and one can generally expect an arbitration provision to be respected by courts,[27] with an exception for any statutory claims for which "Congress itself has evinced an intention to preclude a waiver of judicial remedies. . . ."[28] In general, courts are

---

24. *See* Richard A. Bales, *Normative Consideration of Employment Arbitration at Gilmer's Quinceañera*, 81 Tul. L. Rev. 331 (2006).

25. *See, e.g.*, Owen M. Fiss, *Against Settlement*, 93 Yale L.J. 1073 (1984); Kathryn A. Sabbeth & David C. Vladeck, *Contracting (Out) Rights*, 36 Fordham Urb. L.J. 803 (2009).

26. *See AT & T Techs. v. Commc'ns Workers of Am.*, 475 U.S. 643, 643 (1986) (noting that the district court should have decided whether the parties agreed to submit to arbitration, not the arbitrator); *Janiga v. Questar Capital Corp.*, 615 F.3d 735, 742 (2010) ("[T]he court must decide whether a contract exists before it decides whether to stay an action and order arbitration."); *Spahr v. Secco*, 330 F.3d 1266, 1272-73 (10th Cir. 2003) (holding that the Federal Arbitration Act does not require the arbitrator to determine questions of whether something is subject to arbitration). A challenge to an agreement that contains an exclusive agreement to arbitrate such challenges must be brought in arbitration in accordance with the arbitration provision; however, if the arbitration provision itself is challenged as unenforceable, then a court is the proper forum to resolve this dispute. *See Rent-A-Center, W., Inc. v. Jackson*, 130 S. Ct. 2772, 2778-79 (2010) (holding that where a contract contains an agreement to arbitrate questions of enforceability of the contract, a challenge to the contract's enforceability but not specifically to the severable arbitration provision must be submitted to arbitration).

27. *See Circuit City Stores, Inc. v. Adams*, 532 U.S. 105, 119 (2001) (holding that a clause requiring an employee to submit to exclusive, final, and binding arbitration is enforceable under by the Federal Arbitration Act); *Gilmer v. Interstate/Johnson Lane*, 500 U.S. 20, 35 (1991) (holding that the Age Discrimination in Employment Act ("ADEA") does not preclude arbitration of age discrimination actions).

28. *Mitsubishi Motors Corp. v. Soler Chrysler-Plymouth, Inc.*, 473 U.S. 615, 628 (1985); *see also Gilmer*, 500 U.S. at 23 (agreement to arbitrate claims under the ADEA held enforceable); *Rodriguez de Quijas v. Shearson/Am. Exp., Inc.*, 490 U.S. 477, 479-80 (1989) (agreement to arbitrate claims under the Securities Act of 1933 held enforceable); *Shearson/Am. Express, Inc. v. McMahon*, 482 U.S. 220, 242 (1987) (agreement to arbitrate claims under the Securities Exchange Act of 1934 and the Racketeer Influenced and Corrupt Organizations Act enforceable); *E.E.O.C. v. Luce, Forward, Hamilton & Scripps*, 345 F.3d 742, 744-45 (9th Cir. 2003) (agreement to

extremely deferential to arbitrator decisions.[29] As the Supreme Court has said in the context of a collective-bargaining agreement, "Courts . . . do not sit to hear claims of factual or legal error by an arbitrator as an appellate court does in reviewing decisions of lower courts."[30] The Court went on to say, "[A]s long as the arbitrator is even arguably construing or applying the contract and acting within the scope of his authority, that a court is convinced he committed serious error does not suffice to overturn his decision."[31] In very limited cases, an arbitral award may be subject to review in court for certain defects (e.g., fraud).[32]

Mediation is another common form of dispute resolution but differs from arbitration in that it involves facilitating agreement, rather than resolving disputes, and does not result in a legally binding ruling. Given a varied array of dispute resolution options, companies often institute an internal process of resolving grievances through gradual escalation, involving increasingly senior levels of management until the dispute is resolved. For example, a company and employee might agree upfront to a procedure, where an aggrieved employee first is to notify a supervisor of a concern before notifying a grievance committee, before engaging in informal, internal mediation, before participating in formal, external mediation, and before, then, finally resolving the matter in arbitration. Why might a company wish to institute a gradual-escalation mechanism for dispute resolution?[33]

Under the Agreement, what disputes must be submitted to binding arbitration? Consider the text of § 20, which provides that any dispute that "arises concerning or relating to the Executive's employment" must be submitted to

---

arbitrate claims under Title VII held enforceable). Courts have found that certain statutory claims, at least under certain circumstances, may not be subjected to arbitration, despite an agreement to arbitrate. *See, e.g.,* *Cunningham v. Fleetwood Homes of Georgia, Inc.*, 253 F.3d 611, 617-24 (11th Cir. 2001) (claims under federal Magnuson-Moss Warranty Act, 15 U.S.C. §§ 2301-2312, may be arbitrated but, under the statute, agreement to arbitrate must be disclosed clearly in the same document as all relevant terms of warranty); *Greenwood v. Compucredit Corp.*, 617 F. Supp. 2d 980, 986-87 (N.D. Cal. 2009) (the right to bring suit for claims under the Credit Repair Organization Act is non-waivable and arbitration cannot be compelled).

29. *See, e.g., Gupta v. Cisco Sys., Inc.*, 274 F.3d 1, 3 (1st Cir. 2001) ("Our review of an arbitrator's decision is extremely narrow and exceedingly deferential.") (internal citation and quotation marks omitted); *El Dorado Sch. Dist. No. 15 v. Cont'l Cas. Co.*, 247 F.3d 843, 847 (8th Cir. 2001) ("Our disagreement with an arbitrator's interpretation of the law or determination of facts is an insufficient basis for setting aside his award. . . . [W]hen they contract for arbitration, parties should be aware that they get what they bargain for and that arbitration is far different from adjudication.") (internal citations and quotation marks omitted); *Gingiss Int'l, Inc. v. Bormet*, 58 F.3d 328, 333 (7th Cir. 1995) ("Factual or legal errors by arbitrators—even clear or gross errors—do not authorize courts to annul awards.") (internal citations and quotation marks omitted).

30. *United Paperworkers Int'l Union, AFL-CIO v. Misco, Inc.*, 484 U.S. 29, 38 (1987).

31. *Id.*

32. For example, under the Federal Arbitration Act, a U.S. district court may vacate an arbitral award for various failings of the arbitral process (e.g., corruption, fraud, arbitrator misconduct). 9 U.S.C. § 10(a) (2009). *See also United Paperworkers*, 484 U.S. at 38 ("Of course, decisions procured by the parties through fraud or through the arbitrator's dishonesty need not be enforced. But there is nothing of that sort involved in this case."). Under various state laws, an arbitral award may be similarly reviewed. *See, e.g.,* MINN. STAT. § 572.19 (2006); UNIFORM ARBITRATION ACT § 23 (2000). For further discussion on the judicial review of arbitration awards in the employment context, see Michael H. LeRoy, *Do Courts Create Moral Hazard?: When Judges Nullify Employer Liability in Arbitrations*, 93. MINN. L. REV. 998 (2009).

33. Indeed, grievance arbitration is a hallmark mechanism of dispute resolution in labor contracts.

arbitration. Federal and state courts alike routinely recite that arbitration, in general, enjoys a "favored status" and that "an agreement to arbitration should be read liberally in favor of arbitration."[34] Accordingly, courts will generally read language broadly to include most any claim arguably captured.[35]

> ### *Drafting Note: Arbitration Provisions; "Arising out of" and "Related to"*
>
> This general rule of broad construction is not without its limits. For instance, "courts distinguish 'narrow' arbitration clauses that only require arbitration of disputes 'arising out of' the contract from broad arbitration clauses governing disputes that 'relate to' or 'are connected with' the contract."[36] Claims that "arise out of" a contract are those claims that are *based* on the contract (e.g., breach of the contract), whereas claims that "relate to" or "are connected with" a specified contract are those that—while not necessarily based on the contract—at least "touch" the contract.[37] As an illustration, the Fifth Circuit found a claim of sexual assault against a former employer and co-workers to be outside the scope of an arbitration clause that required all claims "related to" the employment to be arbitrated.[38]
>
> If a party desires a broad arbitration provision, should the party attempt to define the scope of the claims to be submitted to arbitration as those that (i) "arise under" *or* "relate to" (ii) the "employment contract" *or* the "employment"? What are the differences?[39]

---

34. *Garfinkel v. Morristown Obstetrics & Gynecology Assocs., P.A.*, 773 A.2d 665, 670 (N.J. 2001); *see also Moses H. Cone Mem'l Hosp. v. Mercury Constr. Corp.*, 460 U.S. 1, 24-25 (1983) ("Federal law in the terms of the Arbitration Act governs [arbitrability] in either state or federal court" and "any doubts concerning the scope of arbitrable issues should be resolved in favor of arbitration, whether the problem at hand is the construction of the contract language itself or an allegation of waiver, delay, or a like defense to arbitrability").

35. *See, e.g., Pers. Sec. & Safety Sys. Inc. v. Motorola Inc.*, 297 F.3d 388, 392 (5th Cir. 2002) ("[A] valid agreement to arbitrate applies unless it can be said with positive assurance that the arbitration clause is not susceptible of an interpretation which would cover the dispute at issue.") (internal citations and quotations omitted).

36. *Pennzoil Exploration and Prod. Co. v. Ramco Energy Ltd.*, 139 F.3d 1061, 1067 (5th Cir. 1998).

37. *See, e.g., Mitsubishi Motors Corp. v. Soler Chrysler-Plymouth Inc.*, 473 U.S. 614, 625 (1985) (claim under the Sherman Act subject to arbitration because the claim at least "touched" matters covered by the contract); *JLM Indus., Inc. v. Stolt-Nielsen SA*, 387 F.3d 163, 172-73 (2d Cir. 2004) (allegations that price-fixing conspiracy undermined legitimate contractual relations between contractual parties "touched" the contract and were subject to arbitration under contractual provision); *see also Pennzoil Exploration*, 139 F.3d at 1067 (concluding that for matters to be within the scope of an arbitration clause that provided that all claims "related to" the contract must be arbitrated, such matters must have a "significant relationship" to the contract).

38. *Jones v. Halliburton Co.*, 583 F.3d 228, 239 (5th Cir. 2009) (holding that a sexual assault claim did not "relate to" employment because it did not bear a "significant relationship" to the employment); *see also Smith ex rel. Smith v. Captain D's, LLC*, 963 So.2d 1116 (Miss. 2007). *But see Forbes v. A.G. Edwards & Sons, Inc.*, No. 08 Civ. 552(TPG), 2009 WL 424146, at *8 (S.D.N.Y. 2009) ("Because the relevant arbitration agreements clearly require arbitration of 'matters related to or arising from' plaintiff's employment, plaintiff's claims of assault and battery must be submitted to arbitration.").

39. Consider, for example, *Forbes*, 2009 WL 424146, at *8 ("The arbitration clauses at issue here did not limit mandatory arbitration to disputes arising from the employment *contracts;* rather, they explicitly required

Why might the Company prefer arbitration? What risks and benefits does arbitration pose to the Executive? Given your answers to the foregoing, how might each party wish to draft the arbitration provision in the Agreement differently?

How does the "carve-out" found in § 20(c) work with the rest of § 20? What is the purpose and function of this provision? Does it favor the interests of the Company or the Executive (or does it serve both)? Note that, inasmuch as parties intend by contract to empower an arbitrator to award injunctive relief, specific performance, or other equitable remedies, the arbitrator generally will be so empowered, and courts will generally stand behind such an arbitral decree.[40]

5. Waiving the Right to a Jury Trial

Notice that § 20 on arbitration further provides that both "parties expressly waive the right to a jury trial," as agreeing to arbitration as an exclusive means of dispute resolution involves waiving one's right to a jury trial. While the Seventh Amendment to the U.S. Constitution preserves the right to a jury trial in federal courts where the amount in controversy exceeds 20 dollars, this right generally may be waived by contract.[41] Such waiver must be done "knowingly and intentionally" to be effective.[42] Why, then, do you suppose that this clause is bolded in the Agreement? Generally and in addition to other requirements, for a jury-trial waiver to be "knowing and intentional," an agreement should emphasize the provision by, for example, giving the waiver its own paragraph and bolding or enlarging its text.[43] Despite that some commentators have argued that mandatory arbitration provisions should be analyzed as, and held to the standard of, waivers of the right to a jury trial,[44] courts generally have not done so and instead have enforced arbitration provisions regardless of whether they satisfy a "knowing and intentional" standard.[45] A large, corporate employer may wish to forego a jury trial, say, for fear that a jury would view an employee more sympathetically than the corporate entity. Why else might an employer and/or an employee (especially a high-level executive) wish to waive the right to a jury trial?

---

arbitration of matters related to or arising from plaintiff's employment. The language requires arbitration of tort as well as contract claims.") (emphasis in original); *Martindale v. Sandvik, Inc.*, 800 A.2d 87, 883-84 (N.J. 2002) (unlike agreement in previous case that pertained only to claims concerning the *agreement*, the agreement here covered "all disputes relating to . . . employment . . . or termination thereof").

40. Please see Chapter 1 on this topic.

41. *See, e.g., Leasing Serv. Corp. v. Crane*, 804 F.2d 828, 832-33 (4th Cir. 1986) (citing *K.M.C. Co. v. Irving Trust Co.*, 757 F.2d 752, 755-56 (6th Cir. 1985); *Nat'l Equip. Rental Ltd. v. Hendrix*, 565 F.2d 255, 258 (2d Cir. 1977)). Various state constitutions generally also provide for a right to a jury trial, which may be waived.

42. *See supra* note 41.

43. *See, e.g., RDO Fin. Servs. Co. v. Powell*, 191 F. Supp. 2d 811, 814 (N.D. Tex. 2002) (finding a waiver of a jury trial not to be knowingly and intentionally made, where it was "buried in the middle of a lengthy paragraph, not set off from the rest of the text through differential bold, larger print, italics, or any other form of emphasis or distinction").

44. *See, e.g.,* Jean R. Sternlight, *The Rise and Spread of Mandatory Arbitration as a Substitute for the Jury Trial*, 38 U.S.F. L. Rev. 17 (2003).

45. *Id.* at 22-23.

6. Indemnifying a Corporate Officer

Section 11 ("Indemnification") provides that the Company will indemnify the Executive as provided for in the Company's articles of incorporation and bylaws and as provided by Delaware law. "Indemnification" refers to an obligation to pay another person (or, on the other side of the coin, the right of that other person to be paid) for certain damages or losses suffered—in this case, as is provided by the articles of incorporation, the bylaws, and the laws of Delaware.[46] "Articles of incorporation" (sometimes called a "charter" or "certificate of incorporation") refer to the document filed with the state by the organizers of a corporation that forms, and lays out the fundamental governing aspects of, a corporation. "Bylaws" provide a second level of governing provisions that generally need not be filed with the state and that further specify the rules governing the corporation.

Section 145 of Delaware General Corporation Law provides for the indemnification of officers, directors, and employees.[47] Under the provision, a Delaware corporation *may* indemnify any person made party to an action in his capacity as an officer, director, or employee of the corporation for reasonable expenses, fines, judgments, and settlements, as long as that person (1) acted in good faith; (2) in a manner he reasonably believed not to disserve the best interests of the company; and (3), regarding a criminal action, had no reasonable cause to believe his criminal conduct was unlawful.[48] Furthermore, Delaware law provides that a corporation *shall* indemnify an officer or director for any expenses (including attorneys' fees) actually and reasonably incurred by such person in *successfully defending* against any action brought against the person as officer or director of the corporation.[49]

---

46. We revisit indemnification in much greater depth in Chapter 3, where we discuss contractual tools for shifting risk more generally.

47. DEL. CODE ANN. tit. 8, § 145 (2010). Note that, under the "internal affairs doctrine," the law of the state of incorporation will generally govern for matters having to do with officer and director liability and the company's indemnification thereof. *See* RESTATEMENT (SECOND) OF CONFLICT OF LAWS § 309 (1971); *Davis & Cox v. Summa Corp.*, 751 F.2d 1507, 1527 (9th Cir. 1985) ("Claims involving 'internal affairs' of corporations, such as the breach of fiduciary duties, are subject to the laws of the state of incorporation."), *superseded by statute on other grounds as recognized in Northrop Corp. v. Triad Int'l Mktg. S.A.*, 842 F.2d 1154, 1156 (9th Cir. 1988) (per curiam); *Chatlos Found., Inc. v. D'Arata*, 882 So. 2d 1021, 1023 (Fla. Dist. Ct. App. 2004) ("Indemnification of corporate directors, like the fiduciary obligations of corporate directors, is an 'internal affair' of a corporation and is therefore subject to the law of the state of incorporation."). However, this does not mean that an action on such matters must be brought in the state of incorporation. *See Shaffer v. Heitner*, 433 U.S. 186, 215 (1977) ("[W]e have rejected the argument that if a State's law can properly be applied to a dispute, its courts necessarily have jurisdiction over the parties to that dispute."). In addition, the doctrine is limited and another state's law may apply "where, with respect to the particular issue, some other state has a more significant relationship." RESTATEMENT (SECOND) OF CONFLICTS OF LAWS § 309 (1971); CAL. CORP. CODE § 2115 (West Supp. 1977); *Friese v. Superior Court*, 36 Cal. Rptr. 3d 558, 569 (Cal. Ct. App. 2005).

48. DEL. CODE ANN. tit. 8, § 145(a) (2010).

49. *Id.* § 145(c).

Drafting Note: Incorporating Outside Sources of Obligations

Companies will commonly offer to indemnify officers, directors, and certain high-level employees in order to attract the best talent to the posts. This is because these positions become far less attractive when coupled with the potential for significant personal liability. With this in mind, consider whether § 11 provides adequate assurances to the Executive. Does § 11 *require* anything of the Company more than what the Company either has already agreed (or will agree) to do under its articles and bylaws or must do as required by law? If Delaware law *permits* the Company to indemnify the Executive, does § 11 by its terms *require* the Company to do so?

These questions turn on the meaning of "provided" as used in § 11, and, from the section, it is not clear if "provided" means "allowed" (which would yield a broader indemnity) or "required" (which would yield a narrower indemnity). What do you think the parties intended by this provision, and how would you draft this provision more clearly to express this intent? Also, consider that corporate articles and bylaws can be amended (although to do so may be difficult and generally requires shareholder approval) and that the Company's indemnification obligations under § 11, as provided by the Company's articles and bylaws, may be subject to change.

7. Terminating the Employment Relationship

Subsection (a) of § 6 ("Termination") gives the *Company* the right to terminate the Agreement at any time, as long as any of the several, enumerated events and conditions constituting "Cause" occurs and the Company provides the proper notice of, and undergoes the proper procedure for, termination. Similarly, § 6(e) gives the *Executive* the right to terminate for "Good Reason," listing several events that—if uncorrected for 30 days—constitute "Good Reason." Under the Agreement, what is the significance of "Cause" or "Good Reason"? After all, §§ 6(c) and (d) provide that the Executive and the Company, respectively, each have the right to terminate the Agreement *with* or *without* Good Reason or Cause.

Much of the answer lies in § 6(f): If the Company terminates for Cause, or if the Executive terminates *without* Good Reason, then the Executive is only entitled to receive that which he is already due (e.g., earned but unpaid salary, vested benefits). However, if the Company terminates *without* Cause (sometimes referred to as "termination for convenience"), or if the Executive terminates with Good Reason, then the Executive is entitled to receive not only that which is already due but also a lump sum amount and a continuation of benefits. This bundle of pay and benefits due upon termination of employment is commonly called a "severance package."

a. Severance and Release

Subsection 6(g) conditions the Executive's right to severance payment on his executing a waiver and release of claims against the Company. This means that the Executive must agree not to bring suit against the Company for certain claims before the Executive may receive his severance package. Often, at the time of termination, an employer will present an employee with a severance package in exchange for the employee's execution of a waiver of all claims against the employer.[50] This waiver, given by the employee in exchange for severance pay, is likely to be enforced as any other contract (i.e., subject to the classic failings of contracts, e.g., fraud, failure of consideration, duress, unconscionability, mutual mistake).[51] The general rule is that "[o]rdinarily, public policy does not prohibit an otherwise valid release from acting as a waiver of a federal statutory cause of action."[52] However, various federal laws intersect with freedom of contract to prevent waiver of certain claims or to impose certain requirements for such waivers to be effective as to such claims. Note that merely because a waiver fails to satisfy the requirements for waiver of claims under a certain federal statute does not necessarily mean that the waiver fails entirely or as to other claims.[53]

Examples of such federal laws in the employment context include the Employee Retirement Income Security Act ("ERISA"), the Fair Labor Standards Act ("FLSA"), the Family and Medical Leave Act ("FMLA"), the Age Discrimination in Employment Act ("ADEA"), the Workers Adjustment and Retraining Notification Act ("WARN"), and the Americans with Disabilities Act ("ADA"). For example, ERISA regulates employee benefit plans. Claims arising under ERISA *can* be waived, but such waiver must be "knowing and voluntary."[54] Whether a release of ERISA claims is "knowing and voluntary" is a "totality of the circumstances" inquiry that includes the following factors:

> (1) the clarity and specificity of the release language; (2) the plaintiff's education and business experience; (3) the amount of time plaintiff had for deliberation about the release before signing it; (4) whether plaintiff knew or should have known his rights upon execution of the release; (5) whether plaintiff

---

50. Note the distinction between the two scenarios: In the Agreement, the Executive is given the option—at the time of *employment*—to receive severance pay upon termination without Cause or for Good Reason, if he later signs a waiver of claims. Separately, employers commonly present such offers (whether or not *previously* granting the employee an option) at the time of termination. The Executive's option to *compel* severance pay by presenting a waiver of claims may operate as an optional liquidated damages provision. Please see Chapter 1 for more on liquidated damages.

51. *See, e.g., Skirchak v. Dynamics Research Corp.*, 508 F.3d 49, 59-60 (1st Cir. 2007) (finding a class action waiver in employment agreement to be unconscionable); *Shaheen v. B.F. Goodrich Co.*, 873 F.2d 105, 107 (6th Cir. 1989) ("[W]e will examine waivers of employee rights under normal contract principles.").

52. *Shaheen*, 873 F.2d at 107 (citing *Rogers v. Gen. Elec. Co.*, 781 F.2d 452, 454 (5th Cir. 1986)).

53. *See, e.g., Madrid v. Phelps Dodge Corp.*, 211 F. App'x 676, 680 (10th Cir. 2006) ("[T]he fact that a waiver is invalid as to an ADEA claim because it does not meet the minimum requirements established by § 626(f)(1)(A)-(H) does not affect its validity as to other types of claims.").

54. *See Washington v. Bert Bell/Pete Rozelle NFL Ret. Plan*, 504 F.3d 818, 824-25 (9th Cir. 2007); *Madrid*, 211 F. App'x at 679; *Shaheen v. B.F. Goodrich Co.*, 873 F.2d 105, 107 (6th Cir. 1989).

was encouraged to seek, or in fact received benefit of counsel; (6) whether there was an opportunity for negotiation of the terms of the Agreement; and (7) whether the consideration given in exchange for the waiver and accepted by the employee exceeds the benefits to which the employee was already entitled by contract or law.[55]

As an additional illustration, the ADEA forbids employment discrimination against employees who are at least 40 years old. As with ERISA, an employee may waive his ADEA rights, but the waiver must be "knowing and voluntary" to be enforceable.[56] For a waiver of ADEA rights to be "knowing and voluntary," the following criteria must be satisfied:

(A) the waiver is part of an agreement between the individual and the employer that is written in a manner calculated to be understood by such individual, or by the average individual eligible to participate;

(B) the waiver specifically refers to rights or claims arising under this chapter;

(C) the individual does not waive rights or claims that may arise after the date the waiver is executed;

(D) the individual waives rights or claims only in exchange for consideration in addition to anything of value to which the individual already is entitled;

(E) the individual is advised in writing to consult with an attorney prior to executing the agreement;

(F)(i) the individual is given a period of at least 21 days within which to consider the agreement; or

(ii) if a waiver is requested in connection with an exit incentive or other employment termination program offered to a group or class of employees, the individual is given a period of at least 45 days within which to consider the agreement;

(G) the agreement provides that for a period of at least 7 days following the execution of such agreement, the individual may revoke the agreement, and the agreement shall not become effective or enforceable until the revocation period has expired;

(H) if a waiver is requested in connection with an exit incentive or other employment termination program offered to a group or class of employees, the employer (at the commencement of the period specified in subparagraph (F)) informs the individual in writing in a manner calculated to be understood by the average individual eligible to participate, as to—

(i) any class, unit, or group of individuals covered by such program, any eligibility factors for such program, and any time limits applicable to such program; and

---

55. *Madrid*, 211 F. App'x at 679 (internal citation and quotation marks omitted); *see also, e.g., Frommert v. Conkright*, 535 F.3d 111, 121 (2d Cir. 2008) (listing similar factors, as to whether a release of ERISA claims is knowing and voluntary).

56. *See Am. Airlines, Inc. v. Cardoza-Rodriguez*, 133 F.3d 111, 117 (1st Cir. 1998).

(ii) the job titles and ages of all individuals eligible or selected for the program, and the ages of all individuals in the same job classification or organizational unit who are not eligible or selected for the program.[57]

Notice that § 6(g) of the Agreement contemplates the requirements for waiving rights under the ADEA, as 6(g) references the seven-day revocation period required by the statute reproduced above.

b. Material Breach (and Substantial Performance)

Subsection 6(a)(i) provides, among other things, that a "material breach" of the Agreement by the Executive means that the Company has the right to terminate the Agreement for "Cause." Likewise, § 6(e)(iv) provides that a "material breach" by the Company allows the Executive to terminate the Agreement for "Good Reason."

If parties to an employment agreement do not define what constitutes "cause," then a court may find "cause" in any act constituting "material breach" of the agreement.[58] Accordingly, the Agreement defines "cause" more broadly than this judicial inference, as the Agreement includes several enumerated occurrences in addition to material breach.

What qualifies as a material breach? How does a material breach differ from an immaterial breach? The question of whether a breach is material is necessarily an amorphous, "facts and circumstances" inquiry. Courts generally recite some variety of the following standard for what "material" means: "A breach is material if it destroys the essential object of the agreement or deprives the non-breaching party of a benefit that the party reasonably expected."[59] The *Restatement (Second) of Contracts* lists several factors to serve as guideposts:

In determining whether a failure to render or to offer performance is material, the following circumstances are significant:

(a) the extent to which the injured party will be deprived of the benefit which he reasonably expected;

(b) the extent to which the injured party can be adequately compensated for the part of that benefit of which he will be deprived;

(c) the extent to which the party failing to perform or to offer to perform will suffer forfeiture;

---

57. 29 U.S.C. § 626(f) (as amended 2009); *see also Am. Airlines*, 133 F.3d at 117. For further discussion of waiver and federal employment statutes, see *Copeland v. ABB, Inc.*, 521 F.3d 1010, 1014 (8th Cir. 2008) (rights under the FLSA cannot be waived except by payment in full of due wages under the supervision of the Secretary of Labor); 29 C.F.R. § 825.220(d) (2009) (retrospective rights may be waived under the FMLA); *Int'l Ass'n of Machinists and Aerospace Workers, AFL-CIO v. Compania Mexicana de Aviacion, S.A. de C.V.*, 199 F.3d 796, 799 (5th Cir. 2000) (claims under the WARN Act validly waived); *Rivera-Flores v. Bristol-Myers Squibb Caribbean*, 112 F.3d 9, 10 (1st Cir. 1997) (explaining the "knowing and voluntary" standard under the ADA).

58. *See, e.g., Gresham v. Lumbermen's Mut. Cas. Co.*, 404 F.3d 253, 260 (4th Cir. 2005) ("Maryland common law defines cause for termination of employment as a material breach of the terms of the employment agreement.").

59. *Int'l Prod. Specialists, Inc. v. Schwing Am., Inc.*, 580 F.3d 587, 595 (7th Cir. 2009); *see also Rano v. Sipa Press, Inc.*, 987 F.2d 580, 586 (9th Cir. 1993) (a breach is material when it "is of so material and substantial a nature that it affects the very essence of the contract and serves to defeat the object of the parties") (quoting *Affiliated Hosp. Prod. Inc. v. Merdel Game Mfg. Co.*, 513 F.2d 1183, 1186 (2d Cir. 1975)).

(d) the likelihood that the party failing to perform or to offer to perform will cure his failure, taking account of all the circumstances including any reasonable assurances;

(e) the extent to which the behavior of the party failing to perform or to offer to perform comports with standards of good faith and fair dealing.[60]

In light of this factor-laden inquiry, parties can gain some certainty by specifying in the contract how a court will understand material breach of the contract, as a court is likely to find a breach to be material if the parties so contractually specify.[61] A common example is where parties specify that "time is of the essence," which generally makes the failure to perform a contract in a timely manner (as contractually specified) a material breach under the contract.[62]

Examples of a material breach of an employment agreement have included an employer reducing an employee's base salary,[63] an employee's failure "to perform with the customary level of professionalism and competence that is standard in virtually any industry," including recurrent failure to comply with assigned tasks and complicity in altering documents,[64] and an employee violating a non-compete restrictive covenant.[65]

A material breach is significant not only because it may contractually trigger certain rights and obligations (as it does in the Agreement) but also because material breach generally may give the non-breaching party the right not to perform under, and to terminate, the contract.[66]

The mirror image of material breach is "substantial performance." To illustrate, if a party's performance of his contractual obligations is at least substantial, then the party's performance does not constitute a material breach, and the inverse is also true: If a party's performance is less than substantial, then it *is* a material breach.[67] The substantial performance of a party's obligation is sufficient to trigger the other party's obligations that flow from that performance

---

60. RESTATEMENT (SECOND) OF CONTRACTS § 241 (1981).

61. *See, e.g., Finova Capital Corp. v. Richard A. Arledge, Inc.*, No. 07-16384, 2009 WL 166933, at *1 (9th Cir. Jan. 9, 2009) ("Arizona law permits contracting parties to designate certain provisions of a contract as material in the sense that their violation constitutes a material breach."); *Dunkin' Donuts of Am., Inc. v. Middletown Donut Corp.*, 495 A.2d 66, 75 (N.J. 1985) ("[B]ecause the franchise contracts are clear in making the underreporting of sales a material breach of contract, thereby entitling Dunkin' Donuts to terminate the franchise and receive damages due, equity should and must respect these contractual provisions.").

62. *See, e.g., Retrofit Partners I, L.P. v. Lucas Indus., Inc.*, 201 F.3d 155, 160 (2d. Cir. 2000) ("[A 'time is of the essence' clause in a contract means] that insofar as a time for performance is specified in the contract, failure to comply with the time requirement will be considered to be a material breach of the agreement.").

63. *See, e.g., E.E.O.C. v. R.J. Gallagher Co.*, 181 F.3d 645, 651 (5th Cir. 1999).

64. *See, e.g., Carco Grp., Inc. v. Maconachy*, 644 F. Supp. 2d 218, 233 (E.D.N.Y. 2009).

65. *See, e.g., NCMIC Fin. Corp. v. Artino*, 638 F. Supp. 2d 1042, 1069-70 (S.D. Iowa 2009).

66. *See* RESTATEMENT (SECOND) OF CONTRACTS § 237 (1981); *Comedy Club, Inc. v. Improv W. Assocs.*, 553 F.3d 1277, 1289 n.12 (9th Cir. 2009) ("The general rule is that if the breach is a material breach, it may give grounds for the non-breaching party to cancel the contract, but if the breach is a partial breach, the non-breaching party's remedy is for damages.") (internal citations omitted); *Jespersen v. Minn. Mining & Mfg. Co.*, 700 N.E.2d 1014, 1016 (Ill. 1998) ("[A]*ny* contract is terminable upon the occurrence of a material breach.") (emphasis in original).

67. *See Gen. Motors Corp. v. New A.C. Chevrolet, Inc.*, 263 F.3d 296, 317 (3d Cir. 2001) ("[W]e see no real or practical difference between a conclusion that a party materially breached a contract, and a conclusion that the party

(e.g., payment).[68] For example, a party has substantially performed its contractual obligations and is due payment under the contract, even when the party mistakenly installs a brand of pipe equal in quality but different from that specified in the contract.[69] However, if the party less-than-fully performs in *bad faith*, then the doctrine of substantial performance is unlikely to save him, and this breach—while perhaps less than material—*will* excuse the other party's performance.[70]

Realize also what this does not mean. Anything short of a full and complete performance is still a breach—just perhaps not a *material* breach. The non-breaching party is still entitled to damages that proximately result from the less-than-full performance.[71]

The doctrines of material breach and substantial performance present one example of "excuse." Absent contractual specification to the contrary, a party will be excused from performing under a contract, where the other party materially breaches (or, in other words, fails to perform substantially). How may parties influence this analysis by contract? As explained above, parties may define what constitutes material breach under the contract, and, accordingly, parties may specify what amounts to an excuse of performance. As we will discuss in Chapter 3, a party's performance under a contract may also be excused by other events—having nothing to do with the other party's performance or lack thereof. In Chapter 3, we will discuss the doctrines of impossibility and frustration and how the "force majeure" clause enables parties contractually to govern how certain events amount to excuse.

---

failed to substantially comply with its obligations under a contract."); *Bernard v. Las Ams. Commc'ns, Inc.*, 84 F.3d 103, 109 (2d Cir. 1996) ("A finding that Bernard's conduct in representing LAC materially breached his contract with LAC, however, is equivalent to a finding that Bernard did not substantially perform under the contract.").

68. *Riesett v. W.B. Doner & Co.*, 293 F.3d 164, 174 (4th Cir. 2002) ("[T]he doctrine of substantial performance prevents promisee opportunism by forbidding a promisee from walking away from a contract and refusing to perform his reciprocal contractual duties because of a minor breach by the promisor . . ."); *Sununu v. Philippine Airlines, Inc.*, 638 F. Supp. 2d 35, 39 (D.D.C. 2009) ("[S]ubstantial performance occurs, triggering the other party's obligations to perform, where any failure in performance is not material."); *Hoyt v. Hoyt*, 372 S.W.2d 300, 304 (Tenn. 1963) ("The authorities are uniform in holding that where there has been full or substantial performance by one party to a bilateral contract, [even if] invalid for want of mutuality of obligation, the other party cannot refuse performance after receiving the promised benefits.").

69. *Jacob & Youngs v. Kent*, 230 N.Y. 239, 241 (1921) (Cardozo, J.) ("The courts never say that one who makes a contract fills the measure of his duty by less than full performance. They do say, however, that an omission, both trivial and innocent, will sometimes be atoned for by allowance of the resulting damage, and will not always be the breach of a condition to be followed by a forfeiture."). However, if the party less-than-fully performs in *bad faith*, then the doctrine of substantial performance is unlikely to save him, and this breach—while perhaps less than material—*will* excuse the other party's performance. *See Moore's Builder and Contractor, Inc. v. Hoffman*, 409 N.W.2d 191, 192 (Iowa App. 1987).

70. *See Moore's Builder and Contractor, Inc. v. Hoffman*, 409 N.W.2d 191, 192 (Iowa Ct. App. 1987) ("Substantial performance allows only the omissions or deviations from the contract that are inadvertent or unintentional, not the result of bad faith, do not impair the structure as a whole, are remedial without doing material damages to other portions of the building, and may be compensated for through deductions from the contract price."). Note that, while acting in bad faith may give a less-than-material breach the effect of a material breach, acting in good faith will not forgive a material breach and will still excuse the other party's performance under the contract.

71. *See Matador Drilling Co., Inc. v. Post*, 662 F.2d 1190, 1195 (5th Cir. 1981) ("Recovery for substantial performance is the contract price reduced by the amount necessary to compensate for the deficiency."); *Jacob & Youngs*, 230 N.Y. at 247.

c. Constructive Termination

If an employee were to quit, then he may forego many of the benefits he would have received had his employer instead terminated the employment relationship. For instance, in this Agreement, the Executive is better off if the Company were to terminate his employment without Cause than if the Executive were to quit without Good Reason. Indeed, many employment agreements do not include a "Good Reason" provision, and, under these agreements, the employee is likely better off to be fired without cause than to quit *for any reason*. On the flipside, for this reason, an employer generally would rather an employee quit than the employer have to fire him. Accordingly, an employer that wants to terminate an employee might take measures to "motivate" an employee to quit. What is an employee to do should his employer, say, reduce his responsibilities considerably or significantly reduce his pay or assign him to work in an isolated, desert office?

He could quit. If he were afforded the protection of the Good Reason provisions of this Agreement, he would be entitled to a severance package, provided that these occurrences amounted to Good Reason. But what if the employee's agreement contained no such provisions, or what if the employer made the employee's work life intolerable in ways that somehow did not constitute Good Reason? Seemingly, the employee would face the choice of quitting and not receiving a heightened severance package or carrying on despite unsavory conditions.

To provide an employee with some recourse, courts have developed the doctrine of "constructive termination" (or "constructive discharge"). Constructive termination generally occurs when working conditions and arrangements become such that a reasonable employee would be compelled to resign and the employer at least knows of these conditions.[72] The Supreme Court of California has explained:

> In order to amount to a constructive discharge, adverse working conditions must be unusually "aggravated" or amount to a "continuous pattern" before the situation will be deemed intolerable. In general, single, trivial, or isolated acts of misconduct are insufficient to support a constructive discharge claim. Moreover, a poor performance rating or a demotion, even when accompanied by reduction in pay, does not by itself trigger a constructive discharge.[73]

As an example, one court found constructive termination when an employee was taken off an account he spent eight years obtaining, was forced to report his sales activity on a daily basis, and had his monthly take-home pay reduced from $8,000 to $3,000.[74] Another court refused to find constructive termination

---

72. *See, e.g., Moisant v. Air Midwest, Inc.*, 291 F.3d 1028, 1032 (8th Cir. 2002) (requiring that the employer intended to coerce employee to resign in order to find constructive termination); *King v. AC & R Adver.*, 65 F.3d 765, 767 (9th Cir. 1995) (requiring that the employer either intentionally created or knowingly permitted intolerable working conditions to find constructive termination).

73. *Turner v. Anheuser-Busch, Inc.*, 7 Cal. 4th 1238, 1247 (Cal. 1994).

74. *Gower v. IKON Office Solutions, Inc.*, 177 F. Supp. 2d 1224, 1233 (D. Kan. 2001).

when an employee's status was changed to at-will, his managerial responsibilities reduced, and his base salary reduced from $235,000 to $175,000.[75] "[A] constructive discharge is legally regarded as a firing rather than a resignation."[76] Accordingly, all that follows from being fired—rather than quitting—follows from a constructive termination, including any contractual rights and benefits.

Drafting Note: "Notwithstanding" and Statutory Compliance Through Contract

Subsection 21(a) ("Compliance with Section 409A") of the Agreement explains that, "[n]otwithstanding anything in this Agreement to the contrary," distributions to the Executive upon termination are not to be made until a Separation from Service occurs.

"Notwithstanding" is a common convention in contracts that says that a certain provision should be read to "trump" any potentially conflicting provisions. The "order of operations" of contracts and contractual provisions vis-à-vis each other is called "precedence." Here, by beginning with "[n]otwithstanding anything in this Agreement to the contrary" and proceeding to provide certain terms, this clause specifies that these terms take precedence over any other provisions in this Agreement. "Notwithstanding" clauses can be effective tools but can also cause ambiguity as to how particular provisions are to interact with one another, especially when "notwithstanding" is used multiple times as attached to different provisions.

Section 6 further explains that, at least as to terminations triggering a payment upon termination, termination only occurs upon a Separation from Service. What is a Separation from Service, and why does either party care that Separation from Service triggers a payment upon termination?

Section 409A of the U.S. Tax Code imposes various penalties and taxes on certain "nonqualified deferred compensation plans" that do not comport with § 409A's requirements.[77] Among these requirements is paragraph (a)(2), which provides, in part:

(1) Plan failures.—

(A) Gross income inclusion.—

(i) In general.— If at any time during a taxable year a nonqualified deferred compensation plan—

(I) fails to meet the requirements of paragraphs (2), (3), and (4), or

(II) is not operated in accordance with such requirements,

all compensation deferred under the plan for the taxable year and all preceding taxable years shall be includible in gross income for the taxable year to the extent not subject to a substantial risk of forfeiture and not previously included in gross income. . . .

---

75. *King*, 65 F.3d at 766.

76. *Turner*, 7 Cal. 4th at 1245.

77. I.R.C. § 409A(a)(1) (2008). For a definition of "nonqualified deferred compensation plan" and "qualified employer plan," see I.R.C. § 409A(d) (2008).

(2) Distributions.—

(A) In general.— The requirements of this paragraph are met if the plan provides that compensation deferred under the plan may not be distributed earlier than—

    (i) separation from service as determined by the Secretary (except as provided in subparagraph (B)(i)),

    (ii) the date the participant becomes disabled (within the meaning of subparagraph (C)),

    (iii) death,

    (iv) a specified time (or pursuant to a fixed schedule) specified under the plan at the date of the deferral of such compensation,

    (v) to the extent provided by the Secretary, a change in the ownership or effective control of the corporation, or in the ownership of a substantial portion of the assets of the corporation, or

    (vi) the occurrence of an unforeseeable emergency.

(B) Special rules.—

    (i) Specified employees.— In the case of any specified employee, the requirement of subparagraph (A)(i) is met only if distributions may not be made before the date which is 6 months after the date of separation from service (or, if earlier, the date of death of the employee). For purposes of the preceding sentence, a specified employee is a key employee (as defined in section 416(i) without regard to paragraph (5) thereof) of a corporation any stock in which is publicly traded on an established securities market or otherwise.[78]

Note the similarity between the language in the Agreement pertaining to § 409A and the language in the above-excerpted statute. Why do you think this is? Please turn to and reread § 6, § 6(h), and § 21(a) of the Agreement. How is each provision structured so as to protect against running afoul of the statute and triggering tax penalties? In exploring these questions, you should begin to discover how one may use careful drafting to navigate statutory requirements. For instance, with regard to these provisions, does it matter what Separation from Service means? By mirroring the language and providing for the requirements of the statute in the contract (and specifying by use of "notwithstanding" that this provision trumps anything that might contradict it in the Agreement), the employer begins to establish an arrangement that comports with statutory requirements. Of course, mere contractual drafting may not always ensure full compliance with a statutory requirement, but notice that in this case the statute provides that it may be satisfied by a plan that *provides* certain terms. Accordingly, if the Agreement qualifies as a nonqualified deferred compensation plan, then it satisfies the statute by providing these terms. (And, if the Agreement does *not* qualify as a nonqualified deferred compensation plan, then this Agreement itself is outside the scope of these statutory provisions.)

---

78. I.R.C. § 409A(a)(2) (2008).

B. POST-EMPLOYMENT RESTRICTIVE COVENANTS AND THEIR ENFORCEABILITY

1. Covenants, Generally

Generally speaking, a covenant is any promise to perform under a contract. Covenants may be affirmative or negative—that is, a party may covenant *to do* something and a party may covenant *not to do* something. A covenant differs from a representation and from a warranty (each of which we will discuss in greater length in Chapter 3) in that a covenant promises some action—or lack of action. In contrast, a representation is a statement of fact and a warranty is a promise that a statement is true, for the duration of the warranty.[79] While a warranty may incentivize the performance (or non-performance) of an action—as the warrantor may wish to ensure that the warranty remains true so as to avoid breach—a covenant states directly an obligation to perform (or not to perform) an action. For example, if A wishes to hire B to paint A's house, A may pay B for a promise that A's house will be painted—a warranty—but, more to the point, A is likely to pay B for a promise to paint A's house. That is, A will pay B for a covenant to paint A's house. Of course, A may demand additional representations and warranties from B. For example, B may represent that he is licensed and qualified to paint houses and warrant that inclement weather will not damage the paint job.

2. Restrictive Covenants: Obligations Not to Compete, Solicit, or Hire

Section 8 ("Covenant Not to Compete") provides that the Executive will not compete with the Company. There are three principal aspects of the provision: (1) the provision restricts Competitive Activities, listing several acts (e.g., becoming employed, rendering services, acquiring an interest, otherwise assisting) and defining each as a prohibited Competitive Activity when performed for a certain entity (e.g., those engaged in operations involving the transmission, production, syndication, promotion, or marketing of radio entertainment programming); (2) the provision contains a geographic restriction, defining Competitive Activities as only those that assist competitors in North America; and (3) the provision contains a durational restriction, only imposing the non-competition obligation on the Executive during the Restricted Period, which extends one year from the date the Executive's employment terminates.

---

79. As we discuss in greater detail in Chapter 3, some attorneys doubt whether "representation" and "warranty" are meaningfully distinct.

In addition, § 8 contains two covenants not to solicit: (1) the Executive may not solicit *business* from the Company's customers for products or services that compete with those of the Company; and (2) the Executive may not solicit the *employment* of the Company's employees. Note that these covenants, too, only restrict the Executive during the Restricted Period but are not limited in geographical scope. This is likely because competition may pose a threat to a company only in certain geographical areas, whereas solicitation of the Company's customers and employees is dangerous no matter where this solicitation occurs. Might it be difficult to prove who solicited whom? For this reason, an employer may attempt to include a covenant not to employ—along with a covenant not to solicit—the employer's employees in order to provide the company with a more provable breach; the competing concern is that this type of provision is more restrictive.

A Practitioner Perspective:
Retaining Employees and Post-Employment Restrictions

Despite the financial crisis that began in 2007 and the resulting unemployment it has created, the protection of human capital and valuable company trade secrets remains a number one priority for many employers. To succeed in these extraordinarily competitive times, companies face the daunting tasks of creating innovative products and services; developing and maintaining a customer base; recruiting and training an expert and efficient work force; and keeping all of their innovations—and all of their customers and employees—from falling into the hands of their competitors.

These tasks are especially difficult because the most valuable, knowledgeable and highly skilled employees are also the most mobile. When such employees leave their jobs and move on to work for a competitor—or to start their own competitive company—they present an unparalleled risk to their former employer. This risk is further exacerbated by the fact that in the electronic age sensitive data can be misappropriated in milliseconds with unprecedented ease. A departing employee can export important documents and company secrets to external storage devices, PDA's, portable hard drives, and cell phones in mere seconds. Unless the employer does a careful forensic examination of the departing employee's electronic devices, such misappropriation will often go unnoticed.

The employment lawyer plays an important role in helping the company protect itself proactively and then helping the employer to take appropriate steps to move quickly to minimize the damage of the departing employee. Most important to this process are the drafting of enforceable trade secret protections and post-employment restrictions.

Employers frequently attempt to prevent their employees from unfairly competing with them upon termination of their employment by having them covenant, as part of an employment agreement, that they will not compete with their employer after their employment ends. Although many of these disputes end up in federal court under diversity jurisdiction, the enforceability of such agreements is a matter of state common law and statutory law. Many states, including New York, follow the general rule that such agreements are enforceable, provided they are necessary to protect a legitimate interest of the employer and are reasonably limited in time, geography, and the restrictions they place on the employee in pursuing his or her profession.

Other states, including California, Montana, North Dakota, and Oklahoma, do not follow the general rule. For example, California Business & Professions Code § 16600 provides that "every contract by which anyone is restrained from engaging in a lawful profession, trade or business of any kind is to that extent void." California courts have rigorously applied this provision in the employment context and have routinely invalidated agreements purporting to preclude employees (expressly or implicitly through penalties) from working for competitors upon completion of their employment.

Other post-employment restrictions include non-solicitation of employees and customers, and of course, non-retention and non-use of confidential employer information. Employers who want to be proactive about retaining their employees will craft employment and other compensation agreements that create substantial monetary disincentives for employees to leave before certain dates. In some jurisdictions, enforceability of these types of agreements is subject to a similar analysis as the enforceability of non-competes. In other jurisdictions, if an employee resigns his or her employment voluntarily, these kinds of forfeiture provisions may be enforced as ordinary contracts under the "employee choice" doctrine.

Michael Delikat
Partner and Global Chair,
Employment Practice Group
Orrick, Herrington & Sutcliffe LLP

Why might a company (or, the Company) want to impose these restrictive covenants on an employee (or, the Executive)? Companies often invest substantial resources in the training and development of employees. In this way, an employee is similar to any of a company's assets. A company may invest hundreds of thousands of dollars in the development of a piece of heavy machinery. If that machinery could pick itself up, dust itself off, and walk out, straight to a competitor (or into the ocean, for that matter), the company's investment would be largely for naught. Indeed, a company might be hesitant to invest large sums in these assets—at least not without bolting the machinery to the company floor. Of course, the awkwardness of this analogy reveals how we treat and think of human beings and machines differently. Our society may wish to incent companies to invest in labor, and a prospective employee may wish a company to invest heavily in him; however, this desire to motivate companies to invest *ex ante* must be balanced *ex post* against (i) a person's right not to work (under the Thirteenth Amendment) and (ii) a person's right to work elsewhere, in addition to society's need for that person's work.

As for a person's right not to work, a party may not compel another to perform labor: If an employee does not perform under an employment agreement, the company cannot specifically enforce the agreement; a court will not force a person to work.[80] If a company cannot compel performance, then a next-best alternative may be *preventing* the employee from performing for any competitors and/or from taking any company business or competitors—not to mention secrets—with him. Enforcing these covenants may involve requesting a court to issue an injunction so as to stop the employee from working for a competitor or soliciting company customers or employees—but does not involve coercing the employee to act affirmatively. Accordingly, the same Thirteenth Amendment concerns are not at play. Will courts, then, enforce post-employment restrictive convents not to compete, solicit, or hire? The answer lies in the second balancing act: the company's legitimate interest in restricting the future employment of the employee as against the employee's right to work elsewhere, while also considering the public interest at stake.

Omniplex World Servs. Corp. v. U.S. Investigations Servs., Inc.
Supreme Court of Virginia, 2005.
270 Va. 246.

Opinion by Justice Elizabeth B. Lacy.

In this appeal, we consider whether the provisions of a non-competition contract are overbroad and unenforceable.

FACTS AND PROCEEDINGS

Omniplex World Services Corporation (Omniplex) is a highly specialized employment agency that provides a variety of security services to government and private sector customers. In August 2003, Omniplex prevailed in its bid to provide staffing for a government agency, referred to as a "Sensitive Government Customer" or "SGC," in a project entitled "Project Eagle." Staffing of this project required that personnel have a "Top-Secret" security clearance validated by the SGC, regardless of the function performed.

At the time Omniplex won the bid, Kathleen M. Schaffer was working on Project Eagle as an employee of MVM, Inc., another staffing company. Upon learning that MVM no longer had the contract to staff Project Eagle, Schaffer sent out applications for employment to various staffing agencies, including The Smith Corporation. Before receiving a response from The Smith Corporation, Schaffer was offered continued employment at Project Eagle by Omniplex. On August 26, 2003, Schaffer signed a one-year employment agreement with

---

80. *See* Restatement (Second) of Contracts § 367 (1981) ("A promise to render personal service will not be specifically enforced."); *Beverly Glen Music, Inc. v. Warner Commc'ns, Inc.*, 224 Cal. Rptr. 260, 261 (Cal. Ct. App. 1986) (stating that the Thirteenth Amendment prohibits specific enforcement of singer's contract).

Omniplex. The agreement provided for a $2,000 bonus and included a non-competition provision. That provision stated in pertinent part:

> Employee hereby covenants and agrees that, immediately following any termination of employment from OMNIPLEX that occurs before the expiration of the Term, . . . Employee shall not for the remainder of the Term (i) accept employment, become employed by, or perform any services for OMNIPLEX's Customer for whom Employee provided services or for any other employer in a position supporting OMNIPLEX's Customer, if the employment or engagement requires Employee to possess the same level of security clearance Employee relied on during his employment with OMNIPLEX, ...

Schaffer worked for Omniplex in general administrative security support, monitoring alarms and intrusion detection systems at the SGC's general headquarters, an overt location.

On October 23, 2003, The Smith Corporation responded to Schaffer's earlier employment application and offered her a position as an administrative assistant for the SGC at a covert location. This position required her to arrange travel, including obtaining visas and passports and offered a higher hourly wage than Schaffer was currently earning. Schaffer accepted the offer and, on November 4, 2003, resigned from Omniplex and returned the $2,000 bonus.

Omniplex filed a three-count motion for judgment claiming that Schaffer breached her employment contract, that The Smith Company and U.S. Investigation Services, Inc., the parent company of The Smith Company (collectively "USIS"), tortiously interfered with Schaffer's employment contract, and that Schaffer and USIS engaged in a conspiracy to injure Omniplex's business . . . . Omniplex sought injunctive relief and $1,350,000 in damages. The trial court denied Omniplex's motion for a temporary injunction.

Following an *ore tenus* hearing, the trial court struck Omniplex's evidence, concluding that the non-compete provision of Schaffer's employment agreement was overbroad. Based on this conclusion, the trial court entered an order dismissing all three counts of Omniplex's motion for judgment. We awarded Omniplex an appeal.

DISCUSSION

The standards we apply in reviewing a covenant not to compete are well established. A non-competition agreement between an employer and an employee will be enforced if the contract is narrowly drawn to protect the employer's legitimate business interest, is not unduly burdensome on the employee's ability to earn a living, and is not against public policy. Because such restrictive covenants are disfavored restraints on trade, the employer bears the burden of proof and any ambiguities in the contract will be construed in favor of the employee. Each non-competition agreement must be evaluated on its own merits, balancing the provisions of the contract with the circumstances of the businesses and employees involved. Whether the covenant not to compete is enforceable is a question of law which we review *de novo*.

These standards have been developed over the years to strike a balance between an employee's right to secure gainful employment and the employer's legitimate interest in protection from competition by a former employee based on the employee's ability to use information or other elements associated with the employee's former employment. By its very name, a covenant not to compete is an agreement to prevent an employee from engaging in activities that actually or potentially compete with the employee's former employer. Thus, covenants not to compete have been upheld only when employees are prohibited from competing directly with the former employer or through employment with a direct competitor. The restriction in this case is not limited to positions competitive with Omniplex.

Under the provision at issue, Schaffer is prohibited from performing "any services . . . *for any other employer* in a position supporting OMNIPLEX's Customer."* (Emphasis added.) This provision precludes Schaffer from working for *any* business that provides support of any kind to the SGC, not only security staffing businesses that were in competition with Omniplex. Thus, for example, the non-competition agreement precludes Schaffer from working as a delivery person for a vendor which delivers materials to the SGC if such security clearance was required to enter an SGC installation even though the vendor was not a staffing service competing with Omniplex. Because the prohibition in this non-competition provision is not limited to employment that would be in competition with Omniplex, the covenant is overbroad and unenforceable.

Accordingly, for the reasons stated, we will affirm the judgment of the trial court.

Affirmed.

Justice AGEE, with whom Justice KEENAN and Justice KINSER join, dissenting.

The trial court found that the restrictive covenant at issue in this case was overly broad because it had no geographic specification, in effect a worldwide covenant.[1] Not commenting on the trial court's rationale, the majority holds that the covenant is unreasonable because it does not limit the prohibited positions to those of direct competition. Under the specific facts of this case, I cannot agree with either view and therefore respectfully dissent.

[None of the cases we have decided on this issue] establish a rule that noncompete provisions are per se unenforceable if they fail to limit the restriction to those positions in direct competition with the former employer. Rather, in each case we held that under the facts of that case, the restrictive covenant at issue "imposed restraints that exceeded those necessary to protect [the former employer's] legitimate business interests."

---

* It is uncontested that the "customer" referred to in the non-competition provision is the SGC.

1. The noncompetition agreement also contains a provision prohibiting Schaffer from providing "security or security support services . . . within a fifty (50) mile radius of the site or location which Employee primarily provided services during . . . Omniplex employment." Apparently, the trial court did not rule on the applicability of this provision and it is not before us in this appeal.

In a more recent case, *Modern Environments, Inc. v. Stinnett*, we affirmed our view that a court may not determine the enforceability of a restrictive covenant which prohibits a former employee from working for a competitor in any capacity, by the language of the covenant alone. Surveying precedent, we noted that we have "not limit[ed] [our] review to considering whether the restrictive covenants were facially reasonable." Rather, we have "examined the legitimate, protectable interests of the employer, the nature of the former and subsequent employment of the employee . . . and the nature of the restraint in light of all the circumstances of the case."

These considerations form the basis of the three-part test we use to determine the validity of restrictive covenants:

> (1) Is the restraint, from the standpoint of the employer, reasonable in the sense that it is no greater than necessary to protect the employer in some legitimate business interest? (2) From the standpoint of the employee, is the restraint reasonable in the sense that it is not unduly harsh and oppressive in curtailing his legitimate efforts to earn a livelihood? (3) Is the restraint reasonable from the standpoint of a sound public policy?

In examining the reasonableness of the restrictive covenant with regard to the interests of the employer, employee, and the public at large, we pay particular attention to the duration, function, and geographic reach of the covenant. We consider the reasonableness of the covenant on the facts of each particular case. The employer seeking to enforce the restrictive covenant bears the burden of proving that the restraint is reasonable in light of those facts. We review the record *de novo* to determine whether Omniplex has met its burden.

Omniplex argues that it has a legitimate business interest in retaining employees who hold the necessary top-level security clearance during the first year of its contract with the SGC. Neither the trial court nor the majority found that Omniplex' stated interest was not a legitimate business interest, but Schaffer argues on brief that retaining employees is not a legitimate business interest because this Court has never recognized it as such. Such an argument misinterprets the applicable law in this case.

Unlike courts of other jurisdictions, we have never established discrete categories of legitimate business interests which may be the subject of a restrictive covenant. Instead, we have placed the burden on the employer to show that the restrictive covenant is designed to protect an important business interest particular to that employer. Even so, we have recognized Omniplex' stated business interest in an analogous context. The record in this case reflects that Omniplex has shown it has a legitimate business interest in retaining "cleared" employees like Schaffer during the first year of the Project Eagle contract.

At trial, Michael M. Wines, Omniplex' vice president of security services, explained that as part of the SGC's bidding process, a staffing company must describe the steps that it will take to maintain a stable workforce and ensure that the project will be adequately staffed. Once awarded the Project Eagle contract,

Omniplex was required to report staffing levels and plans for future staffing to the SGC on a regular basis. In the past, the SGC has cancelled contracts when a company could no longer provide sufficient "cleared" staff.

> Wines described the impact on Omniplex when a cleared employee departs suddenly:
> [Y]ou have an employee that has institutional knowledge, has the clearance, has goodwill with the client, the client has a comfort level with them . . . .
> But . . . it also creates . . . a serious concern about contract performance . . . [especially] in the first year [of a contract]. As a first-year, a new contractor [is] trying to establish goodwill with the client, . . . a stable workforce, [and] ensure the client that they made the right selection. . . .
> [W]hen [our employee is] working for us today, and the very next day they're working for one of our competitors in the same facility, supporting the same client[,] [t]he client starts to question our ability to retain employees.

Wines noted that while turnover is inevitable in any company, Omniplex has particular concerns about other staffing companies "poaching"[4] employees with top security clearances: "[M]any times our competitors are willing to pay additional funds for an employee [who is] not qualified for a position just because the employee has a clearance." He testified that on a former contract, a competitor of Omniplex "poached five [out of eight] people in one day." Wines noted that if a similar situation occurred on Project Eagle, "the only way [Omniplex] would be able to meet [its] contractual requirements would be [by] forcing our existing staff to work overtime."

USIS has the same concerns. Peter F. Waldorf, an operations director for USIS, agreed that it is "very important for [USIS] to provide an adequate amount of cleared staff to [its] government customers." Waldorf also agreed that adequate staffing was a particularly important concern to the SGC, and that a government contractor such as USIS must maintain adequate staffing levels to be viable. Anthony Gallo, president of USIS professional services division, testified that in order to protect USIS' business interests, Schaffer was required to sign a noncompete[5] agreement similar to that which she signed with Omniplex

---

4. Wines distinguished the problem of "poaching" from the industry practice of hiring the incumbent workforce at a site when a staffing company takes over a contract from an outgoing security firm. When Omniplex was awarded the Project Eagle contract, it offered higher salaries and benefits to the incumbent workforce at the Project Eagle site. Wines testified that this practice is necessary as the incoming staffing company is required to assume contractual duties almost immediately, and the company is not allowed to submit an employee for a security clearance until after that company is awarded the contract. Because the security clearance process takes an average of 12 months, it is unlikely that the contractor could provide enough cleared staff for the crucial first year of the contract without hiring the incumbent employees.

5. The USIS noncompete provision reads in pertinent part:

> Employee agrees that during his or her term of employment and for a six (6) month period commencing on the last day of Employee's employment with Company, whether terminated for cause or otherwise, he or she may not without Company permission, directly or indirectly,
> (a) [provide] services similar to those provided by the Company to any Customer; or
> (b) assist any . . . enterprise in bidding, soliciting or procuring services similar to those provided by the Company to its Customers; . . . .

upon accepting employment.[6] Gallo testified this was necessary "to demonstrate to your customers that your company has the capacity to maintain a stable workforce. . . ."

In order to protect its interest in maintaining a stable, qualified workforce during the crucial first year of the Project Eagle contract, Omniplex required each of its employees to sign a restrictive covenant prohibiting employment with any firm which supports the SGC, within a year from the first day of service with Omniplex, but only if such employment requires the same security clearance the SGC required. Omniplex argues that this restrictive covenant is narrowly tailored to protect its legitimate business interest during the contract's first year. I agree with Omniplex and would find that the restrictive covenant, as drawn in this case, is a reasonable protection of Omniplex' legitimate business interest to maintain a sufficient number of "cleared" employees during Project Eagle's first year.

Omniplex' success on Project Eagle is dependent upon its ability to retain "cleared" employees during the first year of the contract. The restrictive covenant commits an Omniplex employee only during the first year of employment and places no restrictions on an employee who leaves to take another position after that time. For one year after beginning employment with Omniplex, Schaffer was prohibited from working anywhere in the world for any independent contractor of the SGC if the new position required her SGC security clearance. In this case, the restriction on Schaffer would last only nine and one-half months.

This Court has noted that

> [i]n determining the reasonableness and enforceability of restrictive covenants, trial courts must not consider function, geographical scope, and duration as three separate and distinct issues. Rather, these limitations must be considered together.

In my view, the trial court and the majority place undue and exaggerated emphasis on the covenant's lack of geographic restriction and lack of prohibited competitive activities, respectively. Both failed to give due weight to the other narrow aspects of the restriction. As noted above, the covenant applies only to employment with entities servicing the SGC in positions which require Schaffer's top-level security clearance. Schaffer is otherwise free to work for any other employer at any location in the world. She can work for any competitor of Omniplex, even one providing services to the SGC, so long as a lower security clearance is used (subject to other provisions of the noncompetition agreement). The record contained no evidence that Schaffer's work skills could only be used at the SGC as opposed to other potential employers. Considering all these factors in context, the fact that the restrictive covenant does not contain a geographic limitation or a list of prohibited competitive positions does not make it overly broad.

---

6. Significantly, the USIS covenant is longer in duration than that of Omniplex, and prohibits employment with any entity serviced by USIS during the former employee's term of employment.

The majority holds the noncompetition agreement is overbroad because it bars Schaffer from "perform[ing] any services for OMNIPLEX' customer." Such a restriction, the majority argues, would "preclude[ ] Schaffer from working as a delivery person for a vendor which delivers materials to the SGC if such security clearance was required to enter an SGC installation even though the vendor was not a staffing service competing with Omniplex." Even if the majority's analysis of the restrictive covenant is correct on this point, the possible prohibition on Schaffer's employment as an SGC delivery person is not overly broad.

Omniplex has a well-defined, vital business interest in prohibiting Schaffer from seeking other employment using her particular security clearance. Without the ability to enforce the narrowly drawn restriction, Omniplex' legitimate business interest may be vitiated. While it seems unlikely that Domino's Pizza or UPS would need a top level security clearance employee to deliver a pizza or a package to an SGC site, I would not find a restrictive covenant with such an effect to be overly broad under the specific facts of this case. As noted above, the restrictive covenant at issue is limited to only one entity, the SGC, and only in the first year of the contractual relationship. That leaves the rest of the world's entities for the pizza or package delivery person to service. Considering all the circumstances, the covenant is reasonable.

In addition, this Court has upheld restrictive covenants which lack a geographic restriction. In *Foti v. Cook*, we affirmed the trial court's decision to enforce a restrictive covenant which prohibited a former accounting firm partner from performing services for any client of the partnership. The covenant in that case did not contain a geographic restriction, but rather centered on contact with former clients. Like the enforceable restrictive covenant in *Foti*, Schaffer's noncompete agreement is client-specific, rather than geographically based. Schaffer's contract is much more narrowly drawn than the one in *Foti*, because the restrictive limit goes to only one Omniplex client and not to any others.

Similarly in *Advanced Marine Enterprises v. PRC Inc.*, we upheld a noncompete agreement which prohibited a former employee from competing with the employer within 50 miles of any of the employer's offices. We noted that even though the employer had 300 offices worldwide, the geographic restriction was reasonable because other elements of the restriction were more narrowly tailored.

In addition to considering the other narrowly tailored aspects of the restrictive covenant, I believe that our fact-specific inquiry requires us to consider the nature of the employer's business in determining whether any geographic restriction is necessary. I agree with the United States Court of Appeals for the Fourth Circuit that

> [w]ith respect to the territory to which the restriction should apply, the rule has always been that it might extend to the limits wherein the plaintiff's trade would be likely to go. The changes which have marked the course of judicial decisions in modern times seem to consist in conforming the application of the rule to the constant development of the facilities of commerce and the enlargement of the avenues of trade.

Omniplex and its competitors service government agencies both nationally and overseas. A particular government client may have contracts with multiple staffing companies for its various locations. A security clearance specific to such a client is a valuable asset and renders an employee vulnerable to "poaching" by a competitor, who also has a contract with that government client. Without its worldwide scope as to the single client, SGC, the restrictive covenant could not protect Omniplex' interest in protecting its workforce during the crucial first year on Project Eagle.

Likewise, limiting those positions an employee can take after leaving Omniplex does not sufficiently protect Omniplex' interest in maintaining adequate staffing. If Omniplex restricted Schaffer's subsequent employment by the tasks she performed, she would have no incentive not to use her valuable SGC specific security clearance to obtain other employment serving the SGC.

The restrictive covenant at issue in this case, when viewed in the context of the facts of this record, meets the three-part test for the validity of such covenants particularly for purposes of sufficiency on a motion to strike the evidence. The contractual restraint has been amply demonstrated to be reasonable, even essential, to protect Omniplex' contractual interests with the SGC. The restraint is no greater than necessary to protect that interest, particularly when drawn for such a short period of time and without restriction on Schaffer's freedom to seek employment providing services to any employer in the world except one working at the SGC and requiring her level of security clearance.

For these same reasons, it cannot be said the restrictive covenant is unduly harsh in limiting Schaffer's ability to earn a livelihood. Finally, the restraint is reasonable from a public policy standpoint. When drawn as narrowly as in this case, the restrictive covenant safeguards the ability in unique economic circumstances for an employer to maintain the contracts that enable it to be a viable entity, particularly in the areas of national security and defense. Accordingly, I would reverse the judgment of the trial court and therefore respectfully dissent from the majority opinion.

Comments

Would the majority in *Omniplex* likely uphold the Sirius non-compete agreement reproduced earlier in this chapter's employment agreement? Would the dissent? Do you require more information to assess this likelihood? If so, what information? If you predict that the provision would fail under the court's opinion, could you save it by redrafting? If so, how?

---

a. Requirement of Reasonableness

Courts are generally suspicious of "restraints of trade" (e.g., non-competition covenants), as we saw in Chapter 1, and, for this reason, may construe them strictly against the employer.[81] As explained in *Omniplex*, a restrictive covenant not to compete (or to solicit or to hire) must be reasonable to be valid and enforceable.[82] While the exact requirements vary state to state,[83] in general, the question of unreasonableness turns on two independent balancing inquiries: (1) whether the restraint is broader in scope than necessary to protect an employer's legitimate interest; and (2) whether the restraint imposes a hardship on the employee and a likely injury on the public that, together, outweigh the employer's needs for the restraint.[84] That is, the first inquiry asks whether a restraint as written is more restrictive than necessary to serve a legitimate interest of the employer—even if the employer's interest is more important than the harm a narrowly drawn restraint would impose on the employee and the public. By contrast, the second inquiry asks whether a restraint—even if neatly tailored to the employer's interest, under the first prong—imposes an unreasonable burden on the employee and the public.

As for the first inquiry, the breadth of a restrictive covenant is commonly analyzed along three dimensions: geography, duration, and restricted activity.[85] Courts will generally consider these qualifications in the context of each other (e.g., a covenant appropriately narrow in activity and duration might not need to be bounded by geography).[86] Whether a restrictive covenant is appropriately tuned to the legitimate needs of an employer necessarily turns on the particularities of each case.

As for the second inquiry, a post-employment obligation not to compete may also be invalid if it causes the employee undue hardship and/or if it is likely to cause the public injury, either (or the combination) of which outweighs the employer's needs for the restriction. A classic example of a restrictive covenant causing an employee to suffer undue hardship is where the restraint prevents the employee from earning gainful employment elsewhere.[87] The likelihood of injury to the public may outweigh the employer's needs if the employee's not

---

81. *See, e.g., Grant v. Carotek, Inc.*, 737 F.2d 410, 412 (4th Cir. 1984).

82. *See* Restatement (Second) of Contracts § 186(1) (1981) ("A promise is unenforceable on grounds of public policy if it is unreasonably in restraint of trade.").

83. A poignant example is California, which, by statute, does not enforce non-competition agreements in the employment context: "Except as provided in this chapter, every contract by which anyone is restrained from engaging in a lawful profession, trade, or business of any kind is to that extent void." Cal. Bus. & Prof. Code § 16600 (West 2008). However, California does not prohibit non-competition agreements with geographic limitations that are ancillary to a sale of a business or among dissociating partners. *Id.* §§ 16601, 16602, 16602.5.

84. *See* Restatement (Second) of Contracts § 188(1) (1981); *see also Lampman v. DeWolff Boberg & Assocs.*, 319 F. App'x 293, 299-300 (4th Cir. 2009); *Certified Restoration Dry Cleaning Network, LLC v. Tenke Corp.*, 511 F.3d 535, 545-47 (6th Cir. 2007); *Victaulic Co. v. Tieman*, 499 F.3d 227, 235 (3d Cir. 2007).

85. *See* Restatement (Second) of Contracts § 188 cmt. d (1981); *see, e.g., Lampman*, 319 F. App'x at 302; *Certified Restoration Dry Cleaning Network*, 511 F.3d at 545-47; *Victaulic Co.*, 499 F.3d at 235.

86. *See, e.g., Victaulic*, 499 F.3d at 238 ("[W]hether a covenant not to compete is unreasonable is a holistic inquiry."); *Simmons v. Miller*, 544 S.E.2d 666, 678 (Va. 2001).

87. *See* Restatement (Second) of Contracts § 188 cmt. c (1981); *see also, e.g., Lampman*, 319 F. App'x at 299-300 (under South Carolina law, to be enforceable a non-compete covenant must be "not unduly harsh and oppressive in curtailing the legitimate efforts of the employee to earn a living").

working in a particular trade causes the public substantial harm. For example, where a town had only two doctors and a covenant prevented one from providing his services there, the covenant was held to be unenforceable.[88]

Outside of the employment context, restrictive covenants are also commonly used alongside the sale of a business. Courts are generally more lenient in this business-to-business context, when construing the meaning and assessing the reasonableness of a restrictive covenant, than in the employment context.[89]

Note the recitation in § 10 of this chapter's Agreement of the Executive's belief in the reasonableness of the restrictive covenants found in the Agreement and that "the Executive is capable of gainful employment without breaching this Agreement." Similar to the acknowledgment we saw with regard to trade secrets in Chapter 1, an otherwise unreasonable restrictive covenant is not made reasonable merely because the parties characterize it so in their agreement.[90] Contractual recitations of reasonableness may be given some weight, but a court still may inquire into the actual facts and perform the same analysis regarding the reasonableness of a restrictive covenant.[91] Still, that these recitations of reasonableness may be given any weight and that they may persuasively frame a narrative for a future reader and decision-maker may be reason enough to push for inclusion.

b. Lawyer's Agreement Not to Compete

In order to protect the freedom of clients to choose their lawyers,[92] the American Bar Association's Model Rules of Professional Conduct include Rule 5.6:

---

88. *See, e.g.*, *Iredell Digestive Disease Clinic, P.A. v. Petrozza*, 373 S.E.2d 449, 455 (N.C. Ct. App. 1988), *aff'd*, 377 S.E.2d 750 (N.C. 1989) (holding an otherwise reasonable non-compete covenant unenforceable where it would jeopardize public health because it would leave only one gastroenterologist within a 45-mile radius of town). In measuring harm to the public welfare, how important is it that the restricted doctor provides "medically necessary" services? Consider *Weber v. Tillman*, 913 P.2d 84, 95-96 (Kan. 1996) (explaining that the public welfare is not harmed if residents of the town have to travel further for dermatology services). Consider this decision in light of a popular episode of *Seinfeld*, in which Jerry asserts that a dermatologist is not a "life saver" doctor, only to realize that he neglected to consider skin cancer.

89. *See, e.g.*, *Zimmer Melia & Assocs., Inc. v. Stallings*, No. 3:08-0663, 2008 WL 3887664, at *5 (M.D. Tenn. Aug. 21, 2008) ("In contrast, non-competes ancillary to the sale of a business are subjected to less intensive scrutiny. Courts have generally recognized that restrictive covenants are often necessary to secure value in the purchase of a business. . . .") (internal citation omitted); *Centorr-Vacuum Indus., Inc. v. Lavoie*, 609 A.2d 1213, 1215 (N.H. 1992) ("Because our caselaw looks upon contracts in restraint of trade with disfavor, courts normally construe noncompetition covenants narrowly. However, where, as in this case, the noncompetition covenant was ancillary to the sale of a business, it may be interpreted more liberally.") (internal citations omitted). As an extreme example, California, which does not enforce non-compete covenants at all in the employment context, will enforce reasonable non-compete agreements that are ancillary to the sale of an entity or division. CAL. BUS. & PROF. CODE § 16601 (West 2008).

90. *See, e.g.*, *Poole v. U.S. Money Reserve, Inc.*, No. 09-08-137CV, 2008 WL 4735602, at *8 (Tex. App. Oct. 30, 2008) ("[W]e conclude that the language of the agreement at issue here is but one consideration in our analysis to be viewed in conjunction with the record in its entirety."); *Jackson Hewitt Inc. v. Childress*, No. 06-CV-0909 (DMC), 2008 WL 834386 (D.N.J. Mar. 27, 2008) (considering promisor's contractual acknowledgments along with other facts in performing reasonableness analysis).

91. *See supra* note 90.

92. MODEL RULES OF PROF'L CONDUCT R. 5.6 cmt. 1 (2010).

A lawyer shall not participate in offering or making:

(a) a partnership, shareholders, operating, employment, or other similar type of agreement that restricts the right of a lawyer to practice after termination of the relationship, except an agreement concerning benefits upon retirement; or

(b) an agreement in which a restriction on the lawyer's right to practice is part of the settlement of a client controversy.[93]

Accordingly, non-competition agreements for lawyers are per se unenforceable in those states that have adopted Rule 5.6.[94] This rule has its limits; for instance, the rule against lawyer non-competition agreements does not apply to those agreements that are ancillary to a sale of a law practice.[95] In addition, the Supreme Court of California has held that an agreement "imposing a reasonable cost on departing partners who compete with the law firm in a limited geographical area" is not void.[96] However, the Supreme Judicial Court of Massachusetts has recognized, "The strong majority rule in this country is that a court will not give effect to an agreement that greatly penalizes a lawyer for competing with a former law firm."[97] Furthermore, the prohibition on lawyer non-competition agreements does not extend to a condition on a lawyer's retirement benefits: A retiring lawyer's covenant not to compete with his law firm, given in exchange for retirement benefits, is not automatically void.[98]

c. An Employer's Protectable Interest

An employer's legitimate interest in a post-employment restriction usually involves preventing the employee from using or disclosing valuable confidential

---

93. *Id.* at R. 5.6.

94. As of August 15, 2010, every state but California has adopted some version of the Model Rules. *See* Dates of Adoption of the Model Rules of Professional Conduct, http://www.abanet.org/cpr/mrpc/alpha_states.html (last visited Aug. 15, 2010). California has an analog to Model Rule 5.6 in its Rules of Professional Conduct Rule 1-500, which provides:

(A) A member shall not be a party to or participate in offering or making an agreement, whether in connection with the settlement of a lawsuit or otherwise, if the agreement restricts the right of a member to practice law, except that this rule shall not prohibit such an agreement which:

(1) Is a part of an employment, shareholders', or partnership agreement among members provided the restrictive agreement does not survive the termination of the employment, shareholder, or partnership relationship; or

(2) Requires payments to a member upon the member's retirement from the practice of law; or
(3) Is authorized by Business and professions Code sections 6092.5 subdivision (i), or 6093.

(B) A member shall not be a party to or participate in offering or making an agreement which precludes the reporting of a violation of these rules.

95. Model Rules of Prof'l Conduct R. 5.6 cmt. 3 (2010).

96. *Howard v. Babcock*, 863 P.2d 150, 160 (Cal. 1993).

97. *Pettingell v. Morrison, Mahoney & Miller*, 687 N.E.2d 1237, 1239 (Mass. 1997) (expressly disagreeing with the California Supreme Court in *Howard* and noting that most courts have taken a view contrary to that ruling).

98. *See* Model Rules of Prof'l Conduct R. 5.6 cmt. 1 (2010); *Donnelly v. Brown, Winick, Graves, Gross, Baskerville, Schoenebaum, & Walker, P.L.C.*, 599 N.W.2d 677, 681 (Iowa 1999).

information, exploiting the company's goodwill,[99] or stealing the company's customers.[100] In addition, courts often look to whether the covenant reasonably protects the company's investment of specialized training in the employee or, instead, unreasonably prohibits the employee from using his general knowledge and skills elsewhere.[101] Without a legitimate interest at stake, the employer's restrictive covenant will fail.[102] How do courts determine whether such a legitimate interest is at stake? Consider the following case.

Nike, Inc. v. McCarthy
United States Court of Appeals, Ninth Circuit, 2004.
379 F.3d 576.

FISHER, Circuit Judge.

In this case we must determine the validity of a noncompete agreement under Oregon law. Eugene McCarthy left his position as director of sales for Nike's Brand Jordan division in June 2003 to become vice president of U.S. footwear sales and merchandising at Reebok, one of Nike's competitors. Nike sought a preliminary injunction to prevent McCarthy from working for Reebok for a year, invoking a noncompete agreement McCarthy had signed in 1997 when Nike had promoted him to his earlier position as a regional footwear sales manager. . . . We . . . hold that Nike has a legitimate interest in enforcing the agreement, because there is a substantial risk that McCarthy—in shaping Reebok's product allocation, sales and pricing strategies—could enable Reebok to divert a significant amount of Nike's footwear sales given the highly confidential information McCarthy acquired at Nike. Thus, we affirm the district court's preliminary injunction enforcing the agreement.

I. FACTUAL AND PROCEDURAL BACKGROUND

McCarthy began working for Nike in 1993 and became a key account manager in 1995.[1] During the spring of 1997, Nike undertook a major, national reorganization. Out of this came McCarthy's promotion to eastern regional footwear sales manager—and the present dispute as to when that promotion

---

99. "Goodwill" generally refers to the good reputation and brand value a company enjoys. More technically, in accounting, "goodwill" refers to the amount an acquiring company pays to acquire a target company beyond the target company's book value.

100. RESTATEMENT (SECOND) OF CONTRACTS § 188 cmt. b (1981); *see, e.g., Certified Restoration Dry Cleaning Network*, 511 F.3d at 547 ("Reasonable covenants may protect such legitimate interests as trade secrets, confidential information, close contact with the employer's customers or customer lists, or cost factors and pricing. However, an employer may not reasonably prohibit future use of general knowledge or skill."); *Victaulic*, 499 F.3d at 235 (explaining that interests that can be protected through covenants include trade secrets, confidential information, good will, unique or extraordinary skills, and not allowing competitors to benefit from specialized training and skills).

101. *See supra* note 100.

102. *See Victaulic*, 499 F.3d at 235 ("To be reasonably necessary for the protection of the employer, a covenant must be tailored to protect legitimate interests.").

1. McCarthy signed a covenant not to compete as part of his employment agreement for the key account manager position, but that is not the noncompete agreement at issue here.

actually occurred. On February 28, John Petersen, McCarthy's supervisor, called McCarthy and asked, "How would you like to be the regional footwear sales manager for the eastern region?" McCarthy answered, "Absolutely, yes." Petersen mentioned there would be an increase in pay but did not say what the salary would be.[2]

In the following weeks, McCarthy continued to perform some of his old duties while assuming some of the duties of his new position, including leading meetings and preparing a report. In order to perform these duties, McCarthy obtained confidential information he had not seen before that described the top-selling styles in the eastern region. During the week of March 10, Petersen announced to a group of employees that McCarthy was the new regional footwear sales manager. During the remainder of March, McCarthy took several business trips, which were expensed to the cost center for the regional footwear sales manager position.

On March 27, McCarthy received a letter from Petersen confirming the offer for the regional footwear sales manager position ("Offer Letter"). The letter indicated that the "start date" for the new position was April 1, 1997. According to several Nike executives, it is not unusual for an employee to begin to perform the duties of a new position prior to the start date, in order to ensure a smooth transition once he or she "officially" starts in the new position. The Offer Letter also specified that McCarthy's salary would be $110,000, which became effective April 1. Before that date, McCarthy's salary was charged to the cost center for the key account manager position.

In addition, the Offer Letter required McCarthy to sign an attached covenant not to compete and nondisclosure agreement as a condition of acceptance of the offer. The covenant not to compete contained the "Competition Restriction" clause at issue here, stating in relevant part:

> During EMPLOYEE's employment by NIKE . . . and for one (1) year thereafter, (the "Restriction Period"), EMPLOYEE will not directly or indirectly . . . be employed by, consult for, or be connected in any manner with, any business engaged anywhere in the world in the athletic footwear, athletic apparel or sports equipment and accessories business, or any other business which directly competes with NIKE or any of its subsidiaries or affiliated corporations.

McCarthy signed the agreement that day. It is this noncompete agreement that Nike now seeks to enforce.

Two years later, McCarthy was again promoted, this time to the position of director of sales for the Brand Jordan division, the position he held until he resigned from Nike in June 2003. He was not asked to sign a new noncompete agreement. During the spring of 2003, McCarthy accepted a position with Reebok as vice president of U.S. footwear sales and merchandising and tendered his resignation in June. McCarthy began working at Reebok on July 22, 2003.

---

2. Petersen testified that he did not have actual authority to offer McCarthy the position at that time but rather was calling to see if McCarthy would be interested in the position.

On August 18, 2003, Nike filed suit in Oregon circuit court, claiming breach of contract and seeking a declaratory judgment that McCarthy's employment with Reebok violated the covenant not to compete. McCarthy removed the case to the United States District Court for the District of Oregon, which had jurisdiction pursuant to 28 U.S.C. § 1332. Nike then moved for a temporary restraining order, which the district court granted on August 26. After conducting an evidentiary hearing, the court granted Nike's motion for a preliminary injunction on September 24. Specifically, the court enjoined McCarthy from "engaging in any athletic footwear business, athletic apparel business, or any other business which directly competes with Nike or any of its subsidiaries or affiliated corporations," including Reebok, through August 25, 2004. McCarthy appeals the grant of the preliminary injunction. . . .

B. Protectible Interest

Even if the covenant not to compete is not void under [an Oregon statute], it is a contract in restraint of trade that must meet three requirements under Oregon common law to be enforceable:

> (1) it must be partial or restricted in its operation in respect either to time or place; (2) it must be on some good consideration; and (3) it must be reasonable, that is, it should afford only a fair protection to the interests of the party in whose favor it is made, and must not be so large in its operation as to interfere with the interests of the public.

To satisfy the reasonableness requirement, the employer must show as a predicate "that [it] has a 'legitimate interest' entitled to protection." McCarthy argues that Nike has failed to show such a legitimate interest in this case.

McCarthy's general skills in sales and product development as well as industry knowledge that he acquired while working for Nike is not a protectible interest of Nike's that would justify enforcement of a noncompete agreement. "It has been uniformly held that general knowledge, skill, or facility acquired through training or experience while working for an employer appertain exclusively to the employee. The fact that they were acquired or developed during the employment does not, by itself, give the employer a sufficient interest to support a restraining covenant, even though the on-the-job training has been extensive and costly."

Nonetheless, an employer has a protectible interest in "information pertaining especially to the employer's business."

Nike has shown that McCarthy acquired information pertaining especially to Nike's business during the course of his employment with Nike. As Brand Jordan's director of sales, McCarthy obtained knowledge of Nike's product launch dates, product allocation strategies, new product development, product orders six months in advance and strategic sales plans up to three years in the future. This information was not general knowledge in the industry. For instance, McCarthy was privy to information about launch dates—the date Nike plans to introduce a product in the marketplace—for Brand Jordan shoes up through the spring of 2004. According to the undisputed testimony of one of Nike's executives, if a company knew its competitor's launch dates, it could time the launch dates of its own products to disrupt the sales of its competitor.

Nevertheless, McCarthy argues that acquisition of confidential information alone is insufficient to justify enforcement of a noncompete agreement. He contends that Nike must show actual use or potential disclosure of confidential information before a noncompete agreement can be enforced. He attempts to distinguish [Oregon cases that find an employer's interest in protecting confidential information to be a protectable interest] as cases in which the employees actually used the confidential information, for example, to solicit the former employer's customers on behalf of the new employer. These cases do not suggest that actual use is required for a noncompete clause to be enforceable, however. For example, in [one case], the court stated:

> It is clear that if the nature of the employment is such as will bring the employee [i]n personal contact with the patrons or customers of the employer, or enable him to acquire valuable information as to the nature and character of the business and [t]he names and requirements of the patrons or customers, *enabling him . . . to take advantage of such knowledge* of [o]r acquaintance with the patrons or customers of his former employer, and thereby gain an unfair advantage, equity will interfere in behalf of the employer and restrain the breach of a negative covenant not to engage in such competing business. . . .

Thus, the court recognized that an employee's mere ability to take advantage of the employer's confidential information and thereby gain an unfair advantage may be sufficient for equity to restrain the employee from engaging in a competing business.

An employee's knowledge of confidential information is sufficient to justify enforcement of the noncompete if there is a "substantial risk" that the employee will be able to divert all or part of the employer's business given his knowledge. Given the nature of the confidential information that McCarthy acquired at Nike and his new position with Reebok, there is a substantial risk that Reebok would be able to divert a significant part of Nike's business given McCarthy's knowledge. McCarthy had the highest access to confidential information concerning Nike's product allocation, product development and sales strategies. As vice president of U.S. footwear sales and merchandising for Reebok, McCarthy would be responsible for developing strategic sales plans, providing overall direction for product allocation and shaping product lines, including how products are priced. Thus, McCarthy could help choose product allocation, sales and pricing strategies for Reebok that could divert a substantial part of Nike's footwear sales to Reebok based on his knowledge of information confidential to Nike without explicitly disclosing this information to any of Reebok's employees. Accordingly, the potential use of confidential information by McCarthy in his new position with Reebok is sufficient to justify enforcing the noncompete agreement. We conclude that Nike has demonstrated a likelihood of success as to the enforceability of its noncompete agreement with McCarthy. . . .

d. Reasonably in Restraint of Trade: Ancillarity

In addition to a concern for reasonableness, a restrictive covenant not to compete will be found unenforceable as an *unreasonable* restraint of trade (note that "restraints of trade" are not inherently unreasonable or unenforceable), if the covenant is not "ancillary" to a valid transaction or relationship.[103] The *Restatement* neatly explains how this requirement dovetails with the requirement of reasonableness for restraints of trade:

> In order for a promise to refrain from competition to be reasonable, the promisee must have an interest worthy of protection that can be balanced against the hardship on the promisor and the likely injury to the public. The restraint must, therefore, be subsidiary to an otherwise valid transaction or relationship that gives rise to such an interest. A restraint that is not so related to an otherwise valid transaction or relationship is necessarily unreasonable.[104]

Such a valid transaction or relationship is commonly found in an employment agreement to which the restrictive covenant is ancillary.[105] Likewise, restraints of trade are often found valid as ancillary to the sale of a business.[106] Courts have also treated a variety of other transactions or relationships as the legitimate basis to which a restraint of trade may be ancillary, including a landlord-tenant relationship,[107] a gift,[108] and a non-disclosure agreement.[109]

e. Judicial Response to Overly Restrictive Clauses

As with the judicial response to unreasonable non-disclosure covenants, there are three basic judicial approaches for treatment of unreasonably broad covenants not to compete: (1) do nothing; (2) "blue-pencil"; or (3) rewrite to be reasonable.

A few states are unwilling to alter unreasonable restrictive covenants at all, leaving them to fail and severing them from the remainder of the contract so

---

103. *See* RESTATEMENT (SECOND) OF CONTRACTS § 187 (1981).

104. *Id.* § 187 cmt. b (citations omitted).

105. *See, e.g., Ray Mart Inc. v. Stock Bldg. Supply of Tex. LP*, 302 F. App'x 232, 238 (5th Cir. 2008) (applying Texas law); *Siech v. Hobbs Grp., LLC*, 198 F. App'x 840, 842 (11th Cir. 2006) (applying Georgia law); *JAK Prods., Inc. v. Wiza*, 986 F.2d 1080, 1086-87 (7th Cir. 1993) (applying Indiana law).

106. *See, e.g., National-Arnold Magnetics Co. v. Wood*, 46 F. App'x 416, 418 (9th Cir. 2002) (Illinois law); *LDDS Commc'ns, Inc. v. Automated Commc'ns, Inc.*, 35 F.3d 198, 199 (5th Cir. 1994) (Mississippi law).

107. *See, e.g., Red Sage Ltd. P'ship v. DESPA Deutsche Sparkassen Immobilien-Anlage-Gasellschaft mbH*, 254 F.3d 1120, 1132-33 (D.C. Cir. 2001).

108. *See, e.g., Liautaud v. Liautaud*, 221 F.3d 981, 986 (7th Cir. 2000).

109. *See, e.g., Picker Int'l, Inc. v. Blanton*, 756 F. Supp. 971, 982 (N.D. Tex. 1990).

long as appropriate.[110] These courts are unwilling to alter unreasonable restrictive covenants at all because to do so would incent the employer to write overbroad restrictions to later be reduced to reasonableness by a court, if need be.[111] However, these courts may still be willing to sever the unenforceable provision from the rest of the contract.[112]

Some courts are willing to "blue-pencil" an overbroad clause, which means they will enforce a restrictive covenant by *striking* any unreasonable language, provided that this results in a coherent, enforceable provision.[113] In so doing, these courts will not *add* to a restrictive covenant in order to make it valid.[114]

Whether a court is of the do-nothing or the blue-pencil school, it is unlikely to do anything more to abide by a contractual provision like that found in § 10 ("Remedies") of the Agreement, instructing a court that the restrictive covenant "be deemed to be modified to restrict the Executive's competition with the Company to the maximum extent of time, scope and geography which the court or arbitrator shall find enforceable."[115] How might this inform the Company's inclusion and drafting of such a provision (and other relevant provisions) in the Agreement?

The modern trend is the more flexible "rule of reasonableness" (sometimes termed the "partial enforcement") approach.[116] Courts subscribing to this

---

110. *See, e.g.*, *Lampman v. DeWolff Boberg & Assocs., Inc.*, 319 F. App'x 293, 300 (4th Cir. 2009) ("South Carolina courts will not modify or 'blue pencil' a non-competition clause so as to restate its terms in a way to make the agreement enforceable.") (internal citation omitted); *Palmer & Cay, Inc. v. Marsh & McLennan Cos.*, 404 F.3d 1297, 1303-04 (11th Cir. 2005) (observing that Georgia courts will not blue-pencil restrictive covenants in the employment context) (internal citations omitted); *Nalco Chem. Co. v. Hydro Techs., Inc.*, 984 F.2d 801, 806 (7th Cir. 1993) (observing that, under Wisconsin law, a restrictive covenant will not be modified to make enforceable) (citing Wis. Stat. Ann. § 103.465). For further discussion of when courts find it appropriate to sever a provision from a contract, see the discussion of severability in Chapter 1. However, Georgia courts are willing to reform restrictive covenants in the context of the sale of a business. *See Palmer & Cay*, 404 F.3d at 1303.

111. *See, e.g.*, *White v. Fletcher/Mayo/Assocs., Inc.*, 303 S.E.2d 746, 748 (Ga. 1983) (noting that courts altering an employment restrictive covenant to make it more reasonable gives employers the incentive to cast overbroad provisions, which is harmful given the "in terrorem" effects of countless employees abiding by such overbroad provisions without making a fuss).

112. *See, e.g.*, *Lampman*, 319 F. App'x at 300 (4th Cir. 2009). Note that Georgia's approach means that "if an otherwise valid contract contains one overly broad non-solicitation or non-competition covenant, the other non-solicitation or non-competition covenants in the same agreement are automatically rendered unenforceable." *Palmer & Cay*, 404 F.3d at 1304 (internal citations omitted). Please see Chapter 1 for more on severability.

113. *See, e.g.*, *JAK Prods., Inc. v. Wiza*, 986 F.2d 1080, 1087 (7th Cir. 1993) (noting that "[i]n Indiana, the blue pencil doctrine applies to a covenant not to compete that is severable in its terms" and finding that the blue-pencil doctrine could save the restrictive covenants in this case); *Dearborn v. Everett J. Prescott, Inc.*, 486 F. Supp. 2d 802, 810 (S.D. Ind. 2007) (applying Indiana's blue-pencil rule to find that mere striking would not render the provision enforceable); *Tech. Partners, Inc. v. Hart*, 298 F. App'x 238, 243-44 (4th Cir. 2008) (applying North Carolina's blue-pencil rule to find that mere striking would not render the provision enforceable).

114. *See, e.g.*, *Dearborn*, 486 F. Supp. 2d at 810 (stating that "the court may not add terms").

115. *See, e.g.*, *Nalco Chem.*, 984 F.2d at 806 (ruling that, under Wisconsin law, a savings clause instructing a court to enforce a non-compete covenant inasmuch as reasonable is not effective); *Prod. Action Int'l, Inc. v. Mero*, 277 F. Supp. 2d 919, 928-29 (S.D. Ind. 2003) (ruling that, under Indiana law, a court will not add terms to make a provision enforceable even if the provision says "to the extent permitted by law").

116. *See, e.g.*, *A.N. Deringer v. Strough*, 103 F.3d 243, 246 (2d Cir. 1996) (finding that the rule of reasonableness applies under Vermont law); *Ferrofluidics Corp. v. Advanced Vacuum Components, Inc.*, 968 F.2d 1463, 1469 (1st Cir. 1992) (finding that the rule of reasonableness applies under Massachusetts and New Hampshire law);

approach are willing to rewrite an unreasonable clause so as to make it reasonable and, thereby, enforceable.[117] Note, however, that this approach merely permits—and does not require—courts to modify restrictive covenants, and courts may opt not to modify a restrictive covenant.[118]

C. DISTINGUISHING "EMPLOYEE" AND "INDEPENDENT CONTRACTOR"

The difference between an employee and an independent contractor is meaningful in several different contexts—just as a sampling, in the context of vicarious liability for torts, withholding taxes, and rights in copyrighted works. In addition, the substantive rights and obligations imposed by many federal statutes are only triggered when a company's "worker" is an "employee" and not an "independent contractor."[119]

What determines whether someone is an employee or an independent contractor? Courts frequently cite to the factors enumerated by the Supreme Court in *Community for Creative Non-Violence v. Reid*,[120] as a non-exhaustive list of the factors that determine employee classification at common law. As the Supreme Court in *Reid* explained, these factors are:

> [T]he hiring party's right to control the manner and means by which the product is accomplished. Among the other factors relevant to this inquiry are the skill required; the source of the instrumentalities and tools; the location of the work; the duration of the relationship between the parties; whether the hiring party has the right to assign additional projects to the hired party; the extent of the hired party's discretion over when and how long to work; the method of payment; the hired party's role in hiring and paying assistants; whether the work is part of the regular business of the hiring party; whether the hiring party is in business; the provision of employee benefits; and the tax treatment of the hired party. No one of these factors is determinative.[121]

In addition, courts frequently cite to those factors listed in the *Restatement (Second) of Agency*, which include:

> (a) the extent of control which, by the agreement, the master may exercise over the details of the work; (b) whether or not the one employed is engaged in a distinct occupation or business; (c) the kind of occupation, with reference to whether, in the locality, the work is usually done under the direction of the

---

117. *See supra* note 116.

118. *See, e.g., Lamp v. Am. Prosthetics, Inc.,* 379 N.W.2d 909, 910-11 (Iowa 1986) (declining to modify an overly broad restrictive covenant, where it was not properly preserved for appeal, because the *Ehlers* decision does not *require* a court to modify an unreasonable provision).

119. *See generally Nationwide Mut. Ins. Co. v. Darden,* 503 U.S. 318 (1992).

120. 490 U.S. 730, 751-52 (1989).

121. *Id.* (internal citations omitted).

employer or by a specialist without supervision; (d) the skill required in the particular occupation; (e) whether the employer or the workman supplies the instrumentalities, tools, and the place of work for the person doing the work; (f) the length of time for which the person is employed; (g) the method of payment, whether by the time or by the job; (h) whether or not the work is a part of the regular business of the employer; (i) whether or not the parties believe they are creating the relation of master and servant; and (j) whether the principal is or is not in business.[122]

While no single factor is decisive in characterizing a relationship,[123] whether or not the putative employer has the right to control the putative employee's "manner and means" of work has tended to receive the most emphasis by courts.[124] As an illustration, the Supreme Court in *Reid* found a sculptor to be an independent contractor, where an organization commissioned and directed the sculptor to produce a work of certain specifications and the sculptor was skilled, supplied his own tools, worked in his own studio distant from the organization (such that daily supervision was impossible), was retained for less than two months' time, was free to work when and how long he pleased and hire any assistants of his choosing, and was to be paid upon completion of the specific job.[125]

Note that, while what the parties believe is a *Restatement* factor and may be given some weight,[126] contractual specification is not dispositive,[127] and courts will still look to the other relevant factors, especially control.[128] In other words, "an employee does not become an independent contractor simply because a

---

122. RESTATEMENT (SECOND) OF AGENCY § 220(2) (1958). Note that the *Third Restatement of Agency* defines an employee as "an agent whose principal controls or has the right to control the manner and means of the agent's performance of work." RESTATEMENT (THIRD) OF AGENCY § 7.07(3)(a) (2006). The *Third Restatement* retains a list of other factors in comment f.

123. *See N.L.R.B. v. United Ins. Co. of Am.*, 390 U.S. 254, 258 (1968) ("[T]here is no shorthand formula or magic phrase that can be applied to find the answer, but all of the incidents of the relationship must be assessed and weighed with no one factor being decisive.").

124. *See, e.g., Peno Trucking, Inc. v. Comm'r*, 296 F. App'x 449, 455-56 (6th Cir. 2008) ("[A]uthorities seem to be in general agreement that an employer's right to control the manner in which the work is performed is an important if not the master test to be considered.") (citations omitted); *N.L.R.B. v. Friendly Cab Co.*, 512 F.3d 1090, 1096 (9th Cir. 2008) ("[T]he essential ingredient of the agency test is the extent of control exercised by the 'employer.'") (internal quotation marks and citations omitted); *see also* Treas. Reg. § 31.3121(d)-1(c)(2) (as amended 1980) ("Generally such relationship exists when the person for whom services are performed has the right to control and direct the individual who performs the services. . . ."). Consider, also, the *Third Restatement*, which moves the factors to the comments and defines an employee solely in terms of the control factor. *See supra* note 122 and accompanying text. *But see FedEx Home Delivery v. N.L.R.B.*, 563 F.3d 492, 503 (D.C. Cir. 2009) (explaining the court's shift in emphasis from the manner and means of control to whether the putative independent contractor has "a significant entrepreneurial opportunity for gain or loss").

125. *Reid*, 490 U.S. at 751-52.

126. *See, e.g., Weidner v. Sanchez*, 14 S.W.3d 353, 373 (Tex. App. 2000).

127. *See* RESTATEMENT (SECOND) OF AGENCY § 220 (1958) ("It is not determinative that the parties believe or disbelieve that the relation of master and servant exists, except insofar as such belief indicates an assumption of control by the one and submission to control by the other.").

128. *See, e.g., Vizcaino v. Microsoft Corp.*, 120 F.3d 1006, 1009-10 (9th Cir. 1997) (finding workers to be employees despite a contract designating them to be independent contractors); *Hartford Underwriters Ins. Co. v.*

contract describes him as such."[129] What, then, is the value (to any party) of such a contractual designation? As we see throughout this book, a party may wish to include a provision in a contract that gives at least some weight—even if not dispositive weight—to that party's position, whether inside or outside of a courtroom. This rings especially true when including such a provision is virtually costless.

State, Dept. of Human Res., 32 P.3d 1146, 1154 (Kan. 2001) ("The primary concern in determining whether the individual is an employee or an independent contractor is what is done under the contract and not what it states.") (internal citations omitted).

129. *Legeno v. Douglas Elliman, LLC*, 311 F. App'x 403, 405 (2d Cir. 2009) (quoting *In re Shulman Transport Enters., Inc.*, 744 F.2d 293, 295 (2d Cir. 1984)) (applying New York law).

· CHAPTER THREE ·

Services Agreements

Telcove is an internet service provider ("ISP"), which purchases capacity from "up-stream" providers of internet services and sells that capacity to smaller ISPs "downstream," like Asch. Telcove and Asch entered into a three-year agreement ("Agreement") under which Telcove agreed to provide internet services to Asch. Shortly after activating Asch's internet service in February 2004, Telcove began receiving complaints about emails sent from internet protocol ("IP") addresses associated with Asch. Telcove eventually received nearly fifteen hundred complaints about emails sent from these IP addresses. . . . On April 28, 2004, Telcove informed Asch by letter that it was terminating its internet service on April 30, 2004. The letter notified Asch that the Agreement was being terminated in accordance with sections (b) and (g) of the Acceptable Use Policy set forth in the Agreement. However, after a discussion between counsel, Telcove agreed to continue providing internet service to Asch so that it would have time to procure internet services from another provider. On June 10, 2004, Telcove stopped providing internet service to Asch.

Asch did not reach agreement with another internet provider and ceased operations. Asch then initiated this civil action against Telcove. Telcove moved for summary judgment on these claims, arguing that an exculpatory clause in the Agreement prevented Asch from recovering the damages it sought. The District Court granted summary judgment in favor of Telcove and subsequently denied Asch's motion for reconsideration. Asch filed a timely appeal. . . .

In this litigation, Asch argued that Telcove's termination of the Agreement destroyed its business. Accordingly, as damages, it sought the fair market value of its business, allegedly $1.43 million, in consequential damages. If the exculpatory clause is enforceable, by its terms it relieves Telcove of any liability for the damages Asch seeks because Asch agreed to release Telcove from "all liability or responsibility for any direct, indirect, incidental or consequential damages . . . suffered by [Asch] in connection with [its] use of or inability to use the Telcove internet services."

Asch Webhosting, Inc. v. Adelphia Bus. Solutions,
362 F. App'x 310, 311-13 (3d Cir. 2010).

Before entering a services agreement—or any agreement—a party should take care to understand the risks posed by the relationship and the terms contemplated. After all, an agreement essentially consists of two components: potential costs and benefits. After considering the risky scenarios and deciding which potential costs a party wishes to avoid or to minimize, the party may try to structure the agreement to limit its exposure to these risks. As the above-excerpted case illustrates, a party can effectively limit its liability exposure under a services contract (as a party may in most any contract). In the case excerpted above, Telcove accomplished this by including a provision excluding so-called "consequential" damages (and, while the court did not decide the case on this issue, by including a provision allowing for termination upon violation of certain policies).[1] In this chapter, we discuss both the benefits and costs of services agreements and further explore ways in which parties may manage potential costs and shift risk.

We turn our attention in this chapter to agreements for the purchase and sale of services between sophisticated business entities.[2] These agreements include, *inter alia*, independent contractor, consulting, master services, and outsourcing agreements and at a minimum address scope and price of services, term, ownership of any specific goods or products ("deliverables") resulting from the services, and confidentiality undertakings. Most agreements also include pricing assumptions, procedures for determining and specifying changes in scope and

---

1. *Asch Webhosting, Inc. v. Adelphia Bus. Solutions*, 362 F. App'x 310, 313-14 (3d Cir. 2010) (affirming the district court's decision to enforce the exculpatory clause at issue). The exculpatory provision in full provided:

Warranties/Disclaimers
TELCOVE'S INTERNET SERVICE IS PROVIDED ON AN "AS IS, AS AVAILABLE" BASIS UNLESS STATED OTHERWISE IN THE TELCOVE'S SERVICE LEVEL AGREEMENT (SLA). NO WARRANTIES, EXPRESS OR IMPLIED, INCLUDING, BUT NOT LIMITED TO, THOSE OF MERCHANTABILITY OR FITNESS FOR A PARTICULAR PURPOSE, ARE MADE WITH RESPECT TO TELCOVE'S INTERNET SERVICES(S) OR ANY INFORMATION OR SOFTWARE THEREIN. CUSTOMER RELEASES TELCOVE FROM ALL LIABILITY OR RESPONSIBILITY FOR ANY DIRECT, INDIRECT, INCIDENTAL OR CONSEQUENTIAL DAMAGES, INCLUDING BUT NOT LIMITED TO DAMAGES DUE TO LOSS OF REVENUES OR LOSS OF BUSINESS, SUFFERED BY CUSTOMER IN CONNECTION WITH THEIR USE OF OR INABILITY TO USE THE TELCOVE INTERNET SERVICES. WITHOUT LIMITING THE GENERALITY OF THE FOREGOING, TELCOVE DISCLAIMS TO THE FULL EXTENT PERMITTED BY APPLICABLE LAW ANY RESPONSIBILITY FOR (AND UNDER NO CIRCUMSTANCES SHALL BE LIABLE FOR) ANY CONDUCT, CONTENT, GOODS AND SERVICES AVAILABLE ON OR THROUGH THE INTERNET OR TELCOVE SERVICES. IN NO EVENT SHALL TELCOVE'S AGGREGATE LIABILITY EXCEED THE AMOUNT PAID BY CUSTOMER TO TELCOVE FOR THE TELCOVE SERVICES. USE OF ANY INFORMATION OBTAINED VIA TELCOVE'S INTERNET SERVICE IS AT THE CUSTOMER'S OWN RISK. TELCOVE SPECIFICALLY DISCLAIMS ANY RESPONSIBILITY FOR THE ACCURACY OR QUALITY OF THE INFORMATION OBTAINED THROUGH ITS SERVICES.

Id. at 312 (emphasis in original; bold removed).
2. We do not address consumer services contracts, and, accordingly, the Magnuson-Moss Act and other consumer protection laws are outside the scope of this chapter.

for purchasing out-of-scope services, performance standards, warranties, remedies, limitations of liability, indemnifications, and rights around subcontracting and termination.

The particular service offerings and engagements covered by these agreements are of different forms and complexities. They range from relatively straightforward agreements for staff extension (temporary workers) services, to those for the development and installation of complex IT systems, to those for multi-year outsourcings (in which a service provider undertakes to operate one or more often critical areas of a client's business such as data management, customer relationship management, accounting, or payroll).

In this chapter, we examine two services agreements: The first of these involves the provision of consulting services between an individual and a business entity; the second, the provision of Internet services between two business entities.

A. INDEPENDENT CONTRACTOR CONSULTING AGREEMENT

The following agreement sets forth the rights and obligations of an independent contractor to provide consulting services for a corporation.

Things to Consider . . .

As you read through the following agreement, please consider these items. You will want to return to the agreement, as you study the substantive discussion that follows.

> **Context of Relationship.** Notice how this Agreement's recitals (i.e., the "whereas" clauses) explain the context and history of this transaction and the underlying relationship between the parties. What is the historical context and purpose of this Agreement?

> **Agency and Nature of Relationship.** Consider the relationship created and/or evidenced by this Agreement. Do the parties purport to create an employment relationship? What are the similarities and differences between the relationship contemplated by this Agreement and the employment agreement in Chapter 2? Is there an agency relationship between the parties, where, for instance, one may have the authority to bind the other?

CONSULTING AGREEMENT[3]

THIS AGREEMENT is made as of the 6th day of September, 2001 (the "Agreement"), by and between Hewlett-PACKARD COMPANY, a Delaware corporation ("HP", references to HP throughout this Agreement include HP's subsidiaries and affiliates), and BENZION LANDA, a resident of Israel residing at 35 Itamar Ben Avi Street, Nes Ziona, Israel ("Landa").

WHEREAS, Landa is the founder of Indigo N.V., a corporation organized under the laws of The Netherlands ("Indigo"), an inventor of Indigo's core Liquid Electro-Photography technology ("LEP"), and is the prime architect of Indigo's business and product strategies;

WHEREAS, HP and Indigo are parties to an Offer Agreement and other agreements relating thereto (the "Agreements"), dated September 5, 2001, pursuant to which, among other things, HP will offer to purchase all of Indigo's outstanding common shares on the terms and conditions of the Agreements;

WHEREAS, both HP and Landa desire the successful integration of the Indigo business and operations (the "LEP Business") into HP, the growth of the LEP Business following such integration, and the overall future success of HP;

WHEREAS, Landa conceived, made, discovered or developed or was an inventor of intellectual property related to the LEP Business;

WHEREAS, in furtherance of these common interests and in connection with the Agreements (i) HP desires to have access to Landa's experience and knowledge regarding LEP, the LEP Business, and the printing and imaging industry in general, as well as to Landa's insights into potential technological synergies and business opportunities both from within HP and outside of HP (ii) Landa desires to influence HP at the highest levels, both with respect to the LEP Business and to HP's overall business strategy and direction and (iii) Landa and HP desire to confirm that all of Landa's intellectual property rights related to the LEP Business have been assigned to Indigo; and

WHEREAS, Landa is willing to perform Consulting services upon the terms and conditions set forth herein.

NOW, THEREFORE, in consideration of the mutual covenants contained herein and of the mutual benefits provided herein, the parties hereto agree as follows:

1. **Appointment.** HP hereby appoints Landa to the position of a Strategic Advisor to the HP Chief Executive Officer (the "CEO"). In this capacity, he shall advise the CEO of HP, as well as other senior HP executives, on relevant strategic technology, product, market and business matters, particularly regarding HP's printing and imaging business. Landa's primary objectives will be to contribute to the success of the LEP

---

3. Indigo NV, Consulting Agreement (Form SC 14D9), at Exhibit 99(e)(12) (Feb. 21, 2002), *available at* http://www.sec.gov/Archives/edgar/data/920910/000101287002000826/dex99e12.txt.

business within HP and the successful integration of Indigo into HP. Landa's title may be amended during the term of this Agreement as determined by the CEO.

2. <u>Services</u>. Landa hereby agrees that he shall advise HP regarding the following matters (the "<u>Services</u>"):

(a) Identification of technological synergies and business opportunities both from within HP and outside of HP;

(b) Integration of the LEP Business into the operations of HP;

(c) Strategic planning and tactics regarding printing and imaging products and markets; and

(d) Other matters as reasonably requested by HP.

In addition, Landa shall promote the interests of HP and assist its CEO by accepting, in his discretion, suitable industry and public speaking engagements that are mutually acceptable to Landa and HP. These engagements will be arranged by or cleared by the Communications function within Imaging and Printing Systems.

3. <u>Efforts; Exclusivity</u>. Landa will determine, in his sole discretion, the level of effort and time that he shall apply to the performance of the services described herein. Except as provided herein, Landa assumes no specific duties or responsibilities. Subject to the non-compete provisions pursuant to Section 8 below, Landa will be free to pursue any other activities.

4. <u>Compensation; Obligations of HP</u>. Landa's sole compensation for Services rendered pursuant to this Agreement shall be the performance by HP of its obligations and duties under this Agreement. In order to enable Landa to perform the Services described herein, and as consideration for Landa's agreement to perform them, HP will provide the following services and facilities during the term of this Agreement:

(a) <u>Access/Participation</u>. Subsequent to Landa and HP entering into a mutually satisfactory intellectual property agreement, HP agrees in its sole discretion to grant Landa access to HP technical programs, research and development projects (including projects of HP Labs) and HP facilities primarily relating to the printing and imaging business as required to perform the service described in Section 2. Landa may, in HP's sole discretion, participate in technology and design reviews, as well as senior management meetings and strategy sessions related to the LEP Business. HP's CEO shall meet with Landa from time to time at her convenience. Other senior HP executives and senior managers shall meet with Landa at times and venues of mutual convenience.

(b) <u>Consultation</u>. Both parties agree to consult regularly with one another regarding:

(i) significant matters affecting the LEP product offerings and/or the LEP Business;

(ii) significant issues relating to the integration of the LEP Business into HP's operations, including issues of cultural integration; and

(iii) significant issues affecting HP's revenues from the LEP Business.

(c) Office Space, Support Equipment, Staffing. HP will (at its expense) continue to maintain an office for Landa in Israel, comparable to, and adjacent to, the office of the General Manager of the LEP Business and will provide Landa with other services and support, as customarily provided to such General Manager, including, inter alia: (i) reasonable administrative, secretarial and other office support services, (ii) home, office and lap-top computers with access to HP's e-mail network and management information systems, and (iii) reasonable local, long-distance and mobile telephone service for Israel and outside of Israel;

(d) Laboratory Space. HP will, at HP's expense, provide reasonable maintenance and upkeep to Landa's private laboratory at its LEP Business facilities in Israel (the "Laboratory") which shall be (i) at least sixty (60) square meters in area, (ii) reasonably equipped with instrumentation and materials comparable to general research laboratory facilities maintained by HP, and (iii) supported, from time to time as required by Landa, by technical staff, but not to exceed the equivalent of two full-time laboratory technicians/engineers. Landa will have free access to the Israel LEP Business facilities at all times. The Laboratory will be accessible to Landa at all times and to others only as authorized by Landa and HP. Landa will have access to the laboratory while this Agreement is effective or some other period of time mutually agreed upon by Landa and HP, and may use the laboratory for any lawful purpose whatsoever.

(e) Expense Reimbursements. HP will pay or reimburse Landa for all reasonable travel, entertainment or other expenses that he may incur during the term of this Agreement in connection with the performance of Services hereunder.

5. Intellectual Property.

(a) Assignment. Landa agrees that all copyrightable material, models, devices, reports, tooling, schematics and other diagrams, instructional material, notes, records, drawings, algorithms, trade secrets, computer programs, designs, technology, discoveries, ideas, know-how, processes, formulas, compositions, data, techniques, improvements, inventions (whether patentable or not), works of authorship, title, patents, patent rights, copyrights, mask work rights, trade secret rights, and other intellectual property (hereinafter collectively referred to as the "<u>Intellectual Property</u>") in LEP (and improvements to HP's LEP products) which have been or are conceived, made, discovered or developed by Landa, or of which Landa is an inventor, either solely or in collaboration with others, prior to or during the term of this Agreement (the "<u>LEP IP</u>") shall, to the extent such items are subject to the copyright laws of the United States, constitute "work made for hire" under United States and Israeli copyright laws and Indigo, with respect to LEP IP developed or invented prior to the date of this Agreement, and HP, with respect to LEP IP developed or invented on or subsequent to the date of and this Agreement during the term, shall be afforded all rights of ownership incident thereto under such laws, as well as all U.S. and Israeli patent, trademark, trade name and other intellectual property rights related thereto, and all rights of ownership under the patent, trademark, trade name and other intellectual property laws of any other country. Notwithstanding the foregoing, and regardless of whether the LEP IP qualifies as "work made for hire" status and/or treatment under United States and Israeli copyright laws, such LEP IP is the sole property of Indigo or HP, as applicable, and Landa hereby expressly agrees to grant, assign and convey (or cause to be granted, assigned or conveyed) to Indigo or HP, as applicable, all of Landa's right, title, and interest, if any, in and to all LEP IP, and all underlying intellectual property rights including copyright, patent, trademark, mask work, trade name and other proprietary interests related thereto. Landa, at HP's expense, shall do all things, including executing all documents, at the request of HP, reasonably required to vest in Indigo or HP, as applicable, the rights granted, assigned and conveyed to Indigo or HP, as applicable, herein.

(b) <u>Ownership</u>. Landa shall be the sole and exclusive owner of all Intellectual Property, other than that assigned to HP under Section 5(a), conceived, made, discovered or developed independently by Landa, or of which Landa is the sole inventor, beginning on the effective date hereof, and HP shall have no rights whatsoever in or to such Intellectual Property.

(c) <u>Further Assurances</u>. Landa agrees to promptly disclose to HP any LEP inventions or works of authorship made in connection with this Agreement. Landa agrees to assist HP, or its designee, at the expense of HP, in every proper way to secure rights in the LEP IP of HP and any copyrights, patents, mask work rights or other intellectual property rights relating thereto in any and all countries, including the disclosure to HP of all pertinent information and data with respect thereto, the execution of all applications, specifications, oaths, assignments and all other instruments which HP shall deem necessary in order to apply for and obtain such rights and in order to assign and convey to HP, its successors, assigns and nominees the sole and exclusive right, title and interest in and to such LEP IP, and any copyrights, patents, mask work rights or other intellectual property rights relating thereto. Landa further agrees that his obligation to execute or cause to be executed, when it is in his power to do so, any such instrument or papers shall continue after the termination of this Agreement. Landa will deliver all LEP IP to HP upon the earlier of completion of the Services or the request of HP. To the extent permitted by law, Landa waives any moral rights, such as the right to be named as author, the right to modify, the right to prevent mutilation and the right to prevent commercial exploitation, whether arising under the Berne Convention or otherwise.

(d) <u>Maintenance of Records</u>. Landa agrees to keep and maintain adequate and current written records of all LEP IP made by him (solely or jointly with others) during the term of this Agreement. The records will be in the form of notes, sketches, drawings, and any other format that may be specified by HP. The records will be available to and remain the sole property of HP at all times and will be returned to HP upon the earlier of completion of the Services or the request of HP.

(e) <u>Pre-Existing Materials</u>. Landa agrees that if in the course of performing the Services, he incorporates into any LEP IP developed hereunder any invention, improvement, development, concept, discovery or other proprietary information owned by him or in which he has an interest, (i) he shall inform HP, in writing, before incorporating such invention, improvement, development, concept, discovery or other proprietary information into any LEP IP; and, whether or not he complies with the foregoing, (ii) HP is hereby granted and shall have a nonexclusive, royalty-free, perpetual, irrevocable, worldwide license (including the right to sublicense) use, reproduce, distribute, perform, display prepare derivative works of, make, have made, modify, sell and export sell such item as part of or in connection with such LEP IP. Landa shall not incorporate any invention, work of authorship, mask work, protectable design, improvement, development, concept, discovery, trade secret or other proprietary information owned in whole or in part by any third party into any LEP IP without prior written permission of HP.

(f) <u>Attorney-in-Fact</u>. Landa agrees that, if HP is unable because of Landa's unavailability, dissolution, mental or physical incapacity, or for any other reason, to secure Landa's signature for the purpose of applying for or pursuing any application for any United States or foreign patents or mask work or copyright registrations covering the Intellectual Property assigned to HP in Section 5, then Landa hereby irrevocably designates and appoints HP and its duly authorized officers and agents as Landa's agent and attorney-in-fact, to act for and on Landa's behalf to execute and file any such applications and to do all other lawfully permitted acts to further the prosecution and issuance of patents, copyright and mask work registrations with the same legal force and effect as if executed by Landa.

(g) <u>Inventions Assigned to the United States</u>. Landa agrees to assign to the United States government all of his right, title, and interest in and to any and all LEP IP whenever such full title is required to be in the United States by a contract between HP and the United States or any of its agencies.

(h) <u>Representations and Warranties</u>. Landa hereby represents and warrants that (i) all LEP IP will be his original work; (ii) to the best of his knowledge, the LEP IP will not infringe the copyright, patent, trade secret, or any other intellectual property right of any third party; (iii) the LEP IP will not be obscene, libelous, or violate the right of privacy or publicity of any third party; and (iv) the LEP IP will not contain any virus, trap door, worm, or any other device that is injurious or damaging to software or hardware used in conjunction with the LEP IP.

(i) <u>Notice</u>. Landa will give HP notice immediately if at any time he knows or reasonably should know of any third party claim to any intellectual property provided by him to HP pursuant to this Agreement.

6. <u>Confidentiality</u>.

(a) <u>Definition</u>. "<u>Confidential Information</u>" means (i) any proprietary information, technical data, trade secrets or know-how of HP, including, but not limited to, research, product plans, products, services, suppliers, employee lists and employees, customers lists and customers (including, but not limited to, customers of HP on whom Landa called or with whom Landa became acquainted during the term of the consultancy relationship), markets, software, developments, inventions, processes, formulas, technology, designs, drawings, engineering, hardware configuration information, marketing, finances, budgets or other business information disclosed by HP either directly or indirectly in writing, orally or by drawings or inspection of parts or equipment; (ii) any information which HP has identified to Landa as confidential, proprietary or non-public business information and/or trade secrets of HP, and (iii) any information which Landa would reasonably recognize as confidential and proprietary to HP. For the purposes of this Agreement, the term "Confidential Information" shall not include any information which (1) now is or hereafter becomes known or available to the public other than as the result of a disclosure by Landa in breach hereof, (2) becomes known or available to Landa on a nonconfidential basis from a source other than HP which Landa does not reasonably believe is prohibited from disclosing such information to Landa by obligation to HP, (3) is developed by Landa independently of, or was known by or available to Landa prior to, any disclosures made by HP to Landa of such information, (4) is disclosed by HP to a third party without substantially the same restrictions as set forth herein, (5) is required to be disclosed by Landa by order of a court of competent jurisdiction, administrative agency or governmental body, or by any law, rule or regulation, or by subpoena, or any other administrative or legal process, or by applicable regulatory or professional standards, or (6) is disclosed with the consent of HP.

(b) Non-Disclosure. Landa will not, during or subsequent to the term of this Agreement, disclose, sell, license, publish, or otherwise make available Confidential Information for any purpose whatsoever, except to the extent necessary to perform the Services as directed by HP (in which case such disclosure is only permitted to authorized employees of HP). Landa further agrees not to disclose the Confidential Information to any third party. It is understood that said Confidential Information shall remain the sole property of HP. Landa further agrees to take all reasonable precautions to prevent any violation of these provisions (or the other provisions of this Agreement), including, securing and protecting HP's Confidential Information in a manner consistent with the maintenance of HP's confidential and proprietary rights in the information.

(c) Third Party Confidential Information. Landa recognizes that HP has received and in the future will receive from third parties their confidential or proprietary information subject to a duty on HP's part to maintain the confidentiality of such information and to use it only for certain limited purposes. Landa agrees that he owes HP and such third parties, during the term of this Agreement and thereafter, a duty to hold all such confidential or proprietary information in the strictest confidence and not to disclose it to any person, firm or corporation or to use it except as necessary in carrying out the Services for HP consistent with its agreement with such third party.

(d) Former Employer's Confidential Information. Landa agrees that he will not, during the term of this Agreement, improperly disclose any proprietary information or trade secrets of any former or current employer or other person or entity with which he has an agreement or duty to keep in confidence information acquired by him, if any, and that he will not bring onto the premises of HP any unpublished document or proprietary information belonging to such employer, person or entity unless consented to in writing by such employer, person or entity.

7. **Conflicting Obligations**. Landa certifies that he has no outstanding agreement or obligation that is in conflict with any of the provisions of this Agreement, or that would preclude him from complying with the provisions hereof, and further certifies that he will not enter into any such conflicting agreement during the term of this Agreement.

8. <u>Non-Compete</u>. During the term of this Agreement and for a period of twenty-four (24) months after expiration or termination hereof for any reason, Landa will not directly or indirectly (as principal, shareholder, officer, director, employee, Consultant/Employment, partner, agent, advisor or otherwise) own, manage, control, participate in, consult with, render service for, or in any manner engage in any business activity which competes with the commercial printing business of HP anywhere in the world, including, without limitation, the fields of electrophotographic printing or pigment dispersion, provided, that notwithstanding the provisions of this Section, nothing herein shall prevent Landa from acquiring and owning shares of any publicly-traded company.

9. <u>Non-Solicitation</u>. Landa agrees that for the term of this Agreement and for a period of twenty-four (24) months immediately following the termination of this Agreement for any reason, that he will not: (i) either directly or indirectly solicit, induce, recruit or encourage any of HP's directors, officers, employees or consultants to leave their employment, or attempt to solicit, induce or recruit any of the directors, officers, employees or Consultant/Employments of HP, either for Landa or for any other person or entity; or (ii) either directly or indirectly solicit any licensor to or customer of HP or licensee of HP's products that are known to Landa, with respect to any business, products or services that are competitive to the products or services offered by HP's commercial printing business as of the date of termination of this Agreement.

10. <u>Term and Termination</u>.
(a) <u>Term</u>. This Agreement shall become effective upon the Closing Time (as such term is defined in that certain Offer Agreement) of the transactions under the Agreements (the "<u>Effective Date</u>") and shall remain in effect until the first to occur of (i) the termination of this Agreement as provided below, or (ii) the fifth (5th) anniversary of the Effective Date.
(b) <u>Termination</u>. Subsequent to the second anniversary of the Effective Time, this agreement may be terminated by either party at any time, with or without cause, by sixty (60) days' notice to the other party. In the event of either party's breach of this Agreement, this Agreement may be terminated immediately upon reasonable notice.
(c) <u>Survival</u>. Upon such termination all rights and duties of the parties toward each other shall cease except:
(i) HP shall be obliged to pay or reimburse Landa, within thirty (30) days of the effective date of termination, all reasonable expenses owing to Landa relating to Services completed and accepted by HP prior to the termination date in accordance with the provisions of Section 4(e) (Expense Reimbursements) hereof; and

(ii) each of Sections 5, 6, 8, 9 and 10(c) shall survive termination of this Agreement.

11. <u>Notices</u>. Any and all notices hereunder shall, in the absence of receipted hand delivery, be deemed duly given when mailed, if the same shall be sent by registered or certified mail, return receipt requested, and the mailing date shall be deemed the date from which all time periods pertaining to a date of notice shall run. Notices shall be addressed to the parties at the following addresses:
[Notice Information Omitted.]

12. <u>Independent Contractor Status</u>. It is the express intention of the parties that Landa is an independent contractor. The parties hereto acknowledge and agree that this Agreement does not create an employer/employee relationship between the parties.

13. <u>Benefits</u>. Landa acknowledges and agrees and it is the intent of the parties hereto that Landa receive no HP-sponsored benefits from HP either as a Consultant or employee. Such benefits include, but are not limited to, paid vacation, sick leave and medical insurance. If Landa is reclassified by a state or federal agency or court as an employee, Landa will become a reclassified employee and will receive no benefits except those mandated by state or federal law, even if by the terms of HP's benefit plans in effect at the time of such reclassification, Landa would otherwise be eligible for such benefits. Landa shall [hold] HP harmless on account of any insurance premiums or other employment benefits.

14. <u>Amendments</u>. No amendment or waiver of any provision of this Agreement, or consent to any departure by either party from any such provision, shall in any event be effective unless the same shall be in writing and signed by the parties to this Agreement and then such amendment, waiver or consent shall be effective only in the specific instance and for the specific purpose for which given.

15. <u>Assignment</u>. Neither this Agreement nor any right hereunder or interest herein may be assigned or transferred by Landa without the express written consent of HP. Landa warrants that he will not engage the services of independent contractors to provide any Services under this Agreement without the prior written consent of HP. Any assignment without consent is voidable by HP.

16. <u>Entire Agreement</u>. This Agreement shall constitute the entire Agreement and understanding between the parties with respect to the subject matter hereof, and shall supersede and preempt any and all previous oral

and written (and all contemporaneous oral) representations, negotiations, commitments, agreements and understandings relating hereto.

17. <u>Applicable Law</u>. This Agreement shall be construed and enforced in accordance with the internal laws of the State of New York, without reference to conflict of law principles, and shall inure to the benefit of, and be binding upon, Landa and HP and their respective successors and assigns. Each of the parties hereto irrevocably consents to the exclusive jurisdiction and venue of any court within the State of New York, in connection with any matter based upon or arising out of the Agreement or the matters contemplated herein, agrees that process may be served upon such party in any manner authorized by the laws of State of New York for such persons and waives and covenants not to assert or plead any objection which such party might otherwise have to such jurisdiction, venue and process.

18. <u>Attorneys' Fees</u>. In any court action at law or equity which is brought by one of the parties to enforce or interpret the provisions of this Agreement, the prevailing party will be entitled to reasonable attorney's fees, in addition to any other relief to which that party may be entitled.

19. <u>Severability</u>. The invalidity or unenforceability of any provision of this Agreement, or any terms thereof, shall not affect the validity of this Agreement as a whole, which shall at all times remain in full force and effect.

20. <u>No Continuing Waiver</u>. The waiver of any party of any breach of this Agreement shall not operate or be construed to be a waiver of any subsequent breach.

21. <u>Counterparts</u>. This instrument may be executed in one or more counterparts, each of which shall be deemed an original, but all of which together shall constitute one and the same Agreement.
[Signature Page Omitted]

---

1. Familiarity Breeds Fluency: A Review

Prior to this Agreement, you had not encountered a services agreement in this book. Yet, hopefully you found much of the Agreement to be somewhat familiar.

- For instance, you should understand the purpose and the effect of the "whereas" (i.e., recital) clauses in this Agreement. What are recital clauses, and what are their purpose and effect? Do the recitals in this Agreement purport to impose any rights or obligations on Landa or HP? Would it be appropriate or wise for these clauses to do so? (See Chapter 1.)

- Section 6 imposes confidentiality obligations. Are these obligations unilateral or mutual? What is included and what is excluded from the meaning of "Confidential Information"? In whose interest—Landa's or HP's—is a broad definition of Confidential Information? Why, in §§ 6(c) and 6(d), does HP obtain agreement from Landa to hold in the strictest confidence certain confidential information that HP has received from third parties and certain confidential information that Landa has obtained from third parties? That is, what could result if HP did not obtain Landa's promise to keep that information confidential? Consider that HP may be party to contracts requiring HP to maintain third-party information in confidence and to cause others to whom HP reveals such information to do the same. And, what could result if HP did not obtain Landa's promise not to disclose to HP anything that Landa is under a duty to keep confidential? Furthermore, why does HP, in § 7, obtain Landa's certification that this Agreement should not cause Landa to breach a prior agreement? (See Chapter 1.)

- Section 15 contains an anti-assignment provision. Why does the clause prohibit the nonconsensual assignment of "any right hereunder"? Is this provision likely to be enforced as a mere anti-delegation provision or as a provision that forbids the assignment of rights as well? What is HP's likely remedy should Landa violate this provision? Would such a breach void a prohibited assignment and/or entitle HP to damages? (See Chapter 1.)

- Sections 8 and 9 impose restrictive covenants—not to compete and not to solicit—on Landa. Are these likely to be enforceable? What informs this analysis? (See Chapter 2.)

- Section 12 explains that the Agreement creates an independent contractor—and not an employment—relationship and that such is the intent of the parties. What is the utility of this provision? From the information that you have, do you think Landa is likely to be found an independent contractor or an employee? (See Chapter 2.)

You will notice that this Agreement has international dimensions to it. Separate from this Agreement, Landa is the founder of Indigo, a company organized in The Netherlands, and HP has entered into separate agreements to acquire Indigo. Landa is a resident of Israel, and HP is a Delaware corporation. The parties have agreed that New York law governs the Agreement and have consented to exclusive jurisdiction and venue to any court within the State of New York. (Is this likely to include federal courts sitting in New York? *See* Chapter 1.) We have called upon a seasoned practitioner to provide some insight into just a few of the complications that more complex international services agreements may impose.

A Practitioner Perspective: International Services Agreements

It is important to clarify the distinction between "offshoring" and "multinational contracts." I define the former as contracts delivered in one country by a provider to a customer, with the provider using offshore resources for some portion of the delivery from locations like India or the Philippines. I define the latter as a contract that involves delivery of services in more than one country to a multinational customer.

Multinational agreements present unique challenges in terms of project governance and contract structure. Many multinational customers are, to some degree, decentralized by geographic area and may have different business requirements and objectives as it relates to an outsourcing or consulting project. It is essential during negotiations and delivery for the customer and the provider to anticipate and reconcile these differences, particularly when a centralized solution is being delivered. Many "local customizations" come at significant cost in terms of development and timeline, and it is essential that these be anticipated and managed early in the process. In terms of contract structure, if an agreement is intended to provide services in more than one jurisdiction, the parties must take that into account in the structure of the transaction and the agreement. Often one or both parties will have a preference as to the primary signing entity. The ability to enforce the terms of the agreement in various jurisdictions must be addressed, typically through "local country addenda" that deal with local tax and legal issues. In some circumstances a company in the superior ownership chain may not have the legal authority to commit a local entity accepting services so the parties need to provide appropriate due diligence and indemnifications.

If the service provider is an offshore provider or is a local provider that will be offshoring some or all of the services to another location, there are a number of issues to consider. Generally, the market is very mature in terms of offshore delivery. Communications and site security should be carefully assessed during due diligence. The contract should have a clear governance structure as it relates to both onshore and offshore resources, particularly with regard to the transition of services from customer personnel to the offshore provider. The mix of onshore and offshore resources and the rates for each (since offshore rates tend to be significantly lower) is also a key issue. Finally, since the cost of services will be incurred in a currency other than the currency invoiced, foreign exchange issues must be addressed.

Nancy Laben
Senior Vice President
and General Counsel
AECOM

Prior to publication, Ms. Laben left Accenture LLP, where she was Deputy General Counsel, to join AECOM.

---

2. An Attorney-in-Fact Designation and Agency

An attorney-in-fact is synonymous with an agent: someone who has the authority of another (a "principal") to act on that principal's behalf.[4] Under the common law of agency, an agent has the authority to bind a principal when the agent enjoys the principal's "actual" or "apparent" authority.[5]

Actual authority may be express or implied: A principal "expressly" authorizes an agent when the principal grants such authority by words; a principal "impliedly" authorizes an agent when the agent reasonably believes that the principal has so authorized the agent. Implied actual authority often arises when the authority is necessary to accomplish tasks that are expressly authorized, when the agent would be customarily authorized to perform such tasks, or when the agent was so authorized in past dealings with the principal.[6]

An agent enjoys apparent authority when the principal has performed some act that causes a *third party* reasonably to rely on that the agent is authorized.[7] Apparent authority requires that the *principal* manifest some indicia of authority, on which a third party so relies. Notice, then, that apparent authority turns on the reasonable beliefs of third parties, whereas implied actual authority turns on the reasonable beliefs of the agent. Does § 5(f) create an agency relationship? If so, on the basis of what type of authority? To perform what tasks?

What is HP's primary concern in § 5(f)? What future circumstances is HP anticipating—for what is HP attempting to seek protection—in this provision? Normally, a power of attorney to act on the principal's behalf ceases upon the principal's incapacity or death (or, cessation of existence, in the case of a business entity).[8] However, by statute, every state has created what is called a "durable power of attorney."[9] Accordingly, an instrument may create a *durable* power of attorney by complying with the relevant jurisdiction's statutory requirements. Generally, this calls for the instrument to provide that the granted authority does not terminate upon the principal's incapacity.[10] Notice that even

---

4. Note that "attorney," as commonly used to mean "lawyer," refers to an "attorney-at-law" and also speaks to an agency relationship—one with the special fiduciary duties owed by a lawyer to its client.

5. *See* Restatement (Third) of Agency §§ 2.01-2.03 (2006) (discussing actual and apparent authority).

6. *See id.* § 2.01 cmt. b ("'Implied authority' is often used to mean actual authority either (1) to do what is necessary, usual, and proper to accomplish or perform an agent's express responsibilities or (2) to act in a manner in which an agent believes the principal wishes the agent to act based on the agent's reasonable interpretation of the principal's manifestation in light of the principal's objectives and other facts known to the agent.").

7. *See id.* § 3.03 (discussing the creation of apparent authority).

8. *See id.* § 3.07 (discussing the termination of agency upon principal's death); *id.* § 3.08 (discussing the termination of agency upon principal's loss of capacity).

9. *See* Nina A. Kohn, *Elder Empowerment as a Strategy for Curbing the Hidden Abuses of Durable Powers of Attorney*, 59 Rutgers L. Rev. 1, 6-7 (2006).

10. *See* Uniform Durable Power of Attorney Act § 2 (1988) (an instrument granting a durable power of attorney should contain "language, such as 'This power of attorney will continue to be effective if I become disabled, incapacitated, or incompetent,' showing the intent of the principal that the power granted may be exercised notwithstanding later disability, incapacity, or incompetency"); Restatement (Third) of Agency § 3.08 cmt. c (2006) ("The power must contain language expressing the principal's intention that the power shall not be affected by the principal's subsequent disability or loss of capacity, or that the power shall become effective

a durable power of attorney will generally terminate upon the principal's death.[11] Subsection 5(f) provides, in part:

> Landa agrees that, if HP is unable because of Landa's unavailability, dissolution, mental or physical incapacity, or for any other reason, to secure Landa's signature . . . then Landa hereby irrevocably designates and appoints HP and its duly authorized officers and agents as Landa's agent and attorney-in-fact. . . .

Does HP's power of attorney terminate upon Landa's incapacity? Would you draft this provision any differently to make this clearer?[12]

Drafting Note: "Hereby" and Future, Conditional Matters

Note that § 5(f), as it currently reads, states a condition ("if HP is unable because . . .") upon which a designation of authority is to be "hereby" made, as of the effective date of the Agreement. How can a designation be "hereby" (a word that generally refers to the "now") made if the condition that must come before that designation has not yet occurred (presuming that Landa has capacity when entering into this Agreement)? Consider that HP may have intended to effect, as of the Agreement, a designation of a conditional power of attorney—a power of attorney hereby granted but that only "kicks in" when Landa is, say, incapacitated. Does the provision here unambiguously accomplish this? How might you draft this differently?

Separate from addressing whether HP's power of attorney is durable—that is, whether such authority would automatically terminate upon Landa's incapacity—§ 6(f) specifies that the power-of-attorney designation is "irrevocable."[13] The provision states that Landa may not revoke HP's specified powers once granted. Does this mean, at least according to the terms of the Agreement, that HP still has the power to act on Landa's behalf even if Landa were to regain capacity? Do you think the parties intended this, or do you think they intended that HP should have the power to act on Landa's behalf only when Landa is incapacitated and that this *conditional* right is irrevocable? If the latter, how might you draft this provision differently?

Despite what a contract may say, a power of attorney usually must be "coupled with an interest" in order to be irrevocable.[14] That is, a principal may

---

upon the principal's subsequent disability or incapacity."). *But see* UNIFORM POWER OF ATTORNEY ACT § 104 (2006) (explaining that a power of attorney is presumed durable unless expressly provided otherwise).

11. *See* RESTATEMENT (THIRD) OF AGENCY § 3.07 cmt. d (2006).

12. Query whether Landa can "dissolve."

13. To be clear, if a power of attorney is irrevocable, then the incapacity of the principal will not terminate the power. This is because if a power is irrevocable, then even a principal's *willful* attempt to terminate the power will not succeed. *See* RICHARD A. LORD, 12 WILLISTON ON CONTRACTS § 35:32 (4th ed. 2009) ("Unless there is an agreement to the contrary between the parties, the authority or power of an agent, when coupled with an interest, is generally not revocable by the act, condition, or death of the principal before the expiration of the interest.").

14. *See* RICHARD A. LORD, 12 WILLISTON ON CONTRACTS § 35:33 (4th ed. 2009) ("Certainly they mean something more than a contract on the part of the principal that the agency shall not be revoked. For, in spite of such a contract the principal has the power, even if not the right, to revoke the agency with or without reason, even though he may then become liable for damages.").

revoke a power of attorney at her discretion, unless she has transferred to the agent an interest in the subject matter of that power.[15] As one commentator has explained, "Unless there is an agreement to the contrary between the parties, the authority or power of an agent, when coupled with an interest, is generally not revocable by the act, condition, or death of the principal before the expiration of the interest."[16] "Coupled with an interest" refers to "an interest in the property on which the power is to operate."[17] The Third Circuit has explained:

> For example, a power given as security arises when a person manifests consent that the one to whom it is given properly can act to protect a title already in the power holder. Moreover, if an agent has an interest in the subject matter of the agency, as where it engages in a joint enterprise or invests in a business in which another supplies the subject matter, a power given it by the other to protect such interest is a power given as a security.[18]

Accordingly, merely *calling* a power of attorney "irrevocable" is insufficient to *make* the agency irrevocable; to accomplish this, the agent must have an interest in the property that the power affects. Absent a "coupled interest," a contract may still impose a covenant on a principal not to revoke a power of attorney such that revocation constitutes a breach and entitles the other party to any resulting damages.[19] However, despite such a covenant, without a "coupled interest," the principal will generally still have the *power* to revoke the power of attorney, and the agency relationship will still terminate upon the principal's death (or incapacity, if the agency is not durable).[20] Here, Landa has granted HP a power of attorney to effect the transfer of property rights in certain intellectual property, as part of HP's acquisition of Indigo.

3. Intellectual Property Rights and Concerns

As discussed above, much of the Agreement between HP and Landa is concerned with intellectual property and, specifically, Landa's agreement to cooperate in HP's securing of certain intellectual property rights. We have provided the following capsule on the major types of U.S. intellectual property for your general information.

---

15. *See, e.g., Estate of Norman A. Helfan Litig. v. Capital Mgmt. Grp., Inc.*, Nos. CIV. A. 99-CV-6642, CIV. A. 00-1026, 2000 WL 1522857, at *6 (E.D. Pa. Oct. 13, 2000); *see also* RICHARD A. LORD, 12 WILLISTON ON CONTRACTS § 35:32 (4th ed. 2009).

16. RICHARD A. LORD, 12 WILLISTON ON CONTRACTS § 35:32 (4th ed. 2009).

17. *See id.* § 35:33.

18. *Gov't Guarantee Fund of Rep. of Finland v. Hyatt Corp.*, 95 F.3d 291, 300 (3d Cir. 1996) (internal citations omitted).

19. *See* RICHARD A. LORD, 12 WILLISTON ON CONTRACTS § 35:33 (4th ed. 2009).

20. You may wish to return to the discussion of the distinction between "power" and "right" in the context of anti-assignment provisions in Chapter 1.

U.S. Intellectual Property Regimes

The following is a brief overview of the main areas of U.S. intellectual property law: trade secrets, patent, copyright, and trademark.

Trade Secrets

Unlike patents, copyrights, and trademarks, trade secrets law is not rooted in federal law. Rather, state law protects trade secrets. In most states, the state's adopted version of the Uniform Trade Secrets Act provides the basis for trade secrets law; in the remaining states, trade secrets law is based on other state statutory and/or common law. As discussed in greater depth in Chapter 1, a trade secret is generally defined as information that both derives independent economic value from not being generally known and is the subject of reasonable efforts to maintain its secrecy. An owner of trade secrets may enjoy protection in perpetuity—that is, until the trade secret no longer derives independent value from being secret, until it is no longer secret, or until the owner fails to make reasonable efforts to maintain its secrecy.

Patent

Under U.S. patent law, one may obtain a patent in "any new and useful process, machine, manufacture, or composition of matter, or any new and useful improvement thereof."[21] For a patent to issue, the patentable subject matter must be not only useful but also novel (i.e., not already in existence) and non-obvious (i.e., not something that would be obvious to a person having ordinary skill in the art).[22] In general, the United States has a first-to-invent rule, meaning that the first person either to reduce a patent to practice or to file the patent with the U.S. Patent and Trademark Office has priority vis-à-vis competing claims in that patent. However, to obtain rights in a patent, one must "prosecute" that patent, which involves filing a patent application with the patent office and being granted the patent. The term of a patent is 20 years from the date of filing.[23] Unlike trade secrets, this term cannot be abrogated by another's independent invention; however, also unlike trade secrets, there is no risk of the patent persisting in perpetuity. Indeed, a key policy undergirding U.S. patent law is this central quid pro quo: The patent holder discloses the patent to the world in exchange for a 20-year monopoly therein.

Copyright

Under U.S. copyright law, a copyright holder enjoys certain exclusive rights in her copyrighted works. In general, one may obtain copyright protection in "original works of authorship fixed in any tangible medium of expression, now known or later developed, from which they can be perceived, reproduced, or otherwise communicated, either directly or with the aid of a machine or device."[24] Under the "idea-expression" dichotomy, copyright protects the *expression* of ideas

---

21. 35 U.S.C. § 101.
22. *See id.* §§ 102, 103.
23. *Id.* § 154(a).
24. 17 U.S.C. § 102(a).

but not the ideas themselves.[25] In the United States, one obtains rights in copyright upon *fixing* the copyrightable expression in a tangible medium—no filing or registration is required, although registration may be beneficial to the holder. Copyright protection operates by vesting in the copyright holder certain exclusive rights, some of which include the right to make copies of the copyrighted work, to prepare derivative works based on the copyrighted work, and to perform the copyrighted work in public.[26] For instance, the independent creation of a copyrighted work is not actionable under U.S. copyright law because infringement of copyright requires the performance of a copyright holder's exclusive rights (e.g., copying). In general, the term of a copyright is the life of the author plus 70 years.[27] For works made for hire (which are discussed in greater depth below), a copyright endures for either 95 years from its first publication or 120 years from its creation, whichever expires earlier.[28]

Trademark

Under the U.S. Lanham Act, any mark or device that signals the source of a service or good may qualify for trademark protection.[29] As with copyright, one need not register a trademark to own the mark; however, registration may be beneficial to the trademark owner. For example, to enjoy the protection of trademark, one's mark must be distinctive and one must use the mark in commerce. Registering the mark with the U.S. Patent and Copyright office allows one to satisfy the "use in commerce" requirement constructively, so long as one also has the "intent to use" the mark within six months.[30] This "use" requirement may also be satisfied by the actual use of the mark in commerce.[31] Marks are distinctive where consumers associate the mark with the mark's source.[32] For example, upon hearing the NBC chimes, a consumer in the United States is likely to associate that sound with NBC. Where a mark is distinctive and used in commerce, the trademark holder has a claim against those who use the mark, if this use of the mark causes consumer confusion or dilutes the value of the mark.[33] Unlike patents and copyrights, trademarks have no fixed term and registration can be renewed every ten years.[34]

a. *Intellectual Property Ownership and Assignment*

Subsection 5(a) of the Agreement provides that Landa agrees that several items (e.g., models, devices, drawings, notes, data, techniques—indeed, almost

---

25. *Id.* § 102(b) ("In no case does copyright protection for an original work of authorship extend to any idea, procedure, process, system, method of operation, concept, principle, or discovery, regardless of the form in which it is described, explained, illustrated, or embodied in such work.").

26. *Id.* § 106.

27. *Id.* § 302(a).

28. 17 U.S.C. § 302(c).

29. Lanham Act § 45, 15 U.S.C. § 1127.

30. *Id.* § 1051(b).

31. *Id.* § 1051(a).

32. *See Qualitex Co. v. Jacobson Prod. Co., Inc.*, 514 U.S. 159, 164 (1995).

33. Lanham Act § 45, 15 U.S.C. § 1125.

34. *Id.* § 1058.

everything but the kitchen sink, unless of course Landa conceived, made, discovered, or designed a kitchen sink) relating to LEP that Landa has invented (or conceived, made, discovered, etc.) prior to the Agreement constitute "works made for hire" vis-à-vis Indigo and that those which Landa invents as of or subsequent to the Agreement constitute "works made for hire" vis-à-vis HP. In understanding the meaning of this provision, it would be helpful to first understand what a "work made for hire" is (at least under U.S. law),[35] which requires turning to § 101 of the U.S. Copyright Act, which provides, in part:

> A "work made for hire" is —
> (1) a work prepared by an employee within the scope of his or her employment; or
> (2) a work specially ordered or commissioned for use as a contribution to a collective work, as a part of a motion picture or other audiovisual work, as a translation, as a supplementary work, as a compilation, as an instructional text, as a test, as answer material for a test, or as an atlas, if the parties expressly agree in a written instrument signed by them that the work shall be considered a work made for hire. For the purpose of the foregoing sentence, a "supplementary work" is a work prepared for publication as a secondary adjunct to a work by another author for the purpose of introducing, concluding, illustrating, explaining, revising, commenting upon, or assisting in the use of the other work, such as forewords, afterwords, pictorial illustrations, maps, charts, tables, editorial notes, musical arrangements, answer material for tests, bibliographies, appendixes, and indexes, and an "instructional text" is a literary, pictorial, or graphic work prepared for publication and with the purpose of use in systematic instructional activities.[36]

Is the portion of § 5(a) of the Agreement that speaks to "work made for hire" meaningful? Something is a work made for hire if it satisfies the definition in the Copyright Act reproduced above. For example, if the works enumerated in § 5(a) were prepared or are prepared by Landa within the scope of his employment with Indigo or HP, then they qualify as "works made for hire" vis-à-vis Indigo or HP, respectively.[37] While perhaps this Agreement provides evidence that these works were indeed created within the scope of Landa's employment with Indigo, the Agreement is not determinative of this (and § 12 of the Agreement itself does stipulate that no employment relationship exists between the parties). Rather, this is a factual question that first asks whether an employment relationship exists—which is determined by the common-law analysis discussed in Chapter 2—and whether these works were created within the scope of such a relationship.

Absent an employment relationship, a work may still be a "work made for hire" under the second prong of the § 101 definition. However, the second prong is rather narrow, only applying to works commissioned as certain enumerated

---

35. Sections 34 and 35 of the Israeli Copyright Act of 2007 explain who the "first owner" of a copyright is in employment and commissioning situations. Note that the Israeli Copyright Act does not contain the phrase "work made for hire."

36. 17 U.S.C. § 101.

37. Note that this Agreement specifies that the Landa is not an employee of HP but is rather an independent contractor. As discussed in Chapter 2, this contractual designation is not determinative.

items. If a work is the type of work described in the second prong, then it may be considered a work made for hire only if the parties so specify in a writing signed by both parties. While this Agreement does specify that certain works by Landa are to be considered "works made for hire," it would seem unlikely that these works would be specially ordered as any of the types of works enumerated in the second category. Accordingly, it seems that the second type of "work made for hire" is not applicable here.

Why is "work made for hire" status important? For this, we turn back to the U.S. Copyright Act, where § 201 provides:

> (a) Initial Ownership.—Copyright in a work protected under this title vests initially in the author or authors of the work. The authors of a joint work are coowners of copyright in the work.
> (b) Works Made for Hire.—In the case of a work made for hire, the employer or other person for whom the work was prepared is considered the author for purposes of this title, and, unless the parties have expressly agreed otherwise in a written instrument signed by them, owns all of the rights comprised in the copyright.

The party on the "hiring" side of a work made for hire is considered the author *ab initio* of the work. In other words, "work made for hire" presents one way of obtaining rights in a copyrighted work created by another. However, it is not the only way. Look to the remaining portion of § 5(a), which speaks to "regardless of whether the LEP IP qualifies as 'work made for hire' status." Generally, one may transfer or license her intellectual property to a third party.[38] Subsection 5(a) provides that, whether or not the "work made for hire" designation provides Indigo/HP with rights in the LEP IP, Landa agrees to assign to Indigo/HP all such intellectual property that Landa owns. This is an example of what transactional attorneys frequently refer to as "belts and suspenders." The Agreement provides two ways by which Indigo/HP may obtain ownership of certain copyrighted works, and each way, if successful, would be sufficient to accomplish the task.

What is the difference between obtaining ownership of intellectual property through commission as a "work made for hire" and through transfer? For one, the "hiring" party of a work made for hire obtains only *copyright* rights in the work (as the deemed author of the work). As for the rights in the work that are not subject to copyright but rather, for example, sound in patent, trademark, or trade secrets, "work made for hire" status is of no relevance.

Secondly, the "hirer" of a work made for hire is considered the author of the work and enjoys all that entails. The author of a copyrighted work is afforded

---

38. *See, e.g.,* 17 U.S.C. § 204(a) ("Execution of transfers of copyright ownership"); Lanham Act § 45, 15 U.S.C. § 1060(a) (Registered trademark only assignable along with goodwill the associated business); *Taco Cabana Int'l, Inc. v. Two Pesos, Inc.,* 932 F.2d 1113, 1121 (5th Cir. 1991) ("An owner may license its trademark or trade dress and retain proprietary rights if the owner maintains adequate control over the quality of goods and services that the licensee sells with the mark or dress.").

special rights in that work, namely the right to terminate any transfer or license of that work, between the 35th and 40th years after that transfer and to have all rights in the work revert back to the author.[39] This right of reversion is inalienable, meaning no contract may strip the author of the right.[40] Depending on the nature of the work and other circumstances, this right of reversion may be meaningful. For example, suppose the original author of the Mickey Mouse character transferred the rights in the work to The Walt Disney Company (under the U.S. Copyright Act as it currently stands). The author, 35 years later, under the U.S. Copyright Act, would have a valuable right to take back ownership of the iconic character. However, if Disney is the author *ab initio* of the Mickey Mouse character as a "work made for hire" (either because an employee created the work within the scope of employment or because it was commissioned as an enumerated work and expressly characterized as a "work made for hire" in a writing signed by both parties), then Disney owns the copyright free and clear as the deemed author.

Note that, as of the Agreement, Landa has not actually transferred these intellectual property rights but has agreed to do so and to do all that is necessary to do so. However, given that specific performance is an extraordinary remedy and that Landa conceivably could transfer an IP right to another party altogether, might HP wish to obtain a transfer, as of the Agreement, of the intellectual property rights HP wishes to own? In other words, if Landa breaches his agreement to transfer such rights and to do all this is necessary to do so, what will be HP's remedy?

Look to § 5(e) of the Agreement. About what is HP worried in this provision? If Landa incorporates intellectual property into LEP IP, in which HP does not otherwise have rights (namely under § 5(a)), then HP may not be able to use the resulting LEP IP without obtaining permissions from the owner(s) of the incorporated intellectual property. Obtaining permissions can be costly and may result in hold-out problems. Accordingly, to protect against the inclusion of third-party property in LEP IP, § 5(e) prohibits Landa (without HP's written permission) from incorporating any such work in which a third party has any right. Any such inclusion, then, would constitute a breach of this negative covenant by Landa and would entitle HP to those damages proximately resulting. In addition, § 5(e) provides that, with regard to incorporated intellectual property in which Landa has rights, Landa grants HP a royalty-free, irrevocable license to use the intellectual property.[41]

---

39. 17 U.S.C. § 203 ("Termination of transfers and licenses granted by the author.").

40. *See Stewart v. Abend*, 495 U.S. 207, 230 (1990) ("The 1976 Copyright Act provides a single, fixed term, but provides an inalienable termination right.").

41. Query whether such a license can really be "irrevocable" in the context of copyright. Note the discussion above regarding transferring and licensing copyright and the inalienable right of the author-licensor to revoke the rights granted thereby. Please see Chapter 4 for more on IP licensing.

b. Moral Rights of an Author

Note that in § 5(c) of the Agreement, Landa waives "any moral rights." Moral rights refer to the rights of an author of a work—regardless of the owner of the concomitant copyright—to attribution as well as the right to protect the integrity and to prevent the mutilation of the work. The concept and protection of moral rights has generally received stronger endorsement abroad than in the United States. For instance, the Israeli Copyright Act defines a moral right as follows:

> A moral right in relation to a work is the right of its author—(1) To have his name identified with his work to the extent and in the manner suitable in the circumstances; (2) That no distortion shall be made of his work, nor mutilation or other modification, or any other derogatory act in relation to the work, where any aforesaid act would be prejudicial to his honor or reputation.[42]

The Israeli Act further provides, "The moral right is personal and not transferable, and shall be available to the author even if said author does not have copyright in the work or if he has assigned the copyright in the work, partly or wholly, to another person."[43] Under Israeli law, while such rights cannot be transferred, it appears that moral rights may be waived.[44]

In contrast, the U.S. Copyright Act does not generally afford authors with "moral rights"—indeed, the Act never mentions the term. However, the Visual Artists Rights Act of 1990 added § 106A to the U.S. Copyright Act, which provides authors of works of visual art with rights of attribution and the right to maintain the integrity of such works and to prevent the destruction and the mutilation of the original work.[45] Under the U.S. regime, § 106A rights may not be transferred but may be waived "if the author expressly agrees to such waiver in a written instrument signed by the author."[46] For the waiver to be effective, "[s]uch instrument shall specifically identify the work, and uses of that work, to which the waiver applies, and the waiver shall apply only to the work and uses so identified."[47] With the realization that the types of works at issue in this Agreement are unlikely to qualify as works of visual art under the U.S. Copyright Act, could the waiver given by Landa in this Agreement hypothetically satisfy this requirement?[48]

---

42. Israeli Copyright Act of 2007 § 46, *available at* http://www.tau.ac.il/law/members/birnhack/IsraeliCopyrightAct2007.pdf.

43. *Id.* § 45(b).

44. *See* Neil J. Wilkof & Joshua Weisman, *International Copyright Law and Practice: Israel*, § 7 (explaining that the Israeli Copyright Act is silent on waiver of moral rights, leaving the finding of such to the discretion of a court).

45. 17 U.S.C. § 106A(a).

46. *Id.* § 106A(e)(1).

47. *Id.*

48. *See* H.R. Rep. 101-514, at 6929 (1990) ("The author must expressly agree to the waiver in a written instrument, and must sign that instrument. The writing must specifically identify the work and the uses of the work to which the waiver applies. The waiver will apply only to that work and those uses. The bill does not permit blanket waivers.").

Whether an author's moral rights may be waived—and, if so, what is required for this waiver to be valid—varies from country to country.[49]

B. MASTER SERVICES AGREEMENT

Before proceeding to the next agreement in this chapter, a master services agreement between two business entities, we turn the floor over to a seasoned practitioner, experienced in the negotiation of services agreements.

A Practitioner Perspective: The More Contentious Terms in Services Contracts

Each party to a services agreement starts the negotiations from a mutual desire to agree upon the services to be provided by the service provider and to provide a foundation that maximizes the potential for project success. From that point on, each party wants to make sure that they will receive the benefit of the bargain. In addition, they are trying to balance the potential risks with the proposed reward. With that as background, I separate my discussion into two parts: (i) themes I am seeing in the market, and (ii) specific, heavily negotiated issues.

I am seeing a number of counsel advise clients the contract must be used to maintain leverage over the other party. This not only leads them to take aggressive positions in a number of areas; it ignores the notion that a contract should be a platform for resolving issues and challenges in delivery and should provide balanced incentives for each party to perform. An example of an issue I often see in this area is a clear and defined list of responsibilities that each party, including the customer, must perform as a part of making the project successful. Many buyer counsel take the position that the customer should avoid taking on clear accountability, and that the provider should not be given any excuse if the project is not delivered successfully. I understand the appeal of that argument. Unfortunately it ends up taking clear accountability off of the buyer's personnel for getting essential tasks like reviewing and accepting project deliverables in a timely manner. It is a leading cause of projects going off course, which is not good for the buyer or the provider.

There are a number of specific terms and conditions that tend to be contentious as they relate to allocation of risk between the parties. These terms include warranties, damages, indemnifications, and limits of liability. More recently, discussions regarding compliance obligations particularly in the areas of data protection and export compliance are starting to be difficult. While the same terms present issues for outsourcing contracts, given the long-term nature of an

---

49. For a discussion of various regimes, albeit as of a few years ago, please see Neil Netanel, *Alienability Restrictions and the Enhancement of Author Autonomy in United States and Continental Copyright Law*, 12 Cardozo Arts & Ent. L.J. 1 (1994).

> outsourcing transaction, economic terms including benchmarking and termination become heavily negotiated as well.
>
> Nancy Laben
> Senior Vice President
> and General Counsel
> AECOM
>
> *Prior to publication, Ms. Laben left Accenture LLP, where she was Deputy General Counsel, to join AECOM.*

The following agreement sets forth the rights and obligations of two corporations, one to provide Internet services to the other.

Things to Consider . . .

As you read through the following agreement, please consider these items. You will want to return to the agreement, as you study the substantive discussion that follows.

> › **Context of Relationship.** Notice how *this* Agreement's recitals (i.e., the "whereas" clauses) explain the context and history of *this* transaction and the underlying relationship between the parties. What is the historical context and purpose of this Agreement?
> › **Master Structure.** This Agreement is a "master" agreement, which is a framework agreement that provides high-level terms to govern a relationship and that contemplates the use of specific statements (i.e., in this case, "Service Orders") to provide a second level of terms to govern particular transactions to occur within the relationship. Consider what this Agreement opts to address and what it leaves to be decided by Service Orders.
> › **Shifting Risk.** Consider the ways in which certain provisions in this Agreement—including the representation and warranty provisions, the force majeure clause, the indemnification provisions, and the limitation-of-liability provisions—operate to allocate certain risks between the parties.

CONFIDENTIAL
MASTER SERVICES AGREEMENT[50]

THIS MASTER SERVICES AGREEMENT (the "Agreement") is made and entered into on November 16, 2009 and effective as of December 1, 2009 (the

---

50. AOL Inc., Confidential Master Services Agreement (Form 10-12B/A), at Exhibit 10.73 (Nov. 16, 2009), *available at* http://www.sec.gov/Archives/edgar/data/1468516/000119312509235507/dex1073.htm.

"Effective Date"), between AOL Inc., a Delaware corporation with offices at 770 Broadway, New York, New York 10003 (together with its Subsidiaries hereinafter referred to as "AOL"), and Time Warner Inc., a Delaware corporation with offices at One Time Warner Center, New York, NY 10019 ("Time Warner").

WHEREAS, AOL and Time Warner are parties to that certain Separation and Distribution Agreement, dated November 16, 2009, whereby they have agreed that Time Warner shall distribute its entire interest in AOL as a stock dividend to the Time Warner common stockholders with the result that AOL and Time Warner will no longer be affiliated companies (the "Separation").

WHEREAS, prior to the Separation AOL's predecessor, AOL LLC and its Affiliates, have been providing certain Internet services to Time Warner and Time Warner's Affiliates (other than AOL) (each of Time Warner and Time Warner's Affiliates other than AOL, a "TW Company," and together, the "TW Companies") pursuant to a Master Services Agreement between AOL LLC and Turner Broadcasting System, Inc., dated November 1, 2006 and a Managed Hosting Agreement between AOL LLC and Time, Inc., dated October 22, 2008 ("Previous Agreements") and certain other service orders and arrangements.

WHEREAS Time Warner has requested and AOL has agreed to terminate the Previous Agreements and continue to provide such services to the TW Companies (including, for the avoidance of doubt, AOL LLC) pursuant to this Agreement. AOL and each participating TW Company may be referred to herein as a "Party" and collectively the "Parties") [sic].

NOW, THEREFORE, in consideration of the mutual promises set forth herein, AOL and Time Warner hereby agree as follows:

1. **Definitions.** Capitalized terms used but not defined in the body of this Agreement shall have the respective meanings given to such terms in Exhibit A attached hereto.

2. **Provision of Services.**

2.1 <u>Previous Agreements</u>. As of the date of this Agreement, the Parties shall terminate the Previous Agreements; provided, however that notwithstanding the termination of the Previous Agreements, the Service Orders issued thereunder, and attached as Exhibits E and F, shall remain in effect and shall be governed by this Agreement. Time Warner represents and warrants that it has the authority to terminate the Previous Agreements and enter into this Agreement on behalf of itself and the TW Companies.

2.2 <u>Service Orders</u>. The type and scope of the Services to be provided to each TW Company under the terms of this Agreement, including any of the additional Services described in the attached Exhibits, shall be specified in an applicable Service Order. The fees for the Services will be set forth in the Service Order. Notwithstanding anything in this Agreement to the contrary, neither party has any obligation to execute any Service Order, and no Service Order shall be effective (i.e. become a Service Order) unless executed by both Parties; provided, however, that AOL and TW Company shall negotiate all Service Orders in good faith to reach agreement.

2.3 <u>Additional Service Orders</u>. If a TW Company and AOL execute multiple Service Orders, unless otherwise stated in any additional Service Orders, each additional Service Order will supplement rather than replace any prior Service Orders. This will only apply when the Service Orders are for the same Service. For example, if a TW Company has licensed five Licensed Spaces at a particular Collocation Facility and AOL agrees to license four more Licensed Spaces to such TW Company at that Collocation Facility, the second Service Order will specify an order for four Licensed Spaces, and the invoice to TW Company as to that Collocation Facility will reflect that Customer now has licensed nine Licensed Spaces at that Collocation Facility (under two separate Service Orders). It would not apply, if a Service Order was currently in place for Licensed Spaces and a new Service Order was executed for the delivery of a completely different Service. In that case there would be no supplement between the two.

2.4 <u>Use of Services by Affiliates Parties</u>. AOL acknowledges that certain TW Companies are, as of the Effective Date, making the Services available to (i) other Affiliates of Time Warner and (ii) certain joint operations in which such TW Company or its subsidiary is a participant. Such TW Companies may continue to make such Services available to such parties during the term in accordance with this Agreement.

3. AOL Responsibilities. AOL will provide the Services in a manner and with the same level and degree of care from and after the Separation as it has been providing to the TW Companies prior to the Separation.

3.1 <u>Services</u>. AOL shall provide Services to each TW Company as detailed in one or more Exhibits and Service Orders attached to this Agreement setting forth the nature, scope and price of such Services, subject to the terms and conditions contained herein, including all payment obligations. The parties acknowledge and agree that the Exhibits and Service Orders attached hereto shall describe the nature, scope and price of the Services as they have been provided to each TW Company immediately prior to the Separation it being the intention of the Parties that AOL continue to provide such Services from and after the Separation pursuant to the terms hereof. AOL reserves the right not to provide Services to any Customer Site or Customer Domain that AOL determines, in its reasonable discretion, to misappropriate or infringe upon the intellectual property or other rights of AOL or any Third Parties, if a TW Company fails to cure such misappropriation or infringement within five (5) business days of AOL's written notice of such misappropriation or infringement. For avoidance of doubt, in the event of a ruling by a court or agency of competent jurisdiction that a Customer Site or Customer Domain misappropriates or infringes upon the intellectual property rights of AOL or any Third Parties, AOL shall have the right to immediately discontinue Services without further liability to AOL or without further contractual liability by AOL to the affected TW Company under this Agreement, except for amounts payable by the affected TW Company and accrued upon the date of discontinuance of Services.

3.2 Equipment. Each Service Order will set forth the servers, software infrastructure, switches, and associated hardware being provided by AOL to provide the Services. Equipment owned, licensed or leased by AOL and provided to Customer shall hereinafter be referred to as "Equipment". Equipment owned, licensed or leased by a TW Company, including routers on the Customer Site, and provided to AOL shall hereinafter be referred to as "Customer Equipment". As between AOL and the relevant TW Company, AOL shall retain all title, rights and interest in and to the Equipment. AOL shall maintain the Equipment in accordance with its routine maintenance schedule. AOL shall use its Commercially Reasonable Efforts to provide upgrades and patches to maintain the Equipment as necessary for the Equipment to perform its obligations under this Agreement. AOL reserves the right to maintain and/or substitute any Equipment for the Services, as AOL in its sole discretion, deems necessary or reasonable in light of future product releases, industry changes or other events, so long as the Services continue to function materially in accordance with the performance metrics set forth herein; provided that such Equipment is certified by any Third Party whose software is being used on the Host, if necessary.

3.3 Technical Support. AOL shall provide 7x24 technical support for the Services via a network operating center ("NOC") or similar entity. In addition, AOL shall provide technical support, as set forth in the Exhibits, SLAs and the applicable Service Orders attached hereto.

3.4 SLA. The service level agreements ("SLAs") applicable for the Services are attached hereto as Exhibit B.

3.5 Documentation. AOL shall provide Documentation as AOL, in its sole discretion, deems necessary relating to access and use of the Services. Any TW Company may reasonably request information regarding the access to and use of the Services, that may or may not be contained in Documentation, and AOL shall make commercially reasonable efforts to provide such information.

3.6 Reports. As identified in the Exhibits and Service Orders, AOL shall provide to each applicable TW Company reports identifying AOL's service level compliance to such TW Company, any applicable credits due such TW Company in accordance with the SLA, and such TW Company's utilization and billing detail.

3.7 Additional Deliverables. In connection with or in addition to the Deliverables, a TW Company may request Additional Deliverables from AOL. If AOL agrees to provide such Additional Deliverable, the Parties shall mutually agree upon and execute an additional Service Order. Such Service Order shall be executed by both Parties and attached as an Exhibit to this Agreement and shall be deemed to be incorporated herein by this reference.

3.8 Designated Contact. AOL shall provide a designated contact person for each TW Company ordering Services hereunder in the same manner and with the same level of access during the Term as it provided prior to the Separation.

4. Intentionally Omitted.

5. Fees and Payments.

5.1 Payments. Each TW Company will be billed in arrears for monthly and non-monthly Fees and any applicable Taxes for the Services provisioned during the previous calendar month. AOL shall provide itemized billing and separately itemized charges for taxable and non-taxable property and Services. Pursuant to Section 5.4, TW Companies may provide allocation data to be used to determine the tax situs of the Services. The applicable TW Company will pay all amounts owed under the Agreement (including, without limitation, any amounts owed under a Service Order) within forty-five (45) days of the date of each AOL invoice. All payments will be made in U.S. dollars and by wire transfer at the account information specified by AOL. Notwithstanding the foregoing to the contrary, AOL shall maintain the same billing practices from and after the Separation with respect to each TW Company as it maintained prior to the Separation.

5.2 Late Payments. In addition to all due and outstanding amounts, AOL reserves the right to charge and collect a Service fee of one percent (1.0%) over the U.S. prime rate per month, or the highest lawful rate, whichever is less (the "Late Fee"), for all such amounts, whether or not disputed, not paid on or before any due dates set forth in this Agreement. The Late Fee will be computed pro rata for each day any payment is late. In the event that AOL incurs expenses in collecting delinquent amounts from Customer, including reasonable attorneys' fees and court costs, AOL will provide Customer notice and a description of such expenses incurred by AOL and Customer will reimburse AOL for all such documented expenses within thirty (30) days after receiving such notice.

5.3 Disputed Payments. If a TW Company legitimately disputes any invoice amount, such TW Company shall: (i) pay AOL any undisputed portion of the invoice; (ii) provide AOL with a detailed written description of the disputed amount and the basis for such TW Company's dispute concerning such amount; and (iii) cooperate with AOL in promptly resolving any disputed amounts pursuant to Section 12.7.

5.4 <u>Taxes</u>. All Fees required by this Agreement and under the Services Schedules are exclusive of all federal, state, municipal, local or other governmental excise, sales, and use taxes imposed on the sale of the Services provided, now in force or enacted in the future ("Taxes"). Taxes do not include any taxes that are preempted by any Federal law now in force or enacted in the future, including, but not limited to, the Internet Tax Freedom Act currently set forth in the notes to 47 U.S.C. § 151. TW Companies will have sole discretion with respect to the allocation of Services among taxing jurisdictions for purposes of determining tax situs. TW Companies will not be responsible for any taxes or fees not contained within the definition of Taxes, including gross receipts or similar taxes, such as, but not limited to, the Ohio Commercial Activity Tax and the Virginia Business Professional Occupational and License Taxes. TW Companies will tender all such tax payments and reimbursements hereunder to AOL in accordance with Section 5.1 unless otherwise provided by law, such as in the case of an applicable direct pay permit. In addition, if applicable, Customer Equipment, whether or not physically affixed to the Licensed Spaces, will not be construed to be fixtures, and each TW Company is responsible for preparing and filing any necessary ad valorem property tax return for, and paying, any and all taxes separately levied or assessed against the Customer Equipment.

5.5 <u>Changes to Rates, Fees and Charges</u>. AOL has the right to modify any of its rates, fees and charges at any time. Any such modification during the Term of this Agreement will not be effective as to any Service Orders executed by the Parties prior to the modification but will be effective as to any Service Orders (including amendments to Service Orders) executed on or after the date of the modification, unless otherwise stated in a Service Order. Any modification shall take place no later than ten (10) business days after written notice of any such modification.

5.6 <u>Fraudulent Use of Services</u>. Each TW Company is responsible for all charges attributable to such TW Company and incurred respecting Services provided to such TW Company, even if incurred as the result of fraudulent or unauthorized use of Service; except that no TW Company shall be responsible for fraudulent or unauthorized use by AOL or its employees.

5.7 <u>Records Maintenance</u>. AOL shall maintain information, records, and documentation relating to the Services and AOL's performance thereof, including any such records, information, and documentation: (a) required to be maintained under applicable laws and regulations; or (b) necessary to verify AOL's compliance with the SLAs;

or (c) necessary and sufficient to document the Services and Fees paid or payable by any TW Company under this Agreement, in the same manner after the Separation as it has been maintaining prior to the Separation. AOL shall cooperate with the TW Companies to provide records as may be reasonably requested by them.

6. Proprietary Rights.

6.1 <u>Customer Data</u>. Each TW Company shall own any and all data collected from use of the Services the Customer Sites, the content and Customer Domains (collectively, the "Customer Data"). Each TW Company hereby grants AOL and its Affiliates, as applicable, a non-exclusive, limited, revocable, worldwide, royalty-free license to copy, transmit, modify and use the Customer Data solely as necessary to perform its obligations under this Agreement or, with prior written notice by the applicable WT [sic] Company, where practicable, as necessary to comply with applicable laws, regulations, and government orders or requests. Such Customer Data shall not be used by AOL for any marketing or commercial purpose whatsoever and AOL shall not use Customer Data to contact any user of any TW Company products or services without the prior written consent of the applicable TW Company.

6.2 <u>AOL Intellectual Property</u>. Each TW Company acknowledges that all rights to patents, copyrights, trademarks, trade secrets, AOL's name and trademarks, and all intellectual property or proprietary and Confidential Information of any kind or character inherent in or appurtenant to the Services under this Agreement (the "AOL Works") are the sole and exclusive property of AOL. Each TW Company agrees and acknowledges that it is not purchasing title to the AOL Works and that none of the AOL Works or Deliverables shall be considered "works made for hire" within the meaning of the United States Copyright Act. All rights, title and interest in the AOL Works and Services, and derivative works thereof, shall be deemed to vest and remain vested in AOL, including, but not limited to, patents, copyrights, trademarks, trade secrets and other intellectual property rights. All rights, title, and interest in and to the AOL Works not expressly granted herein are reserved to AOL. Notwithstanding the foregoing or any other provision of this Agreement, nothing contained herein shall be construed as granting AOL any right, title or interest in or to any of the TW Companies' intellectual property rights or Confidential Information. Further, the Parties mutually acknowledge that, in providing Services pursuant to this Agreement, AOL and its personnel and agents may become acquainted with certain general ideas, concepts, know-how, methods, techniques, processes, tools, or skills pertaining to the Services and retained in the unaided memory of such personnel and agents (the "Residual Knowledge"). Each TW Company acknowledges and agrees that, excluding such TW Company's intellectual property rights and Confidential Information, AOL may use such Residual Knowledge for any purpose.

7. Insurance.

7.1 <u>Time Warner Required Insurance and Certificates of Insurance</u>. At the TW Companies' expense, during the Term of this Agreement, and with respect to any claims-made policies, for a period of three years thereafter, the TW Companies will maintain in full force and effect with regard to the activities at, or relating to, each of the Collocation or Transit Facilities, (1) Commercial General Liability Insurance in an amount not less than Two Million U.S. Dollars ($2,000,000) per occurrence for bodily injury and property damage, products and completed operations and advertising liability, which policy will include a contractual liability coverage insuring the activities of the TW Companies contemplated by this Agreement; (2) Worker's Compensation and employer's liability insurance in an amount not less than that prescribed by statutory limits; (3) Commercial Automobile Liability Insurance (including owned, non-owned, leased and hired vehicles), which insurance will apply to bodily injury and property damage in a combined single limit of no less than One Million U.S. Dollars ($1,000,000) per accident, if applicable; and (4) Errors and Omissions Liability Insurance covering liability for loss or damage due to an act, error, omission or negligence with a minimum limit per event of Five Million U.S. Dollars ($5,000,000). The TW Companies will ensure that all of the foregoing insurance covers all periods in which this Agreement is in effect, regardless of whether the claims are made during the Term or after this Agreement expires or is earlier terminated. The TW Companies will furnish AOL with certificates of insurance evidencing the minimum levels of insurance set forth herein and shall name AOL as an additional insured on all such policies. Such certificates of insurance will provide that each additional insured must be given at least thirty (30) days prior written notice of any termination, non-renewal, or modification of insurance coverage. All policies shall be primary and non-contributory to any insurance coverage maintained by AOL. Policies shall be written with a licensed insurance company with a Best's Rating of no less than A-VIII. The TW Companies shall, or shall cause their insurance company(ies) to, provide the additional insured thirty (30) days prior written notice of cancellation and/or any material change in any such policy. In the event AOL is providing Services to a Divested Entity in accordance with Section 11.3, such Divested Entity shall obtain or maintain insurance coverage in order to comply with this Section 7.

7.2 <u>AOL Required Insurance and Certificates of Insurance</u>. During the term of this Agreement, and with respect to any claims-made policies, for a period of three years thereafter, AOL shall maintain in full force and effect the following insurance coverage: (i) Commercial General Liability insurance with limits of no less than $2 million per occurrence and $2 million as an annual aggregate, including but not limited to products and completed operations and advertising liability; (ii) Workers' Compensation insurance in compliance with all statutory requirements; (iii) Errors and Omissions liability insurance covering the types of products and services (including all technology products) as well as cyber-liability provided by AOL under this Agreement with limits of no less than $5 million per claim and $5 million as an annual aggregate; and (iv) Business Auto liability insurance with no less than $2 million combined single limit. Time Warner and its Affiliates, successors and assigns existing now or hereafter shall be named as additional insured on all such policies with the exception of workers compensation insurance, as applicable. All policies shall be primary and non-contributory to any insurance coverage maintained by Time Warner. Policies shall be written with a licensed insurance company with a Best's Rating of no less than A-VIII. AOL shall provide a certificate of insurance evidencing all such coverage and a renewal certificate fifteen (15) days prior to the renewal of any such policy. Supplier shall, or shall cause its insurance company(ies) to, provide the additional insured thirty (30) days prior written notice of cancellation and/or any material change in any such policy.

7.3 <u>Customer Waiver and Waiver of Subrogation</u>. Notwithstanding anything in this Agreement to the contrary, Time Warner and each TW Company waives and releases any and all claims and rights of recovery against the AOL Parties for liability or damages if such liability or damage is covered by such insurance policies then in force or the insurance policies required pursuant to this Agreement (whether or not the insurance required pursuant to this Agreement is then in force and effect), whichever is broader. The for[e]going waiver shall not be limited by the amount of insurance then carried by the TW Companies and any deductible shall be deemed to be included in the insurance coverage. The TW Companies will cause and ensure that each insurance policy covering the Customer Equipment, Customer Domain, Customer Site and occurrences thereon, and all other areas of property, or occurrences thereon, will provide that the underwriters waive all claims and rights of recovery by subrogation against the AOL Parties in connection with any liability or damage covered by such insurance policies.

7.4 <u>AOL Waiver and Waiver of Subrogation</u>. Notwithstanding anything in this Agreement to the contrary, AOL waives and releases any and all claims and rights of recovery against the TW Company Parties for liability or damages if such liability or damage is covered by AOL's insurance policies then in force or the insurance policies AOL is required to obtain pursuant to this Agreement (whether or not the insurance AOL is required to obtain is then in force and effect), whichever is broader. AOL's waiver shall not be limited by the amount of insurance then carried by AOL and any deductible shall be deemed to be included in the insurance coverage. AOL will cause and ensure that each insurance policy of AOL covering the AOL Data Centers, AOL Stadium, AOL Works, Collocation Facility, Equipment, Inter-rack-Cabling, Licensed Spaces, Transit Facilities and occurrences thereon, and all other areas of property, or occurrences thereon, will provide that the underwriters waive all claims and rights of recovery by subrogation against the TW Company Parties in connection with any liability or damage covered by AOL's insurance policies.

8. Confidentiality; Data Security.

8.1 <u>Confidential Information</u>. Each Party acknowledges that Confidential Information may be disclosed to the other Party during the course of this Agreement. During the Term and for a period of three (3) years following expiration or termination of this Agreement, each Party shall use at least the same degree of care as it employs to avoid unauthorized disclosure of its own information, but in no event less than a commercially reasonable degree of care and in the same manner and with the same degree of care from and after the Separation as prior to the Separation, to prevent the duplication or disclosure of Confidential Information of the other Party, other than by or to (i) its employees and Permitted Agents who need to know such Confidential Information for the purpose of performing the receiving Party's obligations or exercising its rights under this Agreement and then only to the extent needed to do so, provided that each such employee or Permitted Agent shall agree to comply with confidentiality requirements no less restrictive than those contained in this paragraph and is informed by the receiving Party of the confidential nature of such Confidential Information; and (ii) independent third party auditors that agree in writing to comply with confidentiality requirements no less restrictive than those contained herein. If a disclosure would be deemed a breach of this Agreement if committed by the receiving Party itself, then the receiving Party shall be liable to the other Party for any such disclosure made by its employees or Permitted Agents to whom it has disclosed the other Party's Confidential Information. If a receiving Party is legally compelled to disclose any of the disclosing Party's Confidential Information, then, prior to such disclosure, the receiving Party will (i) assert the confidential nature of the Confidential Information and (ii) cooperate fully with the disclosing Party in protecting against any such disclosure and/or obtaining a protective order narrowing the scope of such disclosure and/or use of the Confidential Information. In the event such protection is not obtained, the receiving Party shall disclose the Confidential Information only to the extent necessary to comply with the applicable legal requirements.

8.2 <u>Reimbursement for Disclosures</u>. The applicable TW Company shall reimburse AOL for any costs incurred by AOL related to disclosures of Confidential Information of such TW Company made by AOL pursuant to a court order, subpoena, or government order, including but not limited to the clean up and repair of any impacted servers and the replacement cost of any affected machines or Equipment. AOL shall reimburse the applicable TW Company for any costs incurred by such TW Company related to disclosures of Confidential Information of AOL made by such TW Company pursuant to a court order, subpoena, or government order, including but not limited to the clean up and repair of any impacted servers and the replacement cost of any affected machines or Customer Equipment.

8.3 <u>Data Security</u>. In order to protect the Confidential Information, AOL shall maintain appropriate standard security measures with respect to the Confidential Information including without limitation, technical, physical and organizational controls, and shall maintain the confidentiality, integrity and availability thereto, in the same manner and with the same level and degree of care from and after the Separation as it has been providing with respect to the Services prior to the Separation. In the event that AOL's systems or property are compromised such that any Confidential Information owned by any TW Company or any employee or customer of a TW Company may have been acquired or is reasonably believed to have been, or is reasonably believed to be at risk of becoming, acquired by unauthorized parties (an "Information Breach"), AOL will, within forty-eight (48) hours of the time it becomes aware of such Information Breach, report any Information Breach to each affected TW Company at the contact information set forth in Schedule 8.3 attached hereto. In the event of an Information Breach, AOL shall cooperate with the applicable TW Company to meet any obligations of such TW Company to notify individuals whose personal information has been compromised as a result of an Information Breach; provided that in no event shall AOL serve any notice or otherwise publicize an Information Breach without the prior written consent of such TW Company.

9. Representations and Warranties.

Each Party represents and warrants to the other Party that: (a) such Party has the full corporate right, power and authority to enter into the Agreement, to grant the rights and licenses granted hereunder and to perform the acts required of it hereunder; (b) such Party shall comply with the provisions of all applicable federal, state, country and local laws, ordinances, regulations and codes; (c) the execution of the Agreement by such Party, and the performance by such Party of its obligations and duties hereunder, do not and will not violate any agreement to which such Party is a party or by which it is otherwise bound; (d) when executed and delivered by such Party, the Agreement will constitute the legal, valid and binding obligation of such Party, enforceable against such Party in accordance with its terms; and (e) such Party acknowledges that the other Party makes no representations, warranties or agreements related to the subject matter hereof that are not expressly provided for in the Agreement.

10. Indemnity and Limitation of Liability.

10.1 <u>Mutual Indemnification</u>. Each of AOL on the one hand and each TW Company on the other hand (the "Indemnifying Party") shall defend, indemnify, save and hold harmless the other and such other's Affiliates and each of its and their officers, directors, agents, affiliates, distributors, franchisees and employees (the "Indemnified Parties"), from any and all Third-Party claims, demands, liabilities, costs or expenses, including reasonable attorneys' fees ("Losses"), resulting from any Third Party claim, suit, action, or proceeding (each, an "Action") brought against one or more of the Indemnified Parties arising out of or resulting from (i) the Indemnifying Party's material breach of any obligation, representation, or warranty of this Agreement; (ii) any injury (including death) to any natural person or damages to tangible property or facilities thereof to the extent arising out of or resulting from the negligence or misconduct of the Indemnifying Party, its officers, employees, servants, affiliates, agents, contractors, licensees, invitees and vendors in connection with the performance by the Indemnifying Party of this Agreement; (iii) any violation by an Indemnifying Party of any regulation, rule, statute or court order of any governmental authority in connection with the performance by the Indemnifying Party of this Agreement.

10.2 <u>Intellectual Property Indemnification</u>. AOL shall defend, indemnify, save and hold harmless the TW Companies and each of their respective . . . officers, directors, agents, Affiliates, distributors, franchisees and Employees from and against any and all Losses arising out of or relating to any claim that the Services infringe a patent, trademark, trade name, trade secret, copyright or any other intellectual property right (an "Intellectual Property Infringement") of any Third Party. In addition to any indemnification payable pursuant to this Agreement, in the event any Third Party claims an Intellectual Property Infringement and without prejudice to any rights of any TW Company, AOL may at its own expense and option either: (i) procure the right for the Services to continue to be used in the manner provided in the Agreement; (ii) make such alterations, modifications or adjustments to the Services so that they become non-infringing without incurring a material diminution in performance or function; or (iii) replace the Services with non-infringing substitutes provided that such substitutes do not produce a material diminution in performance or function, or (iv) if AOL determines that the for[e]going is not commercially practicable, then AOL may terminate the Services without further liability.

Each TW Company shall defend, indemnify, save and hold harmless AOL and its officers, directors, agents, Affiliates, distributors, franchisees and employees from and against any and all Losses arising out of or relating to (a) such TW Company's Customer Site or any Customer Domain (including, any claim by a customer or end-user of the Customer Site); (b) claims related to any authorizations, rights or licenses necessary to provide the Customer Site; (c) claims that the Customer Site, any Updates, the Customer Domain, the registration of the same, and the manner in which a TW Company uses or permits others to use such Customer Site or Customer Domain directly or indirectly, misappropriate or infringe any copyright, trade secret, or trademark or any Patent or other legal rights of any Third Party and (d) claims for reimbursement for any costs arising from or related to the subpoena of any Customer Data, or Customer connection, including but not limited to costs associated with the clean-up of any impacted servers and the replacement cost of any affected machines or Equipment.

10.3 <u>General Provisions</u>. If any Action arises as to which a right of indemnification provided in this Section 10 applies, the Indemnified Party shall promptly notify the Indemnifying Party thereof (provided that any failure to provide timely notice shall not relieve a Party of its obligations under this Section 10 except to the extent actually prejudiced), and allow the Indemnifying Party the opportunity to assume direction and control of the defense against such Action, at the Indemnifying Party's sole expense, including, the settlement thereof at the sole option of the Indemnifying Party to the extent that Indemnified Party's liability is not thereby invoked. The Indemnified Party shall cooperate with the indemnifying Party in the disposition of any such matter (at the Indemnifying Party's expense). The Indemnified Party shall have the right and option to participate in the defense of any Action as to which this Section 10 applies with separate counsel at the Indemnified Party's election and cost. If the Indemnifying Party fails or declines to assume the defense of any such Action within ten (10) days after notice thereof, the Indemnified Party may assume the defense thereof for the account and at the risk of the Indemnifying Party. The Indemnifying Party shall pay promptly to the Indemnified Party any Losses to which the indemnity under this Section 10 relates, as they are incurred.

10.4 <u>Limitation of Indemnity</u>. A Party's indemnity obligations shall be mitigated to the extent of the negligence, recklessness or intentional misconduct of the other Party or the other Party's Affiliates, directors, officers, employees, consultants or agent. The TW Companies agree and acknowledge that AOL shall be in no way responsible for, and each TW Company shall indemnify and hold AOL harmless for, any claims arising from the actions, policies or conduct of the users of the Customer Site of such TW Company. No TW Company shall be obligated under the indemnity provisions in Sections 10.1 or 10.2 for any Losses solely caused by or resulting from the acts or omissions of any other TW Company and AOL shall look only to the applicable TW Company for enforcement of such TW Company's indemnity obligations hereunder.

10.5 <u>SERVICE LEVELS</u>. UNDER NO CIRCUMSTANCES WILL A TW COMPANY RECEIVE A CREDIT FOR ANY NON-RECURRING CHARGES EVEN WHERE SUCH TW COMPANY IS ENTITLED TO A CREDIT FOR RECURRING CHARGES. NOTWITHSTANDING THE FOREGOING, ANY CLAIM BY A TW COMPANY FOR CREDITS WILL BE DEEMED CONCLUSIVELY WAIVED UNLESS, WITHIN THIRTY (30) DAYS AFTER THE DATE OF THE OCCURRENCE OF THE EVENT GIVING RISE TO THE CREDIT, THE APPLICABLE TW COMPANY NOTIFIES AOL THAT SUCH TW COMPANY IS SEEKING A CREDIT AND SPECIFYING THE BASIS FOR THE CLAIM. IN ADDITION, WITHOUT LIMITING THE FOREGOING, ALL OTHER CLAIMS BY A TW COMPANY OF WHATEVER NATURE AGAINST AOL WILL BE DEEMED CONCLUSIVELY TO HAVE BEEN WAIVED UNLESS SUCH TW COMPANY NOTIFIES AOL (SPECIFYING THE NATURE OF THE CLAIM) WITHIN SIX (6) MONTHS AFTER THE DATE OF THE OC-CURRENCE GIVING RISE TO THE CLAIM.

10.6 <u>No Other Warranty</u>. EXCEPT AS EXPRESSLY PROVIDED IN THIS AGREEMENT, THE DELIVERABLES ARE PROVIDED ON AN "AS IS" BASIS, THE TW COMPANIES' USE OF THE DELIVERABLES IS AT ITS OWN RISK. EXCEPT AS EXPRESSLY SET FORTH HEREIN, NO PARTY MAKES, AND EACH HEREBY DISCLAIMS, ANY AND ALL EXPRESS AND/OR IMPLIED WARRANTIES, INCLUDING, BUT NOT LIMITED TO, WARRANTIES OF MERCHANTABILITY, FITNESS FOR A PARTICULAR PURPOSE, AND ANY WARRANTIES ARISING FROM A COURSE OF DEALING, USAGE, OR TRADE PRACTICE. AOL DOES NOT WARRANT THAT THE DELIVERABLES SHALL BE UNINTER-RUPTED, ERROR-FREE OR COMPLETELY SECURE.

10.7 <u>Disclaimer of Actions Caused by and/or Under the Control of Third Parties</u>. AOL DOES NOT AND CANNOT CONTROL THE FLOW OF DATA TO OR FROM AOL'S DATA CENTERS AND THE INTERNET. SUCH FLOW DEPENDS IN LARGE PART ON THE PERFORMANCE

OF INTERNET SERVICES PROVIDED OR CONTROLLED BY THIRD PARTIES. AT TIMES, ACTIONS OR INACTIONS CAUSED BY THESE THIRD PARTIES CAN PRODUCE SITUATIONS IN WHICH A TW COMPANY'S CONNECTIONS TO THE INTERNET (OR PORTIONS THEREOF) MAY BE IMPAIRED OR DISRUPTED. ALTHOUGH AOL SHALL USE COMMERCIALLY REASONABLE EFFORTS TO TAKE ACTIONS IT DEEMS APPROPRIATE TO REMEDY AND AVOID SUCH EVENTS, AOL CANNOT GUARANTEE THAT THEY WILL NOT OCCUR. ACCORDINGLY, AOL DISCLAIMS ANY AND ALL LIABILITY RESULTING FROM OR RELATED TO SUCH EVENTS. AOL DISCLAIMS ANY AND ALL LIABILITY FOR ANY DAMAGES ARISING FROM OR RELATED TO ANY THIRD PARTY SOFTWARE USED BY AOL OR A TW COMPANY, WHETHER PROVIDED BY AOL OR A TW COMPANY, EXCEPT FOR AND LIMITED TO THE SERVICE LEVELS AND CREDITS SET FORTH IN EXHIBIT B.

10.8 Exclusions. EXCEPT AS EXPRESSLY PROVIDED HEREIN, AOL SHALL NOT BE LIABLE TO ANY TW COMPANY, ITS EMPLOYEES, ITS AUTHORIZED REPRESENTATIVES, OR ANY THIRD PARTY FOR ANY CLAIMS ARISING OUT OF OR RELATED TO THIS AGREEMENT, CUSTOMER SITE, CUSTOMER DATA, OR OTHERWISE. EXCEPT FOR (I) ACTS OF GROSS NEGLIGENCE OR WILLFUL MISCONDUCT, (II) BREACHES OF CONFIDENTIALITY OBLIGATIONS AND (II[I]) EACH PARTY'S INDEMNIFICATION OBLIGATIONS HEREUNDER, NO PARTY SHALL BE LIABLE TO ANY OTHER PARTY FOR ANY LOST REVENUE, LOST PROFIT, REPLACEMENT GOODS, LOSS OF TECHNOLOGY, RIGHTS OR SERVICES, INCIDENTAL, PUNITIVE, INDIRECT OR CONSEQUENTIAL DAMAGES, LOSS OF DATA, OR INTERRUPTION OR LOSS OF USE OF SERVICE OR OF ANY EQUIPMENT OR BUSINESS, EVEN IF ADVISED OF THE POSSIBILITY OF SUCH DAMAGE, WHETHER UNDER THEORY OF CONTRACT, TORT (INCLUDING NEGLIGENCE), STRICT LIABILITY OR OTHERWISE.

10.9 Maximum Liability. NOTWITHSTANDING ANYTHING TO THE CONTRARY IN THIS AGREEMENT, EXCEPT FOR (I) ACTS OF GROSS NEGLIGENCE OR WILLFUL MISCONDUCT, (II) BREACHES OF CONFIDENTIALITY OBLIGATIONS AND (II) EACH PARTY'S INDEMNIFICATION OBLIGATIONS HEREUNDER, AS BETWEEN AOL AND EACH TW COMPANY, EACH PARTY'S MAXIMUM AGGREGATE LIABILITY FOR ALL MATTERS RELATED TO, IN CONNECTION WITH, OR ARISING OUT OF, THIS AGREEMENT SHALL NOT EXCEED THE TOTAL AMOUNT PAID BY EACH TW COMPANY TO AOL HEREUNDER FOR THE PRIOR TWELVE (12) MONTH PERIOD.

10.10 Basis of the Bargain; Failure of Essential Purpose. Each TW Company acknowledges that AOL has established its Fees and entered into this Agreement in reliance upon the limitations of liability and the disclaimers of warranties and damages as set forth herein, and that the same form an essential basis of the bargain between the Parties. The Parties agree that the limitations and exclusions of liability and disclaimers specified in this Agreement shall survive and apply even if found to have failed of their essential purpose.

11. Term and Termination.

11.1 <u>Term</u>. The Agreement shall be in effect through the two year anniversary of the Effective Date (the "Term"; and the date of expiration, the "Expiration Date") unless terminated earlier in accordance with this Agreement. The Agreement cannot be renewed by any Party and all Services will cease on the Expiration Date. Each Service Order shall include a term for each Service (the "Service Term"). For the avoidance of doubt, and notwithstanding Section 12.9, in the event that the Service Term or Term of any Service Order conflicts with this Section 11.1, this Section 11.1 shall prevail (i.e., no Service Order shall extend beyond the Term of the Agreement for any reason).

11.2 Termination or Expiration.

11.2.1 For Cause. Either Party shall have the right to terminate this Agreement by giving notice of termination to the other Party, if: (i) the other breaches any material term or condition of this Agreement and fails to cure such breach within thirty (30) days after receipt of notice of the same (other than breaches addressed by Section 11.2.3 or Section 5.1 of Exhibit C); (ii) the other becomes the subject of a voluntary petition in bankruptcy or any voluntary proceeding relating to insolvency, receivership, liquidation, or composition for the benefit of creditors; or (iii) the other Party becomes the subject of an involuntary petition in bankruptcy or any involuntary proceeding relating to insolvency, receivership, liquidation, or composition for the benefit of creditors, if such petition or proceeding is not dismissed within sixty (60) days of filing.

11.2.2 Additional Grounds for Termination by AOL. AOL may terminate this Agreement or any Service Order as to any TW Company and discontinue Service without liability immediately (i) in the event of a ruling by a court or agency of competent jurisdiction that such TW Company violated any law, rule, regulation or policy of any government authority related to the Service; (ii) if such TW Company fails to cure its fraudulent use of the Services after fifteen (15) days' notice from AOL, provided that if such TW Company, in AOL's sole reasonable determination, has taken material steps to cure its fraudulent use of the Services, AOL may not terminate this Agreement or the applicable Service Order as to such TW Company pursuant to this provision of the Agreement; or (iii) if a court or other government authority prohibits AOL from furnishing the Services.

11.2.3 For Non-Payment by a TW Company. Notwithstanding Section 11.2.1, AOL shall have the right to terminate this Agreement (and thereby cease providing all Deliverables under this Agreement) as to a defaulting TW Company only by giving fifteen (15) days notice of non-payment to such defaulting TW Company if any of AOL's undisputed invoices to such TW Company remain unpaid for more than sixty (60) days after the due date indicated on such invoice. No TW Company shall be liable for the fees or charges incurred or payable by any other TW Company and AOL shall look only to the applicable TW Company for payment of such TW Company's invoices.

11.2.4 For Failure to Meet Service Levels. For the purposes of this Section 11.2.4, failure to meet any of the Service Levels in the SLA shall not be deemed a breach of this Agreement by AOL, unless otherwise defined as such in the SLA; provided, however, that if there is any dispute between the applicable Parties as to whether or not such a material breach as described above has in fact occurred, such dispute shall be referred to dispute resolution procedures in accordance with Section 12.7 and this Agreement shall remain in effect until such dispute is resolved in accordance therewith.

11.2.5 Effect of Expiration or Termination. Upon the effective date of expiration or termination of this Agreement or any one or more of the Services: (i) AOL shall cease providing the terminated Services (which may be some or all of the Services); (ii) the applicable TW Companies shall pay AOL (a) any Fees due for Services that have been rendered up to the effective termination/expiration date (provided, that in the event certain Services are terminated prior to others and the Fees for such Services are bundled with Fees for continuing Services, then the Fees shall be reduced pro rata to account for the reduction in Services) and (b) any Out-Of-Pocket Expenses incurred by AOL while providing the Services; and (iii) each Party shall return or destroy all Confidential Information of the other Party in its possession at the time of expiration or termination within forty-five (45) days after such expiration or termination, and shall not make or retain any copies of such Confidential Information except as required to comply with any applicable legal or accounting record-keeping requirement. Upon termination, AOL shall delete Customer Data from its production systems and shall make best efforts to delete or return Customer Data from all other systems and back-ups.

11.2.6 For Convenience. Subject to Section 11.2.5 above, prior to the Expiration Date, any TW Company may terminate this Agreement as to itself and/or any of its Service Orders for any one or more of the Services for any reason. The terminating TW Company shall provide AOL with sixty (60) days notice and shall provide AOL with a project plan for migration of the Services to another provider.

11.3 <u>Divestiture</u>. If Time Warner sells or divests an entity or assets (each, a "Divested Entity"), Time Warner shall inform AOL promptly upon the closing of the divestiture transaction. AOL shall make the Services available to any Divested Entity on the same terms and conditions as stated herein until the end of the Term.

11.4 <u>Transition</u>. Each TW Company shall be responsible for migrating off of all Services and obtaining services from another services provider prior to the expiration of the Term. During the Term, AOL shall cooperate with the TW Companies in the migration of all Services to another provider and shall provide that information and assistance in the transition process as the TW Companies may reasonably request.

12. Miscellaneous.

12.1 <u>Marketing</u>. Neither AOL on the one hand nor any TW Company on the other hand shall use the other Party's name(s), trademark(s), trade name(s) or logo(s), whether or not registered, in publicity releases, marketing materials, or other publicly-available documents (including publicly-available web pages) without securing the prior written approval of the other.

12.2 <u>Assignment</u>. Neither Party shall assign the Agreement or any right, interest or benefit under the Agreement without the prior written consent of the other, such consent not to be unreasonably withheld, conditioned or delayed. Notwithstanding the foregoing, either Party may assign or transfer its rights under this Agreement without the other's consent to: (a) any Subsidiary of such Party; or (b) another business entity in connection with a transaction pursuant to which the business entity acquires all or substantially all of the property or assets of AOL to which this Agreement relates. Subject to the foregoing, this Agreement shall bind and inure to the benefit of each Party's successors and permitted assigns.

12.3 <u>Subcontractors</u>. In providing any of the Deliverables under this Agreement, AOL may, in its sole discretion, subcontract for or otherwise use services provided by Third Parties or any AOL Affiliate, provided that AOL shall remain jointly and severally liable for the performance of such Third Party subcontractor and for all obligations under this Agreement.

12.4 <u>Injunctive Relief</u>. It is understood and agreed that, notwithstanding any other provisions of this Agreement, any breach or threatened breach of the provisions of this Agreement by either AOL on the one hand or any TW Company on the other hand may cause the other irreparable damage for which recovery of money damages would be inadequate and that each Party therefore may seek and obtain timely injunctive relief to protect its rights under this Agreement in addition to any and all other remedies available at law or in equity.

12.5 <u>Force Majeure</u>. No Party will have any liability for any failure or delay in its performance arising from, or relating to, the failure of power, equipment, systems, connections or services not under the control of such party, or the unavailability, inadequate, untimely or poor performance or non-performance of any facilities outside the control of such Party. Without limiting the foregoing, neither Party will be liable for any failure or delay in its performance under this Agreement due to any cause beyond its reasonable control, including, without limitation, national emergencies; acts of war or other civil commotion; acts of God; earthquakes; fires; flood; adverse weather conditions; explosions; other catastrophes; embargo; insurrections; riots; acts of terrorism, sabotage; strikes; lockouts; work stoppages or other labor difficulties; any law, order, regulation or other action of any governing authority or agency thereof; or failure of the Internet (each a "Force Majeure Event") provided that such Party has taken Commercially Reasonable Efforts to resolve or mitigate the effects of such Force Majeure Event. During any period in which Services to any one or more TW Company are reduced, suspended or terminated by AOL pursuant to this Section 12.5, the affected TW Company(ies) shall not be obligated to make payment of Fees with respect to the unfulfilled, suspended or terminated portion of Services until Services are fully resumed. In the event any Force Majeure event shall occur for more than fifteen (15) consecutive business days, the unaffected party shall have the right to terminate the affected Services, upon ten (10) business days written notice to the other party, provided that if an affected TW Company terminates this Agreement, such TW Company shall reimburse AOL for all of AOL's reasonable Out-Of-Pocket Expenses incurred through the date of termination.

12.6 <u>Survival</u>. The provisions of Sections 5, 6, 8, 10, 11.2.5, 12.4, 12.6, and 12.8 of this Agreement shall survive any expiration or termination of this Agreement. In addition, all provisions of this Agreement that can only be given proper effect if they survive the termination of this Agreement will survive the termination of this Agreement. This Agreement will be valid as to any obligation incurred prior to termination of this Agreement. Without limiting the foregoing, the TW Companies will pay all amounts owed to AOL under this Agreement, including, without limitation, any amounts that may become due after the expiration or earlier termination of this Agreement.

12.7 <u>Dispute Resolution</u>. All disputes arising under or relating to this Agreement, except for disputes relating to issues of proprietary rights, including but not limited to intellectual property and confidentiality, shall be governed by this Section 12.7. Any dispute subject to this Section 12.7 will be negotiated between the applicable Parties (at appropriate levels of senior management) commencing upon written notice from one Party to the other for a period of thirty (30) days. Settlement discussions and materials will be confidential and inadmissible in any subsequent proceeding without written consent from all applicable Parties. If the dispute is not resolved by negotiation within thirty (30) days following such notice, the affected Parties may seek remedies in equity or law.

12.8 <u>Legal Construction</u>. Subject to Section 12.7, this Agreement is made under and shall be governed by and construed in accordance with the laws of the State of New York (except that body of law controlling conflicts of law) and specifically excluding from application to this Agreement that law known as the United Nations Convention on the International Sale of Goods. Each Party irrevocably consents to the exclusive jurisdiction of the federal courts located in the Southern District of New York and the local courts located in Manhattan, New York, New York, USA. in connection with any action violating this Agreement. In the event of any conflict between these terms and conditions and those of any Service Order, the Service Order shall prevail.

12.9 <u>Entire Agreement; Counterparts</u>. This Agreement, including all Exhibits and Service Orders, but only as to the Parties to that Service Order, and documents incorporated herein by reference, constitutes the complete and exclusive agreement between the Parties with respect to the subject matter hereof, and supersedes and replaces any and all prior or contemporaneous discussions, negotiations, understandings and agreements, written and oral, regarding such subject matter. This Agreement may be executed in two or more counterparts, each of which shall be deemed an original, but all of which together shall constitute one and the same instrument. In the event of any conflict between the terms of this Agreement, and the terms of any Exhibit or Service Order, the documents shall control in the following order: (1) Service Order; (2) Exhibit; and (3) Agreement.

12.10 <u>Notice</u>. Any notice, approval, request, authorization, direction or other communication under this Agreement will be given in writing and will be deemed to have been delivered and given for all purposes (i) on the delivery date if delivered by confirmed facsimile to a then-valid facsimile number assigned exclusively to the intended recipient; (ii) on the delivery date if delivered personally to the Party to whom the same is directed; (iii) one business day after deposit with a commercial overnight carrier, with written verification of receipt; or (iv) five business days after the mailing date, whether or not actually received, if sent by U.S. mail, return receipt requested, postage and charges prepaid, or any other means of rapid mail delivery for which a receipt is available. In the case of AOL, such notice will be provided to the Deputy General Counsel ([omitted]), each at the address of AOL set forth in the first paragraph of this Agreement. In the case of Time Warner except as otherwise specified herein, the notice address shall be the address for Time Warner set forth in the first paragraph of this Agreement attention to the Vice President, Information Technology, with a copy to the General Counsel ([omitted]). If to any other TW Company, to the address set forth in the Service Order for such TW Company.

12.11 Relationship of Parties. This Agreement shall not constitute, create, or in any way be interpreted as a joint venture, partnership, subsidiary, or formal business organization of any kind. Neither AOL nor the TW Companies have the power to bind the other or incur obligations on the other's behalf without the other's prior written consent, except as otherwise expressly provided herein.

12.12 Amendment and Waiver. The provisions, terms, and covenants of this Agreement may not be amended nor modified and the observance of any provision of this Agreement may not be waived (either generally or in any particular instance and either retroactively or prospectively) without a writing signed by all Parties to which the amendment or modification is intended to apply. The failure of either Party to enforce its rights under this Agreement at any time for any period shall not be construed as a waiver of such rights.

12.13 Severability. In the event that any of the provisions of this Agreement are held unenforceable by a court or other tribunal of competent jurisdiction, the remainder of this Agreement shall remain in full force and effect.

12.14 Non-Exclusivity. Nothing herein shall limit either Party's ability to enter into any agreements with any Third Party for the provision of services similar to those provided and purchased hereunder.

[Signature Page Omitted.]

EXHIBIT A—DEFINITIONS

"*Action*" has the meaning set forth in Section 10.1 of the Agreement.

"*Additional Deliverables*" means any products, services, or documents beyond the Deliverables expressly to be provided by AOL pursuant to this Agreement or any Service Order hereunder.

"*Affiliate*" means, with respect to any Person, any other Person which, directly or indirectly, controls, is controlled by, or is under common control with, such other Person. A Person shall be deemed to "control" another Person if it owns, directly or indirectly, more than fifty percent (50%) of the outstanding voting securities, capital stock, or other comparable equity or ownership interest of such Person.

"*Agreement*" has the meaning set forth in the preamble.

"*AOL*" has the meaning set forth in the preamble.

"*AOL Data Centers*" means AOL owned or controlled facilities used to Host the Customer Site.

"*AOL Employee*" means, for the purposes of this Agreement only, any employee [or] contractor of AOL.

"*AOL Stadium*" (Trademark) is an infrastructure of routers, switches, servers and software required to operate the delivery of static Internet content and accompanying management services.

"*AOL Works*" has the meaning set forth in Section 6.2 of the Agreement.

"*Backup Service Level*" has the meaning set forth in Exhibit B-2.

"*Business Day*" means Monday, Tuesday, Wednesday, Thursday, or Friday, excluding holidays observed in the United States of America.

"*Collocation Facility*" means the building where Licensed Space is located as defined in a Service Order.

"*Collocation Network Service*" has the meaning set forth in Exhibit B-1.

"*Collocation Service Order*" means a request to collocate submitted by Customer in the form of Exhibit C-2.

"*Commercially Reasonable Efforts*" means that degree of skill, effort, expertise, and resources that a business entity's employees with ordinary skill, ability, and experience, under circumstances similar to those addressed herein, would reasonably use and otherwise apply with respect to fulfilling the obligations assumed hereunder.

"*Confidential Information*" means information relating to or disclosed in the course of the Agreement, which is or should be reasonably understood to be confidential or proprietary to the disclosing Party, including, but not limited to, the material terms of this Agreement, Customer Data, information about technical processes and formulas, source codes, product designs, sales, cost and other unpublished financial information, pricing, product and business plans, projections, and marketing data. Confidential Information shall not include information (a) already lawfully known to or independently developed by the receiving Party, (b) disclosed in published materials, (c) generally known to the public, or (d) lawfully obtained by the receiving Party from any Third Party which lawfully was entitled to have and share the information. Notwithstanding anything herein to the contrary, personally identifiable information about a natural person shall be deemed to be Confidential Information for all purposes.

"*Connection Notice*" means written notice from AOL that the Transit Service ordered by a TW Company has been installed by AOL pursuant to the applicable Transit Service Order.

"*Content*" means the digital audio, video, data, text, animation, graphics, photographs, artwork, links, software, applications, other multimedia materials, and combinations of any or all of the foregoing presented in the Customer Site.

"*Customer Data*" has the meaning set forth in Section 6.1 of the Agreement.

"*Customer Domain*" means the domain names to be Hosted by AOL on behalf of a TW Company.

"*Customer Equipment*" has the meaning set forth in Section 3.2 of the Agreement.

"*Customer Notification*" means a communication from AOL to a TW Company informing such TW Company of AOL's acceptance of the Transit Service Order.

"*Customer Premises*" means the location or locations occupied by the TW Companies or its end users to which Transit Services are to be delivered.

"*Customer Site*" means all of the architecture and Content for each of the participating TW Company's website(s) to be located at the Customer Domains.

"*Deliverable*" means any part of the Services or Technical Support, Documentation, Equipment or any other products or services delivered or made available by AOL to any TW Company under this Agreement.

"*Divested Entity*" has the meaning set forth in Section 11.3 of the Agreement.

"*Documentation*" means specifications, descriptions and written instructions, including on-line instructions.

"*Dollar*" and the sign "*$*" mean the lawful money of the United States.

"*ENMP*" has the meaning set forth in section 3.2 of Exhibit B.

"*Effective Date*" has the meaning set forth in the preamble.

"*Employee*" means, for the purposes of this Agreement only, any employee or contractor of a TW Company.

"*Equipment*" has the meaning set forth in Section 3.2 of the Agreement.

"*Expiration Date*" has the meaning set forth in Section 11.1.

"*Fees*" means any fee, pricing, or payment of any type under the Agreement, excluding Taxes.

"*Force Majeure Event*" has the meaning set forth in Section 12.5.

"*Host*" means to provide the software and hardware infrastructure for and the maintenance, operation and administration of certain TW Companies' server software applications.

"*Implement*" means to acquire and install any applicable Equipment and other implementation services agreed upon by the applicable Parties. "*Implementation*" shall be construed accordingly.

"*Include*," "*includes*", and "*including*", whether or not capitalized, mean "include but are not limited to", "includes but is not limited to", and "including but not limited to", respectively.

"*Indemnified Party*" has the meaning set forth in Section 10.1 of the Agreement.

"*Indemnifying Party*" has the meaning set forth in Section 10.1 of the Agreement.

"*Information Breach*" has the meaning set forth in Section 8.3 of the Agreement.

"*Intellectual Property Infringement*" has the meaning set forth in Section 10.2 of the Agreement.

"*Inter-rack Cabling*" means cabling that connects Customer Equipment (i) to electric power sources designated by AOL; (ii) to AOL's routers and distribution network to the extent necessary as determined by AOL; and (iii) upon a TW

Company's request, to other Customer Equipment located in separate Licensed Spaces in the same room.

"*Late Fee*" has the meaning set forth in Section 5.2 of the Agreement.

"*Launch*" means the date on which Implementation has been completed and the Customer Site is launched via the Services.

"*Licensed Spaces*" means the areas licensed by a TW Company under this Agreement as to the amount of spaces. AOL will determine the rooms and the location in the rooms where the Licensed Space(s) will be located, and AOL will notify the applicable TW Company of the locations.

"*Local Loop*" means the connection between Customer Premises and the AOL intercity backbone network.

"*Losses*" has the meaning set forth in Section 10.1 of the Agreement.

"*NOC*" means network operating center.

"*Out-of-Pocket Expenses*" means reasonable, verifiable and actual expenses incurred and paid by AOL to a Third Party, but excluding AOL's overhead costs (or allocations thereof), administrative expenses or other mark-ups and excluding expenses which could reasonably have been avoided or which could reasonably be recouped by AOL.

"*Party*" has the meaning set forth in the recitals.

"*Permitted Agents*" shall mean attorneys, accountants, auditors, lenders and contractors.

"*Person*" means any individual, corporation, partnership, joint venture, trust, unincorporated organization, government or other department or agency thereof or any other entity.

"*PNMP*" has the meaning set forth in Section 3.1 of Exhibit B.

"*Residual Knowledge*" has the meaning set forth in Section 6.2 of the Agreement.

"*Service Level*" has the meaning set forth in Exhibit B.

"*Service Order*" means the service orders executed by the Parties pursuant to the terms of this Agreement.

"*Services*" means the services, functions and responsibilities of AOL as described in the Agreement (including the Exhibits and Service Orders) as such services, functions and responsibilities may evolve during the Term and may be supplemented and enhanced in accordance with the Agreement.

"*Service Outage*" has the meaning set forth in Section [this is mentioned but not defined in Section 3.2 of Exhibit B]

"*Service Term*" means the term for each Service included on each Service Order.

"*SLA*" has the meaning set forth in Exhibit B of the Agreement.

"*Subsidiary*" means an entity in which a Party holds over fifty percent (50%) of the equity or voting interest.

"*Systems Service Level*" has the meaning set forth in Exhibit B-3.

"*Taxes*" has the meaning set forth in Section 5.4 of the Agreement.

"*Technical Specifications*" means the technical specifications communicated by AOL to a TW Company as supported by the Services.

"*Technical Support*" has the meaning set forth in Section 3.3 of the Agreement.

"*Term*" has the meaning set forth in Section 11.1 of the Agreement.

"*Third Party*" means a Person other than an Employee, AOL Employee, AOL or any TW Company.

"*Third Party Software*" means software owned by Third Party vendors.

"*Transit Facility*" or "*Transit Facilities*" means property owned or leased by AOL and used to deliver the Transit Service, including without limitation terminal and other equipment, wires, lines, ports, routers, switches, channel service units, data service units, cabinets, racks, private rooms and the like.

"*Transit Service*" means Internet protocol (IP) transit service offered by AOL pursuant to a Transit Service Order. As part of this IP Transit Service, AOL will advertise all the Internet routes/prefixes which collectively form the Internet Routing Table.

"*Transit Service Order*" means a request for Transit Service submitted by Customer in the form of Exhibit D-1.

"*Transit Service Term*" means the term for Transit Service included on the Transit Service Order.

"*TW Company*" has the meaning set forth in the preamble to this Agreement.

"*Unauthorized Code*" shall mean (i) any virus, Trojan horse, worm, or other software routines designed to permit unauthorized access, or to disable, erase, modify, deactivate or otherwise harm software, hardware, or data or (ii) any back door, time bomb, drop dead device, protect codes, data destruct keys, or other software routines designed to disable a computer program automatically with the passage of time.

"*Update*" has the meaning set forth in Exhibit C to this Agreement.

"*Web Hosting Service Level Identifier*" has the meaning set forth in Exhibit B-8.

[Other Exhibits Omitted]

---

1. Familiarity Breeds Fluency: A Review

Prior to this chapter, you had not encountered a services agreement in this book. Hopefully you found much of this Agreement, in addition to the HP Agreement, to be somewhat familiar.

- Subsection 10.10 provides that certain provisions (e.g., limitations of liability, disclaimers of warranty) are the essential basis of the bargain. If these provisions are found unenforceable, could they be severed from the rest of the Agreement? If these provisions are breached, is the breach likely to constitute a "material breach"? (See Chapters 1 and 2.)

- Subsection 12.12 contains no-oral-modification and no-waiver provisions. How are courts likely to treat these provisions? Is an oral modification likely to be effective? (What law governs this Agreement?) Is a waiver less likely to be found? (See Chapter 2.)

- Under § 11, what is the term, and how may each Party terminate the Agreement? May a Party terminate for convenience? According to § 12.6, what provisions survive the expiration or termination of this Agreement? Why do you think these provisions were selected for survival? (See Chapters 1 and 2.)

2. Relationship of Parties: Agency Revisited

How would you characterize the relationship between AOL and Time Warner, under this Agreement? How does the Agreement characterize this relationship? As we discuss further in Chapter 6, private entities may work together in alliance relationships of various degrees of formality and coordination, from the contracting for the performance of certain services to forming a joint venture to merging into a single entity. What type of arrangement does the Agreement contemplate, according to § 12.11?

Notice that § 12.11 expressly states that AOL and Time Warner do not have the power to bind the other or otherwise to incur obligations on the other's behalf, except as otherwise provided. Compare this to this chapter's earlier discussion of agency in the context of the HP Agreement. Whereas, under certain circumstances, the HP Agreement provides that Landa has granted HP express actual authority to act on Landa's behalf, the AOL Agreement makes clear that no agency relationship is created by the Agreement (again, except where otherwise expressly provided by the Agreement). This provision suggests that no actual authority exists between AOL and Time Warner (for either to act as the agent of the other); however, under what circumstances might a court still find that either Party has bound the other? (See this chapter's earlier discussion of agency.) In addition, does this provision prevent, for example, Time Warner from later bestowing actual authority on AOL to bind Time Warner?

3. Master Agreements: Structure, Precedence, and Incorporation by Reference

As its title attests, this Agreement is a master services agreement (sometimes called an "MSA"). By contrast, this chapter's first agreement, between HP and Landa, is not. What is the difference? Like any services agreement, a master services agreement contemplates a services relationship and provides the terms that will govern that relationship. However, a master services agreement additionally contemplates that for specific services to be provided, the parties will issue a "Service Order" (sometimes called a "work order," a "purchase order," or a "statement of work," often referred to as an "SOW"), which provides the specifications and other details pertinent to the particular services to be performed under the order. For instance, § 2.2 of the Agreement provides, "The type and scope of the Services to be provided to each TW Company under the terms of this Agreement . . . shall be specified in an applicable Service Order. The fees for the Services will be set forth in the Service Order." Accordingly, a master services agreement acts as a global framework agreement, governing the entire services relationship and incorporating by reference (or being incorporated *into*) specific work orders to be issued (contemporaneously with, or subsequent to, the execution of the Agreement) as specific work is commissioned.

What is the legal force of service orders? What is the legal relationship between Service Orders and the Master Services Agreement? As foreshadowed in the previous paragraph, typically either a master services agreement will incorporate work orders into the agreement by reference, or a work order will incorporate a master services agreement into the work order.[51] For example, § 3.7 of the Agreement provides that if the Parties mutually agree and execute an additional Service Order, then the Service Order "shall be deemed to be incorporated herein by this reference." As the Third Circuit has explained, "As a matter of contract law, incorporation by reference is generally effective to accomplish its intended purpose where the provision to which reference is made has a reasonably clear and ascertainable meaning."[52] Moreover, for incorporation to be effective, the incorporating provision should clearly and specifically identify the document (or provision therein) it purports to incorporate.[53] On this, the Federal Circuit has advised:

> Our Circuit likewise does not require "magic words" of reference or of incorporation. However, we stress that parties . . . may easily avoid or at least minimize the risk of having to litigate this issue by simply adopting widely-used and judicially-approved language of incorporation, such as "is hereby incorporated by reference" or "is hereby incorporated as though fully set forth herein," and by including specific and sufficient information identifying a particular document,

---

51. As a general rule, when two or more documents are executed and pertain to the same transaction, they are to be read and construed together, as a whole. RESTATEMENT (SECOND) OF CONTRACTS § 202(2) (1981) ("A writing is interpreted as a whole, and all writings that are part of the same transaction are interpreted together."); *W. United Life Assurance Co. v. Hayden*, 64 F.3d 833, 842 (3d Cir. 1995) ("Under Pennsylvania law, when two or more writings are executed at the same time and involve the same transaction, they should be construed as a whole. If the writings pertain to the same transaction, it does not matter that the parties to each writing are not the same. This general rule also applies where several agreements are made as part of one transaction even though they are executed at different times.") Accordingly, absent a finding that either of a master services agreement and a statement of work is fully integrated and excludes all other documents, a court may understand a statement of work and a master services agreement, executed as part of a single transaction, together to be a single agreement to be read as a whole.

52. *Century Indem. Co. v. Certain Underwriters at Lloyd's, London, Subscribing to Retrocessional Agreement Nos. 950548, 950549, and 950646*, 584 F.3d 513, 534 (3d Cir. 2009) (Pennsylvania law) (internal citations omitted); *see also OBS Co., Inc. v. Pace Constr. Corp.*, 558 So. 2d 404 (Fla. 1990).

53. *See Northrop Grumman Info. Tech., Inc. v. United States*, 535 F.3d 1339, 1345 (Fed. Cir. 2008) ("[T]o incorporate extrinsic material by reference [the contract] must explicitly, or at least precisely, identify the written material being incorporated."); *PaineWebber Inc. v. Bybyk*, 81 F.3d 1193, 1201 (2d Cir. 1996) (under New York law, "a party will not be bound to the terms of any document unless it is clearly identified in the agreement").

such as the title, date, parties to, and section headings of any document to be incorporated.[54]

For those among us who wish to "avoid or at least minimize the risk of having to litigate," take note. Is the above MSA likely to be found to have incorporated a particular Service Order?

Is there a concern where an agreement provides for the incorporation of a *future* document's terms—provisions of a document that does not exist when the original, incorporating agreement is executed? As a general rule, an agreement may incorporate by reference a provision that is to exist in the future.[55] However, there is some authority for just the opposite: "[W]hat is being incorporated must *actually exist at the time of the incorporation*, so the parties can know exactly what they are incorporating."[56] In those jurisdictions where a future provision may be incorporated by reference, for incorporation to be effective, at least one court has required that there be some ascertainable standard for the creation of the future terms "that can provide a substitute for a present knowledge of and assent to the subsequently adopted provisions."[57] For example, where a stock option plan to be incorporated could be modified only in accordance with certain restrictions, including shareholder approval, such future modification was found to be subject to an "ascertainable standard."[58] Another line of authority has required that to enforce a would-be incorporated future provision against a party, that party must have "adopted" the incorporated provision.[59] As an example, where a party performed in accordance with the specifications of a putatively incorporated document that came to exist after incorporation, the party was found to have "adopted" the document and incorporation of the future document was effective.[60] Notice that under §§ 2.2 and 3.7, the Parties under this Agreement must both execute a future Service Order for the

---

54. *Northrop Grumman Info. Tech., Inc.*, 535 F.3d at 1346.

55. *See, e.g., Lamb v. Emhart Corp.*, 47 F.3d 551, 559 (2d Cir. 1995) (under Connecticut law, finding amended stock option agreements to be incorporated into termination agreement); *PB Grp., Inc. v. Proform Thermal Sys., Inc.*, No. 06-CV-15755, 2008 WL 2714426 (E.D. Mich. July 8, 2008); *DVD Copy Control Ass'n v. Kaleidescape, Inc.*, 176 Cal. App. 4th 697 (Cal. Dist. Ct. App. 2009); *Martinson v. Brooks Equip. Leasing, Inc.*, 36 Wis. 2d 209, 217 (Wis. 1967) ("[M]atters not presently in existence may nevertheless be made a part of a contract by reference."); *see also Grandis Family P'ship, Ltd. v. Hess Grp.*, 588 F. Supp. 2d 1319, 1328 (S.D. Fla. 2008) (finding that reference to non-contemporaneous purchase order was not sufficiently specific and direct to effect an incorporation by reference).

56. *Gilbert Street Developers, LLC v. La Quinta Homes, LLC*, 174 Cal. App. 4th 1185, 1194 (Cal. Dist. Ct. App. 2009) (emphasis in original); *see also U.S. for use of Lighting and Power Servs., Inc. v. Interface Constr. Corp.*, 553 F.3d 1150, 1155 (8th Cir. 2009) ("[U]nder Missouri law, a contract cannot incorporate by reference a second contract that is not yet in existence."); *Skouras v. Admiralty Enters., Inc.*, 386 A.2d 674, 678 n.3 (Del. Ch. 1978) ("[S]trict requirements for incorporating by reference an otherwise independent document are that such document be in existence when the incorporating document is executed.").

57. *Lamb*, 47 F.3d at 559 (citing *Housing Auth. of Hartford v. McKenzie*, 412 A.2d 1143, 1146 (Conn. Super. Ct. 1979)).

58. *Id.*

59. *Martinson*, 36 Wis. 2d at 217 ("[P]lans and specifications unagreed upon may [not] be incorporated without some form of adoption by the person sought to be charged with performance.").

60. *See id.* at 217-18.

Agreement to incorporate that Service Order. Is a court likely to find this to satisfy either or both of the "ascertainable standard" and the "adoption" rules? Given that some courts are reluctant to enforce the incorporation by reference of a future provision at all, what might the Parties do to ensure that all the terms of their arrangement are enforceable? One solution is to incorporate the terms of the MSA into each Service Order. Incorporation by reference of the earlier-in-time MSA should pose none of the "future" issues presented by the incorporation of a future Service Order at the time of MSA execution. Do you see any drawbacks to this approach? Do you see any other solutions?

Could a Service Order ever stand on its own as a contract binding the parties thereto? The answer appears to be "yes."[61] Accordingly, could a work order alter a contractual relationship in contravention of a master services agreement that purports to incorporate the work order? A party wishing not to bestow independent contractual force onto an SOW may wish to state as much in the SOW itself and specify its relationship to the master agreement. Please reference the discussion, in Chapter 2, of the modification of contractual rights by future contracts.

The effect of incorporating an external provision by reference is that the incorporated provision is treated as any other term of the agreement.[62] Accordingly, unless otherwise provided by contract, terms incorporated into an agreement by reference have no special favored or disfavored status vis-à-vis the other terms of the agreement. Indeed, just like the other terms of an agreement, the incorporated terms might create ambiguities within a contract and must be considered in determining whether or not a contract is ambiguous.[63] An agreement may specify which provisions (e.g., the provisions incorporated by reference, the agreement's original provisions) should take "precedence" over the other, should there be a conflict between terms. For example, master agreements will often provide that, in the event that a provision in an SOW contradicts a provision within the master agreement, the conflict should be resolved in accordance with the master agreement's terms. Courts will generally respect an order-of-precedence provision as a manifestation of party intent, inasmuch as the provision unambiguously guides the court to a coherent reading of the contract.[64] However, keep in mind that courts, where at all possible, will read

---

61. *See, e.g., Pervel Indus., Inc. v. T.M. Wallcovering, Inc.,* 871 F.2d 7, 8 (2d Cir. 1989) (finding purchase orders to be contracts unto themselves); *Grandis Family P'ship,* 588 F. Supp. 2d at 1334-35 (discussing that a purchase order may be a contract unto itself but declining to find so on the facts of the case). Please also reference the discussion of contract modification in Chapter 2. While a master services agreement may control what it incorporates by reference, could such a master services agreement control what may constitute a future contract or whether a future contract may modify the rights and obligations provided by the master services agreement?

62. *See, e.g., Lamb,* 47 F.3d at 558; *Wilson v. Wilson,* 577 N.E.2d 1323, 1329 (Ill. App. Ct. 1991).

63. *See, e.g., J.E. Hathman, Inc. v. Sigma Alpha Epsilon Club,* 491 S.W.2d 261 (Mo. 1973).

64. *See, e.g., Cessna Aircraft Co. v. Dalton,* 126 F.3d 1442, 1454 (Fed. Cir. 1997). However, what would happen if both the MSA and the statement of work each included a precedence provision that contradicted each other (e.g., the MSA incorporated the SOW by reference, the MSA included a provision that the MSA trumped the SOW, and the SOW included a provision that the SOW trumped the MSA)? Here, there would be a contradiction between the very terms that explain how to resolve contradictions! For the purposes of reading the MSA

contractual terms to be consistent and to avoid finding a conflict (and, so, the need to invoke a precedence provision).[65] Accordingly, an order-of-precedence provision can afford only so much comfort, and a party should not rely on such a provision in lieu of clear and consistent drafting.

As a matter of practice, some service providers will prefer a precedence provision that provides that the master service agreement governs, as the master agreement acts as the core document to govern the relationship and, accordingly, is often negotiated heavily and carefully.[66] By contrast, parties may wish statements of work to control so as to provide the flexibility necessary to tailor the contract for each project. Or, parties may draft a hybrid arrangement, providing, for example, a general precedence provision in the master agreement that the master agreement governs but including a phrase (e.g., "except as provided by a Service Order") in certain provisions indicating that such provisions are the default unless a statement of work provides otherwise.

4. Definitions Sections

Most sophisticated documents will define several terms. A contract may define terms either in a separate definitions section or as each term arises throughout the agreement. There are benefits and costs to each approach. Definitions sections provide a single repository of all defined terms, allowing a future reader of the contract (for instance, a judge or arbitrator) easy reference. However, definitions sections may add to the heft of an agreement, may make an agreement optically more formal (which may be a positive or a negative, depending on the context of the agreement), and do not necessarily make for intuitive reading. An alternative approach involves defining an agreement's meaningful terms as each appears initially in the document (sometimes called "in-line" definitions). This approach may make for relatively simpler reading the first time the definition is used (depending on the length of the definition), but how

---

as incorporating—or incorporated into—the SOW, the terms of the MSA and the SOW must be read as a whole and with equal weight, and neither can resolve the issue. Even if the agreement is fully integrated (see the discussion of integration clauses in Chapter 1), extrinsic evidence may be admitted to resolve this ambiguity.

65. *See, e.g., Pub. Serv. Co. of Oklahoma v. United States*, 88 Fed. Cl. 250, 255 n.5 (2009) ("The court does not, however, see any inconsistency here that requires application of the conflicts or order of precedence clauses of the contract."); *U.S. Fidelity and Guar. Co. v. Stanley Contracting, Inc.*, 396 F. Supp. 2d 1157, 1169 (D. Or. 2005) (where document merely adds an additional term that can be read alongside terms in main document, precedence clause irrelevant to reading of that additional term); *CooperVision, Inc. v. Intek Integration Techs., Inc.*, 794 N.Y.S.2d 812, 818 (N.Y. Sup. Ct. 2005) ("Accordingly, the mere absence of a forum selection clause in the Implementation Agreement does not create a conflict as between it and the Software License Agreement sufficient to invoke the former's order of precedence clause."). In addition, inasmuch as an SOW may stand on its own as a contract between two parties, an order-of-precedence provision in a master agreement—while instructive for how to read the master agreement as incorporating the SOW—might not govern how to read the SOW as a later-in-time contract unto itself.

66. This, of course, is certainly not to suggest that work orders are not or should not be carefully negotiated, as well.

does a reader know where to find a particular definition again without searching through the many pages of the document? One hybrid approach involves defining terms as they first appear but also including an index of defined terms, preceding or following the rest of the agreement, that directs the reader to where each defined term is located in the agreement. Another hybrid approach is to define some terms the first time they appear and other terms in a separate section. As you can see, there are many approaches to defining terms, and certainly creative parties may devise other schemes still. Regardless of the approach taken, a contract will signify that a term is to be given a specific meaning throughout the agreement by enclosing the term in quotation marks where the term is defined and by capitalizing the term each time such term is used as defined in the agreement.

Exhibit A of the Agreement is an example of a definitions section. Notice how each defined term is enclosed in quotation marks where the term is assigned a particular meaning. Also notice that, when the Agreement wishes to use a particular term as so contractually defined, the first letter of each word in the term is capitalized. Even Agreements that include a definitions section are likely to define some basic terms outside of the section. For example, this Agreement defines, *inter alia*, Agreement, Effective Date, and Parties within its first few paragraphs.

Why define terms? Words have several meanings, especially across different contexts. Definitions sections can help ensure that the *parties'* definitions—and only the parties' definitions—will govern the agreement by directing the potential, future reader (imagine an overburdened judge or arbitrator) to the parties' intended meaning for each particular term of importance.[67] However, opting out of Webster's is only one purpose of the definitions section. Sophisticated contractual documents can quickly grow highly technical and nuanced. The parties may be hard-pressed to define a particular term in fewer than 200 words. (For illustration, the Parties use 141 words to explain the meaning of Confidential Information in Exhibit A.) Rather than adding confusion and weight to an already potentially confusing and weighty document, parties may choose to define a term a single time so that they may incorporate that definition by reference throughout the document.

Parties may agree to certain imprecise definitions purposefully. There will be times where parties prefer to leave aspects of their bargain vague: Perhaps articulation with specificity is unduly difficult in the abstract or unduly contentious in negotiations. Parties may prefer to strike the deal with some imprecision, assuming the risk of an unfavorable interpretation down the line, than not to strike the deal at all.

---

67. *See, e.g.*, RESTATEMENT (SECOND) OF CONTRACTS § 202(3) (1981) ("Unless a different intention is manifested, (a) where language has a generally prevailing meaning, it is interpreted in accordance with that meaning; (b) technical terms and words of art are given their technical meaning when used in a transaction within their technical field.").

Definitions sections are only one tool for attaining precision. In the context of services agreements, another place where precision may be desirable is in delineating what is and is not expected of the services provider—that is, the "scope" of the provider's obligations, an important part of services agreements as alluded to in an earlier practitioner comment. To discuss this issue of scope, we have called upon another seasoned practitioner to provide insight.

A Practitioner Perspective: The Perils of "Scope Creep"

Scope creep is one of the top causes of failed services projects (a services project is failing if it either exceeds estimated budget or schedule by more than 25% or fails to deliver material functionality documented in the requirements). As a legal practitioner supporting a services project, it is important to understand what scope creep is, what causes it and what the lawyer can do to assist the project team to deliver the project successfully.

Scope creep occurs when the agreed-upon scope of work is increased without addressing the resulting impact to project schedule, budget and resources. Given the dynamic nature of many projects, scope change is inevitable. Successful project delivery requires project teams to embrace this reality; it is critical that project teams implement the necessary techniques, of which there are many, to properly manage it. Most projects suffer from scope creep for one (or more) of the following reasons:

1) project scope is poorly defined before project is initiated;

2) the duration of the project is long (more than a year);

3) management of project scope during delivery is inadequate;

4) project governance is ineffective; or

5) the project manager is inexperienced.

While the proper management of these five areas of risk rests largely with the project manager, sponsor and key stakeholders, the legal practitioner plays an important role as well.

The legal practitioner can help avoid scope creep by ensuring the project teams are properly focused and equipped to manage it. Below are four techniques a lawyer can employ to manage the potential problem of scope creep:

1) Define scope before work. Ensure project scope is clearly documented and understood by all parties. In addition, all key scope-related project assumptions and dependencies should be documented. All of these points should also be clearly identified in the contract between the parties. This is not easy, as the scope and related dependencies and assumptions are often stated in very technical language filled with acronyms. Do your best to keep it simple, using plain language to describe these items. This will require the lawyer to work closely with

---

the project teams. If the teams are struggling to document the project's scope in sufficient detail, it is usually an indicator that more work is needed to better understand the scope. In these cases, an initial project focusing all parties on determining and documenting the scope is highly recommended before broader project work begins. Parties should avoid beginning work without properly defining scope, as the results are usually poor.

2) Employ shorter project schedule(s). The longer the project, the greater opportunity for change. As a result, a lawyer may encourage the team to reduce the project duration into smaller, more discrete working efforts when possible (no longer than a year is recommended). Using delivery methods that allow for manageable project timelines is strongly recommended.

3) Embrace and manage change. Change is inevitable, so plan for it and effectively manage it. To accomplish this, an effective change management process and committee of professionals must be implemented before work begins. There are many good examples of proven change management processes. Choose the one that is right for the project and its team members. Once it is established, it is equally important to test the process with a real (and insignificant) change to ensure it meets the needs of the project. The change management process should be clearly documented in the contract, together with a change management form noting any impacts to schedule, price and scope, as well as any changes in responsibilities and appropriate approval needed to make the change officially part of the new scope. Additionally, the lawyer should periodically review the change logs (it will reflect the change orders) and be part of the change management board to ensure the changes are carefully considered and documented consistent with the contract. *Note*: If change orders or changes are not reflected in the change logs (the document that records all change orders), it is usually not an indicator that there are no changes (remember change *is* inevitable); it is almost certainly an indicator that the change management process is not being followed and the project may be headed for trouble!

4) Ensure proper governance. Without effective governance from project teams, stakeholders and sponsors, chaos will infect the project making scope creep, among other project ailments, inevitable. Consequently, it is important to ensure the right people are involved in the project at the right levels, providing adequate representation of the project team, users, stakeholders and sponsor. Most governance structures include a sponsor, steering committee and project team, among others. Generally, a project manager is primarily responsible for managing project scope and change management, among many other things. For this reason, a project manager should have a proven track record of successfully delivering projects of similar size, complexity and domain area. Moreover, meeting frequency and communications (e.g., meeting notes, status reports) standards should be implemented as the project begins and rigorously adhered to throughout the life of the project. These elements should all be addressed in the contract—here, the more detail the better. Finally, the lawyer should be involved in the governance of the project and review regular status reports to address early warning signs of scope creep should it appear and to ensure the change management process is being followed.

> Michel Gahard
> General Manager
> Microsoft Corporation
> Lecturer in Law
> The University of Chicago Law School

5. Service Levels and Credits

As we see in § 3.4, the AOL Agreement contemplates the use of "service levels" as agreed to in separate service level agreements.

One of the primary drivers of the decision to retain a service provider or to outsource one or more functional areas of a client's business is to increase the quality and reduce the associated costs to the client of performing the service itself. How one measures quality of performance and service is no small matter and often forms the basis of protracted contractual negotiations.

In what instances would a client seek to impose contractual requirements upon its service provider to meet particular levels of service? From the number of rings a call center takes to answer a call, to the number of matters a customer relations management (CRM) worker successfully handles, to the number of lines of data that can be properly processed in a particular time period, the quality and level of performance of services is of critical importance. Specifying service levels in this way can serve to add articulation and specificity to a perhaps vague "performance standard" (e.g., "best efforts," "commercially reasonable"), which we discuss further in Chapter 4.

Client and service provider alike frequently are concerned with establishing and delineating the particular levels of services required under the contract and with developing and implementing procedures and tools to measure and report the service provider's performance in meeting agreed-upon service levels. Service providers cannot deliver against a "moving target," and clients do not want to pay for deficient services.

As you read the excerpted service level provision below, consider the role service credits play in compensating the client for the service provider's failure to meet established service levels. Do service credits constitute an exclusive remedy (a concept we address later in this chapter) or does the contract permit the client to accept service credits and also sue to recover additional damages? Is benchmarking used to determine the cost of services? Is it necessary to consider service levels when exercising benchmarking rights? Do satisfaction surveys impose additional service level obligations upon the service provider and in this way constitute a "second bite of the apple" for the client?

Section 12. Service Levels[68]

12.1. <u>Service Levels</u>. HP shall perform the Services with promptness and diligence, in a workmanlike manner and in accordance with the Service Levels set forth in Schedule B (and such other service levels as may be agreed upon for those services) and the standards set forth in Section 4.1. HP shall be excused from its obligation to perform the Services in accordance with the applicable Service Levels if, and to the extent that, it cannot meet such Service Levels as a result of SG Cowen failing to perform any obligation hereunder for which the affected Services are dependent; provided that HP promptly notifies SG Cowen of any such failure of SG Cowen to perform an obligation which will or is likely to cause, or has caused, HP to fail to meet the applicable Service Levels.

12.2. <u>Measurement and Monitoring Tools</u>. As of the Services Commencement Date, HP shall implement and utilize the measurement and monitoring tools and procedures set forth in the SOW which are required to measure and report HP's performance of the Services against the Service Levels as specified in Schedule B (and such other service levels as may be agreed upon for those services). HP shall ensure that any measurement and monitoring tools are generally commercially available and that HP's use of such measurement and monitoring tools shall not adversely affect the performance of the Equipment and/or Systems, and will promptly replace any measurement and monitoring tool which degrades or otherwise negatively impacts the Equipment and/or Systems. HP shall further ensure that such measurement and monitoring tools shall permit reporting at a level of detail sufficient to verify compliance with the Service Levels, and HP acknowledges that such measurement and monitoring tools shall be subject to audit by SG Cowen. HP shall provide SG Cowen with information and access to all such measurement and monitoring tools and procedures upon request, for purposes of verification.

12.3. <u>Reports</u>. As part of the Base Services, HP shall provide monthly performance reports to SG Cowen as agreed upon by the Parties from time to time. As one such report, HP shall provide a monthly performance report, which shall be delivered to SG Cowen within seven (7) days after the end of each calendar month, describing HP's performance of the Services in the preceding month (the "Monthly Performance Report"). Such Monthly Performance Report shall:

(a) separately address HP's performance in each area of the Services;

(b) for each area of the Services, assess the degree to which HP has attained or failed to attain the pertinent objectives in that area as described in this Agreement, including with respect to the Service Levels;

(c) explain deviations from the Service Levels and other applicable performance standards and include a plan for corrective action for each such deviation;

---

68. Excerpted from Cowen Holdings, Inc. (formerly Cowen Group, Inc.), Services Agreement (Form S-1/A), at Exhibit 10.7 (May 17, 2006), *available at* http://www.sec.gov/Archives/edgar/data/1355007/000104746906007356/a2168660zex-10_7.htm.

(d) describe the status of problem resolution efforts, ongoing projects, and other initiatives, and the status of HP's performance with respect to change requests; and

(e) include such documentation and other information as SG Cowen may reasonably request for purposes of verifying compliance with, and meeting the objectives of, this Agreement.

12.4. <u>SG Cowen Satisfaction Surveys</u>. No less frequently than twice annually, HP shall perform customer satisfaction surveys acceptable to SG Cowen and shall share the results of those surveys with SG Cowen. All such results shall be deemed the property and Confidential Information of SG Cowen. HP and SG Cowen shall mutually agree upon the form and content of such surveys during Transition.

12.5. <u>Benchmarking</u>. SG Cowen reserves the right from time to time, at its discretion, beginning in the second year of this Agreement and with respect to a complete benchmark no more than once annually, to obtain the services of an independent third party (the "Benchmarker") to benchmark the charges for help-desk Services. The pool of potential benchmarkers shall consist of the following third party firms: (a) Gartner Group; (b) Compass; (c) Meta; and (d) Everest. Additional third parties may be added if one or more of the pre-approved benchmarkers is unavailable, so long as they are independent (i.e., not a competitor of HP or an outsourcing consultant to SG Cowen), are experienced in conducting benchmarking in the relevant industry and region, and possess the information necessary to arrive at an objective and proper result. If none of the pre-approved benchmark service providers is available to perform the benchmark services, then the parties will use best efforts to agree upon a third party qualified to perform the services. If the Parties do not agree within twenty (20) business days of SG Cowen's request, then the third party shall be designated by SG Cowen. SG Cowen will bear the costs and expenses of conducting the benchmark and all results of the benchmark and materials created pursuant to the Benchmark shall be SG Cowen's sole and exclusive property and Confidential Information. The Benchmarker shall perform the benchmarking in accordance with the Benchmarker's documented procedures which shall be provided to the Parties prior to the start of the benchmarking process and to which the Parties may comment prior to the benchmarking, as modified herein. The Benchmarker shall compare the costs, charges and/or performance of the Services under this Agreement, as appropriate, for the Services being benchmarked to the costs, charges, and/or performance in a representative sample of well-managed IT operations performing services similar to the Services. The Benchmarker shall select the representative sample from entities (x) identified by the Benchmarker, and (y) identified by a Party and approved by the Benchmarker. The following conditions apply to the representative sample: (i) it may include entities that have not outsourced IT operations, and (ii) it may include entities that are outsourcing customers of HP. The Benchmarker is to conduct a benchmarking as promptly as is prudent in the circumstances. In conducting the benchmarking, the Benchmarker shall normalize the data used to perform the benchmarking to accommodate, as appropriate, differences in volume of services, scope of services, service levels, financing or payment streams, and other pertinent factors. Each Party shall be provided a reasonable opportunity to review, comment on and request changes in the Benchmarker's proposed findings. Following such review and comment, the Benchmarker shall issue a final report of its findings and conclusions, which final report shall be the property and Confidential Information of SG Cowen. Based upon the final results of such benchmarking, including the aggregate results from the customer satisfaction surveys, HP shall cooperate with SG Cowen to investigate variances, if any, and to take corrective action to respond to any deficiencies; provided that, if such results show that the Fees paid by SG Cowen are higher than the midpoint of fees charged with respect to other well managed outsourcing organizations, HP shall have sixty (60) days to reduce the Fees charged hereunder accordingly. Any dispute as to such deficiencies, variances or reduction shall be resolved pursuant to Section 29.

12.6. Failure to Perform.

(a) Service Level Credits. HP recognizes that SG Cowen is paying HP to deliver the Services at specified Service Levels. Without limiting any other remedy which SG Cowen may have hereunder or otherwise, whether at law, in equity, or otherwise, if HP fails to meet any Service Level(s) (other than due to a Force Majeure event), then HP shall credit to SG Cowen the performance credits specified in Schedule B (the "Service Level Credits") in recognition of the diminished value of the Services resulting from HP's failure to meet the agreed upon level of performance. HP acknowledges and agrees that such Service Level Credits shall not be deemed a penalty.

(b) Failure. If HP fails to meet any Service Levels, HP shall promptly and in accordance with the Service Levels (i) investigate and report on the causes of the problem; (ii) advise SG Cowen, as and to the extent requested by SG Cowen, of the status of remedial efforts that will be and/or are being undertaken with respect to such problems; (iii) correct the problem(s) that led to such failure, and begin meeting the Service Levels; and (iv) take appropriate preventive measures to ensure that the applicable problem(s) do not recur. The foregoing shall not be deemed to limit any other remedy to which SG Cowen may be entitled hereunder or otherwise, whether at law, in equity, or otherwise.

(c) Root Cause Analysis. Within twenty-four (24) hours of any Critical Service Level failure, HP shall: (i) perform a root cause analysis to identify the cause of such failure; (ii) provide SG Cowen with a report detailing the cause of, and procedure for correcting, such failure; and (iii) provide SG Cowen with assurances satisfactory to SG Cowen that such failure will not recur after the procedure has been completed.

(d) Additional Termination Right. In addition to, and without limiting any other rights or remedies of SG Cowen under this Agreement, whether at law, in equity or otherwise, SG Cowen shall have the right to terminate this Agreement, without payment of any termination fee or other liability, if, in any two (2) months in a consecutive three (3) month period, (i) HP fails to perform any Services in accordance with any of the Critical Service Levels, or (ii) HP fails to perform Services in accordance with four (4) or more of the Service Levels.

As you can see, service levels may be the subject of considerable and careful negotiation between parties to services contracts. This may serve the interest of both parties, as the service provider attains clarity as to how it must perform to satisfy its obligations, and the client attains comfort that it is purchasing a certain, measurable quality and type of services. For more on the importance of service levels in practice, we turn again to a seasoned practitioner.

A Practitioner Perspective: The Importance of Service Levels

Service levels are particularly important in services agreements, as they provide a reasonable mechanism to monitor the quality of an ongoing stream of services without having to resort to dispute resolution for small, day-to-day issues. An agreed service level serves to specify the obligations of both parties in a fair and transparent manner. The recipient of the services wants to make sure that the provider is focused on the right performance measures and will want to see some sort of financial payment in the event of a major failure. The service provider wants to be able to demonstrate in a clear fashion that the contractual obligations are being met and that the financial payments for failures are capped and reasonable. There are often two different kinds of service levels. A key service level is a measurement of performance of the services that does not result in financial penalties or credits. A critical service level is a measurement of performance of the base services that may result in financial penalties/credits. Service levels are either negotiated prior to the commencement of services or can be set based upon baselines generated once the service provider has started to provide the services. It is most important that the service levels are limited in number so they can be monitored cost-effectively and simple enough to be executed, agreed upon and transparent to all parties. They should be meaningful to the operation of the contract such that any failure to meet a service legal agreement would actually impact the business of the client.

Nancy Laben
Senior Vice President
and General Counsel
AECOM

Prior to publication, Ms. Laben left Accenture LLP, where she was Deputy General Counsel, to join AECOM.

---

6. Notice and Waiver of Claims; Contractual "Statute of Limitations"

The last sentence of § 10.5 of the AOL Agreement provides that "all other claims by a TW Company of whatever nature" will be waived unless Time Warner provides AOL with notice of the claim within six months of the accrual of the claim. Such a notice provision operates to give AOL an opportunity to remedy the claim or at least to contain the potential damages resulting from the event that gave rise to the claim. In addition, this type of notice provision also works to insulate AOL from liability for any claims where Time Warner, for one reason or another, fails to comply with the notice requirement.

These provisions are not uncommon, and courts are willing to honor them.[69] However, such provisions are generally ineffective where the time limitation is not "reasonable."[70] Similarly, a court will generally enforce a contractual "statute of limitations," where parties in their contract reduce a statute of limitations as applicable to the parties, so long as the contractual period is reasonable.[71] For both notice-requirement provisions and contractual statute-of-limitations provisions, the question of reasonableness turns on the facts and circumstances at issue. For example, a New York court has held that a ten-day period for a notice-requirement provision was unreasonable because, in that case, the party to give notice of a claim could not realistically know of the claim within the ten-day period.[72] However, note that at least one jurisdiction has opted no longer to follow this rule, explaining, "A mere judicial assessment of 'reasonableness' is an invalid basis upon which to refuse to enforce contractual provisions."[73]

In addition to a concern for the reasonableness of the time period, courts have looked to whether a contractual time-bar provision expressly sets forth the consequences of noncompliance.[74] For example, a notice-requirement provision is more likely to bar a claim, where the provision specifically states that the claim will be barred if the notice requirement is not met or that satisfaction of the notice requirement is a condition precedent to bringing such a claim.[75]

---

69. *See, e.g., Cameo Homes v. Kraus-Anderson Constr. Co.*, 394 F.3d 1084, 1088 (8th Cir. 2005) (Minnesota law) ("Cameo failed to give written notice to the architect of its breach of contract claims against the City as required by the contract. It is therefore contractually barred from bringing them here.") (internal citations omitted); *Am. Mfrs. Mut. Ins. Co. v. Payton Lane Nursing Home, Inc.*, No. CV 05-5155(AKT), 2010 WL 144426, at *14 (E.D.N.Y. Jan. 11, 2010) ("Under New York law, courts regularly enforce notice requirements . . . where the relevant provision explicitly states that notice of such a claim is a condition precedent to bringing such a claim. . . .").

70. *See, e.g., Landsman Packing Co., Inc. v. Cont'l Can Co., Inc.*, 864 F.2d 721, 730-31 (11th Cir. 1989) (New York law).

71. *See, e.g., Sarmiento v. Grange Mut. Cas. Co.*, 835 N.E.2d 692, 696 (Ohio 2005). However, under certain statutes, there may be limits to the extent to which the parties may vary the statute of limitations by agreement, if they may at all. *See, e.g.,* U.C.C. § 2-725(1) (2003) ("By the original agreement the parties may reduce the period of limitation to not less than one year but may not extend it. However, in a consumer contract, the period of limitation may not be reduced.").

72. *Weisz v. Parke-Bernet Galleries, Inc.*, 325 N.Y.S.2d 576, 582-83 (N.Y. Civ. Ct. 1971), *rev'd on other grounds*, 351 N.Y.S.2d 911 (N.Y. App. Term 1974).

73. *Rory v. Cont'l Ins. Co.*, 703 N.W.2d 23, 31 (Mich. 2005).

74. *See, e.g., F.D.I.C. v. Kansas Bankers Sur. Co.*, 963 F.2d 289, 294 (10th Cir. 1992) (Oklahoma law) (due to plaintiff's noncompliance with an express time requirement in the notice provision, which expressly barred claims in the event of noncompliance, "no claims exist[ed]").

75. *See, e.g., Smurfit Newsprint Corp. v. Se. Paper Mfg.*, 368 F.3d 944, 951-52 (7th Cir. 2004) (New York law) ("The general language that the obligation of SP to indemnify Smurfit is subject to other terms and conditions of [the Agreement] is not sufficiently precise to make prompt written notice an express condition precedent to indemnification.") (internal quotation marks omitted); *Am. Mfrs. Mut. Ins. Co. v. Payton Lane Nursing Home, Inc.*, No. CV 05-5155(AKT), 2010 WL 144426, at *15 (E.D.N.Y. 2010). For more on "conditions precedent," please see the discussion in Chapter 4.

Accordingly, do you think the penultimate and last sentences of § 10.5 are likely to be effective?

> ### *Drafting Note: Broad Provisions in Specific Sections*
>
> Do you see any issues with placing the last sentence of § 10.5—which purports to apply to "all other claims"—in a section ostensibly about service levels? Imagining you are counsel for AOL in this transaction, might you recommend, as a matter of prudence, that such a provision deserving of conspicuous text might also be deserving of its own section, if the intention indeed is to impose a time limitation on all other claims? Notice that courts, as with the court in *Mobil* presented later in this chapter, may be reluctant to read a broadly worded provision—that affects meaningful or valuable rights—to apply to an entire agreement, where such a provision is tucked away in a section that appears narrow in scope.

7. Representations, Warranties, and Their Differences

Despite that representations and warranties are commonly spoken of and drafted together (as both the HP Agreement and the AOL Agreement demonstrate), representations and warranties are different in their meanings and effects. A "representation" is a statement of fact as of a point in time, usually made to induce someone to enter into a contract.[76] If a representation proves false, then a party may sue the representation-making party for misrepresentation (a tort). On the other hand, a "warranty" is "[a]n express or implied promise that something in furtherance of the contract is guaranteed by one of the contracting parties."[77] If a warranty proves false, then the non-breaching party may sue the warranty-making party for breach of warranty. A contract will usually provide *both* representations and warranties to give a party the rights and benefits afforded by each. With all this said, parties in a complex agreement (e.g., lending, mergers and acquisitions, i.e., "M&A") often specify the universe of rights and remedies that follow from the representations and warranties made in the agreement (and will attempt to exclude those purportedly made outside the agreement), and, accordingly, a contractually designed edifice may wash away much of the significance of any differences in meaning. As we further explore the differences between representations and warranties, please consider the following case.

---

76. BLACK'S LAW DICTIONARY 1415 (9th ed. 2009).
77. *Id.* at 1725.

CBS Inc. v. Ziff-Davis Publishing Co.
Court of Appeals of New York, 1990.
75 N.Y.2d 496.

HANCOCK, Judge.

A corporate buyer made a bid to purchase certain businesses based on financial information as to their profitability supplied by the seller. The bid was accepted and the parties entered into a binding bilateral contract for the sale which included, specifically, the seller's express warranties as to the truthfulness of the previously supplied financial information. Thereafter, pursuant to the purchase agreement, the buyer conducted its own investigation which led it to believe that the warranted information was untrue. The seller dismissed as meritless the buyer's expressions of disbelief in the validity of the financial information and insisted that the sale go through as agreed. The closing took place with the mutual understanding that it would not in any way affect the previously asserted position of either party. Did the buyer's manifested lack of belief in and reliance on the truth of the warranted information prior to the closing relieve the seller of its obligations under the warranties? This is the central question presented in the breach of express warranty claim brought by CBS Inc. (CBS) against Ziff-Davis Publishing Co. (Ziff-Davis).[1] The courts below concluded that CBS's lack of reliance on the warranted information was fatal to its breach of warranty claim and, accordingly, dismissed that cause of action on motion. . . . We granted leave to appeal and, for reasons stated hereinafter, disagree with this conclusion and hold that the warranty claim should be reinstated.

I

The essential facts pleaded—assumed to be true for the purpose of the dismissal motion—are these. In September 1984, Goldman Sachs & Co., acting as Ziff-Davis's investment banker and agent, solicited bids for the sale of the assets and businesses of 12 consumer magazines and 12 business publications. The offering circular, prepared by Goldman Sachs and Ziff-Davis, described Ziff-Davis's financial condition and included operating income statements for the fiscal year ending July 31, 1984 prepared by Ziff-Davis's accountant, Touche Ross & Co. Based on Ziff-Davis's representations in the offering circular, CBS, on November 9, 1984 submitted a bid limited to the purchase of the 12 consumer magazines in the amount of $362,500,000. This was the highest bid.

On November 19, 1984 CBS and Ziff-Davis entered into a binding bilateral purchase agreement for the sale of the consumer magazine businesses for the price of $362,500,000. Under section 3.5 of the purchase agreement, Ziff-Davis warranted that the audited income and expense report of the businesses for the

---

1. Ziff-Davis is a privately held corporation and is a wholly owned subsidiary of defendant Ziff Corporation. Ziff Corp. is the guarantor of the purchase agreement at issue. For ease of reference, when addressing arguments raised by these defendants, I will refer to the defendants collectively as Ziff-Davis.

1984 fiscal year, which had been previously provided to CBS in the offering circular, had "been prepared in accordance with generally accepted accounting principles" (GAAP) and that the report "present[ed] fairly the items set forth". Ziff-Davis agreed to furnish an interim income and expense report (Stub Report) of the businesses covering the period after the end of the 1984 fiscal year, and it warranted under section 3.6 that from July 31, 1984 until the closing, there had "not been any material adverse change in Seller's business of publishing and distributing the Publications, taken as a whole". Section 6.1(a) provided that "all representations and warranties of Seller to Buyer shall be true and correct as of the time of the closing", and in section 8.1, the parties agreed that all "representations and warranties . . . shall survive the closing, notwithstanding any investigation made by or on behalf of the other party." In section 5.1 Ziff-Davis gave CBS permission to "make such investigation" of the magazine businesses being sold "as [it might] desire" and agreed to give CBS and its accountants reasonable access to the books and records pertaining thereto and to furnish such documents and information as might reasonably be requested.

Thereafter, on January 30, 1985 Ziff-Davis delivered the required Stub Report. In the interim, CBS, acting under section 5.1 of the purchase agreement, had performed its own "due diligence" examination of Ziff-Davis's financial condition. Based on this examination and on reports by its accountant, Coopers & Lybrand, CBS discovered information causing it to believe that Ziff-Davis's certified financial statements and other financial reports were not prepared according to GAAP and did not fairly depict Ziff-Davis's financial condition.

In a January 31, 1985 letter, CBS wrote Ziff-Davis that, "[b]ased on the information and analysis provided [to it, CBS was] of the view that there [were] material misrepresentations in the financial statements provided [to CBS] by Touche Ross & Co., Goldman, Sachs & Co. and Ziff-Davis". In response to this letter, Ziff-Davis advised CBS by letter dated February 4, 1985 that it "believe[d] that all conditions to the closing . . . were fulfilled", that "there [was] no merit to the position taken by CBS in its [Jan. 31, 1985] letter" and that the financial statements were properly prepared and fairly presented Ziff-Davis's financial condition. It also warned CBS that, since all conditions to closing were satisfied, closing was required to be held that day, February 4, 1985, and that, if it "should fail to consummate the transactions as provided . . . Ziff-Davis intend[ed] *to pursue all of its rights and remedies as provided by law*." (Emphasis added.)

CBS responded to Ziff-Davis's February 4, 1985 letter with its own February 4 letter, which Ziff-Davis accepted and agreed to. In its February 4 letter, CBS acknowledged that "a clear dispute" existed between the parties. It stated that it had decided to proceed with the deal because it had "spent considerable time, effort and money in complying with [its] obligations . . . and recogniz[ed] that [Ziff-Davis had] considerably more information available". Accordingly, the parties agreed "to close [that day] on a mutual understanding that the decision to close, and the closing, [would] not *constitute a waiver of any rights or defenses either of us may have*" (emphasis added) under the purchase agreement. The deal was consummated on February 4.

CBS then brought this action claiming in its third cause of action that Ziff-Davis had breached the warranties made as to the magazines' profitability. Based on that breach, CBS alleged that "the price bid and the price paid by CBS were in excess of that which would have been bid and paid by CBS had Ziff-Davis not breached its representation and warranties." Supreme Court granted Ziff-Davis's motion to dismiss the breach of warranty cause of action because CBS alleged "it did not believe that the representations set forth in Paragraphs 3.5 and 3.6 of the contract of sale were true" and thus CBS did not satisfy "the law in New York [which] clearly requires that this reliance be alleged in a breach of warranty action." Supreme Court also dismissed CBS's fourth cause of action relating to an alleged breach of condition. The Appellate Division, First Department, unanimously affirmed for reasons stated by Supreme Court. There should be a modification so as to deny the dismissal motion with respect to the third cause of action for breach of warranties.

II

In addressing the central question whether the failure to plead reliance is fatal to CBS's claim for breach of express warranties, it is necessary to examine the exact nature of the missing element of reliance which Ziff-Davis contends is essential. This critical lack of reliance, according to Ziff-Davis, relates to CBS's disbelief in the truth of the warranted financial information which resulted from its investigation *after* the signing of the agreement and *prior to* the date of closing. The reliance in question, it must be emphasized, does not relate to whether CBS relied on the submitted financial information in making its bid or relied on Ziff-Davis's express warranties as to the validity of this information when CBS committed itself to buy the businesses by signing the purchase agreement containing the warranties.

Under Ziff-Davis's theory, the reliance which is a necessary element for a claim of breach of express warranty is essentially that required for a tort action based on fraud or misrepresentation—i.e., a belief in the truth of the representations made in the express warranty and a change of position in reliance on that belief. Thus, because, prior to the closing of the contract on February 4, 1985, CBS demonstrated its lack of belief in the truth of the warranted financial information, it cannot have closed in reliance on it and its breach of warranty claim must fail. This is so, Ziff-Davis maintains, despite its unequivocal rejection of CBS's expressions of its concern that the submitted financial reports contained errors, despite its insistence that the information it had submitted complied with the warranties and that there was "no merit" to CBS's position, and despite its warnings of legal action if CBS did not go ahead with the closing. Ziff-Davis's primary source for the proposition it urges—that a change of position in reliance on the truth of the warranted information is essential for a cause of action for breach of express warranty—is language found in older New York cases. . . .

CBS, on the other hand, maintains that the decisive question is whether it purchased the express warranties as bargained-for contractual terms that were part of the purchase agreement. It alleges that it did so and that, under these circumstances, the warranty provisions amounted to assurances of the existence of facts upon which CBS relied in committing itself to buy the consumer magazines. Ziff-Davis's assurances of these facts, CBS contends, were the equivalent of promises by Ziff-Davis to indemnify CBS if the assurances proved unfounded. Thus, as continuing promises to indemnify, the express contractual warranties did not lose their operative force when, prior to the closing, CBS formed a belief that the warranted financial information was in error. Indeed, CBS claims that it is precisely because of these warranties that it proceeded with the closing, despite its misgivings.

As authority for its position, CBS cites Learned Hand's definition of warranty as "an assurance by one party to a contract of the existence of a fact upon which the other party may rely. It is intended precisely to relieve the promisee of any duty to ascertain the fact for himself; *it amounts to a promise to indemnify the promisee for any loss if the fact warranted proves untrue, for obviously the promisor cannot control what is already in the past.*"

We believe that the analysis of the reliance requirement in actions for breach of express warranties urged by CBS here is correct. The critical question is not whether the buyer believed in the truth of the warranted information, as Ziff-Davis would have it, but whether it believed it was purchasing the seller's promise as to its truth. This view of "reliance"—i.e., as requiring no more than reliance on the express warranty as being a part of the bargain between the parties—reflects the prevailing perception of an action for breach of express warranty as one that is no longer grounded in tort, but essentially in contract. The express warranty is as much a part of the contract as any other term. Once the express warranty is shown to have been relied on as part of the contract, the right to be indemnified in damages for its breach does not depend on proof that the buyer thereafter believed that the assurances of fact made in the warranty would be fulfilled. The right to indemnification depends only on establishing that the warranty was breached.

If, as is allegedly the case here, the buyer has purchased the seller's promise as to the existence of the warranted facts, the seller should not be relieved of responsibility because the buyer, after agreeing to make the purchase, forms doubts as to the existence of those facts. Stated otherwise, the fact that the buyer has questioned the seller's ability to perform as promised should not relieve the seller of his obligations under the express warranties when he thereafter undertakes to render the promised performance. . . .

Viewed as a contract action involving the claimed breach of certain bargained-for express warranties contained in the purchase agreement, the case may be summarized this way. CBS contracted to buy the consumer magazine businesses in consideration, among other things, of the reciprocal promises made by Ziff-Davis concerning the magazines' profitability. These reciprocal promises included the express warranties that the audited reports for the year ending July 31, 1984 made by Touche Ross had been prepared according to GAAP and that the items contained therein were fairly presented, that there had been no adverse material change in the business after July 31, 1984, and that all representations and warranties would "be true and correct as of the time of the closing" and would "survive the closing, notwithstanding any investigation" by CBS.

Unquestionably, the financial information pertaining to the income and expenses of the consumer magazines was relied on by CBS in forming its opinion as to the value of the businesses and in arriving at the amount of its bid; the warranties pertaining to the validity of this financial information were express terms of the bargain and part of what CBS contracted to purchase. CBS was not merely buying identified consumer magazine businesses. It was buying businesses which it believed to be of a certain value based on information furnished by the seller which the seller warranted to be true. The determinative question is this: should Ziff-Davis be relieved from any contractual obligation under these warranties, as it contends that it should, because, prior to the closing, CBS and its accountants questioned the accuracy of the financial information and because CBS, when it closed, did so without *believing in* or *relying on* the truth of the information?

We see no reason why Ziff-Davis should be absolved from its warranty obligations under these circumstances. A holding that it should because CBS questioned the truth of the facts warranted would have the effect of depriving the express warranties of their only value to CBS—i.e., as continuing promises by Ziff-Davis to indemnify CBS if the facts warranted proved to be untrue.[4] Ironically, if Ziff-Davis's position were adopted, it would have succeeded in pressing CBS to close despite CBS's misgivings and, at the same time, would have succeeded in *defeating* CBS's breach of warranties action because CBS harbored these *identical misgivings.*[5] . . .

Comments

The dissenting opinion in *Ziff-Davis* expressed concern that, as a result of the majority's holding, "Predictability and reliability with respect to commercial transactions, fostered by 90 years of precedent, are thus sacrificed."[78] Business

---

4. In this regard, analogy to the Uniform Commercial Code is "instructive." While acceptance of goods by the buyer precludes rejection of the goods accepted, the acceptance of nonconforming goods does not itself impair any other remedy for nonconformity, including damages for breach of an express warranty.

5. We make but one comment on the dissent: in its statement that our "holding discards reliance as a necessary element to maintain an action for breach of an express warranty" the dissent obviously misses the point of our decision. We do not hold that no reliance is required, but that the required reliance is established if, as here, the express warranties are bargained-for terms of the seller.

78. *CBS Inc. v. Ziff-Davis Publ'g Co.*, 75 N.Y.2d 496, 506 (N.Y. 1990) (Bellacosa, J., dissenting).

transactions are negotiated in the shadow of the law. To understand the meaning and effect of an agreement, one must understand the legal world in which the agreement exists and which bestows operative force onto that agreement.

The majority in *Ziff-Davis* believed that CBS and Ziff-Davis entered into their agreement with the expectation that Ziff-Davis's warranty obligation would continue, notwithstanding CBS's knowledge that Ziff-Davis was in breach of the warranty. The court understood this right of CBS's (and, so, obligation of Ziff-Davis's) as "priced into the deal," as something that CBS purchased just the same as it did several consumer magazine businesses. As the high court of New York explained:

> [T]he warranties pertaining to the validity of this financial information were express terms of the bargain and part of what CBS contracted to purchase. CBS was not merely buying identified consumer magazine businesses. It was buying businesses which it believed to be of a certain value based on information furnished by the seller which the seller warranted to be true.[79]

In so explaining, the court in *Ziff-Davis* effectively offered a definition of "warranty" and outlined how warranties are to be enforced. Both the majority and the dissent seem to suggest that party expectation should drive a court's understanding of contractual terms. The majority believed that the parties intended to preserve CBS's right to damages for breach of a promise regardless of CBS's knowledge of the falsity of that promise. In contrast, the dissent believed that reliance on the underlying truth of a promise had always—or, at least for 90 years—been necessary to succeed in an action for breach of warranty and that, accordingly, the parties must have entered into the contract with this understanding and expectation as part of their deal. Does the majority or the dissent's view better comport with party intent in this case? If the dissent's view prevailed, how should CBS have protected itself? Is either view preferable as a rule going forward, or is this a mere "coordination game," where so long as commercial players know the "rules" (e.g., the definition and effect of a "warranty") going into a transaction, they will be able to structure the agreement to allocate their rights and obligations as intended?

---

a. Understanding "Warranty" and "Representation" after Ziff-Davis

Regardless of the rule prior to *Ziff-Davis*, the majority of states are now in accord with the definition of "warranty" attributed to the majority opinion in *Ziff-Davis*.[80] That is, most states do not require reliance on the underlying truth

---

79. *Id.* at 505.

80. *See Vigortone AG Prods., Inc. v. PM AG Prods., Inc.*, 316 F.3d 641, 649 (7th Cir. 2002) (explaining that the "general rule" is that "a party to a contract can enforce an express warranty even if he should believe or even does believe that the mishap warranted against will occur" and that Delaware's high court would subscribe to

of a warranty as an element of proving a breach-of-warranty claim.[81] Implicit in what it means to have a warranty is the right to transfer the risk of the failure of that warranty to the party making the warranty. As the court in *Ziff-Davis* explained, one who obtains a warranty has bought a promise that the warranted statement will be true for the duration of the warranty and the right to damages should that statement prove false.

However, a mere two years after *Ziff-Davis* was decided, the Second Circuit, in *Galli v. Metz*, explained:

> Where a buyer closes on a contract in the full knowledge and acceptance of facts disclosed by the seller which would constitute a breach of warranty under the terms of the contract, the buyer should be foreclosed from later asserting the breach. In that situation, unless the buyer expressly preserves his rights under the warranties (as CBS did in *Ziff-Davis*), we think the buyer has waived the breach.[82]

The court in *Galli* accepted the *Ziff-Davis* definition of "warranty" and that one need not prove reliance on the underlying truth of a warranty in order to prove breach of that warranty. However, the court also narrowed the effect of *Ziff-Davis*, explaining that if a party closes on (i.e., consummates the transaction contemplated by) a contract—presumably when the party is not contractually obligated to close, given the breach—with the full knowledge and acceptance of the falsity of a warranty's underlying facts, then such party will be held to have *waived* the breach of such warranty. Under *Galli*, it is important to ascertain how the party suing for breach of warranty acquired the information that the facts underlying the warranty were untrue. For a party to waive its warranty, the *warranting party* must have disclosed the facts. If the party suing on the warranty acquired such facts elsewhere or as common knowledge, then no waiver will be found.[83]

---

this rule despite "unthinking" lower court case law in Delaware to the contrary); *Mowbray v. Waste Mgmt. Holdings, Inc.*, 189 F.R.D. 194, 200 (D. Mass. 1999) ("A decisive majority of courts that have considered the issue . . . have held . . . that reliance is not an element of a claim for breach of warranty, when the fact that the warranty was created is not in dispute.") (citing cases decided under Illinois, Florida, Pennsylvania, Connecticut, Montana, New York, Indiana, and Massachusetts law). *But see Hendricks v. Callahan*, 972 F.2d 190 (8th Cir. 1992) (Minnesota law); *Land v. Roper Corp.*, 531 F.2d 445, 448 (10th Cir. 1976) (Kansas law).

81. *See supra* note 80.

82. *Galli v. Metz*, 973 F.2d 145, 151 (2d Cir. 1992) (New York law).

83. *See id.; see also Promuto v. Waste Mgmt., Inc.*, 44 F. Supp 2d 628, 648 (S.D.N.Y. 1999) ("The law is clear that in order to conclude that plaintiffs have waived their right to assert a claim for breach of warranty, we must find that, prior to closing, defendants themselves actively disclosed to plaintiffs facts which would have constituted a breach of the warranties under the terms of the Exchange Agreement."). Presumably, this is because, where the warranting party admits that the warranty is false and a false warranty excuses the non-breaching party from any obligation to close, the non-breaching party's choice to close rather than to exercise its right to refuse to close—and to insist on renegotiating price to reflect the diminished value of the contract due to the breached warranty—evidences a waiver of the warranty and the right to sue for breach. Notice, then, this is different from a situation where a party signs a contract with knowledge that a warranty under that contract is untrue. For this warranty to mean anything (and we always try to give meaning to a contractual provision inasmuch as reasonable), we should presume that the receiving party did not intend to "waive" the warranty right by executing the contract with knowledge of the warranty's inaccuracy—indeed, the party did not *have* the right to waive until the contract was executed, and it is nonsensical to think a party intended to gain and waive a right in one fell contractual swoop. Accordingly, *Galli* should be limited to

Furthermore, a party could avoid waiver and preserve its right to bring an action for breach of warranty if the party expressly preserves such a right. This might be accomplished by a provision in the agreement that specifies the exclusive means by which a party may waive a term under the Agreement (e.g., a provision requiring that both parties sign a written waiver).[84] In addition, before closing on an agreement, a party wishing to preserve its warranties under that agreement might insist that a statement of preservation of such warranties be expressly included in the agreement and/or that the warranting party affirmatively state in writing that the facts underlying such warranties remain true. For example, the parties might include a provision in the agreement that states:

> Every warranty set forth in this Agreement and the rights and remedies for any one or more breaches of this Agreement by the Sellers shall not be deemed waived by the Closing and shall be effective regardless of any prior knowledge by or on the part of the Purchaser.[85]

In sum, to bring a breach of warranty action, a plaintiff need not show that she relied on the truth of the warranty but merely that the warranty was breached.[86] A breach of warranty action lies in contract and not tort.[87] As such, punitive damages are ordinarily not available for mere breach of warranty.[88] Unless an agreement provides otherwise, in an action for breach of warranty, one may recover damages generally available for breach of contract, including general and consequential damages.[89] A warranty may be as of a point in time or ongoing into the future, which depends on the nature of the warranty and the language of the contract.[90]

---

situations after the signing of a contract where a party intentionally acts to waive its contractual warranty right, namely by opting to close and consummate the core transaction contemplated by the agreement in lieu of demanding recompense. (We may also understand *Galli* as a decision in favor of judicial economy, as holding out on closing may be a more efficient, non-judicial means of attaining redress.)

84. *See, e.g., NSA Invs. II LLC v. SeraNova, Inc.*, 227 F. Supp. 2d 200, 205 (D. Mass. 2002) (New York law). However, note that some courts may find such a provision itself to be waivable. For more on this, please see the discussion of implied waiver and no-waiver provisions in Chapter 2.

85. *Pegasus Mgmt. Co. v. Lyssa, Inc.*, 995 F. Supp. 29, 38 (D. Mass. 1998) (internal quotation marks omitted) ("In the instant case, there can be no doubt that the buyers expressly reserved their rights [in accordance with *Ziff-Davis*].").

86. *See, e.g., Bank of Am. Corp. v. Lemgruber*, 385 F. Supp. 2d 200, 229 (S.D.N.Y. 2005).

87. *See, e.g., Shurland v. Bacci Café & Pizzeria on Ogden Inc.*, 259 F.R.D. 151, 163 (N.D. Ill. 2009) ("[A]n action for breach of warranty sounds in contract, not tort."); *White v. Holida Kamper & Boats*, No. 7:06-02362-HFF, 2008 WL 4155663, at *5 (D.S.C. Sept. 9, 2008); *RxUSA, Inc. v. Capital Returns, Inc.*, No. 06-C-00790, 2007 WL 2712958, at *10 (E.D. Wis. Sept. 14, 2007); *Barnhill v. Iowa Dist. Court for Polk Cnty.*, 765 N.W.2d 267, 274 (Iowa 2009).

88. *Rosen v. Gupta*, 213 F.3d 626 (2d Cir. 2000) (punitive damages not available for breach of warranty in New York or Texas); *English v. Mentor Corp.*, 67 F.3d 477, 481 (3d Cir. 1995) (punitive damages not available for breach of warranty absent fraud); *Salter v. Al-Hallaq*, No. 02-2406-JWL, 2003 WL 1872991 (D. Kan. Apr. 10, 2003) (punitive damages not available for breach of warranty under U.C.C.).

89. *See, e.g., St. John's Bank & Trust Co. v. Intag, Inc.*, 938 S.W.2d 627, 629 (Mo. App. E.D. 1997) ("[B]reach of warranty case arising out of the performance of a service may recover consequential damages.").

90. *See, e.g., Marvin Lumber and Cedar Co. v. PPG Indus., Inc.*, 223 F.3d 873, 879 (8th Cir. 2000) (Minnesota law).

In contrast, recall that a representation is a statement of fact as of a point in time usually made to induce reliance. If such a representation proves false, one may bring an action for misrepresentation (which lies in tort) unless an agreement provides otherwise.[91] Misrepresentation may be innocent, negligent, or fraudulent. The major difference between these various flavors is the defendant's state of mind. Innocent misrepresentation is a strict liability offense, negligent misrepresentation only requires that a defendant acted—well—negligently, and fraudulent misrepresentation requires that the defendant knowingly or recklessly made a false representation.[92] An action for misrepresentation requires a showing that the plaintiff reasonably relied on the representation.[93] In addition, the general rule is that an action for misrepresentation may only be based on a statement of present or past fact.[94] As the elements vary across the types of misrepresentation, so too do the available remedies. For example, for fraudulent misrepresentation, punitive damages may be available.[95]

While representations are sometimes oral and sometimes expressly written in a contract, a sophisticated party to an agreement may be unable to demonstrate reliance on an oral representation.[96] Indeed, a *sophisticated* party insists on the express inclusion of representations in a written agreement before relying on such.[97] This, then, demonstrates the importance of commercial players receiving express, written representations and the potential futility of relying on mere oral representations. On the flipside, to attempt to avoid responsibility for representations a party wishes not to make, a party may include a provision that expressly states that the party only makes those representations expressly made within the written agreement and that the other party has not relied on any representations made by the party outside of the contract (the latter, a so-called

---

91. However, in New York, a party may not bring a tort action for misrepresentation of a statement of *future* intent unless such representations are "collateral and extraneous" to the contract. *See Int'l CableTel Inc. v. Le Groupe Videotron Ltee*, 978 F. Supp. 483, 487 (S.D.N.Y. 1997). An action for misrepresentation based on representations provided by a contract is not "collateral and extraneous" to the contract. *See GBJ Corp. v. E. Ohio Paving Co.*, 139 F.3d 1080, 1088 (6th Cir. 1998) (New York law). This rule does not apply to false statements of present fact. *See Int'l CableTel Inc.*, 978 F. Supp. at 491. Essentially, then, this New York rule forces claims of misrepresentation based on contractual representations of future intent to be stated in terms of contract or, more specifically, warranty, instead of misrepresentation and tort.

92. For innocent misrepresentation, see RESTATEMENT (SECOND) OF TORTS § 552C (1977). For negligent misrepresentation, see RESTATEMENT (SECOND) OF TORTS § 552 (1977); *see also Dahlgren v. First Nat'l Bank of Holdrege*, 533 F.3d 681, 693 (8th Cir. 2008) (Nebraska law); *Erickson's Flooring & Supply Co. v. Tembec, Inc.*, 212 F. App'x 558, 563 (6th Cir. 2007) (Michigan law). For fraudulent misrepresentation, see RESTATEMENT (SECOND) OF TORTS § 525 (1977); *see also Dahlgren*, 533 F.3d at 692; *Erickson's Flooring & Supply*, 212 F. App'x at 562-63.

93. *See supra* note 92.

94. *See, e.g., Siemens Fin. Servs., Inc. v. Robert J. Combs Ins. Agency, Inc.*, 166 F. App'x 612, 617 (3d Cir. 2006); *Showler v. Harper's Magazine Found.*, 222 F. App'x 755, 765 (10th Cir. 2007).

95. *See, e.g., Spreitzer v. Hawkeye State Bank*, 775 N.W.2d 573, 593 (Iowa 2009).

96. *Century.Pac., Inc. v. Hilton Hotels Corp.*, 354 F. App'x 496, 498-99 (2d Cir. 2009) (New York law).

97. *Id.* In addition, "reliance on the oral representation by a plaintiff can be utterly unjustified in the face of a clear written contradiction." *Spreitzer*, 775 N.W.2d at 585-86 (citing *Marram v. Kobric Offshore Fund, Ltd.*, 809 N.E.2d 1017, 1031 (Mass. 2004)).

"anti-reliance" clause). An integration clause *may* serve this purpose;[98] however, a prudent party will include a provision that expressly disclaims any extra-contractual representations.[99]

A party under a contract may wish to seek both representations and warranties so as to optimize the party's available causes of action and remedies.[100] If a representation proves false, a party may rescind the contract or seek restitution.[101] If the party can prove fraudulent misrepresentation, then the moving party may be able to obtain punitive damages. However, all forms of misrepresentation require a showing that the plaintiff relied on the truth of the representation, and fraudulent misrepresentation requires a hard-to-prove showing of scienter. One need not make a showing of either reliance or scienter, however, to recover for a breach of warranty, but, for a breach of warranty, punitive damages are unavailable.

The two previous agreements (§ 5(h) of the HP Agreement and § 9 of the AOL Agreement) include provisions that address representations and warranties. From the perspective of either party, do you consider the representations and warranties in these agreements to be sufficiently robust? By way of example, is there value in seeking a representation and warranty as to the accuracy and completeness of confidential information exchanged by parties to an agreement? Under what circumstances in particular might this be useful? What other representations and warranties might you consider when negotiating a services agreement?

While parties to a transaction are, of course, free to craft those representations that reflect the facts upon which each party relies and those warranties that reflect the risk each party shall bear, certain representations and warranties are commonplace in the context of certain deals. For instance, the second warranty that Landa provides in the HP Agreement is a variation of a "warranty of non-infringement," which is commonly seen in transactions involving intellectual property. This warranty specifies which party shall bear the risk of infringement of the intellectual property rights of others. While the recipient of the warranty may desire a warranty against infringement of intellectual property rights worldwide, a warrantor may be reluctant take on such broad and

---

98. *See, e.g., Eastman Kodak Co. v. Teletech Servs. Corp.*, No. 05-CV-6594, 2007 WL 2027843, at *3 (W.D.N.Y. July 11, 2007) ("Because, the terms of a written, integrated and enforceable contract must be given effect over purported extra-contractual representations, I find . . . that there were no obligations or promises other than those listed in the contract.").

99. *See, e.g., Kronenberg v. Katz*, 872 A.2d 568, 593 (Del. Ch. 2004) ("Stated summarily, for a contract to bar a fraud in the inducement claim, the contract must contain language that, when read together, can be said to add up to a clear anti-reliance clause by which the plaintiff has contractually promised that it did not rely upon statements outside the contract's four corners in deciding to sign the contract. The presence of a standard integration clause alone, which does not contain explicit anti-reliance representations and which is not accompanied by other contractual provisions demonstrating with clarity that the plaintiff had agreed that it was not relying on facts outside the contract, will not suffice to bar fraud claims.").

100. *See* Tina Stark, *Nonbinding Opinion: Another View on Representations and Warranties*, 15 Bus. L. Today 8 (Jan./Feb. 2006) (explaining the benefits of obtaining both representations and warranties).

101. *See* Restatement (Second) of Contracts § 164 (1981).

unknown risk exposure, given the myriad intellectual property regimes the world over. Accordingly, a warrantor of non-infringement is likely to want to limit such warranty of non-infringement of intellectual property rights to the United States.

Additionally, it is common to find representations akin to the mutual representation made in the AOL Agreement, that each party has the proper authority in the first place to enter into the agreement itself. Picking up on this chapter's earlier discussion of agency, if a signatory to an agreement indeed lacks the authority to bind a supposed party to the agreement—and the principal has not ratified the agreement—then the agreement will not bind the principal, regardless of whether the signing agent makes such a representation. However, for what it may be worth, this representation gives the other party an actionable claim against the party stating the false representation.

b. Use of Representations and Warranties in Practice

Practitioners vary in their understanding and use of "representations" and "warranties."[102] Some (often, M&A attorneys) believe there is no meaningful distinction between the terms and no utility to reciting that a party both "represents and warrants."[103] Others point to cases like *Ziff-Davis* and insist that a "representation" is one thing and a "warranty" is another.[104] To reconcile these positions, it is important to differentiate between the *provision* in a contract called a "representation" or a "warranty," on the one hand, and a "representation" that may give rise to a misrepresentation claim or a "warranty" that may give rise to a breach-of-warranty claim, on the other. That is, something called a "warranty" on a piece of paper may also be a statement of fact made to induce reliance on the truth of the statement (i.e., a "representation"), and something called a "representation" may also be a promise that the truth of a statement is guaranteed by a party (i.e., a "warranty").[105] Still, the simplest way to signal to a future reader of a contract (e.g., a judge, an arbitrator) that a contract states *both* a representation (that may give rise to a claim for misrepresentation) and a warranty (that may give rise to a breach of warranty claim) may be to state expressly that a party *both* "represents and warrants."

Some practitioners do not give much weight to the distinction between the two terms (and may opt, for instance, to use only "represents" and not to use

---

102. *Compare* Kenneth A. Adams, *A Lesson in Drafting Contracts: What's up with 'Representations and Warranties'?*, 15 Bus. L. Today 32 (Nov./Dec. 2005), *with* Stark, *supra* note 100.

103. *See, e.g.*, Adams, *supra* note 102.

104. *See, e.g.*, Stark, *supra* note 100.

105. *See, e.g.*, U.C.C. § 2-313(2) (2003) ("(a) Any affirmation of fact or promise made by the seller which relates to the goods and becomes part of the basis of the bargain creates an express warranty that the goods shall conform to the affirmation or promise. (b) Any description of the goods which is made part of the basis of the bargain creates an express warranty that the goods shall conform to the description."). *See also supra* note 91 and accompanying text.

"warrants") because, for these practitioners, the rights and remedies intended to follow from the contractual representations are all provided and specified by the contract itself. For example, in an M&A agreement, the parties will generally create contractual termination rights and contractual indemnification rights for the failure of a representation/warranty.[106] In this way, the distinction is largely washed away, where the parties specify in the contract completely and exactly how they desire these things called "representations" and/or "warranties" to operate and what rights and remedies are to follow (i.e., the parties *could* call these things "bananas"—although we do not advise it—so long as the contract provided all that the parties desired to follow from their "banana" rights).

c. *Implied Warranties and the Disclaimer Thereof*

As we have seen, a contract may provide *express* warranties—warranties that are affirmatively stated by the contract.[107] However, beyond those warranties specifically offered by each party, certain other warranties may be *implied* by law. In Chapter 4, we will return to the topic of implied warranties in the context of Article 2 of the Uniform Commercial Code ("U.C.C.") and sales transactions. For now, know that where a contract involves both goods and services, most jurisdictions look to the "predominate purpose" of the mixed contract to determine whether Article 2 should apply.[108] Accordingly, even with a contract seemingly for "services," a prudent party will plan for the potentiality of Article 2's application.

Article 2 of the U.C.C. imputes implied warranties to be read into a contract for the sale of goods, even if the parties did not expressly include them. The implied warranty of merchantability warrants that goods to be delivered by a merchant are fit for the ordinary purposes for which such goods are used.[109] The implied warranty of fitness for a particular purpose kicks in when a seller has reason to know that a buyer is relying on the seller to select goods for a particular purpose.[110] In such a situation, an implied warranty arises that these goods are so suited.[111]

Outside of Article 2 and contracts for the sale of goods, it is uncommon for a court to find an implied warranty.[112] However, in certain circumstances, courts

---

106. Please see Chapters 5 and 6 for an examination of the function of representations and warranties in lending and M&A agreements.

107. Express warranties may also arise outside a contract, for instance, in a product manual. *See, e.g., Bell Sports, Inc. v. Yarusso*, 759 A.2d. 582, 592-93 (Del. 2000).

108. *See Novamedix, Ltd. v. NDM Acquisition Corp.*, 166 F.3d 1177, 1182 (6th Cir. 1999).

109. U.C.C. § 2-314(2) (2003).

110. *Id.* § 2-315.

111. *Id.* In addition, Article 2 is the source of a warranty of title, which promises that the seller has adequate title (i.e., sufficient rights to sell the property to be sold and that will not subject the buyer to a lawsuit to protect the title). *Id.* § 2-312. However, this warranty is not considered "implied" for Article 2 purposes, namely its conspicuous disclaimer requirement. *Id.* § 2-312 cmt. 6. Article 2 also provides that the repeated conduct of a party may give rise to additional implied warranties. *Id.* § 2-314(3).

112. *See, e.g., GMA Accessories, Inc. v. ePartners, Inc.*, No. 07 Civ. 8414(LAK), 2008 WL 781188, at *1 (S.D.N.Y. Mar. 19, 2008) ("[T]here is no claim under New York law for breach of an implied warranty for the performance of professional services in service-oriented contracts.").

have done so. For example, the Idaho Supreme Court has "imposed an implied warranty that services will be performed in a workmanlike manner in the context of personal services contracts."[113] Similarly, in contracts for the repair or modification of existing tangible goods or property, Texas has found an implied warranty "that the service will be performed in a good and workmanlike manner."[114] Given that a court may imply warranties beyond that which the parties explicitly provide, how can a commercial party avoid taking on undesirable risk?

Generally, implied warranties may be disclaimed by an agreement. That is, parties to a contract may "opt out" and avoid the application of implied warranties. To be effective, these disclaimers generally must be "conspicuous."[115] To be conspicuous, the disclaimer should be set apart from the contract's other provisions, and the disclaimer's text should appear different from the contract's ordinary text. This is usually accomplished by bolding and/or presenting the text in all caps.[116] Particularly, to disclaim the implied warranty of merchantability, the disclaimer should specifically mention "merchantability."[117] Alternatively, all Article 2 implied warranties may be excluded by specifying that a transaction is "as-is" or "with all faults."[118] Notice that while implied warranties may be disclaimed, most courts are unwilling to give effect to a disclaimer of an *express* warranty.[119] As a matter of prudent drafting, then, while sometimes a contractual provision will state a general rule and then provide exceptions to that general rule, one wishing not to make certain warranties should not provide these warranties in the first place.

8. Force Majeure Provisions and the Doctrine of Excuse

Under the common law, a party may be excused from performing under a contract for a host of reasons. For example, we have already discussed (in

---

113. *Branscum v. 4-J Harvestore, Inc.*, No. 88-3919, 886 F.2d 334, at *3 (9th Cir. 1989) (citing *Hoffman v. Simplot Aviation Inc.*, 539 P.2d 584, 588 (Idaho 1975)).

114. *Walker v. Sears, Roebuck & Co.*, 853 F.2d 355, 360-61 (5th Cir. 1988) (citing *Melody Home Mfg. Co. v. Barnes*, 741 S.W.2d 349, 354 (Tex. 1987)).

115. U.C.C. § 2-316(2) (2003) (disclaiming merchantability and fitness); *see Branscum*, 886 F.2d at *3 ("We need not decide whether this implied warranty would apply in the context of an Article 2 contract because 4-J disclaimed all implied warranties."); *GMA Accessories*, 2008 WL 781188, at *1 (rejecting claim for breach of implied warranty of good and workmanlike performance of services agreement partly because the master services agreement contained an express disclaimer of implied warranties). However, note that to disclaim the warranty of title under Article 2, there are not necessarily "any specific requirements that the disclaimer or modification be contained in a record or be conspicuous." U.C.C. § 2-316 cmt. 6 (2003).

116. *See, e.g., Hornberger v. Gen. Motors Corp.*, 929 F. Supp. 884, 889 (E.D. Pa. 1996) ("Under Pennsylvania law, some characteristics to consider [regarding] a disclaimer of warranty include: (1) the placement of the clause in the document; (2) the size of the disclaimer's print; and (3) whether the disclaimer was . . . in all caps or a different type style or color.").

117. U.C.C. § 2-316(2) (2003).

118. *Id.* § 2-316(3).

119. *See, e.g., L.S. Heath & Son, Inc. v. AT&T Info. Sys., Inc.*, 9 F.3d 561, 570-71 (7th Cir. 1993); *Bell Sports, Inc. v. Yarusso*, 759 A.2d 582, 593 (Del. 2000); *see also* U.C.C. § 2-316(1) (2003).

Chapter 2) that a party may be excused from—that is suffer no liability from not—performing under a contract if the other party has materially breached that contract. Another basic feature of the common law is that a party is excused from performance if some event (through no fault of that party's) either makes that party's performance impracticable or frustrates that party's principal purpose in undertaking the contract, where the non-occurrence of such event was a basic assumption of the contract.[120] However, like much of contract law, the law of excuse is default law, which means that contractual parties may opt out and strike their own accord.[121] This is the basic function of the force majeure provision, a provision commonplace in many agreements and found in § 12.5 of this Agreement.

The force majeure provision will often list several events that excuse a party's performance under the contract. Accordingly, a court need not inquire into what constitutes a "basic assumption" of the contract or what constitutes "impracticable" or "frustration of purpose" under common-law doctrines of excuse; the parties may specify in the force majeure provision what constitutes an excuse of a party's performance.[122] What have the Parties specified as excusing events in this Agreement? Under this Agreement, does a party affected by such an event have an incentive to stop all performance, even if she could otherwise partially or fully perform? Notice that § 12.5 conditions excuse for Force Majeure Events on the affected Party taking Commercially Reasonable Efforts to perform still, despite a Force Majeure Event. Does this condition (and the following provisions in § 12.5) apply to the events enumerated in the first sentence of § 12.5? Do you think the Parties intended them to apply? Where in this Agreement might you first look to understand what Commercially Reasonable Efforts means? Does this provide adequate guidance?[123]

---

120. *See* RESTATEMENT (SECOND) OF CONTRACTS §§ 261, 265 (1981).

121. *See, e.g., Stein v. Paradigm Mirasol, LLC*, 586 F.3d 849, 857 n.6 (11th Cir. 2009) ("It appears to us that force majeure clauses broader than the scope of impossibility are enforceable under Florida law."); *see also* RESTATEMENT (SECOND) OF CONTRACTS §§ 261, 265 (1981) (each providing "unless the language or the circumstances indicate the contrary").

122. *See Wis. Elec. Power Co. v. Union Pac. R.R. Co.*, 557 F.3d 504, 506-07 (7th Cir. 2009) (Wisconsin law). Indeed, while force majeure clauses may commonly provide that an event must be outside the control of a party for such an event to excuse that party, this is up to the parties and not a requirement of law. That is, parties can specify whatever events they like as excusing performance. *See, e.g., PPG Indus., Inc. v. Shell Oil Co.*, 919 F.2d 17 (5th Cir. 1990) (Texas law) ("In support of its position, PPG cites several cases in which courts refused to excuse the non-performing party because the force majeure was found to be within its control. A careful reading of these cases, however, reveals that the reasonable control requirement was supplied by the *terms of the contracts* rather than the *dictates of the law*.") (emphasis in original). However, unless the contract provides otherwise, general doctrines of excuse are available as defenses if the force majeure provision happens not to afford a defense. *See Melford Olsen Honey, Inc. v. Adee*, 452 F.3d 956, 962-64 (8th Cir. 2006) (Minnesota law).

123. Please see Chapter 4 for further discussion of "commercially reasonable" and performance standards generally.

Drafting Note: "Including"

Notice that, where § 12.5 lists the several events that constitute Force Majeure Events, the provision states that such Force Majeure Events are those events beyond a Party's reasonable control, "including, without limitation" and then proceeds to enumerate the several events. The word "including" is generally understood to precede an exemplary or illustrative—*but not exhaustive*—list of items.[124] Accordingly, even without the "without limitation" language, a court is unlikely to find the list of events in § 12.5 to be the only potential Force Majeure Events. However, using language like "without limitation" after the word "including" provides additional clarity, expressly instructing a future reader that the following list of items is intended to be non-exhaustive and merely illustrative.

Notice what excuse and the Force Majeure Provision do not do. The doctrine of excuse and the Force Majeure Provision free the excused party from liability for failure to perform fully; however, they do not allow the excused party, then, to insist on the continued performance of the other party. The *Restatement* makes this clear, explaining that despite that a party may be justified in not performing for impracticability or frustration of purpose, that party's failure to perform may still free the other party from performing.[125] The Agreement makes this clear in § 12.5, providing that an unaffected party may terminate affected Services if the Force Majeure Event shall occur for more than 15 consecutive business days and notice is provided. Is a Force Majeure Event more likely to affect AOL's or TW's ability to perform under this Agreement?

9. Shifting Risk: Indemnification and Limitation of Liability

Much of the enterprise of contracting involves the allocation of "risk" between private parties. All sorts of contractual provisions allocate risks, some of which we have already discussed. As just one example, something as simple as a notice provision may provide what constitutes effective notice, which in turn may trigger certain obligations under a contract. In specifying when notice is effective (e.g., upon receipt, upon five business days after delivery), a notice clause may specify which party bears what kind of risk for failure of delivery.

Representations and warranties both are tools commonly used to spread risk. A representation puts the risk of inaccurate information on the party making the representation, so long as the receiving party has justifiably relied on such information. A warranty puts the risk of failure of a specified promise on

---

124. *See, e.g., Cephalon, Inc. v. Johns Hopkins Univ.*, No. 3505-VCP, 2009 WL 4896227, at *8 (Del. Ch. Dec. 18, 2009); *Nextel Wip Lease Corp. v. Saunders*, 666 S.E.2d 317, 322 (Va. 2008); *Alcoa, Inc. v. Whittaker Corp.*, No. V-02-84, 2007 WL 2900591, at *4 (S.D. Tex. Sep. 30, 2007).

125. Restatement (Second) of Contracts § 267(1) (1981).

the warrantor. We have also looked at how a party may disclaim certain warranties, putting the risk of such a would-be promise failing on the other party. Force majeure provisions allow a party to avoid the risk of having to perform, despite the occurrence of certain critical events in the future. To understand risk and its contractual allocation, one must first appreciate who would suffer the occurrence of a certain cost, in the absence of a contract providing otherwise. With an understanding of this baseline, one may begin to draft contractual provisions to alter this default arrangement and to place the risk of the occurrence of certain costs on the desired party. For instance, drawing on our discussion of implied warranties, absent a disclaimer of implied warranties, a seller assumes the risk of the breach of an implied warranty: If a seller breaches the implied warranty of merchantability, then the seller is liable for the resulting damages to the buyer. However, if the seller effectively disclaims all implied warranties, then the risk of the seller running afoul of the implied warranty of merchantability falls to the buyer, and the buyer will have no legal recourse for any harm she suffers as a result of such "breach." That is, the buyer is "self-insuring" for this risk; she will bear the burden of her own losses.

Accordingly, with this in mind, let's look at two more of the most commonly used contractual tools for allocating risks between parties: indemnification and limitation of liability.

a. Indemnification

Indemnification clauses act to shift the risk of the occurrence of certain specified events, often third-party claims, to one party (the "indemnitor") by requiring this party to compensate the other party (the "indemnitee") for losses arising from such events.[126] At common law and absent a contract addressing the issue, a party may have an obligation to indemnify a second party for the first party's own wrongdoing, where the second party has been held liable (e.g., on a vicarious liability theory) for the first party's wrongdoing.[127] However, parties may wish not to rely on these default rights and laws and may instead wish to specify by contract a party's indemnification obligations.

Courts vary in their suspicion of indemnification provisions. While these provisions are generally enforceable, some states have a general policy of distrust

---

126. *See, e.g., Promuto v. Waste Mgmt., Inc.*, 44 F. Supp. 2d 628, 651 (S.D.N.Y. 1999) (finding an indemnification provision, by its terms, to provide a remedy for breach of a warranty made within that agreement). Indemnification clauses are sometimes referred to as "hold harmless" provisions, and often a provision will include language that a party agrees to "hold harmless" the other party. Indemnification and "hold harmless" language generally will have the same effect. *See* BLACK'S LAW DICTIONARY 837-38 (9th ed. 2009). ("A contractual provision in which one party agrees to answer for any specified or unspecified liability or harm that the other party might incur. Also termed *hold-harmless clause*."); *see, e.g., Ellis v. Landings Assocs., Ltd.*, No. 1:04CV120LG-RHW, 2006 WL 568706, at *2 n.2 (S.D. Miss. Mar. 7, 2006).

127. *See* RESTATEMENT (THIRD) OF TORTS § 22 (2000); RESTATEMENT (SECOND) OF TORTS § 886B (1979).

of indemnification provisions and will construe them strictly against the interests of the indemnitee.[128] On the other hand, other states subscribe to the "modern rule" that "contracts of indemnity are to be fairly and reasonably construed in order to ascertain the intention of the parties and to effectuate the purpose sought to be accomplished."[129] Futhermore, an indemnification provision will generally not operate to indemnify an indemnitee against the indemnitee's *own negligence*, unless the language of the provision clearly and specifically provides as much.[130] In addition, an indemnification provision will generally not be enforceable to indemnify an indemnitee against the indemnitee's intentional misconduct.[131] (Note that an indemnification provision that is unenforceable with respect to an indemnitee's intentional misconduct may still be valid with respect to the indemnitee's negligent act.[132])

Making Sense of Indemnity Agreements

One of the most common features of both tort and contract liability rules is that their terms are more diverse than one might expect. In dealing with the tort side of matters, commentators often say that negligence is the general rule. But in the next breath, they recognize that the law also incorporates large pockets of

---

128. *See, e.g., Akhenaten v. Najee, LLC*, No. 07 CV 970(RJH), 2010 WL 305309, at *1 (S.D.N.Y. Jan. 26, 2010) ("[U]nder New York law indemnity contracts are narrowly construed.").

129. *See, e.g., MacGlashin v. Dunlop Equip. Co.*, 89 F.3d 932, 940 (1st Cir. 1996) (internal quotation marks and citation omitted) ("The rule that indemnity contracts are to be strictly construed against the indemnitee no longer obtains in Massachusetts.").

130. *See United States v. Seckinger*, 397 U.S. 203, 211 (1970) ("[A] contractual provision should not be construed to permit an indemnitee to recover for his own negligence unless the court is firmly convinced that such an interpretation reflects the intention of the parties. This principle, though variously articulated, is accepted with virtual unanimity among American jurisdictions.").

131. *See, e.g., Town of Massena v. Healthcare Underwriters Mut. Ins. Co.*, 779 N.E.2d 167, 171 (N.Y. 2002) ("As a matter of policy, conduct engaged in with the intent to cause injury is not covered by insurance."). *But see Dixon Distrib. Co. v. Hanover Ins. Co.*, 641 N.E.2d 395, 401 (Ill. 1994) ("[W]e recognize that it is generally held that a contract of insurance to indemnify a person for damages resulting from his own intentional misconduct is void as against public policy and courts will not enforce such a contract. [However, no] Illinois case, statute or legislative directive specifically hold[s] that providing insurance coverage against liability for injuries resulting from intentional acts is void as against the public policy of Illinois. . . . ") (internal citations omitted). In addition, some states will not enforce an indemnification provision with regard to an indemnitee's act of "gross negligence." *Compare Caldwell v. Enyeart*, 72 F.3d 129, at *4 (6th Cir. 1995) ("[W]e conclude that under Michigan law a contract to indemnify a party for liability for its own gross negligence violates public policy."), *with St. Paul Fire and Marine Ins. Co. v. Universal Builders Supply*, 409 F.3d 73, 86 (2d Cir. 2005) ("[Indemnity agreements are not contrary to public policy unless they purport to indemnify a party for damages flowing from an injury that was intentional. The New York Court of Appeals has held that a party may obtain insurance as protection against its own gross negligence.") (internal citations omitted). Also to keep in mind, there may be various federal and state statutes that intersect with and alter the effect of these general rules with regard to certain types of indemnification provisions. *See, e.g., O & G Indus., Inc. v. Nat'l R.R. Passenger Corp.*, 537 F.3d 153, 156-63 (2d Cir. 2008) (explaining how a federal statute preempted a Connecticut state statute, which "prohibit[ed], on public policy grounds, indemnity agreements entered into in connection with construction contracts, if they purport[ed] to shield the indemnitee from liability for its own negligence").

132. *See, e.g., Caldwell*, 72 F.3d at *4 ("Further, an indemnity provision which would be invalid if applied to indemnify a person from liability for his wilful [sic] and wanton wrongdoing may, nevertheless, be validly applied to indemnify him from liability for his negligent act.").

strict liability. Take another deep breath, and lo and behold, tort liability in many cases turns on gross negligence or willful neglect. One skeptical view of the tort scene is that the judges or the lawyers, or both, are seeking to juggle too many balls in the air, only to drop them all. But a closer look at the field often suggests that each of these various standards has a peculiar home in which its use makes more sense than any of its rivals.

Linking the different theories of liability to different contexts is what makes for a good lawyer. Here is one partial approximation of how this works on the tort side. Strict liability tends to be the operative norm for harms inflicted against the real property of other individuals, who can scarcely be expected to get out of the way. Negligence, often based on customary care, tends to be the standard of liability in medical malpractice cases, because throwing the risk of adverse events on the physician in difficult cases is too extensive relative to any reasonable fee that could be charged. Recklessness tends to be the standard with athletic injuries because athletes, both professional and amateur, old and young, are all negligent all the time, and the prospect of lawsuits would overwhelm the cooperative venture.

Now note the next move. Of the cases mentioned, only the first is a true tort case. The other two arise out of incompletely defined cooperative arrangements. The variation in their terms reflects the different social setting in which the obligations may be imposed. The object in all cases is to give some protection against misconduct of the other party, without driving them away from the deal altogether. Both sides face the same constraint.

Looking at this complex service arrangement between AOL and Time Warner shows how these same instincts carry over when the requirements of business make deals more formal than they would otherwise be. Some judges look with suspicion on indemnity agreements, thinking that they represent an effort of either, or both, parties to duck out of serious obligations. But the story does not really hold. Just who is exploiting whom when the obligations are so reciprocal?

Most of these agreements contain mutual covenants between parties whose positions are similar in some respect and different in others. That point is clear with this agreement when the general principle of mutual indemnification does not carry over to IP and Customer Site and Customer Domain Agreements. Looking at this agreement, the first task of the outsider is to figure out why, which is not easily done unless one knows the services that each supplies the other. In this case, the indemnity clause arose in the context of a somewhat unusual transaction, the break-up of the highly public but ill-fated merger of Time Warner and AOL. It was a classic case in which the supposed synergies of a content provider and an internet service provider did not pan out. At this point, the indemnity is an attempt to make the separation work cleanly, so that AOL has to defend Time Warner on its home turf of IP rights, while Time Warner has to do the same for AOL on its home turf involving distribution matters. It is hard for anyone to think that either party can exploit the other in the first cause, given its reciprocal nature. And once the asymmetrical positions are identified with respect to IP issues, it is easier to understand why these clauses may require each side to protect the other against its own greatest vulnerabilities.

Yet the story is not finished. It doesn't do quite enough in contract contexts to just identify the covered events. The standards of liability have to be established as well. What is notable about these agreements is how parasitic they are in key particulars on many features of the basic contract law. The agreement talks about mutual indemnification in cases of "material breach," which comes straight out of hornbook contract law. The point seems to be that we do not want to invoke the costly machinery of contract to small breaches that tend to cancel each other out anyway, as part of a "live-and-let-live regime."

Next the tort obligations run pretty deep, and they too reflect the full range of liability standards encountered on the tort side of the line. If those distinctions matter in the one context, they surely must matter in the other. Let negligence or misconduct be used in connection with the primary breach, and we know that liability is a likely prospect in at least some cases, given the volume of anticipated business. But when the indemnity is limited, as in § 10.4, to actions of negligence, recklessness or intentional misconduct, the standards of care are obviously not symmetrical. To pretend that there are no differences is to mock the agreement. So one has to figure out how this deal is organized. In this regard, it is instructive to note that this agreement parallels the common pattern in liability found in the workers' compensation area, where the strict obligation of the employer is met by a duty on the worker only to avoid willful misconduct. Knowing why is key: here is one hint. In the compensation area a worker is subject to bodily risk and the employer is not. Where would you put most of the legal pressure?

And finally, one way to think about all contractual provisions is as a decision tree. At each point in the life of the contract, a party has to know not only the standard of liability but also the consequences in dollar terms of breach. Why? Well if you can't quantify the liability, how do you know whether the future revenue stream will cover the anticipated losses. So it is again common practice to draft provisions that cap liability, just as in ordinary insurance contracts. This contract has a provision of that sort tied to the total consideration paid between the companies, except in cases of gross negligence or willful breach. Once again, ask why this configuration, and reflect that this dual track damage system is nothing novel. It was in fact part of the Roman law of sale, which limited liability to "direct losses" (e.g., the destruction of a thing) for ordinary breaches, but allowed recovery for "consequential losses" (e.g., lost business opportunities) in the event of willful breach.

In the end, therefore, success in both drafting and interpreting contracts requires a high level of respect for both profession and craft. Unless you know the legal tradition in which you work, you cannot piece together the building blocks needed to assemble your overall agreement. Yet once you know these, you have to be attentive to the needs of the business to determine their proper pattern in an individual case. When drafting agreements, your job is first to get the right distribution of liabilities and benefits, and then to determine the pricing terms that makes the deal go. In litigation, knowing how those business elements work

> gives you a leg up in understanding and resolving, hopefully short of litigation, the relevant disputes. There is no room for cynicism in working with, and through, the language of the law.
>
> Professor Richard A. Epstein
> Laurence A. Tisch Professor of Law
> New York University School of Law
> Peter and Kirsten Bedford Senior Fellow
> The Hoover Institution
> Senior Lecturer in Law
> The University of Chicago Law School

Sections 10.1 and 10.2 of the AOL Agreement both provide indemnity obligations. As you may have guessed from its caption, § 10.1 specifies indemnification obligations that, on their face, are equally applicable to both Parties. Specifically, § 10.1 provides that should a Third Party bring an action against a Party resulting from the other Party's material breach of this Agreement, then the breaching Party will indemnify the non-breaching party for Losses resulting from that Action. From either Party's perspective, does this indemnification obligation seem fair? Does it seem sufficient—should Losses from Actions based on *non*-material breaches be included, again from the perspective of either party?

Section 10.1 also provides an indemnity for Losses resulting from an Action brought by a Third Party for the Indemnifying Party's (or its various agents') negligence, misconduct, or violation of law in connection with performing this Agreement that caused injury to natural persons (that is, not to business entities) or damages to tangible property. Is this too broad? Is it too narrow? Why should the indemnification be limited to misconduct only related to the performance of this Agreement? What if a Third Party brings suit against a Party for the other Party's illegal act wholly unrelated to this Agreement?

Section 10.2 imposes an indemnification obligation on only AOL for intellectual property infringement and on only Time Warner for various claims relating to Time Warner's Customer Site. If a Third Party brings a claim against a TW Company because AOL's Service infringes that Third Party's intellectual property rights, what are AOL's obligations and rights under this provision? As we briefly discussed in the context of warranties, a party may sometimes give a warranty of non-infringement, and, as we see now, alternatively, a party may promise to indemnify for third-party infringement. Some view the demand for one over the other in practice to turn on a distinction without a difference and to depend mostly on which is listed on the attorney's standard negotiation "checklist." For deeper insight into how practitioners approach and think about this issue, we turned to a couple seasoned practitioners for their perspective.

A Practitioner Perspective: Warranty vs. Indemnity for IP Infringement

In the context of a service engagement in which the service provider will potentially (i) utilize pre-existing intellectual property ("IP") owned by the provider, the client and/or a third party, (ii) develop new IP, and (iii) include some combination of such pre-existing and newly-developed IP in its deliverables (via grants of ownership or license rights), it is standard practice for the client to negotiate some degree of protection against claims that such activity constitutes IP infringement. Once the general scope of such protection has been defined (e.g., infringement of registered domestic IP rights) and any exceptions thereto have been excluded (e.g., items provided by, on behalf of, or per the specifications of the client; improper usage/modification/combination), the outcome of such negotiation must be documented in a contractual mechanism. Such mechanism typically takes the form of a warranty and/or an indemnity.

There are several key distinctions between the warranty approach and the indemnity approach. Under the indemnity approach, the service provider typically agrees (within the agreed-upon scope and subject to the agreed-upon exceptions) to defend and/or make whole the client if the client faces an infringement claim. In other words, the client seeks protection by causing the service provider to perform an express contractual obligation. Under the warranty approach, the service provider typically warrants (and represents) that there will not be an infringement problem (within the agreed-upon scope and subject to the agreed-upon exceptions). In other words, the client seeks protection by claiming that the service provider committed a breach resulting in a loss. Therefore, at the outset, the warranty approach (i.e., establishing a breach and a related loss) may confront the client with a more difficult burden than the indemnity approach (i.e., demanding performance).

An indemnity-without-warranty approach can offer certain advantages for the service provider (i.e., the indemnitor). For example, it is typical for an obligation to indemnify to be subject to various procedural preconditions (e.g., the indemnitee must provide prompt notice of a claim for which it seeks indemnification; the indemnitee must surrender control of the defense/settlement thereof; the indemnitee must cooperate in such defense) which can often serve to limit or even effectively eliminate the service provider's exposure, whereas it is not typical to see procedural terms (other than a time limit) barring warranty claims. In addition, although a limitation of liability provision (e.g., a cap on aggregate liability; an exclusion of non-direct damages) or an exclusive remedy provision (e.g., reimbursement of losses; rectification of, replacement of, or license to infringing items; refund of amounts paid for infringing items) is always subject to the risk of being held invalid or unenforceable by a court, such a provision might be even more likely to be held invalid or unenforceable if the party seeking to enforce it committed a breach or otherwise has unclean hands. In other words, such a provision might be more likely to be enforceable under the compliance-with-indemnity approach than under the breach-of-warranty approach. However, despite these apparent benefits of the indemnity approach to the service provider, an inadvertently-overbroad indemnity provision might entitle an indemnitee to recover a loss that might not otherwise be recoverable per a warranty claim (e.g., a loss to which the indemnitee contributed).

Although the client may face a more difficult burden seeking a remedy through a prove-a-warranty-breach mechanism than through an enforce-an-indemnity mechanism, the warranty approach can also offer certain advantages for the client. A demonstration of the client's reliance upon a breached non-infringement warranty may not only form the basis for the client's claims for damages arising from the breach—such reliance may also form the basis for claims regarding the formation of the service contract (e.g., fraud). In addition, a demonstration of the client's reliance upon a non-infringement warranty may assist the client in establishing a defense against an infringement claim by a third party.

For these reasons, the client certainly has reasonable justification for seeking a non-infringement warranty in addition to an infringement indemnity. Conversely, if forced to provide protection against infringement, the service provider will typically prefer to provide a tailored and procedurally-conditioned indemnity without a warranty and subject to a limitation of liability provision and an exclusive remedy provision. A common compromise is a linked warranty-and-indemnity in which the service provider provides a non-infringement warranty and, as an exclusive remedy for breach of such warranty, a limited indemnity for damages arising from such breach. In such a situation, the extent to which the compromise actually holds will depend upon the contract drafting, the factual circumstances and the application of the governing law.

Alan A. D'Ambrosio
Partner
Orrick, Herrington & Sutcliffe LLP

Steven Barnett
Senior Associate
Orrick, Herrington & Sutcliffe LLP

What §§ 10.1 and 10.2 giveth, § 10.4 taketh away. Section 10.4 specifically limits the extent of all indemnification obligations provided by the Agreement, providing that a Party's (i.e., the indemnitor's) indemnification obligations are to be reduced to the extent of the other Party's (i.e., the indemnitee's) negligence, recklessness, or intentional misconduct (which, you will notice, is in line with the judicial presumption that an indemnification provision does not operate to indemnify a party for its own negligence). That is, if the indemnitee has contributed to the indemnitor's would-be indemnification obligation (with conduct that is at least negligent), the indemnitor need not indemnify the indemnitee for the amount attributable to this contribution. Does and/or should (and/or could) the Agreement provide clarity as to how this would be measured? Also, notice with this provision that captions do not always capture a provision's entire contents (a lesson for the contract reader, but the lesson for the contract drafter is that captions probably should), as § 10.4 ("Limitation of Indemnity"), in addition to limiting indemnification, also *provides* additional indemnification obligations. As we will soon see, one risks subjecting the scope of a provision to a narrow reading, when one lumps such a provision with other provisions in a section that speaks to a more specific matter.

A Practitioner Perspective: Indemnification Issues in Practice

In contract negotiations, one party frequently seeks to be indemnified against any liabilities and costs that it might incur by virtue of the contractual relationship. The scope of an indemnification provision will thus become a subject of negotiation. At a minimum, any indemnification should be limited to liabilities and costs arising out of the misconduct or negligence of the indemnifying party. Moreover, it should be made reciprocal. In other words, if X is required to indemnify Y against specified developments, Y should be asked to indemnify X against eventualities about which X is concerned. These may, but need not, be the same as those covered by X's indemnifications.

Beyond seeking to minimize the scope of an indemnification and making it reciprocal, it is good practice to avoid giving an indemnification at all. There are two reasons. First, any liability undertaken through an indemnification clause will generally not be covered by the indemnitor's insurance. Thus, if a condition triggering the indemnification arises, the liabilities and costs associated therewith will be the responsibility of the indemnitor—not its insurer. This result can, of course, be devastating if the indemnitor is required to make good on the indemnification.

The risks that an insurance company undertakes are generally limited to negligent and other not-intentionally tortious conduct by the insured. By contrast, indemnification clauses create risks voluntarily undertaken by contract. Underwriters do not factor in such risks in setting premiums. Thus, it is far preferable, if possible, to get the insurance company to add the would-be indemnified party as a named insured to the proposed indemnifier's insurance policy. In this way, the insurer can set premiums based on its valuation of the risk. If the contractual party is added as a named insured, the risk will be on the insurer—not on the contracting party.

The second risk in indemnification clauses is more subtle. Let's say that each party to a contract indemnifies the other against its negligence. Let's say further that something happens that causes injury to a third party. It is foreseeable that each party will take the position that the bad development was the result of the other's negligence—and will seek to be indemnified by the other. The consequence will be a finger-pointing contest that will redound to the benefit of the third party.

The situation can be illustrated by a contract between a hospital and a group of pathologists for the operation of the laboratory at the hospital. Suppose the hospital indemnifies the pathologists against its negligence while the pathology group indemnifies the hospital against its negligence. Now, let's say that a patient suffers an injury allegedly as a result of a laboratory error. There may be a real question as to whether there was any negligence at all. However, if the hospital and the pathology group seek indemnification from the other based on an indemnification against the negligence of the other, they will be rewarded with a huge judgment against each of them.

One final note on indemnification. An indemnification is only as good as the capitalization of the indemnitor. If the indemnitor does not have sufficient assets to cover the indemnification, the indemnified party has bought nothing more than a scrap of paper.

Jack Bierig
Partner
Sidley Austin LLP
Lecturer in Law
The University of Chicago Law School

A classic example of an indemnity agreement is an insurance agreement, as insurance is at its core nothing more than a promise by one party (i.e., the insurer) to pay for the losses of another (i.e., the insured). Contractual parties may sometimes wish to shift the risk of certain losses to a third-party insurer and to obtain an insurance policy to cover this risk. Of course, this insurance is unlikely to come free, and the parties will still have to negotiate about which party (or whether both parties) will pay the cost of this insurance. The viability of third-party insurance as a solution often depends on the specific context, including the type of risk for which insurance is to be obtained, the availability of willing third-party insurers, the type of coverage available, and the cost of obtaining the insurance. On this issue, a seasoned practitioner offers additional insight.

A Practitioner Perspective: Insurance Euphoria

Parties to a contract may feel themselves protected by insurance that they have purchased. However, their sense of security may not be fully justified. This is so for several reasons.

First, insurance policies inevitably contain exclusions. It often happens that an insured party is sued, tenders the claim to the insurer, but finds, to its dismay, that the cause of action asserted against it is excluded by some obscure subparagraph of a multi-page policy. Similarly, sometimes a policy will provide coverage for attorneys' fees but not damages. For these reasons, the exclusions from, and limitations of, any policy need to be clearly understood. It can be disconcerting when the insurer denies coverage—or even when it provides coverage "subject to a reservation of rights."

Second, the insured must be careful to abide by all the conditions of coverage. For example, most policies require prompt reporting of any claim. If the insured does not timely notify the insurer of a threat of litigation, the insured may be deemed to have waived the coverage. In a similar vein, policies generally exclude disputes that existed before the insurance was purchased. If a known dispute was not disclosed in the application form but later ripens into litigation, the company is likely to deny coverage.

Third, almost all policies impose a so-called "retention" or "deductible" threshold. The policyholder must pay all fees and damages until the retention amount is reached. In some policies, the amount can be quite high. It is important to know the retention amount.

Fourth, many policies permit the insurer to designate counsel. This feature can cause difficulties when the insured wants to use lawyers in whom it has confidence but the insurer chooses to assign counsel on its panel. Panel counsel usually have agreed to accept fees significantly lower than those charged by the insured's regular counsel—and may well not have as much experience or skill as counsel that the insured would select. This problem can sometimes be remedied if the insured agrees to pay the difference between the hourly rate of counsel of its choice and that of the insurer's choice. But this solution may not be acceptable to the insurer and, in any event, can result in significant out-of-pocket costs to the insured.

Given these issues in insurance coverage, a party to a contract may want to cap by agreement any liability that it will have to bear arising out of the agreement.

Jack Bierig
Partner
Sidley Austin LLP
Lecturer in Law
The University of Chicago Law School

b. Limitation of Liability

In addition to disclaiming warranties and seeking indemnification, there are several other ways to limit a party's exposure to liability under a contract. Perhaps the simplest way is to place a cap on the dollar amount of a party's liability exposure—such a ceiling may be defined as a stated dollar amount, tied to the purchase price, or defined however else the parties desire. These are commonly referred to as "limitation-of-liability" provisions. Such a provision is found in § 10.9 ("Maximum Liability") of the AOL Agreement. Section 10.9 provides that, regardless of any other provision of the Agreement, each Party's liability for all matters related to the Agreement is limited to the total amount paid by each TW Company to AOL under the Agreement over the course of the prior 12 months. However, notice that this cap does not apply to liability related to (i) acts of gross negligence and willful misconduct; (ii) breaches of confidentiality obligations; and (iii) the indemnification obligations found in the Agreement. Why do you suppose the parties removed these things from the cap, leaving these categories of potential liability effectively boundless? To what extent do these "carve-outs" from the cap reduce the cap's overall effectiveness? Taking the perspective of either party, would you argue that anything else should be excluded from—or included under—the cap?

Another common way of limiting a party's exposure to liability under an agreement is to exclude certain *types* of liability. For instance, § 10.8 of this Agreement provides that no Party is liable for several different kinds of damages, including punitive, indirect, and consequential damages. Excepted from this exclusion (that is, carved out from the exclusion) are, again, (i) acts of gross negligence and willful misconduct; (ii) breaches of confidentiality obligations; and (iii) the indemnification obligations. The net of this provision, then, is that no Party shall be liable for certain types of liability (e.g., consequential damages), except for liability related to three circumstances (i.e., gross negligence or willful misconduct, confidentiality, and indemnification), where those types of liability—not available in general—are fair game.

In general, limitation-of-liability clauses are enforced in both services and sale-of-goods contracts between sophisticated parties.[133] Courts will strictly construe provisions that limit a party's liability for the party's own negligence but will enforce them.[134] While contracts generally may not completely exempt a party from liability under that contract, they may limit a party's liability exposure.[135] Still, a limitation of liability generally will not be enforced as to a party's own acts of *gross* negligence or willful misconduct, which explains why this is often a limitation-of-liability "carve-out."[136]

A Practitioner Perspective: Limitations-of-Liability "Carve-Outs" for Services

Limitations of liability in service agreements typically include both (1) an exclusion of consequential, incidental, special and punitive damages, and (2) a cap on the amount of direct damages for which the service provider would be liable. The liability cap may be a specified dollar amount or a dollar limit that is tied in some manner to the amount of fees paid by the customer to the service provider.

The rationale behind limitations of liability is that they reflect both the limited control that the service provider has in managing the risks in a customer's enterprise and the limited reward the service provider stands to gain from assuming the risks of managing that enterprise. The service provider's perspective is that it is performing a service at an efficient price, which does not factor in the cost of insuring the customer against broad business risks. The service provider argues that the customer would have had the same risk if its own employees were performing the services, and that the customer is actually in a better position by virtue of the liability that the service provider will assume,

---

133. *See Valhal Corp. v. Sullivan Assocs., Inc.*, 44 F.3d 195, 203-04 (3d Cir. 1995) (Pennsylvania law) (observing that limitation-of-liability clauses are "routinely enforced" in sales contracts between sophisticated parties and in services contracts); *Wartsila NSD N. Am., Inc. v. Hill Int'l, Inc.*, 530 F.3d 269 (3d Cir. 2008) (Maryland law) (excluding consequential damages from the available liability under a contract with a provision explicitly excluding consequential damages). Please see Chapter 4 for further discussion of sale-of-goods contracts.

134. *See, e.g., Anunziatta v. Orkin Exterminating Co.*, 180 F. Supp. 2d 353, 359 (N.D.N.Y. 2001).

135. *See, e.g., Elsken v. Network Multi-Family Sec. Corp.*, 49 F.3d 1470, 1475 (10th Cir. 1995) (Oklahoma law); *Mobile Satellite Commc'ns, Inc. v. Intelsat USA Sales Corp.*, 646 F. Supp. 2d 124, 136 (D.D.C. 2009) (New York law).

136. *See, e.g., Elsken*, 49 F.3d at 1475; *Hill Int'l*, 530 F.3d at 274 (Maryland law) ("[A limitation of liability] clause [is] unenforceable . . . when the party protected by the clause intentionally causes harm or engages in acts of reckless, wanton, or gross negligence. . . ."). Under Article 2 of the U.C.C., a contract may disclaim or limit consequential damages; however, this will not be effective as to damages for injury to a person in the context of consumer goods. U.C.C. § 2-719 (2003).

albeit limited. The customer's perspective is that by handing over control of one of its functions to a service provider, the customer becomes dependent on the service provider to properly manage the risk of its performance. The customer further argues that the allocation of risk is essential to maintaining the proper incentive for the service provider, since the financial structure normally creates an adverse incentive by rewarding the service provider with higher profits when it is able to reduce its costs and investments, which can in turn create risks for the customer.

While limitations of liability (including both exclusions and caps) are a staple of service agreements, customers often seek exceptions to these limitations to cover specific risks to which the customer believes the limitations should not apply. The negotiation of these exceptions can be one of the more difficult issues in contracting for services.

Below is a list of exclusions that may be requested by the customer in certain service arrangements.

Representative Exceptions

The limitations of liability shall not apply to:

1. *Losses occasioned by the fraud, willful misconduct, or gross negligence of a party.*
2. *Losses occasioned by service provider's refusal to provide services (where "refusal" means the intentional cessation by service provider, in a manner impermissible under this Agreement, of the performance of all or a material portion of the services then required to be provided by service provider under this Agreement).*
3. *Losses occasioned by any breach of a party's representations or warranties under this Agreement.*
4. *Losses that are the subject of indemnification under this Agreement, including:*
   (a) *Breach of representations and warranties*
   (b) *Death or bodily injury of an agent, employee, business invitee, business visitor or other person or damage, loss or destruction of real or tangible personal property*
   (c) *Infringement*
   (d) *Compliance with laws*
   (e) *Breach of confidentiality*
   (f) *Taxes*
   (g) *Employment claims*
   (h) *Claims under the Agreement by affiliates and subcontractors*

Analysis and Comment

The selection of the particular exceptions that are appropriate for any service agreement, and the weight of each party's argument in negotiating them, depends heavily on the facts and circumstances of the particular services arrangement. Consider some of the issues that can arise for each of the above exceptions:

1. *Fraud, willful misconduct and gross negligence.* Can a party limit its liability for fraud? If not, then is the exception even necessary, and is conceding it

really much of a concession at all? What does *willful misconduct* mean in the selected jurisdiction? That term is not consistently defined and can have very different meanings under different states' laws. For example, in some states willful misconduct includes efficient breaches (i.e., breaches intended only to prevent further economic loss under the contract), while in other states it does not. What does *gross negligence* mean in the applicable jurisdiction? Like willful misconduct, the term gross negligence is not consistently defined under the various state laws. Since gross negligence is a variant of negligence, should it be a complete exception or should it instead only give rise to a higher cap on liability?

2. *Service provider's refusal to provide services.* This exception should only be applicable where the services involve a critical business function of the customer's business. The customer's purpose for having this exception is to ensure that the service provider never has any economic incentive to abandon performance of the services and is never inclined to threaten suspension of mission-critical services as a means of resolving a dispute. Even when the service involves a mission-critical function, consider whether there are instances where the service provider should or must have the right to withhold services given the potential harm to the service provider's interest. Could the customer's concern about abandonment be addressed by adequate notice to allow a transition of responsibility? Is there a higher limit of liability that would be adequate to assure customer that the service provider has no incentive to abandon the services, but which still protects the service provider from unlimited liability?

3. *Breach of a party's representations or warranties under this Agreement.* The appropriateness of this exception depends entirely on the content of the representations and warranties. The exception may be appropriate for some representations and warranties, such as compliance with laws, but may be inappropriate for others, such as representations and warranties regarding the quality of the services, which could have the effect of nullifying the limitations of liability by excluding performance failures that result from simple negligence.

4. *Losses that are the subject of indemnification.* The same analysis as above should be applied to the indemnities since the indemnities are another form of allocating risk. For example, which warranties should be subject to an indemnity? What qualifications and exceptions should apply to the infringement indemnity? What laws should be service provider's responsibility and which should be customer's responsibility? Are there any exceptions to service provider's liability for disclosure of customer's confidential information? Are there any exceptions for service provider's responsibility for employment related claims by its employees against the customer? Are there any exceptions where the service provider's affiliates and subcontractors should be entitled to make a direct claim against the customer? Consider also whether the indemnity is limited to third-party claims or if it also includes direct claims by the customer. In service

agreements, indemnities are more commonly limited to third-party claims. That is often not the case in other corporate M&A agreements(e.g., stock purchase agreements or asset purchase agreements). Finally, if the service provider has unlimited liability for the indemnities, does the service provider get to control the defense and settlement of the third party claim giving rise to the indemnity?

As noted above, one of the principles of limitations of liability is that the service provider's limited control should result in limited liability. In analyzing undertakings in the contract, consider whether the covenants that can give rise to unlimited liability reflect risks over which the service provider exerts complete control. If not, consider how the covenant can be narrowed to reflect what the service provider can control. For example, a service provider may be able to manage its risk for protecting confidential information by requiring that the customer specify the security protocol that each party must follow with regard to any confidential information supplied to the service provider, with the understanding that service provider's compliance with the protocol will serve as a safe harbor protection, even if unauthorized access was obtained despite its compliance. A similar approach may apply to a compliance with laws covenant.

What makes limitations of liability a difficult issue is that it lends itself both to arguments of fairness and accountability (i.e., "Why shouldn't you (service provider) be responsible for the damages you cause?") and arguments of commercial reasonableness (i.e., "I (service provider) am not your insurance company. I am just an efficient provider who doesn't share in the profits of your company."). Finding the allocation of risk that properly reflects the balance of control, responsibility and reward is a critical component of any transaction. It can also affect the sustainability of the service provider's business model and the willingness of customers to enter into service arrangement for sensitive or critical services. As you consider these issues, bear in mind that there is no simple answer to any of these questions, since they are deal-specific and can vary depending on the subject matter of the contract, the relative position of the parties, industry norms, applicable laws and the general business environment.

Paul Roy
Partner
Mayer Brown LLP

(1) Understanding "Consequential" Damages

As in § 10.8 of the AOL Agreement, services agreements will commonly exclude consequential, special, incidental, punitive, and indirect damages from the potential liability to which one or both (or, more, in the case of a multi-party agreement) parties may be exposed under an agreement. As we explore the distinction between these damages terms, take heart in that even seasoned practitioners may have a hard time explaining the distinction between consequential and general damages as well as the distinction between consequential and special, incidental, punitive, and indirect damages.

(a) Distinguishing General and Consequential Damages

"General" (or "direct") damages refer to those damages that result naturally from a breach of a contract.[137] Such damages act to give the non-breaching party the party's expected value of the contract, as if it were fully performed as contractually provided. That is, a breach occurs when a party does not fully perform in accordance with the contract. This departure from full performance results in the non-breaching party receiving less than that which the non-breaching party expected to receive as bargained-for consideration under the contract. Accordingly, general contract damages are generally in the amount of this "benefit of the bargain" or "expectation" interest—to compensate the plaintiff for that which she "should" have received under the contract.[138]

In contrast, consequential damages are those damages, beyond general damages, that proximately result as a consequence of a breach of contract.[139] As a general rule of thumb, while general damages are likely to be suffered by any person in the position of the non-breaching party, consequential damages are often peculiar to an individual non-breaching party.[140] To recover consequential damages, a party generally must show that the breach caused the consequential damages and that such damages were foreseeable at the time the parties entered into the contract.[141] In other words, consequential damages are not the same thing as remote or unforeseeable damages. But, whereas consequential damages turn on the occurrence of various events that may *result* from breach, general damages turn on the value of the contract itself, namely the value of the contract unrealized by the non-breaching party due to the other party's breach.[142]

---

137. *See Hill Int'l*, 530 F.3d at 277 ("[D]amages which a plaintiff may recover for breach of contract include both those which may fairly and reasonably be considered as arising naturally from the breach (general damages).") (internal citation and quotation marks omitted); *TransDulles Ctr., Inc. v. USX Corp.*, 976 F.2d 219, 226 (4th Cir. 1992) (Virginia law) ("Direct damages are those which arise naturally or ordinarily from a breach of contract and which, in the ordinary course of human experience, can be expected to result from the breach.").

138. *See New Valley Corp. v. United States*, 72 Fed. Cl. 411, 414 (2006) ("'[G]eneral damages' are damages measured by the loss of the value of the performance promised by the breaching party."); *see also* RESTATEMENT (SECOND) OF CONTRACTS § 347(a) (1981).

139. *See New Valley Corp.*, 72 Fed. Cl. at 414 ("Consequential damages . . . on the other hand, are those damages that result as a secondary consequence of the defendant's non-performance [and that] arise from the interposition of an additional cause, without which the act done would have produced no harmful result.") (internal citation and quotation marks omitted); *Hill Int'l*, 530 F.3d at 277 ("[D]amages which a plaintiff may recover for breach of contract include . . . those which may reasonably be supposed to have been in the contemplation of both parties at the time of making of the contract (special damages)."); *see also* RESTATEMENT (SECOND) OF CONTRACTS § 347 cmt. c (1981); U.C.C. § 2-715(2) (2003).

140. *See Hill Int'l*, 530 F.3d at 277.

141. *See id.*

142. *See, e.g., New Valley Corp.*, 72 Fed. Cl. at 414 ("Consequential damages are thus distinguishable from general damages in that rather than being based on the value of the promised performance itself, they are based on the value of some consequence that that performance may produce.").

Notice that § 10.8 of the AOL Agreement lists "lost profits" as one of the many things for which no party shall be liable. Are lost profits general or consequential damages? The answer is that they can be both. A party may expect to earn a certain profit *under* a contract: For example, if A expected to pay B 10 dollars for a 20-dollar widget, then A expected to earn a 10-dollar profit under the contract. If B fails to sell the widget to A and if A has not yet paid B, then A's general damages are its lost profits of 10 dollars. By contrast, if A planned to use the widgets to make super widgets and, because of B's failure to perform, A claims it missed an opportunity to make a $10,000 profit from selling super widgets, then A may seek to recover such lost profits from B as consequential damages. Accordingly, lost profits may be a loss in the value of the contract as general damages, and lost profits may be a loss resulting from a breach as consequential damages. Some courts have found that, where a contract excludes "lost profits" from liability, as does § 10.8, such a provision refers only to consequential lost profits and "precludes recovery of only those lost profits and lost revenues beyond direct economic loss or ordinary loss of bargain damages."[143]

(b) Distinguishing Consequential and the Litany

As for the other oft-recited types of damages, "special" and "consequential" damages are synonymous.[144] The term "indirect" damages may be used interchangeably with "consequential"[145] or to mean, more broadly, all damages that are not direct damages (e.g., "incidental" damages are not direct damages).[146] Punitive damages refer to damages that seek to punish—that is, to do more than compensate—the breaching party.[147] A fundamental policy of contract law is the principle of "just compensation," which states that contract law's object is to compensate and not to punish.[148] Accordingly, punitive damages are generally

---

143. *Penncro Assocs., Inc. v. Sprint Corp.*, No. 04-2549-JWL, 2006 WL 416227, at *8 (D. Kan. Feb. 22, 2006) ("The court's conclusion is consistent with other courts that have analyzed similar limitation of damages provisions.") (citing cases decided under California, New York, and Pennsylvania laws). The provision in *Penncro* differed from the provision in § 10.8 of the Agreement in that the *Penncro* provision excluded consequential damages and provided that "lost profits" and "lost revenues" were included in the meaning of consequential damages. However, the court in *Penncro* went on to explain that a reading of the provision that excluded damages for both direct and indirect lost profits and revenues would leave a service provider with no recourse in damages if a buyer refused to pay for services rendered and that such "construction is not reasonable." *Id.*

144. *See, e.g., Hill Int'l*, 530 F.3d at 277 n.6 ("The terms 'special damages' and 'consequential damages' usually are viewed as synonymous.").

145. *See, e.g., Cooper v. Meridian Yachts, Ltd.*, 575 F.3d 1151, 1167 (11th Cir. 2009) (using "consequential" and "indirect" interchangeably); *Washington & O.D. Ry. v. Westinghouse Elec. & Mfg. Co.*, 91 S.E. 646 (Va. 1917) (using "consequential" and "indirect" interchangeably).

146. *Compare Wayne Mem'l Hosp., Inc. Wayne Health Corp. v. Elec. Data Sys. Corp.*, No. 87-905-CIV-5-H, 1990 WL 606686, at *9 n.5 (E.D.N.C. Apr. 10, 1990) ("[I]ncidental damages are not direct but rather indirect damages."), *with Mitsui O.S.K. Lines, Ltd. v. Consol. Rail Corp.*, 743 A.2d 362 (N.J. Super. Ct. App. Div. 2000) (finding "consequential, special, or indirect damages" not to include incidental damages).

147. *See* Restatement (Second) of Contracts § 355 cmt. a (1981).

148. *See id.; see also* Charles J. Goetz & Robert E. Scott, *Liquidated Damages, Penalties and the Just Compensation Principle: Some Notes on an Enforcement Model and a Theory of Efficient Breach*, 77 Colum. L. Rev. 554 (1977).

not available for a pure breach-of-contract claim.[149] However, because punitive damages may be recovered for tortious conduct,[150] liability-exclusion provisions will still commonly disclaim punitive damages. With certain exceptions, these punitive-damages exclusions have generally been enforced.[151] Finally, incidental damages are distinct from consequential damages. Incidental damages refer to the expenses reasonably incurred by a non-breaching party in rejecting goods or in attempting to find replacement performance to substitute for the breaching party's less-than-full performance.[152]

(2) The Economic Loss Doctrine, Actions in Tort, and Limitation of Liability

In general, courts limit the availability of recovery in tort actions by a doctrine called the "economic loss doctrine." As the First Circuit explains, "Like 'duty' and 'proximate clause,' the doctrine cabins what could otherwise be open-ended negligence liability to anyone affected by a negligent act."[153] The economic loss doctrine provides that economic losses are not recoverable in a tort action, unless the action is for personal injury or property damage.[154] Under the doctrine, "property damage" does not include mere injury to a property interest but requires some physical damage to property.[155] Some courts have held that the economic loss doctrine only pertains to contracts for the sale of goods under Article 2 of the U.C.C. and not to services contracts.[156]

So what does a doctrine of tort law have to do with contracts? To avoid a contractual limitation of liability, a plaintiff may seek to frame her claim as an action in tort. However, even if the plaintiff has a bona fide tort claim, the economic loss doctrine operates to limit the efficacy of bringing such a claim.

---

149. *See* RESTATEMENT (SECOND) OF CONTRACTS § 355 (1981) ("Punitive damages are not recoverable for a breach of contract unless the conduct constituting the breach is also a tort for which punitive damages are recoverable."); *Pilot Life Ins. Co. v. Dedeaux*, 481 U.S. 41, 49 (1987) ("[T]he Mississippi Supreme Court explained that punitive damages could be available when the breach of contract was attended by some intentional wrong, insult, abuse, or gross negligence, which amounts to an independent tort.") (citation and internal quotation marks omitted).

150. *See supra* note 149.

151. *See, e.g., Sanderson Farms, Inc. v. Gatlin*, 848 So. 2d 828, 854 (Miss. 2003) ("I am not willing to interpret our Legislature as having established a public policy, favoring punitive damages, of such force as to negate private parties' efforts to mutually waive the opportunity to seek such damages from each other."); *Baravati v. Josephthal, Lyon & Ross, Inc.*, 28 F.3d 704, 709 (7th Cir. 1994) ("For that matter, parties to adjudication have considerable power to vary the normal procedures, and surely can stipulate that punitive damages will not be awarded.") (internal citations omitted). However, note that at least one court has refused to enforce a contractual provision excluding punitive damages as against public policy. *See Ex parte Thicklin*, 824 So. 2d 723 (Ala. 2002), *overruled on other grounds*, *Patriot Mfg., Inc. v. Jackson*, 929 So. 2d 997 (Ala. 2005).

152. *See* RESTATEMENT (SECOND) OF CONTRACTS § 347 cmt. c (1981); U.C.C. § 2-715(1) (2003).

153. *In re TJX Cos. Retail Sec. Breach Litig.*, 564 F.3d 489, 498 (1st Cir. 2009).

154. *See TJX Cos.*, 564 F.3d at 498; *Irwin Seating Co. v. Int'l Bus. Machs. Corp.*, 306 F. App'x 239, 242-44 (6th Cir. 2009).

155. *See TJX Cos.*, 564 F.3d at 498.

156. *See, e.g., Ins. Co. of N. Am. v. Cease Elec. Inc.*, 688 N.W.2d 462, 467-68 (Wis. 2004) (recognizing a split among jurisdictions as to whether the economic loss doctrine applies to services contracts and declining to extend the doctrine to apply to non-U.C.C. contracts).

This is because, under the doctrine, an action purely for economic loss (i.e., not involving physical harm to property or person) cannot be stated in tort. This may apply, for example, to the tort of misrepresentation discussed earlier in this chapter.[157]

In addition, most courts will not allow a party to "dress" a contract claim as a tort claim by "artful pleading."[158] This doctrine attempts to police the line between tort and contract.[159] "Tort actions lie for breaches of duties imposed by law as a matter of social policy, while contract actions lie only for breaches of duties imposed by mutual consensus agreements between particular individuals."[160] Accordingly, even if the economic loss doctrine does not apply, a court is likely to preclude a claim that arises out of a duty provided by contract—or that is otherwise not independent of a contract claim—from being brought in tort.[161]

Moreover, contracts between sophisticated parties will often explicitly provide that limitation-of-liability provisions cover all actions whether stated in contract or tort. For an example, see § 10.8 of the AOL Agreement, which disclaims liability for, among other things, consequential damages "whether under theory of contract, tort (including negligence), strict liability or otherwise." In addition, § 10.9 of the AOL Agreement, in broad language, applies a liability cap to "each party's maximum aggregate liability for all matters related to, in connection with, or arising out of, this agreement." In general, courts will respect these provisions and will give effect to a limitation-of-liability provision between sophisticated parties, regardless of whether the action is pled in contract or tort.[162] However, again, these provisions will generally not insulate a party from liability for gross negligence or willful misconduct.[163]

(3) Exclusive Remedies and Failure of Essential Purpose

In addition to disclaiming warranties and otherwise limiting liability, an agreement may provide that only certain remedies are available as the *exclusive*

---

157. *See, e.g., Irwin Seating Co.*, 306 F. App'x at 242-44.

158. *See, e.g., Clark Motor Co. v. Mfrs. and Traders Trust Co.*, 360 F. App'x 340, 347 (3d Cir. 2010) (Pennsylvania law); *Spengler v. ADT Sec. Servs., Inc.*, 505 F.3d 456, 457-58 (6th Cir. 2007) (Michigan law); *Lewis v. Methodist Hosp., Inc.*, 326 F.3d 851, 854 (7th Cir. 2003) (Indiana law) ("[W]here a contract contains a limiting or qualifying provision, that provision may not be avoided by casting a suit for breach of the contract as a tort."); *Carolina Cas. Ins. Co. v. Sowell*, 603 F. Supp. 2d 914, 927-28 (N.D. Tex. 2009); *Great Earth Int'l Franchising Corp. v. Milks Dev.*, 311 F. Supp. 2d 419, 428 (S.D.N.Y. 2004) ("[T]he basic rule is that a tort claim cannot be a reiteration of a breach of contract claim.").

159. *See, e.g., Clark Motor Co.*, 360 F. App'x at 347.

160. *Id.* (quoting *Bash v. Bell Tel. Co.*, 601 A.2d 825, 829 (Pa. Super. Ct. 1992)).

161. *See, e.g., id.* (finding that a duty to ensure the accuracy of information arose from the implied duty of good faith between contractual parties and, so, that a claim for breach of this duty must be brought in contract and not tort).

162. *See, e.g., Youtie v. Macy's Retail Holding, Inc.*, 653 F. Supp. 2d 612, 630 (E.D. Pa. 2009) ("Both Missouri and Pennsylvania law enforce limitation of liability clauses between sophisticated parties to the extent that they are reasonable . . . , regardless of whether the damages are pled in contract or in tort.").

163. *See, e.g., id.; Doty Commc'ns, Inc. v. L.M. Berry & Co.*, 417 F. Supp. 2d 1355, 1358-59 (N.D. Ga. 2006); *Sommer v. Fed. Signal Corp.*, 79 N.Y.2d 540, 554 (1992).

remedies for certain breaches of the contract. In general, courts will give effect to these exclusivity provisions.[164] A classic example is where an agreement provides that the exclusive remedy for breach of warranty is for the seller either to repair or to replace a defective deliverable or good.[165]

However, at least as to contracts governed by Article 2, where exclusively available remedies fail of their essential purpose, then the limitation restricting the buyer to only those remedies will not be enforced.[166] As an illustration, if the seller fails to act in accordance with a repair-or-replace exclusive-remedy provision (i.e., does not repair or replace a good in a timely or sufficient manner), then a court may make other remedies available to the buyer, under the doctrine of failure of essential purpose.[167] While courts have explained that this doctrine is only applicable in the sale-of-goods context,[168] and, so, does not apply specifically to services contracts, the doctrine is still relevant to our concerns in this chapter. As we discuss in greater length in Chapter 4, contracts are often for both goods and services. For instance, many a "services" contract will be for the provision of services that are to result in a "deliverable" product. A question then arises as to whether such a "mixed" contract is governed by Article 2 of the U.C.C., as a sale-of-goods contract, or by the common law, as a services contract. Accordingly, the parties to a "services contract" may wish to plan for the possibility that a court may ultimately find the contract to be governed by Article 2.

For instance, as discussed in this chapter's earlier presentation of disclaimer of warranty, Article 2 imputes certain implied warranties into contracts, unless the contract specifically disclaims such. Given that a court may characterize an agreement as a sale-of-goods contract, a seller of services may wish to disclaim Article 2 implied warranties so as to avoid their potential application. Likewise, the doctrine of failure of essential purpose might ultimately apply to a contract ostensibly for services. In addition, while some courts have explicitly explained

---

164. *See, e.g., Citadel Grp. Ltd. v. Wash. Reg'l Med. Ctr.*, No. 07-CV-1394, 2009 WL 1329217, at *8 (N.D. Ill. May 13, 2009) (Illinois law) ("Under Illinois law, parties by an express agreement may contract for an exclusive remedy that limits their rights, duties, and obligations.") (citation and internal quotation marks omitted); *Carll v. Terminix Int'l Co., L.P.*, 793 A.2d 921, 924 (Pa. Super. Ct. 2002) ("Thus, under Pennsylvania law in a commercial setting a contractual provision limiting warranties, establishing repair or replacement as the exclusive remedy and excluding liability for special, indirect and consequential damages is generally valid and enforceable."); *see also* U.C.C. § 2-719(1)(b) (2003).

165. *See, e.g., Miss. Chem. Corp. v. Dresser-Rand Co.*, 287 F.3d 359, 366 (5th Cir. 2002) (Mississippi law); *Sunny Indus., Inc. v. Rockwell Int'l Corp.*, 175 F.3d 1021, at *9-10 (7th Cir. 1999) (Illinois law).

166. *See, e.g., Sunny Indus., Inc.*, 175 F.3d 1021, at *9-10.

167. *See, e.g., id.*

168. *See, e.g., Darby Anesthesia Assocs., Inc. v. Anesthesia Bus. Consultants, LLC*, No. 06-1565, 2008 WL 2845587, at *5 (E.D. Pa. July 23, 2008) ("Plaintiff's reliance on the failure-of-the-essential-purpose doctrine is misplaced because the doctrine is grounded in the Uniform Commercial Code (UCC) and its associated case law and thus, applicable only to contracts for the sale of goods."); *Plymouth Pointe Condo. Ass'n v. Delcor Homes-Plymouth Pointe, Ltd.*, No. 233847, 2003 WL 22439654, at *2 (Mich. Ct. App. Oct. 28, 2003) ("Plaintiff . . . encourages this Court to apply the UCC concept of 'failure of essential purpose.' However, there is no need to adopt by analogy a UCC concept . . . because a common law mechanism [of unconscionability] exists for invalidating the contract. . . ."); *see also* U.C.C. § 2-719(2) (2003) ("Where circumstances cause an exclusive or limited remedy to fail of its essential purpose, remedy may be had as provided in this Act.").

that failure of essential purpose is a U.C.C. concept, there is no guarantee that a court will not apply the doctrine by analogy to services contracts.[169] Accordingly, where a seller of services does not act in accordance with the terms of the limited remedies it does afford the buyer, the seller runs the risk of causing a failure of essential purpose of such limited remedies and, as a result, making additional remedies available to the buyer.

With this background on failure of essential purpose in mind, we can begin to digest § 10.10 of the AOL Agreement. This section provides that the limitations and exclusions of liability and disclaimers in the Agreement shall survive despite having been found to fail of their essential purpose. Can such a contractual provision trump the failure-of-essential-purpose doctrine? Based on the limited case law on the subject, it appears that these provisions have not been given effect and that the failure-of-essential-purpose doctrine may still apply when an exclusive remedy fails despite a provision that provides otherwise.[170] Why might a party still wish to include such a provision?

When an exclusive remedy is found to have failed of its essential purpose, should consequential damages then be available, despite a provision excluding consequential damages? While there is a split of authority, it seems that most courts have held that an exclusion-of-consequential-damages provision and a separate exclusive-remedy provision are independent of each other and that the failure of the essential purpose of an exclusive-remedy provision does not invalidate or affect a provision that excludes consequential damages.[171] To help a court find that a certain limitation-of-liability provision is "independent" of an exclusive remedy that may fail, one should be sure to draft the provisions as

---

169. For example, in *CBS v. Ziff-Davis*, discussed earlier in this chapter, the high court of New York did not decide the case based on the U.C.C. because the sale of a magazine business is unlikely to qualify as a sale of goods. However, nonetheless, the court was heavily influenced by the U.C.C. in its understanding of warranties. *See Rogath v. Siebenmann*, 129 F.3d 261, 264 (2d Cir. 1997) ("*CBS* was not decided on the basis of the UCC, probably because the sale of the magazine business at issue did not constitute the sale of goods. Nevertheless, the court relied heavily on UCC authorities, expressly noting that analogy to the Uniform Commercial Code is instructive.") (internal citations and quotation marks omitted).

170. *See, e.g., Evans Indus., Inc. v. Int'l Bus. Machs. Co.*, No. Civ.A. 01-0051, 2004 WL 241701, at *8-9 (E.D. La. Feb. 6, 2004) (denying a motion to vacate an arbitration panel's finding, based on Arkansas law, that "[t]he clause which attempts to void the application of the 'failure of essential purpose' theory is against public policy and unenforceable").

171. *See, e.g., McNally Wellman Co. v. N.Y. State Elec. & Gas Corp.*, 63 F.3d 1188, 1197-98 (2d Cir. 1995) ("Under New York law, however, it is well established that the failure of a limited remedy does not render ineffective all other limitations of liability."); *Razor v. Hyundai Motor Am.*, 222 Ill. 2d 75, 93-99 (Ill. 2006) ("This conclusion [that failure of essential purpose does not invalidate exclusion-of-consequential-damages provisions] is buttressed by the fact that a majority of jurisdictions to consider the issue have adopted the independent approach."); *Int'l Fin. Servs., Inc. v. Franz*, 534 N.W.2d 261, 269 (Minn. 1995) ("We too are of the opinion that the better reasoned approach is to treat the repair or replacement remedy and a consequential damage exclusion as discrete and independent contractual provisions. Accordingly, the consequential damage exclusion is valid unless it is unconscionable."). *But see, e.g., Murray v. Holiday Rambler, Inc.*, 83 Wis. 2d 406, 430-31 (Wis. 1978) (finding that a failure of essential purpose of a limited warranty makes all remedies available, including consequential damages, notwithstanding that the agreement specifically excluded consequential damages).

separate sections in an agreement.[172] In addition, including language that an exclusion of consequential damages "shall be deemed independent of, and shall survive, any failure of the essential purpose of any limited remedy" has assisted in a court's finding that the exclusion provision was independent of an exclusive-remedy provision and insulated from a failure of essential purpose.[173]

(4) The Interaction of Indemnification and Limitation-of-Liability Provisions

While it is clear from the second sentence of § 10.8 and from § 10.9 that the limitation-of-liability provisions therein do not apply to the indemnification obligations otherwise provided in the Agreement, agreements do not always make this explicit. It is not uncommon to find, in the same agreement, a limitation-of-liability provision that purports to limit all liability under that Agreement and an indemnification provision that expressly provides certain payment obligations conditioned on the occurrence of certain events—and for each to make no mention of, or reference to, the other. Accordingly, with such agreements, it is not clear whether a limitation of liability should apply to an indemnification obligation.

The Fifth Circuit has found that a limitation-of-liability provision, excluding "any punitive, indirect, incidental, special or consequential damages of any kind or nature (including, but not limited to, loss of profits, loss of use, loss of hire, and loss of production)," did not apply to an indemnity obligation, where the contract was silent as to the interaction between the two provisions.[174] The Fifth Circuit explained:

> There is nothing in the third paragraph to suggest that it is a restriction on the indemnity provisions in the preceding paragraphs. It references only liability between the parties to the agreement . . . , and does not reference indemnity or liability to third parties or employees. The types of damages referenced in this paragraph are those traditionally associated with contractual claims, and not the personal injury claims which are the subject of the indemnification provision.[175]

---

172. *See, e.g., Hydraform Prods. Corp. v. Am. Steel & Aluminum Corp.*, 498 A.2d 339, 342 (N.H. 1985) ("However, the fact that the terms were placed together confirms what we believe is the more reasonable interpretation, that the parties were agreeing to eliminate a right to consequential damages for the very reason that replacement or refund would operate as effective remedies. Therefore, we are unable to view this as a case in which the status of the limitation of damages clause should be determined independently of the provision for replacement or refund.").

173. *Sheehan v. Monaco Coach Corp.*, No. 04-C-717, 2006 WL 208689, at *13-14 (E.D. Wis. Jan. 25, 2006).

174. *Becker v. Tidewater, Inc.*, 586 F.3d 358, 369 (5th Cir. 2009) (Louisiana law); *see also Howard P. Foley Co. v. Cox*, 679 S.W.2d 58, 63 (Tex. Ct. App. 1984) ("[T]he word 'indemnity' is not even included in the clause. We refuse to find that the contract foreclosed Braun's indemnity claim."); *see also Martin v. Midwest Exp. Holdings, Inc.*, No. 07-55063, 2009 WL 306216, at *1 (9th Cir. Feb. 9, 2006) (explaining that a waiver of consequential damages does not bar an indemnification claim because the clause did not "specifically foreclose indemnity").

175. *Becker*, 586 F.3d at 369.

In contrast, the Sixth Circuit has come down the opposite on similar facts, upholding a district court's finding that a limitation-of-liability provision—capping the total liability between the parties to the service fees charged under the contract—limited an indemnity obligation within that same contract, where the contract was silent as to the interaction between the two provisions.[176]

Given this uncertainty, the best way to avoid forcing a court or an arbitrator to undergo an inquiry into the parties' intent is to draft with clarity. To this end, a contract should explicitly specify whether (and how) provisions that limit liability—either to a certain amount or by excluding certain types of damages—under the contract, limit an indemnity obligation under the same contract.[177] Note that § 10.4, the second sentence of § 10.8, and § 10.9 of the AOL Agreement specifically explain whether the Agreement's limitation-of-liability provisions apply to the Agreement's indemnity provisions.

Drafting Note: "Herein" and Broadly Worded Limitations of Liability

Take a moment to reflect on the lack of clarity in § 10.8. The first sentence says, "Except as expressly provided herein, AOL shall not be liable . . . for any claims arising out of or related to this Agreement. . . . " For one, to what does "herein" refer? According to *Black's Law Dictionary*, "herein" means, "In this thing (such as a document, section, or paragraph)."[178] As *Black's* proceeds to explain, "This term is inherently ambiguous."[179] Are we to read the first sentence except as expressly provided in this *section* or in this *agreement*? Unless the parties would like to leave it up to a court or arbitrator to parse the entire document for uses of "herein," to perhaps look to extrinsic evidence should they find the document ambiguous on its face, and to decide ultimately on the parties' intentions, this provision should lose the "herein" in favor of either "in this section 10.8" or "in this Agreement."

Putting "herein" to the side and assuming it refers to this Agreement, this sentence provides that AOL is not liable for *any claims related to this Agreement*, unless the Agreement *expressly* provides to the contrary. Read literally, this provision essentially says that AOL is liable for nothing, except where the Agreement *expressly* provides that AOL is so liable. Other than AOL's express indemnity obligations, where does the Agreement expressly provide that AOL is liable for anything? Does the Agreement, for example, anywhere expressly provide that AOL is liable for basic general damages for breach of the contract? How does the

---

176. *Moore & Assocs. Inc. v. Jones & Carter Inc.*, 217 F. App'x 430 (6th Cir. 2007) (Texas law).

177. Indeed, a contract may specify that an exclusion of liability applies *only* to indemnification and not to other liability. For example, the Tenth Circuit refused to vacate an arbitrator's decision that a provision that excluded from an indemnification obligation "any direct, indirect, incidental, consequential, special or other damages . . . resulting from loss of actual or anticipated revenues or profits, or loss of business, customers, or goodwill" did not apply to the parties' liability to each other for breach of contract more generally. *Dominion Video Satellite, Inc. v. Echostar Satellite LLC*, 430 F.3d 1269, 1277 (10th Cir. 2005).

178. Black's Law Dictionary 795 (9th ed. 2009).

179. *Id.*

second sentence in § 10.8 comport with the first? For instance, the second sentence excepts breaches of confidentiality obligations from the sentence's liability limitations. Does the Agreement ever expressly provide that AOL shall be liable for breaching its confidentiality obligations? If not, does the first sentence swallow the provisions of the second sentence as applied to AOL?

While it may have been the intent of the Parties strongly to limit AOL's liability exposure under this Agreement, could they have done so with greater clarity to avoid the second-guessing of a judge? (And could they limit AOL's liability *so* strongly?) It is also important to realize that sometimes a party might strategically push for vague or ambiguous aspects in a contract in order to leave certain arguments for litigation or because the party believes that a clear provision would only serve to reduce the party's potential rights under the agreement; however, a litigated result might prove less advantageous than what the party may have been able to achieve in negotiations (not to mention that litigating issues can be expensive). Please consider these issues in the context of the *Mobil* case below.

A drafter of contracts must appreciate her audience and how her contracts will be read. Please consider this in the context of the following case—and please consider the following case in the context of our discussion of limitation of liability, indemnification, and clarity as well as the importance of understanding provisions within a contract together as part of an entire agreement.

Mobil Chemical Co. v. Blount Bros. Corp.
United States Court of Appeals, Fifth Circuit, 1987.
809 F.2d 1175.

GEE, Circuit Judge:

The parties to this action somehow built a chemical plant. They have been trying to figure out who should pay for it ever since. Both the owner and the general contractor have tried to escape all liability, although neither disputes that the subcontractors ended up about $4 million underpaid. We agree with the district court that both are liable. On this and other issues too numerous to summarize here, we affirm in large part, reverse in part, and remand for further proceedings.

A. Facts and Prior Proceedings

This case arises out of a $37 million contract for the construction of a chemical plant. Mobil Chemical is the owner, Blount Brothers the general contractor, and the other parties are subcontractors. Blount Brothers acted as construction manager; it did none of the actual construction. The general contract was for a fixed-price and called for "best efforts" to complete the project by January 1983.

Work began in the fall of 1981. The early phases of the project were significantly delayed by Mobil's failure to provide foundations and to have various components in place at times specified by the contract. Construction fell behind schedule. Blount's planning and scheduling tasks grew more complicated when Mobil failed to meet deadlines for delivery of components. Moreover, Blount's first project manager was not capable of managing such a large and complex construction job. Also, Blount's first construction schedule was prepared by an employee innocent of the ability to prepare such a schedule for a complex project, and Blount did not assign a competent full-time scheduler to the project site until December 1981. The work of the different crafts went uncoordinated, and construction proceeded chaotically and behind schedule.

In the fall of 1982, Mobil and Blount made a joint decision to push the subcontractors to meet the January 1983 completion date by overmanning and acceleration. Mobil knew that the project would not be finished until some months later and told Blount that a later completion would be acceptable. Both Blount and Mobil, however, maintained a united position toward the subcontractors that completion by January was crucial. Mobil threatened to black-ball several subcontractors if they did not add workers and make up time. Mobil's motive for rushing the project is obvious: it wanted a producing plant as soon as possible. Blount's motive is less clear, but apparently its costs as project manager were increased little by acceleration. Indeed, an early completion date would reduce its total overhead costs for managing the project, thereby increasing its profit on the fixed-price contract.

The project was completed in April 1983. Blount submitted claims to Mobil for additional compensation for itself and on behalf of its subcontractors Sauer Industrial Contracting, Inc.; Newtron, Inc.; Andreco Refractory Services, Inc.; B & B Insulation, Inc.; and Riggers and Constructors, Inc. In response, Mobil launched a preemptive strike: it sued Blount and the subcontractors in the Eastern District of Texas for a declaratory judgment that it owed nothing to any of them, and, in the alternative, that it was contractually indemnified by Blount for any amounts it owed Blount and the subcontractors. Blount and the subcontractors filed counterclaims against Mobil and each other.

Shortly before trial, Mobil settled with Sauer, Newtron, B & B, and Riggers. These settlements took the form of "Mary Carter" agreements. The subcontractors accepted payments from Mobil, agreeing to pursue their claims against Blount and to pay Mobil any amount received from Blount up to the amount of Mobil's payment. Excess amounts were to be split fifty-fifty. Only Andreco did not settle with Mobil.

The case was tried to the bench. The district court concluded that the general contract was governed by New York law and that the subcontracts were governed by Texas law. Holding that contract breaches by Mobil and Blount and their negligent joint decision to accelerate were equal causes of the subcontractors' acceleration costs, the court ordered Mobil to release the final $2 million retainage to Blount, awarded the subcontractors virtually all of their claimed

B. Master Services Agreement

damages to be paid by Blount and Mobil in equal shares, and settled several other minor disputes. Both Blount and Mobil appeal.

B. Divvying Up Liability Between Blount and Mobil

The district court found that the subcontractors' acceleration damages were due equally to negligence and contract breaches by Blount and Mobil. Because "the district court's account of the evidence is plausible in light of the record viewed in its entirety," we may not reverse even were we inclined to disagree. And, after reviewing the record, we are not even inclined to disagree.

This case is a paradigm of the inadequacy of legal rules and legal institutions for parsing the messy stuff of life into precise categories. Only God knows to what exact extent the various strategic choices and mistakes of all those concerned in this case eventually caused the damages at stake. And that is exactly why the "clearly erroneous" rule is an appropriate standard of review. It shifts educated guess-work and intuitive justice to the trial court, to the person who was immersed in and who looked most carefully at the mess, from the best vantage point.

No party directly challenges the findings of the district court. Instead, both Blount and Mobil seek to absolve themselves of liability in the face of the facts found by the district court. We take up their arguments in turn. . . .

2. *Mobil's Attempted Escape: The Indemnity Clause*

The contract between Mobil and Blount contains a section entitled "Article 12—Insurance." There are four paragraphs in Article 12. In paragraphs one and two, Mobil assumes the risk of all loss or damage to the plant, materials, and equipment, including those in transit to the construction site. In the third, Blount agrees to maintain insurance for workmen's compensation, comprehensive liability, and automobile liability. The fourth paragraph of Article 12 is an indemnity provision:

> 12.4 CONTRACTOR shall defend, indemnify and hold COMPANY, Mobil Oil Corporation and its subsidiaries and affiliates harmless from and against all losses, expenses, liens, claims, demands and cuases [sic] of action of every kind and character (including those of the parties, their agents and employees) for death, personal injury, property damage *or any other liability,* damages, fines or penalties (except where reimbursement of fines and penalties is prohibited by applicable laws) including costs, attorneys [sic] fees and settlements *arising out of or in any way connected with the WORK whether claimed by (a) CONTRACTOR,* its employees or agents or (b) *any of CONTRACTOR's subcontractors,* its employees or agents or (c) any other contractor, its employees or agents or (d) any third party *and whether resulting from or contributed to by (i) the negligence in any form except sole negligence* of COMPANY, Mobil Oil Corporation and its subsidiaries and affiliates and their agents, employees or independent third parties directly responsible

to COMPANY or (ii) any defect in, or condition of the premises on which the WORK is to be performed or any equipment thereon or any materials furnished by COMPANY.

(Emphasis added.) Mobil argues that the "any other liability" indemnity provision covers any and all of its breaches of the contract. Mobil urges, in the alternative, that even if the clause does not cover contract breaches, it covers Mobil's negligent decision to accelerate because the acceleration was not the result of its "sole negligence."

The language of the provision is so broad that it might be read to indemnify Mobil against every liability related to the work except for "sole negligence." But New York law disapproves of indemnity provisions, so Mobil must make a powerful showing:

> Because it is unnatural that one would agree to indemnify another when otherwise under no such legal obligation, indemnity clauses are strictly construed. In construing such clauses, the court must determine whether "the intention to indemnify can be clearly implied from the language and purposes of the entire agreement, and the surrounding facts and circumstances." Further, the court must consider whether the agreement reflects an unmistakable intent to indemnify.

We must decide if the indemnity clause relied on by Mobil "clearly implies" the intention to indemnify or shows an "unmistakable intent" to make Blount liable for all harms done by Mobil other than "sole negligence."

The district court held: "It is inconceivable that Blount would have agreed to indemnify Mobil for damages resulting from its [Mobil's] own breaches of contract." We agree. Mobil's interpretation is completely artificial in the context of the entire contract. First, the location of the indemnity provision in "Article 12—Insurance" following provisions requiring Blount to maintain liability insurance shows that it was meant to apply to run-of-the-mill tort claims for injury, property damage, and death. It was not intended to alter fundamentally the meaning of the entire contract. Second, in "Article 25—Consequential Damages," the parties explicitly agree that neither should be liable to the other for any indirect or consequential damages. This Article is meaningless if Blount must indemnify Mobil for both direct and indirect damages to Blount itself and everyone else in the world. Finally, if the indemnity provision is given the meaning advanced by Mobil, no contract was formed at all. Under Mobil's reading, the contract would be void for lack of mutuality. Mobil would have no obligations under the contract; it could breach the contract in any way and to any extent and Blount would be liable to itself! This interpretation is ridiculous.

Mobil tries to rescue the argument from the lack of mutuality objection by urging that even if the indemnity provision does not cover its own breaches of contract, it does cover the joint *negligent* decision to accelerate. It is not clear to us why we should treat a negligent breach of contract differently from a deliberate one; but even if we were willing to grant that distinction, the argument will not fly. Either the indemnity clause covers both negligent and non-negligent breach of contract or neither. Negligent acceleration damages must be indemnified, if at all, under a literal reading of the same all-inclusive phrase ("any other liability") that would indemnify breach of contract claims as well. That phrase simply does not support the distinction that Mobil urges.[6]

Although we are lawyers, and although we spend too much of our professional lives listening to this sort of argument, we are nevertheless human beings of average intelligence and average common sense. It is inconceivable that a few words buried in the fourth section of the "Insurance" provisions of the general contract were intended to supersede the normal operation of tort and contract law for the entire agreement, to shift all risks arising out of the contract to Blount, to alter essentially the relationship between the parties. We hold that Mobil is liable for the damages that it caused. . . .

Comments

The court in *Mobil v. Blount* explains that if Mobil were to have no obligations under its contract, then the contract would necessarily fail for lack of mutuality. Most courts now understand the requirement of mutuality as calling for nothing more than consideration.[180] Indeed, as the *Restatement of Contracts* explains, "If the requirement of consideration is met, there is no additional requirement

---

6. Mobil does not attempt to justify its interpretation by pointing to similar contractual language or similar facts in any New York cases. Instead, it cites two of our cases that apply *Texas* law: *Leonard v. Aluminum Co. of Am.*, 767 F.2d 134 (5th Cir. 1985), and *Gulf Oil Corp. v. Burlington N. R.R.*, 751 F.2d 746 (5th Cir. 1985). These cases do not help Mobil's cause.

In *Leonard*, the plaintiff was injured by an exploding soft drink bottle cap. He sued ALCOA, the manufacturer of the capping machine. ALCOA sought indemnity from the bottling company that installed the cap. The district court held that under Texas law a blanket indemnity clause in the contract between the bottler and ALCOA was not to ALCOA's avail. ALCOA was found liable at trial for negligent failure to warn about the risks "that bottle caps might suddenly take flight." Our court reversed. We held that ALCOA was not liable for negligent failure to warn under Texas law. Furthermore, we held that the clause required the bottler to pay ALCOA its costs and attorneys' fees in the suit; negligence was no longer an issue, so it was now immaterial that the indemnity clause did not meet the tough Texas standard for clauses indemnifying one party for its own *negligent* acts. The entire decision in *Leonard* has since been vacated and remanded. *Leonard* relied on *Alm v. Aluminum Co. of America*, which was reversed by the Texas Supreme Court.

In *Gulf Oil*, our court enforced an indemnity provision in a lease of a railroad spur. Cars on the spur had rolled onto the main track and hit a train, damaging property of both the lessor and lessee. The lessor railroad's employees were found negligent in the way they had parked the lessee's cars. We held that a clause indemnifying the railroad for "loss or destruction of or damage to property whatsoever, in any manner caused by, resulting from or incident to storage of private cars on said track" satisfied the Texas requirement that the obligation be expressed in "clear and unequivocal" terms. We relied on a line of Texas cases holding that contracts making one party fully responsible for an "instrumentality, operation, or premises" satisfy the "clear and unequivocal" requirement. Obviously, neither case helps Mobil meet its burden under New York law.

180. *See, e.g., Structural Polymer Grp., Ltd. v. Zoltek Corp.*, 543 F.3d 987, 992 (8th Cir. 2008) (Missouri law); *Riner v. Allstate Life Ins. Co.*, 131 F.3d 530, 536 (5th Cir. 1997) ("Texas law does not require that every right or obligation by one party be met with an identical right or obligation in the other."); *see also* RICHARD A. LORD, 3 WILLISTON ON CONTRACTS § 7:14 (4th ed. 2009) (clarifying the confusion associated with the "supposed requirement of mutuality of obligation" and explaining that such is not required for a contract to have binding effect).

of . . . 'mutuality of obligation.'"[181] Accordingly, inasmuch as a contract is supported by consideration, most courts will not inquire further as to whether obligations under a contract or provision flow both ways.[182]

---

181. Restatement (Second) of Contracts § 79 (1981).

182. *See supra* note 180. For further discussion of the requirement of consideration and that this does not always require mutual obligations within a contract, please see the discussion of consideration in Chapter 1 in the context of non-disclosure agreements.

· CHAPTER FOUR ·

AGREEMENTS FOR THE SALE OF GOODS

Having determined that Florida law applies, we need not decide whether the agreement is a contract for the sale of goods or for services. Though the provisions of the Florida Uniform Commercial Code ("UCC") would apply only if the contract were deemed a sale of goods, the limitation of liability provision governs to bar Meridian's third-party claims regardless of whether the UCC or general Florida contract law applies.

Cooper v. Meridian Yachts, Ltd., 575 F.3d 1151, 1166 (11th Cir. 2009).

In the previous chapter, we began the discussion of how contractual parties may plan for the application of Article 2, even in contracts ostensibly for "services." In this chapter, we continue this discussion. As the above excerpt demonstrates, a prudent drafter can be sure to draft a contract so as to achieve certain results whether Article 2 applies or not and, in this chapter, we further examine the ways in which a drafter may do so. (Indeed, the above excerpt demonstrates the utility of limitation-of-liability provisions, which we discussed in Chapter 3.)

What do we mean by "sale of goods"? What are the important contractual terms applicable to a sale of goods? In the event a contract is silent on one or more of these terms, is there applicable law establishing the rights and obligations of the parties? What role does the Uniform Commercial Code ("U.C.C.") play in this regard? Are parties free to contract around or against particular provisions of the U.C.C.? These are just a few of the questions one encounters when negotiating contracts for the sale of goods.

We turn our attention in this chapter to these and numerous other questions. From dog food to doughnuts, televisions to teapots, toasters to transformers, these are the goods that move commerce.

Many of these goods are often the subject of purchase orders and form contracts; others—particularly those of a unique or bespoke nature—often form the basis of heavily negotiated standalone agreements. In most cases, these contracts rely upon and showcase the building blocks of many commercial contracts, namely: term and termination, price and payment, warranty, and liability. How these component terms best serve each party's interests—and the degree of leverage each party brings to the negotiation table—informs the art of commercial negotiation.

We begin our analysis with a discussion of the scope of Article 2 of the U.C.C. and the sometimes unclear meaning of "goods" and the "transactions" therein.

A. THE SCOPE OF ARTICLE TWO OF THE UNIFORM COMMERCIAL CODE

1. Some Background on the U.C.C.

We already have encountered Article 2 of the Uniform Commercial Code in Chapter 3, with our discussion of services contracts. There, we discussed that Article 2 ostensibly applies only to contracts for the sale of goods[1] but that a prudent party will always plan for the possibility that Article 2 may apply. Here, before we look at this chapter's agreement and the various issues that arise therein, we delve further into the world of the Uniform Commercial Code.

Though we have discussed the U.C.C. some throughout this book, we should take a moment to explore the background and nature of the Uniform Commercial Code. The U.C.C. is a joint collaboration between the American Law Institute ("ALI") and the National Conference of Commissioners on Uniform State Laws ("NCCUSL"). An overarching purpose of the U.C.C. is to harmonize commercial law throughout the United States.[2] Accordingly, the U.C.C. is a uniform, model act, which does not have the effect of law in any given state until that state adopts the U.C.C. by statute. A state legislature may adopt the U.C.C. wholesale or make various substantive changes before passing the uniform code as state law (or, as in the case of Louisiana and Article 2 of the U.C.C., the state may

---

1. Some courts find that Article 2 applies not merely to sales but more broadly to "transactions" in goods, as we discuss below.

2. *See* U.C.C. § 1-103(a)(3) (2003) ("[The Uniform Commercial Code] must be liberally construed and applied to promote its underlying purposes and policies, which [include] . . . to make uniform the law among the various jurisdictions.").

decline to adopt the uniform code altogether). The U.C.C. contains nine primary articles, addressing ten areas of commercial law: Article 2 (sales), Article 2A (leases), Article 3 (negotiable instruments), Article 4 (bank deposits), Article 4A (fund transfers), Article 5 (letters of credit), Article 6 (bulk transfers), Article 7 (warehouse receipts, bills of lading, and other documents of title), Article 8 (investment securities), and Article 9 (secured transactions). Article 1 of the U.C.C. contains "general provisions," which apply generally to the other articles that comprise the U.C.C. In addition to Article 1, we discuss Article 2 (primarily in this chapter) and Article 9 (primarily in Chapter 5) inasmuch as they apply to the transactions and agreements in this book.

A fundamental policy underlying the U.C.C. is freedom of contract between commercial parties. Consistent with this policy, Article 2 is deferential to the contractual arrangements of private parties. Frequently, a provision within Article 2 will state that the provision applies "unless otherwise agreed" by contract and the like. Moreover, the U.C.C. expressly provides that, even where a provision of the U.C.C. is silent as to whether it may be altered by contract, parties may generally alter the effect of the statutory provision by agreement.[3] This means that most of the U.C.C. is "default" law as opposed to "mandatory" law. Default laws may be altered; they are the stand-in rules unless the parties agree otherwise. In contrast, mandatory laws may not be altered by private arrangement. For example, Article 1 explains, "The obligations of good faith, diligence, reasonableness, and care prescribed by [the Uniform Commercial Code] may not be disclaimed by agreement."[4] In addition, as we discuss later in this chapter, whenever the U.C.C. "requires an action to be taken within a reasonable time, a time that is not manifestly unreasonable may be fixed by agreement."[5] Accordingly, the U.C.C. gives the parties the freedom to stipulate what constitutes a "reasonable time" but reserves a mandatory rule that a contractually specified reasonable time that is manifestly unreasonable is not sufficient to satisfy a U.C.C. reasonable-time requirement.

The ALI and NCCUSL adopted Revised Article 2 in 2003. While the revisions did not mark a complete overhaul of the previous version, there are some substantive and meaningful departures. Because, as of this publication, states have not yet widely adopted Revised Article 2, we address both versions. In this book, when we refer to Article 2 without providing further specification, we are referring to the revised version of Article 2. When we discuss a matter on which the two versions meaningfully diverge, we discuss both the pre-revised and the revised versions. Accordingly, when we speak of Article 2 generally, without

---

3. *Id.* § 1-302(a) ("Except as otherwise provided in subsection (b) or elsewhere in [the Uniform Commercial Code], the effect of provisions of [the Uniform Commercial Code] may be varied by agreement."); *id.* § 1-302(c) ("The presence in certain provisions of [the Uniform Commercial Code] of the phrase 'unless otherwise agreed', or words of similar import, does not imply that the effect of other provisions may not be varied by agreement under this section.").

4. *Id.* § 1-302(b).

5. *Id.*

further adieu, you can assume that we are speaking of the revised version of Article 2 and that both versions are in at least basic accord on the matter.

An International Focus with Domestic Implications: The United Nations Convention on Contracts for the International Sale of Goods

As of January 1, 1988, and the United States' adoption of the United Nations Convention on Contracts for the International Sale of Goods ("CISG"), the CISG is *domestic* American contracts law—no less than the U.C.C. or the common law.[6] Indeed, in some respects, it is *more*. As a ratified treaty, the CISG is U.S. federal law that preempts state law (e.g., the U.C.C. as adopted by state legislatures and state common law) where the CISG applies.[7] So, where does the CISG apply? And, what substantive law does the CISG provide?

For starters, as with the U.C.C. generally, the CISG applies only to the sale of goods and adopts a predominate-purpose test to address mixed contracts.[8] Furthermore, the CISG applies only to transactions between parties with places of business in *different* signatory countries (i.e., countries that have adopted the CISG as law). If a party has more than one place of business, then the party's place of business with the "closest relationship to the contract and its performance" is its place of business for the purposes of the CISG and its application.[9] The CISG expressly excludes many types of transactions from its scope, including sales of goods for personal or household use, sales by auction, sales of investment securities or negotiable instruments, sales of ships or aircraft, and sales of electricity.[10] In addition, parties may "opt out" of the CISG entirely (as evident in the AOL Agreement in Chapter 3);[11] however, merely designating that "domestic" law governs is insufficient to avoid the CISG's application because the CISG

---

6. United Nations Convention on Contracts for the International Sale of Goods, *reprinted in* 15 U.S.C.A. App. (West. Supp. 1995), *available at* http://www.uncitral.org/pdf/english/texts/sales/cisg/CISG.pdf [hereinafter "CISG"]. The U.S. Senate ratified the CISG in 1986. *See BP Oil Int'l, Ltd. v. Empresa Estatal Petroleos de Ecuador*, 332 F.3d 333, 336 n.6 (5th Cir. 2003).

7. *See, e.g., Caterpillar, Inc. v. Usinor Industeel*, 393 F. Supp. 2d 659, 673 (N.D. Ill. 2005) ("As a treaty to which the United States is a signatory, the CISG is federal law; thus, under the Supremacy Clause, it preempts inconsistent provisions of Illinois law where it applies."). Note, however, that the CISG does not apply to claims against persons not party to an agreement that falls within the scope of the CISG. *Id.* at 676. In addition, the CISG does not apply to non-contract claims, such as promissory estoppel or misrepresentation. *See, e.g., Miami Valley Paper, LLC v. Lebbing Eng'g & Consulting GmbH*, No. 1:05-CV-00702, 2006 WL 2924779, at *3 (S.D. Ohio Oct. 10, 2006) ("[T]he CISG does not prevent Plaintiff from pleading negligent misrepresentation and fraudulent inducement."); *Caterpillar*, 393 F. Supp. 2d at 676 ("[T]he court declines to extend the preemptive force of the CISG to state law claims for promissory estoppel.").

8. CISG, *supra* note 6, at art. 3 ("This Convention does not apply to contracts in which the preponderant part of the obligations of the party who furnishes the goods consists in the supply of labour or other services.").

9. CISG, *supra* note 6, at art. 10(a) (considering the "circumstances known to or contemplated by the parties at any time before or at the conclusion of the contract" when determining the place of business).

10. CISG, *supra* note 6, at art. 2.

11. CISG, *supra* note 6, at art. 6 ("The parties may exclude the application of this Convention or . . . derogate from or vary the effect of any of its provisions.").

is domestic law where adopted.[12] Accordingly, contractual parties can be sure to avoid the CISG by *expressly* saying so in their contract. Do you think the CISG is likely to govern the agreement in this chapter?

The CISG deals much with contract *formation*, a topic that is not a focus of this book. In short, the CISG adopts rules that differ from the much feared "battle of the forms" found in pre-revised U.C.C. § 2-207 and that are closer to the U.S. common law and its "mirror image" rule.[13] In addition, the CISG does away with the "statute of frauds" by not requiring that any contract be in writing, so long as its existence may be proved.[14] Like the U.C.C., the CISG departs from U.S. common law by giving real effect to no-oral-modification clauses, providing parties may not orally modify contracts that contain such clauses but that the clauses may still be waived.[15]

The CISG also contains implied warranty provisions similar to those found in the U.C.C., including implied warranties that goods are fit for their ordinary purpose ("merchantability," in U.C.C. parlance) and that goods are fit for a particular purpose made known to the seller, where the buyer reasonably relied on the seller's skill and judgment (i.e., "fitness").[16] However, unlike the U.C.C. and the common law (at least after *Ziff-Davis*), the CISG will not enforce a "breach of warranty" (note that the CISG does not use this terminology) where the buyer knew or should have known of the "breach" at the time of the conclusion of the contract.[17] Also unlike the U.C.C., the CISG does not require conspicuous disclaimers or "magic words" to disclaim implied warranties effectively—although, the CISG may be less concerned with consumer protection, as personal and household goods are excluded from its scope.

These are just a sampling of the variations between the CISG and the U.C.C. We proceed to focus our discussion on the implications of the U.C.C. and this chapter's agreement, between two companies with their places of business in the U.S.

2. The Scope of Article Two

To determine when Article 2 does and does not apply, we look first to Article 2 itself, which defines its own scope in § 2-102:

Unless the context otherwise requires, this Article applies to transactions in goods; it does not apply to any transaction which although in the form of an

---

12. *See, e.g., BP Oil Int'l*, 332 F.3d at 337 ("Given that the CISG is Ecuadorian law, a choice of law provision designating Ecuadorian law merely confirms that the treaty governs the transaction.") (emphasis in original).

13. CISG, *supra* note 6, at art. 19.

14. CISG, *supra* note 6, at art. 11 ("A contract of sale need not be concluded in or evidenced by writing and is not subject to any other requirement as to form. It may be proved by any means, including witnesses.").

15. CISG, *supra* note 6, at art. 29(2).

16. CISG, *supra* note 6, at art. 35(2).

17. CISG, *supra* note 6, at art. 35(3).

unconditional contract to sell or present sale is intended to operate only as a security transaction nor does this Article impair or repeal any statute regulating sales to consumers, farmers or other specified classes of buyers.

Right from the start, we know that Article 2 applies to "transactions in goods." Accordingly, before turning to this chapter's agreement, we briefly explore, in turn, three basic questions:

(1) What is a "good"?

(2) What is a "transaction in goods"?

(3) How does Article 2 apply to a transaction in both goods and non-goods?

a. What Is a "Good"?

Section 2-103(k) of the U.C.C. defines "goods" as follows:

"Goods" means all things that are movable at the time of identification to a contract for sale. The term includes future goods, specially manufactured goods, the unborn young of animals, growing crops, and other identified things attached to realty as described in Section 2-107. The term does not include information, the money in which the price is to be paid, investment securities under Article 8, the subject matter of foreign exchange transactions, or choses in action.[18]

The definition of "goods" within the meaning of Article 2, then, turns on whether the subject of a transaction is a movable thing. Examples of such movable things that have been found to meet the definition of a good under

---

18. The pre-revised version of Article 2 similarly defines "goods" in § 2-105 as:

[A]ll things (including specially manufactured goods) which are movable at the time of identification to the contract for sale other than the money in which the price is to be paid, investment securities (Article 8) and things in action. "Goods" also includes the unborn young of animals and growing crops and other identified things attached to realty as described in the section on goods to be severed from realty (Section 2-107).

Article 2 include: animals,[19] cars,[20] trees,[21] equipment,[22] and ships.[23] Courts have split as to whether utilities such as electricity[24] and water[25] are goods.

What about software? Consistent with the excerpted case below, several courts have found software to fall within the meaning of "goods" under Article 2 and accordingly have found Article 2 to govern transactions in software.[26] In chewing over whether software should be considered a good within the meaning of Article 2, please consider the following case. (And please pay particular attention to—and revisit—the *facts* below, as additional excerpts from this same case appear throughout this chapter.)

---

19. *See, e.g., Flanagan v. Consol. Nutrition*, 627 N.W.2d 573, 577 (Iowa Ct. App. 2001) (holding that pigs were "goods" within the meaning of Article 2); *Trad Indus., Ltd. v. Brogan*, 805 P.2d 54, 58 (Mont. 1991) (holding that elk were "goods" under Article 2).

20. *See, e.g., Hodges v. Johnson*, 199 P.3d 1251, 1259 (Kan. 2009).

21. *See, e.g., Kaitz v. Landscape Creations, Inc.*, No. 1271, 2000 WL 694274, at *2 (Mass. App. Div. May 24, 2000) (finding that "trees, shrubs and plants provided by the defendant are 'goods' within the meaning of the U.C.C." because they were grown in a nursery for the purpose of replanting on a third party's property).

22. *See, e.g., Boyle v. Douglas Dynamics, LLC*, 292 F. Supp. 2d 198, 211 (D. Mass. 2003).

23. *See, e.g., Benetic v. Alexander*, No. CV 00-06845 ABC (EX), 2001 WL 1843781, at *3 (C.D. Cal. Aug. 13, 2001).

24. *Compare New Balance Athletic Shoe, Inc. v. Boston Edison Co.*, No. 95-5321-E, 1996 WL 406673, at *2 (Mass. Super. Ct. Mar. 26, 1996) ("The decision to expose public utilities to liability for their 'products' is best left in the capable hands of the legislative body that is charged with regulating those utilities. Accordingly, this court finds that electricity is not a 'good' as defined in the Uniform Commercial Code."), *with Helvey v. Wabash Cnty. REMC*, 278 N.E.2d 608, 610 (Ind. Ct. App. 1972) (finding electricity to be a "good" within the meaning of the U.C.C.).

25. *Compare Mattoon v. City of Pittsfield*, 775 N.E.2d 770, 784 (Mass. App. Ct. 2002) (finding water sold by a city not to be a "good" within the meaning of the U.C.C.), *with Zepp v. Mayor of Athens*, 348 S.E.2d 673, 677-78 (Ga. Ct. App. 1986) (finding water sold by a city to be a "good" within the meaning of the U.C.C.).

26. *See, e.g., Micro Data Base Sys., Inc. v. Dharma Sys., Inc.*, 148 F.3d 649, 654 (7th Cir. 1998) ("But as Colonial Life is consistent with the weight of authority, and reaches the right result—for we can think of no reason why the UCC is not suitable to govern disputes arising from the sale of custom software—we'll follow it.") (internal citations omitted); *SoftMan Prods. Co. v. Adobe Sys., Inc.*, 171 F. Supp. 2d 1075, 1084 (C.D. Cal. 2001) ("A number of courts have held that the sale of software is the sale of a good within the meaning of Uniform Commercial Code."); *Colonial Life Ins. Co. of Am. v. Elec. Data Sys. Corp.*, 817 F. Supp. 235, 239 (D.N.H. 1993) (New Hampshire law) ("Computer software has been held to fall within the definition of a 'good' under the Code.") (citing *Advent Sys. Ltd. v. Unisys Corp.*, 925 F.2d 670, 675-76 (3d Cir. 1991); *RRX Indus., Inc. v. Lab-Con, Inc.*, 772 F.2d 543, 546-47 (9th Cir. 1985); *Triangle Underwriters, Inc. v. Honeywell, Inc.*, 604 F.2d 737, 742-43 (2d Cir. 1979)); *Wachter Mgmt. Co. v. Dexter & Chaney, Inc.*, 144 P.3d 747, 750 (Kan. 2006) ("Computer software is considered to be goods subject to the UCC even though incidental services are provided along with the sale of the software."). *But see, e.g., Conwell v. Gray Loon Outdoor Mktg. Grp., Inc.*, 906 N.E.2d 805, 812 (Ind. 2009) ("On the surface, these cases might suggest that customized software is a service while pre-made software is a good, but when courts try to pour new wine into old legal bottles, we sometimes miss the nuances. It would be a mistake, for instance, to treat software as a good simply because it was contained in a tangible medium that fits within that category.") (citing *Olcott Int'l & Co., Inc. v. Micro Data Base Sys., Inc.*, 793 N.E.2d 1063, 1071 (Ind. Ct. App. 2003); *Data Processing Servs., Inc. v. L.H. Smith Oil Corp.*, 492 N.E.2d 314, 318-20 (Ind. Ct. App. 1986)); *Liberty Fin. Mgmt. Corp. v. Beneficial Data Processing Corp.*, 670 S.W.2d 40, 49 (Mo. Ct. App. 1984) (holding that a sale of custom software is not a transaction in goods within the meaning of Article 2).

Advent Systems Ltd. v. Unisys Corp.
United States Court of Appeals, Third Circuit, 1991.
925 F.2d 670.

WEIS, Circuit Judge.

In this diversity case we conclude that computer software is a good within the Uniform Commercial Code. . . . Because the district court ruled that the Code did not apply, we will grant a new trial on a breach of contract claim. . . .

Plaintiff, Advent Systems Limited, is engaged primarily in the production of software for computers. As a result of its research and development efforts, by 1986 the company had developed an electronic document management system (EDMS), a process for transforming engineering drawings and similar documents into a computer data base.

Unisys Corporation manufactures a variety of computers. As a result of information gained by its wholly-owned United Kingdom subsidiary during 1986, Unisys decided to market the document management system in the United States. In June 1987 Advent and Unisys signed two documents, one labeled "Heads of Agreement" (in British parlance "an outline of agreement") and, the other "Distribution Agreement."

In these documents, Advent agreed to provide the software and hardware making up the document systems to be sold by Unisys in the United States. Advent was obligated to provide sales and marketing material and manpower as well as technical personnel to work with Unisys employees in building and installing the document systems. The agreement was to continue for two years, subject to automatic renewal or termination on notice.

During the summer of 1987, Unisys attempted to sell the document system to Arco, a large oil company, but was unsuccessful. Nevertheless, progress on the sales and training programs in the United States was satisfactory, and negotiations for a contract between Unisys (UK) and Advent were underway.

The relationship, however, soon came to an end. Unisys, in the throes of restructuring, decided it would be better served by developing its own document system and in December 1987 told Advent their arrangement had ended. Unisys also advised its UK subsidiary of those developments and, as a result, negotiations there were terminated.

Advent filed a complaint in the district court alleging, *inter alia*, breach of contract, fraud, and tortious interference with contractual relations. The district court ruled at pretrial that the Uniform Commercial Code did not apply because although goods were to be sold, the services aspect of the contract predominated. . . .

On appeal Advent argues that the Distribution Agreement prohibited Unisys from pressuring its UK subsidiary to terminate negotiations on a corollary contract. Unisys contends that the relationship between it and Advent was one for the sale of goods and hence subject to the terms of statute of frauds in the

Uniform Commercial Code. Because the agreements lacked an express provision on quantity, Unisys insists that the statute of frauds bans enforcement. In addition, Unisys contends that the evidence did not support the damage verdict. . . .

II. SOFTWARE AND THE UNIFORM COMMERCIAL CODE

The district court ruled that as a matter of law the arrangement between the two parties was not within the Uniform Commercial Code and, consequently, the statute of frauds was not applicable. As the district court appraised the transaction, provisions for services outweighed those for products and, consequently, the arrangement was not predominantly one for the sale of goods.

In the "Heads of Agreement" Advent and Unisys purported to enter into a "joint business collaboration." Advent was to modify its software and hardware interfaces to run initially on equipment not manufactured by Unisys but eventually on Unisys hardware. It was Advent's responsibility to purchase the necessary hardware. "[I]n so far as Advent has successfully completed [some of the processing] of software and hardware interfaces," Unisys promised to reimburse Advent to the extent of $150,000 derived from a "surcharge" on products purchased.

Advent agreed to provide twelve man-weeks of marketing manpower, but with Unisys bearing certain expenses. Advent also undertook to furnish an experienced systems builder to work with Unisys personnel at Advent's prevailing rates, and to provide sales and support training for Unisys staff as well as its customers.

The Distribution Agreement begins with the statement, "Unisys desires to purchase, and Advent desires to sell, on a non-exclusive basis, certain of Advent hardware products and software licenses for resale worldwide." Following a heading "Subject Matter of Sales," appears this sentence, "(a) Advent agrees to sell hardware and license software to Unisys, and Unisys agrees to buy from Advent the products listed in Schedule A." Schedule A lists twenty products, such as computer cards, plotters, imagers, scanners and designer systems.

Advent was to invoice Unisys for each product purchased upon shipment, but to issue separate invoices for maintenance fees. The cost of the "support services" was set at 3% "per annum of the prevailing Advent user list price of each software module for which Unisys is receiving revenue from a customer." Services included field technical bulletins, enhancement and maintenance releases, telephone consultation, and software patches, among others. At no charge to Unisys, Advent was to provide publications such as installation manuals, servicing and adjustment manuals, diagnostic operation and test procedures, sales materials, product brochures and similar items. In turn, Unisys was to "employ resources in performing marketing efforts" and develop "the technical ability to be thoroughly familiar" with the products.

In support of the district court's ruling that the U.C.C. did not apply, Advent contends that the agreement's requirement of furnishing services did not come within the Code. Moreover, the argument continues, the "software" referred to in the agreement as a "product" was not a "good" but intellectual property outside the ambit of the Uniform Commercial Code.

Because software was a major portion of the "products" described in the agreement, this matter requires some discussion. Computer systems consist of "hardware" and "software." Hardware is the computer machinery, its electronic circuitry and peripheral items such as keyboards, readers, scanners and printers. Software is a more elusive concept. Generally speaking, "software" refers to the medium that stores input and output data as well as computer programs. The medium includes hard disks, floppy disks, and magnetic tapes.

In simplistic terms, programs are codes prepared by a programmer that instruct the computer to perform certain functions. When the program is transposed onto a medium compatible with the computer's needs, it becomes software. . . .

The increasing frequency of computer products as subjects of commercial litigation has led to controversy over whether software is a "good" or intellectual property. The Code does not specifically mention software.

In the absence of express legislative guidance, courts interpret the Code in light of commercial and technological developments. The Code is designed "[t]o simplify, clarify and modernize the law governing commercial transactions" and "[t]o permit the continued expansion of commercial practices." As the Official Commentary makes clear:

> "This Act is drawn to provide flexibility so that, since it is intended to be a semi-permanent piece of legislation, it will provide its own machinery for expansion of commercial practices. It is intended to make it possible for the law embodied in this Act to be developed by the courts in the light of unforeseen and new circumstances and practices."

The Code "applies to transactions in goods." Goods are defined as "all things (including specially manufactured goods) which are moveable at the time of the identification for sale." The Pennsylvania courts have recognized that "'goods' has a very extensive meaning" under the U.C.C.

Our Court has addressed computer package sales in other cases, but has not been required to consider whether the U.C.C. applied to software per se.

Computer programs are the product of an intellectual process, but once implanted in a medium are widely distributed to computer owners. An analogy can be drawn to a compact disc recording of an orchestral rendition. The music is produced by the artistry of musicians and in itself is not a "good," but when transferred to a laser-readable disc becomes a readily merchantable commodity. Similarly, when a professor delivers a lecture, it is not a good, but, when transcribed as a book, it becomes a good.

That a computer program may be copyrightable as intellectual property does not alter the fact that once in the form of a floppy disc or other medium, the program is tangible, moveable and available in the marketplace. The fact that some programs may be tailored for specific purposes need not alter their status as "goods" because the Code definition includes "specially manufactured goods."

The topic has stimulated academic commentary[2] with the majority espousing the view that software fits within the definition of a "good" in the U.C.C.

Applying the U.C.C. to computer software transactions offers substantial benefits to litigants and the courts. The Code offers a uniform body of law on a wide range of questions likely to arise in computer software disputes: implied warranties, consequential damages, disclaimers of liability, the statute of limitations, to name a few.

The importance of software to the commercial world and the advantages to be gained by the uniformity inherent in the U.C.C. are strong policy arguments favoring inclusion. The contrary arguments are not persuasive, and we hold that software is a "good" within the definition in the Code.

[This case is continued on page 234.]

Comments

The court in *Advent Systems* contends that software, once embodied in some tangible form, becomes a good. When the Third Circuit authored this opinion in 1991, the Internet was in its infancy relative to its present incarnation, and companies largely sold software on diskettes and other forms of tangible media. Should the mode of delivery—by electronic download or by physical delivery of a CD-ROM—determine whether or not Article 2 applies to a software transaction? Does it make sense to apply Article 2 to software sold on tangible media but not to software transmitted online?[27] While this is hardly a settled question, the Second Circuit has opined on the matter:

> The district court concluded that the SmartDownload transactions here should be governed by "California law as it relates to the sale of goods, including the Uniform Commercial Code in effect in California." It is not obvious, however, that UCC Article 2 ("sales of goods") applies to the licensing of software that is downloadable from the Internet. There is no doubt that a sale of tangible goods over the Internet is governed by Article 2 of the UCC. Downloadable software, however, is scarcely a "tangible" good, and, in part because software may be

---

2. Among the articles and notes that have reviewed extant caselaw are: Boss & Woodward, *Scope of the Uniform Commercial Code; Survey of Computer Contracting Cases*, 43 Bus. Law. 1513 (1988); Owen, *The Application of Article 2 of the Uniform Commercial Code To Computer Contracts*, 14 [N. Ky.] L. Rev. 277 (1987); Rodau, *Computer Software: Does Article 2 of the Uniform Commercial Code Apply*, 35 Emory L.J. 853 (1986); Holmes, *Application of Article Two of the Uniform Commercial Code to Computer System Acquisitions*, 9 Rutgers Computer & Technology L.J. 1 (1982); Note, *Computer Software As A Good Under the Uniform Commercial Code: Taking a Byte Out of the Intangibility Myth*, 65 B.U. L. Rev. 129 (1985); Note, *Computer Programs as Goods Under the U.C.C.*, 77 Mich. L. Rev. 1149 (1979).

27. *See, e.g., Youngtech, Inc. v. Beijing Book Co., Inc.*, 2006 WL 3903976, at *5 (N.J. Super. Ct. App. Div. Dec. 29, 2006) ("However, most jurisdictions treat computer software development and sales not as a service but as goods subject to the UCC, both for the sake of uniformity and clarity of the law and because software is on discs and is a tangible and moveable item rather than an intangible idea.").

obtained, copied, or transferred effortlessly at the stroke of a computer key, licensing of such Internet products has assumed a vast importance in recent years. Recognizing that "a body of law based on images of the sale of manufactured goods ill fits licenses and other transactions in computer information," the National Conference of Commissioners on Uniform State Laws has promulgated the Uniform Computer Information Transactions Act. . . . We need not decide today whether UCC Article 2 applies to Internet transactions in downloadable products. The district court's analysis and the parties' arguments on appeal show that, for present purposes, there is no essential difference between UCC Article 2 and the common law of contracts. We therefore apply the common law, with exceptions as noted.[28]

b. What Is a "Transaction in Goods"?

Courts subscribe to one of two schools of thought with regard to the meaning of "transaction" under Article 2. First, all jurisdictions agree that Article 2 applies to the sale of goods. Under Article 2, a "sale" occurs upon "the passing of title from the seller to the buyer for a price."[29] And, "[u]nless otherwise explicitly agreed title passes to the buyer at the time and place at which the seller completes performance with reference to the delivery of the goods. . . ."[30] We further discuss the concept of "title" along with "risk of loss" and delivery later in this chapter, but, for our purposes, an Article 2 "sale" occurs when the seller, in exchange for a price, satisfies its obligations to deliver goods. A seller's delivery obligations are generally set by contract; for example, a contract may require the seller to deliver the goods to the buyer's location or not to deliver the goods at all.

Some courts have held that Article 2 may apply to transactions in goods other than pure sales. These courts justify their position by making some combination of two arguments: (1) that the word "transaction" is plainly broader than the word "sale"; and (2) that transactions similar to sales should be treated as sales by analogy.[31] In contradistinction, other courts have noticed that

---

28. *Specht v. Netscape Commc'ns Corp.*, 306 F.3d 17, 30 n.13 (2d Cir. 2002) (internal citations omitted) (California law).

29. U.C.C. § 2-106(1) (2003).

30. *Id.* § 2-401(2).

31. *See, e.g., Imaging Fin. Serv., Inc. v. Lettergraphics/Detroit, Inc.*, No. 97-1930, 1999 WL 115473, at *5 (6th Cir. Feb. 9, 1999) ("The use of the term transaction rather than sale in U.C.C. § 2-102 is significant in that it makes clear that the reach of Article 2 goes beyond those transactions where there is a transfer of title. Thus, Article 2 sections have been applied in decisions involving transactions that are not sales, but which are used as substitutes for a sale or which have attributes analogous to a sale, such as leases, bailments, or construction contracts.") (quoting *Wells v. 10-X Mfg. Co.*, 609 F.2d 248, 254 n.3 (6th Cir. 1979)); *Embryo Progeny Assocs. v. Lovana Farms*, 416 S.E.2d 833, 835 (Ga. Ct. App. 1992) ("'[T]ransactions in goods' to which the sales article of the Uniform Commercial Code applies, has been given a broader meaning than the sale of goods."); *Xerox Corp. v. Hawkes*, 475 A.2d 7, 9 (N.H. 1984) ("Although a 'lease' and not a 'sale' was contemplated by the parties to the service agreements, the Uniform Commercial Code still applies to the warranty provisions of the two service agreements. [U.C.C. § 2-102] does not refer to 'sales,' but instead to 'transactions in goods.'").

Article 2 defines "goods" as movable things subject to a contract for *sale* and have held, then, that a "transaction in goods" requires an actual sale of goods.[32] Even where a transaction takes the form of a non-sale transaction, a court may characterize the transaction, based on its economic substance, as a sale.[33] Accordingly, whether Article 2 governs a particular non-sale transaction in goods largely depends on the jurisdiction, a court's willingness to read Article 2 broadly, and the economic substance of a transaction.

For example, software publishers usually characterize the exchange of software for cash consideration as a "license" and not as a "sale."[34] These license agreements often take the form of so-called "shrink-wrap" or "click-wrap" license agreements. "Shrink-wrap" license agreements require a user to agree to license terms before tearing open the shrink-wrap plastic that covers a software box, and "click-wrap" license agreements require a user to click a dialog box on a computer screen indicating the user's assent to certain license terms before the user may access the software. Courts generally enforce these agreements.[35] However, enforceability notwithstanding, some courts will look past an agreement's self-identification as a "license" to find the transaction to be a "sale" for Article 2 purposes.[36] Even without recasting the parties' transaction as a sale, many courts have been willing—if begrudgingly—to apply Article 2 to software license transactions.[37] In so doing, some courts have found comfort in precedent for a broad reading of "transaction in goods," while others have applied Article 2 for lack of a better alternative.[38]

---

32. *See, e.g., Neuhoff v. Marvin Lumber and Cedar Co.*, 370 F.3d 197, 205 (1st Cir. 2004) ("Article 2 of the U.C.C. applies to all 'transactions in goods.' Typically, the U.C.C. only implies warranties in connection with goods that are involved in a 'sale.' In contrast, gifts do not receive implied warranties under Article 2.") (internal citations omitted); *Computer Servicenters, Inc. v. Beacon Mfg. Co.*, 328 F. Supp. 653, 654-55 (D.S.C. 1970) ("'Goods' as used in the section means 'all things (including specially manufactured goods) which are movable at the time of identification to the contract for sale. . . .' That definition is indeed broad, however, it must be noted that the article deals with, and the definition of goods is cast in terms of, the contract for sale.") (internal citations omitted).

33. *See, e.g., Neilson Bus. Equip. Ctr., Inc. v. Italo V. Monteleone, M.D., P.A.*, 524 A.2d 1172, 1175 (Del. 1987) ("Here, the parties cast their agreement in terms of a lease with an option . . . to purchase the computer system later. Although structured as a lease, it is clear that the parties intended to enter into the equivalent of a purchase and sale. . . . Though structured as a lease, the substance of the transaction was a sale. . . .").

34. A major reason software publishers license, instead of sell, their software is to avoid the so-called "first sale doctrine," which gives the first purchaser of certain intellectual property (most notably, copyrighted works) the right to resell the work without risk of infringement.

35. *See, e.g., ProCD, Inc. v. Zeidenberg*, 86 F.3d 1447, 1449 (7th Cir. 1996) ("Shrinkwrap licenses are enforceable unless their terms are objectionable on grounds applicable to contracts in general.").

36. *See, e.g., Sagent Tech., Inc. v. Micros Sys., Inc.*, 276 F. Supp. 2d 464, 467 n.1 (D. Md. 2003) ("[T]he U.C.C. should apply to a transaction that, although labeled a license, is for all practical purposes a sale of computer software.").

37. *See, e.g., i.Lan Sys., Inc. v. Netscout Serv. Level Corp.*, 183 F. Supp. 2d 328, 332 (D. Mass. 2002) ("For the time being, Article 2's familiar provisions—which are the inspiration for UCITA—better fulfill those expectations than would the common law. Article 2 technically does not, and certainly will not in the future, govern software licenses, but for the time being, the Court will assume it does."); *Colonial Life Ins. Co. of Am. v. Elec. Data Sys. Corp.*, 817 F. Supp. 235, 239 (D.N.H. 1993) ("The Court holds that the Uniform Commercial Code, as adopted in New Hampshire, applies to the contract between EDS and Chubb, the principal object of which was to provide for a license to use computer software."); *Schroders, Inc. v. Hogan Sys., Inc.*, 522 N.Y.S.2d 404, 406 (N.Y.

In fact, the National Conference of Commissioners on Uniform State Laws proposed, in 1999, that a uniform act be added to the U.C. C., as Article 2B. The proposal for U.C.C. Article 2B called for a more comprehensive and tailored approach to addressing computer information transactions generally, software licenses especially. However, this proposal was met with meaningful opposition, and the American Law Institute refused to cast its necessary vote in favor of creating the proposed Article 2B. The NCCUSL went on to release the model act on its own as the Uniform Computer Information Transactions Act ("UCITA"). Accordingly, while not a part of the U.C.C., UCITA has gone on to become statutory law in two states: Virginia and Maryland.[39]

The next event in this saga occurred in 2010, when the ALI published the Principles of the Law of Software Contracts, the purpose of which is to present "legal principles to guide courts in deciding disputes involving transactions in software and to guide those drafting software contracts."[40] Accordingly, the Principles do not represent a model code or uniform act, along the lines of the U.C.C. or UCITA, to be adopted by state legislatures as statutory law. Rather, the Principles are similar to the Restatements of the Law (which, incidentally, the ALI also promulgates), a body of "soft law" published to influence and guide common law courts—in the case of the Principles, in deciding contract matters involving software. What level of prominence and influence the Principles of the Law of Software Contracts attains remains to be seen.

c. "Mixed" Contracts for Both Goods and Services

The real world features a variety of worthwhile business transactions that happen not to fit the sort of tidy boxes that sometimes preoccupy the minds of lawyers. The reality is that sometimes transactions are for goods, sometimes they

---

App. Div. 1987) ("Although the parties' agreement in the instant matter did not involve sale of computer hardware, but simply a licensure of software, the arrangement should nevertheless be construed to fall within the provisions of UCC Article 2."). *See also Cytyc Corp. v. DEKA Prod. Ltd. P'ship*, 439 F.3d 27, 35-36 (1st Cir. 2006) ("Indeed, it is hopelessly unclear whether this provision, which appears in New Hampshire's version of Article 2 of the Uniform Commercial Code, governs agreements to license patented intellectual property."); *Arbitron, Inc. v. Tralyn Broad., Inc.*, 400 F.3d 130, 138 (2d Cir. 2005) ("It is not clear whether, under New York law, a license agreement of the sort at issue in this case [of copyrighted radio listener data] constitutes a contract for the sale of goods, or is otherwise governed by the U.C.C.").

38. *See supra* note 37.

39. Md. Code Ann., Com. Law I § 22-101 (West 2000); Va. Code. Ann. § 59.1-501.1 (Michie 2001). In response to the passage of UCITA, several states passed "bomb shelter" acts that void a choice-of-law and/or forum provision that would result in the application of UCITA. *See, e.g.,* Iowa Code § 554D.104 (2000); Iowa Code § 554D.125 (2005); N.C. Gen. Stat. § 66-329 (2001); Vt. Stat. Ann. tit. 9, § 2463a (2003); W. Va. Code § 55-8-15 (2001).

40. The American Law Institute, Principles of the Law of Software Contracts, http://www.ali.org/index.cfm?fuseaction=projects.proj_ip&projectid;=9 (last visited July 23, 2010); *see also* The American Law Institute, Principles of the Law of Software Contracts, http://www.ali.org/index.cfm?fuseaction=publications.ppage&node_id =121 (last visited July 23, 2010).

are for services, and sometimes they are for both goods and services. For example, as we see in this chapter's agreement, a buyer of computer-related products may wish to purchase not only the products but also, as part of the same transaction, any services necessary to use, support, and maintain the products. Certainly you can relate: When was the last time you bought a computer or television (or just about anything) without a sales associate trying to sell you additional support services? Other examples abound: If a buyer commissions a painter to produce a painting, is the buyer purchasing the painter's services or the resulting painting? If a buyer pays a carpeting manufacturer to install carpeting in the buyer's building, is the buyer purchasing the manufacturer's carpeting or the manufacturer's installation services? The answer is both; the question is whether and how Article 2 applies to these contracts for both goods and services.

The majority of states answer this question by applying what is called the "predominate-factor" test.[41] Under the predominate-factor test, "the court determines whether [the parties'] predominant factor, their thrust, their purpose, reasonably stated, is the rendition of service, with goods incidentally involved (e.g., contract with artist for painting) or is a transaction of sale, with labor incidentally involved (e.g., installation of a water heater in a bathroom)."[42] In determining the primary purpose of a contract, courts will look to the contract's language, the parties' purpose for entering the contract (i.e., to produce goods or services), the relative costs of the goods and services involved, whether the contract charges separately for goods and services, and, if so, the relative contract price of the goods and services.[43] A drafter can help guide a court's framing and understanding of a contract by prominently (e.g., in the title of the contract) and consistently specifying throughout a contract that the contract is really

---

41. *See BMC Indus. v. Barth Indus.*, 160 F.3d 1322, 1329 (11th Cir. 1998) ("Most courts follow the 'predominant factor' test to determine whether such hybrid contracts are transactions in goods, and therefore covered by the UCC, or transactions in services, and therefore excluded."); *Care Display, Inc. v. Didde-Glaser, Inc.*, 589 P.2d 599, 605 (Kan. 1979) ("The test for inclusion or exclusion is not whether they are mixed, but, granting that they are mixed, whether their predominant factor, their thrust, their purpose, reasonably stated, is the rendition of service.").

42. *BMC Indus.*, 160 F.3d at 1330 (Florida law).

43. *See, e.g., Paramount Aviation Corp. v. Agusta*, 288 F.3d 67, 72 (3d Cir. 2002) (New Jersey law) ("In making this determination, a court must examine the whole transaction and . . . main objective of the parties' agreement. Courts look to the language and circumstances surrounding the contract, the relationship between the goods and services, the compensation structure and the intrinsic worth of the goods provided.") (internal citations and quotation marks omitted); *BMC Indus.*, 160 F.3d at 1330 ("Although courts generally have not found any single factor determinative in classifying a hybrid contract as one for goods or services, courts find several aspects of a contract particularly significant. First, the language of the contract itself provides insight into whether the parties believed the goods or services were the more important element of their agreement. Contractual language that refers to the transaction as a 'purchase,' for example, or identifies the parties as the 'buyer' and 'seller,' indicates that the transaction is for goods rather than services. Courts also examine the manner in which the transaction was billed; when the contract price does not include the cost of services, or the charge for goods exceeds that for services, the contract is more likely to be for goods.") (internal citations and quotation marks omitted).

about the sale of goods or really about the provision of services, as the case may be.[44]

In further considering the application of the "predominate-factor" test, we return to the case of *Advent Systems*.

Advent Systems Ltd. v. Unisys Corp.
United States Court of Appeals, Third Circuit, 1991.
925 F.2d 670.

[This case is continued from page 229.]

The relationship at issue here is a typical mixed goods and services arrangement. The services are not substantially different from those generally accompanying package sales of computer systems consisting of hardware and software.

Although determining the applicability of the U.C.C. to a contract by examining the predominance of goods or services has been criticized, we see no reason to depart from that practice here. As we pointed out in [in a previous case], segregating goods from non-goods and insisting "that the Statute of Frauds apply only to a portion of the contract, would be to make the contract divisible and impossible of performance within the intention of the parties."

We consider the purpose or essence of the contract. Comparing the relative costs of the materials supplied with the costs of the labor may be helpful in this analysis, but not dispositive.

In this case the contract's main objective was to transfer "products." The specific provisions for training of Unisys personnel by Advent were but a small part of the parties' contemplated relationship.

The compensation structure of the agreement also focuses on "goods." The projected sales figures introduced during the trial demonstrate that in the contemplation of the parties the sale of goods clearly predominated. The payment provision of $150,000 for developmental work which Advent had previously completed, was to be made through individual purchases of software and hardware rather than through the fees for services and is further evidence that the intellectual work was to be subsumed into tangible items for sale.

We are persuaded that the transaction at issue here was within the scope of the Uniform Commercial Code and, therefore, the judgment in favor of the plaintiff must be reversed. . . .

[This case is continued on page 281.]

---

44. *See, e.g., Old Country Toyota Corp. v. Toyota Motor Distribs., Inc.*, 966 F. Supp. 167, 169 (E.D.N.Y. 1997) ("The prominence of the word 'sales' and its location in the Agreement's title . . . are revealing."); *Conopco, Inc. v. McCreadie*, 826 F. Supp. 855, 868 (D.N.J. 1993) ("The initial engagement letter . . . unmistakably contemplates a services agreement, referring in its opening to 'the management consulting services you requested' and indicating elsewhere that 'we will serve as facilitators and implementors.'").

Under the majority "predominate-factor" test, the court determines whether the contract is predominately about goods or not. If the contract is predominately about goods, then the court applies Article 2 to the whole contract; if not, then Article 2 does not apply at all.[45] In general, this is an all-or-nothing endeavor. However, where a contract is "divisible," some courts have applied Article 2 to the goods portion of a contract and the common law to the non-goods portion.[46] A willingness to "bifurcate" contracts and to apply Article 2 only to a portion of a contract has been attributed to a "minority" position; however, it seems even "predominate-factor" courts have found occasion to divide contracts and to apply Article 2 only to its goods-related parts.[47] Warranties present a prominent example of this. As Article 2 is the source of certain implied warranties that may not otherwise be available, plaintiffs often argue for Article 2's broad application so as to support a claim for breach of warranty.

---

45. *See, e.g.*, *United States v. City of Twin Falls*, 806 F.2d 862, 871 (9th Cir. 1986), *cert denied*, 482 U.S. 914 (1987) ("[W]e find that the predominant factor, thrust, and purpose of the contract . . . was for the sale of goods, with a necessary, non-divisible, but incidental services component. We . . . hold that as a matter of Idaho law, this contract was governed by the Idaho Uniform Commercial Code."); *Wheeler Peak, LLC v. L.C.I.2, Inc.*, No. CIV 07-1117 JB/WDS, 2009 WL 1329115, at *3 (D.N.M. Apr. 13, 2009) ("While '[a] minority of jurisdictions divide a mixed contract for goods and services into its component parts and apply Article 2 solely to the transaction for the sale of goods,' in New Mexico such mixed contracts are governed by one body of law determined according to the primary purpose test.") (quoting *Kirkpatrick v. Introspect Healthcare Corp.*, 845 P.2d 800, 803 (N.M. 1992)); *Respect, Inc. v. Comm. on Status of Women*, 781 F. Supp. 1358, 1364 (N.D. Ill. 1992) ("If the contract is predominantly for goods, then the entire contract falls within the ambit of UCC Article 2. If it is primarily a contract for services, then the entire contract must be tested by common-law standards.") (internal citations omitted).

46. *See BMC Indus.*, 160 F.3d at 1329 n.13 ("A few courts do not categorize hybrid contracts as either transactions in goods or services, but rather apply the UCC only to the sale of goods elements of the contract.") (citing *Foster v. Colorado Radio Corp.*, 381 F.2d 222, 226 (10th Cir. 1967)); *TK Power, Inc. v. Textron, Inc.*, 443 F. Supp. 2d 1058, 1064 (N.D. Cal. 2006) ("A number of courts have held that where a transaction involves a mix of 'goods' covered by the UCC and non-goods such as service or real estate, the court may apply non-UCC law to that portion of the contract that does not involve 'goods.'"). In *TK Power*, the court explained that whether or not a contract is "divisible" for Article 2 purposes turned on three factors:

1. Whether the non-goods aspect of the transaction is clearly distinct and easily separable from the goods aspect. . . .
2. Whether the alleged performance or non-performance pertains solely to the non-goods aspect of the transaction.
3. Whether it makes sense to apply the UCC to the non-goods aspect of the transaction and whether applying non-UCC law accords with the parties' intent.

433 F. Supp. 2d at 1064. The court went on to find, "All three factors are present here. Under these circumstances, even if it is assumed that there was a larger agreement of which the prototype development was only a part, applying the common law to this segregable portion of the transaction comports with the purposes of the UCC. . . ." *Id.* at 1064-65.

47. *See, e.g., TK Power*, 433 F. Supp. 2d at 1062-65 (reciting the predominate-factor test and then proceeding to apply the common law to the non-Article-2 portion of an arguably larger contract).

Some courts have refused to extend Article 2 warranties to the services component of a contract predominately for the sale of goods.[48]

As we turn our attention to this chapter's agreement, please consider whether or not Article 2 is likely to apply. Is this agreement for goods? Is this agreement for services? If it is for both, is a court applying the predominate-factor test likely to find the agreement to be within the scope of Article 2? As we began to discuss in Chapter 3, a prudent drafter will plan for the possibility that a court may find Article 2 to govern his contract.

B. MASTER PURCHASE AGREEMENT

The following Master Purchase Agreement contains the terms pursuant to which Dell Products L.P. and Dell Computer Corporation's other subsidiaries and affiliates (collectively, "Dell") will purchase products from Adaptec, Inc., the manufacturer of a range of products for data centers and cloud computing environments.

Things to Consider . . .

As you read through the following agreement, please consider these items. You will want to return to the agreement, as you study the substantive discussion that follows.

> **Price.** What price or pricing mechanism have the parties agreed to for the goods to be sold under this Agreement? Is price determined as of this Agreement? If not, have the parties agreed as to how price will be determined?

> **Quantity.** How many goods are to be sold under this Agreement? Is this determined as of this Agreement? Does the Agreement impose any obligations on the parties with respect to the quantity of goods to be sold, or at least with respect to the determination of the quantity of goods to be sold under this Agreement?

> **Acceptance.** How does this Agreement provide that the buyer may accept or reject goods that the seller delivers to the buyer? Are there certain restrictions (e.g., time period) on what constitutes effective acceptance or rejection under this Agreement? What rights of the buyer are triggered (and what rights of the buyer are lost) by the buyer's acceptance of goods?

---

48. *See, e.g., Lemley v. J & B Tire Co.*, 426 F. Supp. 1378, 1379 (W.D. Pa. 1977) ("Even in those hybrid sale-service transactions . . . , that liability is limited to defects in the product supplied and does not include nonnegligent mistakes in the service.").

[Note that a footnote to the following agreement as published on EDGAR states: "Confidential treatment requested: Certain portions of this agreement have been omitted pursuant to a request for confidential treatment and, where applicable, have been marked with an asterisk to denote where omissions have been made. The confidential material has been filed separately with the Securities and Exchange Commission."[49] In the following agreement, these omissions generally relate to specific business terms, and the authors have generally edited this agreement around these omissions.]

DELL SUPPLIER MASTER PURCHASE AGREEMENT[50]

This Master Purchase Agreement by and between Adaptec, Inc. ("SUPPLIER"), a corporation registered in Delaware and located for the purposes of this Agreement at 691 S. Milpitas Boulevard, Milpitas, California 95035 and Dell Products L.P., a Texas limited partnership located at One Dell Way, Round Rock, Texas 78682, is effective as of September 27, 2002 ("Effective Date"). This Master Purchase Agreement and its Schedules, Addenda, Exhibits and Attachments, as so identified, will be hereinafter collectively referred to as the "Agreement."

1.0 Introduction

This Agreement sets forth the only terms and conditions under which Dell Products L.P. and Dell Computer Corporation's other subsidiaries and affiliates (collectively, "Dell") will purchase products from SUPPLIER. The terms and conditions of this Agreement will apply to all products purchased by Dell from SUPPLIER. For the purpose of this Agreement, products include required service, and any software and/or documentation that accompany the products (collectively, "Products"). Unless specifically stated otherwise, all references to Product will include, without limitation, all services and spare parts necessary for SUPPLIER to meet the terms of this Agreement. The terms and conditions of this Agreement will apply to all purchase orders ("Dell PO(s)") issued by Dell for the purchase of Products.

2.0 Term and Termination

The initial term of this Agreement will be three (3) years beginning on the Effective Date. This Agreement will automatically renew for additional successive one-year terms unless one party informs the other of its intent to let the Agreement expire one hundred and eighty (180) days before the end of the then-current term. Either party may terminate this Agreement based on the material breach of the other party, provided that the party

---

49. Adaptec Inc, Dell Supplier Master Purchase Agreement (Form 8-K), at Exhibit 99.1 (Jan. 24, 2003), *available at* http://www.sec.gov/Archives/edgar/data/709804/000104746903002474/a2100825zex-99_1.htm.
50. *Id.*

alleged to be in material breach receives written notice stating the cause and sixty (60) days to cure.

3.0 Price

3.1 SUPPLIER agrees to work with Dell to develop a mutually agreed-upon pricing model for each Product no less than ninety (90) days prior to planned first shipment that meets Dell's price/ performance objectives and provides an agreed-upon level of return for SUPPLIER. The unit price for each Product may be reviewed on a quarterly basis or as otherwise required by Dell. . . . Worldwide prices will be negotiated between SUPPLIER and Dell Worldwide Procurement at Dell's corporate headquarters in Austin, Texas.

3.2 Dell expects material cost reductions to be worked aggressively by SUPPLIER. . . . SUPPLIER will review with Dell, on an ongoing basis [details omitted]. All prices will be in United States dollars and are exclusive of applicable sales taxes, but are inclusive of all other charges including any charges for freight, freight insurance, labeling, packing and crating, any finishing or inspecting fees, any applicable royalties, duties and all other taxes. Dell will have no liability for any tax for which it has an appropriate exemption.

3.3 . . . SUPPLIER agrees to provide service spare part pricing on a monthly basis as requested by Dell Service. Dell shall have the right, but not the obligation, to have the pricing audited by a mutually agreed independent third party upon five (5) days notice to SUPPLIER. Dell agrees that the exclusive remedy of Dell and sole liability of SUPPLIER for any failure by SUPPLIER to comply with this Section 3.3 shall be the right of Dell to receive the payment, if any, determined by such audit to be owed to Dell and/or the right of Dell to terminate this Agreement.

4.0 Payment

4.1 Unless otherwise agreed in writing, all payments will be stated (and payments made) in United States dollars and are exclusive of applicable sales, use or similar taxes for which Dell will be obligated to pay SUPPLIER. All invoices for Products received by Dell will be accumulated, upon receipt, for a period from the 16th day of a month to the 15th day of the following month (the "Accumulation Period"). Dell will pay invoices received during the Accumulation Period net [x] days from the end of such Accumulation Period. . . . No invoice can be dated prior to the date the Products reflected in such invoice are received or in the case of products shipped directly to Dell factories, the date of such shipment.

4.2 SUPPLIER acknowledges and agrees that Dell has the right to withhold any applicable taxes from any royalties or other payments due under this Agreement if required by any government authority.

5.0 Delivery of Products

5.1 The parties recognize that Products may be provided to Dell in two ways: (i) from an approved Supplier Logistics Center ("SLC"), or (ii) directly to Dell without use of an SLC. The parties recognize that some terms and conditions will be the same in both situations and others terms may vary depending on the method by which Dell receives the Products. The parties, therefore, agree that the applicable provisions will be as follows:

5.2 Provisions applicable to Products whether or not an SLC is used:

5.2.1 SUPPLIER will exert commercially reasonable efforts to meet scheduled delivery dates. Subject to the provisions of Section 5.2.4, SUPPLIER agrees to fill all Dell POs and will use commercially reasonable efforts to reduce the lead-time during the term of this Agreement. SUPPLIER will not ship Products to Dell that were manufactured in locations not approved in advance and in writing by Dell.

5.2.2 SUPPLIER will handle, pack, mark and ship the Products in accordance with Dell's packaging and labeling specifications (P/N's 11500 and 13190, respectively). SUPPLIER will meet additional packaging and labeling requirements of Dell Service, as stated in Dell Document #40.09.SQ.0055. Upon request, Dell will provide a copy of these specifications and requirements to SUPPLIER.

5.2.3 All Products are subject to inspection and acceptance at destination, notwithstanding any prior payments or inspection. This inspection and acceptance process may include the following, without limitation:

(a) Dell may perform those tests it deems necessary to determine if the Products are acceptable. If, upon inspection, Dell reasonably determines that the Products are defective or otherwise fail to comply with SUPPLIER'S Product specifications, Dell may reject an entire lot based upon a sampling or inspect all units of the lot. Any such lot may be returned to SUPPLIER for one hundred percent (100%) retesting within forty-eight (48) hours at SUPPLIER'S cost. After the retesting, the lot may be reinspected by Dell.

(b) Dell's acceptance of any Products will in no way be construed as a representation by Dell that Dell has completely tested the Products or that such Products comply with their specifications or conform to any other warranties made by SUPPLIER under this Agreement. Dell's acceptance of any Product will in no way negate any warranty provided under this Agreement or affect any other provision of this Agreement.

Acceptance is only to be used to determine whether SUPPLIER is entitled to receive payment for the Products.

(c) Dell will be deemed to have accepted the Products only in the event that Dell: (i) fails to accept or reject the Products within two (2) days of delivery to Dell, (ii) explicitly accepts the Products in writing, (iii) uses the Products in Dell's manufacturing process and the Products successfully complete final test, or (iv) delivers the Products to any customer.

5.2.4 On approximately a monthly basis, Dell will provide rolling six (6) month forecasts of projected purchases of Products for AMF, NCC, EMF, APCC, CCC, BCC and potentially other delivery locations, but any such forecasts provided by Dell are for planning purposes only and do not constitute a commitment of any type by Dell. No later than three (3) days after receipt of the Dell six (6) month forecast, SUPPLIER shall advise Dell whether or not it can confirm supply for the rolling six (6) month period (current month plus five) and if not, SUPPLIER shall advise Dell of the supply to which it can commit. Confirmation of the forecast by SUPPLIER shall constitute a commitment by SUPPLIER to provide the forecasted quantities to Dell, if ordered by Dell.

5.2.5 Dell will transmit Dell PO(s) by facsimile or other agreed upon means to cover Dell's forecasted requirements for the next two (2) months. Such Dell PO(s) will be continually updated to reflect Dell's next two (2) month forecast. SUPPLIER will send Dell an acknowledgement within two (2) business days of receipt of the Dell PO confirming the quantity, delivery date and delivery location(s). . . . Upon Dell's request, SUPPLIER will execute a monthly reconciliation of open Dell POs. SUPPLIER will perform this reconciliation within three (3) business days of Dell's request.

5.2.6 Except as expressly set forth in this Agreement, any expenditures or commitments by SUPPLIER in anticipation of Dell's requirements will be at SUPPLIER'S sole risk and expense.

5.3 Delivery to Dell using an SLC:

5.3.1 Unless Dell specifically requests that Product be delivered directly to Dell, all Product delivered under this Agreement to Dell for manufacturing and service will come from inventory held by SUPPLIER at an approved SLC ("Revolver Inventory"). SUPPLIER agrees to maintain an SLC for American Manufacturing Facility ("AMF") in Austin, Texas, Nashville Customer Center ("NCC") in Nashville, Tennessee, and the European Manufacturing Facility ("EMF") in Limerick, Ireland. As reasonably requested by Dell, SUPPLIER agrees to maintain an SLC for Asia Pacific Customer Center ("APCC") in Penang, Malaysia, China Configuration Center in Xiamen, China ("CCC"), Brazil Customer Center ("BCC") in

Eldorado do Sul, Brazil and, any other major delivery locations reasonably requested by Dell. If the Product volume in a particular region does not warrant the use of an SLC, Dell may provide SUPPLIER with a written waiver relieving the SUPPLIER of its revolver obligations for that particular region until such time as the volumes warrant reinstatement or implementation of an SLC.

5.3.2 SUPPLIER agrees to maintain Revolver Inventory at each SLC in quantities equal to Dell's most recent two (2) week forecasted demand requirements for the applicable Dell location unless otherwise agreed to in writing by the applicable Dell region. After four weeks of operation, the two (2) week inventory will be calculated as follows: one (1) week based on the average of Dell PO(s) for the preceding four weeks and the second week based on the most recent Dell forecast. The parties will work together to determine the appropriate Revolver Inventory required for End of Life ("EOL") situations. SUPPLIER agrees to replenish the Revolver Inventory as necessary to ensure the required Revolver Inventory is on hand at all times. Dell and SUPPLIER will meet periodically for an inventory pipeline assessment. At this meeting, inventory status at both Dell and SUPPLIER will be reviewed, along with any changes in Dell demand.

5.3.3 Dell's transmission of a Pull Order is SUPPLIER'S only authorization to deliver Products to Dell and invoice Dell for the part numbers and quantities set forth in the Pull Order. Title and risk of loss will not pass to Dell until the Products are pulled from the SLC and Dell takes physical possession and control of the Products at the applicable Dell manufacturing facility. . . .

5.3.4 In the event that Dell requests that SUPPLIER utilize used or repaired parts to meet the needs of Dell Service, such used or repaired parts will be clearly marked as used and will be segregated from new Product inventory.

5.4 Delivery directly to Dell without using an SLC:

5.4.1 If Dell authorizes SUPPLIER to deliver Product directly from SUPPLIER to Dell without using a SLC, the following terms will apply. SUPPLIER will schedule delivery of each Product to the delivery location on the delivery date listed in the Dell PO. Delivery will not be deemed to be complete until all Products have been actually delivered to the applicable delivery location. SUPPLIER will not make deliveries more than three (3) days earlier than the delivery date. If Products are delivered more than three (3) days early, Dell may: (i) refuse to take possession of all or some of the Products in which case Products that are returned will be redelivered only upon Dell's instructions or (ii) store the Products at

SUPPLIER'S risk and expense and delay processing the corresponding invoice until the agreed to delivery date. SUPPLIER will inform Dell immediately if late deliveries become likely in which case SUPPLIER will ship the Products by air-freight or other expedited routing, at SUPPLIER'S expense. Dell reserves the right to cancel deliveries on Dell PO(s) that are at least [x days] past-due unless delayed shipment is mutually agreed in advance. If only a portion of the Products are available for shipment to meet the delivery date, SUPPLIER will notify Dell and ship the available Products unless otherwise directed by Dell. Dell may return any unauthorized under-shipment or any over-shipment or any portions thereof, at SUPPLIER'S expense and without charge to Dell. If a complete delivery is not made after Dell receives confirmation of the shipment, SUPPLIER will pay to Dell the sum of $ (to be discussed) for each unit not delivered.

5.4.2 Dell's transmission of a Dell PO is SUPPLIER'S only authorization to deliver Products to Dell and invoice Dell for the part numbers and quantities set forth in the Dell PO. Title and risk of loss will not pass to Dell until Dell takes physical possession and control of the Products at the applicable Dell manufacturing facility. . . .

6.0 Acceleration . . . and Cancellation

6.1 Acceleration:

6.1.1 Dell may, without cost or liability, increase the pull quantities scheduled to be delivered to Dell, over and above its confirmed six (6) month rolling forecast as follows:

Days From Planned delivery to Dell	Acceleration Amount
0-10	15%
11-30	30%
31-60	75%
61+	100%

(By way of example, if on January 1 Dell wanted to increase the quantities scheduled to be delivered on January 20, SUPPLIER agrees to increase the originally scheduled delivery quantity by up to 30%.)

6.1.2 In order to ensure that SUPPLIER can meet the upside requirements, SUPPLIER will maintain a safety stock for certain Product components, which will include without limitation any Dell unique components, as follows:

Component	Weeks of Supply
All of IOPs Memory, and Controllers, and any other components experiencing increasing lead-times or industry allocation	8

6.2 [Omitted]

6.3 Cancellation:

6.3.1 Dell may, without cost or liability, cancel Dell PO(s) as follows:

[Schedule of Dell's Cancellation Rights and Obligations Omitted]

To be entitled to consideration under this Agreement, SUPPLIER must meet the following conditions: (i) provide documentation of its actual incurred costs as a result of Dell's cancellation, (ii) limit such costs to Dell-unique components that cannot be utilized by other customers, and (iii) use commercially reasonable efforts to mitigate Dell's liability.

6.3.2 If SUPPLIER'S quality does not meet the agreed-upon quality metrics set forth in the applicable Schedule, Dell may terminate (in whole or in part) any or all outstanding Dell PO(s) without liability or charge.

6.3.3 SUPPLIER acknowledges and agrees that the remedies set forth in this Section 6.3 represent the sole and exclusive remedies of SUPPLIER, and Dell's sole liability for, cancellation of Dell PO(s).

7.0 Documentation, Software and Trademarks

7.1 Documentation. SUPPLIER agrees to provide Dell with clear and accurate Product documentation ("Documentation"). The structure and content of the Documentation will be as specified by the applicable Dell commodity STR (Shared Technology Resource) [DEFINE]. The Documentation will be provided in hard copy, PDF and HTML formats unless otherwise requested by Dell. Dell may reproduce and distribute the Documentation in hard copy or softcopy form as well as in electronic form (e.g., on Dell's website). SUPPLIER agrees to provide such national language versions as are required by Dell. Supplier agrees to comply with Dell's Supplier E Docs (HTML) and Double-byte Language Testing Requirement.

7.2 Software. For all device drivers, firmware, and all necessary software for the proper operation and support of the Product (collectively "Software"), Dell is granted a non-exclusive, non-transferable . . . worldwide right and license to use, reproduce, and distribute the Software solely in connection with Dell's distribution and support of the Products including without limitation distribution in electronic form (e.g., via Dell's website). Dell may not prepare derivative works of Software accept as authorized by SUPPLIER in writing. SUPPLIER agrees to provide all updates to the Software to Dell during the term of this Agreement.

7.3 Trademarks. SUPPLIER hereby grants Dell a non-exclusive, non-transferable . . . worldwide right and license to utilize the SUPPLIER Trademarks in connection with advertising, promotion, and sale of Products. "SUPPLIER Trademarks" will mean those trademarks, trade names, service marks, slogans, designs, distinctive advertising, labels, logos, and other trade-identifying symbols as are or have been developed and used by SUPPLIER or any of its subsidiaries or affiliate companies anywhere in the world. Dell shall use the SUPPLIER Trademarks only in strict accordance with SUPPLIER's trademark and logo use guidelines as outlined in Schedule C. SUPPLIER shall provide Dell with notice prior to modifications to the SUPPLIER'S trademark and logo use guidelines. Dell agrees to implement such modifications into any materials created and distributed after receipt of such notice. Dell shall properly attribute the SUPPLIER Trademarks to SUPPLIER in any materials that reference or contain a SUPPLIER Trademark.

8.0 Product Withdrawal

SUPPLIER will provide Dell with at least [x days] written notice prior to the last date of manufacture of any Product. SUPPLIER will provide Product sufficient to meet Dell's forecasted pulls that SUPPLIER has confirmed before the last day of manufacture. SUPPLIER will provide Dell a one time, non-cancelable last time buy opportunity . . . prior to the last day of manufacture. SUPPLIER agrees to inventory last time buy quantities in an SLC for a period not to exceed [x days] from the last day of manufacture. All Product not pulled by the end of the [specified time period] will be shipped to Dell and invoiced at the PO price, subject to the parties' joint good faith efforts to otherwise dispose of the Products. Additionally, SUPPLIER will retain spare parts for the Products . . . from the last date of manufacture. If spares or repairs are not available, SUPPLIER will use reasonable efforts to provide similar product with equivalent or better functionality, subject to approval by Dell. SUPPLIER will allow Dell to make a final purchase in order to provide support for such Products. Dell may assign its rights to warranty replacement parts or end of life parts to a third party.

9.0 Warranties

9.1 SUPPLIER represents and warrants on an ongoing basis that:

(a) Dell will acquire good and marketable title to the Products, and that all Products will be free and clear of all liens, claims, encumbrances and other restrictions;

(b) All Products will be new and unused and will not contain used or repaired parts unless requested by Dell in writing, in which case such Products will be clearly labeled as refurbished;

(c) all Products will be free from defects in design, materials and workmanship, including but not limited to, cosmetic defects, and will conform to SUPPLIER'S Product specifications and specifications provided by Dell . . . from the Product manufacturing date code. SUPPLIER agrees to use a first-in/first-out inventory method for finished goods, and further agrees that the Product manufacturing date code will not be more than [x days] prior to shipment to Dell;

(d) Notwithstanding the foregoing, Batteries provided to Dell by SUPPLIER for use with SUPPLIER's Products will be free from defects in design, materials and workmanship, including but not limited to, cosmetic defects, and will conform to SUPPLIER'S Product specifications and specifications provided by Dell for thirteen (13) months from the Product manufacturing date code.

(e) it has all the rights and licenses in the Products necessary to allow Dell to distribute and resell Products without restriction or additional charge; and

(f) SUPPLIER will pass through warranty coverage from its suppliers, whenever allowable by (c) suppliers, upon the request of Dell Service.

9.2 SUPPLIER is responsible for reasonable out of pocket liability, cost and expense . . . with respect to defects in design, manufacturing process or material that constitute epidemic defects ("Epidemic Defects"). A defect is an Epidemic Defect when found in [x] or more of the units delivered during any three (3) month period.

9.3 Return Product. SUPPLIER agrees to fulfill the following terms and conditions.

9.3.1 The following provisions are applicable to return Product, whether returned from Dell manufacturing facilities or from the customer installed-base (field):

(a) At SUPPLIER's expense, Dell or Dell's designated service provider will return Product to a commercially reasonable location designated by SUPPLIER. Dell, at its sole option, will declare a credit (or demand a refund) equal to the last purchase price of the returned Product, which credit will be applied no later than five (5) days after Dell's notice of Product return. Dell may, at its sole option, apply such credit to the purchase of new Product, or repaired or replacement Product.

(b) In support of Dell's manufacturing and service organizations and to facilitate return of Products to SUPPLIER for credit or exchange, SUPPLIER will issue Return Material Authorization numbers ("RMA") in rolling blocks of up to fifty (50) for each Dell manufacturing facility and Dell Service organization. Dell or Dell's designated service provider will notify SUPPLIER when they have fifteen (15) pre-approved RMAs remaining and SUPPLIER will provide another block of fifty (50) pre-approved RMAs within two (2) business days of such request. If the additional RMAs are not provided within two business days, and no block RMAs remain, Dell will ship return Product to SUPPLIER without an RMA at SUPPLIER's expense. For each return shipment from Dell Service, a pre-shipment notification form will be provided to SUPPLIER communicating the Return PO number, part number, quantity, price, and extended value of that shipment. No additional information will be provided to return in-warranty Products to the SUPPLIER.

(c) SUPPLIER will establish and maintain an extended testing process for returned Products. This testing process will be subject to audit and approval by Dell's worldwide Supplier Quality Engineer. SUPPLIER will provide an initial failure analysis of the returned Product within forty-eight (48) hours of its receipt, and a failure analysis to the component level within ten (10) days of receipt. SUPPLIER will segregate and separately report returns by region.

9.3.2 The following provisions are applicable to Product returned from Dell's manufacturing facility:

(a) SUPPLIER will validate each returned Product, and will report the results of its testing to Dell on a weekly basis. This weekly report will reflect, by Product type and part number, the number of units returned, number of CND Manufacturing Products (as defined below), and number and type of defective parts. Additionally, SUPPLIER will validate that returned Product is not a result of a production test escape. For purposes of this Agreement, "CND Manufacturing Product" will refer to returned Product that has not yet been shipped to a Dell customer, for which SUPPLIER is unable to duplicate reported failures after thorough testing.

(b) Dell may (at its sole option) repurchase such CND Manufacturing Product for use in new product manufacturing, provided that such CND Manufacturing Product has completed extended testing. SUPPLIER will ensure that CND Manufacturing Product to be returned to Dell has completed such testing, and meets the latest Product revision and BIOS levels. SUPPLIER will warrant such returned Product in accordance with the terms of the full new Product warranty outlined above in this Section 9.0.

9.3.3 The following provisions are applicable to Product returned from the customer installed-base (the field):

(a) If Dell Service determines that a Product that has been shipped to a Dell customer must be returned to SUPPLIER, Dell or Dell's designated service provider will return such Product, untested, directly to the location designated by the SUPPLIER, documenting the transaction with a Dell return purchase order ("Return PO"). Dell Service will return all such Products to the SUPPLIER at SUPPLIER's expense, and will debit SUPPLIER's worldwide account in an amount equal to the last purchase price of the Product at the time of shipment from Dell or Dell's designated service provider. SUPPLIER agrees to provide to Dell these Return for Credit terms ("RFC", as further described below in this Section 9.3.3) on all Products returned from the field unless otherwise mutually agreed in writing. Dell will not be required to re-purchase the returned Product.

(b) For purposes of this Section, Product for which SUPPLIER cannot duplicate failures after thorough testing will be referred to as "CND Field Product". Dell may (at its sole option) repurchase CND Field Product (if any) for use by Dell Service, provided that such CND Field Product has completed extended testing. SUPPLIER will ensure that CND Field Product to be returned to Dell meets the latest Product revision and BIOS levels prior to being returned for Dell Service inventory. CND Field Product will be covered by the longer of (i) the remainder of the original warranty (as described in Section 9.1 above), or (ii) one hundred eighty (180) days. SUPPLIER will validate each returned Product, and will report the results of its testing to Dell on a weekly basis. This weekly report will reflect, by Product type and part number, the number of units returned, number of CND Field Products, and number and type of defective parts.

9.3.4 The following provisions are applicable to Product returned for repair using Dell Service's Exchange Process:

(a) Product that will be returned to SUPPLIER for repair will be referred to as "Return for Repair" or "RFR" Product. SUPPLIER will exchange all RFR Product with new or repaired Product within twenty-four (24) hours of receipt at SUPPLIER's facility. This mechanism will be referred to as the "Return for Exchange" or "RFE" Process.

(b) To support this RFE Process, SUPPLIER will SUPPLIER [sic] establish and maintain a finished goods exchange inventory ("FG Inventory") based on Dell Service's forecast. SUPPLIER will ensure that Product to be returned to Dell through the RFE Process has completed, thorough testing, and meets the latest Product revision and BIOS levels.

(c) SUPPLIER will perform all repairs within three (3) to five (5) business days of receipt of RFR Product. As the repaired Product is completed, it will be used to replenish the FG Inventory at the SUPPLIER'S facility. If at any point the required FG Inventory falls below seventy five percent (75%) of the inventory target (based on Dell Service's forecast and the RFE Process), SUPPLIER will meet the FG Inventory target requirements with new Product, at SUPPLIER's expense.

(d) All repaired or replacement Product being returned by SUPPLIER to Dell Service will be shipped at the expense of Dell Service. . . .

(e) To facilitate tracking and control of RFR Product return, Dell will debit SUPPLIER's worldwide account by means of a Return PO. This debit will reflect amounts consistent with the most recent purchase price of the Product, at the time of RFR Product shipment from Dell or Dell's designated service provider. Upon shipment by SUPPLIER of the repaired Product to Dell (for use by Dell Service), SUPPLIER will re-invoice Dell for the quantity and price specified on the applicable Return PO.

(f) At Dell's request, SUPPLIER will use Dell Service's capacity management process. If SUPPLIER'S repair capacity is insufficient to meet the requirements of this Section 9.3.4, SUPPLIER agrees to work diligently with Dell Service to certify a third-party repair center acceptable to Dell and agrees to authorize such center to perform in-warranty repair of Products on SUPPLIER'S behalf and expense.

(g) SUPPLIER will continue to support the RFE Process throughout the Product life cycle (i.e., while the Product is in-production, at end of production and during end of life).

9.4 SUPPLIER will provide [a certain type of] service to Dell at commercially reasonable prices for a period of [x days] after the last date of manufacture of a Dell system containing the Product. SUPPLIER agrees to provide three (3) to five (5) day turn around time (TAT) on all [such] repair unless instructed otherwise by Dell Service. Supplier will use commercially reasonable efforts to reduce the total cost of [such] service, while meeting Dell Service quality requirements.

10.0 Indemnification

10.1 SUPPLIER agrees to defend, indemnify and hold harmless Dell, Dell Computer Corporation, and all their respective directors, officers, employees agents and OEM distributors from and against any and all claims, actions, demands, legal proceedings, liabilities, damages, losses, judgments, authorized settlements, costs and expenses, including without limitation attorney's fees, arising out of or in connection with any alleged or actual:

(i) infringement by SUPPLIER and/or a Product(s), alone or in combination with SUPPLIER authorized hardware or software, of a copyright, patent, trademark, trade secret or other intellectual property right of any third party;

(ii) claim that a Product provided under this Agreement has caused bodily injury (including death) or has damaged real or tangible personal property;

(iii) claim arising out of or relating to SUPPLIER'S provision of repaired Products that contain used or refurbished parts that are not clearly and conspicuously labeled as such;

(iv) any violation by SUPPLIER of any governmental laws, rules, ordinances or regulations; and/or

(v) claim by or on behalf of SUPPLIER'S subcontractors, materialmen, providers, employees or agents.

10.2 SUPPLIER will provide the above indemnity even if losses are due, or alleged to be due, in part to Dell's concurrent negligence or other fault, breach of contract or warranty, violation of the Texas Deceptive Trade Practices Act, or strict liability without regard to fault; provided, however, that SUPPLIER'S contractual obligation of indemnification will not extend to the percentage of the third party claimant's damages or injuries or the settlement amount attributable to Dell's negligence or other fault, breach of contract or warranty, or breach of the Texas Deceptive Trade Practices Act, or to strict liability imposed upon Dell as a matter of law.

10.3 In the event of any such claims, Dell will: (i) promptly notify SUPPLIER, (ii) cooperate with SUPPLIER in the defense thereof and (iii) not settle any such claims without SUPPLIER'S consent, which SUPPLIER agrees not to unreasonably withhold.

10.4 In addition to SUPPLIER'S obligations and liabilities above, if an infringement claim is made or appears likely to be made about a Product, SUPPLIER will, at SUPPLIER'S option, either procure for Dell the right to continue to market the Product, modify the Product so that it is no longer infringing or replace it with a non-infringing Product. If the parties determine that none of these alternatives is commercially reasonable, Dell will return any Products in inventory freight-collect to SUPPLIER'S designated location for a credit or refund of the purchase price.

11.0 Liability

11.1 EXCEPT AS SET FORTH BELOW in Sections 11.2 and 11.3, NEITHER PARTY WILL BE LIABLE FOR ANY LOST PROFITS, LOST SAVINGS OR ANY OTHER INCIDENTAL, INDIRECT, PUNITIVE, SPE-CIAL, OR CONSEQUENTIAL DAMAGES UNDER ANY PART OF THIS AGREEMENT EVEN IF ADVISED OR AWARE OF THE POSSIBILITY OF SUCH DAMAGES.

11.2 SUPPLIER'S entire cumulative liability to Dell arising out of or in connection with or relating to this Agreement, the sale of Products, license of software, and the use, performance, receipt or disposition of such Products or software, from any cause whatsoever, whether based upon warranty, contract, tort, statute, or otherwise, shall not exceed all sums paid by Dell to SUPPLIER in the twelve (12) month period preceding the date of claim.

11.3 Notwithstanding the foregoing, the limitation set forth in Section 11.1 and 11.2 above will not apply to SUPPLIER'S obligations and liabilities under section 10.1(i) (Indemnification) and 18.4 (Confidentiality). SUPPLIER'S entire liability for each claim or cause of action for section 10.1(i) (Indemnification) and 18.4 (Confidentiality) shall not exceed the greater of all sums paid by Dell to SUPPLIER in the twelve (12) month period proceeding [sic] the date of claim. . . .

12.0 Quality, Product Safety, Regulatory Compliance and Engineering Changes

12.1 SUPPLIER agrees to meet or exceed the quality requirements set forth in the Schedule B.

12.2 In the event either SUPPLIER or Dell becomes aware of any information that reasonably supports a conclusion that a hazard may exist in any Product and the defect could cause death or bodily injury to any person or property damage (a "Hazard"), the party becoming aware of this information will notify the other of the potential Hazard. Whenever possible, notification to the other party will precede notice to any governmental agency, unless required by law. SUPPLIER and Dell will promptly exchange all relevant data and then, if practical, as promptly as possible, meet to review and discuss the information, tests, and conclusions relating to the alleged Hazard. At this meeting the parties will discuss the bases for any action, including a recall, and the origin or causation of the alleged Hazard. SUPPLIER will be responsible for the costs of effecting a recall including, but not limited to, the reasonable out-of-pocket costs to Dell directly related to the recall Each party will, on request, provide to the other reasonable assistance in (i) determining how best to deal with the Hazard; and (ii) preparing for and making any presentation before any governmental agency which may have jurisdiction over Hazards involving Products.

12.3 SUPPLIER is responsible for obtaining and maintaining all necessary U.S. and foreign regulatory approvals for the Product(s). Additionally, SUPPLIER will assist Dell in addressing problems with its Products that contribute to a Dell system's failure to meet any regulatory requirement due to SUPPLIER Products being integrated into the Dell system. Notwithstanding the foregoing, to the extent SUPPLIER provides sufficient detail to Dell that the Hazard is due to the interoperability of the Product with a Dell system, Dell agrees to meet with SUPPLIER to mutually agree on the cost allocation, between the parties, to execute a recall.

12.4 SUPPLIER may issue "Mandatory Changes," which are changes required to satisfy governmental standards or for safety. SUPPLIER will provide Dell with prior written notice of Mandatory Changes prior to implementing such changes. SUPPLIER will provide, at SUPPLIER'S expense, all necessary materials, reasonable labor and instructions if Mandatory Changes must be installed on Products already delivered to Dell. SUPPLIER will also provide ninety (90) days prior written notice of changes that affect any Product's (including Software or drivers) form, fit or function to allow Dell to evaluate such changes. . . . SUPPLIER agrees to supply Dell for evaluation purposes with up to twenty-five (25) samples of Product that incorporate the agreed-to ECO.

13.0 Compliance

13.1 Dell is an Affirmative Action/Equal Opportunity Employer. Since Dell transacts business with the United States Government, the Equal Opportunity Clauses at 41 CFR sections 60-1.4(a), 60-250.5(a) and 60-741.5(a) are hereby incorporated and SUPPLIER will, if applicable, comply with FAR 52.212-3, Offer or Representations and Certifications-Commercial Items, and FAR 52-219-8, Utilization of Small Business Concerns.

13.2 SUPPLIER agrees to give full consideration to use minority and women owned businesses to provide components to SUPPLIER for subsequent integration into Product sold to Dell.

14.0 Import/Export Requirements

14.1 SUPPLIER acknowledges that the Products licensed or sold under this Agreement, and the transaction contemplated by this agreement, which may include technology and software, are subject to the customs and export control laws and regulations of the United States ("U.S.") and may also be subject to the customs and export laws and regulations of the country in which the Products are manufactured and/or received. SUPPLIER agrees to abide by those laws and regulations. Further, under U.S. law, the Products may not be sold, leased or otherwise transferred to restricted end-users or to restricted countries. In addition, the Products may not be sold, leased or otherwise transferred to, or utilized by an end-user engaged in activities related to weapons of mass destruction, including without limitation, activities related to the design, development, production or use of nuclear weapons, materials, or facilities, missiles or the support of missile projects, and chemical or biological weapons.

14.2 SUPPLIER agrees not to provide any written regulatory certifications or notifications on behalf of Dell without first seeking prior written approval from Dell's Export Compliance Representative. When applicable and necessary, Dell will provide SUPPLIER with all U.S. export licenses, license designations, National Defense Authorization Act ("NDAA") authorizations and commodity classifications unless otherwise agreed to in writing by SUPPLIER and Dell and unless SUPPLIER is obligated to obtain the license under U.S. law.

14.3 SUPPLIER is prohibited from diverting any Dell shipment without first securing written approval from Dell's Export Compliance Representative. SUPPLIER agrees not to support or engage in any boycott related transaction and/or requests in order to execute a transaction on behalf of Dell.

14.4 In addition, SUPPLIER agrees to indemnify, defend and hold Dell harmless from any loss, expense, penalty or claim against Dell due to SUPPLIER'S violation or alleged violation of any such applicable laws and regulations.

14.5 Further, regarding processing Shippers Export Declarations (SED) or the Automated Export System (AES), Dell will retain the right to name its own Freight Forwarder in all transactions. Dell may, at its sole discretion, permit the SUPPLIER to name its own Freight Forwarder for the purpose of clearing outbound Customs from the United States. In such cases, SUPPLIER must provide the name, address, contact person, telephone number, and email address of that Freight Forwarder and must indicate in the order that it has authorized its Freight Forwarder to prepare to prepare and file the Shipper's Export Declaration (SED) with the Bureau of the Census. In no circumstances will Dell rely upon the Freight Forwarder of SUPPLIERS to obtain export licenses from the United States Government even if the SUPPLIER has authorized its Freight Forwarder to act as the exporter for purposes of the Export Administration regulations. Instead, Dell will obtain the necessary export license with reliance upon the transaction information that the SUPPLIER has made available to Dell.

14.6 Neither SUPPLIER, nor Dell shall, directly or indirectly, export, re-export or transship Products in violation of any applicable U.S. export control laws and regulations or any other applicable export control laws promulgated and administered by the government of any country having jurisdiction over the parties or the transactions contemplated herein. In accordance with the US Export Administration Regulations, SUPPLIER will provide required classification information by completing the Global Export Compliance Questionnaire attached hereto as Schedule ___.

15.0 Continuity of Supply

15.1 SUPPLIER shall within sixty (60) calendar days from the Effective Date of this Agreement identify an escrow custodian ("Escrow Custodian") acceptable to both parties and contract with such Escrow Custodian ("Escrow Agreement") for the pre-arranged holding and releasing of materials required to produce or have produced the Products ("Escrow Material"). Escrow Material shall include, but is not limited to, all materials, specifications, and other items necessary to enable Dell, or a third party designated by Dell, to manufacture, support, distribute, license, and sell the Products. Within thirty (30) calendar days after the execution of the Escrow Agreement, SUPPLIER shall deposit with the Escrow Custodian the most current production level of the Escrow Material, as defined in the Escrow Agreement. Thereafter, SUPPLIER shall within ten (10) days after the release of an update to a Product, deposit updated Escrow Material with the Escrow Custodian. SUPPLIER agrees to bear the cost of establishing and maintaining the escrow account for the Products and the costs associated with its compliance with this Section, including without limitation the costs of any and all document preparation necessary to meet the requirements of this Section and the Escrow Agreement. If due to the occurrence of any of the following events SUPPLIER is unable to or fails to provide Products for Dell: (a) any bankruptcy, reorganization, or other case or proceeding under any bankruptcy or insolvency law or any dissolution or liquidation proceeding is commenced by or against SUPPLIER, and if such case or proceeding is not commenced by SUPPLIER, it is acquiesced in or remains undismissed for ninety (90) days; or (b) SUPPLIER ceases active operation of its business for any reason; or (c) SUPPLIER applies for or consents to the appointment of a trustee, receiver or other custodian for SUPPLIER or makes a general assignment for the benefit of its creditors; or (d) SUPPLIER does not remedy any supply issue within ninety (90) days of receipt of notice from Dell that a supply issue exists, then Dell shall have the right to receive possession of the Escrow Materials pursuant to the provisions of the Escrow Agreement and SUPPLIER agrees that it authorizes Dell to use the Escrow Material to produce or have produced the Products by sources other than SUPPLIER. Such authorization consists of a worldwide, non-exclusive manufacturing rights license to make or have made the Products only for use consistent with the terms of this

Agreement. Such license shall be in force until such time as SUPPLIER is able to resume manufacturing of the Products; provided, however, that if Dell has commenced manufacturing the Products, it shall be entitled to continue manufacturing the Products despite SUPPLIER's ability to resume doing so, for [x days] after SUPPLIER is able to resume manufacturing the Products. Dell may not sell, lease, or otherwise distribute Products other than as intended in this Agreement. Following the Escrow License Period, Dell shall return all of SUPPLIER's Escrowed Material and documentation to SUPPLIER or its successor or trustee within thirty (30) calendar days.

15.2   In the event that Dell has the Products manufactured directly for Dell in accordance with Subsections 15.1, SUPPLIER will be liable to Dell under Section 10.0 "Indemnification" for such Products. Not withstanding [sic] the foregoing, SUPPLIER will be liable to Dell for design defects under Section 9.1 (c) and Section 9.2. SUPPLIER will also provide Dell with a list of those Manufacturers used by SUPPLIER for custom components. SUPPLIER agrees that Dell may use such component Manufacturers as well as any SUPPLIER-owned or -unique tooling used by such Manufacturer. In addition, SUPPLIER will provide an on-site expert engineer at Dell, at no charge, to assist Dell in the manufacturing, design and validation of the Product.

15.3   If SUPPLIER reasonably anticipates that Section 15.1 will be invoked and SUPPLIER does not manufacture the Products itself, SUPPLIER will make best efforts to execute written agreements with each Manufacturer naming Dell as a third party beneficiary. SUPPLIER will provide copies of such agreement to Dell. Such agreements) will contain provisions that:

(a)   obligate the Manufacturer to provide the applicable Products to Dell at the same price that the Manufacturer charges SUPPLIER in the event that Section 15.1 is invoked;

(b)   grant the Manufacturer a license to manufacture and sell the Products directly to Dell in the event that Section 15.1 is invoked;

(c)   allow Dell to use any SUPPLIER-owned or -unique tooling used by the Manufacturer to manufacture the Products in the event that Section 15.1 is invoked;

(d)   require the Manufacturer to comply with Sections 5.0, 6.0, 9.0, 10.0, 11.0, 12.0, 13.0, 14.0, 15.0, 17.0, 18.0 and Schedule B of this Agreement.

16.0 Capacity Constraints

SUPPLIER shall reasonably inform Dell on an ongoing basis of any negative impact on SUPPLIER'S production capacity as a result of large orders SUPPLIER receives from third parties. SUPPLIER will make best efforts to ensure Dell that such additional sales will in no way impact SUPPLIER'S ability to provide to Dell the quantities of the applicable Product set forth in Dell's six (6) month forecast for such Product.

17.0 New Products

17.1   During the term of this Agreement or for a period of three (3) years, whichever is greater, SUPPLIER agrees to offer to sell to Dell all products developed, manufactured, distributed or sold by SUPPLIER. If Dell agrees to purchase such products, such sale will be pursuant to the terms and conditions of this Agreement at a price equivalent to or lower than the price paid by other customers purchasing similar quantities. The terms of this Subsection 17.1 will survive any termination of this Agreement.

17.2   Prior to offering for sale any new standard SUPPLIER product (hereafter "new product"), SUPPLIER will first consult with Dell and allow Dell to place Dell PO(s) for such new product no later than when SUPPLIER extended a similar offer to any other customer. Prior to the addition of a new product to a Schedule, the parties will mutually agree on a new product program schedule which will include the appointment of business and technical contacts for each party to monitor compatibility issues and product release issues with Dell systems. SUPPLIER agrees that Dell will receive limited quantities of pre-release versions of all new products that are added to this Agreement.

17.3   Prior to the general availability of Dell's systems containing any new SUPPLIER product, SUPPLIER will provide mutually agreed-upon training to Dell for its sales, customer support and technical support organizations. Following Dell's award of business to SUPPLIER with respect to a new product, SUPPLIER will obtain Microsoft's certification for the products to the applicable current PC specification and WHQL standards and all other government and regulatory certifications required by Dell.

17.4   SUPPLIER will provide Dell with detailed silicon and board ramp-up plans. Dell will be entitled to participate in hardware and software design reviews for all new products. Dell will be entitled to participate in the formulation and direction of SUPPLIER'S future product and technology roadmaps.

17.5   Following Dell's award of new product business to SUPPLIER, SUPPLIER will provide manufacturing, customer and field diagnostics, as agreed, to Dell for testing and evaluation at least ninety (90) days prior to Dell's shipment of a new Product. These diagnostics must comply with the Dell Diagnostics specification.

17.6   Upon Dell's award of new product business to SUPPLIER, SUPPLIER will provide Dell with a minimum of one hundred (100) samples of new Products for Dell's validation, compatibility, and test processes. Such Products will be delivered to Dell as directed by the Dell Strategic Commodity Manager. If a new product does not meet Dell's requirements, Dell may return some or all of the new product samples for a credit of the price paid.

17.7 SUPPLIER agrees to support Dell Service's requirements with respect to spare parts availability. SUPPLIER will provide new Product information reasonably requested by Dell at least ninety (90) days in advance of Dell's shipment of new Product, and will stock Revolver Inventory of spare parts as requested by Dell at least fifteen (15) days prior to Dell's shipment of new Product.

18.0 General

18.1 Before initiating a lawsuit against the other relating to this Agreement, the parties agree to work in good faith to resolve between them all disputes and claims arising out of or relating to this Agreement. To this end, either party may request that each party designate an officer or other management employee with authority to bind the party to meet to resolve the dispute. During their discussions, each party will honor the other's reasonable requests for non-privileged and relevant information. This paragraph will not apply if: (i) the expiration of the statute of limitations for a cause of action is imminent, or (ii) injunctive or other equitable relief is necessary to mitigate damages.

18.2 The provisions of Sections 9.0, 10.0, 11.0 and 18.0 will survive any termination or expiration of this Agreement and will continue to bind the parties and their permitted successors and assigns.

18.3 SUPPLIER will not use the name of Dell nor any Dell trademarks, trade names, service marks, or quote the opinion of any Dell employee in any advertising or otherwise without first obtaining the prior written consent of Dell.

18.4 Any confidential information that will be disclosed by either party related to this Agreement will be pursuant to the terms and conditions of the (9/21/98) (date) Non-disclosure Agreement between Dell and Adaptec. The terms and conditions of this Agreement will be deemed to be confidential information. Notwithstanding the terms of the Non-disclosure Agreement, SUPPLIER agrees that Dell may provide information related to SUPPLIER'S Product roadmaps and other related information to certain Dell customers provided such Dell customers have executed a non-disclosure agreement with Dell that requires the customer not to disclose the information to a third party. SUPPLIER may not publicly release any information relating to this Agreement, including the existence of this Agreement, or use the Dell name or names of Dell officials, without first receiving the prior written approval of Dell's Corporate Communications department.

No other department within Dell is authorized to consent to public releases of information.

18.5 SUPPLIER will maintain accurate and legible records for a period of three (3) years records of its quality programs, test documentation and any other documents related that pertain to this Agreement. SUPPLIER will grant Dell reasonable access to and copies of such records.

18.6 Except as may be otherwise provided in this Agreement, the rights or remedies of the parties hereunder are not exclusive, and either party will be entitled alternatively or cumulatively, subject to the other provisions of this Agreement, to damages for breach, to an order requiring specific performance, or to any other remedy available at law or in equity.

18.7 The parties are independent contractors and neither party is an agent, servant, representative, partner, joint venturer or employee of the other or has any authority to assume or create any obligation or liability of any kind on behalf of the other.

18.8 No waiver of any term or condition is valid unless in writing and signed by authorized representatives of both parties, and will be limited to the specific situation for which it is given. No amendment or modification to this Agreement will be valid unless set forth in writing and signed by authorized representatives of both parties. No other action or failure to act (including inspection, failure to inspect, acceptance' of late deliveries, or acceptance of or payment for any Products) will constitute a waiver of any rights.

18.9 This Agreement may not be assigned by SUPPLIER in whole or in part, even by operation of law in a merger or stock or asset sale, without the express written permission of Dell. Such consent will not be unreasonably withheld. Any attempt to do so will be null and void.

18.10 This Agreement will be governed and construed in accordance with the laws of the State of New York, U.S.A., exclusive of any provisions of the United Nations Convention on the International Sale of Goods and without regard to its principles of conflicts of law. SUPPLIER hereby irrevocably submits to the jurisdiction of the federal and state courts of the State of Texas U.S.A. and hereby agrees that any such court will be a proper forum for the determination of any dispute arising hereunder.

18.11 Any notice required or permitted by this Agreement will be in writing in English and delivered by certified or registered mail, return receipt requested, postage prepaid and addressed as follows or to such other addresses as may be designated by notice from one party to the other, all such notices being effective on the date received or, if mailed as set forth above, three (3) days after the date of mailing:

[Notice Information Omitted]

18.12 Whenever possible, each provision of this Agreement will be interpreted in such a manner as to be effective and valid under applicable law, but if any provision of this Agreement is found to violate a law, it will be severed from the rest of the Agreement and ignored and a new provision deemed added to this Agreement to accomplish to the extent possible the intent of the parties as evidenced by the provision so severed. The headings used in this Agreement have no legal effect.

18.13 Dell will have full freedom and flexibility in its decisions concerning the distribution and marketing of the Product(s), including without limitation the decision of whether or not to distribute or discontinue distribution of the Product(s). Dell does not guarantee that its marketing, if any, of the Product(s) will be successful. . . .

18.14 Nothing in this Agreement will require Dell to purchase from SUPPLIER a minimum quantity or any or all of its requirements for products that are the same or similar to the Products. Dell may also purchase similar or identical products from others. Furthermore, SUP-PLIER agrees to cooperate and work with Dell and any other providers that Dell may engage in connection with the provision of Products.

18.15 With the exception of the ROMB software letter agreement dated 3/15/2001 and attachment A to that agreement dated 6/26/01, and with the exception of the Indirect Purchase agreement dated October 16, 2000, This Agreement, and its attached Addenda, Exhibits, Attachments and Schedules, as so designated, set forth the entire agreement and understanding of the parties relating to the subject matter contained herein, and merges all prior discussions and agreements, both oral and written, between the parties. Each party agrees that use of pre-printed forms, such as purchase orders or acknowledgments, is for convenience only and all terms and conditions stated thereon, except as specifically set forth in this Agreement, are void and of no effect. Unless otherwise expressly set forth in an Addendum, Exhibit, Attachment or Schedule, as so designated, in the event of a conflict between this Master Purchase Agreement and any Addenda, Exhibit, Attachment or Schedule, the terms of this Master Purchase Agreement will prevail.

18.16 SUPPLIER agrees that for the term of this Agreement and any extensions thereof it will not seek orders in any legal or administrative proceeding that would prevent Dell from shipping any Dell or third party products.

18.17 Orders issued by Dell pursuant to this Agreement are placed with the expectation of potential acquisition of credit for current and/or anticipated future offset obligations of Dell, Dell Computer Corporation or Dell Computer Corporation's subsidiaries or affiliates, or their designated assignees to various governments around the world. Supplier agrees to reasonably assist Dell, Dell Computer Corporation or Dell Computer Corporation's subsidiaries or affiliates, or their designated assignees in their efforts to secure offset credit from these governments in an amount equal to the value of the applicable in-country content of the orders placed under this Agreement.

18.18 Throughout this Agreement, any reference to "days" means calendar days unless otherwise specified.

18.19 SUPPLIER will ensure that all specifications, prints and other documentation will be provided to Dell in the English language.

[Signature Page Omitted]

How "balanced" is the preceding Master Purchase Agreement? If you were counsel to Adaptec, what would you tell your client about the Agreement? Would you draw a line between identifying risk issues and advising your client whether to sign the Agreement? If so, how and where would you draw this line?

Assume for our purposes that you are an attorney in Adaptec's General Counsel's Office and your business leaders ask you to identify the risk issues in the Agreement. What would you say? To what extent would business considerations inform your analysis? How closely would your findings come to those in the following fictitious risk memorandum?

RISK MEMORANDUM (FICTIONAL)

September 20, 2002

TO: ADAPTEC MANAGEMENT

FROM: ADAPTEC OFFICE OF GENERAL COUNSEL

SUBJECT: DELL SUPPLIER MASTER PURCHASE AGREEMENT— RISK ASSESSMENT

We have reviewed Dell's proposal for a Master Purchase Agreement pursuant to which Dell Products L.P. and unspecified other subsidiaries and affiliates of Dell Computer Corporation (collectively, "Dell") would purchase Adaptec's products through issuance of purchase orders. The Agreement appears to be a Dell form document and, accordingly, is heavily weighted in favor of Dell. In particular, we have the following concerns, *viz.*:

(i) The agreement imposes upon Adaptec burdens typically associated with a requirements contract (e.g., Adaptec has obligations with respect to meeting Dell's possibly changing needs for products) without any of the benefits (e.g., Dell's commitment to purchase a minimum quantity or any or all of its requirements for the same or similar products);

(ii)   The agreement requires Adaptec to be aggressive in delivering material reductions in its pricing and appears to require "most favored nations" pricing.

We address these and other concerns in the balance of this memorandum. For ease of reference and to facilitate discussions with Dell, our analysis proceeds sequentially through the 18 sections of the agreement.

Section 1.0—Introduction

The agreement contemplates the sale of Adaptec products to Dell Products L.P. and unnamed other subsidiaries and affiliates of Dell Computer Corporation. Greater clarity around the subsidiaries and affiliates would be helpful for purposes of understanding the particular Dell entities against which Adaptec will have recourse to enforce payment and other contractual obligations and to plan product development and inventory.

Beyond this, the particular services, software, and documentation subsumed in the definition of "Products" should be specified and, as necessary, priced.

Section 2.0—Term and Termination

The initial three-year term of the Agreement automatically renews for additional successive one-year terms absent 180 days' notice of either party prior to end of the then-current term. We recommend the addition of a mechanism providing for price increases (perhaps tied to the Consumer Price Index).

Section 3.0—Price

The agreement contains an "agreement to agree" upon a "pricing model" for each Product meeting "Dell's price/performance objectives" and providing for "an agreed-upon level of return" to Adaptec. This is at best vague and is likely to lead to misunderstandings. (Insofar as Dell has the unfettered right to distribute or discontinue distribution of the Products, we caution against any pricing model that is tied to distribution. See subsection 18.13.)

We recommend against sharing margin information with Dell to meet the level-of-return approach.

Additionally, subsections 3.2 and 3.3 require, among other things, "material cost reductions" and pricing audits—the latter, we suspect, in connection with a most-favored-nations clause. (Portions of the text have been omitted for our review.)

Lastly, subsection 3.3 makes reference to "Dell Service"; the precise corporate entity, state of incorporation, and principal place of business should be specified.

Section 4.0—Payment

We recommend the inclusion of an interest provision to serve as a disincentive to late payment. Also, the approach of accumulating invoices for payment will have the effect of increasing the terms of invoices received prior to the last day of the "Accumulation Period."

Section 5.0—Delivery of Products

Dell's rights around acceptance are broad and have the potential to lead to delayed or withholding of payments to Adaptec. Beyond this, Dell has the right to dictate the locations at which Products are produced; this strikes us as overreaching and may have cost implications. Lastly, the Agreement imposes stringent inventory requirements upon Adaptec (in this regard, see subsection 5.3.2).

Section 6.0—Acceleration and Cancellation

Dell's ability to increase quantities of Product upon limited notice will have inventory and cost implications for Adaptec. Additionally, the Agreement imposes stringent mitigation requirements upon Adaptec as a precondition to receiving payment for cancelled Products and limits Dell's liability to Adaptec to payment of still-to-be- determined cancellation sums.

Section 7.0—Documentation, Software and Trademarks

The Agreement grants various IP rights to Dell without regard to restrictions (nonpayment, etc.); at a minimum, rights should be tied to payment.

Section 8.0—Product Withdrawal

Adaptec is required to maintain inventories of cancelled products and spare parts for a period still to be determined. Beyond this, we strongly recommend against permitting Dell to assign to third parties its rights to warranty replacement and end-of-life parts, given the costs associated with meeting these warranty obligations.

Section 9.0—Warranties

We recommend against offering warranties associated with cosmetic defects. We also recommend against warranting batteries against non-compliance with specifications for 13 months from the Product manufacturing date code. This period seems excessive, and there may be factors outside of Adaptec's control that bear upon compliance.

We believe Dell should be required to specify the reasons for return of in-warranty Products; the Agreement does not currently require this.

The testing process for returned Products seems unnecessarily burdensome.

We recommend that the Agreement make clear that Adaptec's satisfaction of its warranty obligations constitutes Dell's exclusive remedy in connection with deficient Products. (See also subsection 18.6.)

Section 10.0—Indemnification

Adaptec's indemnity obligations appear to extend to unnamed Dell subsidiaries and affiliates (given the use of the defined "Dell"); this universe of potential claimants needs to be limited.

Section 11.0—Liability

To the extent possible, we recommend seeking to limit liability for Adaptec's indemnification obligations. Also, Dell should agree that the liability limitations of the Agreement apply in the aggregate to its subsidiaries and affiliates, and Dell should indemnify Adaptec for any damages Adaptec sustains in excess of this amount. In addition, the last sentence of section 11.3, which limits Adaptec's liability for certain matters, is unclear and appears to be missing language.

Section 12.0—Quality, Product Safety, Regulatory Compliance and Engineering Changes

Adaptec's obligation to obtain Product approvals should be limited to approvals necessary only through the time the Products leave Adaptec's control; Dell should bear responsibility for obtaining any approvals that may be necessary in connection with Dell's use of the Products.

Section 13.0—Compliance

The cost of compliance with all governmental requirements must be factored into pricing.

Section 14.0—Import/Export Requirements

Dell should acknowledge and agree to abide by all applicable import and export laws and regulations applicable to its use of the Products.

Section 15.0—Continuity of Supply

Dell should bear the costs associated with maintaining Escrow Material. The "best efforts" requirement in subsection 15.3 is unacceptable; we recommend substituting a "commercially reasonable" standard in its place.

Section 16.0—Capacity Constraints

Likewise, the "best efforts" standard (to ensure that sales to third parties will not impact Adaptec's ability to provide Dell with Product) is unduly burdensome; we should replace this with a "commercially reasonable" standard. Moreover, we question why Adaptec should agree to capacity constraints absent Dell's agreement to purchase minimum quantities of the Products.

Section 17.0—New Products

Similarly, we question why Adaptec should agree to "most favored nations" pricing of new products, absent Dell's minimum purchase of new products or agreement to other favorable commercial terms. Beyond this, we recommend that all costs associated with the undertakings of section 17.0 be carefully considered.

Section 18.0—General

We recommend eliminating subsection 18.14 (which confirms, for the avoidance of doubt, that Dell is not required to purchase any minimum quantities or requirements), and, instead, imposing minimum purchase requirements upon Dell.

We recommend seeking clarification from Dell as to its reasons for requiring agreement to subsection 18.16 (preventing Adaptec from seeking orders in legal or administrative proceedings that prevent Dell from shipping any Dell or third-party products).

Likewise, we recommend seeking clarification as to the expectation language in subsection 18.17 (Dell's orders are placed with the expectation of potential acquisition of credit and/or anticipated future offset obligations of Dell for Dell's acquisition of credit and/or anticipated future offset obligations), and the reasons for requiring Adaptec's reasonable assistance to Dell to secure offset credit. (Among other concerns, what is meant by "reasonable"?) Certainly, Adaptec should not be exposed to the consequences of Dell's failure to obtain such offset credit.

FICTIONAL

1. Familiarity Breeds Fluency: A Review

While prior to reading this chapter you may not have seen or read an agreement for the sale of goods, hopefully you found this Agreement's structure and many of its terms to be familiar.

- To review, does this Agreement contain a definitions section? How does this Agreement define its terms? What are the benefits and drawbacks of the method this Agreement has adopted? (See Chapter 3.)

- According to § 18.11 of this Agreement, what is required for notice to be effective? Who bears the risk of the failure of delivery? That is, if notice is sent but not received, will such notice be considered "effective" so as to constitute the notice required or contemplated by various terms of the Agreement? (See Chapter 3.)

- Consider the structure of this sale-of-goods agreement. Section 1.0 of this Agreement contemplates, "The terms and conditions of this Agreement will apply to all purchase orders ("Dell PO(s)") issued by Dell for the purchase of Products." How might the parties wish to be sure that the terms of this Agreement do indeed govern future Dell purchase orders? (See Chapter 3.)

- According to § 18.15 of the Agreement, if there is a conflict between the Master Agreement and any Addendum, Exhibits, Attachments, or

Schedules, the terms of which document will prevail? What are the effect and the limits of such order-of-precedence provisions? (See Chapter 3.)

- Section 9.1 presents various representations and warranties made by SUPPLIER. Review the difference between representations and warranties. How would it affect the warranty presented in § 9.1(a) if, before entering into the Agreement, Dell had knowledge that Products would necessarily be encumbered? Do these representations and warranties seem to favor SUPPLIER or Dell? Taking the perspective of SUPPLIER's counsel, what representations and/or warranties would you advise your client not to make? What, if anything, would you ask that Dell represent and/or warrant? Taking the perspective of Dell's counsel, for what, if anything, would you advise your client to negotiate in addition to the representations and/or warranties already made? (See Chapter 3.)

- Sections 11.1 and 11.2 of the Agreement act to limit the liability of the parties. What types of damages and other liability are excluded from each party's potential liability? Is the total liability of each party capped at a certain maximum amount? If so, how is that maximum amount figured? As provided by § 11.3, what are excluded from these limitation-of-liability provisions? We have discussed that it may be unclear whether a limitation-of-liability provision applies to limit indemnification obligations under the same Agreement. Can you discern from this Agreement whether or not such limitations of liability are intended to apply to the Agreement's indemnity obligations? Are all of these indemnity obligations unbounded? (See Chapter 3.)

- Sections 10.0 and 14.4 specify the indemnity obligations provided by the Agreement. For what does SUPPLIER indemnify Dell? For what does Dell indemnify SUPPLIER? From the perspective of each party, do these indemnification obligations appear overly broad or narrow? Are these indemnity obligations broader or narrower than the indemnity obligations found in the AOL Agreement in Chapter 3? Is either party taking on "too much" risk? (See Chapter 3.)

Notice that issues of intellectual-property infringement are not unique to services transactions (as evidenced by § 10.1 of the Agreement); indeed, IP infringement presents concerns in transactions pertaining to goods, as well. Accordingly, we asked two seasoned practitioners to help us revisit indemnification provisions and IP infringement but this time in the context of transactions involving goods and with respect to patent infringement.

A Practitioner Perspective: Indemnification and Patent Infringement

Over the past several years, intellectual property infringement indemnity has become the most contentiously negotiated issue in technology-related commercial negotiations. This increased focus parallels the significant growth in volume and scope of patent litigation. In the United States, the number of patent cases has increased from just over 1,000 in 1991 to nearly 3,000 in 2008. In addition, damage awards have been growing—prior to 1990, only one damage award exceeded $100 million, but, in just the three years between 2005 and 2008, district courts issued nine awards exceeding $100 million. Increasingly, litigation is brought by entities that acquire patents solely to obtain license fees, not by inventors seeking to commercialize their creations or manufacturers seeking to retain the benefits of commercialization. By threatening expensive litigation against any company that is not willing to enter into a license and by relying on legal impediments to reexamination or invalidation of questionable patents and a lack of clear standards for the basis of damages calculations, these "non-practicing entities" are able to use the litigation system to gain negotiating leverage regardless of the strength of either the underlying patent or the infringement claim being asserted.

Because of the high cost of patent litigation (the cost of defending a case through trial and appeal currently costs upwards of $10 million), the increasing number of claims, and the increasing amount of damage awards, both vendors and customers now focus on liability for IP litigation as a real financial cost to be addressed with appropriate risk allocation in technology contracts.

The two main areas of debate (other than the overall limit of liability for the vendor's defense and indemnity obligation, where the buyer typically seeks unlimited liability) in IP infringement indemnity negotiations are (1) the vendor's obligation to pay damages or royalties based upon the customer's usage or revenue generated from use of the vendor's product, and (2) the vendor's obligation to defend and indemnify a customer when the claim arises from the customer's use of the vendor's product—which alone does not infringe—in combination with products the customer purchases from other vendors.

With respect to the first issue, if a vendor is sued directly for infringement and its product is found to infringe, a "reasonable royalty" is likely to be determined (at a minimum) based on the value of the infringing component or (at a maximum) based on the overall value of the product in which the infringing component resides. In either case, the vendor's liability is limited to a royalty that is proportional to the revenue the vendor receives from the sale of its product, although the damages in the latter case could be wildly disproportionate to the value of the novelty reflected in the patent. However, when a customer is sued for infringement, and the claim is based upon the customer's recurring use or the customer's revenue generated from using the vendor product, the vendor's potential liability is wholly disproportionate to the price paid by the customer for the vendor's product.

For example, if the vendor sells products to a telecom service provider enabling the service provider to offer a home video solution to its customers, the vendor typically will receive a one-time payment for those products. The service provider, however, will generate recurring monthly revenue by selling video service to its customers. The patent holder making an infringement claim against the service provider will likely seek a royalty based upon the service provider's recurring revenue for that service, and not a royalty based upon the products themselves that enable the service. The recurring revenue, and associated royalty payment to the patent holder, could exponentially exceed the vendor's revenue from selling those products to the service provider. Customers, however, expect their vendors to accept liability regardless of the method of damage or royalty calculation because in their view the vendor's product caused the infringement. Determining the appropriate risk allocation for this type of liability as between vendor and customer often depends on the type of customer, the strategic nature of the vendor/customer relationship, and the relative bargaining power of each.

The risk allocation for so-called "combinations claims" is similarly challenging. From the vendor perspective, it is a difficult financial proposition to accept liability for defending and indemnifying a customer when the claim is based not on an infringement by the vendor's product alone (where the vendor's product alone is not infringing), but on a solution architected by the customer that utilizes multiple vendors' products. The vendor may have no control over what third-party products the customer chose in order to create the solution or the purpose or use for which that ultimate solution is offered. The vendor's contribution to the combination may be immaterial to the infringement claim itself (patent claims increasingly are written very broadly to sweep in prior art), and/or may be a small portion of the value of the overall solution. From a practical perspective, a vendor cannot effectively defend the claim because it does not have information on the third parties' products essential to the defense; also, in the open standards world which characterizes the telecom industry, products from multiple vendors frequently are combined in a single network, further complicating an already challenging multi-party defense of a claim. Vendors, therefore, typically seek to exclude liability for combinations claims in the indemnity provision, at least where they have not had the express ability to review the combination in advance. Customers, on the other hand, prefer to have all of their vendors on the hook to defend and indemnify against combinations claims to ensure that they are fully protected from liability and rely on arguments that a vendor should share liability for any "reasonable" or "anticipatable" use of a product.

Continuing the example above of a home video solution to illustrate the combinations scenario, suppose the customer purchases video-on-demand servers from one vendor (Vendor 1) and purchases set-top boxes from another (Vendor 2). Suppose a patent holder asserts an infringement claim against the service provider based on a patent where the invention relates to the way videos are served up on a video-on-demand server. The claim specifies a video-on-demand server in combination with a set-top box. The functionality of the set-top box has long been part of the prior art (e.g., simply receiving signals at the customer premises), and the truly inventive element of the claim relates to the video-on-demand server. In this scenario, Vendor 2 will not want to accept liability because the set-top box is not the truly novel element of the patent claim.

Negotiating the indemnity terms regarding combinations requires consideration of a number of issues to arrive at an equitable allocation of risk: who specified the combination (customer or vendor), which components of the combination are material to the inventive elements of the claim, what the relative value of a particular component is to the overall solution, and the contribution of all parties to the value of the combination (including the customer). In the final analysis, many customers attempt to use purchasing leverage to obtain an indemnity for a risk that is beyond the vendor's control or visibility.

Improvements to the patent system to ensure that only strong patents are granted, that damages are apportioned fairly, and that weak patents can be challenged more easily to reduce unfair leverage, are essential. Until these changes are made, it is likely that the IP indemnity clause will continue to be the main source of contention in technology contract negotiations.

Julia Hickey
Director of Legal Services
US Service Providers
Cisco Systems, Inc.

Mark Chandler
Senior Vice President and General Counsel
Cisco Systems, Inc.

The content of this piece reflects the personal views of the authors of this piece and is not an official position of Cisco Systems, Inc. [Note: Ms. Hickey and Mr. Chandler specifically requested this disclaimer. The inclusion of this disclaimer in no way speaks to this book's other contributions or the authors or affiliations thereof.]

2. Revisiting No-Oral-Modification Provisions Under Article Two

Notice that § 18.8 of the Agreement provides that no amendment or modification to the Agreement will be valid unless it is in writing and signed by both parties. In Chapter 2, we explored the issues of "no-oral-modification" provisions. There we discussed that the general rule has been that a contract cannot prevent or govern its own modification. However, Chapter 2 also discussed significant limitations on this general rule. Namely, by statute, some states (e.g., New York, California) have given no-oral-modification provisions some bite.[51]

Article 2 presents yet another important exception to the general rule regarding no-oral-modification provisions. The U.C.C. provides, "An agreement in a signed record which excludes modification or rescission except by a signed

---

51. *See* Cal. Civ. Code § 1698 (West 1985); N.Y. Gen. Oblig. Law § 15-301 (Consol. 2001).

record may not be otherwise modified or rescinded. . . . ."[52] Accordingly, unlike the rule for contracts generally (and similar to the New York and California rules), a contract for the sale of goods may indeed effectively prevent its own oral modification.[53]

Also of note is another departure Article 2 makes from the common law of contracts: A modification to a contract for the sale of goods need not be supported by additional consideration to be effective. Under the common law, a modification must be supported by consideration to create contractual rights and obligations, and, under the common law's pre-existing duty rule, rights and obligations already owed under an original contract do not constitute consideration for a subsequent modification.[54] Article 2 summarily does away with this, expressly providing, "An agreement modifying a contract within this Article needs no consideration to be binding."[55] Accordingly, parties may modify their contracts for the sale of goods in a subsequent agreement, without so much as a consideration for—well—consideration.

Accordingly, because § 18.8 requires it and Article 2 likely governs, a modification to this Agreement will need to be in writing—but will not need consideration—in order to be of effect.

3. Conditions

We have already encountered several "conditions" throughout the agreements explored thus far throughout this book. A "condition" generally refers to something that must happen (or happen to be the case) in order to trigger a party's rights or obligations.[56] This type of condition is also commonly called a "condition precedent," as it precedes the activation of certain rights. A "condition subsequent," on the other hand, refers to an event that terminates or discharges a contractual right or a duty.[57] In other words, a condition precedent states a logical relationship where the condition is generally necessary (although, not necessarily sufficient) to activate the rights that follow the condition—in the case of a condition subsequent, to terminate the rights that

---

52. U.C.C. § 2-209(2) (2003).

53. However, consider that the U.C.C. explicitly provides that a no-oral-modification provision does not operate to prevent a finding that a party later waived a right under the contract. U.C.C. § 2-209(4) (2003). The official comment to § 2-209(4) states, "Subsection (4) is intended, despite the provisions of subsections (2) and (3), to prevent contractual [no-oral-modification] provisions . . . from limiting in other respects the legal effect of the parties' actual later conduct." *Id.* § 2-209(4) cmt. 4. For more on the topic of no-oral-modification provisions, please see Chapter 2; for more on the topic of waiver, please also see Chapter 2.

54. *See* Restatement (Second) of Contracts § 73 cmt. c (1981).

55. U.C.C. § 2-209(1) (2003).

56. *See* Restatement (Second) of Contracts § 224 (1981) ("A condition is an event, not certain to occur, which must occur, unless its non-occurrence is excused, before performance under a contract becomes due.").

57. *Id.* § 224 cmt. e ("Parties sometimes provide that the occurrence of an event, such as the failure of one of them to commence an action within a prescribed time, will extinguish a duty after performance has become due, along with any claim for breach. Such an event has often been called a 'condition subsequent,' while an event of the kind defined in this section has been called a "condition precedent.").

precede the condition.[58] For instance, a condition might require one party to perform some act before the other party will be obligated to perform certain obligations. Likewise, a condition may require certain circumstances to be true or certain events to occur before a party's obligations will "kick in." Conditions may be conditions precedent to the entire agreement, or they may be conditions precedent to certain specific obligations within the agreement.[59] Accordingly, agreements may contain (i) conditions nestled within provisions and/or (ii) entire conditions sections, providing that all (or certain) obligations under the agreement are premised on certain conditions enumerated within the section. A condition precedent to an entire agreement generally must be satisfied before the contract itself comes into existence.[60]

Drafting Note: The Language of Conditions

Courts will find conditions to exist where the parties so intended: "the inclusion of words such as 'if,' 'provided,' 'on condition that,' or some similar phrase of conditional language indicate that the parties intended there to be a condition precedent."[61] However, courts often will err on the side of construing a provision as a promise (that is, an ordinary covenant) rather than as a condition, where there is any uncertainty.[62] Accordingly, a prudent drafter will take care to create conditions expressly and clearly, for instance, by calling a provision a "condition."

For examples of conditions, we need turn no further than this chapter's Agreement. Section 2.0 essentially provides that the Agreement will endure indefinitely, *unless* one party provides 180-day notice of termination for a given year. Accordingly, "unless" signals that effective notice is a condition of the Agreement's not automatically renewing (i.e., a party's termination right). Section 4.2 provides that Dell has the right to withhold certain taxes, *if* required by a governmental authority. "If" signals that governmental authority is sufficient to give Dell the right to withhold certain taxes. While governmental authority may not be the exclusive source of such a right, the "if" clause operates to state a condition upon which Dell's rights arising out of § 4.2 depend. (That is, Dell may find the right to withhold taxes outside of § 4.2, and, so, we do not know that satisfaction of the "if" clause is *necessary* for Dell to withhold taxes. However, the "if" clause found in § 4.2 restricts Dell's ability to access § 4.2 *rights* to the

---

58. *Id.* § 224 cmt. d ("A duty may be subject to any number of conditions, which may be related to each other in various ways. They may be cumulative so that performance will not become due unless all of them occur. They may be alternative so that performance may become due if any one of them occurs. Or some may be cumulative and some alternative. Furthermore, a condition may qualify the duties of both parties.").

59. *See, e.g., John M. Floyd & Assocs. Inc. v. Star Fin. Bank,* 489 F.3d 852, 855 (7th Cir. 2007) (Indiana law) ("We recognize, however, that the term 'condition precedent' carries multiple meanings, and can refer to a condition precedent to the formation of a contract, or a condition precedent to an obligation that arises under an already existing contract.").

60. *Id.* (explaining that the term "condition precedent" has many meanings, including "a condition precedent to the formation of a contract").

61. *Cedyco Corp. v. PetroQuest Energy, LLC,* 497 F.3d 485, 488 (5th Cir. 2007).

62. *See, e.g., Sahadi v. Cont'l Ill. Nat'l Bank & Trust Co. of Chicago,* 706 F.2d 193, 198 (7th Cir. 1983) ("In general, contractual terms are presumed to represent independent promises rather than conditions.").

if-clause's satisfaction.) In order to state a right that a party will have upon, but *only* upon, the satisfaction of a condition, "if" should be replaced with "if and only if." If § 4.2 provided that "Dell has the right to withhold any applicable taxes, if and only if required by any government authority," then § 4.2 would not only provide Dell with a source for its right to withhold taxes but it also would restrict Dell to look only to § 4.2 for such a right. As a final illustration, § 6.3.1 contains a list of several so-named "conditions," providing that SUPPLIER "must" satisfy such conditions in order for SUPPLIER to be entitled to payment in the event of cancellation (within the meaning of § 6.2). Perhaps there is no clearer way to signal a condition than expressly to label a provision a "condition" and to specify that for certain rights to be available, a party "must" satisfy these "conditions."

Notice that conditions differ from covenants and warranties. Both covenants and warranties impose obligations on the party making them. A covenant states an obligation of a party to act. A warranty states a party's promise that a statement is true and to provide a remedy for any breach of the warranty. By contrast, a condition is not framed as an *obligation* of a party; rather, a condition states what *is necessary to trigger* an obligation under the contract. A condition—inasmuch as it turns on the behavior of one party—poses a "take it or leave it" scenario. Imagine that party B's obligation to sell 100 widgets to party A is conditioned on party A producing a third-party audit report detailing party A's financial condition. Party A has a choice: He may cause the report's production and satisfy a necessary precursor to party B's obligation to sell the widgets, or party A may opt not to have the report produced and to lose the right to purchase the widgets. While conditions are framed as options and covenants and warranties are framed as obligations, notice that in the end all contractual obligations are in some sense "options." A party may choose to perform its contractual obligations, or a party may choose not to perform its contractual obligations and, instead, to pay the damages that result from this breaching non-performance. The difference here is that *within* the contractual arrangement, both covenants and warranties impose obligations, *the non-performance of which amounts to a breach of that contract*, whereas the non-performance of a condition does not result in a breach of contract but leaves certain rights and obligations on the table un-triggered.[63]

Subject to certain exceptions, generally one must *precisely* meet an express condition in order to unlock any rights and obligations that flow from the satisfaction of the condition.[64] As one well-known commentator has explained: "The promisor can only be held liable according to the terms of the promise

---

63. *See, e.g., Frost Constr. Co. v. Lobo, Inc.*, 951 P.2d 390, 397 (Wyo. 1998) ("The assertion that the nonperformance of a condition precedent constitutes a breach of the agreement is incorrect. A breach of contract is the nonperformance of some duty created by a promise.").

64. *See, e.g., In re Krueger*, 192 F.3d 733, 738 (7th Cir. 1999) ("In Illinois, courts generally demand strict compliance with the requirement that a condition precedent be satisfied.").

which he or she makes. . . . [I]f he or she makes a promise to do an act on condition that he or she receives $5.01, the promisor cannot be required to perform on being paid $5.00."[65] In contrast, recall from Chapter 2 that contractual *obligations* need not be precisely performed in order to bind the other party to his contractual obligations. If a party, in good faith, fails to perform his contractual obligations fully but still performs substantially, then the non-breaching party may sue for damages but is not excused from performing his obligations under the contract. Conditions, then, are different. If party A's obligations to perform under a contract are conditioned on party B's use of Reading brand pipes and party B uses a different but equal brand of pipe, then party B will have failed to have satisfied the condition.[66] Accordingly, any rights and obligations that were premised on such condition's satisfaction remain dormant. A pushback on this general rule requiring strict satisfaction of conditions is that a court may be unwilling to cause a party to forfeit rights under a contract, where a condition has fallen short of complete satisfaction.[67] Courts generally disfavor the forfeiture of rights so as to avoid unjust results.[68] As the Fifth Circuit has explained:

> Texas courts excuse non-performance of a condition precedent if the condition's requirement (a) will involve extreme forfeiture or penalty, and (b) its existence or occurrence forms no essential part of the exchange for the promisor's performance.[69]

This is necessarily a soft standard that leaves much discretion to the court.[70] Courts have been more willing to enforce a condition by its strict terms, despite a resulting forfeiture of rights, where the condition is part of a contract negotiated between sophisticated parties.[71]

---

65. Richard A. Lord, 13 Williston on Contracts § 38:6 (4th ed. 2009).

66. This is a play on the famous case of *Jacob & Youngs, Inc. v. Kent*, 230 N.Y. 239 (1921), where a contractor agreed to build a house according to certain specifications, including that all pipes in the house were to be Reading brand pipe. The contractor built the house but mistakenly—neither fraudulently nor willfully—failed to use Reading pipe and instead used a pipe identical in all but its name. The defendant refused to pay the contractor the remaining, unpaid balance of the price. The contractor sued to recover this amount. Then Judge Cardozo found that the contractor had substantially performed his obligations and, so, had not forfeited his right to payment under the contract.

67. *See* Restatement (Second) of Contracts § 229 (1981) ("To the extent that the non-occurrence of a condition would cause disproportionate forfeiture, a court may excuse the non-occurrence of that condition unless its occurrence was a material part of the agreed exchange.").

68. *See, e.g.*, *Klipsch, Inc. v. WWR Tech., Inc.*, 127 F.3d 729, 737 (8th Cir. 1997) ("Indiana law generally disfavors forfeitures; however, forfeiture may be appropriate under circumstances in which it is found to be consonant with notions of fairness and justice under the law.") (internal citations and quotation marks omitted); *Varel v. Banc One Capital Partners, Inc.*, 55 F.3d 1016, 1018 (5th Cir. 1995) ("Texas courts disfavor forfeitures.").

69. *Varel*, 55 F.3d at 1018 (internal citations and quotation marks omitted).

70. *See* Restatement (Second) of Contracts § 229 cmt. b (1981) ("The rule stated in the present Section is, of necessity, a flexible one, and its application is within the sound discretion of the court.").

71. *See, e.g.*, *Klipsch*, 127 F.3d at 737 ("Forfeiture based on the facts of this case is in keeping with the concepts of fairness and justice. In negotiating the License Agreement, [the relevant parties] were all represented by counsel and freely agreed to the clear and unambiguous language contained in the termination provision.").

4. Open-Price Terms

Section 3.0 is the portion of this Agreement devoted to price. Having reviewed the section, can you determine how much Dell must pay for the Products it receives under this Agreement? The answer, of course, is "no," and this is not because *this* information has been redacted for confidentiality reasons. Because this is a master agreement, where Dell plans to purchase various Products from the SUPPLIER under separate purchase orders (i.e., Dell POs), the parties lack the knowledge necessary to designate in the master contract the price of these Products to be purchased in the future. Accordingly, the price of each such Product is to be agreed upon by the parties and presumably specified in the corresponding Dell PO. As we discussed in Chapter 3, this is the nature of a master agreement, which provides the global terms governing a relationship to involve the future purchase of services and/or goods by a work order. Indeed, Article 2 of the U.C.C. anticipates commercial contracts with open-price terms, providing in § 2-305, "The parties if they so intend may conclude a contract for sale even if the price is not settled."[72]

In this Agreement, SUPPLIER agrees to work with Dell to develop a mutually agreeable price for each Product. What if the parties fail to agree on a price? Article 2 not only contemplates that commercial arrangements may include open-price terms but also provides for what happens if the parties later fail to agree on an open-price term. Article 2 resolves the situation where "the price is left to be agreed by the parties and they fail to agree," by providing that "the price is a reasonable price at the time for delivery."[73] Article 2 often plays a gap-filling role, providing substantive terms where parties otherwise neglect to do so. Under this Agreement, if the parties fail to agree on a price, must SUPPLIER still fill Dell POs? Does SUPPLIER have any protection or recourse other than whatever confidence may be attained from a right to receive a "reasonable" price?

As we discuss further in the context of letters of intent in Chapter 6, parties will sometimes agree—either within a larger contract or as the subject of an entire document—to agree in the future to certain terms. These so-called "agreements to agree" occur when parties have not yet come to agreement on the issue in question as of the time of the contract but do agree that they *will* come to an agreement on the issue in the future. As of the contracting time, the parties may not have sufficient information or the desire to overcomplicate the present contract negotiations so as to come to agreement on the additional issue. Courts

---

72. U.C.C. § 2-305(1) (2003).
73. *Id.* § 2-305(1).

routinely hold that these agreements to agree in the future are *not* enforceable contractual obligations.[74] Accordingly, in general, the failure of parties to agree, despite an agreement to do so, does not constitute a breach of contract.[75] However, courts have generally found that attaching a performance standard (which we discuss in further detail below) to negotiate an agreement (e.g., in good faith) *can* create an enforceable obligation to negotiate in conformance with that standard. To illustrate, some courts have found an agreement to negotiate in "good faith" or with "best efforts" creates an enforceable obligation to negotiate—although not necessarily to agree—accordingly.[76] As the Seventh Circuit has explained:

> The obligation to negotiate in good faith has been generally described as preventing one party from, renouncing the deal, abandoning the negotiations, or insisting on conditions that do not conform to the preliminary agreement. For instance, a party might breach its obligation to bargain in good faith by unreasonably insisting on a condition outside the scope of the parties' preliminary agreement, especially where such insistence is a thinly disguised pretext for scotching the deal because of an unfavorable change in market conditions. The full extent of a party's duty to negotiate in good faith can only be determined, however, from the terms of the letter of intent itself.[77]

Still, some courts have held that an agreement to negotiate in good faith or with best efforts, while perhaps creating a contractual obligation *in theory*, does not result in an obligation that courts can practically enforce, "[u]nless the parties delineate in the contract objective standards by which their efforts are to be measured."[78] This is because "the very nature of contract negotiations renders it

---

74. *See, e.g., Diamond Elec. Inc. v. Pace Pac. Corp.*, 346 F. App'x 186, 187 (9th Cir. 2009) ("An agreement to agree on contract terms at a later date is not a binding contract in Nevada."); *Specialized Transp. of Tampa Bay, Inc. v. Nestle Waters N. Am., Inc.*, No. 09-12807, 2009 WL 3601606, at *7 (11th Cir. Nov. 3, 2009) (Florida law) ("An agreement to agree in the future is an agreement for which there is no remedy and which is thus unenforceable.") (internal citations and quotation marks omitted); *Tractebel Energy Mktg., Inc. v. AEP Power Mktg., Inc.*, 487 F.3d 89, 95 (2d Cir. 2007) ("'[A] mere agreement to agree, in which a material term is left for future negotiations, is unenforceable.'") (quoting *Joseph Martin, Jr., Delicatessen, Inc. v. Schumacher*, 417 N.E.2d 541, 543 (N.Y. 1981)) (alteration in original).

75. *See supra* note 74.

76. *See, e.g., Dual, Inc. v. Symvionics, Inc.*, No. 97-1228, 1997 WL 565663, at *4 (4th Cir. Sept. 12, 1997) ("[U]nder California law . . . parties may contract to create the obligation to negotiate in good faith with one another, so long as the obligation does not go so far as to require an agreement on a subsequent contract.").

77. *A/S Apothekernes Laboratorium for Specialpraeparater v. I.M.C. Chem. Group, Inc.*, 873 F.2d 155, 158 (7th Cir. 1989) (internal citations and quotation marks omitted).

78. *Pinnacle Books, Inc. v. Harlequin Enters., Ltd.*, 519 F. Supp. 118, 122 (S.D.N.Y. 1981); *see also Precision Indus., Inc. v. Tyson Foods, Inc.*, No. 8:09CV195, 2009 WL 4377558, at *4 (D. Neb. Nov. 25, 2009) ("It is particularly difficult to enforce this provision as there is no way to measure the breach, if any, or to give a particular remedy."). As the Seventh Circuit has explained:

> [W]e are mindful of the powerful argument that the parties' undertakings were too vague to be judicially enforceable. . . . This is the approach taken in some states. But interpreting Illinois law, we

impossible to determine whether the parties have used their 'best' efforts."[79] If parties wish, then, to create an enforceable obligation to negotiate, at least according to these courts, they should consider imposing definite obligations: "For instance, the parties could agree in the contract that 'best efforts' means that they would not negotiate with others for a specific period of time or that one party has the right to match any offer received from another."[80]

Accordingly, the work of Article 2 here is to address a particular instance of "agreements to agree"—agreements to agree to a price term in the future. A failure to agree to price in accordance with an agreement's provision does not cause the contract to fail nor does it amount to a breach of contract; Article 2 merely fills the gap with a "reasonable" price.

A Practitioner Perspective: The "Manufacturer's Suggested Retail Price"

The manufacturer's suggested retail price, often referred to as the "MSRP" or just the "suggested retail price," is a concept that pervades virtually all categories of retail sales. Although the MSRP for a given product originates at the manufacturer level, every retailer employs the MSRP to a greater or lesser extent, depending upon the category of retail sales in which they operate. Indeed, the MSRP plays a critically important role in the advertising and promotional cadence of the retailer from the time products are received from the manufacturer to their final sale or disposition.

For example, retailers selling exclusive or semi-exclusive merchandise view the MSRP almost as a pricing standard and only vary significantly from that standard during end-of-season promotions to exhaust residual inventories or when economic circumstances dictate. In determining what price to offer these products to their customers, these retailers generally apply more liberal mark-ups from their cost to acquire the merchandise and, thus, may decide to equal or even exceed the MSRP depending upon the scarcity of the product involved and the perceived level of customer demand. This phenomenon is clearly illustrated when an automobile dealership raises the retail price of a given vehicle to exceed the MSRP based upon the vehicle's limited availability.

Other retailers use the MSRP more as a high-water mark against which to compare their pricing structure. These retailers generally deal in merchandise that is freely available at competing retailers which, in turn, restricts their ability to benefit from generous mark-ups. Said another way, retailers that are forced to

---

have held that agreements to negotiate toward the formation of a contract are themselves enforceable as contracts if the parties intended to be legally bound.

Venture Assocs. Corp. v. Zenith Data Sys. Corp., 96 F.3d 275, 277 (7th Cir. 1996) (internal citations and quotation marks omitted).

79. *Pinnacle Books*, 519 F. Supp. at 122.
80. *Id.* at 122 n.4.

compete with other retailers selling virtually the same items at outlets just as convenient to their target customers must be willing to accept lower mark-ups and purchase larger quantities from manufacturers in order to maximize profitability. Thus, "30% off MSRP" is a common phrase used by discount retailers accustomed to driving traffic into stores or websites through comparisons to the MSRP.

Of course, only certain retailers are granted the right to distribute a particular manufacturer's products, and the identification of qualified retailers in any given market is a function of how that manufacturer intends to go to market and the type of products involved. Mass marketers look to grow their volume over time by opening as many distribution sites as possible and, thus, tend to be less concerned about adherence to the MSRP. Higher-end manufacturers, on the other hand, are more concerned about maintaining the quality, reputation or mystique of their products at a very high level. Therefore, they seek to maintain more control over the pricing of their products at retail, as well as the manner in which their products are merchandised, by limiting the number of retailers granted the right to sell their products in a given geographical area.

The degree to which manufacturers can actually require retailers to price merchandise at the MSRP is governed by antitrust considerations. Over the last few decades, there has been a gradual relaxation of the prohibition against agreements between manufacturers and retailers concerning pricing at the retail level, which, in turn, has emboldened manufacturers to seek more control over the manner and timing of their retailers' promotional efforts. Conversely, retailers have generally resisted these efforts by seeking greater freedom in the manner in which they exhaust inventories. Until the current antitrust framework is clarified through case precedent or legislation, there seems to be ample ammunition on both sides of this argument to prevent manufacturers or retailers from gaining the upper hand.

In addition to the protections afforded consumers by antitrust law, a fairly complicated web of consumer protection legislation has developed, at both the state and federal level, to prevent unscrupulous retailers from enticing customers to make retail purchases through inappropriate price comparisons to the MSRP. Strict requirements governing the description, timing and prominence of comparisons to the MSRP form the basis of these laws, which are enforced by state attorneys general and at the federal level by the Federal Trade Commission. Monetary penalties and injunctive relief are the typical forms of remedies available under these laws, but in some states so-called "private attorneys general" are also empowered to enforce these laws.

Tony Bangs
Senior Vice President and General Counsel
The Neiman Marcus Group, Inc.
Lecturer in Law
The University of Chicago Law School

5. Most-Favored-Nations Clauses

Often department stores will pay customers if a reduction in price occurs within a certain number of days after the purchase of an item. While it is unlikely that the customer came upon this right through active negotiations with the store, the store is concerned that the customer may be less willing to buy something now—and may become dissatisfied later—given the possibility that the item may go down in price in the future. Certainly, from the vantage point of the buyer, one can appreciate the value of such a right—it can only mean a better price (although perhaps it creates some incentive for the store not to offer cheaper prices in the future). Similarly, a commercial buyer of goods benefits from a provision that entitles the buyer to a price reduction, if the seller ever makes a better price available to another buyer. These provisions are commonly called "most-favored-nations" clauses and can be found not only in agreements for the sale of goods but also in almost any type of commercial agreement, where one party has the right to float its "deal" to the level of the best terms made available by the other party.

From the language in §§ 3.2 and 3.3 of the Agreement, it appears that Dell has the right to cause SUPPLIER to review prices on an ongoing basis. We do not know the details to inform these reviews and the associated reductions in price, but, if Dell's prices are to be reduced to match the price offerings made to others for similar products, then we have here a most-favored-nations provision. Indeed, the party wishing to enforce a most-favored-nations provision needs access to information regarding what terms the other party has given to third parties in order to know if the party's most-favored-nations provision has been implicated. Including an auditing mechanism along with the most-favored-nations provision in the agreement is one means of causing the production of such information and, so, of facilitating the enforcement of a most-favored-nations provision. Section 17.0 of the Agreement presents a variation on most-favored-nations terms, providing that SUPPLIER must make available to Dell any products sold by SUPPLIER to a third party "at a price equivalent to or lower than the price paid by other customers purchasing similar quantities." Accordingly, § 17.0 differs from a standard most-favored-nations provision in that § 17.0 addresses Dell's pricing rights not for products already the subject of a Dell PO but, rather, those products that Dell has not yet ordered and that SUPPLIER has made available to another customer.

As a brief aside, notice further that, while § 17.0 addresses the *advent* of *new* Products, § 8.0 of the Agreement provides Dell with certain rights upon SUPPLIER's *cessation* of production of *old* Products. Among these, SUPPLIER must give Dell notice before the last date of manufacture and continue to supply Dell with the quantity of Products that SUPPLIER has committed to supply to meet

Dell's forecasted needs as provided by § 5.2.4.[81] Before discontinuing a Product, SUPPLIER must give Dell a single opportunity to order the Product and must warehouse these quantities. In exchange, Dell must pay for all such Product at the price specified in the associated purchase order, provided that both parties make a good faith effort otherwise to sell the Product.[82]

Returning to most-favored-nations clauses, a primary concern with such provisions is the scope of third-party transactions that may trigger adjustment rights under the provision. That is, a contract for the purchase of apples is unlikely to include a most-favored-nations clause that gives the buyer the right to purchase apples for the price at which the seller sells oranges to a third-party customer. A major point of negotiations, then, is defining what types of transactions are "similar" enough to the transaction at hand so as to be within the scope of a most-favored-nations clause and to cause adjustments to price and, perhaps, other terms. A buyer (or, borrower, or whatever party stands to benefit from a most-favored-nations provision) will want to define what constitutes a triggering transaction broadly because the buyer will want to cast a wide net around what may allow him to reduce prices. Of course, then, in contrast, a seller (or, again, whatever party must offer the better deal in the event that a most-favored-nations provision is triggered) will want to define the scope of a most-favored-nations provision narrowly so as to minimize the types of deals that will cause the seller to reduce the price of goods. Looking to the Agreement, as we mention above, § 17.1 provides a variation of a most-favored-nations clause. What is the scope of this provision? Why is the concern, as discussed in this paragraph, for what constitutes a "similar" transaction not at play here? From the language found in § 17.1, what limits the types of transactions that may trigger Dell's pricing rights? Which party—SUPPLIER or Dell—does the inclusion of this limitation benefit? Is this limitation vague or well defined in the text of § 17.1? Which party does such vagueness or definiteness benefit?

6. Quantity: Output and Requirements Contracts

Along with price, quantity is some of the basic information a contract for the sale of goods might include. There are a number of ways for contracts to address quantity. Straightforwardly, sale-of-goods contracts may simply state the number of goods to be sold under the contract. Alternatively, a contract may be for all the goods that the buyer requires or, as another example, all the goods that the seller produces. The former is commonly called a "requirements" contract and

---

81. Please see the discussion of quantity below.
82. For more on "good faith," please see the discussion of the implied covenant of good faith and fair dealing below.

the latter, an "output" contract. As these are common modes of doing business, Article 2 contemplates their use and offers its own gloss for their interpretation. The U.C.C. provides that where a contract defines the quantity of goods to be sold as the seller's output or the buyer's requirements, this quantity term "means such actual output or requirements as may occur in good faith."[83] What does it mean for output or requirements quantities to occur in "good faith"? As the Fourth Circuit has explained:

> Although there is no established standard for determining whether a buyer acted in good faith, courts focus on whether the buyer's reduction of its requirements stemmed from second thoughts about the terms of the contract and the desire to get out of it. Thus, if the buyer had a legitimate business reason for eliminating its requirements, as opposed to a desire to avoid its contract, the buyer acts in good faith.[84]

The Fourth Circuit went on to find that a buyer that closed its plant facility "as part of its overall restructuring" and "because of its low profitability" and, thus, eliminated its requirements under a requirements contract did so based on "a legitimate business decision" and in good faith.[85] In addition, the U.C.C. expresses concern for the situation where the quantity (i.e., the amount required or the amount produced) is "unreasonably disproportionate" to the parties' stated estimate or—if no estimate is stated—"to any normal or otherwise comparable prior output or requirements."[86] Despite an output or requirements quantity provision, in these cases where a "disproportionate" quantity results from the goods required or produced, such a quantity will not be forced upon, say, a buyer (by a seller in an output contract) or a seller (by a buyer in a requirements contract). Many courts have held that this concern for disproportionately is asymmetrical—that it only applies when the quantity term would be disproportionately *greater* than an estimated or reasonable amount and that good faith *reductions* that result in disproportionately low quantities do not violate Article 2.[87]

---

83. U.C.C. § 2-306(1) (2003). Please note that we discuss below the implied covenant of good faith, which permeates all contractual relationships.

84. *Brewster of Lynchburg, Inc. v. Dial Corp.*, 33 F.3d 355, 365-66 (4th Cir. 1994) (internal citations and quotation marks omitted).

85. *Id.* at 366.

86. U.C.C. § 2-306(1) (2003).

87. *See, e.g., Brewster*, 33 F.3d at 365 ("[U]nder Arizona law, a requirements contract allows a buyer to reduce the quantity demanded to any amount, including zero, so long as it does so in good faith. If the seller wishes to reallocate some of the inherent risks in such a contract, it may specify some minimum requirement."); *Empire Gas Corp. v. Am. Bakeries Co.*, 840 F.2d 1333, 1339 (7th Cir. 1988) ("The ['unreasonably disproportionate'] proviso does not apply, though the requirement of good faith does, where the buyer takes less rather than more of the stated estimate in a requirements contract."). *But see Simcala, Inc. v. Am. Coal Trade, Inc.*, 821 So.2d 197 (Ala. 2001) ("We conclude that the interpretation supported by the plain meaning of the language of the statute and by the official comments is that [U.C.C § 2-306(1)] prohibits unreasonably disproportionate decreases made in good faith.").

Does this Agreement contemplate a requirements or output arrangement? In other words: Must SUPPLIER supply all the Products that Dell requires, or must Dell purchase all the Products that SUPPLIER produces? Subsection 5.2.4 speaks to the quantity of Products that SUPPLIER will supply Dell, stating that Dell will give SUPPLIER notice of a six-month-advance quantity amount and that SUPPLIER will respond, in kind, with whether or not SUPPLIER will meet the forecasted quantity. Subsection 5.2.4 further specifies that it is SUPPLIER's confirmation of its commitment to meet Dell's forecasted quantity that will bind SUPPLIER to do so. Subsection 5.2.1 provides, "Subject to the provisions of Section 5.2.4, SUPPLIER agrees to fill all Dell POs. . . ." In addition, notice that § 18.14 provides explicitly that the Agreement itself imposes no obligation on Dell to purchase any minimum quantity from SUPPLIER. Accordingly, it would seem that SUPPLIER is not obligated to supply all of Dell's requirements and that Dell is not obligated to purchase all of SUPPLIER's output. This Agreement provides specific mechanisms by which Dell and SUPPLIER may agree to the purchase and supply of certain quantities of goods.

Section 2-201 is the U.C.C. version of the statute of frauds and requires that a contract for the sale of goods over $5,000 contain a quantity term in order to be enforceable.[88] If the Agreement does not require Dell to purchase and/or SUPPLIER to sell any certain quantity of goods, does this Agreement run afoul of the statute of frauds? Does it matter that a purchase order (presumably incorporated with the Agreement by reference) is likely to include a specific quantity term? The official comments to § 2-201 provide some guidance:

> A term indicating the manner by which the quantity is determined is sufficient. Thus, for example, a term indicating that the quantity is based on the output of the seller or the requirements of the buyer satisfies the requirement. The same reasoning can be extended to a term that indicates that the contract is similar to, but does not qualify as, an output or requirement contract. Similarly, a term that refers to a master contract that provides a basis for determining a quantity satisfies this requirement.[89]

Please consider this official comment along with the case excerpted below (we return again to *Advent Systems*) in determining whether you think the Agreement is likely to be enforceable under the U.C.C.

---

88. U.C.C. § 2-201(1) (2003) ("[A] contract is not enforceable under this subsection beyond the quantity of goods shown in the record."). Note the pre-revised version of § 2-201 sets the threshold at $500, which the revised version increased to $5,000.

89. *Id.* § 2-201 cmt. 1 (internal citations omitted).

Advent Systems Ltd. v. Unisys Corp.
United States Court of Appeals, Third Circuit, 1991.
925 F.2d 670.

[This case is continued from page 234.]

III. THE STATUTE OF FRAUDS

This brings us to the Unisys contention that the U.C.C. statute of frauds bars enforcement of the agreement because the writings do not contain a quantity term.

Section 2-201(a) provides that a contract for the sale of goods of $500 or more is not enforceable unless in writing. "[A] contract . . . is not enforceable . . . unless there is some writing sufficient to indicate that a contract for sale has been made. . . . A writing is not insufficient because it omits . . . a term agreed upon but the contract is not enforceable . . . beyond the quantity of goods shown in such writing." The comment to this section states that although the "required writing need not contain all the material terms" there are "three definite and invariable requirements as to the memorandum," one of which is that "it must specify a quantity."

The statute of frauds has been frequently criticized as a means for creating rather than preventing fraud, and there have been calls for its total repeal. Serious considerations therefore counsel courts to be careful in construing its provisions so that undesirable rigidity does not result in injustice.

The limited scope of section 2-201 should not be overlooked. "It is also clear that a sufficient writing merely satisfies the statute of frauds under the Code, i.e., it does not, in itself, prove the terms of the contract."

Moreover, compliance with the statute of frauds must be distinguished from enforcement of a remedy. At this point we focus on the statute of frauds, reserving for discussion enforcement under § 2-204.

Courts have generally found that a quantity term must be stated for compliance with the Code, and commentators have agreed.

A contrary view, however, has been advanced. In her article *The Weed and the Web: Section 2-201's Corruption of The U.C.C.'s Substantive Provisions—The Quantity Problem*, Professor Bruckel argues that the quantity section of the statute of frauds should be construed so that the contract is not enforceable beyond the quantity shown in the writing—if a quantity is specified. If no quantity is mentioned, the omission should not be fatal.

Respected scholars concede some force to this argument. As White and Summers state, "All commentators say the memo must state a quantity term. However, a close reading of section 2-201 indicates that all commentators may be wrong. An alternative explanation is that only if the writing states a quantity term is that term determinative."

This liberal approach found an interested audience in *Riegel Fiber Corp. v. Anderson Gin Co.*, 512 F.2d 784 (5th Cir. 1975), where the Court described that reasoning as "plausible," noting that the quantity term offers little aid in the primary purpose of the statute of frauds. Once a party alleges that the agreement took place and proves a signed writing, "surely he is no more likely to lie about the agreed quantity term than about price, time of performance, or any other material term." A Pennsylvania court also struck a sympathetic chord in discussing the effect of a memorandum that refers to an oral agreement.

The circumstances here do not require us to adopt an open-ended reading of the statute but permit us to apply a narrower holding. Nothing in the Code commands us to ignore the practicality of commercial arrangements in construing the statute of frauds. Indeed, the Code's rule of construction states that the language "shall be liberally construed and applied to promote its underlying purposes and policies." As noted earlier, Comment 1 to that section observes that the Code promotes flexibility in providing "machinery for expansion of commercial practices." Following this guidance, we look to the realities of the arrangement between the parties.

In the distribution agreement, Unisys agreed to engage in the business of selling identified document systems during the two-year term of the contract and to buy from Advent on stated terms the specified products necessary to engage in that venture. The detailed nature of the document, including as it does, such provisions as those for notice of breach, opportunity for cure, and termination leaves no doubt that the parties intended to create a contract.

The parties were obviously aware that they were entering a new, speculative market and some uncertainty was inevitable in the amount of sales Unisys could make and the orders it would place with Advent. Consequently, quantity was not stated in absolute terms. In effect, the parties arrived at a non-exclusive requirements contract, a commercially useful device. We do not consider that in the circumstances here the arrangement raises the statute of frauds bar.

The Code recognizes exclusive requirements contracts in section 2-306, and imposes on the parties to such agreements a duty of good faith. For present purposes, the salient factor is that exclusive requirements contracts satisfy the quantity requirements of the statute of frauds, albeit no specific amount is stated.

The reasons for excepting exclusive requirements contracts from the strictures of the statute of frauds are strong. The purchasing party, perhaps unable to anticipate its precise needs, nevertheless wishes to have assurances of supply and fixed price. The seller, on the other hand, finds an advantage in having a steady customer. Such arrangements have commercial value. To deny enforceability through a rigid reading of the quantity term in the statute of frauds would run contrary to the basic thrust of the Code—to conform the law to business reality and practices.

By holding that exclusive requirements contracts comply with the statute of frauds, courts have decided that indefiniteness in the quantity term is acceptable. If the agreement here does not satisfy the statute of frauds because of indefiniteness of a quantity term, then neither does an exclusive requirements contract. We find no reason in logic or policy to differentiate in the statute of frauds construction between the contract here and an exclusive requirements arrangement.

The same reasons that led courts to dispense with a specific and certain quantity term in the exclusive requirements context apply equally when a continuing relationship is non-exclusive. The same regulating factor—good faith performance by the parties—applies and prevents the contracts from being illusory. The writings here demonstrate that the parties did not articulate a series of distinct, unrelated, simple buy and sell arrangements but contemplated what resembles in some respects a joint venture or a distributorship.

A construction of the statute of frauds that does not recognize the quite substantial difference between a simple buy and sell agreement and what occurred here is unduly restrictive. Section 2-306 in recognizing exclusive requirements and output contracts does not purport to treat them as the only permissible types of open quantity agreements. We do not read section 2-306 as an exclusionary measure, but rather as one capable of enlargement so as to serve the purposes of the Code.

We emphasize once again that our focus has been on a technical requirement of the statute of frauds whose *raison d'etre* is dubious. We have not yet considered the importance of evidence to support a remedy, an issue we consider to be addressed by section 2-204 rather than being comprehensively covered by the statute of frauds.

The separation of the concepts advanced by the statute of frauds and section 2-204 has a very practical significance. If the statute of frauds was not satisfied, this case would be dismissed on the complaint, but by surmounting that threshold, the litigation proceeds to a point where the terms of the contract and its enforcement may be determined. This disposition comports with the goals of the Code and gives due recognition to legitimate business practices.

In sum, we hold that the writings here satisfy the statute of frauds. . . .

[This case is continued on page 303.]

Comments

The official comments to revised § 2-201 cite *PMC Corp. v. Houston Wire & Cable Co.*[90] In that case, the Supreme Court of New Hampshire found that an agreement for the sale of goods did not fail the statute of frauds because the agreement "was not totally silent as to quantity because it referred to [a party's] expectation to purchase a 'major share'" of its products from the other party.[91] The comments also cite *Riegel Fiber Corp. v. Anderson Gin Co.*[92] There, the court focused its inquiry on whether commercial buyers and sellers in the relevant

---

90. 797 A.2d 125 (N.H. 2002).
91. *Id.* at 129.
92. 512 F.2d 784 (5th Cir. 1975).

industry would view the approach to the agreement's determination of quantity to be acceptable.[93] Accordingly, the court found a master contract for the sale of cotton with an undefined quantity term to be enforceable because the approach to contracting conformed to "acceptable practices in the cotton trade."[94] How do these cases inform your understanding of the Dell Agreement and its enforceability under § 2-201 of the U.C.C.?

---

7. Delivery, Transfer of Title, and Risk of Loss

a. *"Title" and "Risk of Loss"*

"Title" refers to "the legal right to control and dispose of property."[95] "Risk of loss" refers to "[t]he danger or possibility of damage to, destruction of, or misplacement of goods or other property."[96] While title and risk of loss often move together from a seller to a buyer, the transfer of one does not always coincide with the other.[97] Understanding how and when risk of loss passes is important: The party bearing the risk of loss for certain goods at a given moment suffers any harm that befalls those goods through no fault of either party. For example, if the risk of loss has already transferred from the seller to the buyer when goods are damaged, then the buyer must still pay for the goods, as agreed upon in the contract. If the seller still holds the risk of loss when goods are damaged and the seller is unable to deliver conforming goods as required by the contract, then the seller is liable to the buyer for failure to deliver conforming goods.

For how and when risk of loss passes from a buyer to a seller, we first look to Article 2. And Article 2 makes it clear that the first step is to look at what the parties to the contract specified.[98] If the contract provides specific terms for how and when risk of loss is transferred, then, as we discuss below, this governs. Absent the parties' so providing, Article 2 fills this gap with a host of its own rules. As an illustration, if the contract provides for delivery by a common carrier, then the risk of loss transfers to the buyer upon the seller's completion of its delivery obligations.[99] Either party's breach of contract may change when the risk of loss passes from the seller to the buyer. In short, the seller retains the risk

---

93. *Id.* at 790 ("[W]e view our inquiry as limited to the question whether these contracts contained quantity terms acceptable to the majority of buyers and sellers knowledgeable in the cotton trade.").

94. *Id.* at 792.

95. Black's Law Dictionary 1622 (9th ed. 2009).

96. *Id.* at 1443.

97. *See, e.g., Commonwealth Propane Co. v. Petrosol Int'l, Inc.*, 818 F.2d 522, 526-27 (6th Cir. 1987) ("It is true that the person with title will also (and incidentally) often bear the risk that the goods may be destroyed or lost; but the seller may have title and the buyer the risk, or the seller may have the risk and the buyer the title."); *see also* U.C.C. § 2-509 cmt. 1 (2003) ("The underlying theory of this section on risk of loss is in conformity with common commercial and insurance practice, to base the risk of loss on the physical location of the goods and not by shifting of the risk with the 'property' in the goods.").

98. U.C.C. § 2-509(4) (2003).

99. *Id.* § 2-509(1). Note that the 2003 revisions of Article 2 altered some of the default risk-of-loss rules under Article 2.

of loss if the seller has not satisfied all conditions necessary for the seller to obligate the buyer to accept the goods (e.g., the seller has not delivered conforming goods).[100] If the buyer has breached the contract, the buyer is liable to the seller for any damage to the goods beyond what the seller's insurance covers.[101] To be clear, if a party causes damage to the other party's goods, the aggrieved party has the same rights it always does to seek to recover in contract or tort from the party causing such damage.[102] "Risk of loss" refers to the risk of loss or damage that occurs through no fault of either party.

If you found the above paragraph dizzying (or, if not, feel free to review U.C.C. § 2-509 in further detail), take heed of the wondrous power of contracts to alter "default" law. As with much of contract law, the U.C.C. provides default risk-of-loss terms that designate how and when the risk of loss passes from the seller to the buyer in the absence of contractual provisions providing otherwise.[103] Parties to a contract for the sale of goods may specify in that contract how the risk of loss may (or may not) pass from the seller to the buyer.[104] Accordingly, to understand when Dell assumes the risk of damage befalling Products, Article 2 instructs us first to look to the Agreement itself.

Subsections 5.3.3 and 5.4.2 explain how risk of loss may pass under two mutually exclusive scenarios. As § 5.1 explains, SUPPLIER may deliver Products to Dell in either of two ways: (i) from certain Supplier Logistic Centers (SLCs); or (ii) directly to Dell. As § 5.3.1 clarifies, SUPPLIER will provide all Products from an SLC, unless Dell specifically requests direct delivery. Subsection 5.3.3 addresses risk of loss in the context of delivery from an SLC, and § 5.4.2 provides the risk-of-loss rules for direct delivery. For delivery from an SLC, SUPPLIER is only "authorized" to deliver Products to Dell, once Dell has given Supplier a "Pull Order." (Notice that the Agreement nowhere provides a definition of "Pull Order.") Absent a Pull Order, risk of loss cannot pass for any Products to be delivered from an SLC. If Dell issues a Pull Order, then the risk of loss passes once Dell takes physical possession and control of the Products at a Dell facility. Similarly, with regard to Products to be delivered directly to Dell, the risk of loss does not pass until Dell takes physical possession and control of the Products at a Dell facility. In addition, recall that Products, under this Agreement, do not attain "direct delivery" status (and so § 5.4.2 does not apply) unless Dell specifically authorizes SUPPLIER to deliver the Products directly. Test yourself: If Dell has transmitted a Pull Order for the Product but has not specifically requested direct delivery and a Product is damaged while en route to Dell (through no fault or doing of either party), which party bears this loss? Is it Dell or SUPPLIER who bears the costs of the damaged goods?

---

100. *Id.* § 2-510(1).

101. *Id.* § 2-510(3).

102. As we discussed in Chapter 3, the contract may seek to insulate a party from such liability. Please see the discussion in Chapter 3 on indemnification and limitation-of-liability provisions.

103. *See, e.g.,* U.C.C. §§ 2-509, 2-510 & 2-327 (2003).

104. *See supra* note 103. For example, § 2-509(4) provides, "The provisions of this section are subject to contrary agreement of the parties. . . ."

b. Terms of Delivery

Revised Article 2 did away with §§ 2-319 through 2-324, which provided various terms and rules for the delivery of goods. Under the pre-revised Article 2, § 2-319 addresses "F.O.B" (free on board) and "F.A.S" (free alongside) terms, and § 2-320 addresses "C.I.F." (cost, insurance, and freight) and "C. & F." (cost and freight) terms. For example, under pre-revised § 2-319, when a contract specifies that goods are to be delivered F.O.B. place of shipment, then the seller must deliver the goods to a common carrier and arrange for their shipment to the buyer. When a contract specifies that goods are to be delivered F.O.B. place of destination, then the seller must deliver the goods to this specified destination. Under the pre-revised Article 2, the parties are free to vary the meaning and obligations associated with these terms as used in their contract. Absent such variation, pre-revised Article 2 steps in to specify delivery obligations and the transfer of risk of loss, when the parties specify one of these delivery terms of art.

The revised version of Article 2 does not provide particular meaning or rules for the use of these delivery terms, but the use of terms, such as "F.O.B" or "F.A.S.," in a contract governed by Revised Article 2 will be interpreted as any other term. If the parties do not define the terms within their contract, the course of performance between the parties under that contract, the course of dealing between the parties under previous contracts, and the usage of trade by those in the relevant industry may inform the interpretation of these terms.[105]

In addition, the International Chamber of Commerce ("ICC") has promulgated International Commercial Terms (or "Incoterms") for the delivery of goods within the international commercial community.[106] Contractual parties may signal their intention to subscribe to the rights and responsibilities (e.g., delivery obligations, insurance obligations, transfer of risk of loss) afforded to certain Incoterms by expressly incorporating "Incoterms" by reference into their contract. As the ICC releases updated versions of Incoterms (e.g., "Incoterms 2010"), parties should specify the year of the Incoterms they wish to incorporate. As with Article 2 delivery terms, the parties may alter or change the incorporated meaning of Incoterms by so providing in their contract.

Where the sale of goods has an international dimension, parties will want to be sure to comply with any applicable U.S. export control laws. On this topic, we asked a couple seasoned practitioners to share their knowledge and experience.

A Practitioner Perspective: Overview of U.S. Export Control Laws

Export control laws regulate *what* is exported, *where* it is exported, to *whom* it is exported, and *how* the exported goods, service, or technology will be used. Some exports require licensing from the U.S. government based on these *what*, *where*,

---

105. U.C.C. § 1-303 (2003).
106. *See generally* Incoterms, http://www.iccwbo.org/incoterms/ (last visited Aug. 15, 2010).

whom, and *how* factors. Several U.S. regulatory agencies have export control authority. The principal agencies in this regard are the Commerce Department and the State Department, but more specialized U.S. export controls are administered, for instance, by the Drug Enforcement Administration (drugs, chemicals, and precursors), the Nuclear Regulatory Commission (nuclear materials and equipment), the Department of Energy (nuclear technology), and the Department of Agriculture (certain plants, plant products, and live animals).

A. Commerce Department Regulations

1. Overview

Through the Export Administration Regulations ("EAR," 15 C.F.R. Pts. 730 to 774), the Commerce Department's Bureau of Industry and Security ("BIS") has broad authority to regulate virtually all exports from the United States and authority to regulate "reexports" of U.S.-origin and U.S.-content items from one non-U.S. country to another. Nearly all exports from the United States require authorization under the EAR. In practice, however, prior authorization—in the form of a license issued by BIS—is required for only a narrow subset of items or end-uses.

The EAR focus on sensitive or so-called "dual-use" items, including goods, technology, and software, that could be used for military purposes or in weapons, even though the items may have predominately commercial applications. The EAR also prohibit certain activities or exports that support terrorists; nuclear, chemical, or biological weapons proliferation; and other prohibited "end-uses."

The EAR apply to exports and reexports, which include:

- Physical shipments or transfers out of the United States of goods, software, or technology;
- Cross-border electronic transmissions of software or technology (including e-mail or downloading from a remote computer server);
- "Deemed exports": disclosures of technology or software source code to a foreign national (i.e., someone who is not a U.S. citizen or green-card holder) that occur within the United States;
- Reexports: transfers of U.S.-origin goods, software, or technology from one foreign country to another, including the transfer of items that contain more than a certain amount of U.S.-origin content (10% or 25% by value, depending on the country to which the goods are being exported); and
- "Deemed reexports": the release or disclosure of U.S.-origin technology or source code in one foreign country to a national of a second foreign country.

2. The Commerce Control List

The Commerce Control List ("CCL") is part of the EAR that identifies and describes "dual-use" items that are considered sensitive and, therefore, require a U.S. license for export to some or all destinations. The CCL consists of ten categories numbered 0 to 9: (0) Nuclear Materials, Facilities and Equipment; (1) Materials, Chemicals, Microorganisms and Toxins; (2) Materials Processing; (3) Electronics; (4) Computers; (5) Telecommunications, Information Security; (6) Sensors and Lasers; (7) Navigation and Avionics; (8) Marine; and (9) Propulsion Systems, Space Vehicles and Related Equipment.

Each category of the CCL is arranged into Export Control Classification Numbers ("ECCN"), each of which contains detailed technical parameters and performance characteristics and identifies one or more reasons that the export of the item is controlled, such as "AT" for antiterrorism and "NP" for nuclear nonproliferation. Identifying the appropriate ECCN to apply to an item to be exported can be a highly complex and technical exercise requiring the cooperation of scientists, engineers, and lawyers.

Once a company, sometimes with the assistance of a Commerce Department ruling, has determined which ECCN applies to a particular good, software, or technology, it can determine whether export of the item requires a license. This determination is made by consulting the ECCN entry to determine the reason or reasons that the export of the item is controlled and then referring to the "country chart" in the EAR—a grid that lists the controls that apply to exports to each country and that helps the exporter determine whether a license is required. Narrow exceptions to licensing requirements may apply. Commercial items that are not included in a particular entry on the CCL (so-called "EAR99" items) do not require licensing for export unless the export is to an embargoed country or government or to a prohibited end-use or end-user.

3. Prohibited End-Use/End-Users

Exports of all items subject to the EAR that are for certain end-uses and end-users are prohibited. This includes even non-sensitive EAR99 items. The prohibitions include exports to embargoed countries or blocked parties, activities supporting the Arab boycott of Israel, activities supporting weapons proliferation (chemical, biological, nuclear, missiles), dealing with items that have been unlawfully exported, and exporting an item when the exporter knows or has reason to know that an EAR violation will occur.

In addition, exports may not be sent to individuals or entities on the Commerce Department's Denied Persons List (export violators), Entity List (individuals or entities believed to be engaged in weapons proliferation), or Unverified Users List (entities that raise a red flag requiring additional vigilance).

4. Violations of the EAR

Violations of the EAR can result in significant penalties. Penalties include criminal fines of up to $1 million and/or jail terms of up to 20 years. Violators also may be assessed civil fines of up to $250,000 per violation or twice the value of the transaction, whichever is higher, and may have their export privileges suspended or revoked. This last sanction can severely disrupt the ongoing transactions of a U.S. company and its affiliates outside the United States. Finally, violations of the EAR also can also result in negative publicity that may damage the exporter's reputation.

B. State Department Regulations

The State Department's Directorate of Defense Trade Controls ("DDTC") administers the International Traffic in Arms Regulations ("ITAR"). The ITAR are a complex body of regulations that govern the export of defense articles and defense services, and the temporary import of defense articles. (Permanent imports of certain defense articles are regulated by the U.S. Department of Justice, Bureau of Alcohol, Tobacco, Firearms and Explosives.)

1. Overview

The ITAR regulate the export of "defense articles" and "defense services," both of which are broadly defined. A "defense article" includes any product or technical data that could have significant military or intelligence applicability. A "defense service" is provided when technical data are furnished to foreign persons, whether inside or outside the United States. "Defense services" also include providing a foreign person with training or other assistance in the design, manufacture, testing, modification, demilitarization, etc. of defense articles—even when no technical data are disclosed or the information is in the public domain. "Foreign persons" includes foreign nationals, foreign companies, foreign governments (including their embassies and diplomatic missions), and international organizations.

As with the Commerce Department's EAR, an export under the ITAR may include taking or shipping a controlled product or technical data out of the United States, disclosing or transferring technical data to a foreign government or foreign person (whether in the United States or abroad), or performing a defense service on behalf of or for the benefit of a foreign person within or outside the United States. In addition, an "export" includes the transfer of ownership, registration, or control of an aircraft, vessel, or satellite controlled by the ITAR. Under the ITAR, manufacturers of defense articles are required to register with DDTC even if they do not export defense articles. The ITAR also regulate the brokering of defense articles.

With limited exceptions, a license is required from DDTC to export or reexport any defense article. Under the ITAR, an exporter can obtain an individual license for a proposed export, or it can seek DDTC approval of a Technical Assistance Agreement or a Manufacturing License Agreement with a non-U.S. entity.

2. The U.S. Munitions List

Defense articles controlled for export purposes by the State Department are enumerated on the U.S. Munitions List ("USML"), which is part of the ITAR. This list consists of 21 categories. The listed articles range from guns and ammunition to chemical weapons and associated equipment to tanks, naval vessels, and aircraft. Because determining whether an item fits on the USML may be complicated, companies can apply to the State Department for a "commodity jurisdiction" ruling that indicates whether the State Department views the company's product, data, or service as regulated by the ITAR.

Significantly, items need not be deemed "classified" for national security purposes (i.e., secret), nor need they be state-of-the-art, high-performance, or sophisticated technology to be controlled by the ITAR. Indeed, even seemingly minor modifications to off-the-shelf commercial items in order to meet the requirements of a defense contractor or military customer can result in the modified item being subject to the ITAR rather than the EAR.

The fact that a product modified for military use also is sold for commercial applications is generally not enough, by itself, to remove that item from ITAR control. If an item was specially designed or modified for a military application

but also has commercial applications, a person can submit a commodity jurisdiction request to DDTC asking that the item be removed from ITAR regulation.

3. Violations of the ITAR

Violations of the ITAR can result in significant penalties. Criminal ("willful")
violations are punishable by fines up to $1 million and/or 20 years in prison. Civil
violations are punishable by fines up to $500,000 per violation. Violations can
also result in the denial of export privileges or debarment, which can have
significant financial consequences and can impair the company's ability to
contract with the U.S. government.

Stephen P. Anthony
Partner
White Collar Defense and Investigations
Covington & Burling LLP

Peter L. Flanagan
Partner
International Trade and Finance
Member of the Management Committee
Covington & Burling LLP

8. Acceptance and Rejection: Triggering Payment and Warranties

As with the risk-of-loss rules described above, the rules for acceptance and
rejection are largely default law, which means that the parties may alter them by
contract.[107] However, some rules are mandatory, namely that a buyer generally
have a "reasonable time" to inspect the goods before having accepted them.

The default rules of rejection under Article 2 are as follows. In general, when
a buyer receives goods from a seller that "fail in any respect to conform" to
contractual specifications, the buyer has the right (i) to reject all of the goods,
(ii) to accept all of the goods, or (iii) to accept some of the goods, rejecting the
rest.[108] This is commonly called the "perfect-tender" rule, as the buyer has the
right to reject the whole delivery for any nonconformity whatsoever. However,
the perfect-tender rule does not apply to "installment contracts."[109] An installment contract is defined broadly as a contract for multiple goods that allows for
delivery in separate groups, each of which is to be separately accepted.[110] Indeed,

---

107. *See* U.C.C. § 1-302 (2003) ("Except as otherwise provided in subsection (b) or elsewhere in [the
Uniform Commercial Code], the effect of provisions of [the Uniform Commercial Code] may be varied by
agreement.").

108. *Id.* § 2-601.

109. *Id.*

110. *Id.* § 2-612(1); *see also Midwest Mobile Diagnostic Imaging v. Dynamic Corp. of Am.*, No. 97-1673, 1998 WL
537592, at *2 (6th Cir. Aug. 7, 1998) (Michigan law) ("An installment sale is a contract for multiple items that
permits delivery in separate groups and at different times.").

even if such a contract contains language that each delivery constitutes its own contract, the entire contract will still be treated as an "installment contract" for the purposes of Article 2.[111] As follows, this chapter's Agreement is likely to be treated as an installment contract. With installment contracts, "The buyer may reject any installment that is nonconforming if the nonconformity substantially impairs the value of that installment to the buyer. . . ."[112] Accordingly, an installment contract allows a buyer to reject goods for nonconformity only where the nonconformity constitutes a "substantial impairment," whereas any nonconformance of goods whatsoever is sufficient grounds for rejection under a non-installment contract (under the perfect-tender rule and subject to the seller's assurance of cure).

Assuming that a buyer has a right to reject, in order to effect such a rejection, the buyer must "seasonably" notify the seller of the rejection and such rejection must be within a reasonable time after delivery.[113] An action occurs "seasonably" if it occurs within a contractually specified time; if the contract does not so specify, an action occurs "seasonably" if it occurs within a "reasonable time."[114] What constitutes a "reasonable time" depends on the "nature, purpose, and circumstances" of the particular context.[115] Parties may fix a "reasonable time" by contract; however, a contractually agreed upon "reasonable time" that is "manifestly unreasonable" is not a "reasonable time" under the U.C.C, notwithstanding the agreement to the contrary.[116] If the buyer effectively rejects the goods, the seller under certain circumstances may still have the right to cure any nonconformity; this means the seller is allowed to fix any problems with the goods and re-deliver them to the buyer for acceptance but may still be liable to the buyer for any reasonable expenses caused by the breach and delayed performance.[117]

The buyer's alternative to rejecting goods is to accept them. Under Article 2, acceptance occurs in one of three ways: (1) the buyer notifies the seller, after a reasonable opportunity to inspect them, that the goods are conforming or that the buyer will take them despite their nonconformity; (2) the buyer fails to reject the goods and the buyer has had a reasonable opportunity to inspect the goods;

---

111. U.C.C. § 2-612(1) (2003) (A contract is an installment contract "even if the contract contains a clause 'each delivery is a separate contract' or its equivalent.").

112. *Id.* § 2-612(2). Note that a "defect in the required documents" (e.g., required insurance documents, a bill of lading) is also a sufficient basis to reject any installment. *Id.* However, if a seller gives adequate assurance that the seller will cure the defect (i.e., nonconformity constituting substantial impairment of value, defect in the required documents), then the buyer must accept the installment, unless the nonconformity substantially impairs the value of the *whole* contract. *Id.* § 2-612(2) & (3).

113. *Id.* § 2-602(1).

114. *Id.* § 1-205(b).

115. *Id.* § 1-205(a).

116. *Id.* § 1-302(b).

117. *Id.* § 2-508.

or (3) the buyer acts in any way inconsistent with the seller's owning the goods.[118] Note that payment alone is generally not conclusive of acceptance.[119]

Two competing concerns are at play regarding what constitutes a "reasonable time" in the context of acceptance and rejection: (1) the buyer's right to have a reasonable opportunity to inspect the goods before accepting them; and (2) the seller's right to have rejection occur, if it is to occur, within a reasonable time. The easy cases are when the buyer expressly accepts the goods or expressly rejects the goods right away. The more difficult cases are when the buyer does not expressly reject the goods immediately, and it becomes a question of fact whether a reasonable time for rejection has passed and whether the buyer has had a reasonable chance to inspect the goods, such that a failure to reject is a deemed acceptance. Again, as with the "reasonable time" that sets the outer bound for a timely rejection, what constitutes a reasonable time for a buyer's inspection may be fixed by contract, unless the contractual time limit has left the buyer with a "manifestly unreasonable" opportunity to inspect.[120] This is one place where a contract generally cannot completely alter a party's rights under Article 2, as the official comments explain: "However, no agreement by the parties can displace the entire right of inspection except where the contract is simply for the sale of 'this thing.'"[121] For example, the Eighth Circuit has held that a requirement that a notice of rejection be provided within five days after delivery did not prevent a later rejection because the buyer could not know within the contractual time period of the nonconformity.[122] In that case, the buyer of a tower received a warped base plate, which the seller assured would not affect the performance of the tower, and the buyer could not discover that the warped base plate affected the tower's conformance to specifications until after the buyer had erected the tower.[123]

In addition, even if a buyer has accepted goods, the buyer may still be able to "revoke" the acceptance. Revocation gives the buyer the same rights the buyer would have had if the buyer had rejected the goods in the first place.[124] A buyer may revoke an acceptance of goods when a "nonconformity substantially impairs [the goods'] value" to the buyer.[125] In addition, revocation requires that the buyer has accepted the goods "on the reasonable assumption that its nonconformity would be cured and it has not been seasonably cured" or "without

---

118. *Id.* § 2-606(1); *see also id.* § 2-513(1).

119. *Id.* § 2-606 cmt. 3.

120. *See, e.g., Nw. Airlines, Inc. v. Aeroservice, Inc.,* 168 F. Supp. 2d 1052, 1054-55 (D. Minn. 2001) ("The reasonable inspection time is here defined by the contract: ten days. Aeroservice did not notify Northwest of any possible lack of conformance of the goods until *at least* eleven days after delivery of the second shipment. Thus, as a matter of law, Aeroservice accepted the goods—conforming or not—and yet has not fully performed its obligations under the contract.") (emphasis in original).

121. U.C.C. § 2-513 cmt. 1 (2003).

122. *Trinity Prods., Inc. v. Burgess Steel, LLC,* 486 F.3d 325, 332 (8th Cir. 2007) (Missouri law).

123. *Id.* at 331.

124. U.C.C. § 2-608(3) (2003).

125. *Id.* § 2-608(1).

discovery of the nonconformity," in the latter case such acceptance being "reasonably induced either by the difficulty of discovery before acceptance or by the seller's assurances."[126] Note that wrongful rejection or revocation of goods is a breach of contract that leaves the seller with the full panoply of remedies available as with any breach of contract.[127]

What is the meaning of all this talk of rejection and acceptance (and, then, revocation still)? Rejection and revocation are important because they generally allow the buyer to return the goods to the seller without liability or having to pay.[128] Moreover, as discussed above, absent a contract to the contrary, the seller retains the risk of loss for certain goods if the buyer has a right to reject such goods.[129] In addition, absent a contract to the contrary, acceptance triggers the buyer's payment obligations.[130] Indeed, this Agreement provides as much: § 5.2.3(b) provides that acceptance triggers SUPPLIER's right to payment for delivered Products. Acceptance forecloses rejection (although, revocation may be available) of goods for nonconformity,[131] but acceptance generally triggers or, at least preserves, the buyer's right to sue for breach of warranty for the nonconformity of goods. Under § 5.2.3(b) of the Agreement, acceptance preserves Dell's warranty rights, as the provision makes clear that Dell's acceptance of the Products in no way waives a claim for breach of warranty or an argument that Products comport with specifications or warranties. To preserve a remedy for breach of warranty the buyer must generally notify the seller of the breach within a reasonable time of discovery.[132] Indeed, parties may contractually agree that the buyer will have waived all remedies for a nonconformity, where the notice of such is not given within a contractually stipulated number of days, and this contractual waiver will be enforced so long as the stipulated number of days reasonably allows for the buyer to discover the defect.[133]

What constitutes acceptance and rejection under this Agreement? Recall that the U.C.C. generally defers to a contract, except where the U.C.C. provides otherwise.[134] Also, recall that one example of the U.C.C. "providing otherwise" is with regard to a "reasonable time" to inspect goods before acceptance. As Article 2 requires, then, § 5.2.3 of the Agreement affords the buyer, Dell, an opportunity to inspect the Products before accepting them. Section 5.2.3(c)

---

126. *Id.* § 2-608(1); *see, e.g., Trinity*, 486 F.3d at 331-32.

127. U.C.C. § 2-703(1) (2003); *see also id.* § 2-602(3) (citing U.C.C. § 2-703 for remedies generally available to the seller).

128. *Id.* § 2-602(2)(c).

129. *See id.* § 2-510(1).

130. *Id.* § 2-607(1) ("The buyer must pay at the contract rate for any goods accepted.").

131. *Id.* § 2-607(2).

132. *Id.* § 2-607(3)(a). Under pre-revised Article 2, failure to notify within a reasonable time for a breach of warranty bars any remedy, whereas, under Revised Article 2, failure to notify within a reasonable time bars the buyer from a remedy if the seller is prejudiced by the failure.

133. *See, e.g., Traffic Safety Devices, Inc. v. Safety Barriers, Inc.*, No. 3:02-CV-636, 2006 WL 2709229 (E.D. Tenn. Sept. 20, 2006). See Chapter 3 for more on notice-requirement provisions and contractual "statute of limitations" provisions.

134. *See* U.C.C. § 1-205(a) (2003).

specifies how acceptance may occur under this Agreement. Recall that acceptance may occur under Article 2 upon the buyer's giving notice of acceptance to the seller.[135] This is the easy instance of acceptance, and § 5.2.3(c)(ii) of the Agreement provides that Dell may explicitly accept the Products in writing. The more difficult scenario turns on the question of when "silence" amounts to acceptance. Section 2-606(1)(b) of the Revised U.C.C. tells us that a buyer will be deemed to have accepted goods when the buyer fails to make an effective rejection and has had a reasonable opportunity to inspect the goods. And we know from § 2-602(1) that the buyer must "seasonably notify" (recall, parties may set by contract what constitutes a "seasonable" duration of time) the seller of the rejection for it to be effective. If the buyer has not "seasonably notified" the seller of rejection and the buyer has had a reasonable opportunity to inspect the goods, then the buyer will be deemed to have accepted the goods. Section 5.2.3(c)(i) provides that if Dell does not reject the Products within two days of delivery, then Dell will be deemed to have accepted the Products. As long as this provides Dell with a reasonable opportunity to inspect, then such deemed acceptance will be effective. (However, Dell still would retain the right to revoke its acceptance, if the requirements for such, as discussed above, are satisfied.) The last two methods of acceptance under § 5.2.3(c) of the Agreement are consistent with U.C.C. § 2-606(1)(c), as Dell's use of the Products in its manufacturing process or delivering of such Products to a customer each likely constitutes an "act inconsistent with seller's ownership."[136]

9. Revisiting Warranties and Disclaimers under Article Two

We have already discussed warranties at length in Chapter 3. In the context of goods sold, warranties often speak to the quality or nature of the goods and are promises that such goods will meet certain specifications. Warranties may be express or implied, and Article 2 is a source of implied warranties. We first explore the requirements for the creation of express warranties under Article 2, and then we reexamine the implied warranties Article 2 imputes into a contract for the sale of goods, absent an effective disclaimer.

a. *Express Warranties*

Under Article 2, a seller makes an express "warranty" to a buyer when the seller makes a promise, which relates to the goods and which "becomes part of

---

135. *Id.* § 2-606(1)(a).
136. *Id.* § 2-606(1)(c).

the basis of the bargain."[137] The official comments explain that this requirement dispenses with the requirement of reliance.[138] The question, then, is similar to that posed by the court in *Ziff-Davis*: Did the buyer purchase the warranty as part of the bargain? A seller's description of goods in a written agreement is likely to steer a court to find the description of fact to be a basis of the bargain.[139] Another question is whether such warranty is as of a point in time or ongoing into the future. Courts will generally look to the nature of the promise, usually requiring some explicit statement extending the warranty to future performance in order to find a warranty of future performance.[140] Accordingly, § 9.1 provides express warranties from SUPPLIER to Dell, the breach of which occurs if such warranties prove untrue. Notice that § 9.1 removes doubt that such warranties are "ongoing" and speak not only to the state of the goods at the point of delivery but also going forward into the future. What warranties does SUPPLIER provide?

b. Implied Warranties

Recall that Article 2 is the source of two types of implied warranties: merchantability and fitness. Article 2 supplies implied warranties as "gap fillers," as warranties that will attend any sale of goods unless the parties otherwise provide. As to the implied warranty of merchantability, which applies if the seller is a "merchant,"[141] Article 2 provides:

---

137. *Id.* § 2-313(2).

138. *Id.* § 2-313 cmt. 5 ("In actual practice affirmations of fact and promises made by the seller about the goods during a bargain are regarded as part of the description of those goods; hence no particular reliance on these statements need be shown in order to weave them into the fabric of the agreement."). Please see Chapter 3 for further discussion of the requirement of reliance in the context of breach of warranty actions. Note that some courts still require some showing of reliance to make out a claim for breach of warranty. *See, e.g., McManus v. Fleetwood Enters.*, 320 F.3d 545, 550 (5th Cir. 2003) ("The Texas Supreme Court has concluded that basis of the bargain loosely reflects the common-law express warranty requirement of reliance and that therefore an express warranty claim requires *a form of reliance*.") (emphasis in original) (internal citations and quotation marks omitted).

139. *See, e.g., Martin v. Am. Med. Sys., Inc.*, 115 F.3d 102, 105 (4th Cir. 1997) ("Any description of the goods, other than the seller's mere opinion about the product, constitutes part of the basis of the bargain and is therefore an express warranty."); *see also* U.C.C. § 2-313 cmt. 8 (2003) ("In general, the presumption is that . . . any affirmation of fact . . . is intended to become a basis of the bargain.").

140. *See, e.g., Marvin Lumber & Cedar Co. v. PPG Indus., Inc.*, 223 F.3d 873, 879 (8th Cir. 2000) (Minnesota law) ("Moreover, an express warranty of the present condition of goods without a specific reference to the future is not an explicit warranty of future performance, even if the description implies that the goods will perform a certain way in the future.").

141. Under Article 2:

"Merchant" means a person that deals in goods of the kind or otherwise holds itself out by occupation as having knowledge or skill peculiar to the practices or goods involved in the transaction or to which the knowledge or skill may be attributed by the person's employment of an agent or broker or other intermediary that holds itself out by occupation as having the knowledge or skill.

U.C.C. § 2-104(1) (2003). Is SUPPLIER likely to be found a merchant?

Goods to be merchantable must be at least such as:
(a) pass without objection in the trade under the contract description;
(b) in the case of fungible goods, are of fair average quality within the description;
(c) are fit for the ordinary purposes for which goods of that description are used;
(d) run, within the variations permitted by the agreement, of even kind, quality and quantity within each unit and among all units involved;
(e) are adequately contained, packaged, and labeled as the agreement may require; and
(f) conform to the promise or affirmations of fact made on the container or label if any.[142]

Accordingly, merchantability generally warrants that the goods will be what they are supposed to be—that they will be fit for the ordinary purpose for which such goods are used. As for the implied warranty of fitness for a particular purpose, Article 2 provides:

Where the seller at the time of contracting has reason to know any particular purpose for which the goods are required and that the buyer is relying on the seller's skill or judgment to select or furnish suitable goods, there is unless excluded or modified under [§ 2-316] an implied warranty that the goods shall be fit for such purpose.[143]

Do you think that the warranty of fitness is likely to apply to the Agreement? What additional information might be helpful in drawing this conclusion?

When we last visited these concepts (in Chapter 3) we discussed that these implied warranties may be disclaimed by contract. Again, implied warranties mark another instance of Article 2 acting as a friendly filler of contractual gaps: If a contract effectively tells Article 2 "thanks, but no thanks," Article 2 will happily defer and refrain from imputing implied warranties. Still, to be sure the parties so intended, Article 2 requires that such disclaimers meet certain criteria in order to be effective.[144] Indeed, in Chapter 3, we saw an example of a contract's conspicuous—and likely effective—disclaimer of Article 2's implied warranties. Does this chapter's Agreement disclaim any of these implied warranties? If so, is such disclaimer effective?

10. Licensing Intellectual Property

Sections 7.2 and 7.3 of the Agreement grant Dell, respectively: (i) a license to use, reproduce, and distribute Software (a defined term) solely in connection with Dell's distribution and support of Products; and (ii) a license to use

---

142. *Id.* § 2-314(2).
143. *Id.* § 2-315.
144. U.C.C. § 2-316 explains what makes for an effective exclusion of Article 2 implied warranties. Note that the warranty of title is not considered an "implied warranty," at least with respect to disclaimer. U.C.C. § 2-312(3) cmt. 5 (2003). For further discussion of this, please see Chapter 3. Please also see Chapter 3 for a discussion of exclusive remedies and the failure of essential purpose, both concepts that arise under Article 2.

SUPPLIER Trademarks (again, as defined) in connection with advertising, promotion, and sale of Products. In the context of intellectual property, a license grants the licensee the right to do certain specified things with the licensor's intellectual property.[145] Here, the license grants Dell the right to engage in certain activities (with respect to Software: to use, to reproduce, and to distribute; with respect to SUPPLIER Trademarks: to use) and limits the scope of such permissible activities to Dell's promotion and sale of the Products. In addition, both licenses are non-exclusive, meaning Dell has no right to exclude, or to expect the exclusion of, others (including SUPPLIER) from engaging in the same activities with respect to Software and SUPPLIER Trademarks, and both licenses are non-transferable, meaning that Dell may not sell, assign, or otherwise convey the rights granted to Dell under the license to another party.[146] That both licenses are "worldwide" is perhaps self-explanatory: Dell may exercise its rights under the license anywhere in the world. It is also common for such license provisions to specify the term and revocability of the license. The term of the license may be perpetual or fixed in length, and the license may be revocable or irrevocable, which speaks to the licensor's right to terminate the license and, so, the licensee's right to engage in the licensed activities. For illustration, a license may be perpetual but subject to the licensor's right to revoke the license, or, as another example, a license may be fixed in length but not subject to a right of the licensor to revoke.

Accordingly, here, SUPPLIER has given Dell limited permission to use SUPPLIER's intellectual property by granting Dell non-exclusive license rights to exploit such intellectual property in connection with the sale and distribution of Products. This serves both parties' interests, as both SUPPLIER and Dell have a financial stake in Dell's reselling of the Products. Dell may be better positioned to make sales if Dell has permission to use SUPPLIER's Trademarks in the advertising, promotion, and sale of the Products and to use and pass along the software necessary to the proper operation and support of the Products. Absent such license rights, Dell risks infringing SUPPLIER's intellectual property rights and potential future lawsuits, despite that litigation may seem unrealistic at the time of contracting. If nothing else, without a license, Dell would be treading in uncertain waters in its use of another's property, left to argue that it had an implied license or rights under fair use to use the property.[147] Accordingly, when feasible, a prudent party will obtain express license rights to use another party's intellectual property. For more on the licensing of intellectual property, we turn the floor over to a couple seasoned practitioners.

---

145. For more on intellectual property in general, please see the discussion of intellectual property in Chapter 3.

146. For more on the transfer, assignment, and the delegation of rights and duties, please see Chapter 1.

147. "Fair use" refers to a doctrine found in both copyright and trademark and that allows persons to use (or otherwise exploit) the copyright or trademark of another without permission in certain narrow and "fair" manners, such that this use does not constitute infringement of the intellectual property.

A Practitioner Perspective: Intellectual Property License Agreements

In many ways, intellectual property license agreements are similar to other commercial contracts and include many of the same provisions (e.g., representations and warranties, term and termination provisions, limitations of liability, and dispute resolution provisions). They are unique, though, because they also include licenses to one or more of the four main types of intellectual property: patents, trademarks, copyrights, and trade secrets. Under a license, the licensor agrees that it will not sue the licensee for certain activities that would otherwise be prohibited due to the licensor's ownership of certain intellectual property.

Licenses can be granted or limited in many different ways, including: (a) geographically (e.g., a license for the United States but not Australia, or for Chicago but not New York); (b) temporally (e.g., a license for 10 years or a perpetual license); (c) by field of use (e.g., a license for veterinary but not human medical purposes); or (d) numerically (e.g., a license to make 5,000 widgets per year). The ways in which intellectual property rights can be subdivided, especially with respect to fields of use, are limited only by your imagination. In a license we handled for the movie rights to a comic book character, the field-of-use provisions went on for pages—which party had rights to coloring books, lunch boxes, toys accompanying children's fast-food meals, computer games, and much more.

Unlike public M&A agreements and syndicated loan agreements, the terms of which are often driven significantly by market conditions, the terms of license agreements are typically not public, tend to be unique and are highly dependent on the facts and circumstances of each transaction, especially the relative bargaining power of the licensor and licensee. A lawyer who works on a license agreement should find out first what the business dynamics of the transaction are. Who needs the transaction less? That party will likely have the upper hand when difficult issues arise.

License agreements often mix state and federal law. Rights in a patent or copyright arise under federal law, and trademark rights can arise under both state and federal law. Only trade secrets are solely based on state law. In each case, though, state law governs the general interpretation and enforcement of the license. State law, however, can be preempted by federal law if the application of state law would run counter to the purposes of federal intellectual property laws. For example, under most states' contract law, if a contract is silent as to whether or not it can be assigned, the contract is freely assignable without the consent of the other party. However, for patent, copyright, and trademark licenses, the default rule is the opposite (i.e., absent an express provision permitting assignment, the contract cannot be assigned without the licensor's consent).

A license may contain royalty provisions, pursuant to which the licensee agrees to make ongoing payments to the licensor based on what the licensee makes or sells using or under the intellectual property. When drafting royalty provisions, the lawyer should pay careful consideration to the way royalties will be measured (e.g., what deductions from gross sales will be included before the royalty is applied), when and how royalties will be paid, and how the calculation of the royalties will be verified by the licensor. If there is ambiguity as to which products are covered by a royalty provision and which are not, or as to which costs of sale may be deducted from gross sales before the royalty is applied, the client may find itself in a dispute down the road.

Trademark and trade secret licenses require special provisions. A trademark license agreement must contain quality control provisions that give the licensor a meaningful way to monitor and control the quality of products and services sold under its trademark. Without those provisions, the licensor risks the abandonment of the mark. A trade secret license must require the licensee to maintain the trade secret in confidence. Since a trade secret is only protectable as long as the owner is using appropriate means to keep it secret, providing the trade secret to a third party without an obligation to keep it confidential could cost the owner its right to prevent others from using it.

A licensor often indemnifies its licensee against infringement claims arising from the licensee's use of the licensed intellectual property. In other words, if a third party sues the licensee for the use of material provided by the licensor, the licensor will pay all of the attorneys' fees, court costs, and damages resulting from such suit, and often assume the defense of the suit as well. In certain circumstances, a licensee may indemnify the licensor for claims arising from the licensee's use of the licensed intellectual property. These indemnities are often among the most heavily negotiated provisions in a license. Again, the scope of each indemnity is highly dependent on the dynamics of the transaction.

The best licensing lawyers understand the technology they are licensing, and they use that knowledge to advance their clients' interests. A Ph.D. is not necessary, but a licensing lawyer must understand the nature of the technology, how it was developed, how it is made and used, and how it interrelates with other technology. A lawyer should not be shy about asking questions. It is usually not hard to find a scientist or engineer at the client company who will be delighted to teach. This detailed knowledge will enable the lawyer to think through how each provision of the agreement needs to be customized to fit the client's needs, and it will give the lawyer the background to develop practical and creative ways to resolve the issues that will arise during negotiations.

Jeffrey S. Rothstein
Partner
Sidley Austin LLP

Timothy M. Swan
Associate
Sidley Austin LLP

11. The "Ipso Facto" Clause: Anticipating Bankruptcy

Provisions that terminate or alter a party's interests in certain property, as triggered by the occurrence of a bankruptcy case, the party's insolvency, or the appointment of a custodian (before bankruptcy) or trustee (in bankruptcy), are often called "ipso facto" clauses.[148] As a matter of federal law (i.e., the Bankruptcy Code), these provisions are generally of no effect.[149] Accordingly, why are these provisions so commonly included in contracts, if they are not enforceable?

Part of the answer is found in a theme that runs throughout this book: While a provision may be unlikely to have legal effect in court, a party may still wish to include the provision if to do so is virtually costless. In other words, the answer is essentially another question: "Why not?" In addition, there are specific exceptions where an ipso facto clause may be enforceable (if still redundant as Professor Baird explains below); for example, the Bankruptcy Code allows a creditor to enforce an ipso facto clause (e.g., to accelerate payment under a loan agreement upon bankruptcy) in "a contract to make a loan, or extend other debt financing or financial accommodations, to or for the benefit of the debtor."[150]

Understanding the "Ipso Facto" Clause

Contracts of every sort commonly contain what is known as an "ipso facto" clause. It provides that the mere fact of filing a bankruptcy petition constitutes a default that terminates the contractual relationship.

A party to a contract may want such a clause for entirely defensive reasons. If the other a party files for bankruptcy, one wants to be able to come into court and assert one's rights, even if no obligations are then owing. If you make a long-term loan, you do not want to be left helpless while other creditors whose loans are overdue go after whatever assets are available.

Ipso facto clauses also serve an offensive purpose. Even if the other side is not behind on any obligations, the bankruptcy filing signals information. The operations of a business often suffer when someone is in financial distress. At the very least, it raises doubts about the business's long-term viability. News of a bankruptcy filing wakes everyone up and makes them take stock. It is useful to have the ability to bail out if, on investigation, the warning signal proves justified.

Notwithstanding their logic, ipso facto clauses present something of a mystery, as they represent parts of a contract that do no work. Ipso facto clauses are either redundant or unenforceable. They could disappear from a contract and the legal rights of the parties would be entirely unaffected.

A defensive ipso facto clause is part of the background rules built into every contract. Under bankruptcy law, the filing of a bankruptcy petition automatically accelerates obligations, regardless whether the contract provides for it. A creditor whose loan is due in ten years time is treated the same as someone whose loan is due today.

Moreover, the Bankruptcy Code prohibits the offensive use of an ipso facto clause. The rules governing the treatment of executory contracts are among the

---

148. *See* 11 U.S.C.A. § 365(e)(1) (West Supp. 2005); 11 U.S.C.A. § 541(c)(1)(B) (West Supp. 2010).

149. *See supra* note 148.

150. *See* 11 U.S.C.A. § 365(e)(2)(B) (West Supp. 2005); *see also, e.g., Mims v. Fid. Funding, Inc.*, 307 B.R. 849, 858 (N.D. Tex. 2002) ("[I]t is clear that the Bankruptcy Code's invalidation of *ipso facto* clauses does not apply in this situation involving a contract to make a loan for the benefit of the debtor.").

most complicated in all of bankruptcy. A debtor in bankruptcy may or may not be able to assume an executory contract. The debtor in some cases can even reinstate loans. But the debtor's ability to do so exists independently of whether the contract contains an ipso facto clause. This idea is one of the few that are clear.

The pervasiveness of ipso facto clauses likely exists for a combination of reasons. Path dependence explains much. These clauses were generally enforceable before a dramatic revision of the bankruptcy law in 1978. Though they have long ceased to do any work, they do no harm either. There is no evolutionary pressure to eliminate them, especially as they often appear in conjunction with other language—such as a reference to state insolvency proceedings—which might still be effective.

There is one qualification to all of this, however. While the inclusion of an ipso facto clause for offensive purposes is wholly ineffective, their defensive use may bring a small benefit at the margin. The concept that the filing of a petition constitutes a default that accelerates the obligations owing under a contract is imminent in the structure of the Bankruptcy Code, but it is not stated in so many words. Ever cautious, lawyers do not want to take the chance that some judge might misunderstand. The chance that a judge would do so is low, but the costs of including the clause in a contract are lower still.

Professor Douglas Baird
Harry A. Bigelow Distinguished
Service Professor of Law
The University of Chicago Law School

12. The Implied Covenant of Good Faith and Fair Dealing

Last but certainly not least, is an important concept that affects every contract in this book—and every contract outside this book. We have spoken a bit about implied warranties, and, so, the concept of implied contractual terms should be familiar to you by now. An "implied" term is one that is not expressly written in a contract but that is nonetheless found to be a part of the contract's terms. Warranties are not the only type of contractual provisions impliedly found in an agreement. Indeed, courts also impute a special covenant: the "implied covenant of good faith and fair dealing." While implied warranties are not frequently found outside contracts governed by the U.C.C., the implied covenant of good faith and fair dealing is ubiquitous, found in every contractual agreement, including those between sophisticated parties.[151] As the *Restatement*

---

151. *See, e.g., Anthony's Pier Four, Inc. v. HBC Assocs.*, 583 N.E.2d 806, 821 (Mass. 1991) ("Anthony's asks us to hold that, in contracts between sophisticated businesspeople, no covenant of good faith and fair dealing is implied. We decline so to hold. . . . Indeed, the rule is clear in Massachusetts that every contract is subject to an implied covenant of good faith and fair dealing.").

explains: "Every contract imposes upon each party a duty of good faith and fair dealing in its performance and its enforcement."[152] The U.C.C. echoes the *Restatement*: "Every contract or duty within [the Uniform Commercial Code] imposes an obligation of good faith in its performance and enforcement."[153]

We have already encountered the concept of "good faith" a few times. Earlier in this chapter we discussed output and requirements contracts and that a quantity term tied to the seller's output production or the buyer's requirements requires that the seller produce its output or that the buyer determine its requirements in "good faith." Indeed, as discussed in the *Advent Systems* excerpt below, the implied covenant of good faith and fair dealing works to impose this duty of good faith even in *non-exclusive* "output" and "requirements" contracts.[154] We also discussed "good faith" earlier in this chapter in the context of "agreements to agree," specifically with regard to agreements to negotiate in good faith.

What is this omnipresent covenant to act in good faith and to deal fairly? The official comments to the *Restatement* explain:

> Subterfuges and evasions violate the obligation of good faith in performance even though the actor believes his conduct to be justified. But the obligation goes further: bad faith may be overt or may consist of inaction, and fair dealing may require more than honesty. A complete catalogue of types of bad faith is impossible, but the following types are among those which have been recognized in judicial decisions: evasion of the spirit of the bargain, lack of diligence and slacking off, willful rendering of imperfect performance, abuse of a power to specify terms, and interference with or failure to cooperate in the other party's performance.[155]

The implied covenant is a duty to perform the express provisions of the contract in consonance with the spirit of the agreement. In this way, the implied covenant of good faith and fair dealing offers a thick understanding of contractual provisions: The implied covenant tells us to understand contractual duties to perform not as reduced to their barest terms. Accordingly, the implied covenant

---

152. RESTATEMENT (SECOND) OF CONTRACTS § 205 (1981); *see O'Tool v. Genmar Holdings, Inc.*, 387 F.3d 1188, 1195 (10th Cir. 2004) ("Under Delaware law, an implied covenant of good faith and fair dealing inheres in every contract.") (citation omitted); *see also In re Ocwen Loan Servicing, LLC*, 491 F.3d 638, 645 (7th Cir. 2007) ("Most state laws impose a duty of good faith performance of contracts, meaning that a party to a contract cannot engage in opportunistic behavior.").

153. U.C.C. § 1-304 (2003).

154. Query what it means to have a "non-exclusive" output or requirements contract. Under a non-exclusive output contract, the seller must sell and the buyer must buy some of the seller's output but not all of its output—to require the seller to sell all of its output to the buyer would amount to requiring the seller to deal exclusively with the buyer. Under a non-exclusive requirements contract, the buyer must purchase and the seller must sell some of the buyer's requirements but not all of its requirements—to require the buyer to buy all of its requirements from the seller would amount to requiring the buyer to deal exclusively with the seller. Is there any difference between such an arrangement and just a regular agreement to buy or sell an undetermined amount?

155. RESTATEMENT (SECOND) OF CONTRACTS § 205 cmt. d (1981).

suggests that parties enter contracts with an expectation of good-faith performance. In thinking about what is required and meant by the implied covenant of good faith and fair dealing, please consider the following case.

Advent Systems Ltd. v. Unisys Corp.
United States Court of Appeals, Third Circuit, 1991.
925 F.2d 670.

[This case is continued from page 283.]

IV. ENFORCEABILITY

Having concluded that the statute of frauds is not a bar, we now confront the issue of enforceability.

Section 2-204 [of the Uniform Commercial Code] provides that a contract does not fail for indefiniteness even though one or more terms have been left open if the parties intended to make a contract and there is a reasonably certain basis for giving an appropriate remedy. As Professor Murray has explained:

> "Rather than focusing upon what parties failed to say, the Code and RESTATE-MENT 2d focus upon the overriding question of whether the parties manifestly intended to make a binding arrangement. If that manifestation is present, the only remaining concern is whether the terms are definite enough to permit courts to afford an appropriate remedy. The second requirement assists courts to determine the degree of permissible indefiniteness."

J. Murray, *Murray On Contracts* § 38, at 85 (3d ed. 1990).

Unlike the statute of frauds issue discussed earlier, the definiteness required to provide a remedy rests on a very solid foundation of practicality. A remedy may not be based on speculation and an award cannot be made if there is no basis for determining if a breach has occurred.

Unisys argues that because there are specific non-exclusive stipulations in the agreement, they negate the implication found in most exclusive requirements contracts that a "best efforts clause" is included. That may be so, but that does not nullify the obligation of the parties to deal in good faith.

Section 1-203 of the Code [section 1-304 of the revised version of Article 1] provides that contracts require a "good faith performance." This requires the parties to observe "reasonable commercial standards of fair dealing in the trade."

The Pennsylvania Superior Court has concluded that in the absence of any express language, the law will imply an agreement by the parties to do those things that "according to reason and justice they should do in order to carry out the purposes for which the contract was made and to refrain from doing anything that would destroy or injure the other party's right to receive the fruits of the contract." One commentator opines that when the contract does not have a "best efforts" clause, "the law will usually imply . . . that the dealer must act in good faith and use 'reasonable efforts' to sell. This implied obligation requires the distributor to do more than the bare minimum to comply with a contract; the distributor must really make some attempt to sell."

The terms of the agreement between Unisys and Advent lend themselves to imply a good faith obligation on the parties of at least some minimal effort: "A fundamental assumption of both parties is that throughout the term of this agreement, Unisys will employ resources in performing marketing efforts involving Advent Products and will develop the technical capability to be thoroughly familiar with these products."

On remand, Advent may be able to show that it was inconsistent with good faith for a party that has committed itself to engage in particular business for a specified period of time to cease devoting any resources to that venture prior to the end of the stated period. We leave open the possibility that the performance of the parties following signing of the documents and perhaps pre-contractual expectations will provide evidence to satisfy the requirements of section 2-204.

On the other hand, it may be that the reason Unisys decided to devote no resources to the project of selling document systems is relevant to whether the standard of fair dealing in the trade was breached. Simply because no resources were devoted, does not mean in and of itself that there was a breach of the covenant of good faith.

Whether Advent can establish the definiteness required to sustain a remedy is a serious question. The record before us consists of evidence submitted on the basis of the pretrial ruling denying application of the U.C.C. Our contrary holding will require the parties to reassess the proofs necessary to meet the Code. We are in no position to anticipate the evidence that may appear in further proceedings and, thus, at this juncture cannot rule whether the agreement between Unisys and Advent is enforceable. . . .

. . . The judgment in favor of the plaintiff on the breach of contract claim will be reversed and the case will be remanded for further proceedings.

---

a. The Implied "Fruits" of Express Provisions

The implied covenant of good faith and fair dealing only operates when attached to, or rooted in, an express provision.[156] A breach of the implied covenant occurs when one party deprives the other of the "fruits" of the express provisions of an agreement.[157] This comports with our earlier discussion of the

---

156. *See, e.g., Metro. Life Ins. Co. v. NJR Nabisco,* 716 F. Supp. 1504, 1519 (S.D.N.Y. 1989) ("These plaintiffs do not invoke an implied covenant of good faith to protect a legitimate, mutually contemplated benefit of the indentures; rather, they seek to have this Court create an additional benefit for which they did not bargain.").

157. *See id.* at 1518 ("The appropriate analysis, then, is first to examine the indentures to determine 'the fruits of the agreement' between the parties, and then to decide whether those 'fruits' have been spoiled—which is to say, whether plaintiffs' contractual rights have been violated by defendants."); *Warner Ins. Co. v. Comm'r of Ins.,* 548 N.E.2d 188, 471 (Mass. 1991) ("The implied covenant of good faith and fair dealing provides that

essential nature of the implied covenant, which imposes a duty on parties to perform in good faith their already existing contractual duties. Accordingly, the covenant does not impose independent substantive duties beyond those expressly provided in a contract but, rather, provides a standard for how parties are to perform such duties.[158]

In deciding how to impute the implied covenant, courts sometimes will ask whether the parties would have provided as much in their contract had they contemplated the question at issue.[159] Indeed, courts will not find the *implied* covenant to contravene the *express* provisions of a contract.[160] Accordingly, parties may wish to provide expressly in their contract what is and is not expected of a party in performing its contractual duties. Otherwise, if the contract ends up in litigation or arbitration, a court or arbitrator will have to discern the contours of what constitutes appropriate party behavior.

For example, in *O'Tool v. Genmar Holdings, Inc.*,[161] the Tenth Circuit found that a reasonable finder of fact could find that a company, acquiring another company, violated the implied covenant of good faith and fair dealing when it made decisions that minimized the payment under an "earnout" provision. We take up the topic of earnout provisions in greater detail when we discuss mergers and acquisitions in Chapter 6; however, for now, an earnout provision provides a way for owners of an acquired company to earn additional consideration for the acquisition of the company. An earnout provision is generally tied to some earnings metric (e.g., revenue, net income) of the acquired line of business. In *O'Tool*, a large boat-manufacturing company, Genmar, acquired another boat-manufacturing company, Horizon, in exchange for: (i) cash consideration of $2.3 million; and (ii) an earnout with the potential to pay $5.3 million over five years based on the annual gross revenues from the sale of Horizon (or any successor) brand boats and boats manufactured in Horizon's plant facility. However, after the acquisition, Genmar immediately changed the name of the Horizon-line boats to Nova, saddled the Horizon facility with the production of a new and expensive-to-produce line of boats, and implemented a policy giving

---

neither party shall do anything that will have the effect of destroying or injuring the right of the other party to receive the fruits of the contract.") (internal citations and quotation marks omitted).

158. *See, e.g.*, U.C.C. § 1-304 cmt. 1 (2003). Please see below for the discussion of "good faith" in the context of "agreements to negotiate in good faith," as part of the earlier discussion of "agreements to agree."

159. *See, e.g., Third Story Music, Inc. v. Waits*, 48 Cal. Rptr. 2d 747, 750 (Cal. Ct. App. 1995) ("[A] promise can be implied only where it can be rightfully assumed that it would have been made if attention had been called to it.") (internal citation and quotation marks omitted); *Fashion Fabrics of Iowa, Inc. v. Retail Investors Corp.*, 266 N.W.2d 22, 28 (Iowa 1978) ("[An implied covenant] can arise only when it can be assumed it would have been made part of the agreement if attention had been called to it."); *O'Tool*, 387 F.3d at 1197.

160. *See, e.g., Uno Rests., Inc. v. Boston Kenmore Realty Corp.*, 805 N.E.2d 957, 964 (Mass. 2004) ("The covenant may not, however, be invoked to create rights and duties not otherwise provided for in the existing contractual relationship, as the purpose of the covenant is to guarantee that the parties remain faithful to the intended and agreed expectations of the parties in their performance."); *Dalton v. Educ. Testing Serv.*, 663 N.E.2d 289, 291-92 (N.Y. 1995) ("The duty of good faith and fair dealing, however, is not without limits, and no obligation can be implied that would be inconsistent with other terms of the contractual relationship.") (internal citations and quotation marks omitted).

161. 387 F.3d 1188 (10th Cir. 2004) (Delaware law).

production priority to non-Horizon/Nova-line boats. Genmar also eventually caused its dealers to change from selling Horizon/Nova-brand boats to other Genmar brands, stopped the manufacture of Horizon/Nova-brand boats, and closed the Horizon plant facility. All of these acts hampered the gross revenues from the sale of Horizon/Nova-line boats and from the boats manufactured in the Horizon plant facility, reducing payment available under the earnout provision. The acquisition agreement between Genmar and Horizon neither authorized nor prohibited any of these acts. The Tenth Circuit explained:

> [W]e conclude that a reasonable finder of fact could have concluded the parties (had they actually thought about it) would not have simultaneously included within the agreement provisions expressly allowing Genmar to: (1) immediately change the brand name of the boats designed and produced by GMK [the subsidiary that acquired Horizon]; (2) set production schedules or priorities that effectively reduced the maximum earn-out consideration available to Pepper [an owner of Horizon, whom Genmar hired as president of GMK]; (3) impose significant design and production costs upon GMK for other Genmar brands of boats . . . ; or (4) "flip" Horizon dealers to other brands of Genmar boats.[162]

b. Performance Standards: "Commercially Reasonable" and "Best Efforts"

Quoting a commentator, the court in *Advent Systems* explained that even when a contract does not have a "best efforts" clause, the law implies that a party must act in good faith and that, in the context of an (exclusive or non-exclusive) requirements contract that does not expressly speak to the purchaser's obligation to sell or otherwise to maintain minimum requirements, a purchaser must "do more than the bare minimum to comply with a contract; [the purchaser] must really make some attempt to sell."[163] Accordingly, absent some contractually provided standard for the performance of a party's duties, the implied covenant of good faith and fair dealing steps in to provide a "reasonableness" standard.[164] Parties desiring to lower or to heighten (or to be confident in) a standard of performance may wish to specify in the contract the standard by which one must perform his obligations.

Examples of performance standards commonly found in agreements include "commercially reasonable" and "best efforts." That is, a contract may require that one perform some obligation in a "commercially reasonable" manner or that one use "best efforts" in so performing.

---

162. *Id.* at 1197 (citing *Katz v. Oak Indus., Inc.*, 508 A.2d 873, 880 (Del. Ch. 1986)).

163. The court in *Advent Systems* quoted and cited Theodore Banks, Distribution Law, 226-2 (1990) for this proposition. *Advent Sys. Ltd. v. Unisys Corp.*, 925 F.2d 670, 680 (3d Cir. 1991).

164. *See* Restatement (Second) of Contracts § 205 cmt. 1 (1981) ("Good faith performance or enforcement of a contract emphasizes faithfulness to an agreed common purpose and consistency with the justified expectations of the other party; it excludes a variety of types of conduct characterized as involving 'bad faith' because they violate community standards of decency, fairness or reasonableness.").

What meaning do these standards have? "Best efforts" intuitively calls for something more than a "commercially reasonable" performance—but how *much* more? How can we give measure to these necessarily vague concepts? Are these standards too amorphous to impose enforceable obligations?[165] In general, courts will enforce "best efforts" and "commercially reasonable" standards for performance,[166] but what does this mean? These are necessarily imprecise, "facts-and-circumstances" standards and do not lend themselves to precise definition.

A "best efforts" standard does not require efforts of Herculean proportions,[167] nor does it require that a party disregard his own interests.[168] Indeed, at least one court has equated "best efforts" with the level of performance required by the implied covenant of good faith.[169] Still, a party agreeing to perform his "best efforts" should take note that courts have often required something more than mere good faith.[170] In addition, many practitioners representing the performing party will seek to avoid a "best efforts" standard at all costs.

In contrast, courts have seemed not to require anything more of a "commercially reasonable" standard than what is required by the implied covenant of good faith.[171]

Even if parties have agreed to a performance standard requiring no more than the implied covenant of good faith, a prudent party may still wish to write a performance standard into the contract. As judges or arbitrators may be uneasy and reluctant to use a legal rule of implication to impose a standard of duty on contractual parties,[172] stating the standard expressly instructs the

---

165. See this chapter's earlier discussion of agreements to negotiate in good faith and that some courts have found these agreements to be enforceable in the abstract but too imprecise to allow for enforcement in practice.

166. *See, e.g., NBC Capital Mkts. Grp., Inc. v. First Bank*, 25 F. App'x 363, 365 (6th Cir. 2002) ("[Defendant] argues the 'best efforts' clause is so ambiguous as to be unenforceable. Yet, applying Tennessee law, which undisputedly applies to the construction and enforcement of this contract, this Court has enforced the contractual 'best efforts' promise.").

167. *See, e.g., Triple-A Baseball Club Assocs. v. Ne. Baseball, Inc.*, 832 F.2d 214, 228 (1st Cir. 1987) (Maine law) ("We have found no cases, and none have been cited, holding that 'best efforts' means every conceivable effort.").

168. *See, e.g., Baron Fin. Corp. v. Natanzon*, 509 F. Supp. 2d 501, 514 (D. Md. 2007) ("Indeed, courts recognize that a promise to use best efforts does not require that a party disregard its own interests.") (internal citations and quotation marks omitted).

169. *See, e.g., Triple-A Baseball*, 832 F.2d at 225 (1st Cir. 1987) (Maine law) ("We have been unable to find any case in which a court found, as here, that a party acted in good faith but did not use its best efforts.").

170. *See, e.g., Nat'l Data Payment Sys., Inc. v. Meridian Bank*, 212 F.3d 849, 854 (3d Cir. 2000) ("The duty of best efforts has diligence as its essence and is more exacting than the usual contractual duty of good faith.") (internal citation and quotation marks omitted); *Olympia Hotels Corp. v. Johnson Wax Dev.*, 908 F.2d 1363, 1373 (7th Cir. 1990).

171. *See, e.g., Subaru Distrib. Corp. v. Subaru of Am., Inc.*, 47 F. Supp. 2d 451, 462 (S.D.N.Y. 1999) (good faith performance requires that a party exercise its contractual discretion in a commercially reasonable manner); *Wilson v. Amerada Hess Corp.*, 168 A.2d 1121, 1131 (N.J. 2001) (quoting approvingly the lower court's explanation that a breach of the implied covenant of good faith and fair dealing turns on a party's bad faith or violation of a commercially reasonable standard).

172. *See Fashion Fabrics*, 266 N.W.2d at 27 ("Courts are slow to find implied covenants.").

reader that the parties entered into their contract having contemplated and with the expectation that a party's performance would meet at least *some* level or standard.

Notice that §§ 5.2.1, 6.3.1, 9.3.1(a), 9.4, and 10.4 of the Agreement each use a "commercially reasonable" standard, whereas §§ 15.3 and 16.0 impose a potentially more stringent "best efforts" standard. Look back to each of these sections and seek to determine which party would benefit from switching a "commercially reasonable" standard to a "best efforts" standard (or vice versa, in the cases of §§ 15.3 and 16.0).

· CHAPTER FIVE ·

LENDING AGREEMENTS

—————————————•———————————————————————•—————————————

There are two oft-conceived notions about lending agreements and transactions: (i) that most deals are "cookie cutter," needing only to be "papered" with "off-the-shelf" contracts; and, given this, (ii) that lending deals are necessarily dry and uninteresting. To combat these (mis)conceptions, enter Gary ("Skip") Stern, whose practice includes the financing of big-budget studio films.

A Practitioner Perspective: A Colorful Side of Lending Agreements

I received a call from a hedge fund client to which we had provided assistance from time to time with investments in various financial products. He knew that I had been involved in numerous transactions involving the financing of motion pictures so he was very excited to tell me that he had a great opportunity to invest in movies to be made by a director who had recently had a couple of big "hits." After he was done gushing about how "cool" it would be to be associated with this popular director, I started asking him questions about how he planned to structure this investment in movies and, more importantly, how he thought he would get his money back, hopefully with a return on his investment. Our client was fairly sophisticated in financial matters and quickly realized that the risk/return profile of an equity investment in a slate of films was not consistent with the fund's investment objectives. On the other hand, a loan to the director's company secured by the copyrights and distribution rights for the films would be repaid prior to payments to the holders of equity in the company. Although taking less risk would mean less upside as the loan would bear interest at a specified rate (even if the movies broke records at the box office), our client decided that investing in these movies by using a loan structure was an acceptable risk.

After deciding to document this investment as a secured loan, my next series of questions to our client tried to flush out the terms of the loan and the scope of the required documentation. "Let's just use one of your form loan agreements for film financings," was the client's response to many of my inquiries. I had to explain that I had seen loans for these types of transactions documented with a five-page note, a 150-page credit agreement, and a lot in between. For sophisticated business financings, there is no such thing as a "one-size-fits-all" loan agreement. Gathering as much information from a client (such as internal deal memos and term sheets and other correspondence with the borrower) as early as possible in the documentation process is critical to meeting the expectations of the parties. In this case, the client ultimately wanted something relatively simple that protected his primary interests but did not have all of the "bells and whistles" that might be contained in the documents used by a money-center bank.

Skip Stern
Partner
Sidley Austin LLP

As Mr. Stern demonstrates, a prudent lender, as assisted by counsel, in most any context will consider the risk she is willing to tolerate and, in exchange, the reward (e.g., interest) she wishes to obtain—that is, how the borrower is to pay the lender back and how likely the lender is to be left out in the cold.

Money makes the world go around, or so they say.[1] It moves commerce and is often the object of desire by those hoping to use it toward a variety of ends. Who has it, who wants it, and the methods and means of transferring it between these two groups through lending is the subject of considerable complexity and this chapter.

In this chapter, our review centers upon a commercial loan agreement between a wholesaler and its parent company, as borrower and guarantor, respectively, and a national retailer, as lender. We also examine the various devices that operate to provide a lender with additional comfort that a loan and its agreed-upon interest will be repaid. On this score, we look at Article 9 of the U.C.C.,[2] along with the security and guaranty agreement used in this chapter's sample transaction as well as legal opinion letters, generally. In addition, we explore the competing interests of the several players often involved in a loan transaction, including the several creditors competing for rights against a single debtor's—perhaps limited—assets. Accordingly, we look at a subordination agreement and examine how this document operates to order the relative priority of creditors. Please note that, while bankruptcy law looms with tremendous importance behind lending transactions and agreements in general, a full discussion of the

---

1. On this point, see the musical *Cabaret* (1966) by Kander and Ebb.
2. This book's—and, in particular, this chapter's—references to Article 9 of the U.C.C. are to Revised Article 9 (2000), which took effect on July 1, 2001. *See* U.C.C. § 9-701 (2000).

complexities of the U.S. bankruptcy regime as applicable to lending agreements is outside the scope of this chapter.

We take as our sample transaction for this chapter a basic business-to-business loan. Depending on the nature of one's transactional practice, one may commonly encounter loan transactions between a *bank*, as lender, and a company, as borrower. These may involve more complicated arrangements, such as loan syndication (where other lenders may participate in the loan) or asset securitization (a financial structure that involves the creation of a special purpose subsidiary to which the parent sells assets (e.g., receivables) against which the special purpose entity borrows money (e.g., issues debt securities)). Throughout this chapter, we call on expert practitioners to help shed light on these and other concerns that commonly arise in the practice of lending transactions.

A. COMMERCIAL LENDING AGREEMENT

We begin with commentary from a seasoned practitioner, Martin D. Jacobson, who highlights the various provisions found in lending agreements, specifically previewing this chapter's agreement and offering insight into the various ways in which this agreement might differ and overlap with a loan agreement between a bank and a sophisticated borrower. Following Mr. Jacobson's note, please find this chapter's loan agreement preceded by a few focus points for your consideration.

A Practitioner Perspective: Loan and Related Agreements

Although financial instruments are numerous and have evolved into diverse and complex financial products, none is more fundamental than the loan agreement. An understanding of the structure and typical provisions of a loan agreement is immensely useful in analyzing, structuring, and negotiating the terms of other financial products involving an extension of credit. The sample loan agreement, with accompanying promissory note, subordination agreement and security, pledge and guaranty agreement, is broadly illustrative of loans entered into between business parties, and more particularly of the category of loans made by non-bank businesses in furtherance of an underlying relationship or transaction. In the sample agreement, the underlying transaction appears to be an equity investment by the lender in the parent company of the borrower. In this practice note, I will comment on selected provisions of the sample loan documents and will also broaden the discussion to include observations about some of the significant differences between the terms of the sample loan transaction and those of the typical bank credit agreement arranged on market terms.

Article I of the sample loan agreement provides for the amount and other monetary terms of the loans. In the sample, a fixed dollar amount commitment is established under which the borrower may borrow and prepay without penalty, but the borrower does not have the right to re-borrow prepaid amounts as it would in a bank revolving credit agreement. Also, the lender does not charge a commitment fee for making funds available during the commitment period, as bank lenders normally would. Finally, interest in the sample loan documents is calculated based upon "LIBOR" (the interbank lending rate for short term deposits in the London interbank market), which is typically used by commercial banks as one of the bases of pricing floating rate loans, because it is assumed to measure the banks' cost of matching borrowed funds. The lender in the sample loan transaction appears to be using LIBOR plus a margin as a proxy for its own cost of funds, perhaps because it is using a LIBOR-based loan agreement with a commercial bank as its source of funds. However, the typical LIBOR provisions in commercial bank loan agreements are more favorable to the lender than in the sample. Provisions are typically included whereby the borrower assumes substantial responsibility for preserving the banks' effective yield on the loan, notwithstanding the occurrence of a LIBOR market disruption or the imposition after the closing of reserve requirements with respect to the loan, for example. The sample loan agreement contains a gross-up for the risk of withholding taxes, which would typically be more extensively dealt with in a cross-border loan among international parties.

Article II of the sample loan agreement contains the conditions of lending. The main documentary and legal conditions precedent are typically required to be satisfied on or before the first drawdown, and thereafter are largely confirmatory in nature. Conditions precedent are to some extent customary, such as those regarding corporate matters, legal authority, due authorization and execution of documents, absence of a conflict with legal requirements or other agreements, and confirmatory legal opinions, and to some extent, are tailored to the business circumstances of the particular loan transaction. The borrower will normally seek to avoid subjective and judgmental conditions precedent to the extent possible. The lender will normally be keen to incorporate a "material adverse change" condition precedent, pursuant to which the lender is excused from its obligation to lend if the borrower has suffered a defined "material adverse change" with respect to its financial condition (or other measures) from a specified date, often the date of the borrower's most recent financial statements preceding the first closing. In the sample loan agreement there is no material adverse change clause, indicating that in the context of the business relationship between the parties the lender will take the risk of deterioration in credit standing of the borrower during the five-year commitment period.

Article III of the sample loan agreement contains the borrower's (and the guarantors') representations and warranties as to the factual and legal matters upon which the extension of credit is based. The representations and warranties speak only as of the date when made, normally the closing date or in some cases a specified earlier date, and are therefore distinguished from ongoing covenants. Representations and warranties and conditions precedent are complementary in the sense that the conditions precedent are structured to validate and confirm the accuracy of many of the representations and warranties made at closing. In these clauses the borrower is called upon to represent and warrant to the lender, at the risk of an event of default if materially incorrect, the truthfulness and accuracy of a comprehensive list of legal, documentary, and factual matters. These typically cover (i) legal matters, such as the existence and good standing of the borrower, corporate organization, corporate power and authority, the due authorization and execution of the loan documents, enforceability of the loan documents, the absence of conflicts with other agreements, applicable law or constituent documents, and governmental approvals; (ii) broader corporate matters, such as the accuracy of financial statements, the status of litigation, payment of taxes, and environmental compliance; and (iii) transaction specific matters, such as the use of proceeds, the completion of a related corporate transaction, and in a secured credit, the validity and perfection of security interests in collateral, among others. The parties will be concerned to provide for adequate breadth in these matters on the one hand, while incorporating appropriate exceptions and exclusions, on the other hand. The borrower should avoid "taking the risk" in these representations, because if they prove to be materially inaccurate an event of default will occur, and there is also the risk of illegal conduct if materially inaccurate representations are made to a lender to induce it to make a loan.

Article IV of the sample loan agreement contains the ongoing covenants of the borrower (and the guarantors) which if not observed will form the basis for an event of default. Covenants are structured, in general, to complement the representations and warranties made at closing (confirmed in the closing conditions) by obligating the borrower to a series of contractual promises, which are applicable beginning on the closing date and applicable thereafter during the term of the loan. Thus, the lender will want the borrower to affirmatively promise to do certain things (i.e., affirmative covenants), and to promise not to do or permit to occur or to be continuing certain other things (i.e., negative covenants). Affirmative covenants as to maintenance of corporate existence, financial and other reporting, compliance with law, and use of proceeds, to name a few, are customary. Other affirmative covenants are tailored to the particular loan transaction, such as the maintenance of financial ratios and the continuance of perfection of liens. Negative covenants contain restrictions and limitations on the borrower and its activities and are tailored to reflect the particular transaction. The sample loan agreement contains tight and restrictive covenants concerning liens and debt, sale of assets, mergers, changes of ownership and other fundamental corporate changes, executive compensation, capital expenditures, payment of dividends and others. Restrictive negative covenants vest substantial control rights in the lender with respect to the relevant business activities of the borrower because the borrower would be required to obtain a waiver, or to prepay the indebtedness, in the event that at any time during the loan term it wishes to engage in a transaction which is prohibited by the terms of negative covenants contained in a loan agreement. In syndicated loan agreements, the covenant package is at the very heart of the financial arrangements and can be the subject of intense competition and negotiation in the placement and execution process. Especially sensitive are financial covenants and covenants concerning change of control, mergers and other fundamental corporate changes.

Article V of the sample loan agreement contains the events of default, which entitle the lender to terminate the lending commitment, accelerate the loans outstanding and/or exercise remedies under the loan documents and applicable law. Events of default due to nonpayment when due, material misrepresentation or breach of covenant, and bankruptcy or the like, are standard in loan agreements. Grace periods are usually negotiated, although grace periods for voluntary bankruptcy and breach of negative covenants may be limited or nonexistent in the typical bank credit agreement. In the sample "cross default" clauses, the other indebtedness of the borrower (and the guarantor) have been incorporated in the events of default, the purpose being to give the lender a seat at the table if another significant debt of the borrower falls into default or has been or may be accelerated even though the sample loan is not independently in default.

Article VI of the sample loan agreement provides for subordination of the loans provided for in the sample loan agreement to specified credit facilities of a named bank lender. Subordination agreements can involve considerable complexity, but in general subordination involves an intercreditor agreement by the subordinated lender covering, among other things, priority of payment, exercise of remedies and control over collateral.

Article VI of the sample loan agreement also provides for the security, pledge and guaranty agreement, which supports payment of the loans made in these documents. The provision of collateral serves a number of purposes, and only the most general comments can be offered. By taking collateral security, and properly perfecting its interests therein, a secured lender obtains enforcement and other rights with respect to the collateral and with respect to the secured loan, as provided for in the applicable security documents and applicable law, but subject to the inhibitions of applicable law including bankruptcy law. From the borrower's perspective, overly broad granting clauses in security agreements can easily lead to an unintended loss of financial flexibility or even to default with other lenders. The words and phrases used in typical granting clauses in security agreements are highly technical, often referring to the defined terms of the Uniform Commercial Code, so caution is warranted on the part of the borrower with respect to the scope and content of these granting clauses. The pledge of stock provided for in the sample security documents raises important questions about the voting and other rights of the lender under various scenarios—for example, the voting rights of the lender before an actual enforcement of the lien against the pledged stock following the occurrence of an event of default, and the circumstances under which the lender becomes entitled to receive any dividends or distributions on the pledged stock. Remedy clauses such as these deserve careful consideration by the borrower.

The guaranty by the parent company and an affiliated company of the borrower provided for in the sample security, pledge and guaranty agreement does not require that the borrower first default or that collection attempts be made by the lender before resort is made to the guaranty. The guarantors waive all defenses to their liabilities, which are stated to be absolute and unconditional, irrespective of any circumstance that might otherwise constitute a defense available to, or a discharge of, the borrower. The terms of the sample guaranty effectively convert the borrowing into a corporate family loan because the stated obligations of the guarantors are tantamount to each of them co-signing the loan documents. However, third-party guarantees, such as those extended by an insurance company or governmental entity, typically differ significantly in their terms and provisions and legal effect.

Article VII of the sample loan agreement contains the miscellaneous and "boilerplate" provisions. These deserve special attention by the parties because they can assume great significance in an enforcement or default situation. Among the more significant provisions typically found in this section of a loan agreement are the choice of law and venue provisions. Banks and financial institutions often have strict policies with regard to these matters, often favoring their home jurisdiction. Arbitration and other forms of alternative dispute resolution are not common in commercial bank and institutional loan, security, and guaranty agreements. A clause allocating financial responsibility for payment of the expenses of closing, including those of counsel to the lender, is customary in bank credit transactions, but its absence in the sample indicates that each party will bear its own expenses. Although the sample loan agreement requires borrower consent to any transfer by the lender, in commercial bank loans the ability of the banks to transfer or assign—or to sell participations in—the loans without borrower consent is often at the very heart of the transaction from the banks' perspective. However, the borrower's interests in controlling the numbers and characteristics of its lenders are also important, especially if an amendment is ever sought or a dispute should arise, or if a bank seeks to transfer its lending commitment. Accordingly, exceptions and limitations recognizing the borrower's interests in these matters will normally be negotiated.

In conclusion, the sample loan agreement and accompanying documents provide an instructive introduction to the typical structure and main provisions of commercial loan agreements. Although the sample loan falls into the category of loans made by non-bank businesses in furtherance of an underlying relationship or transaction, the sample loan and the typical commercial bank loan are close relatives. They share the same general transaction structure, document organization, and many standard terms and provisions and in practice involve consideration of many of the same legal, structural, and documentary issues by the parties and their advisors. Thus, the sample loan is a bridge to understanding and analyzing commercial bank loans and the broader field of credit extensions generally.

Martin D. Jacobson
Retired Partner
Simpson Thacher & Bartlett LLP
Lecturer in Law
The University of Chicago Law School

Things to Consider . . .

As you read through the following agreement, please consider these items. You will want to return to the agreement, as you study the substantive discussion that follows.

> **Background and Purpose.** Who are the various parties to this Agreement? From the Agreement, what can you tell about the relationship between these parties? Why do you suppose they entered into this transaction—
> what is the Agreement's purpose? Does the Agreement restrict the use of any lent money to this purpose?

> **Contractual Recourse.** What levers does the Agreement give the lender if the borrower breaches certain provisions of the Agreement or if certain representations or warranties prove untrue? How do conditions to lending mitigate certain of the lender's risks in this Agreement? What recourse does the lender have with respect to money already lent under this Agreement?

> **Ancillary Documents.** What other agreements does the following Agreement contemplate as part of this transaction? What function do these Agreements serve? What ensures these various documents will be executed? What issues do you believe the lender is likely to request for inclusion in an opinion letter from the borrower's counsel?

LOAN AGREEMENT[3]

This LOAN AGREEMENT (this "AGREEMENT") is entered into as of May 1, 2001 by and among: (i) L.S. Wholesale, Inc., a Massachusetts corporation (the "BORROWER"), Little Switzerland, Inc., a Delaware corporation (the "PARENT" and the "GUARANTOR" hereunder; and collectively with the Borrower, the "BORROWER PARTIES"), on the one hand, and (ii) Tiffany and Company, a New York corporation (the "LENDER"), on the other hand.

RECITALS

A. The Borrower is a direct wholly-owned subsidiary of the Guarantor.

B. The Lender is willing to make Advances (as hereinafter defined), and the Borrower wishes to receive and repay Advances, all as more fully set forth herein.

C. The Borrower Parties and the Lender will enter into a Security, Pledge and Guaranty Agreement (the "SECURITY, PLEDGE AND

---

3. Little Switzerland, Inc., Loan Agreement (Form 8-K), at Exhibit 10.14 (May 30, 2001), *available at* http://www.sec.gov/Archives/edgar/data/875523/000091205701517915/a2050252zex-10_14.txt.

GUARANTY AGREEMENT" and collectively with this Agreement, the Subordination Agreement and the Note, the "LOAN DOCUMENTS") with respect to the Advances.

D. Certain affiliates of the Borrower Parties and the Lender are entering into a Loan Agreement and a Security, Pledge and Guaranty Agreement of even date herewith (collectively, the "AFFILIATE LOAN DOCUMENTS").

NOW, THEREFORE, in consideration of these premises and the mutual consideration set forth herein, the Lender and the Borrower Parties hereby agree as follows:

ARTICLE I
AMOUNTS AND TERMS OF THE ADVANCES

SECTION 1.1 DEFINITIONS. The following terms have the following meanings for purposes of this Agreement:

"ADVANCES" has the meaning ascribed to that term in Section 1.2.

"AFFILIATE" means, as to a Person, any other Person that, directly or indirectly, through one or more intermediaries controls, is controlled by or is under common control with the first-mentioned Person.

"AFFILIATE LOAN DOCUMENTS" has the meaning ascribed to that term in the Recitals.

"AGREEMENT" has the meaning ascribed to that term in the Header.

"APPLICABLE LAW" means with respect to any Person, any international, national, regional, federal, state or local treaty, statute, law, ordinance, rule, administrative action, regulation, order, writ, injunction, judgment, directive, decree or other requirement of any Governmental Authority, and any requirements imposed by common law or case law, applicable to such Person or any of its Affiliates or any of their respective properties, assets, officers, directors, employees, consultants or agents (in connection with their activities on behalf of such Person or one of its Affiliates).

"BNS" means The Bank of Nova Scotia.

"BORROWER" has the meaning ascribed to that term in the Header.

"BORROWER PARTIES" has the meaning ascribed to that term in the Header.

"BUSINESS DAY" means any day that is not a Saturday, Sunday or other day on which banks in New York, New York are authorized or obligated to close.

"CHASE" means The Chase Manhattan Bank, N.A.

"CHASE LOAN AGREEMENTS" means (i) the Loan Agreement, dated May 1, 2001, by and among L.S. Wholesale, Inc., the Parent and

Chase, providing for a revolving credit facility in an aggregate principal amount of $700,000, (ii) the Loan Agreement, dated May 1, 2001, by and among L.S. Holding, Inc., the Parent, L.S. Wholesale, Inc. and Chase, providing for a revolving credit facility in an aggregate principal amount of $2,950,000, and (iii) the Loan Agreement, dated May 1, 2001, by and among L.S. Holding (USA), Inc., the Parent, L.S. Wholesale, Inc. and Chase, providing for a revolving credit facility in an aggregate principal amount of $100,000.

"COMMITMENT" means Four Hundred Seventy Five Thousand Dollars ($475,000.00).

"DEBT" has the meaning ascribed to that term in Section 4.2(a).

"ERISA" means the Employee Retirement Income Security Act of 1974, as amended.

"EVENT OF DEFAULT" has the meaning ascribed to that term in Section 5.1.

"EXCHANGE ACT" means the Securities Exchange Act of 1934, as amended.

"FINANCIAL STATEMENTS" has the meaning ascribed to that term in Section 3.1(d).

"GAAP" means U.S. generally accepted accounting principles.

"GOVERNMENTAL AUTHORITY" has the meaning ascribed to that term in Section 3.1(h).

"GOVERNMENTAL CONSENT" has the meaning ascribed to that term in Section 3.1(h).

"GUARANTOR" has the meaning ascribed to that term in the Header.

"KNOWLEDGE" means actual knowledge after reasonable inquiry.

"LENDER" has the meaning ascribed to that term in the Header.

"LOAN DOCUMENTS" have the meaning ascribed to that term in the Recitals.

"MATERIAL ADVERSE EFFECT" means a material adverse effect on the business, properties, prospects, financial condition or results of operations of the Borrower and the Subsidiaries, taken as a whole.

"NOTE" has the meaning ascribed to that term in Section 1.4.

"PARENT" means Little Switzerland, Inc., a Delaware corporation.

"PARENT SECURITIES FILINGS" has the meaning ascribed to that term in Section 3.1(g).

"PERSON" means an individual, corporation, partnership, limited liability company, association, trust, unincorporated organization or other legal entity.

"SEC" means the U.S. Securities and Exchange Commission (or any successor thereto).

"SECURITY, PLEDGE AND GUARANTY AGREEMENT" has the meaning ascribed to that term in the Recitals.

"SUBSIDIARY" means each corporation, partnership, limited liability company and other entity with respect to which a Borrower Party (i) beneficially owns, directly or indirectly, 10% or more of the outstanding stock or other equity interests, (ii) otherwise controls, directly or indirectly, because of factors or relationships other than the percentage of equity interests owned or (iii) is required to account for its ownership under the equity method. For avoidance of doubt, "Subsidiary" shall include L.S. Holdings, Inc., a U.S. Virgin Islands corporation, and its respective Subsidiaries.

"SUBORDINATION AGREEMENT" means the Subordination Agreement, dated May 1, 2001, by and among the Borrower, certain affiliates of the Borrower, the Lender and Chase.

"TERMINATION DATE" has the meaning ascribed to that term in Section 1.2.

"TRANSACTIONS" has the meaning ascribed to that term in Section 3.1(b).

SECTION 1.2 THE ADVANCES. The Lender agrees, on the terms and conditions hereinafter set forth, to make advances (the "ADVANCES") to the Borrower from time to time on any Business Day during the period from the date hereof until April 30, 2006 (such date, or the earlier date of termination of the Commitment pursuant to Section 5.1, being the "TERMINATION DATE") in an aggregate amount not to exceed at any time outstanding the Commitment. Each Advance shall be in an amount not less than $200,000 or an integral multiple of $200,000 in excess thereof. Within the limits of the Commitment, the Borrower may borrow and prepay pursuant to Section 1.6, but may not reborrow such prepaid amounts.

SECTION 1.3 MAKING THE ADVANCES. (a) Each Advance shall be made on notice, given not later than 11:00 A.M. (New York City time) on the third Business Day prior to the date of the proposed Advance, by the Borrower to the Lender, specifying the date and amount thereof and wire instructions for delivery thereof. Not later than 11:00 A.M. (New York City time) on the date of such Advance and upon fulfillment of the applicable conditions set forth in Article II, the Lender will make such Advance available to the Borrower in same day funds pursuant to the wire instructions so provided.

(b) Each notice from the Borrower to the Lender requesting an Advance shall be irrevocable and binding on the Borrower. The Borrower shall indemnify the Lender against any loss, cost or expense incurred by the Lender as a result of any failure to fulfill on or before the date specified in such notice for such Advance the applicable conditions set forth in Article II, including any loss (including loss of anticipated profits), cost or expense incurred by reason of the liquidation or reemployment of deposits or other funds by the Lender to fund the Advance when the Advance, as a result of such failure, is not made on such date.

SECTION 1.4 REPAYMENT. The Borrower shall repay the aggregate unpaid principal amount of all Advances in accordance with a promissory note of the Borrower, in the form of Exhibit A hereto (the "NOTE"), evidencing the indebtedness resulting from such Advances and delivered to the Lender pursuant to Article II.

SECTION 1.5 INTEREST. The Borrower shall pay interest on the unpaid principal amount of each Advance from the date of such Advance until such principal amount shall be paid in full as set forth in the Note.

SECTION 1.6 OPTIONAL PREPAYMENTS. The Borrower may, upon at least two Business Days' notice to the Lender stating the proposed date and principal amount of the prepayment, and if such notice is given the Borrower shall, prepay the outstanding principal amount of the Advances in whole or in part, together with accrued interest to the date of such prepayment on the principal amount prepaid, PROVIDED, HOWEVER, that each partial prepayment shall be in an aggregate principal amount not less than $250,000. There shall be no prepayment penalty, fee or premium.

SECTION 1.7 PAYMENTS AND COMPUTATIONS. (a) The Borrower shall make each payment under any Loan Document not later than 2:00 p.m. (New York City time) on the day when due in U.S. dollars to the Lender at its address referred to in Section 7.1 in same day funds pursuant to wire instructions provided by the Lender upon request.

(b) All computations of interest shall be made by the Lender on the basis of a year of 360 days for the actual number of days occurring in the period for which such interest is payable. Determination by the Lender of an interest rate hereunder shall be conclusive and binding for all purposes, absent manifest error.

(c) Whenever any payment under any Loan Document shall be stated to be due on a day other than a Business Day, such payment shall be made on the next succeeding Business Day, and such extension of time shall in such case be included in the computation of payment of interest; provided, however, if such extension would cause payment of interest on or principal to be made in the next following calendar month, such payment shall be made on the Business Day next preceding the due date.

(d) All payments under any Loan Document shall be made without withholding and, to the extent that Applicable Law requires such withholding, such payment shall be increased in order that the net amount received by Lender after making such withholding shall be equal to the amount otherwise required to be paid to Lender under the applicable Loan Document.

ARTICLE II
CONDITIONS OF LENDING

SECTION 2.1 CONDITION PRECEDENT TO INITIAL ADVANCE. The obligation of the Lender to make its initial Advance is subject to the condition precedent that the Lender shall have received on or before the day of such Advance the following, each dated such day, in form and substance satisfactory to the Lender:

(a) The Note.

(b) The Security, Pledge and Guaranty Agreement.

(c) Certified copies of the resolutions of the Board of Directors of each Borrower Party approving each Loan Document to which it is a party, and of all documents evidencing other necessary corporate action and governmental approvals, if any, with respect to each such Loan Document.

(d) A certificate of the Secretary or an Assistant Secretary of each Borrower Party certifying the names and true signatures of the officers of such Borrower Party authorized to sign each Loan Document to which it is a party and the other documents to be delivered hereunder.

(e) A favorable opinion of Proskauer Rose LLP, counsel for the Borrower Parties, as to such other matters as the Lender may reasonably request.

(f) Evidence satisfactory to the Lender that there are no amounts owed by any of the Borrower Parties to BNS, or, if any amount is so owed, appropriate documentation (including pay-off letters, lien releases and receipts) to demonstrate that a sufficient portion of such initial Advance will be, contemporaneous with such Initial Advance, paid directly to BNS so that any such balance outstanding prior to the initial Advance is paid in full.

(g) Evidence satisfactory to the Lender that there are no amounts owed by the Borrower Parties to Chase, other than a maximum aggregate principal amount of $3,750,000 pursuant to the Chase Loan Agreements (including pay-off letters, lien releases and receipts).

(h) The Subordination Agreement.

(i) Evidence of the completion of all recordings and filings of or with respect to the Borrower that the Lender may deem necessary or desirable in order to perfect the security interests created by the Security, Pledge and Guaranty Agreement.

(j) The Affiliate Loan Documents.

(k) Such other approvals, opinions or documents as the Lender may reasonably request.

SECTION 2.2 CONDITIONS PRECEDENT TO ALL ADVANCES. The obligation of the Lender to make each Advance (including the initial Advance) shall be subject to the following further conditions precedent:

(a) On the date of such Advance the following statements shall be true and the Lender shall have received a certificate signed by a duly authorized officer of each Borrower Party (as to each Loan Document to which it is a party), dated the date of such Advance, stating that:

(i) The representations and warranties contained in Section 3.1 of this Agreement and in Section 4.01 of the Security, Pledge and Guaranty Agreement are correct on and as of the date of such Advance, before and after giving effect to such Advance and to the application of the proceeds therefrom, as though made on and as of such date, and

(ii) No event has occurred and is continuing, or would result from such Advance or from the application of the proceeds therefrom, which constitutes an Event of Default (as defined in Section 5.1 hereof) or would constitute an Event of Default but for the requirement that notice be given or time elapse or both.

(b) Receipt by the Lender of such other approvals, opinions or documents as the Lender may reasonably request.

ARTICLE III
REPRESENTATIONS AND WARRANTIES

SECTION 3.1 REPRESENTATIONS AND WARRANTIES OF THE BORROWER PARTIES. The Borrower Parties jointly and severally represent and warrant as follows:

(a) ORGANIZATION AND GOOD STANDING. Each of the Borrower Parties and its Subsidiaries is duly organized, validly existing and in good standing under the laws of the jurisdiction of its incorporation. Each Borrower Party and its Subsidiaries is qualified to do business and is in good standing in each jurisdiction in which the ownership of property or the conduct of business requires each to be so qualified, except where the lack of such qualification would not reasonably be expected to have a Material Adverse Effect.

(b) CONFLICTS, DEFAULTS. The execution and delivery of this Agreement and the other agreements and instruments contemplated hereby by the Borrower Parties do not, and the performance of the Borrower Parties' obligations hereunder and thereunder and the consummation by the Borrower Parties of the transactions contemplated hereby (the "TRANSACTIONS") will not: (i) violate, conflict with or constitute a breach or default under the certificate of incorporation or bylaws or equivalent organizational document of any Borrower Party; (ii) require any authorization, approval, consent, registration, declaration or filing with (other than a report on Form 8-K and a filing of a Form D), from or to any Governmental Authority; (iii) violate any Applicable Law; (iv) result in the creation of any lien, security interest, charge or encumbrance upon any of the properties or assets of any Borrower Party or their Subsidiaries (other than as contemplated hereby); or (v) after giving effect to the satisfaction of the condition set forth in Section 2.1(f), conflict with or result in a breach of, create an event of default (or event that, with the giving of notice or lapse of time or both, would constitute an event of default) under, or give any third party the right to terminate, cancel or accelerate any obligation under, any contract, agreement, note, bond, guarantee, deed of trust, loan agreement, mortgage, license, lease, indenture, instrument, order, arbitration award, judgment or decree to which any Borrower Party is a party or by which any Borrower Party is bound. There is no pending or, to the Knowledge of the Borrower Parties, threatened action, suit, claim, proceeding, inquiry or investigation before or by any Governmental Authority against or affecting any Borrower Party or their Subsidiaries, involving or seeking to restrain or prevent the consummation of the Transactions.

(c) CORPORATE POWER AND AUTHORIZATION. The Borrower Parties have all requisite and legal corporate power to execute and deliver this Agreement and to carry out and perform their other obligations under this Agreement and the Transactions. All corporate action on the part of the Borrower Parties and their directors necessary for the performance of their obligations under this Agreement have been taken. This Agreement is a legal, valid and binding obligation of the Borrower Parties, enforceable in accordance with its terms. The Transactions do not require the consent of the stockholders of the Borrower Parties. The Borrower Parties have provided their stockholders with any notice of the Transactions required by Applicable Law. Each of the Borrower Parties has, independently and without reliance upon the Lender and based on documents and information as it has deemed appropriate, made its own credit analysis and decision to enter into this Agreement.

(d) FINANCIAL STATEMENTS.

(i) The Borrower has provided the Lender with the following financial statements of the Parent and its Subsidiaries (collectively, the "FINANCIAL STATEMENTS"):

(A) the audited consolidated balance sheet of the Parent and its Subsidiaries as of May 27, 2000, and the related audited consolidated statements of income and cash flows of the Parent and its Subsidiaries for the fiscal year then ended, and

(B) the unaudited consolidated balance sheet of the Parent and its Subsidiaries as of February 27, 2001, and the related unaudited consolidated statements of income and cash flows of the Parent and its Subsidiaries for the 9-month period then ended.

(ii) The Financial Statements: (A) have been prepared in all material respects in accordance with the books and records of the Parent and its Subsidiaries; (B) have been prepared in accordance with GAAP; (C) reflect and provide adequate reserves and disclosures in respect of all liabilities of the Parent and its Subsidiaries, including all contingent liabilities; and (D) present fairly the consolidated financial position of the Parent and its Subsidiaries at such dates and the results of operations and cash flows of the Parent and its Subsidiaries for the periods then ended.

(iii) Each of the Parent and its Subsidiaries: (A) keeps books, records and accounts that, in reasonable detail, accurately and fairly reflect the transactions and dispositions of assets; and (B) maintains a system of internal accounting controls sufficient to provide reasonable assurance that (1) transactions are executed in accordance with management's general or specific authorization, (2) transactions are recorded as necessary to permit preparation of financial statements in accordance with GAAP to maintain accountability for assets, (3) access to assets is permitted only in accordance with management's general or specific authorizations and (4) the recorded accountability for assets and inventory is compared with existing assets and inventory at reasonable intervals and appropriate action is taken with respect to any differences.

(e) COMPLIANCE WITH LAW. The Borrower Parties and their Subsidiaries are in compliance in all material respects with all Applicable Law; PROVIDED, HOWEVER, that this Section 3.1(e) does not apply to the requirements of the Exchange Act to the extent that compliance with the Exchange Act is covered by Section 3.1(g) hereof.

(f) ABSENCE OF UNDISCLOSED LIABILITIES. None of the Borrower Parties or their Subsidiaries has any indebtedness or liability, whether accrued, fixed or contingent, whether or not required by GAAP to be disclosed on the Financial Statements, other than (a) liabilities reflected in the Financial Statements, (b) liabilities, none of which individually or in the aggregate is material to the assets, properties, business or business prospects any of the Borrower Parties or their Subsidiaries, and (c) liabilities incurred in the ordinary course of business of each of the Borrower Parties or their Subsidiaries (consistent with past practice in terms of both frequency and amount) subsequent to February 24, 2001.

(g) SECURITIES FILINGS. The Parent has made available to the Lender true and complete copies of (a) its Annual Reports on Form 10-K, as amended for each of the last three fiscal years as filed with the SEC, (b) its proxy statements relating to all of the meetings of stockholders (whether annual or special) of the Parent since January 1, 1998 as filed with the SEC, (c) its Quarterly Report on Form 10-Q for the quarterly periods ended August 27, 2000, November 29, 2000 and February 24, 2001 as filed with the SEC, and (d) all other reports, statements and registration statements and amendments thereto filed by the Parent with the SEC since May 27, 2000. The reports and statements set forth in clauses (a) through (d) are collectively referred to herein as the "PARENT SECURITIES FILINGS"). As of their respective dates, or as of the date of the last amendment thereof, if amended after filing, each of the Parent Securities Filings was prepared in all respects in accordance with the requirements of the Exchange Act, as the case may be, and none of the Parent Securities Filings contained any untrue statement of a material fact or omitted to state a material fact required to be stated therein or necessary to make the statements contained therein, in light of the circumstances under which they were made, not misleading.

(h) GOVERNMENTAL APPROVALS. No material consent, approval, waiver or authorization of, notice to or declaration of filing with (each, a "GOVERNMENTAL CONSENT") any nation or government, any state or other political subdivision thereof or any entity, authority or body exercising executive, legislative, judicial or regulatory functions of or pertaining to government, including any governmental or regulatory authority, agency, department, board, commission or instrumentality, any court or tribunal (each, a "GOVERNMENTAL AUTHORITY"), on the part of the Borrower or any subsidiary is required in connection with the execution of this Agreement and the consummation of the Transactions.

(i) LITIGATION. Except as set forth on Schedule 3.1(i), there is no pending or, to the Knowledge of the Borrower Parties, threatened litigation, action, suit, proceeding, arbitration, claim, investigation or administrative proceeding, by or before any Governmental Authority or dispute resolution panel, involving or affecting any of the Borrower Parties or their Subsidiaries, or the assets, properties or business of any of the Borrower Parties or their Subsidiaries, or relating to or involving the transactions contemplated by the Loan Documents. No litigation, action, suit, proceeding, arbitration, claim, investigation or administrative proceeding, whether or not set forth on Schedule 3.1(i), reasonably could be expected to have a Material Adverse Effect or to result in the imposition of a lien, security interest or other encumbrance on any of the assets of any of the Borrower Parties or their Subsidiaries. None of the Borrower Parties or their Subsidiaries has received any opinion or memorandum or legal advice or notice from legal counsel to the effect that it is exposed, from a legal standpoint, to any liability or disadvantage that may be material to its assets, properties, business or business prospects. None of the Borrower Parties or their Subsidiaries is in default with respect to any material order, writ, injunction or decree known to or served upon any of the Borrower Parties or their Subsidiaries. Except as set forth on Schedule 3.1(i), there is no pending action or suit brought by any of the Borrower Parties or their Subsidiaries against others.

(j) USE OF PROCEEDS. No proceeds of any Advance will be used to acquire any equity security of a class which is registered pursuant to Section 12 of the Exchange Act. The Borrower Parties and their Subsidiaries are not engaged in the business of extending credit for the purpose of purchasing or carrying margin stock (within the meaning of Regulations T, U and X of the Federal Reserve Board, as amended from time to time), and no proceeds of any Advance will be used to purchase or carry any margin stock or to extend credit to others for the purpose of purchasing or carrying any margin stock.

ARTICLE IV
COVENANTS OF THE BORROWER

SECTION 4.1 AFFIRMATIVE COVENANTS. So long as the Note shall remain unpaid or the Lender shall have any Commitment hereunder, each of the Borrower Parties will, unless the Lender shall otherwise consent in writing:

(a) COMPLIANCE WITH LAWS, ETC. Comply, and cause each of its Subsidiaries to comply, in all material respects with all Applicable Law, such compliance to include, without limitation, paying before the same become delinquent all taxes, assessments and governmental charges imposed upon it or upon its property except to the extent contested in good faith.

(b) REPORTING REQUIREMENTS. Furnish to the Lender

(i) as soon as available and in any event within 45 days after the end of each of the first three quarters of each fiscal year of the Parent, the unaudited consolidated balance sheet of the Parent and its Subsidiaries and the related unaudited consolidated statements of income and cash flows of the Parent and its Subsidiaries for the 3-month period then ended for the period commencing at the end of the previous fiscal year and ending with the end of such quarter, certified by the chief financial officer of the Parent;

(ii) as soon as available and in any event within 90 days after the end of each fiscal year of the Parent, a copy of the annual report for such year for the Parent and its Subsidiaries, containing the audited consolidated balance sheet of the Parent and its Subsidiaries as of each fiscal year end, and the related audited consolidated statements of income and cash flows of the Parent and its Subsidiaries for the fiscal year then ended, certified by PricewaterhouseCoopers LLP or other independent public accountants reasonably acceptable to the Lender with no qualifications as to the scope of the audit;

(iii) as soon as possible and in any event within five days after the occurrence of each Event of Default known to a Borrower Party and each event which, with the giving of notice or lapse of time, or both, would constitute an Event of Default, continuing on the date of such statement, a statement of the chief financial officer or chief executive officer of such Borrower Party setting forth details of such Event of Default or event and the action which such Borrower Party has taken and proposes to take with respect thereto;

(iv) promptly after the sending or filing thereof, copies of all reports which any of the Borrower Parties sends to any of its security holders, and copies of all reports and registration statements which the Parent files with the SEC or any national securities exchange;

(v) promptly after the filing or receiving thereof, copies of all reports and notices which any of the Borrower Parties files under ERISA with the Internal Revenue Service or the Pension Benefit Guaranty Corporation or the U.S. Department of Labor or which any of the Borrower Parties receives from such entity;

(vi) promptly after the commencement thereof, notice of all actions, suits and proceedings before any Government Authority, or arbitrations affecting the Borrower Parties which, if determined adversely to the Borrower Parties and their Subsidiaries could reasonably be expected to have a Material Adverse Effect on the Borrower Parties or their Subsidiaries; and

(vii) such other information respecting the condition or operations, financial or otherwise, of any of the Borrower Parties as the Lender may from time to time reasonably request.

(c) USE OF PROCEEDS. The proceeds of the Advances shall be used by the Borrower Parties only for repayment of indebtedness for borrowed money and for working capital purposes. No part of the proceeds of the Advances shall be used directly or indirectly for the purpose, whether immediate, incidental or ultimate, of purchasing or carrying any margin stock or maintaining or extending credit to others for such purpose or for any other purpose that otherwise violates Regulations T, U and X of the Federal Reserve Board, as amended from time to time.

(d) MAINTENANCE OF CORPORATION AND PROPERTIES. The Borrower Parties shall, and shall cause their Subsidiaries, to preserve and maintain their respective corporate existence and good standing in their respective jurisdiction of incorporation and in every other jurisdiction in which such qualification is required, unless the failure to qualify would not have a Material Adverse Effect on such respective corporation, and maintain all of their respective properties and assets in good working order and condition, ordinary wear excepted.

SECTION 4.2 NEGATIVE COVENANTS. So long as the Note shall remain unpaid or the Lender shall have any Commitment hereunder, each of the Borrower Parties will not, and shall cause their Subsidiaries to not, without the written consent of the Lender:

(a) LIENS. Create or suffer to exist, or permit any of its Subsidiaries to create or suffer to exist, any lien, security interest or other charge or encumbrance, or any other type of preferential arrangement, upon or with respect to any of its properties, whether now owned or hereafter acquired, or assign, or permit any of its Subsidiaries to assign, any right to receive income, in each case to secure or provide for the payment of any Debt of any Person or entity, other than (i) liens securing the Advances; (ii) liens securing the credit facilities provided by Chase pursuant to the Chase Loan Agreements; (iii) liens existing on the date hereof as described on Schedule 4.2(a) hereto; (iv) purchase money liens or purchase money security interests upon or in any property acquired or held by any of the Borrower Parties and their Subsidiaries in the ordinary course of business to secure the purchase price of such property or to secure indebtedness incurred solely for the purpose of financing the acquisition of such property, (v) liens or security interests existing on such property at the time of its acquisition (other than any such lien or security interest created in contemplation of such acquisition), PROVIDED that the aggregate principal amount of the indebtedness secured by the liens or security interests referred to in clauses (iii), (iv) and (v) above shall not exceed an amount not inconsistent with the Company's business plan as approved by its Board of Directors from time to time. "DEBT" means (i) indebtedness for borrowed money, (ii) obligations evidenced by bonds, debentures, notes or other similar instruments, (iii) obligations to pay the deferred purchase price of property or services, (iv) obligations as lessee under leases which shall have been or should be, in accordance with generally accepted accounting principles, recorded as capital leases, (v) obligations under direct or indirect guaranties in respect of, and obligations (contingent or otherwise) to purchase or otherwise acquire, or otherwise to assure a creditor against loss in respect of, indebtedness or obligations of others of the kinds referred to in clause (i) through (iv) above, and

(vi) liabilities in respect of unfunded vested benefits under plans covered by Title IV of ERISA.

(b) INDEBTEDNESS. (i) Directly or indirectly create, incur, assume, guarantee, or otherwise become or remain liable with respect to any Debt except:

> (A) the Advances, indebtedness existing as of the date hereof as described on Schedule 4.2(b) hereto and capitalized leases obligations in an amount not to exceed $250,000 per annum at any time outstanding; and

> (B) indebtedness in an aggregate principal amount not to exceed $3,750,000 pursuant to the Chase Loan Agreements.

(c) GUARANTY. Assume, guaranty, endorse or otherwise be or become directly or contingently responsible or liable to assure the creditors of any third party against loss, for the obligations of any Person (other than (i) one or more of the Borrower's Subsidiaries or (ii) endorsements of instruments for collection in the ordinary course of business), including an agreement to purchase any obligation, stock, assets, goods or services or to supply or advance any funds, assets, goods or services or an agreement to maintain or cause any such person to maintain a minimum working capital or net worth.

(d) SALES OF ASSETS. Sell, lease, assign, transfer, abandon, or otherwise dispose of, directly or indirectly, whether voluntary or involuntary, any of its now owned or hereafter acquired assets, including without limitation inventory, capital stock and receivables, except (i) inventory disposed of in the ordinary course of business consistent with past practice, (ii) obsolete, outmoded or worn-out machinery, equipment, furniture or fixtures or (iii) leases or subleases granted by the Borrower Parties to third persons which such leases or subleases do not interfere in any material respect with the business of the Borrower Parties and their Subsidiaries.

(e) MERGERS. Merge or consolidate with, or sell, assign, lease or otherwise dispose of (in one transaction or in a series of related transactions) all or substantially all of its assets (whether now owned or hereafter acquired) to any Person (other than another Borrower Party), or acquire all or substantially all of the assets of the business of any Person (other than another Borrower Party), or enter into any agreement to do any of the foregoing.

(f) OFFICER/EMPLOYEE DISTRIBUTIONS. Except as occurs in the ordinary course of business consistent with past practice, grant or pay any extraordinary distributions, including bonuses or extraordinary salary increases; or make loans or other forms of cash payments to employees or officers or directors; or, make any payments of principal or interest on any shareholder loans existing on its books (except as set forth on Schedule 4.2(f)); or give any preferential treatment, directly or indirectly, to any officer, director or employee.

(g) DIVIDENDS. Declare or pay any dividend or make any distribution upon its capital stock (preferred or common), or purchase or retire, or otherwise acquire for value any of its capital stock now or hereafter outstanding, or make any distribution of assets or loans to its stockholders, whether in cash, assets or obligations, or allocate or otherwise set aside any sum for the payment of any dividend or distribution by reduction of capital or otherwise in respect of any shares of its capital stock.

(h) CAPITAL EXPENDITURES. Purchase any assets, vehicles or equipment or make any other capital expenditures in excess of $75,000 per annum, except in the ordinary course of business consistent with past practice.

(i) TRANSACTIONS WITH AFFILIATES. Enter into any transaction, including, without limitation, the purchase, sale or exchange of property or the rendering of any service, with any Affiliate (other than another Borrower Party), except in the ordinary course of and pursuant to the reasonable requirements of its business and upon fair and reasonable terms.

(j) STOCK. Change the number of authorized shares, voting rights of shares, class of shares, engage in any "split-ups", revisions, reclassifications or other like change of its stock.

(k) CHANGE IN OWNERSHIP. Cause, permit or suffer the transfer of its shares to an entity which, following such transfer, then holds a majority of its shares or cause, permit or suffer any change of control whatsoever, without the prior written consent of the Lender. The term "control" means the possession, directly or indirectly, of the power to direct or cause the direction of the management policies of a Person, whether through the ownership of voting securities, by contract, or otherwise.

(l) BUSINESS. Change the general character of its business as conducted as of the date hereof or engage in any type of business not reasonably related to its business as normally conducted, or change its corporate name.

ARTICLE V
EVENTS OF DEFAULT

SECTION 5.1 EVENTS OF DEFAULT. If any of the following events ("EVENTS OF DEFAULT") shall occur and be continuing:

(a) The Borrower shall fail to pay any principal of, or interest on, the Note when the same becomes due and payable (after giving effect to applicable grace periods, if any); or

(b) Any representation or warranty made by any Borrower Party (or any of its officers) under or in connection with any Loan Document shall prove to have been incorrect in any material respect when made; or

(c) Any Borrower Party shall fail to perform or observe any term, covenant or agreement contained in any Loan Document on its part to be performed or observed if such failure shall remain unremedied for 10 days after written notice thereof shall have been given to such Borrower Party by the Lender; or

(d) Any Borrower Party or any of its Affiliates shall fail to pay any principal of or premium or interest on any Debt (including the indebtedness to Chase pursuant to the Chase Loan Agreements and indebtedness to the Lender pursuant to the Affiliate Loan Documents, but excluding Debt hereunder as evidenced by the Note) of such Borrower Party or such subsidiary (as the case may be), when the same becomes due and payable (whether by scheduled maturity, required prepayment, acceleration, demand or otherwise), and such failure shall continue after the applicable grace period, if any, specified in the agreement or instrument relating to such Debt; or any other event shall occur or condition shall exist under any agreement or instrument relating to any such Debt and shall continue after the applicable grace period, if any, specified in such agreement or instrument, if the effect of such event or condition is to accelerate, or to permit the acceleration of, the maturity of such Debt; or any such Debt shall be declared to be due and payable, or required to be prepaid (other than by a regularly scheduled required prepayment), prior to the stated maturity thereof; or

(e) Any Borrower Party or any of its Subsidiaries shall generally not pay its debts as such debts become due, or shall admit in writing its inability to pay its debts generally, or shall make a general assignment for the benefit of creditors; or any proceeding shall be instituted by or against any Borrower Party or any of its Subsidiaries seeking to adjudicate it a bankrupt or insolvent, or seeking liquidation, winding up, reorganization, arrangement, adjustment, protection, relief, or composition of it or its debts under any law relating to bankruptcy, insolvency or reorganization or relief of debtors, or seeking the entry of an order for relief or the appointment of a receiver, trustee, custodian or other similar official for it or for any substantial part of its property and, in the case of any such proceeding instituted against it (but not instituted by it), either such proceeding shall remain undismissed or unstayed for a period of 30 days, or any of the actions sought in such proceeding (including, without limitation, the entry of an order for relief against, or the appointment of a receiver, trustee, custodian or other similar official for, it or for any substantial part of its property) shall occur; or any Borrower Party or any of its Subsidiaries shall take any corporate action to authorize any of the actions set forth above in this subsection (e); or

(f) Any judgment or order for the payment of money in excess of $75,000 shall be rendered against any Borrower Party or any of its Subsidiaries and either (i) enforcement proceedings shall have been commenced by any creditor upon such judgment or order or (ii) there shall be any period of 10 consecutive days during which a stay of enforcement of such judgment or order, by reason of a pending appeal or otherwise, shall not be in effect; or

(g) Any provision of the Security, Pledge and Guaranty Agreement after delivery thereof pursuant to Section 2.01 shall for any reason cease to be valid and binding on any Borrower Party, or a Borrower Party shall so state in writing; or

(h) The Security, Pledge and Guaranty Agreement after delivery thereof pursuant to Section 2.01 shall for any reason (other than pursuant to the terms thereof) cease to create a valid and perfected security interest in any of the collateral purported to be covered thereby;

then, and in any such event, the Lender (1) may, by notice to the Borrower, declare its obligation to make Advances to be terminated, whereupon the same shall forthwith terminate, and (2) may, by notice to the Borrower, declare the Note, all interest thereon and all other amounts payable under this Agreement to be forthwith due and payable, whereupon the Note, all such interest and all such amounts shall become and be forthwith due and payable, without presentment, demand, protest, or further notice of any kind, all of which are hereby expressly waived by the Borrower Parties; provided, however, that in the event of an actual or deemed entry of an order for relief with respect to any of the Borrower Parties under the Federal Bankruptcy Code, (A) the obligation of the Lender to make Advances shall automatically be terminated and (B) the Advances, the Note, all such interest and all such amounts shall automatically become and be due and payable, without presentment, demand, protest or any notice of any kind, all of which are hereby expressly waived by the Borrower.

ARTICLE VI
SUBORDINATION

SECTION 6.1 SUBORDINATION OF ADVANCES. The Advances are subordinated to the credit facilities provided by Chase pursuant to the Chase Loan Agreements as set forth herein, in the Security, Pledge and Guarantee Agreement and in the Subordination Agreement. Except as set forth in the Subordination Agreement, no payment of principal or interest will be made with respect to the Advances.

SECTION 6.2 SECURITY FOR THE ADVANCES. As set forth in the Security, Pledge and Guaranty Agreement, the Advances are secured, subject to the rights of Chase pursuant to the Subordination Agreement, by a security interest in the Collateral (as defined in the Security, Pledge and Guaranty Agreement) in favor of the Lender.

SECTION 6.3 APPLICATION OF COLLATERAL PROCEEDS. All proceeds from the sale of other disposition of Collateral shall be applied as provided by the terms of the Security, Pledge and Guaranty Agreement, the Subordination Agreement and Section 4.1(c) above.

ARTICLE VII
MISCELLANEOUS

SECTION 7.1 NOTICES. All notices, requests and other communications under this Agreement will be in writing and will be deemed to have been duly given if delivered personally, or sent by either certified or registered mail, return receipt requested, postage prepaid, by overnight courier guaranteeing next day delivery or by telecopier (with telephonic or machine confirmation by the sender), addressed as follows:

   (a) If to the Borrower Parties:
       [Borrower Notice Information Omitted]
       With a copy to:
       [Counsel Notice Information Omitted]
or at such other address or telecopy number as the Borrower may have advised the Lender in writing; and

   (b) If to the Lender:
       [Lender Notice Information Omitted]
       With a copy to:
       [Counsel Notice Information Omitted]
or at such other address or telecopy number as the Lender may have advised the Borrower in writing. All such notices, requests and other communications shall be deemed to have been received on the date of delivery thereof (if delivered by hand), on the third day after the mailing thereof (if mailed), on the next day after the sending thereof (if by overnight courier) and when receipt is confirmed as provided above (if telecopied).

SECTION 7.2 WAIVERS AND AMENDMENTS. No amendment or waiver of any provision of this Agreement, nor consent to any departure therefrom, will be effective unless the same shall be in writing and signed by an officer of each party hereto, and then such waiver or consent will be effective only in the specific instance and for the specific purpose for which given. No failure on the part of a party hereto to exercise, and no delay in exercising, any right hereunder will operate as a waiver thereof; nor will any single or partial exercise of any right hereunder preclude any other or further exercise thereof or the exercise of any other right. The remedies provided in this Agreement are cumulative and, unless otherwise expressly provided herein, not exclusive of any remedies provided by law.

SECTION 7.3 BINDING EFFECT. This Agreement will be binding upon and inure to the benefit of the parties and their respective heirs, executors, administrators, personal representatives, successors and permitted assigns. No party may assign his or its rights hereunder or any interest herein without the prior written consent of the other parties and such attempted assignment shall be void and without effect, provided however, that the Lender may assign, to one or more of its Affiliates, all or any part of, or any interest in, the Lender's rights and benefits hereunder. To the extent of such assignment, such assignee will have the same rights and benefits against the other parties as it would have had if it were a named party hereunder. No party will be released of any of its obligations under this Agreement by virtue of such assignment.

SECTION 7.4 EXHIBITS AND SCHEDULES. The Exhibits and Schedules attached hereto or referred to herein are incorporated herein and made a part hereof for all purposes. As used herein, the expression "this Agreement" includes such Exhibits and Schedules.

SECTION 7.5 GOVERNING LAW. THIS AGREEMENT, THE TRANSACTIONS CONTEMPLATED HEREBY THE RIGHTS AND OBLIGATIONS OF THE PARTIES HERETO, AND ANY DISPUTES OR CONTROVERSIES ARISING THEREFROM SHALL BE GOVERNED BY AND CONSTRUED AND ENFORCED IN ACCORDANCE WITH THE LAWS OF THE STATE OF NEW YORK, WITHOUT REGARD TO ITS PRINCIPLES OF CONFLICT OF LAWS THAT WOULD PROVIDE FOR THE APPLICATION OF ANY OTHER LAW.

SECTION 7.6 CAPTIONS. The captions, headings and arrangements used in this Agreement are for convenience only and do not in any way affect, limit or amplify the provisions hereof.

SECTION 7.7 ENTIRETY. This Agreement contains the entire agreement and understanding between the parties with respect to the matters addressed herein and supersedes all prior representations, inducements, promises or agreements, oral or otherwise, which are not embodied herein.

SECTION 7.8 COUNTERPARTS. This Agreement may be executed in multiple counterparts, each of which will be deemed an original for all purposes and all of which will be deemed collectively to be one agreement. Execution may be effected by delivery of facsimiles of signature pages, followed by delivery of originals of such pages.

SECTION 7.9 THIRD PARTY BENEFICIARIES. Nothing contained herein, express or implied, is intended to confer upon any Person or entity other than the parties and their heirs, executors, administrators, personal representatives, successors and permitted assigns any rights or remedies under or by reason of this Agreement, except as otherwise expressly provided in this Agreement.

SECTION 7.10 ACCOUNTING TERMS. All accounting terms not specifically defined herein shall be construed in accordance with generally accepted accounting principles consistent with those applied in the preparation of the financial statements referred to in Section 3.1(d).

SECTION 7.11 COSTS, EXPENSES AND TAXES. The Borrower agrees to pay on demand all costs and expenses, if any (including reasonable counsel fees and expenses), in connection with the enforcement (whether through negotiations, legal proceedings or otherwise) of the Loan Documents and the other documents to be delivered under the Loan Documents, including, without limitation, reasonable counsel fees and expenses in connection with the enforcement of rights under this Section 7.11.

IN WITNESS WHEREOF, the parties hereto have caused this Agreement to be executed by their respective officers thereunto duly authorized, as of the date first above written.

[Signature Page Omitted]

EXHIBIT A
PROMISSORY NOTE

$_____   Dated: May 1, 2001
                                               New York, New York

FOR VALUE RECEIVED, the undersigned, _____ (the "BORROWER"), hereby unconditionally promises to pay to the order of Tiffany and Company, a New York corporation (the "LENDER"), the principal amount of _____ Dollars ($_____) (or, if less, the aggregate principal amount of all Advances made by the Lender to the Borrower pursuant to the Loan Agreement (the "LOAN AGREEMENT") among the Borrower, certain of its affiliates and the Lender), in lawful money of the United States of America in immediately available funds on April 30, 2006 (or, if earlier, the Termination Date as defined in the Loan Agreement).

The Borrower promises to pay interest on the principal amount hereof from time to time outstanding, in like funds, at a rate per annum compounded annually during the time that this Promissory Note is outstanding until such principal is paid in full equal to a fluctuating interest rate determined in advance of each interest payment period as hereinafter provided and equal at all times to three percent (3%) per annum above LIBOR (the "INTEREST RATE"). "LIBOR" means the rate per annum (rounded upwards if necessary to the nearest 1/16 of 1%) quoted by the British Bankers' Association for the offering to leading banks in the London Interbank market of Dollar deposits in immediately available funds and in an amount comparable to the principal amount outstanding hereunder.

LIBOR shall be determined in advance of each interest payment period as of approximately 11:00 A.M. London time on each date which is two Business Days prior to the start of such interest payment period and such determination shall govern throughout such interest payment period. LIBOR shall be determined by reference to Bloomberg LP on page BBAM. Interest payment periods shall commence on February 1 and August 1 of each calendar year. All accrued and unpaid interest hereunder shall be due and payable as of January 31st and July 31st of each calendar year until the principal and all accrued interest are paid in full. All computations of interest based on the Interest Rate shall be made by the Lender on the basis of a year of 360 days for the actual number of days occurring in the period for which such interest is payable. Determination by the Lender of an interest rate hereunder shall be conclusive and binding for all purposes, absent manifest error.

Both principal and interest are payable in lawful money of the United States of America to the Lender at 600 Madison Avenue, Eighth Floor, New York, New York 10022 in same day funds on the Termination Date. Each Advance made by the Lender to the Borrower and the maturity thereof, and all payments made on account of the principal amount thereof, shall be recorded by the Lender and, prior to any transfer hereof, endorsed on the grid attached hereto which is a part of this Promissory Note.

The Borrower promises to pay interest, on demand, on any overdue principal and, to the fullest extent permitted by law, on any overdue interest and on any overdue amount under any instrument now or hereinafter evidencing or securing the indebtedness evidenced hereby, at a rate equal to the Interest Rate plus 3% per annum, from the date such principal or interest was due to the date or payment in full.

If any payment under this Promissory Note is not made when due, whether at maturity or by acceleration, the Borrower shall pay all costs of collection (including reasonable attorneys' fees) whether or not suit is filed hereon, on the Loan Documents (as defined in the Loan Agreement) or otherwise, and all expenses incurred in connection with the protection or realization of any collateral.

This Promissory Note is the Note referred to in, and is entitled to the benefits of, the Loan Agreement and Security, Pledge and Guaranty Agreement referred to therein and entered into pursuant thereto. The Loan Agreement, among other things, (i) provides for the making of Advances by the Lender to the Borrower from time to time in an aggregate amount not to exceed at any time outstanding the U.S. dollar amount first above mentioned, the indebtedness of the Borrower resulting from each such Advance being evidenced by this Promissory Note, and (ii) contains provisions for acceleration of the maturity hereof upon the happening of certain stated events and also for prepayments on account of principal hereof prior to the maturity hereof upon the terms and conditions therein specified.

The Borrower hereby waives (to the extent permitted by law) diligence, presentment, demand, protest and notice of any kind whatsoever except as expressly required herein. The non-exercise by the Lender of any of its rights hereunder or under the Security, Pledge and Guaranty Agreement in any particular instance shall not constitute a waiver thereof in that or any subsequent instance. The Borrower shall at all times have the right to proceed against any portion of the security held therefor in such order and in such manner as the Borrower may select, without waiving any rights with respect to any other security. No delay or omission on the part of the Borrower in exercising any right hereunder or under the Security, Pledge and Guaranty Agreement or other agreement shall operate as a waiver of such right or of any other right under this Promissory Note.

This Promissory Note, the transactions contemplated hereby the rights and obligations of the parties hereto, and any disputes or controversies arising therefrom shall be governed by and construed and enforced in accordance with the laws of the State of New York, without regard to its principles of conflict of laws that would provide for the application of any other law.

[Signature Page Omitted]

[Other Schedules and Exhibits Omitted]

---

1. Familiarity Breeds Fluency: A Review

The above Agreement marks this book's first encounter with an agreement for the lending of money. However, despite your potential unfamiliarity, it is our hope that you found many of this Agreement's concepts and provisions—and even its structure—to be familiar.

- How is the structure of this particular Agreement similar to those we have seen in previous chapters? Does the Loan Agreement itself extend monies to the Borrower and a right of payment to the Lender—that is, does the loan "happen" as of the execution of the Loan Agreement? In this case, the answer is "no." The Loan Agreement states the global terms of the lending relationship, in much the same way as the master agreements we have encountered in previous chapters do. Similar to a work order in this respect, then, the Note here states the specific terms (e.g., interest rate, principal) of the loan. Please do note that generally, in commercial lending transactions, it is quite common for loan agreements to state all payment terms and for promissory notes not to be used. (See Chapters 3 and 4.)

- In § 5.1(e), we find an "ipso facto" clause. What makes this provision an "ipso facto" clause? Is this likely to be enforceable in bankruptcy? (See Chapter 4.)

- Is there any provision in this Agreement or the Note that provides that the Borrower may receive an interest rate or other terms comparable to (or more favorable than) other similar notes made available by the Lender? Would such a most-favored-nations provision benefit the Borrower or the Lender? How might the Lender wish to define what qualifies as a similar loan that would trigger such a provision? (See Chapter 4.)

- Does this Agreement stipulate what monetary damages are available in the event of a breach of contract? Does an Event of Default amount to a breach? Are the remedies provided by § 5.1 in the occurrence of an Event of Default liquidated damages, penalties, or something altogether outside the law of liquidated damages? While we have discussed liquidated damages previously, we take up these questions in the context of loan agreements below. (See Chapter 1.)

- In addition, you should by now be familiar with several of the types of provisions—the "building blocks"—that make up this Loan Agreement. The Agreement makes use of conditions, representations, warranties, and covenants (both affirmative and negative) to lay out the rights and obligations of the parties to the Agreement. We further discuss each of these below in the context of lending agreements. (See Chapters 1-4.)

2. The Basic Terms and Structure of Loan Agreements

Loan agreements come in various structures and forms, depending on the capital needs of the borrower and the willingness and flexibility of the lender. Perhaps the most intuitive and straightforward loan is a simple exchange of a certain amount of money in consideration for a promise to pay that money back by a certain date with interest. The amount borrowed is called the "principal" or the "face" amount of the loan. The amount that the borrower must pay in addition to the borrowed principal is called the "interest" (often understood as the "cost of capital"). Interest is likely to be stated in terms of an "interest rate." A loan's stated interest rate will usually be an *annual* rate, which means that the rate reflects the percentage of the outstanding principal owed as interest for a one-year period. The loan agreement and/or promissory note will state how and when interest payments are due; for example, interest may be due quarterly or only once at the end of the loan period. While partial principal payments may be due throughout the term of the loan, a loan must be paid back in its entirety upon the "maturity date," as provided by the agreement.

This simple arrangement described above is a basic "term loan," where a party lends a certain amount of money to be paid back on specified terms.[4] As we have seen, commercial parties may enter into a relationship at a time when they may not know the specific details of their future needs as pertains to that relationship. We have seen this dynamic with master services and supply agreements, where parties have entered into framework agreements pursuant to which they may agree to the provision of specific goods and/or services in the future. Similarly in the interest of flexibility, parties may enter into a "revolving" credit agreement. A revolving credit facility makes a certain lending commitment available to the borrower, under which the borrower may borrow, repay, and "re-borrow" in accordance with the specific terms and procedures of the agreement.[5] A familiar example of a revolving credit facility is a credit card, which allows a consumer the ability to borrow up to a certain credit limit, and to repay and re-borrow from time to time, so long as the credit limit is not exceeded. A revolving credit agreement will state the global terms of the arrangement, but the actual loans occur when the borrower draws from the available commitment. As with any other loan, the borrower must pay interest and must pay back the borrowed principal according to the terms of the agreement. It is not uncommon for a lending agreement to contemplate both types of credit facilities, lending a fixed amount at the time of contracting (or, upon a specified date in the future) and extending a revolving credit facility from which the borrower may draw if more funds are needed.

Please note that the above Loan Agreement contemplates a variation of a term loan, with "multiple draw" features that resemble a revolving loan in part. How can you tell this from the Loan Agreement? Under § 1.2 of this Agreement, the Borrower may not "re-borrow" the loans it pays back; the right to re-borrow is generally considered a basic feature of a revolving loan.[6] That is, a revolving loan allows a borrower to draw from a credit pool for a certain period of time, where any amounts paid back act to replenish the pool available to the borrower.

Notice that the Note provided in Exhibit A attached to the Loan Agreement above does not state a fixed-percentage interest rate. Rather, the Note provides that the interest rate is "equal to a fluctuating interest rate determined in advance of each interest payment period as hereinafter provided and equal at all times to three percent (3%) per annum above LIBOR (the 'INTEREST RATE')." The interest rate attached to a debt instrument may be fixed or it may be variable (sometimes called "floating" or "fluctuating"). Fixed rates generally do not change over time, whereas variable rates do. How is a variable rate to be determined, then, as of any given time? Often, parties will tie a variable rate to a "reference rate," such as "LIBOR," typically including a "spread" or "margin" (in this case, 3%) above the reference rate. LIBOR generally refers to the London

---

4. 1 Sandra Schnitzer Stern, Structuring and Drafting Commercial Loan Agreements ¶ 1.02[3] (rev. ed. 2010).

5. Id. ¶ 1.02[2].

6. Id.

Interbank Offered Rate, which is the rate at which banks borrow money from each other on the London interbank market. A prudent party will be careful to define a reference rate precisely as intended for use in a particular lending agreement. In addition, a prudent borrower might shy away from the use of a reference rate that the lender may affect and, thus, may prefer a third-party-determined reference rate, such as LIBOR. Also, for this reason, loan agreements will sometimes reference a composite rate based on several large U.S. banks, such as the Wall Street Journal Prime Rate published by the *Wall Street Journal*. Similarly, to provide an "objective" source for the reference rate, notice that the parties in this Agreement specify that LIBOR is to be determined by reference to Bloomberg's publication.

These are some basic features commonly found in loans, as illustrated by this chapter's simple loan agreement. However, in practice, loan agreements may be very complicated, contemplating sophisticated lending structures with many players involved. For this reason, we asked a seasoned practitioner to shed some light on a relatively common feature of sophisticated lending arrangements: syndication.

A Practitioner Perspective: Syndicated Lending Arrangements

The sample Loan Agreement featured in this chapter evidences a simple lending arrangement made available by a corporate lender to a borrower. More often than not, however, loans and other extensions of credit are provided by commercial banks or other financial institutions, and it is quite common for a credit facility to be made available by a collection of lenders acting severally but in concert. A credit facility that is coordinated by one or more lead institutions but made available to a borrower by multiple lenders is referred to as a "syndicated" loan transaction. Among other advantages, loan syndication allows regulated banks to reduce required capital reserves associated with loans and allows lenders and borrowers alike to reduce risk exposure to one another. The following discussion provides a broad introduction to certain elements of syndicated lending.

General Description of the Players and Process in a Syndicated Lending Transaction

The consortium of lenders in a syndicated loan transaction is referred to as the "syndicate." While all of the lenders in a syndicate (as distinguished from participants, see below) have contractual privity with the borrower, in a syndicated deal, a lead financial institution will be appointed as the "administrative agent" for the facility and will assume primary responsibility for structuring, negotiating, documenting and administering the transaction and, following a default, enforcing rights and remedies. Accordingly, the borrower will typically communicate with the lenders through the administrative agent. The administrative agent views its role as truly administrative, and credit agreements will go to great lengths to define the administrative agent's duties narrowly, including an express disclaimer of any fiduciary duty owing from the administrative agent (or any other agent for that matter) to the borrower or any lender. Additional agent titles may be awarded to other lenders in the transaction, at times reflecting actual duties (for example, a "collateral agent" that acts as the "secured party" for the lenders and potentially other creditors in a secured transaction) or sometimes simply giving nominal agent status to a lender in recognition of a substantial commitment (for example, "syndication agents," "documentation agents" or other "co-agents").

An investment bank or other non-bank affiliate of the administrative agent (referred to as an "arranger" and/or "bookrunner," although this discussion uses the term "arranger") will assume responsibility for actually syndicating the transaction—that is, selling the commitments to lend to other lenders.[1] A threshold question relates to exactly what portion of the commitments an arranger needs to sell. Syndicated deals can be underwritten on a "best efforts" basis, which means that the arranger (or, more accurately, its lender affiliate) commits to a portion of the facility and will use "commercially reasonable efforts" to syndicate the balance of the commitments. In a best efforts deal, success in syndicating the balance of the commitments is a stated condition to the administrative agent's and arranger's commitments and agreements; the deal is not required to close if the commitments are not fully syndicated. Alternatively, a deal may be fully underwritten, which means that the arranger (or, more accurately, its lender affiliate) commits to the full amount of the facility but in reality the arranger expects to sell a significant portion of the commitments. In such instances, the arranger has an obligation to close the deal whether or not the desired portion, or indeed any, of the commitments can be syndicated, assuming that the other conditions to closing are satisfied. An arranger in a fully underwritten deal will often seek protections to help it achieve what it considers to be a "successful syndication" (defined differently within the context of each transaction). One such tool is a "market flex" provision, which allows the arranger to adjust the transaction terms and conditions (including pricing), generally subject to negotiated limitations, in order to achieve a successful syndication.[2]

In terms of documentation process, at the outset of a syndicated transaction, the administrative agent and arranger will negotiate a commitment letter with the borrower, evidencing their respective commitments and agreements on the terms and conditions set forth in the commitment letter and in a "term sheet" or outline of the deal. In that letter, the arranger will state its intention to syndicate

---

1. For simplicity's sake, this discussion refers to a single arranger, although oftentimes more than one institution has that title. The arranger who is truly in charge of the syndication process will have "lead left" status (referring to its placement on the left-hand side of the commitment letter and marketing materials). Similarly, other portions of this discussion refer to a single borrower, notwithstanding that credit facilities can be in favor of multiple borrowers.

2. A similar tool is a "market MAC" condition, which makes the commitments subject to the absence of a material adverse change in the relevant financial markets that could impair syndication of the facility. The "market MAC" is to be distinguished from the "business MAC," which pertains to material adverse changes specific to the borrower and its subsidiaries (as seen in the sample Loan Agreement).

the deal and the borrower will agree to provide certain information and otherwise assist with the syndication process. The borrower will also agree to reimburse the agent and arranger for costs and expenses, and to indemnify the agent and arranger for losses, claims, damages and liabilities associated with these undertakings. The borrower, administrative agent and arranger will separately enter into a confidential fee letter documenting supplemental fees payable to the administrative agent and arranger (in addition to fees that may be earned by the lenders) in consideration for their respective commitments and agreements. Upon execution and delivery of the commitment and fee letters, counsel for the administrative agent and arranger will draft the credit agreement and other definitive loan documentation, which will first be negotiated with the borrower and its counsel, and thereafter will be presented to other members of the syndicate and their respective counsel for review, comment and ultimately signature.

Structural Variations in Syndicated Lending Transactions

The size and composition of a syndicate will vary widely depending on the size and structure of the underlying transaction. Syndicated credit facilities can have as few as two or three "relationship" lenders that often provide cash management, derivative and other services to the borrower and its subsidiaries (frequently referred to as "club" deals), or as many as several hundred lenders comprised of a wide array of commercial banks, finance companies and institutional investors such as funds and CLOs.[3] This latter type of syndicate is often found in "leveraged" transactions[4] featuring both revolving and often sizable term loan facilities. In the years leading up to the credit crunch that commenced in the second half of 2007, large syndicates such as these became commonplace in leveraged transactions, as institutional investors readily deployed capital into syndicated term loans.[5] As institutional lenders are driven primarily by return on their investments, the expanded presence of such lenders in syndicated deals has given rise to a robust loan trading market, and has intensified the role of trade

---

3. CLO stands for "collateralized loan obligation" and refers to a special purpose bankruptcy-remote entity established to purchase loans from a bank and in turn issue securities backed by those loans. CLOs represented a significant portion of the institutional investor liquidity that fueled the financing boom witnessed between 2005 and 2007.

4. Though the term "leverage" can be used in a variety of ways with slightly different implications, leverage generally refers to the incurrence of a substantial amount of debt, which ends up translating to a riskier credit profile of the borrower. A common example of a leveraged financing is a leveraged buy-out (LBO) in which a target company incurs debt for the purpose of funding the acquisition of its own shares. The leveraged syndicated loan market typically refers to the segment of the syndicated loan market populated by less credit-worthy borrowers that are labeled as non-investment grade (referring to the credit rating assigned to a company or its debt by rating agencies such as Moody's Investors Service, Inc. (which defines non-investment grade as below Baa3) and Standard & Poor's Ratings Services (which defines non-investment grade as below BBB-)).

5. The slowdown in syndicated and other lending that began in the third quarter of 2007 is sometimes referred to as the "credit crunch." This credit crunch precipitated into a full-blown credit crisis in September 2008 in the wake of the Lehman Brothers bankruptcy filing. While the credit markets still face challenges and investor demand has hardly returned to pre-2007 levels, the credit markets began to show signs of thawing by the latter portion of 2009 and this trend has continued during the first half of 2010.

organizations such as the Loan Syndications and Trading Association (LSTA), which "promotes a fair, orderly and efficient corporate loan market and provides leadership in advancing the interests of all market participants" through the promulgation of standard market practices documentation.[6]

Syndicated loan facilities can reflect a variety of structural features, depending on the borrower's needs and credit position. Many include a revolving loan facility[7] that is available for working capital or general corporate purposes and/or a term loan facility that is available in one or more draws for a specific purpose (for example, to fund an acquisition). It is fairly common for the revolving facility to include subfacilities for letters of credit (bank guarantees of a borrower's payment obligations to third parties) and/or swingline loans (quick-access, short-term loans) that are fronted by one lender but risk participated to all lenders. That is, a portion of the aggregate revolving loan commitment can be utilized for certain extensions of credit that are made by one lender acting as the letter of credit issuing bank or swingline lender, as the case may be, but if the borrower fails to reimburse the fronting lender on time, all revolving lenders must fund their ratable share of the unreimbursed amount to the fronting lender.

Furthermore, syndicated loans can be denominated in U.S. dollars or foreign currencies and can be made available to U.S. or foreign borrowers, all of which dictates the composition of the lender group and, in some cases, necessitates the creation of additional sub-facilities to navigate currency and tax issues. In addition, syndicated loans can be secured or unsecured, and can be structured as asset-based loans (which make loans available based on the lesser of the commitment amount and a percentage of the value of certain of the borrower's assets having realizable collateral value) or cash-flow loans (which make loans available up to the commitment amount), all of which, when considered with other factors such as the purpose of the facility and the credit quality of the borrower, will influence what pricing and other terms are necessary or appropriate to attract lenders into the syndicate.

Certain Significant Issues in Syndicated Lending Transactions

Beyond the substantive facility terms (including prices and fees) that facilitate the syndication process, certain issues are either unique to syndicated deals or are featured more prominently in syndicated deals than in single-lender transactions. Perhaps the most fundamental concept to a multi-lender syndicate

---

6. *See* LTSA Home Page, http://www.lsta.org (last visited Aug. 9, 2010).

7. Note that the various facilities and subfacilities in a syndicated lending transaction (for example, a revolving facility, one or more term loan facilities, a multicurrency subfacility, etc.) are frequently referred to as "tranches" or "subtranches." In deals with multiple term loan tranches, each tranche may be assigned a letter designation. A "tranche A" term loan will be comprised of lenders whose identity is similar to lenders that participate in the revolver (i.e. more traditional lenders like commercial banks and finance companies). By contrast, a "tranche B" (or C, D, etc.) term loan will be funded largely by institutional investors. Among other possible differences, institutional term loans usually have slower amortization, a longer maturity, and higher pricing than tranche A term loans.

is that of voting rights. Whose approval is needed to amend or otherwise consent to a deviation from the original terms of, or to waive a default under, the facility? What percentage of lenders can direct the exercise of rights and remedies following a default? The answer to these and other similar questions will be found in the underlying loan documents and will differ depending on the nature of the issue, the size of the deal and other idiosyncrasies in the particular transaction. Many syndicated transactions will establish a minimum percentage threshold of commitments and loans necessary to effect most amendments, consents and waivers (for example, a simple majority of greater than 50%). The lenders whose commitments and loans satisfy such threshold are commonly referred to as the "Required Lenders." Certain other changes or consents are so basic that the administrative agent may be able to act to implement them alone, whereas others are so sacred to the lenders that they cannot be implemented without the consent of a supermajority of the lenders (for example, 66⅔% or 80%), a majority or supermajority of a class of lenders (for example, revolving or term) or 100% of the lenders or each lender *affected*, *directly affected* or *adversely affected* thereby.[8]

In larger deals where the borrower may not have as much control over the composition of the syndicate (see the assignment discussion below), the borrower strives to achieve as much flexibility as possible at the outset of the transaction so as to avoid the time-consuming and potentially costly process of seeking lender consent in the future.[9] However, it is often impossible to foresee precisely what type of flexibility may be desired at a transaction's inception.[10] It is worth noting that in addition to creating tension between lenders and borrowers, voting provisions can also give rise to intra-lender conflict, particularly in the context of a distressed credit where the interests of the lenders may not be aligned in connection with a proposed restructuring or remedial action and the stakes of action/inaction may be high.

---

8. With certain exceptions, a lender's consent is almost always required in order to increase or extend the maturity of its commitment, to postpone any date fixed for payment of obligations owing to that lender, or to reduce the amount of any obligations owing to that lender. The consent of all lenders is often required to modify the provisions providing for pro rata sharing of payments, to modify any provision specifying the number or percentage of lenders required to take action under the facility (including the definition of Required Lenders), or to release all or substantially all of the guarantees or collateral in a transaction.

9. In addition to having to reimburse the cost of preparing and administering an amendment, waiver or consent, a borrower may have to pay a fee to the approving lenders.

10. Several trends inspired by recent market conditions have necessitated intense scrutiny of voting provisions. One example is the "amend-and-extend" phenomenon, in which borrowers have sought non-pro rata extensions of the commitments and/or loans of consenting lenders in a tranche (often accompanied by increased pricing), while non-consenting lenders retain their existing maturity and pricing. This structure is one of several market responses to the "refinancing cliff" expected to occur between 2012 and 2014, when numerous leveraged loans that were issued in the years leading up to 2007 are set to mature in the face of a sharp decrease in the sources of market liquidity that financed the initial loans (namely, CLOs). Another such trend is allowing "debt buybacks" by borrowers who wish to repurchase their loans at a discount in the open market when those loans are trading below par. While a discussion of the specific issues associated with such transactions is beyond the scope of this overview, whether or not they can be accomplished with something less than unanimous consent is a question that needs to be analyzed under the voting provisions of the specific loan documents, and recently some syndicates have acknowledged these trends by adopting provisions in credit agreements that establish ground rules to enable such conduct in the future.

Another topic somewhat unique to syndicated deals that has regained prominence since late 2008 as a result of the Lehman Brothers bankruptcy filing is the notion of a defaulting lender. A lender will focus on what circumstances can cause that lender to be branded as a defaulting lender under a deal (for example, failure to fund its loans or participations in letters of credit and swingline loans, insolvency events, and in a number of cases, other potential indicators of default), and what the consequences should be (for example, loss of voting rights and fees). Credit agreements vary in their treatment of defaulting lenders and also as to the impact of a defaulting lender's presence on other lenders in the facility. A somewhat less controversial analogue to the defaulting lender dilemma is the "costly lender" scenario. As a general rule, the borrower is expected to indemnify members of the syndicate for taxes and other losses or costs suffered as a result of post-closing changes in law or circumstances. However, many credit agreements include a "yank-a-bank" provision that entitles the borrower to replace lenders who have suffered such costs (assuming the borrower can identify a suitable assignee). Similar provisions may also provide for replacement of lenders who do not consent to certain amendments or waivers to the credit facility.

While the topic of assignability is not limited to syndicated loan agreements, it does have special significance in syndicated transactions. On the one hand, there is a desire on the part of the borrower (as well as the administrative agent and lenders with fronting obligations) to retain some control over the composition of the lender group for a variety of reasons, including voting matters and risk exposure to the lenders. On the other hand, lenders often want or need to sell their positions, and, as alluded to above, there is a particular interest in promoting and preserving the liquidity of the institutional term loan market. Lenders also expect a fair amount of flexibility in being able to sell participation interests in the loans to persons who receive certain limited rights but do not actually become lenders under the Credit Agreement. In recent years, the LSTA has contributed to the standardization of both assignment and participation terms (including which parties have veto rights over new assignees), and the related trading documentation, by proposing model documentation that has been widely, though not universally, accepted in the syndicated loan market.

****

As the foregoing summary reveals, the procedural and substantive issues affecting syndicated lending arrangements will differ depending on the particular features of the underlying transaction, and it is difficult to summarize each and every one of the issues that may arise within a deal structure that can take so many variations and appears in so many segments of the market. Perhaps the one certainty is that syndicated lending in its many forms will continue to evolve in response to ever-changing market conditions and the available pool of willing market participants.

Allison J. Satyr
Partner
Sidley Austin LLP

3. Conditions to Closing (i.e., Lending)

As we have seen thus far and will see further in the context of mergers and acquisitions, agreements often contemplate a timeline of events. Commonly in lending and M&A transactions, the agreement will be structured around a "closing." That is, the parties may enter into the agreement before the agreement's critical event (e.g., the lending of money, the acquisition of a company) has occurred. The agreement is likely to state various representations, warranties, and covenants, some of which may apply as of signing, some of which may reapply at closing, some of which may apply from signing to closing, and some of which may even survive after the parties close. In addition, the agreement is likely to provide conditions that must be satisfied (strictly, if you recall from the discussion of conditions in the previous chapter) before a party is obligated to close. If such conditions are satisfied, the agreement generally obligates the parties to consummate the transaction, regardless of a change in preferences or an emergence of regrets since the time of contracting.

Notice that this Agreement does not speak in terms of a "closing," as there is not a single core transfer of funds to occur, but instead speaks in terms of lending "Advances." Section 1.2 defines Advances, providing that the Lender agrees to make Advances to the Borrower from time to time until April 30, 2006, unless the Agreement is terminated earlier due to an Event of Default (under § 5.1). Under the Agreement, Advances may not exceed the Commitment, which is defined in § 1.1 as $475,000. According to § 1.3, the Lender is obligated to make an Advance available to the Borrower, *if* both the Borrower provides proper notice and all of the applicable conditions set forth in Article II of the Agreement are satisfied.

Accordingly, before the Lender has any obligation to lend money (i.e., to make an Advance), the conditions of §§ 2.1 and 2.2 must be satisfied. Section 2.1 provides conditions that precede only the first Advance, whereas § 2.2 provides conditions that precede all Advances. According to § 2.1, the Lender's obligation to make the first Advance to the Borrower is conditioned on several events, including the Borrower's delivery of certain basic transaction documents. These include the Note and the Security, Pledge and Guaranty Agreement (hereinafter "SPG Agreement" and which we explore and discuss below). These also include certified copies of resolutions by the board of directors of the Borrower Parties (which, as defined, includes the Guarantor) approving each Loan Document and a certificate from the Secretary of each Borrower Party verifying that the signatories of the Loan Document are authorized to bind each Borrower Party. The certificate helps the Lender to mitigate the risk that a party purporting to bind a Borrower Party is not so authorized. Recall our discussion of agency and authority to bind a principal from Chapter 3. There, we saw a representation that a party had the authority to enter into an agreement. Such provisions may only provide a party with so much comfort: If the representation proves untrue, there may be a cause of action for misrepresentation against the representing party; however, the provision cannot work to cause an unauthorized "agent" to bind an innocent "principal." Here, however, the Lender has no obligation to transfer any monies without further assurances of the signatories' authorization and without each Borrower Party board indicating its assent to the terms, which itself may act to bind each respective Borrower Party.[7]

The Lender also has no obligation to make the initial Advance without first receiving a legal opinion from the Borrower Parties' legal counsel on matters the Lender may reasonably request. We delve a bit deeper into legal opinions later in this chapter. From the Borrower Parties' perspective, does this condition give the Lender too much discretion so that the Lender too easily may avoid making the initial Advance? Do any of the other conditions provide the Lender with too easy an "out" from making the initial or a subsequent Advance?

Subsections 2.1(f)-(h) address the Lender's potential concern regarding competing debts owed by the Borrower to third parties. Subsection 2.1(f) provides that, before the Lender has an obligation to make the initial Advance, either the Borrower Parties must owe no debt to BNS or the Borrower must use the initial Advance to pay off the debt to BNS directly and entirely. In addition, the Lender requires that the Borrower Parties show that they owe nothing to Chase, except for an amount (not to exceed $3,750,000) under the Chase Loan Agreements. Furthermore, the Borrower must deliver the Subordination Agreement as a condition of the initial Advance. Subordination agreements are between two or more of a debtor's creditors and state the rights of each creditor vis-à-vis each other as against the debtor. Here, the Subordination Agreement appears to subordinate the Lender's debt and liens to the Chase debt and liens. We discuss subordination agreements in greater detail later in this chapter.

Section 2.2 states the conditions that must be satisfied before the Lender is obligated to make any Advance, including the initial Advance, to the Borrower. Each Borrower Party to a Loan Document must certify that the representations and warranties of the Loan Agreement and the SPG Agreement are correct as of the date of the Advance, and the representations and warranties must actually be true. Importantly, this conditions the obligation to lend on the truth of the representations and warranties as of this later date.

In addition, recall the discussion in Chapter 3 of representations and warranties following *Ziff-Davis* and regarding *Galli*. Having a warranting party reaffirm the underlying truth of warranties made helps the party receiving the warranties show that she has not waived the warranties by closing (i.e., lending) with notice from the warranting party of the warranties' untruth. In addition, as we saw in Chapter 3, a party must show that she relied on the underlying truth of a representation in order to make out a claim for misrepresentation: A party's reaffirmation of a representation's truth prior to closing helps show that the

---

7. *See, e.g., Sea Lion Corp. v. Air Logistics of Ala., Inc.*, 787 P.2d 109, 118 (Alaska 1990) (holding company bound by contract notwithstanding agent's lack of authority to bind the company because board of directors ratified the contract); *see also* RICHARD A. LORD, 12 WILLISTON ON CONTRACTS § 20:38 (4th ed. 2010).

other party closed without knowledge of the representation's untruth and so in reliance on its truth.[8] Accordingly, the condition precedent of § 2.2(a)(i) helps preserve some of the Lender's rights under the representation and warranty provisions.

How does the condition stated in § 2.2(a)(ii) serve the interests of the Lender? Notice what kind of event would prevent the satisfaction of this condition as stated in § 2.2(a)(ii). Could the occurrence of an event that does not qualify as an Event of Default still allow the Lender to avoid its putative obligation to make an Advance?

4. Representations and Warranties of a Borrower

We have discussed at length the purpose and use of representations and warranties as contractual tools, namely for allocating the risk of the accuracy or inaccuracy of certain statements. Beyond understanding "reps and warranties" as tools in the abstract, the reader's task is to begin to appreciate how commercial parties may wish to employ these tools in various business contexts. To this end, we explore the representations and warranties of this chapter's Loan Agreement. Recall that, under § 2.2(a)(i), the correctness of the representations and warranties in the Loan Agreement (and in § 4.01 of the SPG Agreement) is a condition precedent to the Lender's obligation to make an Advance. And, under § 5.1(b), any material incorrectness of a representation or warranty, as of when the representation or warranty was made, constitutes an Event of Default, giving rise to the Lender's right to terminate its obligation to make Advances and the Lender's right to declare any outstanding principal and interest on the Note due and payable.

Notice that these representations and warranties are made by the Borrower Parties and not by the Lender—that is, they are not mutual nor reciprocal. Why do you think this is? What are the risks and concerns attendant to each party in this transaction for which representations and warranties may provide comfort?

a. Avoiding the Breach of Third-Party Contracts

In § 3.1(b), the Borrower Parties represent and warrant that the execution of the Loan Documents and the performance of the obligations thereunder will not cause any of several concerns. Beyond representing and warranting that the Transactions will not violate the Borrower Parties' governing corporate documents or any applicable laws, the Borrower Parties represent and warrant that the Transactions will not result in a breach, an event of default, or a termination right under a contract with a third party. Breaches of contract may be pricy, and

---

8. For a more in-depth discussion of these topics, please see the discussion in Chapter 3.

the Lender may wish not to lend money if so doing will cause the Borrower to incur such additional costs. In addition, the Lender may wish to avoid a claim that the Lender intentionally interfered with another contract by intentionally causing the Borrower to breach a contract with a third party.[9] Having the Borrower represent that the Lender is not causing the Borrower to breach third-party contracts helps the Lender to demonstrate that it did not have sufficient intent to have tortiously interfered with a third party's contract.[10] Furthermore, the Lender may want the Borrower to be in default on this Loan in the event that the Borrower is in default on any of its other loans with third parties. We discuss this further below in the context of an express "cross-default" provision. A cross-default clause provides that a borrower has defaulted on a loan upon defaulting on any of its other (or certain specified) loans. Why does § 3.1(b) not amount exactly to a cross-default provision? In other words, under § 3.1(b) and the provisions that it triggers (e.g., §§ 2.2(a)(i) & 5.1(b)), is the Borrower deemed to default under this Agreement for any default under another loan agreement occurring at any time throughout the term of the Agreement?[11]

b. Disclosing Financial Information; Accounting Terms

Under § 3.1(d)(ii), the Borrower Parties represent and warrant that the Financial Statements previously provided by the Borrower have been prepared in accordance with "GAAP." These Financial Statements include: the audited consolidated balance sheet of the Parent and its Subsidiaries as of May 27, 2000; the audited consolidated income statement and the statement of cash flows of the Parent and its Subsidiaries for the year ended May 27, 2000; the unaudited consolidated balance sheet of the Parent and its Subsidiaries as of February 27, 2001; and the unaudited consolidated income statement and the statement of cash flows of the Parent and its Subsidiaries for the year ended February 27, 2001. Notice that the Borrower Parties agree to provide additional financial statements into the future, in §§ 4.1(b)(i) and 4.1(b)(ii). Here we meet a bevy of new terms and concepts, which we walk through in turn.

"GAAP" (sometimes referred to as "U.S. GAAP") refers to "generally accepted accounting principles" in the United States. Under the Securities Exchange Act of 1934, the Securities and Exchange Commission ("SEC") has the authority to establish financial accounting and reporting standards to govern publicly held companies.[12] In turn, the SEC has delegated its authority to the Financial

---

9. Please see Chapter 1 for more on tortious interference with contract.

10. *See, e.g.*, RESTATEMENT (SECOND) OF TORTS § 767 (1979) (explaining that an "actor's motive" is one factor for determining tortious interference with contract); *see also generally Green v. Racing Ass'n of Cent. Iowa*, 713 N.W.2d 234, 244 (Iowa 2006); *Dykstra v. Page Holding Co.*, 766 N.W.2d 491, 499 (S.D. 2009).

11. For an example of a cross-default provision, see § 5.1(d) of the Agreement, and, for more on the topic, please see the relevant commentary later in this chapter.

12. *See* 15 U.S.C. § 78c(b) (2006).

Accounting Standards Board ("FASB"), a private organization, as the body responsible for promulgating accounting rules and standards.[13] In addition, the American Institute of Certified Public Accountants has recognized FASB and its accounting standards as authoritative.[14] That is, FASB determines the rules and standards that make up U.S. GAAP. Outside of the United States, the International Accounting Standards Board ("IASB") is the body in charge of promulgating the International Financial Reporting Standards ("IFRS"), which are the international analog to GAAP. As of this publication, FASB and the IASB are currently working to harmonize the two regimes—GAAP and IFRS—into a single set of global accounting standards.

The "balance sheet" is a financial statement that reflects a company's asset, liability, and stockholders' equity (or, just "equity") accounts as of a point in time; it is a "snapshot" of a company's financial position. Assets are those things a company owns that confer future benefit to the company (e.g., cash, inventory, equipment), liabilities are obligations the company owes to outsiders, and stockholders' equity is the residual value conceptualized to be owned by the stockholders. Equity is also known as "net assets" because a company's equity always equals its assets less its liabilities. The "income statement" reflects a company's net income—its revenues and gains minus its expenses and losses—over a period of time. The "statement of cash flows" reports how cash has moved in and out of a company over a period of time. For this reason, § 3.1(d)(i) refers to the balance sheets "as of" a certain date (i.e., the balance sheet is a "snapshot" statement) but refers to the income statements and the statements of cash flows "for the fiscal year then ended." Subsection 3.1(d)(i) also references "consolidated" financial statements. A consolidated statement of a parent company includes the financial information of the parent's subsidiaries (which, for consolidated statement purposes, are generally those companies in which the parent owns more than 50 percent of the voting stock), as if the subsidiaries and the parent company comprised a single company. A consolidat*ing* (as opposed to a consolidat*ed*) financial statement reports the information for the parent company's subsidiaries separately in addition to the total consolidated amounts.

c. Revealing Liabilities: Off-Balance-Sheet Liabilities and Litigation

Subsection 3.1(f) attempts to fill the gaps that § 3.1(d) may not adequately address. The Borrower Parties are required to produce financial statements current as of February 27, 2001, under § 3.1(d)(i)(B). Might the Lender be concerned that the Borrower Parties have debts or obligations beyond what is

---

13. SEC Statement of Policy Reaffirming the Status of the FASB as a Designated Private-Sector Standard Setter, 68 Fed. Reg. 23,333 (May 1, 2003).

14. *See* RULES OF PROF'L CONDUCT R. 203 (Am. Inst. of Certified Pub. Accountants 1979).

disclosed in their Financial Statements, as required by GAAP? Accordingly, the Borrower Parties represent and warrant in § 3.1(f) that they have not incurred any liabilities not reflected in their Financial Statements, except for certain liabilities (that might not terribly concern the Lender): (i) liabilities that the Borrower Parties have incurred as part of the ordinary course of business (consistent with the past incurrence of liabilities); and (ii) liabilities that, in the aggregate, are not material to the business or business prospects of any of the Borrower Parties.

In § 3.1(i), the Borrower Parties represent and warrant that to their Knowledge (query: How is Knowledge defined?) there is no pending or threatened litigation involving or affecting any of the Borrower Parties, *except* as set forth in a schedule attached to the Agreement. Additionally, the Borrower Parties represent and warrant that no litigation at all (whether set forth in the schedule or not) reasonably could be expected (i) to have a Material Adverse Effect (a defined term and a concept to which we return below) or (ii) to result in an encumbrance of any of the assets of the Borrower Parties. Notice the different layers of protection, then, afforded to the Lender by this subsection.

As an aside, § 3.1(j) provides that monies from the Advances will not be used for certain purposes. Is this provision a representation, a warranty, and/or a covenant? Which should it be, or does it not matter? Regulations T, U, and X of the Federal Reserve Board impose registration and other requirements and restrictions on persons who lend or borrow for the purpose of purchasing or carrying margin stock.[15] For the purpose of these regulations, margin stock includes stock registered on a national stock exchange (e.g., the New York Stock Exchange), stock traded "over the counter" (e.g., on the Nasdaq Stock Market's National Market), debt that may be converted into margin stock, and most mutual funds.[16] Subsection 3.1(j) states a representation and warranty that the Borrower will not use the borrowed funds in a way that triggers the requirements of these federal regulations. In addition, this subsection provides evidence that the Lender is not extending credit for the purpose of acquiring or carrying margin stock and that such Federal Reserve Board regulations (namely Regulation U, which applies to credit extended by persons other than brokers or dealers for the purpose of purchasing or carrying margin stock) do not apply.[17] As Regulation U explains:

---

15. *See* 12 C.F.R. parts 220, 221, 224 (2010).

16. *See id.* § 221.2.

17. *See, e.g., Amalgamated Bank of N.Y. v. Pa. Cos.*, No. CIV.A. 93-6703, 1995 WL 429130, at *2 n.2 (E.D. Pa. July 19, 1995) ("The elements of a Reg. U claim are as follows: 1) A bank must extend credit to the borrower for the purpose of buying and carrying registered securities; 2) *the bank knew the loan was made for such purposes*; 3) the loan was secured directly or indirectly by any stock; and 4) the loan was in excess of margin requirements.") (emphasis added) (citing *Freeman v. Marine Midland Bank-N.Y.*, 494 F.2d 1334, 1338 (2d Cir. 1974)); *see also Goldman v. Bank of Commonwealth*, 467 F.2d 439, 444 (6th Cir. 1972) (holding a lender may recover against a borrower for misrepresentation regarding the borrower's secret intention to use the borrowed money to purchase stock).

This part imposes credit restrictions upon persons other than brokers or dealers (hereinafter lenders) that extend credit for the purpose of buying or carrying margin stock if the credit is secured directly or indirectly by margin stock. . . . Lenders may not extend more than the maximum loan value of the collateral securing such credit, as set by the Board in § 221.7 (the Supplement).[18]

We return again to the topic of "use of proceeds" restrictions below in our discussion of loan covenants.

5. Covenants of a Borrower

We turn to the covenants made by the Borrower in this Agreement. Recall that covenants are the "action" components of any contract. As the Loan Agreement states each of the Borrower Parties' covenants either affirmatively or negatively and sorts them accordingly, we do the same. Affirmative covenants are promises to perform some act; they are promises to do. Negative covenants—of which the "restrictive covenants" we discussed in Chapters 1 and 2 are examples[19]—are promises *not* to perform some act; they are promises not to do.

a. Affirmative Covenants of the Borrower

What is the scope of the Borrower Parties' affirmative covenant obligations? The Borrower Parties need only perform the covenants of § 4.1 inasmuch as (1) any portion of the Note is unpaid; *or* (2) the Lender has any Commitment under the Agreement.

Drafting Note: Defining Terms for Use Throughout an Agreement

What is the definition of "Commitment"? Section 1.1 tells us that Commitment means "Four Hundred Seventy Five Thousand Dollars ($475,000.00)." One "rule-of-thumb" test for whether you are using a defined term properly in drafting a contract—or have defined a term properly for use throughout a contract—is to substitute its entire definition word for word and, then, to read the resulting sentence, asking whether it makes sense and whether it states the terms of the agreement as you intend them to read. Employing this test here with § 4.1 and "Commitment," we read that the Borrower Parties' affirmative obligations apply "[s]o long as . . . the Lender shall have any [Four Hundred Seventy

---

18. 12 C.F.R. § 221.1(b)(1).

19. The terms "restrictive covenant" and "negative covenant" are often used interchangeably. "Negative covenant" is the more generic of the two terms, whereas "restrictive covenant" is often used to refer to non-disclosure and non-competition covenants in addition to real covenants that restrict the use of real property.

Five Thousand Dollars ($475,000.00)] hereunder. . . ." Does this make any sense? Is this what the parties intended—that these covenants apply so long as the Lender has $475,000 under the Agreement? Presumably, this provision is intended to mean that these affirmative covenant obligations apply to the Borrower Parties so long as the Lender has an obligation to make all or any portion of the $475,000 credit facility available to the Borrower under the Agreement. How would you draft this provision differently?

(1) Compliance with Law

As the Borrower Parties represent and warrant under § 3.1(e) that they and their Subsidiaries[20] are in compliance with Applicable Law, the Borrower Parties covenant under § 4.1(a) that they will comply and cause their Subsidiaries to comply with Applicable Law. Is this "belts and suspenders," or does each provision do something that the other does not?

For one, § 3.1(e) states a representation and a warranty as of the effective date of the Agreement and does not create an ongoing obligation, whereas § 4.1(a) states a continuing obligation to perform going forward. (Note, however, that under § 2.2(a)(i) each Borrower Party must confirm that each representation and warranty in § 3.1 remains true before the Lender has an obligation to make an Advance.)

Secondly, as we have seen, the conditions precedent to the Lender's obligation to make any Advance under § 2.2 include that all representations and warranties made in § 3.1 are true as of the Advance and that no event that would amount to an Event of Default, if time were to elapse and/or proper notice given, is continuing as of the Advance. As we discuss in a moment, a failure to observe a covenant constitutes an Event of Default (under this Agreement) if gone uncured for ten days after the Lender provides notice. Accordingly, § 3.1(e) and § 4.1(a) seem to have similar effects under § 2.2 as conditions precedent to Advances.

Lastly, notice that an incorrect representation or warranty may constitute an Event of Default. Under § 5.1(b), a representation or warranty that is materially incorrect *when made* amounts to an Event of Default. In contrast, a failure of a Borrower Party to observe any term, covenant, or agreement in any Loan Document constitutes an Event of Default, if gone uncured for ten days after written notice is provided by the Lender. (Query how the Lender is to know that a Borrower Party has failed to comply with the law.) Under this Agreement, representations and warranties on the one hand and covenants on the other are treated differently in how they may give rise to the Lender's remedies, including the

---

20. Note how the Agreement defines "Subsidiary." A party may wish to restrict its representations and warranties regarding the conduct of another to those over which the representing party has control or otherwise the ability to ensure compliance with the representation and warranty.

Lender's right to terminate its obligation to make Advances and the Lender's right to accelerate payment of the Note (rights we discuss in greater detail below).

Because all of this may be confusing, we recap:

(1) the Lender need not make a particular Advance if:

> (a) any of the representations and warranties stated in the Agreement are inaccurate *as of the time of the would-be Advance*; or

> (b) any breach of covenant (i.e., an Event of Default or "unmatured" event of default) has occurred and is continuing *as of the time of the would-be Advance*;

(2) the Lender may terminate its overarching obligation to make any Advances and may accelerate any outstanding loans under the Agreement if:

> (a) any representation or warranty was materially incorrect *when made* (where each is made as of the Agreement and is required to be reasserted prior to the Lender's obligation to make any Advance); or

> (b) any covenant (or term or agreement) is breached and uncured for ten days following notice from the Lender (or any other Event of Default has occurred and is continuing);

(3) the Lender may recover any additional damages (if any are available) for misrepresentation or breach of warranty if a representation or warranty, respectively, is inaccurate and the other elements of each cause of action are proven (see Chapter 3); and

(4) the Lender may recover any additional damages (if any are available) for breach of contract if a Borrower Party breaches a covenant (or any other part of the contract).

(2) Reporting Requirements

We have discussed financial statements and the Borrower's reporting requirements in the representations and warranties section. Subsection 4.1(b) states the ongoing reporting obligations of the Borrower Parties. In other words, § 4.1(b) imposes a continuing duty on the Borrower Parties to communicate with the Lender. Subsection 4.1(b)(i) requires each Borrower Party to produce unaudited financial statements following each of the first three fiscal quarters, and § 4.1(b)(ii) requires the furnishing of annual reports, containing the financial statements for the fiscal year (i.e., following the fourth fiscal quarter). In addition to financial statements, the Borrower Parties must provide the Lender with a statement detailing any Event of Default or any occurrence that would amount to an Event of Default if time were to pass or proper notice given (e.g., a failure to perform a covenant does not amount to an Event of Default without the Lender providing written notice and the Borrower Party failing to cure). The

Borrower Parties must also provide the Lenders with copies of any report sent to shareholders (or bondholders) and any reports or registration statements filed with the SEC or a national securities exchange (e.g., the New York Stock Exchange). What else must the Borrower Parties communicate to the Lender? As the Lender, is there any other information you might wish to receive? Is there some information that would be more important for you to receive than others? Which information and why?

(3) Restricting Use of Loan Proceeds

Subsection 4.1(c) restricts how the Borrower Parties may use the proceeds of the Advances and imposes two covenants. First, § 4.1(c) provides that the Borrower Parties must use the Advance proceeds only for the repayment of debt or for "working capital" purposes. Working capital generally refers to the short-term assets and liabilities involved in a business's day-to-day ongoing operations. Accordingly, we might expect it to be okay for a Borrower Party to use the Advances to pay sales persons to sell jewelry or to purchase inventory but not okay to use the Advances to purchase a new store or new jewelry manufacturing equipment. Could the Borrower take out new loans from a third party to purchase new equipment such that the repayment of this new loan would constitute "repayment of indebtedness for borrowed money," which is a permissible use of proceeds? Is this a loophole? Does § 4.2(b) affect your answer?

Drafting Note: Consistency in Series

Notice that, while subsections (a) and (b) begin by neatly and properly following the "each of the Borrower Parties will . . ." text from the header in § 4.1, subsection (c) fails to do so. That is, § 4.1(c) technically states that "each of the Borrower Parties will . . . [t]he proceeds of the Advances shall be used. . . ." On the other hand, § 4.1(a) provides that "each of the Borrower Parties will . . . [c]omply, and cause each of its Subsidiaries to comply. . . ." With a "series" structure (like the one § 4.1 employs) with lead-in language that is to distribute to each subsection that follows, a drafter should be careful that each subsection dovetails properly and follows the syntax and format of the lead-in paragraph. Otherwise, a reader may be left with technically nonsensical language. While the reader may be able to figure out what the drafters were "going for," this is never a desirable scenario and may sometimes leave a contract subject to more than one plausible interpretation—that is, ambiguous.

Second, § 4.1(c) provides that the Borrower Parties may use no part of Advance proceeds for the purpose of purchasing or carrying any margin stock or for extending credit to others for such purpose. (In the context of the Borrower's representations and warranties above, we discussed briefly Regulations T, U, and X of the Federal Reserve Board. Please see that discussion for definitions and background and an overview of the purpose of the regulations.) While in the "affirmative covenant" section of the Agreement, is this covenant affirmative or negative?

Proving a breach of a covenant restricting the borrower's use of loan proceeds can be difficult. For instance, if the Borrower has several sources of cash inflows (e.g., from sales), how do we determine if the Borrower used sales-generated cash or loan-generated cash for a particular purpose? While perhaps an interesting philosophical question, this is a practical matter where a loan agreement, such as this Agreement, restricts the use of loan proceeds and where courts routinely enforce such restrictions.[21] If funds are commingled, courts will generally engage in methods of "tracing" in order to discern whether certain funds were used. A common method of tracing is the "lowest-intermediate-balance" rule, which looks to see if the balance of an account containing several sources of cash ever fell below the amount of the sum in question.[22] If the account in fact fell below this amount, then this sum must have been at least partially used. A borrower may wish to avoid confusion by keeping restricted loan proceeds in a separate account. Similarly, a lender may wish the borrower to covenant that loan proceeds will not be commingled with other monies such that commingling itself would constitute a breach.

b. Negative Covenants

Subsection 4.2 enumerates a host of behaviors the Borrower Parties are *not* to do and which the Borrower Parties are to cause their Subsidiaries not to do.

(1) Negative Pledges

[Note: Please see this chapter's discussion preceding and following the SPG Agreement below regarding security interests, perfection, and priority for some basic background information on these topics.]

As evidenced by § 6.1 of this Agreement, the loans made by the Lender to the Borrower and the liens granted by the Borrower in favor of the Lender are intended to be "subordinate" to the loans provided by Chase and the liens granted by the Borrower in favor of Chase pursuant to a separate lending transaction between Chase and the Borrower. This means that Chase has certain rights against the Borrower and the Borrower's assets that are superior to the rights of the Lender, including in the event that the Borrower defaults or declares bankruptcy. We discuss these rights in greater detail below in the context of security agreements and creditor remedies. While the Lender is

---

21. *See, e.g., Boatmen's Nat'l Bank of St. Louis v. Smith*, 835 F.2d 1200, 1202 (7th Cir. 1987) (Illinois law).

22. *See, e.g., C.O. Funk & Sons, Inc. v. Sullivan Equip., Inc.*, 431 N.E.2d 370, 372 (Ill. 1982) ("The rule, which operates on a common-sense view that dollars are fungible and cannot practically be earmarked in an account, provides a presumption that proceeds remain in the account as long as the account balance is equal to or greater than the amount of the proceeds deposited.").

willing to take a backseat to Chase, the Lender does not wish to be subordinate to other creditors. The Lender also does not want the Borrower to encumber its assets to secure debt owing to other creditors, regardless of the priority of those liens. One way to help prevent this from happening is to elicit a so-called "negative pledge" provision from the Borrower, an example of which is found in § 4.2(a) of the Agreement.

Negative pledges are covenants like any other. To act in contravention of a covenant is to breach the contract and may additionally trigger other provisions within the contract (e.g., § 5.1 of this Agreement). Here, § 4.2(a) prohibits the Borrower from granting or allowing to exist a "security interest" in or other encumbrances on any of its (or its Subsidiaries') assets to secure Debt (as defined in § 4.2(a)), save for several carved-out exceptions. These exceptions include: the liens that are to secure the loans contemplated by the Agreement (of course); the liens related to the Chase Loan Agreements (which is consistent with the Lender's contemplation that Chase will have a superior secured position vis-à-vis the Lender); the liens that are disclosed in an attached schedule; the existing liens on acquired property; and purchase money security interests. The first four carve-outs listed above are self- (or parenthetically) explanatory. A purchase money security interest (or a purchase money lien) refers to a security interest granted in an asset in order to secure financing for the purchase of *that* asset. For example, if a department store allows you to purchase a laundry machine by making several payments over time so long as you grant the department store a security interest in that laundry machine as collateral, then this security interest is a purchase money security interest or "PMSI." A party that holds a PMSI in an asset may enjoy certain superior rights (indeed, often called "super-priority" rights) in that asset as compared to other secured parties, if it has taken the requisite action under the U.C.C., even if another secured party "perfected" or "filed" first (as we discuss further below). Similarly, in § 4.2(b), the Borrower covenants not to incur any Debt, except for the Advances and the Chase Loan indebtedness, not to exceed a certain amount.

Negative pledges, however, are no substitute for perfecting a security interest in an asset. In this case, what may seem like half a dozen in the one hand and six in the other can have very different results. A negative pledge is a mere *promise* not to incur or permit to exist any other liens in an asset, whereas a holder of a security interest, if properly perfected, *has* superior rights vis-à-vis certain other secured parties. When is a negative pledge not adequate to protect a lender against superior claims against a borrower's collateral by third parties? For one, even a borrower with the best of intentions of honoring its contractual provisions may cause injury to a third party. Injured parties with a claim against the borrower are so-called "involuntary creditors" because, while they may not have negotiated and documented a creditor-debtor relationship with the borrower, such a relationship was thrust upon them. The borrower caused them injury and, as a result, may owe them money. Such parties may recover against the borrower's assets, despite that the borrower had previously signed an agreement with another creditor that contained a negative pledge. Secondly, imagining we have a not-so-noble borrower on our hands, the borrower may simply violate the negative pledge provision and grant a third party a security interest in the collateral. As discussed, this would amount to a breach of the contract and may entitle the lender to certain remedies; however, this does not nullify the transfer of the security interest to the third party.[23]

In addition, in bankruptcy, a secured creditor with a properly perfected security interest generally can recover on its claim against the bankruptcy estate before subordinate secured creditors (which we discuss further below in the context of priority and subordination agreements) and unsecured creditors.[24] A party who obtains a security interest in the debtor's assets and properly perfects this security interest may achieve secured-creditor status in bankruptcy.[25] As follows, a creditor does not achieve secured-party status in bankruptcy by virtue of a negative pledge.[26] In bankruptcy, such an unsecured party must get in line with the "riff raff" of other unsecured creditors and might only recover pennies on the dollar—if anything at all—on its claim. Negative pledges are covenants ubiquitously found in loan agreements, and they serve to provide a cause of action for breach of contract should the borrower run afoul; however, they do not serve the same ends as a perfected security interest.

On the history and purpose of a clause that is similar to a negative pledge in that, in both cases, the borrower makes certain promises concerning the preservation of the lender's rank and priority, we asked a seasoned practitioner to share his expertise on the "pari passu" clause.

A Practitioner Perspective: The "Pari Passu" Clause and Cross-Border Lending

The Clause

"The Notes rank, and will rank, *pari passu* in right of payment with all other present and future unsubordinated External Indebtedness of the Issuer."

---

23. *See* U.C.C. § 9-401(b) (2000) ("An agreement between the debtor and secured party which prohibits a transfer of the debtor's rights in collateral or makes the transfer a default does not prevent the transfer from taking effect.").

24. *See, e.g., In re Darnell*, 834 F.2d 1263, 1265 (6th Cir. 1987) ("[A]s a general rule, if a lien is perfected, it must be satisfied out of the asset(s) it encumbers before any proceeds of the asset(s) are available to unsecured claimants. . . .").

25. *See* 11 U.S.C. § 506 (2006).

26. *See* Carl S. Bjerre, *Secured Transactions Inside Out: Negative Pledge Covenants, Property and Perfection*, 84 CORNELL L. REV. 305, 312 (1999) ("The covenants usually confer on the negative pledgee nothing more than the rights to sue for damages and, assuming the loan agreement is correctly drafted, to accelerate the original debt.").

The Context

A *pari passu* (Latin for "in equal step") clause similar to the above text appears in most cross-border financial instruments, both loans and bonds. When used in an agreement with a corporate borrower, the clause is intended to assure the lender on two important points. First, that no class of senior lenders lurks somewhere in the company's capital structure waiting to uncloak itself once a bankruptcy proceeding starts. Second, that the borrower will not attempt in the future to bestow such senior status on any other lender.

But since the late 1970s, a version of the *pari passu* clause has also appeared in cross-border debt instruments issued by sovereign borrowers. Sovereign borrowers are not subject to domestic bankruptcy regimes so the fear of subordination in bankruptcy cannot have been the motivation for including such a clause in sovereign debt instruments. Although a few commentators had speculated over the years about what purpose the clause was intended to serve in the sovereign context, these were just conjectures. The truth is that the legal profession had for several decades been routinely including a standard clause in its financial contracts without remembering, in its collective consciousness, exactly why or how the provision had gotten there in the first place.

The Controversy

It was probably inevitable that the plaintiffs' bar would eventually try to exploit this instance of professional amnesia. In 2000, a New York hedge fund—a judgment creditor of the Republic of Peru—filed an *ex parte* motion in Belgium seeking to enjoin the Brussels-based Euroclear System from processing payments on certain Republic of Peru bonds. In support of this motion, the hedge fund offered an affidavit from a New York law professor stating that the *pari passu* clause in the debt instrument held by the hedge fund justified it in ensuring that no other creditor of Peru could be paid while the hedge fund's own claim remained unsatisfied. In effect, the professor opined, this clause required all creditors of a borrower to be paid ratably; none could be paid while others remained in default.

The Brussels lawsuit was quickly settled, but the "ratable payment" interpretation of the *pari passu* clause in a sovereign debt instrument sparked a major controversy. Among other problems with this theory (and there were many other problems), sovereign borrowers in financial distress had never behaved in this way. Some creditors (like the IMF), for example, were invariably paid while others (like banks, bondholders and government-to-government creditors) were routinely restructured. None of this was consistent with a ratable payment interpretation of the *pari passu* clause.

The Chase

Branding the ratable payment theory a fallacy, however, required an intensive search into the origins of the clause in sovereign debt instruments. The hunt for *pari passu* was on.

After several years of this chase, the clause was traced back to some syndicated loan agreements for the Republic of the Philippines circa 1979. The lending banks in those deals had discovered to their horror that under Philippine law one lender could elevate itself to a senior creditor status simply by registering its debt instrument with a special notary. In other words, an unwary creditor could find itself insensibly and involuntarily subordinated by an action of some other lender to the same borrower. A few other countries, it turned out, had similar legal mechanisms. The fear was that in a financial emergency, even a sovereign borrower might feel itself legally obliged to pay its senior creditors ahead of the subordinated variety. The *pari passu* representation and covenant was intended as the solution to this problem.

But while the motivation for including the clause in a sovereign debt instrument was eventually forgotten by practitioners and academics alike, the clause itself became embedded into a fossilized boilerplate.

> Lee C. Buchheit
> Partner
> Cleary Gottlieb Steen & Hamilton LLP

(2) Depletion or Distribution of Assets

The Lender is likely to be concerned that the Borrower may sell its assets and, thus, reduce the available collateral against which the Lender may recover if the Borrower cannot pay back its debt.

Subsection 4.2(d) of the Agreement in part looks to address this concern. The Lender ideally wants the Borrower to maximize the value of its collateral assets and surely would like to avoid the minimization of such value. However, the Lender also has an interest in the Borrower succeeding as an ongoing concern; the Borrower will be far better positioned to pay back its loan if the Borrower can operate its business profitably. Accordingly, the Lender has received a covenant from the Borrower not to sell, lease, or otherwise dispose of its assets, with certain exceptions to address the Lender's and the Borrower's mutual concern not to hamstring the Borrower's operations. These exceptions include that each of the Borrower Parties may: dispose of its inventory in the ordinary course of business consistent with past practice; dispose of used-up machinery and equipment; and lease property to third parties so long as such leases do not materially interfere with the business operations of the Borrower Parties. These exceptions reflect a balance struck by both parties: The business vitality of the Borrower likely turns on its selling inventory; used-up assets are presumably of no value to either of the Borrower Parties or the Lender, and any cash generated by their salvage sale may go toward otherwise operating the business; and leases that do not interfere in any material way with the business probably should not hamper—indeed, if the Borrower Parties are profit-maximizing, presumably should help—the Borrower Parties' profitable operations.[27] As the Borrower, what, if any, additional exceptions to this covenant might you like so that you may be free to operate your business as you see fit?

Subsections 4.2(f)-(i) of the Agreement address similar concerns. Subsections 4.2(f) and (g) restrict the distribution of assets to employees and to stockholders. Ideally, the Lender would like to keep all of the Borrower Parties' assets with the Borrower Parties. The more assets that are dispersed to third parties, the fewer assets from which the Lender may recover its loan. As follows, the Lender may be concerned with any out-of-the-ordinary payments to the Borrower Parties' employees. This may occur in a multitude of forms, including the payment of bonuses and the increase of salaries. In addition, the Lender may see dividends as another opportunity for cash to escape the Borrower Parties. In order to patch up this potential hole, § 4.2(g) provides that the Borrower Parties may not pay any dividends to any of its stockholders. Dividends refer to any distribution of assets from a company to its stockholders as an incident of holding a share of stock in the company. While cash dividends are the most common, dividends may involve the distribution of cash, other assets, additional shares of stock in the company, or any combination thereof. In addition, a company may buy some of its shares back from its stockholders. Repurchasing stock is distinct from paying a dividend, as the stockholder must give up certain shares in exchange for receiving cash (or other consideration). However, repurchasing stock may have the same effect as declaring and paying dividends. For example, imagine a company has a total of 10 shareholders, each with 10 shares in the company for a total of 100 shares outstanding. At this point in time, each shareholder holds a 10 percent stake in the company. If the company repurchases 5 shares from each shareholder for $10 per share, then the company will have paid out $50 to each shareholder ($10/share × 5 shares/shareholder) and will be left with 50 shares outstanding (5 shares/shareholder × 10 shareholders). As of *this* moment, each shareholder only has 5 shares; however, each shareholder has maintained its 10 percent stake in the company, as the total number of shares outstanding has grown proportionately smaller. Accordingly, the company effectively distributed $50 to each of its shareholders without reducing their individual stakes in the company—a "de facto" dividend. We can see that the Agreement anticipates this concern by providing that the Borrower Parties may not "purchase or retire, or otherwise acquire for value any of its capital stock now or hereafter outstanding."

Just as the Lender may be concerned with the Borrower's *disposing* of assets, the Lender may be concerned with the Borrower's *purchasing* of assets. In § 4.2(e), the Borrower Parties covenant not to acquire all or substantially all of the assets

---

27. Do note that like buyers in the ordinary course, lessees in the ordinary course also take free of a security interest in goods leased. U.C.C. § 9-321(c) (2000) ("A lessee in ordinary course of business takes its leasehold interest free of a security interest in the goods created by the lessor, even if the security interest is perfected and the lessee knows of its existence.").

of the business of any Person, and, in § 4.2(h), the Borrower Parties covenant not to make certain "capital expenditures." Capital expenditures ("CAPEX") refer to the purchase of long-term assets, which generally are to confer future benefit to the company for more than one year.[28] Examples include the purchase of machinery, equipment, buildings, or land. Here, the Borrower Parties have promised not to make any capital expenditures that exceed $75,000 per year; however, excepted from this restriction are those capital expenditures that are in the ordinary course of business as evidenced by past practice.

What does it mean for a transaction to occur in the "ordinary course of business"? As we have seen, parties may draw upon such language in drafting covenants limiting the borrower's behavior. Please consider the following case and what may qualify as a transaction occurring within or outside a borrower's "ordinary course of business."

Medigroup, Inc. v. Schildknecht
United States Court of Appeals, Seventh Circuit, 1972.
463 F.2d 525.

SPRECHER, Circuit Judge.

This diversity action is for damages for breach of warranty in connection with the sale of the stock of two corporations which owned and operated Parkview Manor, a nursing home in O'Fallon, Illinois.

During January, 1969, plaintiff's president negotiated with defendants for sale of the stock. Defendants furnished him the most recent balance sheets available, which listed each corporation's assets and liabilities as of November 30, 1968.

Plaintiff's offer of purchase contained the following language:

> It is understood that in accepting this offer you make the following warranties: . . .
>
> That balance sheets for both corporations as of November 30, 1968 being given the undersigned are true and correct, and that as of the time of closing there will have been no changes except in the ordinary course of business.

Defendants accepted the offer in writing on February 15, 1969. The closing took place on April 30, 1969.

Plaintiff's claim is based on the alleged omission or understatement of five debts of the Parkview Manor corporations on the November 30, 1968, balance sheets. Four of the obligations remain unpaid; the allegations of the complaint relating to them were dismissed without prejudice by the district court at the close of plaintiff's case. The fifth obligation, described in part II of this opinion, was paid with three checks by Parkview Manor in December, 1968, and January,

---

28. Generally, a long-term asset is an asset that is not expected to be used within one year or within the company's operating cycle, if the company's operating cycle is longer than one year. *See* WALTER T. HARRISON JR. ET AL., FINANCIAL ACCOUNTING 167 (8th ed. 2010).

1969. The allegation relating to the fifth debt was submitted to the jury, which returned a verdict in favor of defendants. Plaintiff appeals as to all debts. . . .

II

The fifth claim was for $40,000 paid to James Schmitt of the Mississippi Mortgage Co. as a fee for obtaining a commitment for a construction loan of $1,450,000. Schmitt began looking for a lender in March, 1968, but the letter of commitment was not written until December 20, 1968. By Schmitt's agreement with Parkview, he was not entitled to his fee until Parkview had received a letter of commitment. The $40,000 does not appear on the November 30, 1968, balance sheets, perhaps because the liability did not become definite until receipt of the letter of commitment the following month.

The jury found defendants not liable for this claim. Plaintiff raises two issues on appeal, both centering on defendants' warranty that the balance sheets were accurate and that there would be no changes before the closing "except in the ordinary course of business."

Since it is clear from the offer of purchase that plaintiff was aware of the loan commitment at the end of negotiations, the question arises whether the parties intended that transactions incidental to the loan be considered "in the ordinary course of business." Defendants introduced substantial testimony that plaintiff's officers were told about the finder's fee during the initial negotiations. They did not object to its payment nor to its omission from the balance sheets. Plaintiff objected to the admission of this testimony as parol evidence which varied the terms of the written contract.

The validity of plaintiff's objection depends on whether the phrase, "in the ordinary course of business," is ambiguous. If it is, parol evidence is admissible to establish the practical interpretation of the parties. Parol evidence has been admitted to interpret such phrases as "[changes] resulting from normal station operations" and "good will."

If a buyer did not know the selling corporation had made arrangements to construct a large addition to its plant, "the ordinary course of business" might refer to such transactions as billing customers and purchasing supplies. But a buyer aware of expansion plans would intend "the ordinary course of business" to include whatever transactions are normally incurred in effectuating such plans. Therefore it was proper for the district judge to admit testimony about the parties' discussions of the construction loan and the finder's fee.

The cases plaintiff relies on are instances of the exclusion of parol evidence which would change or contradict the terms of the written contract. They do not govern here, because admission of the negotiation discussions merely gives definition and context to the ambiguous phrase, "in the ordinary course of business."

Plaintiff's second allegation of error is an attack on two instructions given to the jury. The first was a definition of "ordinary course of business" as "that course of conduct that reasonable prudent men would use in conducting business affairs as they may occur from day to day." Plaintiff also claims the following instruction was incorrect:

> In determining whether a given transaction is made in the ordinary and usual course of business of a party, the question is not whether such transactions are usual in the general conduct of business throughout the community, but whether they are according to the usual course of business of the particular person whose transaction is subject to investigation.

Plaintiff's objection to the first instruction is that the district judge either should have refused to define "ordinary course of business" or should have instructed the jury that the payment of a finder's fee for a large loan commitment was such an unusual transaction that it could not have occurred "in the ordinary course of business." Plaintiff has not shown that the definition given varies in any important element from the definitions it cites. Its real complaint seems to be that the district judge did not direct a verdict against defendants on this aspect of the case. Under the unusual circumstances, however, it was proper to let the jury decide, whether the parties intended that defendants should continue to take whatever steps were proper and necessary to further the construction project.

. . . [T]he instruction is consistent with our analysis of "ordinary course of business" above; defendants cite authority for it; and it is difficult to see how the jury's conclusion would have been altered by focusing on the general business community rather than on the particular business. . . .

Comments

In light of the reasoning in this case, how might you advise a client about the use of "in the ordinary course of business" language in a contract? Does the phrase create unnecessary or undesirable ambiguity, or is the phrase useful for its flexibility? In what ways might you, as drafter, be able to enhance the clarity of the phrase? From the perspective of the party restricted to activity within the ordinary course of business, how might you draft to address concerns that certain activities might be found to be outside the ordinary course of your business?

---

(3) Financial Covenants

A lending agreement sometimes will contain covenants—either stated affirmatively or negatively—that a borrower will maintain certain financial positions, often expressed as ratios. These covenants frequently draw upon the language of accounting and GAAP concepts. Financial covenants act as proxies, signaling whether the borrower is financially healthy and likely to be able to pay its debts. For example, a loan agreement may contain a covenant that a borrower's "retained earnings" or "current ratio" will never fall below a certain amount (or will always be above a certain amount). As a general matter, retained earnings refers to the amount of net income a company has earned since the company's inception, minus any dividends the company has declared. In other words, retained earnings captures a company's accumulated net income that the company has retained and not paid out as dividends over the years. The "current ratio" is one of a myriad financial ratios used to measure company performance and solvency. The current ratio is a company's current assets divided by the company's current liabilities. Generally, current assets are those assets to be used or converted to cash within one year, and current liabilities are those liabilities due within one year. The current ratio, then, attempts to get at a company's ability to pay its debts as they come due, measuring a company's relatively liquid assets against the company's soon-to-be-due debts.

In addition, financial covenants commonly refer to a creature called "EBITDA." EBITDA is an acronym for earnings before interest, taxes, depreciation, and amortization. EBITDA is basically used as a substitute for "net income" (another term for "earnings"), as some feel that EBITDA is a more accurate or, under certain circumstances, relevant indicator of company performance. Net income is literally the "bottom line" of an income statement and is a measure of a company's financial performance for a given period. Net income is a company's revenues (and any gains) minus its expenses (and any losses). Under GAAP, expenses include many things, including our expenses of the moment: interest expense, tax expense, depreciation expense, and amortization expense. Interest expense and tax expense are perhaps self-explanatory; they are the expenses associated with the interest owed on debt obligations and the taxes owed on income.

Depreciation and amortization expenses perhaps require further explanation. Most large companies own certain assets called "plant assets" (also called "property, plant, and equipment" or "PPE," for short), which are long-term tangible assets. Examples of PPE include land, buildings, furniture, equipment, and machinery. Most PPE will decline in usefulness to the company over time, and the PPE will eventually be salvaged or scrapped. Accordingly, GAAP requires that a company record a periodic expense to reflect the use of a plant asset—with the exception of land—over its useful life. In other words, instead of expensing the entire price of an asset upon purchase, a company spreads the cost of the asset (minus any salvage value) across the useful life of this asset. This expense is called "depreciation" expense. Like many expenses, depreciation expense has nothing to do with the use of cash in a given year. A company generally has discretion in computing its annual depreciation expense, as it must choose one of several depreciation methods (e.g., straight-line, accelerated) and must make several assumptions, including the length of an asset's useful life and the asset's market value at the end of this useful life. For these reasons, some feel that depreciation is subject to manipulation in a problematic way and prefer EBITDA to net income. Quite similar to the depreciation of PPE, "amortization" spreads the cost of certain *intangible* assets (e.g., copyrights, patents) over their useful lives.

Some also feel that EBITDA captures the cash flow of a company; however, under GAAP, the earnings of a company (the "E" in EBITDA) are recorded on an "accrual" basis (as opposed to a cash basis), to which the cash flow of a company is essentially irrelevant. Adding back these certain expenses does not fairly reconcile an accrual-basis net income with a cash-basis one.

In order to understand and appreciate the implications of a financial covenant, one must understand the covenant's meaning and also how onerous or realistic the covenant is for the particular borrower to satisfy. A prudent party will define exactly what is meant by a particular ratio or term used in its financial covenants so as to avoid any doubt or ambiguity regarding the intended meaning. What might constitute a "reasonable" or a "good" ratio or financial position varies from industry to industry and company to company, and, so, one must consider the particulars of a borrower before calibrating certain financial covenants.

Note that the Loan Agreement in this chapter does not contain a financial covenant. Accordingly, for illustration we reproduce a sample provision, excerpted from a $6,000,000 term loan agreement between a bank and a corporation.

SECTION 5 FINANCIAL COVENANTS[29]

The Borrower covenants and agrees that from the date hereof until payment in full of all indebtedness and the performance of all obligations under the Loan Documents, the Borrower shall at all times maintain the following financial covenants and ratios all in accordance with GAAP unless otherwise specified:

Minimum Tangible Net Worth. A minimum tangible net worth of not less than $6,000,000.00 as of December 31, 2005, and increasing annually by 50% of all net income, plus 100% of all new equity, minus $0 for net losses. Tangible Net Worth is defined as net worth, plus obligations contractually subordinated to debts owed to Bank, minus goodwill, contract rights, and assets representing claims on stockholders or affiliated entities.

EBITDA Ratio. Ratio of EBITDA to the preceding twelve months interest expense plus the projected maturities of long-term debt for the next succeeding twelve months on a rolling basis, of not less than 1.25:1.00, to be measured annually.

Debt/Tangible Net Worth. Maximum of 4.00: 1.00, to be measured annually.

---

29. Industrial Services of America, Inc., Loan Agreement (Form 8-K), at Exhibit 10.1 (May 22, 2008), *available at* http://www.sec.gov/Archives/edgar/data/4187/000089230308000045/isa8kex10_1.htm.

(4) Change in Ownership and Business

Much of a lender's appetite for a loan transaction turns on the specific borrower with whom the lender expects to do business. The Lender presumably has done its due diligence and has familiarized itself with the business operations and credit history of the Borrower and has priced the riskiness of lending to the Borrower into the deal. The Lender, then, presumably has entered into this Agreement with the expectation that the Borrower will be the party drawing and paying Advances—and not some unknown third party or reconstituted entity hardly resembling the Borrower whom the Lender had grown to know and perhaps trust. We can see evidence of these concerns of the Lender in §§ 4.2(e) and 4.2(j)-(l).

Subsections 4.2(e) and 4.2(j)-(k) address the issue of "change in control." Under § 4.2(e), each Borrower Party may not merge with a third party or sell substantially all of its assets to a third party. Subsection 4.2(j) speaks to issues of control by restricting the right of each Borrower Party to alter its equity capital structure. State law generally restricts the shares of stock a corporation may issue to the number authorized by the corporation's articles of incorporation—the corporation's "authorized shares."[30] In order to issue more than the number of shares currently authorized by its articles, a corporation must amend its articles to authorize more shares to be issued, an act that generally requires stockholder approval. The holders of outstanding stock have certain abilities to exercise control of a corporation—for example, electing members of the board and approving fundamental transactions.[31] Accordingly, the issuance of additional shares and the alteration of voting rights can affect how a corporation is governed and controlled. For this reason, the Lender in § 4.2(j) restricts the Borrower Parties from changing the number of authorized shares and restricts each Borrower Party from otherwise altering the rights and abilities of its current stockholders to control the company.

In addition to § 4.2(j), which restricts each Borrower Party from altering the rights of current stockholders to control the Borrower Party, and to § 4.2(e), which restricts each Borrower Party from engaging in merger activity, § 4.2(k) restricts each Borrower Party from allowing a third party to acquire control of the Borrower Party's stock (or other means of controlling the Borrower Party). Under § 4.2(k), each Borrower Party may not allow an entity to obtain a majority of the Borrower Party's shares or the power to control the Borrower Party, without the consent of the Lender. An entity may obtain "control" of a Borrower Party without obtaining a majority of the Borrower Party's shares. As § 4.2(k) contemplates, control involves the power to direct the management of a Borrower Party, which may be achieved by contract or through acquisition of less

---

30. *See, e.g.*, DEL. CODE ANN. tit. 8, § 151 (1998); MODEL BUSINESS CORPORATION ACT § 6.01 (2002).

31. *See, e.g.*, DEL. CODE ANN. tit. 8, §§ 141, 242, 251 (2010); DEL. CODE ANN. tit. 8, § 211 (2009); MODEL BUSINESS CORPORATION ACT §§ 7.21, 7.28, 11.04 (2002).

than a majority of the company's voting shares. For instance, if the ownership of a company is diffusely spread across several shareholders, one person's acquisition of a minority bloc of the company's voting stock may be enough to control the company's management. As we discuss further in Chapter 6, where we discuss the various forms of mergers and acquisitions, a statutory merger, a purchase of substantially all of a company's assets, and the acquisition of a controlling stake of a company's stock are all methods of merging with or acquiring a company. In order to restrict a Borrower Party's right to combine with, or be acquired by, another company, then, the Lender must anticipate all such potential forms of business combination. Such change-of-control (or "fundamental change") covenants are commonly found in lending and other commercial agreements, and courts generally have enforced them.[32]

Notice that § 4.2(e) expresses a concern not only with a third party acquiring a Borrower Party's operations but also with a Borrower Party acquiring a third party's operations. Similarly, § 4.2(l) reflects a concern that each Borrower Party not change its business or engage in a line of business not related to the Borrower Party's business as of the Agreement. Again, the Lender presumably wishes to loan money to the Borrower at the interest rate and the other terms provided by the Agreement, given the Borrower's current character and operations. The alteration of the Borrower's business might yield a company to which the Lender is less eager to lend money—at least on the terms provided in the Agreement. Accordingly, the Lender has obtained a covenant from the Borrower not to change the conduct of its business operations in a meaningful way throughout the term of the Agreement. Similarly, the Lender has agreed to lend money to the Borrower as currently constituted—and not as constituted after having acquired substantially all of the assets of a third-party entity. Acquiring "substantially all of the assets" generally involves the acquisition of an additional line of business or a sizeable expansion of a current line.[33] Integrating a separate company can be costly—at least early on—and detract from a company's current operations and profitability. Accordingly, the Lender has obtained a covenant from each of the Borrower Parties to stay basically as it is and not to acquire third-party operations.

6. Events of Default and (Some of) Seller's Remedies Upon Default

Under a loan agreement, a default generally refers to a contractually specified event that generally gives the Lender certain specified remedies. A basic example of a default is the failure of a borrower to pay according to an agreement's terms.

---

32. *See, e.g., MJCM, L.L.C. v. United Cmty. Banks, Inc.*, 212 F. App'x 323, 325 (5th Cir. 2007) (Texas law).
33. We discuss the legal definition of this phrase and its implications in Chapter 6.

The term "default," in the context of a loan agreement, can be both broader and narrower than "breach," as under a loan agreement it may be the case (i) that only certain breaches rise to the level of a default (e.g., uncured, material breaches) and/or (ii) that certain non-breach events rise to the level of a default (e.g., default under a third-party loan agreement). As previewed throughout this chapter, § 5.1 defines what events amount to "Events of Default" under the Loan Agreement and provides the Lender with certain recourse in the event of such an event. As § 7.2 makes clear, the remedies provided to the Lender upon an Event of Default are "cumulative" and not "exclusive." As we have learned through our previous encounters with exclusive remedies, contractual parties may provide that certain remedies are the exclusive recourse of an aggrieved party under the contract. In general, courts will honor these provisions and limit a party to its bargained-for exclusive remedies.[34] In the absence of a provision affirmatively stating that a remedy is exclusive, a court will try to discern the parties' intent with regard to whether the provision is exclusive or cumulative.[35] Accordingly, a prudent party wanting contractually specified remedies to be cumulative or exclusive will clearly and expressly state as much in her contract.[36] With this in mind, we turn to what constitutes an Event of Default under the Agreement and (some of) the Lender's rights upon such an Event of Default.

a. Events of Default

The following are several of the Events of Default provided and defined by § 5.1 of the Loan Agreement. As you review these Events of Default, consider whether you would define any of these events any differently and/or negotiate for any additional or fewer events, adopting the perspective of each of the Lender and the Borrower.

(1) Defaulting on the Note; Payment Default

In its most basic form, a loan agreement involves a lender's promise to transfer money to a borrower in exchange for the borrower's promise to pay that money back, plus an additional amount of interest. As we might expect, then,

---

34. *See, e.g., Price Dev. Co. v. Redevelopment Agency of Chino, Cal.*, 852. F.2d 1123, 1127 (9th Cir. 1988) (California law) ("A clear and unambiguous contractual provision providing an exclusive remedy for breach will be enforced."). However, we have also seen that at least in the context of Article 2 transactions, courts will sometimes cast aside an exclusive remedy provision and make all potential remedies available, where an exclusive remedy fails of its essential purpose. Please see Chapter 3 for further discussion of this doctrine.

35. *See, e.g., Intrastate Piping & Controls, Inc. v. Robert-James Sales, Inc.*, 733 N.E.2d 718, 725 (Ill. App. Ct. 2000) ("Illinois courts have recognized and enforced exclusive remedy provisions, even without the word 'exclusive,' when the contract as a whole warrants such a construction."); *see also* U.C.C. § 2-719(1)(b) (2003) ("[R]esort to a remedy as provided is optional unless the remedy is expressly agreed to be exclusive, in which case it is the sole remedy.").

36. *See, e.g., In re Homeowners Mortg. & Equity, Inc.*, 354 F.3d 372, 374-75 (5th Cir. 2003) (Texas law) ("This provision is non-exclusive, because it provides that Fannie Mae can 'also enforce any other available remedy.' ").

§ 5.1(a) provides that the failure of the Borrower to make a payment in accordance with the terms of the Note amounts to an Event of Default under the Agreement. This is the most basic way to default under any loan agreement. Oftentimes payment default will extend to a failure to pay fees, expenses, and other amounts due under a loan agreement, usually with some grace period allowed for these types of delayed payment.

(2) Incorrect Representation or Warranty

As we have seen, § 5.1(b) provides that if a representation or warranty made by any Borrower Party under—or in connection with—any Loan Document proves to be false in any material respect when made, then an Event of Default will have occurred. There is much to unpack in this sentence. First, note that the provision does not explicitly reference § 3.1 of the Agreement or the representations and warranties made therein. Rather, the provision speaks to *any* representation or warranty made by *any* Borrower Party or *any* of its officers not only within the Loan Documents but also "in connection" with any Loan Document. On its face, then, the provision is quite broad and includes representations and warranties made outside (but still in connection with, e.g., in a closing certificate) the Loan Documents. While broad in this respect, the language of § 5.1(b) is also narrow in that it only applies to representations and warranties that were incorrect *when they were made*. So, for instance, a warranty that the Borrower is validly organized and in good standing that was true when it was made but later becomes false—say, because the Borrower does not pay its annual dues to its state of incorporation—would not be an Event of Default under § 5.1(b) according to its language. Recall, when are representations and warranties "made" as contemplated by this Agreement?

(3) Failure of Covenant

Likewise, § 5.1(c) provides that the failure of a Borrower Party to perform or to observe a term of the Loan Documents constitutes an Event of Default, *if* the Lender has given the Borrower Party notice of the failure and the Borrower Party has not cured the failure within ten days of the written notice. A contract may define what is required for a party to have "cured" a breach or failure; otherwise, a court may find that a party has "cured" by substantially performing the obligation owed within the cure period.[37] For this reason, if they intend as much, parties may wish to define "cure" to require—in addition to mere performance of the unperformed promise—that the curing party compensate the other for *any loss* resulting from the delay in performance. Even failing this, while

---

37. *See, e.g., Volvo Trucks N. Am. v. State Dep't of Transp.*, 779 N.W.2d 423, 433 (Wis. 2010) (to "cure" under contract law generally does not require "restoration to the *status quo ante* or repair of all harm done by the breach"); *Anacapa Tech., Inc. v. ADC Telecomm., Inc.*, 241 F. Supp. 2d 1016, 1020-21 (D. Minn. 2002)). *But see* Uniform Computer Information Transactions Act § 703 cmt. 5 ("Cure requires a party to perform the contract obligation and to compensate fully for loss.").

a party may have "cured" a defect within the meaning of a contract, the other party may generally still sue for any resulting damages, for instance, for losses incurred due to a delayed performance, unless the contract provides otherwise.[38] For example, a contract might "provide otherwise" by providing that a "breach" only occurs when a party fails to cure, with the result being that a cured performance of the contract is no breach at all under the contract.[39] In other words, by defining "breach" as an uncured failure to perform, a party may only sue for damages for breach of contract when a failure to perform goes uncured (which might only require performance within the specified cure period) and cannot recover damages that result from delayed, but cured performance because there has been no breach of the agreement. Under the Agreement here, a Borrower that cures a failure to perform under the Agreement may avoid giving rise to an Event of Default under § 5.1(c); however, the Borrower will still have breached the Agreement by its initial failure to perform according to the terms of the Agreement.

What right does the Lender have to terminate its obligations under the Loan Agreement and to declare the Note immediately due if the Lender does not provide written notice of such a Default? Do you suppose that the Lender will always be in a position to know of a failure of a Borrower Party to perform an obligation of the Agreement? What incentives does this create for the Borrower Parties? Under this arrangement, is a Borrower Party likely to act forthright if it has knowledge of a failure of covenant?

(4) Cross-Default Provisions

As provided in § 5.1(a) and discussed above, you might expect that if anything were to be considered an event of default in a loan agreement, it would be the failure to pay back a loan as required by the agreement. However, oftentimes a loan agreement will not stop there. It is common for a loan agreement to provide that a default under any *other* loan agreement—or certain other loan agreements as specified—also constitutes a default under the loan agreement. As we touched on earlier and as seen in § 5.1(d) of the Agreement, this is commonly called a "cross-default" provision. (A "cross-acceleration" provision is quite similar, triggering default under an agreement when a creditor under another agreement *actually* accelerates payment.[40] This is distinct from a cross-default

---

38. *See, e.g., Allan Block Corp. v. Cnty. Materials Corp.*, 512 F.3d 912, 919 (7th Cir. 2008) ("[Under the parties' contract, a] declaration of default is a condition precedent not to suing for a breach of contract but to being authorized to terminate the contract immediately without liability to the other party."); *Volvo*, 779 N.W.2d at 433 n.27 ("In certain circumstances, contract law may provide that the non-breaching party recovers damages from the breaching party to repair past harm.") (citing RESTATEMENT (SECOND) OF CONTRACTS § 237 cmt. b (1981)).

39. *See, e.g., Hypergraphics Press, Inc. v. Cengage Learning, Inc.*, No. 08 C 5102, 2009 WL 972823, at *3 (N.D. Ill. Apr. 8, 2009) ("[I]n order for notice and opportunity to cure to be a condition precedent to filing suit on the claim, the contract must so state. Other parties have done so successfully by defining, within the contract, a 'breach' as occurring only after notice and opportunity to cure.").

40. *See* LEE C. BUCHHEIT, HOW TO NEGOTIATE EUROCURRENCY LOAN AGREEMENTS 102 (2d ed. 2006).

provision, which triggers default under an agreement when a creditor under another agreement *may* accelerate payment (presuming that this remedy is available).[41] In other words, a cross-default clause turns upon a default under another loan, and a cross-acceleration clause turns upon the exercise of an acceleration remedy following a default under another loan.) Because cross-default provisions are common across loan agreements, the default of a debtor under one of its loan agreements may have a domino effect, as an initial default cascades into default after default under several of the debtor's other loan agreements.

Why do lenders insist on the inclusion of cross-default provisions? A lender whose borrower has defaulted on its loan is likely to have rights to immediate payment of the loan and any outstanding principal and may have additional remedies if the loan is secured (as we discuss below). In addition, a borrower that is not paying one of its loans as payments come due may have limited resources. That is, the debtor might be unable to pay back all of its debts to all of its creditors. No lender wants to get left out in the cold with a claim against a debtor already picked clean by other creditors with earlier accruing claims. By including a cross-default provision in its lending agreement with a debtor, a lender helps ensure that it will have a claim against the debtor contemporaneously with any other of the debtor's lenders and can look to enforce its rights against the debtor alongside these other creditors (i.e., the lender will have a "seat at the table") with an accrued claim, outside or inside bankruptcy. The question then becomes who gets to take what and when, as among a debtor's various creditors with claims of default. With respect to competing secured creditors, the first to perfect (e.g., file) its security interest generally has priority, with certain exceptions. As between a secured creditor and an unsecured creditor, the secured creditor will generally have priority. Outside of bankruptcy, as between unsecured creditors, it may become a race to the courthouse, as the first to reduce the default to a judgment may have the first right to recover from the debtor's assets.[42]

b. Lender's Rights upon Event of Default

If any Event of Default occurs, § 5.1 provides the Lender with two rights. Under § 7.2, as we have seen, the Lender's rights upon an Event of Default are cumulative and not exclusive. Accordingly, the Lender may have other rights in addition to the two provided by § 5.1, some of which we discuss further in the discussion of secured creditor remedies following the SPG Agreement below. The Lender's rights under § 5.1 include that: (1) the Lender may terminate its obligations to make Advances to the Borrower by giving notice to the Borrower;

---

41. *Id.*
42. *See, e.g.,* 735 Ill. Comp. Stat. 5/12-136 (2008); N.Y. C.P.L.R. § 5234 (McKinney 2008).

and (2) the Lender may make all outstanding principal and interest due immediately by providing the Borrower with notice. The right to terminate obligations is a familiar one we have seen throughout this book. However, this is our first encounter with the Lender's latter right—the right to "accelerate" payment. Lenders commonly reserve the right to accelerate payment in the event of a borrower's default under a loan. Notice that acceleration makes immediately due any remaining amount of principal and any unpaid interest that has accrued over time until the present—but does not include any unearned interest that would be earned under the loan into the future. Why is acceleration limited in this way? Recall the discussion of liquidated damages in Chapter 1. "Penalties" are not enforceable, and courts generally regard the acceleration of unearned interest as an unenforceable penalty.[43]

In addition, loan agreements will sometimes give the lender the right to continue the loan upon an event of default but at an increased interest rate. This post-default rate is typically called a "default rate" and the interest, "default interest." Whether a court will enforce the increased default rate generally turns on whether the default rate amounts to a penalty. Courts have found a default rate enforceable, for instance, where the increased rate reflected losses incurred as a result of the default,[44] and where the increased rate reflected the increased risk of lending to a borrower who has defaulted.[45] In addition, as with any interest rate, the default rate generally must not be usurious—that is, exceed the maximum rate allowed—under state law. The effect of a loan being found usurious depends on the state, as (i) some states require the borrower to pay the loan at the legal interest rate but allow the borrower to avoid paying the excess above the legal maximum, (ii) others require the borrower to pay only the principal back with no interest, while (iii) a handful relieve the borrower of having to repay anything at all.[46] Whether a state's usury statute restricts the interest chargeable on a particular type of loan depends on the statute.[47]

The flipside of acceleration is prepayment. While a *lender* may have the right to demand payment of a note before its original maturity date, a *borrower* may have the right to pay off the note prematurely. Why would a borrower want to do

---

43. *See, e.g., Justine Realty Co. v. Am. Nat'l Can Co.*, 976 F.2d 385, 389-90 (8th Cir. 1992) (noting that under Illinois law, an acceleration clause that makes unearned interest due operates as a penalty).

44. *See, e.g., GFL Advantage Fund, Ltd. v. Colkitt*, 272 F.3d 189, 216 (3d Cir. 2001) (Pennsylvania law) ("In contrast, the 'default interest' is intended to compensate GFL for damages it incurred since Colkitt's breach—namely, the deprivation of its money over the past four and a half years."). By statute, Ohio has provided that default rates are not penalties and are enforceable so long as they do not exceed the maximum set by the state usury statute. *See LTV Corp. v. Gulf States Steel, Inc. of Ala.*, 969 F.2d 1050, 1063 (D.C. Cir. 1992) ("A special default rate of interest is permitted under Ohio law.") (citing Ohio Rev. Code. Ann. § 1343.03(A) (Anderson Supp. 1991)).

45. *See, e.g., Citibank, N.A. v. Nyland (CF8) Ltd.*, 878 F.2d 620, 625 (2d Cir. 1989) ("The default rate was simply part of Nyland's bargain.").

46. *See* Richard A. Lord, 9 Williston on Contracts § 20:38 (4th ed. 2009).

47. *See, e.g., Whirlpool Fin. Corp. v. Sevaux*, 96 F.3d 216, 227 (7th Cir. 1996) (explaining that Illinois usury statute left the interest rates on "business loans" uncapped) (citing 815 Ill. Comp. Stat. Ann. 205/4(1)(c)) (2007).

this? The circumstances that caused a borrower to take out a loan may change. The borrower may have become flush in cash and no longer have the need to pay for capital. Or, the borrower may be able to borrow more cheaply on the market than under the particular loan. A common example of this is when a homeowner "refinances" her home loan by borrowing money at a lower rate and using that money to pay off the original loan obligation. A prudent borrower that wants this right will negotiate for the inclusion of a provision in the loan agreement that allows for prepayment, as some courts find silence to mean that a lender has no obligation to accept prepayment.[48] Just the same, a prudent lender that wants to prohibit the prepayment of a loan should include a provision explicitly providing such.[49] Section 1.6 of the Loan Agreement above allows the Borrower to prepay the loan and to suffer no penalty. Lenders are not always keen on borrowers prepaying their payment obligations. Lenders make their money on loans from the interest earned over time, and the prepayment of a loan obligation cuts short this stream of cash—not to mention, the timing of a prepayment may be important to the lender who itself may be borrowing money under certain other terms. Accordingly, it is not uncommon to see "prepayment fees" (sometimes termed "call protection" or less shrewdly named "prepayment penalties")—additional sums due in the event of prepayment—in a loan agreement. Courts have enforced these prepayment provisions where they have been found not to be punitive or grossly disproportionate to the losses the lender would suffer.[50]

7. Material Adverse Change or Effect

"Material adverse change" (or, for short, "MAC"), which is also sometimes framed in terms of a "material adverse event" or a "material adverse effect" (as in this Agreement and, for short, "MAE"), is language commonly found in business

---

48. *See, e.g., Parker Plaza W. Partners v. UNUM Pension and Ins. Co.*, 941 F.2d 349, 352 (5th Cir. 1991) ("Under Texas law, a borrower has no right to prepay a loan in the absence of the contract permitting it."); *Metro. Life Ins. Co. v. Promenade Towers Mut. Hous. Corp.*, 581 A.2d 846, 849 (Md. Ct. Spec. App. 1990) (discussing the "majority" and "minority" approaches to prepayment rights in real estate loan contracts that are silent on the matter, with the "majority rule" being the rule of "perfect tender in time," which is a common law presumption that a "payee is under no obligation to accept payment prior to maturity").

49. *See, e.g., River E. Plaza, L.L.C. v. Variable Annuity Life Ins. Co.*, 498 F.3d 718, 723 (7th Cir. 2007) ("Under Illinois law, the loan could have explicitly prohibited any prepayment whatsoever.").

50. *See, e.g., id.* at 723 (7th Cir. 2007) ("[W]e find nothing to suggest that the clause is an unenforceable penalty."). *But see Auto. Fin. Corp. v. Ridge Chrysler Plymouth L.L.C.*, 219 F. Supp. 2d 945, 955-56 (N.D. Ill. 2002) ("What Automotive stood to receive by way of the prepayment penalty was grossly disproportionate to any reasonably anticipatable and legitimate loss. While Automotive is entitled to protect itself against the loss of its bargain if interest rates were to decline prior to Ridge's prepayment, it is not entitled to do so through terms that amount to an unenforceable penalty.") (internal citations omitted). In addition, several states have various statutes that govern the enforceability of prepayment penalties in various contexts. *See, e.g.*, Tenn. Code Ann. § 47-14-108 (2000) (requiring that prepayment penalty or prohibition provisions be set in conspicuous type in consumer loans).

agreements. An agreement may tie various rights and obligations to the occurrence of a MAC event. A party to a merger agreement may be able to avoid going through with the merger (i.e., "closing"), if the other company suffers a MAC. A lending party to a loan agreement may be able to avoid lending money to a borrower if the borrower incurs a MAC. Because it is not always easy to discern what constitutes a MAC and whether such an event has occurred giving rise to certain rights, a contract will usually define the term or what constitutes such an event. However, despite the parties' attempt to define the term, it still may not be clear what amounts to a MAC, and parties often litigate about whether such an event has occurred.

How does this Agreement define a "Material Adverse Effect" and what rights and obligations are trigged by the occurrence of an MAE? The definitions section in § 1.1 defines Material Adverse Effect as "a material adverse effect on the business, properties, prospects, financial condition or results of operations of the Borrower and the Subsidiaries, taken as a whole." What does this definition add to your understanding of what a Material Adverse Effect is under the Agreement? Does this benefit the Borrower or the Lender? Does this definition resolve the vagueness of the concept, or is much discretion left to a court or arbitrator to determine whether an event amounted to a Material Adverse Effect?

Material Adverse Effect is used throughout the Agreement to different ends. For instance, Material Adverse Effect is used in § 3.1(a) to narrow the provision. There, the Borrower Parties represent and warrant that they are qualified to do business where they own property or conduct business, except if lacking such qualification would not reasonably be expected to cause a Material Adverse Effect. That is, if the lack of qualification is not an MAE, then the representation and the warranty do not apply. Is this particular use of Material Adverse Effect beneficial to the Borrower Parties or the Lender? How is Material Adverse Effect used in § 3.1(i), § 4.1(b)(vi), and § 4.1(d), and does each of these uses benefit the Borrower Parties or the Lender?

Notice that this Agreement does not use MAE in one of the ways MAE is most commonly used: as a condition to closing. MAE clauses are commonly used as conditions to closing in both the lending and the mergers-and-acquisitions contexts. Please see Chapter 6 and the *In re IBP* case, in that chapter, for further articulation of what constitutes an MAE, particularly in the context of mergers and acquisitions.

B. SECURITY AND GUARANTY AGREEMENT

A lender of money engages in a risk calculation before agreeing to lend money to a borrower. Ideally, the lender would like to be paid back and within a certain specified time. Other opportunities exist for the lender to earn a rate of return on its money without incurring any practical risk (e.g., U.S. Treasury bills). Accordingly, the lender will want at least this "risk-free" rate of return from the borrower. In addition, because the borrower poses some risk of non-payment, the lender will want at least an additional amount of return on its loan to compensate for this increased risk. The riskier the loan, the higher the interest rate the lender will demand. However, there are also ways to reduce the riskiness of a particular loan and, so, to reduce the interest rate at which one borrows. One common means is secured lending.

A lender may secure the performance of its loan by taking a "security interest" (a particular kind of property interest) in some of the borrower's assets (i.e., collateral). If a borrower defaults on its loan with a secured lender, then the secured lender will have certain rights it may exercise against the debtor's collateral in which the lender holds a security interest. If the loan is expressly "non-recourse," the creditor will be limited to recovering only against the debtor's collateral.[51] Otherwise, the lender may additionally bring an action to recover any deficiency not realized from foreclosing on the debtor's collateral.[52] In addition, a secured lender will generally have superior rights in the debtor's collateral as against the unsecured creditors of the debtor and as against other secured creditors with lower or subordinate "priority." In the United States, Article 9 of the Uniform Commercial Code generally governs security interests in personal property.[53] However, Article 9 does not apply to liens taken in real property (e.g., a home mortgage) other than fixtures, and other law applies instead.[54] We limit the discussion in this chapter to security interests in personal property and governed by Article 9 of the U.C.C.

On this score, we asked a seasoned practitioner with first-hand insight into the evolution of Article 9 of the Uniform Commercial Code to share with us this process and what we might expect in the way of changes in the near future.

A Practitioner Perspective: Article Nine and the Revision Process

Under U.S. Law, secured transactions involving personal property are governed by Article 9 of the Uniform Commercial Code, as adopted in each of the 50 states. The first version of the Uniform Commercial Code (the "UCC" or the "Code"), published in 1952, was a masterful achievement. Even its most ardent supporters, however, realized that it may need to change over time. As a result, they ensured that the Code had both protective guardians and able interpreters permanently tasked with assuring its well-being.

---

51. *See, e.g., Bernard Nat. Loan Investors, Ltd. v. Traditions Mgmt., LLC,* 688 F. Supp. 2d 347, 353-54 (S.D.N.Y. 2010); *see also* U.C.C. § 9-608 cmt. 3 (2000).

52. U.C.C. § 9-608(a)(4) (2000).

53. *See id.* § 9-109(a).

54. *See generally id.* § 9-109.

Today, the American Law Institute (the "ALI") and the Uniform Law Commission (the "ULC", officially known as the National Conference of Commissioners for Uniform State Laws) share responsibility for protecting the Code. When changes in market practice, erroneous judicial interpretations, or state-level efforts to promulgate non-uniform amendments threaten the Code, both the ALI and ULC spring into action. One line of defense is the Permanent Editorial Board for the UCC, a joint committee of the ALI and ULC that provides interpretive support in the form of commentaries on the Code. Another line of defense, one with greater consequences and involving much greater effort, is proposing amendments to the Code, which must then be adopted in each of the 50 states and the various territories that have enacted the UCC.

At the time of this writing, the most recent significant changes to Article 9 of the Code were those that took effect in 2001. The resulting version of Article 9 is commonly referred to as "Revised Article 9." The 2001 revisions constituted a major overhaul of Article 9, driven by many factors. Among other things, the revisions expanded the scope of Article 9, simplified choice of law rules, provided for paperless electronic transactions, boosted consumer protections, responded to erroneous court decisions, and reorganized the code into a more rational order. The revisions were generally positively received.

As the tenth anniversary of the revisions approached, both the ALI and ULC took the opportunity to review the performance of Revised Article 9 and determine whether there was a need for technical or other corrections. This effort was prompted in part by a wave of non-uniform amendments in states concerning how best to reflect individual debtor names on UCC financing statements—the public records that are filed to evidence a security interest. A Joint Review Committee was formed in 2008 by the ALI and ULC to identify any other issues that needed to be addressed, with the understanding that the committee would not revisit policy decisions made in connection with the 2001 revisions. After a series of several meetings, the Joint Review Committee proposed—and in 2010 the ALI and ULC approved—a relatively minor series of changes to Revised Article 9. The changes include use of driver's license names for individual debtors as either a safe harbor or required name; clarifying the debtor naming rules for registered organizations, trusts and decedent's estates; and responses to a limited number of troubling judicial decisions reached since the 2001 revisions. The proposed changes are expected to be considered in state legislatures in the 2010 and 2011 legislative sessions and are intended to have a uniform effective date of 2013.

Teresa Harmon
Partner
Sidley Austin LLP
Lecturer in Law
The University of Chicago Law School

A lender will often require that a borrower promise some of its assets as collateral before the lender will lend money to the borrower. Indeed, in the Loan Agreement above, the execution of the SPG Agreement is a condition precedent to the Lender's obligation to make an initial Advance to the Borrower. This is but one means of "credit enhancement," a term that refers to the reduction of the risk that a lender's right to receive payment will go unsatisfied (or, stated positively, the enhancement of the "creditworthiness" of a borrower). Another common method of credit enhancement is to require that one or more third parties "guarantee" a borrower's obligations, which means generally that the third-party "guarantor" promises to pay the borrower's obligation. Guaranties themselves can be secured or unsecured. Other ways to enhance a borrower's credit that may be available depending on the circumstances include obtaining a "monoline" insurance policy (used to increase the credit rating of debt securities, i.e., bonds), purchasing so-called "credit-default swaps" (which are contracts between private parties agreeing to pay a sum of money if there is a default on a separate, specified contract obligation), and isolating the borrower's collateral assets, often as part of a "securitization" (which involves selling the borrower's collateral assets to a newly formed special entity, which acts as the borrower, removing the risk of the parent company's bankruptcy). Depending on their cost (and their efficacy), credit-enhancing measures may be desirable to both lenders and borrowers alike. A lender may wish that a borrower undergo one or several credit-enhancing measures so as to reduce the risk that the lender will not be paid on its loan. A borrower may wish to enhance its own credit so that it may borrow money more cheaply and more easily.

A Practitioner Perspective: What Are Asset Securitization and Structured Finance?

Notwithstanding widespread public criticism in the wake of the global financial crisis that began in 2007, asset securitization was not invented in 2005 by greedy investment bankers looking to unload "toxic" sub-prime mortgage loans to unsuspecting investors. Securitization and structured finance have been around for decades and have provided very useful forms of financing to real companies and ultimately to American consumers and businesses. And while that criticism portrayed securitization as smoke and mirrors that can mysteriously convert those toxic assets into highly rated securities, structured finance actually uses sound and well-established legal principles to enable securitization transactions to issue securities with credit profiles that are better than that of the seller of the assets, and even of the assets themselves.

The history of asset securitization in the United States dates back to as early as 1938, when the Federal Housing Administration (FHA) chartered the Federal National Mortgage Association (today known as Fannie Mae) to purchase, hold and sell FHA-insured mortgage loans that had been originated by private lenders. Several decades later, as part of a national commitment to housing, Fannie Mae was joined by the Government National Mortgage Association (now known as Ginnie Mae) and the Federal Home Loan Mortgage Corporation (now known as Freddie Mac) in the goal of creating a secondary mortgage market to ensure a reliable supply of mortgage credit throughout the country. These "government

---

sponsored enterprises" (GSEs) were given the authority to issue mortgage-backed securities (MBS) guaranteed by the GSEs[1] and the first such MBS was issued in 1970. Through the GSEs, lenders are able to sell loans to generate cash to make more loans, as opposed to holding those loans until maturity.

By the late 1970's, private lenders started to use securitization to finance their residential mortgage loans that were not eligible for sale to the GSEs, starting what is now called the "private label" MBS market. In the mid 1980's, the non-mortgage, asset-backed securities (ABS) market was launched with the issuance of auto-loan backed securities by General Motors Acceptance Corporation (GMAC). Today, the ABS market issues securities backed not only by auto loans and leases (and loans to auto dealers themselves), but also credit card receivables, student loans, equipment loans and leases, insurance premiums, small business loans, trade receivables, royalty streams, among many other types of financial assets. In the early 1990's, MBS backed by commercial mortgage loans (secured by mortgages on multifamily residential properties and commercial properties, such as office buildings, shopping malls and industrial properties) began to be issued and CMBS became another significant part of the securitization market.

So what is securitization and why do companies engage in it? Generally, securitization is a method of financing financial assets, such as loans or receivables, by selling interests in such assets through the capital markets in the form of securities. Originators of financial assets can finance their business activities in a number of ways. They can raise equity in the private or public equity markets. They can also borrow through banks or other lenders or through the corporate bond market. The cost of borrowing in the debt markets can vary significantly depending on the credit rating of the company and whether the financing is secured or unsecured. Securitization is a form of secured financing in that an originator can transfer the loans that it originates into a securitization and sell ABS backed by those loans. It then takes the proceeds of the ABS and uses those proceeds to originate more loans. Using GMAC as an example, GMAC makes loans or leases to buyers of General Motors cars. It can sell those loans or leases into securitizations and realize proceeds that it can use to continue to finance its business of making auto loans and leases, and that in turn facilitates the sale of more GM cars. That is how securitization can help increase the flow of credit to both consumers and businesses. That is also why the collapse of the securitization markets starting in late 2007 and early 2008 resulted in less credit available over all.

What can make securitization a more cost-effective means of financing than other forms of secured borrowings is the ability to use structured finance techniques to achieve a higher credit rating on the ABS than what could be achieved through the issuance of corporate secured or unsecured debt. Debt that is rated

---

1. Ginnie Mae's guarantee is backed by the full faith and credit of the U.S. government and is limited to mortgage loans insured by the FHA and the Veterans Administration. Fannie Mae, which was privatized in 1968, and Freddie Mac impose eligibility restrictions and risk sharing requirements on the mortgages they can buy from private originators and they then guarantee their MBS, but their guarantees are not direct obligations of the U.S. government.

in the highest rating categories by nationally recognized statistical rating organizations, such as Standard & Poor's or Moody's Investors Service, carry lower interest rates than lower rated or unrated debt. So how does a company (such as GMAC) that is not AAA rated take assets that are not AAA rated and issue AAA rated ABS? It uses structured finance techniques that (1) isolate the performance of the assets from the credit risk of the seller of the assets and (2) use forms of credit enhancement that would absorb losses on the assets before those losses would affect the investors in the AAA ABS.

Since even secured creditors are ordinarily subject to the general credit risk of the borrower in insolvency[2] and can be subject to costly delays in exercising their remedies against the collateral, isolating the credit risk of the assets in a securitization from the credit risk of the seller is critical. In order to achieve that, you need to do two things: (1) create a securitization entity that is "bankruptcy remote" and would not be consolidated with the seller in the event of the seller's insolvency (referred to as "non-consolidation") and (2) transfer the assets to that securitization entity such that the assets have been legally isolated from the seller and cannot be re-characterized as assets of the seller in the event of the seller's insolvency (referred to as "legal isolation").[3]

In order for the securitization entity to be considered "bankruptcy remote," the entity needs to be "special purpose" (a "special purpose entity", or "SPE"). In other words, it should be established with the sole limited purpose of holding the assets to be securitized (as opposed to a general-purpose corporation, for example). This limits the SPE from engaging in other business that would subject it to liabilities other than the securitization, which reduces the risk of any involuntary insolvency proceedings being commenced against it. In addition, any documentation entered into by the SPE in connection with the transaction should also contain "non-petition covenants" under which the other parties to the transaction agree not to commence insolvency proceedings against the SPE. In order to achieve non-consolidation, the SPE needs to have covenants in its organizational documents that establish its separateness from its organizational parent. Those include requirements such as having separate books and records, accounts, offices and phone numbers, and independent directors. Those independent directors would be required to vote to commence any voluntary insolvency proceeding of the SPE. If the SPE has been established correctly, counsel would be able to give an opinion (referred to as a "non-consolidation opinion") that, in the event of an insolvency of the seller, the SPE to which the seller transferred the assets would not be consolidated with the seller.

---

2. For purposes of this article, I will use the term insolvency as the general term, but the technical details I am discussing will vary depending on whether the seller is an entity subject to the U.S. Bankruptcy Code or is subject to another insolvency regime, such as banks and insurance companies.

3. For purposes of this article, I am just focusing on the legal requirements for isolating the assets in the event of insolvency. There are also accounting, tax and regulatory capital implications as to how securitizations are structured that dictate whether a securitization is treated as a sale for accounting and tax purposes or whether a regulated seller must continue to hold capital against those assets, but those are outside the scope of this article (though in practice they are very closely intertwined).

Once you establish your bankruptcy remote SPE and have received a non-consolidation opinion, there are a number of factors that are important to determining whether the transfer of the assets to the SPE is characterized as a sale or a secured financing; in other words, whether you have achieved legal isolation.[4] One is to determine whether the seller has retained any recourse to the assets in connection with the transfer. For example, has the seller guaranteed the performance of the assets or remains otherwise responsible for any losses on the assets after they have been transferred. If any such recourse is limited to a *de minimis* amount, counsel would still be able to give a legal isolation opinion; in other words an opinion that the transfer of the assets would be considered to be a sale and not a secured financing in the event of the insolvency of the seller.[5] Another factor is whether the risks and rewards of ownership have been transferred such that the transfer is irrevocable; in other words, the seller has no ongoing right to repurchase the assets and the transferee has no ability to "put" the assets back to the seller. Other factors include the intent of the parties and the tax and accounting treatment of the transaction by the seller.

Legal isolation is usually best achieved in a "two-step" process. The seller would first transfer the assets to an intermediate bankruptcy remote SPE that is typically a subsidiary of the seller and as to which counsel has given a non-consolidation opinion. That SPE would then "deposit" the assets (and as a result is referred to as the "depositor") into a second SPE, which is often a trust[6] with an independent trustee. The trust issues the securities and uses the proceeds to pay the depositor for the assets, and the depositor in turn uses those proceeds to pay the seller for the assets. The trust is managed by the independent trustee, and the assets are serviced[7] by a servicer (which may be an affiliate of the seller). The two steps are helpful in achieving legal isolation because it interposes a bankruptcy remote SPE, the depositor, in between the trust holding the assets and the seller. The first step of the transfer would be a clean sale transaction to the depositor. The second step can then either be a sale or a secured financing (if the SPE retains any interests in the assets, for example) but that does not impact the securitization because the depositor is bankruptcy remote and unlikely to become insolvent.

Isolating the securitization SPE and the assets from the credit risk of the seller enables the securitization to have ratings that are independent from the rating of the seller of the assets. In order to issue securities that have ratings that are higher than the credit risk of the assets themselves, credit enhancement is

---

4. There are some securitizations that are intentionally structured as a secured financing by the seller, but the vast majority of securitizations are meant to be structured a legal sale.

5. These opinions are often referred to as "true sale" opinions but that is really only applicable to sellers that are subject to the U.S. Bankruptcy Code. For non-Bankruptcy Code entities, such as banks, the term "legal isolation" opinion is more precise.

6. A trust is often used for tax purposes. It is important that the issuer of the securitization not be subject to entity-level taxes that would decrease the cash flow on the securities. As a result, trusts or other vehicles that have "pass-through" tax treatment is a preferred choice.

7. "Serviced" means that the servicer collects payments on the assets and manages defaults and other activities that require interaction with the obligors on the assets.

used to cover losses on the assets before those would be borne by investors in the AAA securities. In order to avoid the recourse issues that might jeopardize legal isolation, credit enhancement is usually structured as either internal enhancement built into the transaction structure or external enhancement provided by a third party that is paid for taking some or all of the credit risk on the assets. Internal credit enhancement can include reserve funds but the primary form is subordination. Subordination involves issuing multiple classes, or tranches,[8] of securities such that a junior class of securities is allocated credit losses on the underlying assets (by writing down the principal balance of such class) before losses are allocated to a more senior class.[9] Only when and if the losses on the assets exceed the principal balance of the subordinated classes are any losses borne by the more senior classes. Since the subordinated classes are taking more credit risk on the assets, they will carry lower credit ratings and higher yields than the more senior classes.

External credit enhancement may be in the form of guarantees, letters of credit or surety bonds provided by banks or insurance companies. These third-party enhancement providers will perform credit reviews of the assets and then will be paid a fee for insuring the credit risk on those assets. The ratings on the securitization will then be dependent on the rating assigned to the credit enhancement provider itself.

The amount of credit enhancement necessary to achieve the required ratings on the securitization will be dictated by the credit rating agencies after their reviews of the assets and the transaction structure, and their estimates of the worst-case scenarios for losses on the pool of assets.

The above is a brief, high level and, frankly, very simplified explanation of the core principals of securitization and structured finance. These transactions are complex and have many legal and structural issues that intertwine and make these transactions fascinating and very challenging. There are many other benefits to securitization that I have not been able to cover in any detail, such as transforming illiquid assets into tradable (and presumably more liquid) securities and the diversification of risk by pooling assets together. There are also many other structured finance transactions that have been developed aside from asset securitization, such at collateralized debt obligations, which are managed pools of corporate debt or loans. While some of these structures may have been abused in the market exuberance that began in 2006 and ended with the ensuing

---

8. The word *tranche* is French for slice, section or portion. In a securitization, each class of securities is a different tranche, or slice, of the deal's risk.

9. Subordination is a form of "credit tranching." Securitizations can also be "time tranched" so that the cash flow on the assets gets paid to a class before it is paid to the next class in the "waterfall." For example, you might have two classes of securities, Class A and Class B. All the cash flow that comes in from the assets would be paid to Class A until Class A is paid in full and then any remaining cash flow is then paid to Class B. This is used to structure securities that have different maturity dates and can be sold to investors with different investment needs. It also mitigates a significant risk of holding mortgages themselves. Homeowners tend to prepay their mortgages when interest rates decline, giving the lenders their money back at a time when they can only reinvest it at lower prevailing interest rates. Tranching allocates this prepayment risk to investors willing to assume, and be compensated for, that risk.

financial crisis, many of these structures have very valuable and legitimate business purposes. But this does give you some insight into the huge asset securitization market,[10] which finances many of the homes, cars, credit cards and student loans and much of the commercial real estate across the country, and which provides real value to American consumers and businesses.

> Bianca A. Russo
> Managing Director and
> Associate General Counsel
> JPMorgan Chase & Co.[11]

We turn our focus to the SPG Agreement executed as part of the Tiffany-Little Switzerland loan transaction. In this agreement, we encounter the granting of a security interest and the execution of a guaranty agreement. Under Article 9 of the Uniform Commercial Code, one method of creating an enforceable security interest in the debtor's collateral requires the debtor to execute a security agreement that adequately describes the collateral.[55] A lender that wishes to obtain a security interest in a borrower's assets to secure payment of the borrower's loan obligation, then, will commonly obtain a security agreement from the borrower.

SECURITY, PLEDGE AND GUARANTY AGREEMENT[56]

This SECURITY, PLEDGE AND GUARANTY AGREEMENT (this "AGREEMENT") is entered into as of May 1, 2001 by and among: (i) L.S. Holding (USA), Inc., an Alaska corporation (the "BORROWER"), Little Switzerland, Inc., a Delaware corporation (the "PARENT" and a "GUARANTOR") and L.S. Wholesale, Inc., a Massachusetts corporation (also a "GUARANTOR"; and collectively with the Borrower and Parent, the "BORROWER PARTIES"), on the one hand, and (ii) Tiffany and Company, a New York corporation (the "LENDER"), on the other hand.

---

10. At the end of 2009, there was approximately $11.6 trillion of outstanding MBS and ABS, including those issued by the GSEs.

11. The writer is not necessarily representing the views or opinions of JPMorgan Chase & Co. [Note: Ms. Russo specifically requested this disclaimer. The inclusion of this disclaimer in no way speaks to this book's other contributions or the authors or affiliations thereof.]

55. U.C.C. § 9-203(b)(3)(A) (2000).

56. Little Switzerland, Inc., Security, Pledge and Guaranty Agreement (Form 8-K), at Exhibit 10.18 (May 30, 2001), *available at* http://www.sec.gov/Archives/edgar/data/875523/000091205701517915/a2050252zex-10_18.txt.

RECITALS

A. The Borrower, Guarantor and the Lender have entered into a Loan Agreement dated as of May 1, 2001 (as it may hereafter be amended or otherwise modified from time to time, the "LOAN AGREEMENT").

B. Borrower is an indirect wholly-owned subsidiary of the Parent.

C. L.S. Wholesale, Inc. is a direct wholly-owned subsidiary of the Parent.

D. It is a condition precedent to the making of Advances by the Lender under the Loan Agreement that the Borrower Parties shall have executed and delivered this Agreement and taken the action contemplated hereby.

NOW, THEREFORE, in consideration of the premises and in order to induce the Lender to make Advances under the Loan Agreement, the Lender and the Borrower Parties hereby agree as follows:

ARTICLE 1
DEFINITIONS

SECTION 1.01. DEFINITIONS. Capitalized terms used but not defined herein shall have the meanings ascribed to such terms in the Loan Agreement.

"AGREEMENT" has the meaning ascribed to that term in the Header.

"BORROWER" has the meaning ascribed to that term in the Header.

"BORROWER PARTIES" has the meaning ascribed to that term in the Header.

"CHASE" means The Chase Manhattan Bank, N.A.

"CHASE LOAN AGREEMENTS" means (i) the Loan Agreement, dated May 1, 2001, by and among L.S. Wholesale, Inc., the Parent and Chase, providing for a revolving credit facility in an aggregate principal amount of $700,000, (ii) the Loan Agreement, dated May 1, 2001, by and among L.S. Holding, Inc., the Parent, L.S. Wholesale, Inc. and Chase, providing for a revolving credit facility in an aggregate principal amount of $2,950,000, and (iii) the Loan Agreement, dated May 1, 2001, by and among L.S. Holding (USA), Inc., the Parent, L.S. Wholesale, Inc. and Chase, providing for a revolving credit facility in an aggregate principal amount of $100,000.

"CODE" has the meaning ascribed to that term in Section 2.11(a).

"COLLATERAL" has the meaning ascribed to that term in Section 2.01(a).

"DEBT" has the meaning ascribed to that term in Section 3.05(a).

"FINANCIAL STATEMENTS" has the meaning ascribed to that term in Section 4.01(g).

"GUARANTORS" has the meaning ascribed to that term in the Header.

"IMPLEMENTING AGREEMENTS" has the meaning ascribed to that term in Section 2.01(b).

"INVENTORY" has the meaning ascribed to that term in Section 2.01(a)(i).

"ISSUER" has the meaning ascribed to that term in Section 2.01(a)(v).

"LENDER" has the meaning ascribed to that term in the Header.

"LOAN AGREEMENT" has the meaning ascribed to that term in the Recitals.

"OBLIGATIONS" has the meaning ascribed to that term in Section 2.02.

"PARENT" means Little Switzerland, Inc., a Delaware corporation.

"PLEDGED STOCK" has the meaning ascribed to that term in Section 2.01(a)(iv).

"RECEIVABLES" has the meaning ascribed to that term in Section 2.01(a)(ii).

"SUBSIDIARY" means each corporation, partnership, limited liability company and other entity with respect to which a Borrower Party (i) beneficially owns, directly or indirectly, 10% or more of the outstanding stock or other equity interests, (ii) otherwise controls, directly or indirectly, because of factors or relationships other than the percentage of equity interests owned or (iii) is required to account for its ownership under the equity method. For avoidance of doubt, "Subsidiary" shall include L.S. Holdings, Inc., a U.S. Virgin Islands corporation, and its respective Subsidiaries.

"SUBORDINATION AGREEMENT" means the Subordination Agreement, dated May 1, 2001, by and among the Borrower, certain affiliates of the Borrower, the Lender and Chase.

"TRANSACTIONS" has the meaning ascribed to that term in Section 4.01(b).

ARTICLE 2
SECURITY AND PLEDGE

SECTION 2.01. PLEDGE, ASSIGNMENT AND GRANT OF SECURITY.

(a) The Borrower Parties hereby grant, assign and pledge a security interest in and lien on all of their right, title and interest in and to the following, whether now owned or hereafter acquired (the "COLLATERAL"):

(i) all inventory in all of its forms, wherever located, now or hereafter existing including, but not limited to, goods in which the Borrower Parties have an interest in mass or a joint or other interest or right of any kind and goods which are returned to the Borrower Parties, and all accessions thereto and products thereof and documents therefore (any and all such inventory, accessions, products and documents being the "INVENTORY");

(ii) all accounts, contract rights, chattel paper, instruments, deposit accounts, general intangibles and other obligations of any kind of the Borrower Parties, now or hereafter existing, whether or not arising out of or in connection with the sale or lease of goods or the rendering of services, and all rights now or hereafter existing in and to all security agreements, leases, and other contracts securing or otherwise relating to any such accounts, contract rights, chattel paper, instruments, deposit accounts, general intangibles or obligations (any and all such accounts, contract rights, chattel paper, instruments, deposit accounts, general intangibles and obligations being the "RECEIVABLES")

(iii) all or a portion of the issued and outstanding capital stock owned by the Borrower Parties issued by the Borrower Parties and certain Subsidiaries, as set forth on Schedule II hereto, and all of the capital stock of any additional Subsidiary organized within the U.S. and 65% of the capital stock of any additional Subsidiary organized outside the U.S. of any of the Borrower Parties organized or acquired after the date hereof and all stock dividends granted thereon (the "PLEDGED STOCK;" each issuer of Pledged Stock is referred to herein as an "ISSUER");

(iv) all proceeds of any and all of the foregoing Collateral (including, without limitation, proceeds which constitute property of the types described in clauses (i)-(iii) of this Section 2.01(a)) and, to the extent not otherwise included, all (A) payments under insurance, or any indemnity, warranty or guaranty, payable by reason of loss or damage to or otherwise with respect to any of the foregoing Collateral, (B) cash and (C) all dividends, distributions, option or rights granted on Pledged Stock, whether in addition to, in substitution of, as a conversion of, or in exchange for such Pledged Stock, and any sums paid upon or in respect of the Pledged Stock upon the liquidation or dissolution of any Issuer.

Notwithstanding anything in this Section 2.01(a) to the contrary, the grant, assignment and pledge of a security interest by the Borrower Parties hereunder of all of their respective right, title and interest in and to the Collateral is subject, pursuant to the terms and conditions of the Subordination Agreement, to the prior lien on the Collateral in favor of Chase as security for the credit facilities provided by Chase pursuant to the Chase Loan Agreements.

(b) The Borrower Parties hereby covenant and agree to execute and deliver in favor of the Lender such documents (the "IMPLEMENTING

AGREEMENTS") as the Lender shall reasonably determine from time to time are necessary to perfect, grant, assign and pledge a security interest in and lien on all of the Borrower Parties' right, title and interest in and to the Collateral, subject, pursuant to the terms and conditions of the Subordination Agreement, only to the prior lien on the Collateral in favor of Chase as security for the credit facilities provided by Chase pursuant to the Chase Loan Agreements.

SECTION 2.02. SECURITY FOR OBLIGATIONS. This Agreement and the Implementing Agreements shall secure the payment of all obligations of the Borrower now or hereafter existing under the Loan Agreement and the Note, whether for principal, interest, fees, expenses or otherwise, and all obligations of the Borrower now or hereafter existing under this Agreement (all such obligations of the Borrower being the "OBLIGATIONS"). Without limiting the generality of the foregoing, this Agreement and the Implementing Agreements shall secure the payment of all amounts which constitute part of the Obligations and would be owed by the Borrower to the Lender under the Loan Agreement and the Note but for the fact that they are unenforceable or not allowable due to the existence of a bankruptcy, reorganization, insolvency or similar proceeding involving the Borrower.

SECTION 2.03. THE BORROWER PARTIES REMAIN LIABLE. Anything herein to the contrary notwithstanding: (a) each Borrower Party shall remain liable under the contracts and agreements to which it is a party included in the Collateral to the extent set forth therein to perform all of its duties and obligations thereunder to the same extent as if the Loan Documents had not been executed (subject to any limitations on such performance contained in the Loan Documents); (b) the exercise by the Lender of any of the rights hereunder shall not release the Borrower Parties from any of their duties or obligations under the contracts and agreements included in the Collateral; and (c) the Lender shall not have any obligation or liability under the contracts and agreements included in the Collateral by reason of the Loan Documents, nor shall the Lender be obligated to perform any of the obligations or duties of the Borrower Parties thereunder or to take any action to collect or enforce any claim for payment assigned hereunder.

SECTION 2.04. FURTHER ASSURANCES. (a) The Borrower Parties agree that from time to time, at their expense, they shall promptly execute and deliver all further instruments and documents, and take all further action, that may be necessary, or that the Lender may reasonably request, in order to consummate the Transactions, perfect and protect any pledge, assignment or security interest granted or purported to be granted under this Agreement or to enable the Lender to exercise and enforce its rights and remedies hereunder or under the Implementing Agreements with respect to any Collateral. Without limiting the generality of the foregoing, the Borrower Parties will: (i) if any Collateral shall be evidenced by a promissory note or other instrument, deliver and pledge to the Lender hereunder such note or instrument duly indorsed and accompanied by duly executed instruments of transfer or assignment, including delivery of stock certificates representing any shares of the Pledged Stock and an undated stock power covering each such certificate, duly executed in blank by the pertinent Borrower Party, all in form and substance reasonably satisfactory to the Lender; and (ii) execute and file such financing or continuation statements, or amendments thereto, and such other instruments or notices, as may be necessary, or as the Lender may reasonably request, in order to perfect and preserve the pledge, assignment and security interest granted or purported to be granted hereunder or under the Implementing Agreements.

(b) The Borrower Parties hereby authorize the Lender to file one or more financing or continuation statements, and amendments thereto, relating to all or any part of the Collateral without the signature of any of the Borrower Parties where permitted by law. A photocopy or other reproduction of this Agreement or any financing statement covering the Collateral or any part thereof shall be sufficient as a financing statement where permitted by law.

(c) The Borrower Parties will furnish to the Lender from time to time statements and schedules further identifying and describing the Collateral and such other reports in connection with the Collateral as the Lender may reasonably request, all in reasonable detail.

SECTION 2.05. AS TO INVENTORY. The Borrower Parties shall keep the Inventory (other than Inventory sold in the ordinary course of business) at the places set forth on Schedule I hereto or, upon 30 days' prior written notice to the Lender, at such other places in a jurisdiction where all action required by Section 2.04 shall have been taken with respect to the Inventory. The Borrower Parties shall pay promptly when due all property and other taxes, assessments and governmental charges or levies imposed upon, and all claims (including claims for labor, materials and supplies) against, the Inventory, except to the extent that any of the foregoing are being contested by any of the Borrower Parties and no lien is imposed on the Inventory.

SECTION 2.06. AS TO PLEDGED STOCK.

(a) The Borrower Parties covenant and agree that, from and after the date of this Agreement until this Agreement is terminated and the security interests created hereby are released and subject to the Subordination Agreement:

(i) If a Borrower Party shall, as a result of its ownership of the Pledged Stock or otherwise, become entitled to receive or shall receive any capital stock (including, without limitation, any stock dividend or a distribution in connection with any reclassification, increase or reduction of capital or any certificate issued in connection with any reorganization), option or rights, whether in addition to, in substitution of, as a conversion of, or in exchange for any shares of the Pledged Stock, or otherwise in respect thereof, the pertinent Borrower Party shall accept certificates representing the same as the agent of the Lender, hold the same in trust for the Lender and deliver the same forthwith to the Lender in the exact form received duly endorsed by the pertinent Borrower Party to the Lender, together with an undated stock power covering such certificate duly executed in blank by the pertinent Borrower Party to be held by the Lender, subject to the terms hereof, as additional Collateral. Any sums paid upon or in respect of the Pledged Stock upon the liquidation or dissolution of any Issuer shall be paid over to the Lender to be held by it hereunder as additional Collateral, and in case any distribution of capital shall be made on or in respect of the Pledged Stock or any property shall be distributed upon or with respect to the Pledged Stock pursuant to the recapitalization or reclassification of the capital of any Issuer or pursuant to the reorganization thereof, the property so distributed shall be delivered to the Lender to be held by it hereunder as additional Collateral. If any sums of money or property so paid or distributed in respect of the Pledged Stock shall be received by a Borrower Party, it shall, until such money or property is paid or delivered to the Lender, hold such money or property in trust for the Lender, segregated from other funds of such Borrower Party, as additional Collateral.

(ii) Without the prior written consent of the Lender, the Borrower Parties will not vote to enable, or take any other action to permit, any Issuer to issue any capital stock or other equity securities of any nature or to issue any other securities convertible into or granting the right to purchase or exchange for any capital stock or other equity securities of any nature of any Issuer.

(b) Unless an Event of Default shall have occurred and is continuing and the Lender shall have given notice to the Borrower Parties of the Lender's intent to exercise its rights pursuant to this Section 2.06(b), the Borrower Parties shall be permitted to receive all cash dividends paid in the normal course of business of the Issuers and consistent with past practice in respect of the Pledged Stock and, except as set forth in Section 2.06(a)(ii), to exercise all voting and corporate rights with respect to the Pledged Stock; PROVIDED, HOWEVER, that no vote shall be cast or corporate right exercised or other action taken which would impair the Collateral or which would be inconsistent with or result in any violation of any provision of the Loan Documents. If an Event of Default shall occur and is continuing and the Lender has given notice to the Borrower Parties of its intent to exercise its rights pursuant to this Section 2.06(b), and subject, pursuant to the terms and conditions of the Subordination Agreement, to the prior rights of Chase: (i) the Lender shall have the right to receive any and all cash dividends or other payments paid in respect of the Pledged Stock and apply all or any part thereof against the Obligations or any part thereof and (ii) any or all shares of the Pledged Stock shall be registered in the name of the Lender or its nominee, and the Lender or its nominee may thereafter exercise (A) all voting, corporate and other rights pertaining to such Pledged Stock at any meeting of shareholders of any Issuer or otherwise and (B) any and all rights of conversion, exchange, subscription and any other rights, privileges or options pertaining to such Pledged Stock as if it were the absolute owner thereof (including, without limitation, the right to exchange at its discretion any and all of the Pledged Stock upon the merger, consolidation, reorganization, recapitalization or other fundamental change in the corporate structure of any Issuer, or upon the exercise by any Borrower Party or the Lender of any right, privilege or option pertaining to such Pledged Stock, and in connection therewith, the right to deposit and deliver any and all of the Pledged Stock with any committee, depositary, transfer agent, registrar or other designated agency upon such terms and conditions as the Lender may determine), all without liability except to account for property actually received by it, but the Lender shall have no duty to the Borrower Parties to exercise any such right, privilege or option and shall not be responsible for any failure to do so or delay in so doing.

(c) The Borrower Parties hereby acknowledge and agree that the Lender may exercise its right to sell any or all of the Pledged Stock pursuant to Section 2.06(b) hereof in one or more private sales thereof to a restricted group of purchasers which will be obliged to agree, among other things, to acquire such securities for their own account for investment and not with a view to the distribution or resale thereof. The Borrower Parties further acknowledge and agree that any such private sale may result in prices and other terms less favorable than if such sale were a public sale and, notwithstanding such circumstances, agrees that any such private sale shall be deemed to have been made in a commercially reasonable manner. The Lender shall be under no obligation to delay a sale of any of the Pledged Stock for the period of time necessary to permit the Issuer thereof to register such securities for public sale under the Securities Act of 1933, as amended, or under applicable state securities laws, even if such Issuer would agree to do so. The Borrower Parties agree to use their best efforts to do or cause to be done all such other acts as may be necessary to make such sale or sales of all or any portion of the Pledged Stock pursuant to this

Section 2.06(c) valid and binding and in compliance with any and all other Applicable Law.

(d) The Borrower Parties further agree that a breach of any of the covenants contained in this Section 2.06 will cause irreparable injury to the Lender, that the Lender have no adequate remedy at law in respect of such breach and, as a consequence, that each and every covenant contained in this Section 2.06 shall be specifically enforceable against the Borrower Parties, and the Borrower Parties hereby waive and agree not to assert any defenses against an action for specific performance of such covenants, except for a defense that no Event of Default has occurred.

(e) The Borrower Parties hereby authorize and instruct each Issuer of any Pledged Stock pledged by the Borrower Parties hereunder to (i) comply with any instruction received by it from the Lender in writing that (A) states that an Event of Default has occurred and is continuing and (B) is otherwise in accordance with the terms of this Agreement, without any other or further instructions from the Borrower Parties, and the Borrower Parties agree that each Issuer shall be fully protected in so complying, and (ii) upon an Event of Default, unless otherwise expressly permitted hereby, pay any dividends or other payments with respect to the Pledged Stock directly to the Lender. Concurrently with the delivery of any Pledged Stock hereunder, the Issuer of such Pledged Stock shall deliver to the Lender an Acknowledgement and Consent, in the form attached hereto as Annex A, certifying, among other things, that it will be bound by the terms of this Agreement and will comply with such terms insofar as such terms are applicable to it.

SECTION 2.07. PLACE OF PERFECTION; RECORDS; COLLECTION. (a) The Borrower shall keep its chief place of business and chief executive office and the office where it keeps its and other Borrower Parties' records concerning the Receivables and the Pledged Stock at the address specified in Section 5.02 or, upon 30 days' prior written notice to the Lender, at any other locations in a jurisdiction where all actions required by Section 2.04 shall have been taken with respect to the Receivables and the Pledged Stock. The Borrower will hold and preserve such records and will permit representatives of the Lender at any time during normal business hours to inspect and make abstracts from such records, provided that so long as no Event of Default shall have occurred or be continuing, no more than one such visit per calendar year shall be at the expense of the Borrower Parties.

(b) Except as otherwise provided in this Section 2.07(b), the Borrower Parties shall continue to collect, at their own expense, all amounts due or to become due them under the Receivables and/or to adjust, settle or compromise the amount thereof. In connection with such collections, the Borrower Parties may take (and, following the occurrence and during the continuance of an Event of Default at the

Lender's direction, shall take) such action as the Borrower Parties or the Lender may deem necessary or advisable to enforce collection of the Receivables; PROVIDED, HOWEVER, that the Lender shall have the right following the occurrence and during the continuance of an Event of Default, upon 10 days' written notice to the Borrower Parties of its intention to do so, to notify the account debtors or obligors under any Receivables of the assignment of such Receivables to the Lender and to direct such account debtors or obligors to make payment of all amounts due or to become due to the Borrower Parties thereunder directly to the Lender and, upon such notification and at the expense of the Borrower Parties, to enforce collection of any such Receivables, and to adjust, settle or compromise the amount or payment thereof, in the same manner and to the same extent as the Borrower might have done. After receipt by the Borrower of the notice from the Lender referred to in the proviso to the preceding sentence, (i) all amounts and proceeds (including instruments) received by the Borrower Parties in respect of the Receivables shall be received in trust for the benefit of the Lender hereunder, shall be segregated from other funds of the Borrower Parties and shall be forthwith paid over to the Lender in the same form as so received (with any necessary indorsement) to be held as cash collateral and either (A) released to the Borrower Parties so long as no Event of Default shall have occurred and be continuing or (B) if any Event of Default shall have occurred and be continuing, applied as provided by Section 2.11(b), and (ii) the Borrower Parties shall not adjust, settle or compromise the amount or payment of any Receivable, release wholly or partly any account debtor or obligor thereof, or allow any credit or discount thereon.

SECTION 2.08. TRANSFERS AND OTHER LIENS. The Borrower Parties shall not (i) sell, assign (by operation of law or otherwise) or otherwise dispose of, or grant any option with respect to, any of the Collateral, except as permitted in accordance with the Loan Agreement, or (ii) create or permit to exist any lien, security interest, option or other charge or encumbrance upon or with respect to any of the Collateral, except for the security interests under the Chase Loan Agreements or the Implementing Agreements or as otherwise permitted in accordance with the Loan Documents.

SECTION 2.09. LENDER APPOINTED ATTORNEY-IN-FACT. Each Borrower Party hereby irrevocably appoints the Lender its attorney-in-fact, with full authority in the place and stead of such Borrower Party and in the name of such Borrower Party or otherwise, from time to time in the Lender's discretion, to take any action and to execute any instrument which the Lender may deem necessary or advisable to accomplish the purposes of this Agreement, including, without limitation:

(a) to ask, demand, collect, sue for, recover, compromise, receive and give acquittance and receipts for moneys due and to become due under or in connection with the Collateral,

(b) to receive, indorse, and collect any drafts or other instruments, documents and chattel paper, in connection therewith, and

(c) to file any claims or take any action or institute any proceedings which the Lender may deem necessary for the collection of any of the Collateral or otherwise to enforce the rights of the Lender with respect to any of the Collateral.

Notwithstanding anything herein to the contrary, unless an Event of Default shall exist and be continuing, the Lender shall not exercise any of the rights set forth in this Section 2.09.

SECTION 2.10. LENDER MAY PERFORM. If any Borrower Party fails to perform any agreement contained herein, the Lender may, upon notice to the applicable Borrower Party, itself perform, or cause performance of, such agreement, and the expenses incurred in connection therewith shall be payable by such Borrower Party.

SECTION 2.11. REMEDIES. If any Event of Default shall have occurred and be continuing, subject to the prior rights of Chase under the Subordination Agreement:

(a) The Lender may exercise in respect of the Collateral, in addition to other rights and remedies provided for herein, in the Loan Agreement, the Implementing Agreements or otherwise available to it at law or in equity, all the rights and remedies of a secured party on default under the Uniform Commercial Code in effect in the State of New York at that time (the "CODE") (whether or not the Code applies to the affected Collateral), and also may (i) require the Borrower Parties to, and the Borrower Parties hereby agree that they will, at their expense and upon request of the Lender, forthwith, assemble all or part of the Collateral as directed by the Lender and make it available to the Lender at a place to be designated by the Lender which is reasonably convenient to both parties and (ii) without notice except as specified below, sell the Collateral or any part thereof in one or more parcels at public or private sale, at any of the Lender's offices or elsewhere, for cash, on credit or for future delivery, and upon such other terms as the Lender may deem commercially reasonable. The Borrower Parties agree that, to the extent notice of sale shall be required by law, at least ten days' notice to the Borrower Parties of the time and place of any public sale or the time after which any private sale is to be made shall constitute reasonable notification. The Lender shall not be obligated to make any sale of Collateral regardless of notice of sale having been given. The Lender may adjourn any public or private sale from time to time by announcement at the time and place fixed therefor, and such sale may, without further notice, be made at the time and place to which it was so adjourned.

(b) Any cash held by the Lender as Collateral and all cash proceeds received by the Lender in respect of any sale of, collection from, or other realization upon all or any part of the Collateral may, in the discretion of the Lender, be held by the Lender as collateral for, and/or then or at any time thereafter be applied in whole or in part by the Lender against all or any part of the Obligations in such order as the Lender shall elect. Any surplus of such cash or cash proceeds held by the Lender and remaining after payment in full of all the Obligations shall be paid over to the Borrower Parties or to whomsoever may be lawfully entitled to receive such surplus.

(c) The Lender may exercise any and all rights and remedies of the Borrower Parties under or in respect of the Collateral.

(d) All payments received by the Borrower Parties under or in connection with any of the Collateral shall be received in trust for the benefit of the Lender, shall be segregated from other funds of the Borrower Parties.

SECTION 2.12. CONTINUING SECURITY INTEREST. This Agreement shall create a continuing security interest in the Collateral and shall remain in full force and effect until the later of (x) the payment in full of the Obligations and all other amounts payable under this Agreement and (y) the expiration or termination of the Commitment. Upon the later of the payment in full of the Obligations and all other amounts payable under this Agreement and the expiration or termination of the Commitment, the security interest granted hereunder shall terminate and all rights to the Collateral shall revert to the Borrower Parties.

ARTICLE 3
GUARANTY

SECTION 3.01. GUARANTY. (a) The Guarantors hereby, jointly and severally, unconditionally irrevocably guaranty the punctual payment when due, whether at stated maturity, by acceleration or otherwise, of all Obligations and agree to pay any and all expenses (including reasonable counsel fees and expenses) incurred by the Lender in enforcing any rights under this Agreement. Without limiting the generality of the foregoing, the Guarantors' liability shall extend to all amounts which constitute part of the Obligations and would be owed by the Borrower under the Loan Agreement and the Note but for the fact that they are unenforceable or not allowable due to the existence of a bankruptcy, reorganization or similar proceeding involving the Borrower.

(b) The Guarantors jointly and severally guaranty that the Obligations will be paid strictly in accordance with the terms of the Loan

Agreement and the Note, regardless of any law, regulation or order now or hereafter in effect in any jurisdiction affecting any of such terms or the rights of the Lender with respect thereto. The obligations of the Guarantors under this Article 3 are independent of the obligations of the Borrower under the Loan Agreement and the Note, and a separate action or actions may be brought and prosecuted against the Guarantors to enforce this Article 3 irrespective of whether any action is brought against the Borrower or whether the Borrower is joined in any such action or actions. The liability of the Guarantors under this Article 3 shall be absolute and unconditional irrespective of:

(i) any lack of validity or enforceability of the Loan Agreement, the Note or any other agreement or instrument relating thereto;

(ii) any change in the time, manner or place of payment of, or in any other term of, all or any of the Obligations, or any other amendment or waiver of or any consent to departure from the Loan Agreement or the Note, including, without limitation, any increase in the Obligations resulting from the extension of additional credit to the Borrower or any of its Subsidiaries or otherwise;

(iii) any taking, exchange, release or non-perfection of any collateral, or any taking, release or amendment or waiver of or consent to departure from any other guaranty, for all or any of the Obligations;

(iv) any manner of application of collateral, or proceeds thereof, to all or any of the Obligations, or any manner of sale or other disposition of any collateral for all or any of the Obligations or any other assets of any of the Borrower Parties;

(v) any change, restructuring or termination of the corporate structure or existence of any of the Borrower Parties;

(vi) any other circumstance which might otherwise constitute a defense available to, or a discharge of, any of the Borrower Parties; or

(vii) any bankruptcy, reorganization or similar proceeding commenced by or against any of the Borrower Parties.

This Guaranty shall continue to be effective or be reinstated, as the case may be, if at any time any payment of any of the Obligations is rescinded or must otherwise be returned by the Lender upon the insolvency, bankruptcy or reorganization of the Borrower or otherwise, all as though such payment had not been made.

SECTION 3.02. WAIVER. The Guarantors hereby waive promptness, diligence, rights of set-off, presentment, protest, notice of acceptance and any other notice with respect to any of the Obligations and this Article 3 and any requirement that the Lender protect, secure, perfect or insure any security interest or lien or any property subject thereto or exhaust any right or take any action against the Guarantors or any other person or entity or any Collateral.

SECTION 3.03. SUBROGATION. The Guarantors will not exercise any rights which they may acquire by way of subrogation under this Article 3, by any payment made hereunder or otherwise, until all the Obligations and all other amounts payable under this Guaranty shall have been paid in full and the Commitment shall have expired or terminated. If any amount shall be paid to the Guarantors on account of such subrogation rights at any time prior to the later of (x) the payment in full of the Obligations and all other amounts payable under this Article 3 and (y) the expiration or termination of the Commitment, such amount shall be held in trust for the benefit of the Lender and shall forthwith be paid to the Lender to be credited and applied upon the Obligations, whether matured or unmatured, in accordance with the terms of the Loan Agreement or to be held by the Lender as Collateral for any Obligations thereafter existing. If (i) the Guarantors shall make payment to the Lender of all or any part of the Obligations, (ii) all the Obligations and all other amounts payable under this Guaranty shall be paid in full and (iii) the Commitment shall have expired or terminated, the Lender will, at the Guarantors' request, execute and deliver to the Guarantors appropriate documents, without recourse and without representation or warranty, necessary to evidence the transfer by subrogation to the Guarantors of an interest in the Obligations resulting from such payment by the Guarantors.

SECTION 3.04. AFFIRMATIVE COVENANTS. The Guarantors covenant and agree that, so long as any part of the Obligations shall remain unpaid or the Lender shall have any Commitment, the Guarantors will, unless the Lender shall otherwise consent in writing:

(a) COMPLIANCE WITH LAWS, ETC. Comply, and cause each of their Subsidiaries to comply, in all material respects with all Applicable Law, such compliance to include, without limitation, paying before the same become delinquent all taxes, assessments and governmental charges imposed upon it or upon its property except to the extent contested in good faith.

(b) REPORTING REQUIREMENTS. Furnish to the Lender:

(i) as soon as available and in any event within 45 days after the end of each of the first three quarters of each fiscal year of the Parent, the unaudited consolidated balance sheet of the Parent and the Subsidiaries and the related unaudited consolidated statements of income and cash flows of the Parent and the Subsidiaries for the 3-month period then ended for the period commencing at the end of the previous fiscal year and ending with the end of such quarter, certified by the chief financial officer of the Parent;

(ii) as soon as available and in any event within 90 days after the end of each fiscal year of the Parent, a copy of the annual report for such year for the Parent and its Subsidiaries, containing the audited consolidated balance sheet of the Parent and the Subsidiaries as of each fiscal year end, and the related audited consolidated statements of income and cash flows of the Parent and the Subsidiaries for the fiscal year then ended, certified by PricewaterhouseCoopers LLP or other independent public accountants reasonably acceptable to the Lender with no qualifications as to the scope of the audit;

(iii) as soon as possible and in any event within five days after the occurrence of each Event of Default known to a Borrower Party and each event which, with the giving of notice or lapse of time, or both, would constitute an Event of Default, continuing on the date of such statement, a statement of the chief financial officer or chief executive officer of the Borrower Party setting forth details of such Event of Default or event and the action which the Borrower Party has taken and proposes to take with respect thereto

(iv) promptly after the sending or filing thereof, copies of all reports which any of the Borrower Parties sends to any of its security holders, and copies of all reports and registration statements which the Parent files with the SEC or any national securities exchange;

(v) promptly after the filing or receiving thereof, copies of all reports and notices which any of the Borrower Parties files under ERISA with the Internal Revenue Service or the Pension Benefit Guaranty Corporation or the U.S. Department of Labor or which any of the Borrower Parties receives from such entity;

(vi) promptly after the commencement thereof, notice of all actions, suits and proceedings before any Government Authority, or arbitrations affecting the Borrower Parties which, if determined adversely to the Borrower Parties and their Subsidiaries could reasonably be expected to have a Material Adverse Effect on the Borrower Parties or their Subsidiaries; and

(vii) such other information respecting the condition or operations, financial or otherwise, of any of the Borrower Parties as the Lender may from time to time reasonably request.

(c) MAINTENANCE OF CORPORATION AND PROPERTIES. The Borrower Parties shall, and shall cause their Subsidiaries, to preserve and maintain their respective corporate existence and good standing in their respective jurisdiction of organization and in every other jurisdiction in which such qualification is required, unless the failure to qualify would not have a Material Adverse Effect on such respective corporation, and maintain all of their respective properties and assets in good working order and condition, ordinary wear and tear excepted.

SECTION 3.05. NEGATIVE COVENANTS. The Borrower Parties covenant and agree that, so long as any part of the Obligations shall remain unpaid or the Lender shall have any Commitment, each of the Borrower Parties will not, and shall cause their Subsidiaries to not, without the written consent of the Lender:

(a) LIENS. Create or suffer to exist, or permit any of its Subsidiaries to create or suffer to exist, any lien, security interest or other charge or encumbrance, or any other type of preferential arrangement, upon or with respect to any of its properties, whether now owned or hereafter acquired, or assign, or permit any of its Subsidiaries to assign, any right to receive income, in each case to secure or provide for the payment of any Debt of any Person or entity, other than (i) the liens created hereunder; (ii) liens securing the credit facilities provided by Chase pursuant to the Chase Loan Agreements; (iii) liens existing on the date hereof as described on Schedule 3.05(a) hereto; (iv) purchase money liens or purchase money security interests upon or in any property acquired or held by any of the Borrower Parties and their Subsidiaries in the ordinary course of business to secure the purchase price of such property or to secure indebtedness incurred solely for the purpose of financing the acquisition of such property, (v) liens or security interests existing on such property at the time of its acquisition (other than any such lien or security interest created in contemplation of such acquisition), PROVIDED that the aggregate principal amount of the indebtedness secured by the liens or security interests referred to in clauses (iii), (iv) and (v) above shall not exceed an amount not inconsistent with the Company's business plan as approved by its Board of Directors from time to time. "DEBT" means (i) indebtedness for borrowed money, (ii) obligations evidenced by bonds, debentures, notes or other similar instruments, (iii) obligations to pay the deferred purchase price of property or services, (iv) obligations as lessee under leases which shall have been or should be, in accordance with generally accepted accounting principles, recorded as capital leases, (v) obligations under direct or indirect guaranties in respect of, and obligations (contingent or otherwise) to purchase or otherwise acquire, or otherwise to assure a creditor against loss in respect of, indebtedness or obligations of others of the kinds referred to in clause (i) through (iv) above, and (vi) liabilities in respect of unfunded vested benefits under plans covered by Title IV of ERISA.

(b) INDEBTEDNESS. The Borrower Parties shall not directly or indirectly create, incur, assume, guarantee, or otherwise become or remain liable with respect to any Debt other than the Advances, indebtedness existing as of the date hereof as described on Schedule 3.05(b) hereto, capitalized leases obligations in an amount not to exceed $250,000 per annum at any time outstanding, and indebtedness to Chase for up to an aggregate principal amount of $3,750,000 pursuant to the Chase Loan Agreements, if any.

SECTION 3.06. CONTINUING GUARANTY; ASSIGNMENTS UNDER LOAN AGREEMENT. This Article 3 provides for a continuing guaranty and shall (i) remain in full force and effect until the later of (x) the payment in full of the Obligations and all other amounts payable under this Article 3 and (y) the expiration or termination of the Commitment, (ii) be binding upon the Guarantors, their successors and assigns, and (iii) inure to the benefit of, and be enforceable by, the Lender and its successors, transferees and assigns. Without limiting the generality of the foregoing clause (iii), the Lender may assign or otherwise transfer all or any portion of its rights and obligations under the Loan Agreement (including, without limitation, all or any portion of its Commitment, the Advances and the Note) to any other person or entity, and such other person or entity shall thereupon become vested with all the benefits in respect thereof granted to the Lender by this Agreement.

ARTICLE 4
REPRESENTATIONS AND WARRANTIES

SECTION 4.01. REPRESENTATIONS AND WARRANTIES OF THE BORROWER PARTIES. The Borrower Parties jointly and severally represent and warrant to the Lender as follows:

(a) ORGANIZATION AND GOOD STANDING. Each of the Borrower Parties and its Subsidiaries is duly organized, validly existing and in good standing under the laws of the jurisdiction of its incorporation. Each Borrower Party and its Subsidiaries is qualified to do business and is in good standing in each jurisdiction in which the ownership of property or the conduct of business requires each to be so qualified, except where the lack of such qualification would not reasonably be expected to have a Material Adverse Effect.

(b) CONFLICTS, DEFAULTS. The execution and delivery of this Agreement and the other agreements and instruments contemplated hereby by the Borrower Parties do not, and the performance of the Borrower Parties' obligations hereunder and thereunder and the consummation by the Borrower Parties of the transactions contemplated hereby (the "TRANSACTIONS") will not: (i) violate, conflict with or constitute a breach or default under the certificate of incorporation or bylaws or equivalent organizational document of any Borrower Party; (ii) require any authorization, approval, consent, registration, declaration or filing with, from or to any Governmental Authority; (iii) violate any Applicable Law; (iv) result in the creation of any lien, security interest, charge or encumbrance upon any of the properties or assets of any Borrower Party or their Subsidiaries (other than as contemplated hereby); or (v) after giving effect to the satisfaction of the condition set forth in Section 2.1(f) of the Loan Agreement, conflict with or result in a breach of, create an event of default (or event that, with the giving of notice or lapse of time or both, would constitute an event of default) under, or give any third party the right to terminate, cancel or accelerate any obligation under, any contract, agreement, note, bond, guarantee, deed of trust, loan agreement, mortgage, license, lease, indenture, instrument, order, arbitration award, judgment or decree to which any Borrower Party is a party or by which any Borrower Party is bound. There is no pending or, to the Knowledge of the Borrower Parties, threatened action, suit, claim, proceeding, inquiry or investigation before or by any Governmental Authority against or affecting any Borrower Party or their Subsidiaries, involving or seeking to restrain or prevent the consummation of the Transactions.

(c) CORPORATE POWER AND AUTHORIZATION. The Borrower Parties have all requisite and legal corporate power to execute and deliver this Agreement and to carry out and perform their other obligations under this Agreement and the Transactions. All corporate action on the part of the Borrower Parties and their directors necessary for the performance of their obligations under this Agreement have been taken. This Agreement is a legal, valid and binding obligation of the Borrower Parties, enforceable in accordance with its terms. The Transactions do not require the consent of the stockholders of the Borrower Parties. The Borrower Parties have provided their stockholders with any notice of the Transactions required by Applicable Law. Each of the Borrower Parties has, independently and without reliance upon the Lender and based on documents and information as it has deemed appropriate, made its own credit analysis and decision to enter into this Agreement.

(d) APPROVALS AND CONSENTS. Except as set forth on Schedule 3.01(d), no license or other authorization, approval or other action by, and no notice to or filing with, any Governmental Authority or other Person is required (i) for the pledge of the Collateral pursuant to this Agreement, for the grant of the assignment, lien and security interest granted hereby or for the execution, delivery or performance of this Agreement and the Transactions, (ii) for the perfection or maintenance of the pledge, assignment and security interest created thereby (other than filings contemplated hereby) or (iii) for the exercise of the remedies in respect of the Collateral pursuant to this Agreement (other than a sale of any Pledged Stock which may have to be registered under the Securities Act of 1933, as amended, and other applicable securities laws). There are no conditions precedent to the effectiveness of this Agreement that have not been satisfied or waived.

(e) LIEN AND SECURITY IN THE COLLATERAL.

(i) All of the Inventory is located at the places specified in Schedule I hereto. The chief place of business and chief executive office of the Borrower and the office where the records concerning the Collateral, including current statements regarding Receivables, the stock ledger recording the Pledged Stock, the originals of all chattel paper that evidence Receivables and the original stock certificates representing the Pledged Stock, is located at the address specified in Section 5.02.

(ii) The Borrower Parties are the legal and beneficial owner of the Collateral, free and clear of any lien, security interest, option or other charge or encumbrance except for the security interest created by this Agreement and the prior lien on the Collateral in favor of Chase as security for the credit facilities provided by Chase pursuant to the Chase Loan Agreements. The Borrower Parties have exclusive possession and control of the Inventory and the stock certificates representing the Pledged Stock. No effective financing statement or other document similar in effect covering all or any part of the Collateral is on file in any recording office (other than those in favor of Chase as security for the credit facilities provided by Chase pursuant to the Chase Loan Agreements). The Borrower Parties own and operate under the trade name "Little Switzerland" and variations thereof. None of the Receivables is evidenced by a promissory note or other instrument.

(iii) Upon delivery to the Lender of the stock certificates evidencing the Pledged Stock and the taking of any further actions as contemplated in Section 2.05 with respect to the Collateral, the security interest created by this Agreement will constitute a valid, perfected security interest in the Collateral securing the payment of the Obligations, enforceable in accordance with the terms of this Agreement and the Loan Agreement against all creditors of the Borrower Parties and any Persons purporting to purchase any of the Collateral from the Borrower Parties, except (i) as affected by bankruptcy, insolvency, fraudulent conveyance, reorganization, moratorium and other similar laws relating to or affecting creditors' rights generally, general equitable principles (whether considered in a proceeding in equity or at law) and an implied covenant of good faith and fair dealing and (ii) the prior lien on the Collateral in favor of Chase as security for the credit facilities provided by Chase pursuant to the Chase Loan Agreements.

(f) THE PLEDGED STOCK.

(i) The shares of Pledged Stock constitute all the issued and outstanding shares of all classes of the capital stock of each Issuer. There are no outstanding options, warrants or other rights to purchase any shares of capital stock of any Issuer.

(ii) All the shares of the Pledged Stock are, and all other Pledged Stock in which the Borrower Parties shall hereafter grant a security interest pursuant to this Agreement will be, duly and validly issued, fully paid and non-assessable. An appropriate notation has been placed on the stock ledger or other books and records of each Issuer of the Pledged Stock (and, in the case of Pledged Stock hereafter acquired by the Borrower Parties, will be so placed on the stock ledger or other books and records of the Issuer of such stock pledged hereunder) in order to reflect the pledge in favor of the Lender securing the payment of the Obligations.

(g) FINANCIAL STATEMENTS. The financial statements of the Borrower Parties (collectively, the "FINANCIAL STATEMENTS") have been provided to the Lender. The Financial Statements: (i) have been prepared in accordance with the books and records of the Borrower Parties; (ii) have been prepared in all material respects in accordance with GAAP; (iii) reflect and provide adequate reserves and disclosures in respect of all liabilities of the Borrower Parties, including all contingent liabilities; and (iv) present fairly the financial position of the Borrower Parties at such dates and the results of operations and cash flows of the Borrower Parties for the periods then ended. The Borrower Parties: (i) keep books, records and accounts that, in reasonable detail, accurately and fairly reflect the transactions and dispositions of assets; and (ii) maintain a system of internal accounting controls sufficient to provide reasonable assurance that (A) transactions are executed in accordance with management's general or specific authorization, (B) transactions are recorded as necessary to permit preparation of financial statements in accordance with GAAP to maintain accountability for assets, (C) access to assets is permitted only in accordance with management's general or specific authorizations and (D) the recorded accountability for assets and inventory is compared with existing assets and inventory at reasonable intervals and appropriate action is taken with respect to any differences.

(h) COMPLIANCE WITH LAW. Each Borrower Party and its Subsidiaries is in compliance in all material respects with all Applicable Law. No Borrower Party has received any notification of any asserted present or past failure to comply with Applicable Law.

(i) ABSENCE OF UNDISCLOSED LIABILITIES. None of the Borrower Parties or their Subsidiaries has any indebtedness or liability, whether accrued, fixed or contingent, whether or not required by GAAP to be disclosed on the Financial Statements, other than (a) liabilities reflected in the Financial Statements, (b) liabilities, none of which individually or in the aggregate is material to the assets, properties, business or business prospects any of the Borrower Parties or their Subsidiaries, and (c) liabilities incurred in the ordinary course of business of each of the Borrower Parties or their Subsidiaries (consistent with past practice in terms of both frequency and amount) subsequent to February 24, 2001.

(j) LITIGATION. Except as set forth on Schedule 4.01(j), there is no pending or, to the Knowledge of the Borrower Parties, threatened litigation, action, suit, proceeding, arbitration, claim, investigation or administrative proceeding, by or before any Governmental Authority or dispute resolution panel, involving or affecting any of the Borrower Parties or their Subsidiaries, or the assets, properties or business of any of the Borrower Parties or their Subsidiaries, or relating to or involving the transactions contemplated by the Loan Documents. No litigation, action, suit, proceeding, arbitration, claim, investigation or administrative proceeding, whether or not set forth on Schedule 4.01(j), reasonably could be expected to have a Material Adverse Effect or to result in the imposition of a lien, security interest or other encumbrance on any of the assets of any of the Borrower Parties or their Subsidiaries. None of the Borrower Parties or their Subsidiaries has received any opinion or memorandum or legal advice or notice from legal counsel to the effect that it is exposed, from a legal standpoint, to any liability or disadvantage that may be material to its assets, properties, business or business prospects. None of the Borrower Parties or their Subsidiaries is in default with respect to any material order, writ, injunction or decree known to or served upon any of the Borrower Parties or their Subsidiaries. Except as set forth on Schedule 4.01(j), there is no pending action or suit brought by any of the Borrower Parties or their Subsidiaries against others.

ARTICLE 5
MISCELLANEOUS

SECTION 5.01. INDEMNITY AND EXPENSES. (a) The Borrower Parties agree to jointly and severally indemnify the Lender from and against any and all claims, losses and liabilities (including reasonable attorneys' fees) growing out of or resulting from this Agreement (including, without limitation, enforcement of this Agreement), except for those claims, losses and liabilities attributable to the willful misconduct or bad faith of Lender.

(b) The Borrower Parties will upon demand pay to the Lender the amount of any and all reasonable expenses, including the reasonable fees and expenses of its counsel and of any experts and Lenders, which the Lender may incur in connection with (i) the custody, preservation, use or operation of, or the sale of, collection from, or other realization upon, any of the Collateral, (ii) the exercise or enforcement of any of the rights of the Lender hereunder or under the Implementing Agreements or (iii) the failure by the Borrower Parties to perform or observe any of the provisions hereof or thereof.

SECTION 5.02. NOTICES. All notices, requests and other communications under this Agreement will be in writing and will be deemed to have been duly given if delivered personally, or sent by either certified or registered mail, return receipt requested, postage prepaid, by overnight courier guaranteeing next day delivery or by telecopier (with telephonic or machine confirmation by the sender), addressed as follows:

(a) If to the Borrower Parties:

[Borrower Notice Information Omitted]

With a copy to:

[Counsel Notice Information Omitted]

or at such other address or telecopy number as the Borrower may have advised theLender in writing; and

(b) If to the Lender:

[Lender Notice Information Omitted]

With a copy to:

[Counsel Notice Information Omitted]

or at such other address or telecopy number as the Lender may have advised the Borrower Parties in writing. All such notices, requests and other communications shall be deemed to have been received on the date of delivery thereof (if delivered by hand), on the third day after the mailing thereof (if mailed), on the next day after the sending thereof (if by overnight courier) and when receipt is confirmed as provided above (if telecopied).

SECTION 5.03. WAIVERS AND AMENDMENTS. No amendment or waiver of any provision of this Agreement, nor consent to any departure therefrom, will be effective unless the same shall be in writing and signed by an officer of each party hereto, and then such waiver or consent will be effective only in the specific instance and for the specific purpose for which given. No failure on the part of a party hereto to exercise, and no delay in exercising, any right hereunder will operate as a waiver thereof; nor will any single or partial exercise of any right hereunder preclude any other or further exercise thereof or the exercise of any other right. The remedies provided in this Agreement are cumulative and, unless otherwise expressly provided herein, not exclusive of any remedies provided by law.

SECTION 5.04. BINDING EFFECT. This Agreement will be binding upon and inure to the benefit of the parties and their respective heirs, executors, administrators, personal representatives, successors and permitted assigns. No party may assign his or its rights hereunder or any interest herein without the prior written consent of the other parties and such attempted assignment shall be void and without effect, provided however, that the Lender may assign, to one or more of its Affiliates, all or any part of, or any interest in, the Lender's rights and benefits hereunder. To the extent of such assignment, such assignee will have the same rights and benefits against the other parties as it would have had if it were a named party hereunder. No party will be released of any of its obligations under this Agreement by virtue of such assignment.

(SECTION 5.05 INTENTIONALLY OMITTED)

SECTION 5.06. GOVERNING LAW. THIS AGREEMENT, THE TRANS-ACTIONS CONTEMPLATED HEREBY THE RIGHTS AND OBLIGATIONS OF THE PARTIES HERETO, AND ANY DISPUTES OR CONTROVERSIES ARISING THEREFROM SHALL BE GOVERNED BY AND CONSTRUED AND ENFORCED IN ACCORDANCE WITH THE LAWS OF THE STATE OF NEW YORK, WITHOUT REGARD TO ITS PRINCIPLES OF CONFLICT OF LAWS THAT WOULD PROVIDE FOR THE APPLICATION OF ANY OTHER LAW.

SECTION 5.07. CAPTIONS. The captions, headings and arrangements used in this Agreement are for convenience only and do not in any way affect, limit or amplify the provisions hereof.

SECTION 5.08. ENTIRETY. This Agreement contains the entire agreement and understanding between the parties with respect to the matters addressed herein and supersedes all prior representations, inducements, promises or agreements, oral or otherwise, which are not embodied herein.

SECTION 5.09. COUNTERPARTS. This Agreement may be executed in multiple counterparts, each of which will be deemed an original for all purposes and all of which will be deemed collectively to be one agreement. Execution may be effected by delivery of facsimiles of signature pages, followed by delivery of originals of such pages.

SECTION 5.10. THIRD PARTY BENEFICIARIES. Nothing contained herein, express or implied, is intended to confer upon any person or entity other than the parties and their heirs, executors, administrators, personal representatives, successors and permitted assigns any rights or remedies under or by reason of this Agreement, except as otherwise expressly provided in this Agreement.

IN WITNESS WHEREOF, the Borrower Parties and the Lender have caused this Agreement to be duly executed and delivered by the officer of each thereunto duly authorized as of the date first above written.

[Signature Page Omitted]

[Schedules and Exhibits Omitted]

1. Credit Enhancement: Third-Party Guaranties

A party enters into a guaranty agreement when it promises to pay the debts of another. Under Article 3 of the U.C.C., which governs negotiable instruments, one may agree to guarantee a note merely by signing the note itself.[57] However, sophisticated commercial entities are likely to execute a separate guaranty agreement that clearly specifies the rights and obligations of the guarantor and guarantee parties. The SPG Agreement includes an example of this.

As a brief aside, a device that is similar to a guaranty is the "letter of credit." Commonly, a bank issues a letter of credit, under which the bank is to pay a specified sum upon presentation of the letter by a third party (the "beneficiary"), as long as any specified conditions are satisfied. A letter of credit is broadly similar to a guaranty in that, in both cases, a lender causes a borrower to obtain the promise of a third party to pay in the event that the borrower does not and, so, both are devices that a lender may use to help ensure that it will ultimately be paid. Article 5 of the U.C.C. governs letters of credit. For a brief overview of letters of credit and for an international perspective focused on one of the world's major centers of banking, we asked a seasoned practitioner to offer her insight.

A Practitioner Perspective: Standby Letters of Credit and Swiss Law

The standby letter of credit has its origin in American banking legislation, which prohibits U.S. credit institutions from assuming guarantee obligations vis-à-vis third parties and has as a consequence propelled the introduction and use of the standby letter of credit. The standby letter of credit is not a construct of Swiss law; it can, however, be used in lieu of a traditional Swiss bank guarantee. It is prevalent mainly in the context of import and export business with the U.S. but increasingly also in trade transactions with the Far East and, of course, wherever the contracting parties decide to opt for this legal form.[1]

Under Swiss law, the term "bank guarantee" is generically used for the following constructs: surety (simple surety, joint and several surety), guarantee, confirmed payment order and standby letter of credit. These legal forms are used to secure performance and provide the contracting parties with the assurance that the transaction they have entered into will actually be carried out. To properly assess the expertise or financial prospects of a supplier is a difficult task for most customers purchasing goods or services, which is why a guarantee for the purpose of securing performance is often required.[2] In international trade, the use of a bank guarantee as a means of securing payment is basically restricted

---

57. See U.C.C. § 3-419 (2002).

1. UBS AG, 1998-2010, BANK GUARANTEES: EXPLOITING KNOW-HOW IS CRUCIAL TO KEEP THE WHEELS OF BUSINESS TURNING 4, 8.

2. UBS AG, 1998-2010, DOCUMENTARY CREDITS AND COLLECTIONS: IN-DEPTH KNOWLEDGE IS DECISIVE FOR THE FLOW OF INTERNATIONAL COMMERCE 83.

to a (default) payment guarantee. In international transactions, non-Swiss parties hardly ever accept sureties and demand guarantees governed by Swiss law, as they are unwilling to familiarize themselves with the intricacies of the Swiss Code of Obligations.

Standby letters of credit are used instead of documentary credits and guarantees to secure both payment and performance—i.e., to secure any claims by the obligee against the obligor due to a failure of contractual delivery or performance by the agreed date. In the context of securing performance of the contract, letters of credit are a means to secure payment as well. The main difference between a letter of credit and a guarantee is that letters of credit are used as a payment instrument whereas guarantees provide assurance that contractual obligations will be fulfilled. As with a traditional bank guarantee, the standby letter of credit covers numerous scenarios: tender guarantee, advance payment guarantee, performance guarantee and retention money guarantee.

Like the guarantee, the standby letter of credit is legally separated from the underlying transaction.[3]

In the case of a standby letter of credit, the documents stipulated in the claim must be submitted within the specified period. These documents should show that the client (exporter) has not met or has insufficiently fulfilled his/her performance obligations or that the debtor has not made a payment on time. The standby basically fulfills the same purpose as a guarantee: it is payable upon first demand and without objections or defenses on the basis of the underlying transaction. The bank does not need to verify whether a claim is justified. The minimum document required when payment is demanded is the declaration from the beneficiary stating the principal's default. All the bank has to do is to ensure that the demand for payment made by the beneficiary as well as any other documents described in the standby letter of credit appear to correspond to the terms thereof.

If the documents based on which payment is made are forged, the erroneously paid amount can be claimed back (based on Art. 63, para. 1 of the Swiss Code of Obligations and as confirmed by the Swiss Supreme Court[4]). The abstract nature of the standby as well as the mechanism of payment on demand have led to numerous attempts by parties to claim payment without the covered risk having materialized; a fact which is illustrated by numerous cases concerning non-justified and legally abusive payment demands.[5]

Swiss courts have been reluctant to determine bad faith and legally abusive claims for payment on demand by the beneficiary. The fraudulent claim has to be proven in order for a bank to deny payment. If the beneficiary severely breaches his/her contractual obligations, proactively prevents performance, or explicitly

---

3. Mark R. Richter, *Eine systematische Darstellung unter besonderer Berücksichtigung des US-amerikanischen Rechts* 121 (1990).
4. BGE 131 III 222 ff; Heinrich Honsell, *Schweizerisches Obligationenrecht, Besonderer Teil* 382 (2006).
5. Norbert Horn, *Die Bankgarantie im internationalen Umfeld, in* PERSONALSICHERHEITEN 87 (1997); Richter, *supra* note 3, at 242.

renounces said secured performance, he/she is deemed to be acting in bad faith and in a legally abusive way.[6]

In general, standby letters of credit are to contain: (i) an introduction/ preamble to set out the contractual relationship between the obligor in the underlying transaction and the beneficiary, (ii) a "guarantee" clause, and (c) an expiration clause at the minimum.[7] The "guarantee" clause obligates the bank on behalf of the principal obligor (bank client) to pay a sum of money to the beneficiary (generally a contracting partner of the principal obligor in the underlying transaction). The clause contains an amount of the letter of credit (aggregate amount, currency denomination) and defines the conditions under which the bank can be required to pay.

The expiration clause governs the duration of the obligation entered into and as a result any demand for payment must be lodged with the guarantor named in the deed on or before the specified date; if not, the beneficiary is deemed to have forfeited his/her rights under the guarantee. The beneficiary is responsible for the mailing risk and any other delays (e.g., force majeure). This is not to be confused with the fact that since the standby letter of credit is independent of the underlying relationship, an incident of force majeure which concerns the underlying relationship (e.g., earthquake in the country of the beneficiary) does not affect the payment obligation of the bank in general and hence demanding payment is not considered to be an act of bad faith on the part of the beneficiary.[8] The same holds true in case a deficiency exists at the time of entering into the contract, if the underlying relationship is illegal or gets dissolved.

The letter of credit amount and the term both depend on the purpose of the security. The standby letter offers usually a credit in the amount of 5% to 20% of the value of the contract, the amount of the contract price or part thereof, or the amount of the loan.[9]

In contrast to the guarantee, a standby can be confirmed immediately, provided the standby conditions permit it, and thus the country and credit risk can be deferred.

On January 1, 1999, the International Chamber of Commerce introduced the International Standby Practices ("ISP 98"), new guidelines, which were drawn up especially for standby letters of credit business.[10] In practice, however, standbys are generally still subject to the Uniform Customs and Practice for Documentary Credits ("UCP 600"). Both of these regulations provide an interpretation of the regulations that are common in the different countries that utilize standby letters of credit. Both the ISP 98 and the UCP 600 have to be explicitly agreed on and referenced to in the standby letter of credit to be applicable.

---

6. Franziska Löw, *Missbrauch von Bankgarantien und vorläufiger Rechtsschutz, Eine rechtsvergleichende Untersuchung des US-amerikanischen, englischen und Schweizer Rechts* 109 (2002).

7. UBS AG, Bank Guarantees, *supra* note 1, at 11.

8. Löw, *supra* note 6, at 91.

9. UBS AG, Bank Guarantees, *supra* note 1, at 15.

10. BSK OR Thomas Koller, *Anhang zum 18. Titel: Das Dokumentenakkreditiv, Basler Kommentar zum Schweizerischen Privatrecht, Obligationenrecht I, Art. 1 – 529 OR*, (Honsell et al. eds., 2007).

As a general rule, and unless otherwise agreed, the applicable law is the one of the issuing bank. Under Swiss law the parties are free to determine the contents and form of a letter of credit. Issues not provided for will be determined on the basis of Art. 111 Swiss Code of Obligations.[11]

In December 1995, the UN General Assembly passed Resolution 50/48 and introduced the United Nations Convention on Independent Guarantees and Stand-by Letters of Credit to unify the law. This Convention equates bank guarantees and standby letters of credit by using the technical term of "independent undertakings."[12] This convention has not yielded the success envisaged, as countries such as the U.S., the UK and Switzerland are not willing to abandon their case law, in particular in the area of abuse of law and injunctive relief in favor of a unified body of law.[13]

Anne M. Wildhaber, lic.iur., LL.M.
Attorney-at-Law (admitted to the bar in
Switzerland and New York)
UBS AG, Litigation & Investigations

From a discussion of international law and letters of credit, we turn to U.S. domestic law and guaranties.

a. Types of Guaranty: Payment and Collection

The law generally distinguishes between two types of guaranties: (1) a "guaranty of payment"; and (2) a "guaranty of collection." A guarantor of payment promises to pay another's obligation immediately upon the borrower's default, regardless of any action taken by the creditor as against the debtor.[59] A guarantor of collection promises to pay another's obligation only after the creditor has taken all reasonable efforts to collect against the primary obligor, usually including judicial enforcement.[60] Courts will look to the language used in a guaranty agreement to discern whether it is a guaranty of payment or collection,

---

11. Susan Emmenegger & Andrea Zbinden, *Die Inanspruchnahme der Bankgarantie, in* Kreditsicherheiten 145 (Susan Emmenegger ed., 2008).

12. Horn, *supra* note 5, at 96.

13. Löw, *supra* note 6, at 171.

59. *See, e.g., Perry Drug Stores v. NP Holding Corp.*, 243 F. App'x 989, 996 (6th Cir. 2007) ("[U]nder Michigan law, whether the guarantee must first sue the primary obligor depends upon the type of guaranty. While the guarantee may proceed immediately against the guarantor if it is a guaranty of payment, if it is a guaranty of collection, the guarantee must first sue the primary obligor.") (internal citation and quotation marks omitted); *Sterling Prop. Mgmt., Inc. v. Tex. Commerce Bank, Nat'l Ass'n*, 32 F.3d 964, 967-68 (5th Cir. 1994) ("[Under Texas law, a] guaranty of payment, which is also known as an absolute guaranty, requires the guarantor to pay immediately upon the principal obligor's default.") (internal citation and quotation marks omitted).

60. *See, e.g. Perry Drug Stores*, 243 F. App'x at 996; *United States v. Vahlco Corp.*, 800 F.2d 462, 466 (5th Cir. 1986) ("A conditional guaranty, also termed a 'guaranty of collection', is one under which the creditor can seek performance from the guarantor only after the occurrence of some condition such as the condition that the creditor has unsuccessfully and with reasonable diligence sought to collect the debt from the principal debtor.").

and, accordingly, parties should clearly state as much in the contract. Which type of guaranty does the SPG Agreement contemplate in Article 3 of the SPG Agreement, and how do you know?

b. Rights of a Guarantor upon Payment

When a guarantor performs its guaranty obligation, it commonly gains a "right of reimbursement" against the debtor to collect the amount paid to the creditor on the debtor's behalf.[61] In addition, when the guarantor satisfies the creditor's rights under the debt in full, the guarantor, as a general rule, becomes "subrogated" as a matter of law to the rights of the creditor.[62] This means that the guarantor "steps into the shoes" of the creditor and obtains the creditor's rights to recover as against the debtor. Against this backdrop, we see that, in § 3.03 of the SPG Agreement, the Lender has received a covenant from the Guarantors not to exercise any of their subrogation rights until all amounts owed to the Lender are paid in full and the Lender no longer has any obligation to make Advances. Here, it appears the Lender does not want the Guarantors to siphon money away from the Borrower until the Lender has no outstanding loans or potential to have outstanding loans to the Borrower.

c. Waiving the Defenses of a Guarantor

As a general rule, a guarantor may raise any defense of the primary obligor (i.e., the borrower).[63] However, this rule is subject to certain exceptions; for example, a guarantor cannot raise as a defense—and thereby avoid its guaranty obligation—that the primary obligor lacked capacity (e.g., was a minor) or that the primary obligor's obligations were discharged in bankruptcy.[64] These exceptions make good sense, as a lender will often require a guaranty for these precise reasons. In these situations, a lender will commonly look to a guarantor (e.g., a minor's parent) before agreeing to make the loan. In addition to these exceptions, a defense of the primary obligor may be unavailable to a guarantor because the guarantor has waived the defense. A guarantor may waive a defense of the borrower by stating so in the guaranty agreement, and, in this way, a guarantor may take on even more liability than the borrower.[65] Courts have found a waiver of specific defenses in broad language waiving all defenses of the

---

61. *See, e.g.,* Restatement (Third) of Suretyship & Guaranty § 22 (1996).

62. *See, e.g., id.* § 27 (1996); *Putnam v. Comm'r of Internal Revenue*, 352 U.S. 82, 85 (1956) ("[U]pon the payment by the guarantor of the debt, the debtor's obligation to the creditor becomes an obligation to the guarantor, not a new debt, but, by subrogation, the result of the shift of the original debt from the creditor to the guarantor who steps into the creditor's shoes.").

63. *See, e.g.,* Restatement (Third) of Suretyship & Guaranty § 34(1) (1996).

64. *See, e.g., id.*

65. Peter A. Alces, The Law of Suretyship and Guaranty § 7:6 (2010) ("[T]he secondary obligation may in fact exceed the principal obligation, as, for instance, when the secondary obligor explicitly waives the benefit of any defenses available to the principal.").

borrower,[66] including language that a guaranty is "absolute and unconditional."[67] Please notice that § 3.01(b) provides that the Guarantors' Obligations are "absolute and unconditional" and are independent of the obligations of the Borrower, and that the Guarantors guarantee that the Obligations will be paid irrespective of any defense available to any of the Borrower Parties.

A lender may be found liable to a guarantor if the lender impairs the value of the debtor's collateral securing the loan. "In limited circumstances, an obligee . . . may be held liable for impairment of suretyship status if it acts 'to increase the secondary obligor's . . . risk of loss by increasing its potential cost of performance or decreasing its potential ability to cause the principal obligor . . . to bear the cost of performance.'"[68] Examples of ways in which a creditor may impair the underlying collateral include:

> (a) failure to obtain or maintain perfection or recordation of the interest in collateral;
> (b) release of collateral without substitution of collateral of equal value or equivalent reduction of the underlying obligation;
> (c) failure to perform a duty to preserve the value of collateral owed to the principal obligor or the secondary obligor; and
> (d) failure to comply with applicable law in disposing of collateral.[69]

As with the defenses of a guarantor, the right of a guarantor to recover against a creditor for its impairment of the collateral may be waived by the guarantor.[70] Where the guarantor has given an unconditional guaranty of payment, the guarantor may be found to have waived the defense of impairment.[71] Accordingly, in § 3.02, notice that the Guarantors have waived any notice rights they may have and any right to avoid a guaranty obligation for the Lender's failure to perfect (a concept which we discuss below) or otherwise to protect its security interest in the collateral.

---

66. *See, e.g., Compagnie Financiere de CIC et de L'Union Europeenne v. Merrill Lynch, Pierce, Fenner & Smith Inc.*, 188 F.3d 31, 36 (2d Cir. 1999) ("The waiver also reached any defense that would relate to the underlying debt. . . . The waiver of defenses in this case was thus broad enough to encompass release of the primary debtor."); *see also* RESTATEMENT (THIRD) OF SURETYSHIP & GUARANTY § 48(1) (1996) ("Such consent, agreement, or waiver, if express, may be effectuated by specific language or by general language indicating that the secondary obligor waives defenses based on suretyship.").

67. *See, e.g., First N.Y. Bank for Bus. v. DeMarco*, 130 B.R. 650, 654 (S.D.N.Y. 1991) ("Indeed, unconditional guaranties have been held to foreclose, as a matter of law, guarantors from asserting any defenses or counterclaims.").

68. *McWane, Inc. v. Fid. & Deposit Co. of Md.*, 372 F.3d 798, 804 (6th Cir. 2004) (quoting RESTATEMENT (THIRD) OF SURETYSHIP AND GUARANTY § 37(1) (1996)).

69. RESTATEMENT (THIRD) SURETYSHIP & GUARANTY § 42(2) (1996).

70. *See, e.g., Joslin v. Beavert*, No. 96-2665WA, 1997 WL 434038, at *1 (8th Cir. 1997) (finding waiver of defense of impairment of collateral to be effective under Texas law).

71. *See, e.g., Istituto Mobiliare Italiano, S.p.A. v. Motorola, Inc.*, 689 F. Supp. 812, 817 (N.D. Ill. 1988) ("[Under New York law, although] impairment of security resulting from a creditor's unreasonable conduct, negligence or bad faith normally discharges a surety from liability to the extent of the impairment, the defense of impairment of collateral is not available to one who has given an unconditional guarantee of payment.").

2. Requirements of a Security Agreement Under Article Nine

Under Article 9 of the Uniform Commercial Code, a creditor obtains a security interest in the debtor's assets enforceable against the debtor and third parties only if (1) value has been given; (2) the debtor has sufficient rights in the collateral, or otherwise has the power, to grant the security interest; and (3) one of several evidentiary conditions are met, the most basic of which is that the debtor has authenticated a security agreement that provides a description of the collateral.[72] In most any commercial loan, value will be given to the debtor, satisfying the first prong, in the commitment to lend money or the money lent to the debtor. The second prong states the simple proposition that the debtor cannot give the creditor a security interest if the debtor does not have sufficient rights to grant it.[73] For example, if the debtor has the rights of a mere "bailee" in certain assets, then the debtor generally does not have sufficient rights to grant a security interest in those assets.[74] A "bailment" refers to "the delivery of personal property by one person to another in trust *for a specific purpose,* with a contract, express or implied, that the trust shall be faithfully executed and the property returned or duly accounted for when the special purpose is accomplished."[75]

Lastly, to obtain a security interest in the debtor's collateral and satisfy the third prong, the creditor may want the debtor to execute a security agreement. On this score, Article 9 does not require much. According to Article 9, a security agreement is any agreement that provides for the creation of a security interest.[76] For the security agreement to be effective, the debtor—that is, the person granting the security interest in the property—must sign the security agreement, and the security agreement must sufficiently describe the collateral in which the security interest is granted. A surefire way for a security agreement to describe most collateral sufficiently, under Article 9, is to identify the collateral by one of the categories of collateral that Article 9 provides (e.g., inventory, equipment, payment intangible).[77] (Now, of course, describing collateral at the categorical level might be overbroad vis-à-vis the security interest one wishes to grant as part

---

72. U.C.C. § 9-203(b) (2000).

73. *See id.* § 9-203 cmt. 6.

74. *See, e.g., Evergreen Marine Corp. v. Six Consignments of Frozen Scallops,* 4 F.3d 90, 98 (1st Cir. 1993) ("Although the term 'rights in the collateral' is not defined in the Code, and has been viewed broadly by courts on occasion, it clearly contemplates some *property interest* in goods, not mere bare possession acquired from a bailee under a transaction of entrustment.") (emphasis in original) (internal citation omitted); *GMAC Bus. Credit, L.L.C. v. Ford Motor Co.,* 100 F. App'x 404, 408-09 (6th Cir. 2004) (finding that the debtor had sufficient rights to grant a security interest and was not a mere bailee).

75. *GMAC Bus. Credit, L.L.C.,* 100 F. App'x at 407-08 (Michigan law) (emphasis in original) (internal citations omitted).

76. U.C.C. § 9-102(a)(73) (2000).

77. *Id.* § 9-108(b); *see also id.* § 9-108(e) ("A description only by type of collateral defined in [the Uniform Commercial Code] is an insufficient description of: (1) a commercial tort claim; or (2) in a consumer transaction, consumer goods, a security entitlement, a securities account, or a commodity account.").

of a particular transaction.) In contrast, referring to the debtor's collateral "supergenerically" in a security agreement—for example, by identifying the collateral as "all the debtor's assets"—is a surefire way *not* to describe collateral sufficiently for Article 9 purposes.[78] A security agreement may grant a security interest in collateral that the debtor has not yet come to possess—so-called "after-acquired collateral."[79] With after-acquired collateral, the security interest attaches when the debtor acquires sufficient rights in the collateral (presuming the other requirements are satisfied). Under Article 9, a security interest also automatically continues in the identifiable proceeds of collateral, for instance, if the debtor sells or otherwise disposes of the collateral.[80] Section 2.01 of the SPG Agreement provides that the Borrower Parties grant a security interest in several assets. Are these sufficiently described in the Agreement so as to create an enforceable security interest?

While a security agreement must describe collateral with at least some degree of specificity, the security agreement need not, as a general rule, describe the secured loan amount with any specificity whatsoever in order to be enforceable. As the official comments to Article 9 provide, "Indeed, the parties are free to agree that a security interest secures any obligation whatsoever. Determining the obligations secured by collateral is solely a matter of construing the parties' agreement under applicable law."[81] Accordingly, most courts are in accord that so-called "dragnet" clauses—provisions that broadly state that a security agreement secures all current and future obligations that the debtor owes the creditor—are enforceable.[82] We need look no further than § 2.02 of the SPG Agreement for an example of such a clause.

3. Perfection of Security Interests

In general, a secured party with a "perfected" security interest in collateral enjoys a position senior to a secured party with an "unperfected" security interest in that same collateral.[83] In addition, in bankruptcy, a perfected secured party generally enjoys secured status superior to any unperfected secured

---

78. *Id.* § 9-108(c) ("A description of collateral as 'all the debtor's assets' or 'all the debtor's personal property' or using words of similar import does not reasonably identify the collateral.").

79. *Id.* § 9-204(a). However, under U.C.C. § 9-204(b) (2000), a security interest will not attach to collateral acquired after a security agreement is executed, despite a security agreement providing for a security interest to attach in after-acquired collateral, as to: (1) collateral that is consumer goods, unless the debtor acquires sufficient rights in the consumer goods within ten days after giving value; and (2) a commercial tort claim.

80. *Id.* § 9-315(a)(2).

81. *Id.* § 9-204 cmt. 5.

82. *See, e.g., Universal Guar. Life Ins. Co. v. Coughlin*, 481 F.3d 458, 463 (7th Cir. 2007) ("Dragnet clauses are not favored in Illinois, but they are enforceable if they are clear and unambiguous."); *Pride Hyundai, Inc. v. Chrysler Fin. Co.*, 369 F.3d 603, 612-15 (1st Cir. 2004); *Horob v. Farm Credit Servs. of N.D. ACA*, 777 N.W.2d 611, 615-16 (N.D. 2010).

83. U.C.C. § 9-322 (2000).

parties, and an unperfected secured party is generally given the same treatment as any other general unsecured creditor in bankruptcy.[84] As between perfected secured parties, the general rule is that the first to perfect enjoys the senior-most priority in collateral.[85] Accordingly, it behooves a secured party to perfect its security interest and to perfect first. A common method of perfecting a security interest is by the filing of a financing statement (sometimes called a "U.C.C. filing").[86]

For most financing statements to be filed effectively, the debtor must have authorized the filing.[87] A debtor may authorize a filing of a financing statement in collateral by signing a security agreement that describes that collateral.[88] By signing a security agreement covering certain collateral, a debtor also authorizes the filing of a financing statement covering proceeds in that collateral.[89] Even though Article 9 provides that the security agreement itself is authorization enough, notice that § 2.04(b) of the SPG Agreement explicitly provides that the Borrower Parties authorize the Lender to file financing and continuation statements relating to the Collateral. For a financing statement to be sufficient, it must provide the names of the debtor and the secured party, and it must indicate the collateral covered by the financing statement.[90] A *financing statement* may effectively indicate collateral by describing the collateral "super-generically."[91] Recall that this was not the case with a *security agreement*, which must describe collateral more specifically to be effective. For example, a financing statement may sufficiently indicate the collateral it covers by providing "an indication that the financing statement covers all assets or all personal property."[92] A financing statement should also include the address of the debtor, or else the filing office is entitled to reject the filing.[93]

Note that § 9-521 of Article 9 provides a model financing statement. As the official comments provide, "A filing office that accepts written communications may not reject, on grounds of form or format, a filing using these forms."[94]

---

84. *See* JAMES J. WHITE & ROBERT S. SUMMERS, UNIFORM COMMERCIAL CODE (HORNBOOK SERIES) § 31-4, at 4 (5th ed. 2000) ("Thus a secured creditor who perfects prior to bankruptcy usually enjoys a solitary feast, but an unperfected secured party will invariably have to eat from the general creditors' trough in bankruptcy.").

85. U.C.C. § 9-322(a) (2000).

86. For a discussion of perfection by filing, see U.C.C. § 9-310 (2000).

87. *Id.* § 9-509(a)(1). U.C.C. § 9-509(a)(2) (2000) provides a separate rule for agricultural liens.

88. *Id.* § 9-509(b)(1).

89. *Id.* § 9-509(b)(2).

90. *Id.* § 9-502(a).

91. *Id.* § 9-504(2).

92. *Id.*

93. *Id.* § 9-516(b). Notice that § 9-516(b) provides a host of other factors, each of which allows the filing office to reject a financing statement.

94. *Id.* § 9-521 cmt. 2.

4. Remedies Available to a Secured Lender

Article 9 provides a secured party with certain rights and remedies upon default. What constitutes default is left to the parties to decide in their agreement.[95] This underscores the importance of defining what constitutes "default," as the Loan Agreement does in § 5.1 (where it defines Events of Default). Absent the parties' contractual definition, a court may opt to find default only in a borrower's failure to pay the loan.[96]

A secured party may enforce a security interest by any available judicial procedure;[97] however, this may be costly and take time. The secured party may also exercise "self-help" by taking possession of the collateral and may even render equipment unusable.[98] In so doing, a secured party need not go through judicial channels but must proceed without breaching the peace.[99] This duty to avoid breaching the peace while enforcing its remedies is one that the secured party cannot avoid or alter by contract—it is an example of mandatory law.[100]

In addition, upon a debtor's default, a secured party may sell, lease, license, or otherwise dispose of collateral, as long as such disposition is commercially reasonable in all respects.[101] However, before doing so, the secured party generally must give notice to the debtor, any secondary obligors (e.g., a guarantor), and any other secured parties that are perfected or that have given the disposing secured party notice of a claim of an interest in the collateral.[102] Proceeds from a sale or other disposition are paid out to secured creditors in the order of their priority: The secured party that disposed of the collateral receives proceeds up to the amount of its secured obligation and, then, subordinate secured parties receive proceeds up to the amount of their secured obligations, in the order of their respective priority.[103] The baseline rule is that after all proceeds from a disposition are paid out, any remaining surplus goes to the debtor,[104] and, if the proceeds are insufficient to satisfy all secured claims, then the obligor—the party liable for the secured obligations—remains liable for any such deficiency.[105] The parties may vary their rights and obligations with respect to a potential deficiency by agreement, for example, providing a creditor has no right to a deficiency and limiting the creditor's recourse to the collateral alone.[106]

---

95. *Id.* § 9-601 cmt. 3.
96. *See, e.g., Cofield v. Randolph Cnty. Comm'n,* 90 F.3d 468, 471 (11th Cir. 1996).
97. U.C.C. §9-601(a)(1) (2000).
98. *Id.* § 9-609(a).
99. *Id.* § 9-609(b)(2).
100. *Id.* §§ 9-602(6), 9-603(b).
101. *Id.* §§ 9-610(a), (b).
102. *Id.* § 9-611(c).
103. *Id.* § 9-615(a).
104. *Id.* § 9-608(a)(4); *see also id.* § 9-615(d)(1).
105. *Id.* § 9-608(a)(4); *see also id.* § 9-615(d)(2).
106. *See id.* § 9-608 cmt. 3.

When a secured party disposes of collateral after default, the secured party's security interest is discharged and all subordinate security interests are discharged.[107] However, any security interests senior to the disposing secured party's interest remain in the collateral.[108] This underscores the value of a creditor's inclusion of a cross-default provision in its loan agreement. A senior secured party can ensure control of the disposition of collateral and obtain the right to be the first to satisfy its secured loan from the proceeds of such disposition by providing in its agreement with the debtor that the debtor's default under any other loan agreement is a default under the senior secured party's agreement. With the debtor's default, the senior secured party obtains the rights of a secured party upon default, and a junior party must turn the disposition of the collateral over to the senior party.[109] (If the junior party fails to do so, it will be liable for having committed the tort of conversion.[110]) Accordingly, perfection and the resulting priority rights are important for deciding who gets first dibs with respect to the debtor's collateral. In addition, perfection and priority are important if the debtor ends up in bankruptcy, as these rules also generally inform which creditors are first in line to recover from the debtor's bankruptcy estate, except, as noted above, an unperfected secured party is treated as a regular unsecured party in the bankruptcy pecking order. A more complete and nuanced discussion of bankruptcy law is outside the scope of this chapter.

C. SUBORDINATION AGREEMENT

Under Article 9 of the U.C.C., the relative priority of creditors may be altered by contract.[111] Indeed, to "subordinate" is to do just this—to make one's priority rights in the debtor's collateral junior to those of another.[112] A subordination agreement is a common "inter-creditor agreement"—that is, an agreement between several of a borrower's lenders—that may operate to affect the lien priority rights (e.g., rights upon default) of each creditor and/or to affect each creditor's rights to receive payment as lenders of the same borrower.

---

107. *Id.* § 9-617(a).

108. *Id.*

109. *See id.* § 9-609 cmt. 5 ("Thus, a senior secured party is entitled to possession as against a junior claimant. Non-UCC law governs whether a junior secured party in possession of collateral is liable to the senior in conversion. Normally, a junior who refuses to relinquish possession of collateral upon the demand of a secured party having a superior possessory right to the collateral would be liable in conversion.").

110. *See, e.g., In re Mach., Inc.*, 337 B.R. 368, 375 (Bankr. E.D. Mo. 2005) ("If the junior secured creditor refuses the senior secured creditor's demand to return the collateral, the junior creditor is liable in conversion to the senior.").

111. U.C.C. § 9-339 (2000).

112. *See* BLACK's LAW DICTIONARY 1562 (9th ed. 2009) (defining to "subordinate" as "to assign a lower priority," as in to "subordinate the debt to a different class of claims").

This chapter's Loan Agreement contemplates a Subordination Agreement between Chase, the Lender, and the Borrower. Under § 2.1, execution of the Subordination Agreement is a condition precedent to the Lender's obligations to lend, and Article VI provides a basic framework understanding of the subordination arrangement between the parties. Section 6.1 provides that the Lender's right to payment under the Advances are subordinated to the Chase credit facility, as provided by the Subordination Agreement, and that no payment may be made by the Borrower to the Lender, except as permitted by the Subordination Agreement. Because both Lender's obligation under the sample Loan Agreement and Chase's obligations under its loan arrangement appear to be secured by common assets of the Borrower Parties', one would expect the Little Switzerland Subordination Agreement (by contrast to the subordination agreement below) to include lien subordination provisions, as well. At a minimum, the Lender has likely agreed that its liens on, and enforcement rights with respect to, the common collateral will be subordinated to Chase's liens and enforcement rights.[113] As this Subordination Agreement is not publicly available, we take this as an opportunity to look at a different subordination agreement as part of a different lending transaction.

Please find below a simple subordination agreement between three parties: a senior creditor (JPMorgan Chase Bank, N.A.), a subordinate creditor (Blackwater Midstream Corp.), and a borrower (Blackwater New Orleans, L.L.C.). Subsection 1(a) of this agreement subordinates the junior creditor's payment priority to the senior creditor. Subsection 1(c) of this agreement specifies when and how the borrower may make payments to the junior creditor. This is similar to a provision we might envision in the Little Switzerland Subordination Agreement, explaining how and when payments may be made to a junior creditor. The subordination agreement below includes an additional covenant from the borrower and the junior creditor that the borrower will not grant the junior creditor a security interest in the borrower's assets. Similar to the negative-pledge covenant, which we have examined in this chapter, this covenant gives the senior creditor a cause of action for breach of contract as against a breaching party—in this case, the borrower *and* the junior creditor.

SUBORDINATION AGREEMENT[114]

THIS SUBORDINATION AGREEMENT (this "Agreement"), dated as of February 12, 2010 is among BLACKWATER NEW ORLEANS, L.L.C. ("Borrower"),

---

113. Lien subordination agreements can be quite complex and include, among other provisions, prospective waivers of a number of rights in a bankruptcy proceeding (the enforceability of which have not been fully tested).

114. Blackwater Midstream Corp., Subordination Agreement (Form 8-K), at Exhibit 10.4 (Feb. 18, 2010), *available at* http://www.sec.gov/Archives/edgar/data/1292518/000101968710000685/blackwater_ex1004.htm.

BLACKWATER MIDSTREAM CORP. ("Midstream"), and JPMORGAN CHASE BANK, N.A. ("Bank"), who agree as follows:

RECITALS

A. Borrower and Bank have entered into that certain Credit Agreement dated as of December 23, 2008 (as it may from time to time be amended, modified or supplemented, the "Credit Agreement"), pursuant to which the Bank agreed to make credit facilities available to Borrower upon and subject to the terms and conditions thereof.

B. Midstream has heretofore loaned Borrower $3,000,000 (the "Subordinated Advance"), which loan proceeds were derived from a subordinated debt issuance of Midstream (the "Subordinated Advance").

C. As a condition to increasing the Credit Facilities, Bank requires that Borrower subordinate the Subordinated Advance to all indebtedness of Borrower to Bank, now existing and hereafter arising, including the Credit Facilities.

AGREEMENT

1. <u>Subordination</u>. The parties hereto agree as follows:

(a) Midstream hereby subordinates the Subordinated Advance to the payment and performance in full of all indebtedness of the Borrower to the Bank, now existing and hereafter arising.

(b) Midstream and Borrower agree that they will not amend the terms of the Subordinated Advance in any respect without the consent of the Bank.

(c) Midstream and Borrower agree that so long as any indebtedness of the Borrower to the Bank pursuant to the Credit Agreement is outstanding, the Borrower will not make and Midstream will not receive any payments of principal on the Subordinated Advance. So long as no Event of Default (as defined in the Credit Agreement) exists, Borrower may pay and Midstream may receive payments of interest on the Subordinated Advance, but following the occurrence and during the continuance of an Event of Default, Borrower will not make and Midstream will not receive any payments of interest on the Subordinated Advance.

(d) Borrower and Midstream represent that the Subordinated Advance is unsecured as of the date of this Agreement and agree that Borrower will not grant (and Midstream will not accept) a security interest in or pledge of any assets of the Borrower as security for the Subordinated Advance.

2. <u>Continuance of Agreement</u>. This Agreement shall continue until the payment in full of the indebtedness of the Borrower to the Bank.

3. <u>WAIVER OF JURY TRIAL</u>. BORROWER, MIDSTREAM AND BANK HEREBY WAIVE TRIAL BY JURY IN ANY ACTION OR PROCEEDING TO WHICH, THE BORROWER, MIDSTREAM AND BANK MAY BE PARTIES, ARISING OUT OF OR IN ANY WAY PERTAINING TO THIS AGREEMENT. IT IS AGREED AND UNDERSTOOD THAT THIS WAIVER CONSTITUTES A WAIVER OF TRIAL BY JURY OF ALL CLAIMS AGAINST ALL PARTIES TO SUCH ACTIONS OR PROCEEDINGS. THIS WAIVER IS KNOWINGLY, WILLINGLY AND VOLUNTARILY MADE BY BORROWER, MIDSTREAM AND BANK, AND BORROWER, MIDSTREAM AND BANK HEREBY REPRESENT THAT NO REPRESENTATIONS OF FACT OR OPINION HAVE BEEN MADE BY ANY INDIVIDUAL TO INDUCE THIS WAIVER OF TRIAL BY JURY OR TO IN ANY WAY MODIFY OR NULLIFY ITS EFFECT. BORROWER, MIDSTREAM AND BANK FURTHER REPRESENT THAT THEY HAVE BEEN REPRESENTED IN THE SIGNING OF THIS AGREEMENT AND IN THE MAKING OF THIS WAIVER BY INDEPENDENT LEGAL COUNSEL, SELECTED OF THEIR OWN FREE WILL, AND THAT THEY HAVE HAD THE OPPORTUNITY TO DISCUSS THIS WAIVER WITH COUNSEL.

4. <u>Amendments, Etc</u>. No amendment or waiver of any provision of this Agreement nor consent to any departure by Borrower, Midstream or the Bank therefrom shall in any event be effective unless the same shall be in writing and signed by Borrower, Midstream and the Bank, and then such waiver or consent shall be effective only in the specific instance and for the specific purpose for which given.

5. <u>Counterparts</u>. This Agreement may be executed in separate counterparts, each of which when so executed and delivered shall be deemed to be effective and all of which when taken together shall constitute one and the same instrument. Delivery by any party of telecopied copies of executed counterparts shall constitute delivery hereof by such party.

[Remainder of Agreement Omitted]

Comments

How does the above subordination agreement differ and how does it match up with what you would expect of the Subordination Agreement between Little Switzerland, Tiffany, and Chase? Does it contemplate a transaction that is at all different from the Little Switzerland transaction? If so, what are these differences, and how do you know?

D. LEGAL OPINION LETTERS

A party to a commercial transaction will often require that the other party's counsel provide a legal opinion letter (sometimes referred to as an "opinion," an "opinion letter," or a "legal opinion") with regard to certain matters pertaining to the transaction.[115] Legal opinion letters may be used in all sorts of commercial transactions, and their production is commonly a condition to closing in lending and mergers-and-acquisitions transactions. A legal opinion letter will generally state opinions of law relevant to the transaction at hand, usually pertaining to a specified jurisdiction—and sometimes may also include representations of fact (sometimes called "confirmations of fact," in the context of legal opinion letters[116]). For example, in an opinion letter, a lawyer may state her legal opinion that a contract is valid and enforceable against her client under the laws of a specified jurisdiction.[117] As another example, a lawyer may represent as factually true that there is no pending litigation against her client.[118]

What is the exposure of the giver of an opinion letter? An opinion letter—given by the lawyer for the guidance of the recipient and on which the recipient justifiably relies—presents the recipient of the letter with an additional party against whom the recipient may have a claim, should either legal opinions or factual assertions in the letter prove to have been false and given without exercising reasonable care (i.e., negligently or, worse yet, fraudulently).[119] As we have seen how a contract may be the source of a representation and concomitant misrepresentation claim, a letter may also be a source of a representation and a misrepresentation claim for information asserted in the letter. A letter may also provide the basis for a potential claim for legal malpractice (i.e., professional negligence). On these issues, please consider the following case.

Greycas, Inc. v. Proud

United States Court of Appeals, Seventh Circuit, 1987.
826 F.2d 1560.

POSNER, Circuit Judge.

Theodore S. Proud, Jr., a member of the Illinois bar who practices law in a suburb of Chicago, appeals from a judgment against him for $833,760, entered

---

115. For more on legal opinion letters, see generally ABA Committee on Legal Opinions, *Guidelines for the Preparation of Closing Opinions*, 57 BUS. LAW. 875 (2002) [hereinafter "ABA Guidelines"]; TriBar Opinion Committee, *Third-Party "Closing" Opinions: A Report of the TriBar Opinion Committee*, 53 BUS. LAW. 591 (1998), *available at* http://www.abanet.org/buslaw/ tribar/materials/20050303000003.pdf [hereinafter "TriBar Report"].

116. *See* TriBar Report, *supra* note 115, at 606.

117. *See* TriBar Report, *supra* note 115, at 619-21.

118. *See* TriBar Report, *supra* note 115, at 663-65.

119. *See* RESTATEMENT (SECOND) OF TORTS § 552 (1976) (A professional is liable for the damages caused by the justifiable reliance of third parties on his supplying of false information for their guidance, "if he fails to exercise reasonable care or competence in obtaining or communicating the information."); *id.* § 525 (explaining fraudulent misrepresentation of fact, opinion, intention, or law).

after a bench trial. The tale of malpractice and misrepresentation that led to the judgment begins with Proud's brother-in-law, Wayne Crawford, like Proud a lawyer but one who devoted most of his attention to a large farm that he owned in downstate Illinois. The farm fell on hard times and by 1981 Crawford was in dire financial straits. He had pledged most of his farm machinery to lenders, yet now desperately needed more money. He approached Greycas, Inc., the plaintiff in this case, a large financial company headquartered in Arizona, seeking a large loan that he offered to secure with the farm machinery. He did not tell Greycas about his financial difficulties or that he had pledged the machinery to other lenders, but he did make clear that he needed the loan in a hurry. Greycas obtained several appraisals of Crawford's farm machinery but did not investigate Crawford's financial position or discover that he had pledged the collateral to other lenders, who had perfected their liens in the collateral. Greycas agreed to lend Crawford $1,367,966.50, which was less than the appraised value of the machinery.

The loan was subject, however, to an important condition, which is at the heart of this case: Crawford was required to submit a letter to Greycas, from counsel whom he would retain, assuring Greycas that there were no prior liens on the machinery that was to secure the loan. Crawford asked Proud to prepare the letter, and he did so, and mailed it to Greycas, and within 20 days of the first contact between Crawford and Greycas the loan closed and the money was disbursed. A year later Crawford defaulted on the loan; shortly afterward he committed suicide. Greycas then learned that most of the farm machinery that Crawford had pledged to it had previously been pledged to other lenders.

The machinery was sold at auction. The Illinois state court that determined the creditors' priorities in the proceeds of the sale held that Greycas did not have a first priority on most of the machinery that secured its loan; as a result Greycas has been able to recover only a small part of the loan. The judgment it obtained in the present suit is the district judge's estimate of the value that it would have realized on its collateral had there been no prior liens, as Proud represented in his letter.

That letter is the centerpiece of the litigation. Typed on the stationery of Proud's firm and addressed to Greycas, it identifies Proud as Crawford's lawyer and states that, "in such capacity, I have been asked to render my opinion in connection with" the proposed loan to Crawford. It also states that "this opinion is being delivered in accordance with the requirements of the Loan Agreement" and that

> I have conducted a U.C.C., tax, and judgment search with respect to the Company [i.e., Crawford's farm] as of March 19, 1981, and except as hereinafter noted all units listed on the attached Exhibit A ("Equipment") are free and clear of all liens or encumbrances other than Lender's perfected security interest

therein which was recorded March 19, 1981 at the Office of the Recorder of Deeds of Fayette County, Illinois.

The reference to the lender's security interest is to Greycas's interest; Crawford, pursuant to the loan agreement, had filed a notice of that interest with the recorder. The excepted units to which the letter refers are four vehicles. Exhibit A is a long list of farm machinery—the collateral that Greycas thought it was getting to secure the loan, free of any other liens. Attached to the loan agreement itself, however, as Exhibit B, is another list of farm machinery constituting the collateral for the loan, and there are discrepancies between the two lists; more on this later.

Proud never conducted a search for prior liens on the machinery listed in Exhibit A. His brother-in-law gave him the list and told him there were no liens other than the one that Crawford had just filed for Greycas. Proud made no effort to verify Crawford's statement. The theory of the complaint is that Proud was negligent in representing that there were no prior liens, merely on his brother-in-law's say-so. No doubt Proud *was* negligent in failing to conduct a search, but we are not clear why the *misrepresentation* is alleged to be negligent rather than deliberate and hence fraudulent, in which event Greycas's alleged contributory negligence would not be an issue (as it is, we shall see), since there is no defense of contributory or comparative negligence to a deliberate tort, such as fraud. Proud did not merely say, "There are no liens"; he said, "I have conducted a U.C.C., tax, and judgment search"; and not only is this statement, too, a false one, but its falsehood cannot have been inadvertent, for Proud knew he had not conducted such a search. The concealment of his relationship with Crawford might also support a charge of fraud. But Greycas decided, for whatever reason, to argue negligent misrepresentation rather than fraud. It may have feared that Proud's insurance policy for professional malpractice excluded deliberate wrongdoing from its coverage, or may not have wanted to bear the higher burden of proving fraud, or may have feared that an accusation of fraud would make it harder to settle the case—for most cases, of course, are settled, though this one has not been. In any event, Proud does not argue that either he is liable for fraud or he is liable for nothing.

He also does not, and could not, deny or justify the misrepresentation; but he argues that it is not actionable under the tort law of Illinois, because he had no duty of care to Greycas. (This is a diversity case and the parties agree that Illinois tort law governs the substantive issues.) He argues that Greycas had an adversarial relationship with Proud's client, Crawford, and that a lawyer has no duty of straight dealing to an adversary, at least none enforceable by a tort suit. In so arguing, Proud is characterizing Greycas's suit as one for professional malpractice rather than negligent misrepresentation, yet elsewhere in his briefs he insists that the suit was solely for negligent misrepresentation—while Greycas insists that its suit charges both torts. Legal malpractice based on a false representation, and negligent misrepresentation by a lawyer, are such similar legal concepts, however, that we have great difficulty both in holding them apart in our minds and in understanding why the parties are quarreling over the exact characterization; no one suggests, for example, that the statute of limitations might have run on one but not the other tort. So we shall discuss both.

Proud is undoubtedly correct in arguing that a lawyer has no general duty of care toward his adversary's client; it would be a considerable and, as it seems to us, an undesirable novelty to hold that every bit of sharp dealing by a lawyer gives rise to prima facie tort liability to the opposing party in the lawsuit or negotiation. The tort of malpractice normally refers to a lawyer's careless or otherwise wrongful conduct toward his own client. Proud argues that Crawford rather than Greycas was his client, and although this is not so clear as Proud supposes—another characterization of the transaction is that Crawford undertook to obtain a lawyer for Greycas in the loan transaction—we shall assume for purposes of discussion that Greycas was not Proud's client.

Therefore if malpractice just meant carelessness or other misconduct toward one's own client, Proud would not be liable for malpractice to Greycas. But in *Pelham v. Griesheimer*, the Supreme Court of Illinois discarded the old common law requirement of privity of contract for professional malpractice; so now it is possible for someone who is not the lawyer's (or other professional's) client to sue him for malpractice. The court in *Pelham* was worried, though, about the possibility of a lawyer's being held liable "to an unlimited and unknown number of potential plaintiffs," so it added that "for a nonclient to succeed in a negligence action against an attorney, he must prove that the primary purpose and intent of the attorney-client relationship itself was to benefit or influence the third party." That, however, describes this case exactly. Crawford hired Proud not only for the primary purpose, but for the sole purpose, of influencing Greycas to make Crawford a loan. The case is much like *Brumley v. Touche, Ross & Co.*, where a complaint that an accounting firm had negligently prepared an audit report that the firm knew would be shown to an investor in the audited corporation and relied on by that investor was held to state a claim for professional malpractice. In *Conroy v. Andeck Resources '81 Year-End Ltd.*, in contrast, a law firm that represented an offeror of securities was held not to have any duty of care to investors. The representation was not intended for the benefit of investors. Their reliance on the law firm's using due care in the services it provided in connection with the offer was not invited.

All this assumes that *Pelham* governs this case, but arguably it does not, for Greycas, as we noted, may have decided to bring this as a suit for negligent misrepresentation rather than professional malpractice. We know of no obstacle to such an election; nothing is more common in American jurisprudence than overlapping torts.

The claim of negligent misrepresentation might seem utterly straightforward. It might seem that by addressing a letter to Greycas intended (as Proud's counsel admitted at argument) to induce reliance on the statements in it, Proud made himself prima facie liable for any material misrepresentations, careless or deliberate, in the letter, whether or not Proud was Crawford's lawyer or for that matter anyone's lawyer. Knowing that Greycas was relying on him to determine whether the collateral for the loan was encumbered and to advise Greycas of the results of his determination, Proud negligently misrepresented the situation, to Greycas's detriment. But merely labeling a suit as one for negligent misrepresentation rather than professional malpractice will not make the problem of indefinite and perhaps excessive liability, which induced the court in *Pelham* to place limitations on the duty of care, go away. So one is not surprised to find that courts have placed similar limitations on suits for negligent misrepresentation— so similar that we are led to question whether . . . these really are different torts, at least when both grow out of negligent misrepresentations by lawyers. For example, the *Brumley* case, which we cited earlier, is a professional-malpractice case, yet it has essentially the same facts as *Ultramares Corp. v. Touche, Niven & Co.*, where the New York Court of Appeals, in a famous opinion by Judge Cardozo, held that an accountant's negligent misrepresentation was not actionable at the suit of a lender who had relied on the accountant's certified audit of the borrower.

The absence of a contract between the lender and the accountant defeated the suit in *Ultramares*—yet why should privity of contract have been required for liability just because the negligence lay in disseminating information rather than in designing or manufacturing a product? The privity limitation in products cases had been rejected, in another famous Cardozo opinion, years earlier. Professor Bishop suggests that courts were worried that imposing heavy liabilities on producers of information might cause socially valuable information to be underproduced. Many producers of information have difficulty appropriating its benefits to society. The property-rights system in information is incomplete; someone who comes up with a new idea that the law of intellectual property does not protect cannot prevent others from using the idea without reimbursing his costs of invention or discovery. So the law must be careful not to weigh these producers down too heavily with tort liabilities. For example, information produced by securities analysts, the news media, academicians, and so forth is socially valuable, but as its producers can't capture the full value of the information in their fees and other remuneration the information may be underproduced. Maybe it is right, therefore—or at least efficient—that none of these producers should have to bear the full costs. (Similar reasoning may explain the tort immunity, now largely abrogated, of charitable enterprises, and the tort immunities of public officers.) At least that was once the view; and while *Ultramares* has now been rejected, in Illinois as elsewhere—maybe because providers of information are deemed more robust today than they once were or maybe because it is now believed that auditors, surveyors, and other providers of professional services were always able to capture the social value of even the information component of those services in the fees they charged their clients—a residuum of concern remains. So when in *Rozny v. Marnul*, the Supreme Court of Illinois, joining the march away from *Ultramares*, held for the first time that negligent misrepresentation was actionable despite the absence of a contract, and thus cast aside the same "privity of contract" limitation later overruled with regard to professional malpractice in *Pelham*, the court was careful to emphasize facts in the particular case before it that limited the scope of its holding—facts such as that the defendant, a surveyor, had placed his "absolute guarantee for accuracy" on the plat and that only a few persons would receive and rely on it, thus limiting the potential scope of liability.

Later Illinois cases, however, influenced by section 552 of the Second Restatement of Torts (1977), state the limitation on liability for negligent misrepresentation in more compact terms—as well as in narrower scope—than *Rozny*. These are cases in the intermediate appellate court, but, as we have no reason to think the Supreme Court of Illinois would reject them, we are bound to follow them. They hold that "one who in the course of his business or profession supplies information for the guidance of others in their business transactions" is liable for negligent misrepresentations that induce detrimental reliance. Whether there is a practical as distinct from a merely semantic difference between this formulation of the duty limitation and that of *Pelham* may be doubted but cannot change the outcome of this case. Proud, in the practice of his profession, supplied information (or rather misinformation) to Greycas that was intended to guide Greycas in commercial dealings with Crawford. Proud therefore had a duty to use due care to see that the information was correct. He used no care.

Proud must lose on the issue of liability even if the narrower, *ad hoc* approach of *Rozny* is used instead of the approach of section 552 of the Restatement. Information about the existence of previous liens on particular items of property is of limited social as distinct from private value, by which we mean simply that the information is not likely to be disseminated widely. There is consequently no reason to give it special encouragement by overlooking carelessness in its collection and expression. Where as in this case the defendant makes the negligent misrepresentation directly to the plaintiff in the course of the defendant's business or profession, the courts have little difficulty in finding a duty of care.

There is no serious doubt about the existence of a causal relationship between the misrepresentation and the loan. Greycas would not have made the loan without Proud's letter. Nor would it have made the loan had Proud advised it that the collateral was so heavily encumbered that the loan was as if unsecured, for then Greycas would have known that the probability of repayment was slight. Merely to charge a higher interest rate would not have been an attractive alternative to security; it would have made default virtually inevitable by saddling Crawford with a huge fixed debt. To understand the astronomical interest rate that is required to make an unsecured loan a paying proposition to the lender when the risk of default is high, notice that even if the riskless interest rate is only 3 percent, the rate of inflation zero, the cost of administering the loan zero, and the lender risk-neutral, he still must charge an annual interest rate of 106 percent if he thinks there is only a 50 percent chance that he will get his principal back.

Proud argues, however, that his damages should be reduced in recognition of Greycas's own contributory negligence, which, though no longer a complete defense in Illinois, is a partial defense, renamed "comparative negligence." It is as much a defense to negligent misrepresentation as to any other tort of negligence. On the issue of comparative negligence the district court said only that "defendant may have proved negligence upon the part of plaintiff but that negligence, if any, had no causal relationship to the malpractice of the defendant or the damages to the plaintiff." This comment is not easy to fathom. If Greycas was careless in deciding whether to make the loan, this implies that a reasonable investigation by Greycas would have shown that the collateral for the loan was already heavily encumbered; knowing this, Greycas would not have made the loan and therefore would not have suffered any damages.

But we think it too clear to require a remand for further proceedings that Proud failed to prove a want of due care by Greycas. Due care is the care that is optimal given that the other party is exercising due care. It is not the higher level of care that would be optimal if potential tort victims were required to assume that the rest of the world was negligent. A pedestrian is not required to exercise a level of care (e.g., wearing a helmet or a shin guard) that would be optimal if there were no sanctions against reckless driving. Otherwise drivers would be encouraged to drive recklessly, and knowing this pedestrians would be encouraged to wear helmets and shin guards. The result would be a shift from a superior method of accident avoidance (not driving recklessly) to an inferior one (pedestrian armor).

So we must ask whether Greycas would have been careless not to conduct its own UCC search had Proud done what he had said he did—conduct his own UCC search. The answer is no. The law normally does not require duplicative precautions unless one is likely to fail or the consequences of failure (slight though the likelihood may be) would be catastrophic. One UCC search is enough to disclose prior liens, and Greycas acted reasonably in relying on Proud to conduct it. Although Greycas had much warning that Crawford was in financial trouble and that the loan might not be repaid, that was a reason for charging a hefty interest rate and insisting that the loan be secured; it was not a reason for duplicating Proud's work. It is not hard to conduct a UCC lien search; it just requires checking the records in the recorder's office for the county where the debtor lives. So the only reason to backstop Proud was if Greycas should have assumed he was careless or dishonest; and we have just said that the duty of care does not require such an assumption. Had Proud disclosed that he was Crawford's brother-in-law this might have been a warning signal that Greycas could ignore only at its peril. To go forward in the face of a known danger is to assume the risk. But Proud did not disclose his relationship to Crawford. . . .

A final point. The record of this case reveals serious misconduct by an Illinois attorney. We are therefore sending a copy of this opinion to the Attorney Registration and Disciplinary Commission of the Supreme Court of Illinois for such disciplinary action as may be deemed appropriate in the circumstances. AFFIRMED.

BAUER, Chief Judge, concurring.

I am in agreement with the majority opinion. I believe that Proud would be liable without reference to legal malpractice or negligent misrepresentation. The evidence in this case indicates that he is guilty of fraud or intentional misrepresentation. He was lying when he represented that he had made U.C.C., tax and judgment searches on his brother-in-law's farm. He intended the misrepresentation to induce Greycas to make a loan to his brother-in-law; Greycas justifiably relied upon the misrepresentation in making the loan and was injured as a result. Under these facts, Proud's misrepresentation was indefensible.

Comments

As the Seventh Circuit in *Greycas* explained, lawyers may incur liability on the basis of asserted information in opinion letters rendered to third parties—that is, *non-clients*. Jurisdictions vary in their allowance of claims of professional malpractice brought by non-clients against lawyers (i.e., where there is a lack of "privity").[120] In contrast, a non-client may generally bring a claim for negligent (or fraudulent) misrepresentation based on the non-client's justifiable reliance on information asserted by a lawyer in an opinion letter, provided the other elements of the cause of action are satisfied.[121] That is, while the court in *Greycas* suggested that these torts—(i) professional malpractice and (ii) negligent misrepresentation—might overlap and explained that Illinois no longer requires privity for either, some jurisdictions have allowed non-clients to bring claims against lawyers for misrepresentation but not for malpractice.[122]

---

120. *Compare, e.g., Lucas v. Hamm*, 364 P.2d 685 (Cal. 1961) (finding lawyer liable to non-client for malpractice on "balancing of factors" theory), *cert. denied*, 368 U.S. 987 (1962), *and Guy v. Liederbach*, 459 A.2d 744, 749 (Pa. 1983) (finding lawyer liable to non-client for malpractice on "intended beneficiary" theory), *with Banc One Capital Partners Corp. v. Kneipper*, 67 F.3d 1187, 1198 (5th Cir. 1995) ("Under Texas law, there is no attorney-client relationship absent a showing of privity of contract, and an attorney owes no professional duty to a third party or non-client."). For a nice description of the various judicial approaches to attorney liability to non-clients for malpractice and the "requirement" of privity, please see *Flaherty v. Weinberg*, 492 A.2d 618, 621-26 (Md. 1985).

121. *See, e.g., McCamish, Martin, Brown & Loeffler v. F.E. Appling Interests*, 991 S.W.2d 787, 793 (Tex. 1999) ("Several jurisdictions have held that an attorney can be liable to a nonclient for negligent misrepresentation, as defined in section 552 [of the *Restatement (Second) of Torts*], based on the issuance of opinion letters.").

122. *See supra* notes 120, 121.

As an example of a legal opinion letter, please review the document reproduced below from a stock purchase transaction and consider how its language may have been structured to limit potential lawyer liability.

LEGAL OPINION LETTER FROM COUNSEL FOR MAYFLOWER[123]

1. Mayflower has the requisite corporate power and authority to enter into the Agreement, to perform its obligations thereunder and to consummate the transactions contemplated thereby.

2. The execution and delivery of the Agreement by Mayflower, the performance by Mayflower of its obligations thereunder and the consummation by Mayflower of the transactions contemplated thereby (a) have been duly authorized by all necessary corporate action on the part of Mayflower, (b) do not contravene any provision of Mayflower's articles of incorporation or bylaws and (c) do not contravene any present law, or present regulation of any governmental agency or authority, of the State of Indiana.

3. Assuming that all consents, approvals, authorizations and other actions have been obtained and all filings, notifications, approvals and other actions referred to in Article V and Sections 6.1(a) and 6.1(b) of the Purchase Agreement have been made or obtained, the execution and delivery of the Agreement by Mayflower, the performance by Mayflower of its obligations thereunder and the consummation by Mayflower of the transactions contemplated thereby will not violate (a) any present law, or present regulation of any governmental agency or authority, of the United States of America or (b) any agreement binding upon Mayflower or its property that is listed on Annex _____ to the Officer's Certificate of Mayflower delivered to us in connection with this opinion. [Copy of Officer's Certificate to be attached to opinion with list of material agreements.]

4. The Purchase Agreement has been duly executed and delivered by Mayflower and, assuming that the Agreement constitutes a valid and binding obligation of Citizens, constitutes a legal, valid and binding obligation of Mayflower, enforceable against Mayflower in accordance with its terms.

---

123. Excerpted from Alterwoods Group Inc., Stock Purchase Agreement Exhibit B (Form 10-Q), at Exhibit 2.7 (June 19, 2004), *available at* http://www.sec.gov/Archives/edgar/data/927914/0001047469040 24176/a2138514zex2_7.txt.

> 5. SPL is validly existing and in good standing under the laws of the State of Louisiana. Security Fire is validly existing and in good standing under the laws of the State of Louisiana.
>
> The opinions expressed herein are limited to (a) with respect to the opinions expressed in paragraphs 1 and 2 above, the laws of the State of Indiana and (b)with respect to the opinions expressed in paragraphs 3 and 4 above, the federal laws of the United States of America and the Texas Business Corporation Act. In connection with the opinions expressed in paragraph 5 above, we have relied solely upon certificates of public officials as to the factual matters and legal conclusions set forth therein, copies of which have been provided to you. With respect to the opinions expressed in paragraphs 2(c) and 3(a) above, our opinions are limited to only those laws and regulations that, in our experience, are normally applicable to transactions of the type contemplated by the Agreement.
>
> [Remainder Omitted]

Notice that one way a lawyer drafting a legal opinion letter may hedge her exposure is to premise an opinion or confirmation on stated assumptions.[124] A drafter may also expressly limit the scope and applicability of a statement, including with regard to what applicable law. As a drafting lawyer may be presumed to have established diligently the factual basis of a legal opinion, the lawyer may wish to specify expressly in the letter the factual investigation that the lawyer *did* undertake and that the lawyer performed no further investigation (or, if the lawyer performed no investigation at all, that the lawyer's opinion is "without investigation").[125] Simply stating "to my knowledge" might not be enough to communicate that the drafting lawyer did not undertake a customary level of investigation to inform the lawyer's "knowledge" in the first place.[126] In addition, in order to help prevent unexpected parties from justifiably relying on an opinion and from perhaps recovering on a claim for malpractice or misrepresentation, a lawyer may wish to limit expressly in the opinion letter the persons to whom the letter is intended to address and, accordingly, who may justifiably rely on the opinion as an addressee.[127] Where and how does the above legal opinion letter limit the exposure of its drafter?

---

124. *See* TriBar Report, *supra* note 115, at 615-16.

125. *See* TriBar Report, *supra* note 115, at 619.

126. *See* ABA Guidelines, *supra* note 115, at 878-79; TriBar Report, *supra* note 115, at 618-19.

127. *See, e.g.,* ABA Guidelines, *supra* note 115, at 876-77 ("On occasion, a closing opinion expressly authorizes persons to whom it is not addressed (for example, assignees of notes) to rely on it. Those persons are permitted to rely on the closing opinion to the same extent as—but to no greater extent than—the addressee.").

· CHAPTER SIX ·

AGREEMENTS FOR MERGER AND ACQUISITION

· ·

We begin our introduction to this chapter on agreements related to mergers and acquisitions with a comment from Justice Jack B. Jacobs of the Delaware Supreme Court. For some time, Delaware has enjoyed a special relationship with corporate law, in general, and mergers and acquisitions (as well as the agreements that memorialize these transactions), in particular. Justice Jacobs offers his perspective on Delaware's unique relevance to this sphere.

Delaware's Continued Primacy as a Source of Corporate Law

Since the 1930s, U.S. corporations have been concurrently regulated at both the state and federal levels. At the state level, for over a century the corporate law of Delaware, both statutory and judge-made, has been regarded as preeminent.[1] There is no single, overarching reason for that; there are several causes, some the product of historical circumstance and others, of design. What follows is a modest effort to summarize the principal causes in a chronological setting.

Delaware's primacy in the corporate governance area is rooted in the fact that since the 1920s, Delaware has been the principal state of incorporation of this country's largest business enterprises, and also of numerous smaller, "start up" companies that elect to "go public."[2] Delaware is the corporate home to over 60% of Fortune 500 companies and a majority of companies listed on the New York Stock Exchange; and in 2007, over 90% of all United States-based public offerings were made by issuers incorporated in Delaware.[3]

That fact is legally important because by operation of the "internal affairs" doctrine, all disputes involving the internal governance of Delaware corporations are governed by Delaware law. The "internal affairs" doctrine is a

---

1. *See* WILLIAM L. CARY, CASES AND MATERIALS ON CORPORATIONS 26-27 (4th ed. 1969).

2. *Id.* at 26; I DAVID A. DREXLER, LEWIS S. BLACK, JR. & A. GILCHRIST SPARKS, III, DELAWARE CORPORATION LAW AND PRACTICE 1-4 (Matthew Bender 2009).

3. HARRIET SMITH WINDSOR, DEL. DEP'T OF STATE, DIV. OF CORPS., 2007 ANNUAL REPORT 1 (2008), *available at* http://corp.delaware.gov/2007DivCorpAR.pdf.

choice-of-law rule mandating that disputes over matters that are peculiar to the relationships among or between the corporation and its directors, officers and shareholders are governed by the laws of its state of incorporation.[4] In the case of Delaware, the applicable law includes the Delaware General Corporation Law ("DGCL") and the decisions of the Delaware Supreme Court and the Delaware Court of Chancery, which interpret that statute and that also apply judge-made principles of fiduciary law to specific internal corporate disputes. Over the past century this has resulted in the development of an extensive body of state corporate law, which has furthered stability and predictability in planning corporate transactions and internal governance structures. Because Delaware law applies even if the corporation has no physical presence in, or relationship to, Delaware, law firms throughout the country routinely advise clients on Delaware corporate law matters, and courts outside of Delaware apply Delaware law in litigations presenting internal governance issues.[5]

That fact triggers a more fundamental question: how did Delaware come—and continue—to be the favored state of incorporation in a country comprising 49 other states, each with its own corporate laws, for over a century? As noted, there were multiple causes, including historical accident, the evolution of the Delaware Court of Chancery as a preferred forum for litigating intracorporate disputes, and the continued commitment of the Delaware legislature to keep the DGCL as responsive, progressive, and flexible as possible.[6]

Although Delaware's first General Corporation Law was enacted in 1897, Delaware was not immediately successful in attracting incorporation business. What began Delaware's trajectory to its current position as the major corporate domicile were reforms in New Jersey, prompted by Governor Woodrow Wilson. Those reforms led to amendments of New Jersey's corporate statute in 1913, to restrict the economic activities of New Jersey corporations perceived to be conducting predatory business practices. In response, New Jersey's largest corporations (then called "trusts") reincorporated from New Jersey to Delaware, a neighboring state with lower franchise taxes and a similar corporate statute, but without the newly enacted business practices. Gradually, the number of incorporations increased until by the 1920s, Delaware had become the incorporation venue of choice by much of the American business community.[7]

That historic accident, however, does not explain how Delaware has continued to maintain that position for almost a century. That explanation must be found elsewhere, specifically, in the evolution of the Delaware Court of Chancery

---

4. *See generally McDermott Inc. v. Lewis*, 531 A.2d 206, 214-15 (Del. 1987); *Vantage Point Venture Partners 1996 v. Examen, Inc.*, 871 A.2d 1108, 1112-13 (Del. 2005); RESTATEMENT (SECOND) OF CONFLICT OF LAWS § 302 cmt. a. (1971); Note, *The Internal Affairs Doctrine: Theoretical Justifications and Tentative Explanations for its Continued Primacy*, 115 HARV. L. REV. 1480 (2002).

5. I DONALD J. WOLFE, JR. & MICHAEL A. PITTENGER, CORPORATE AND COMMERCIAL PRACTICE IN THE DELAWARE COURT OF CHANCERY § 1.03 (Lexis Law Publishing 2009).

6. *Id.*

7. CARY, *supra* note 1, at 26; DREXLER, BLACK & SPARKS, *supra* note 2, at 1-4.

as the nation's first (and preferred) "business court,"[8] and the continued commitment of the Delaware legislature to the responsiveness, currency, and flexibility of the DGCL to the changing needs of American business enterprises.

The Court of Chancery, which was created in 1897, was not established as a "business court" as that term is now understood, but rather as Delaware's constitutional court of equity jurisdiction. Because that court (modeled after the English Court of Chancery) sits without a jury and has limited jurisdiction, it was well positioned to adjudicate complex business disputes on a timely basis. In the 1920s and 1930s, the Court of Chancery began to develop a reputation for expertise in corporate matters, resulting in part from a series of equity receiverships of certain utility empires of holding companies and other businesses that collapsed under the weight of economic bad times and mismanagement. The 1930s and 1940s saw the flowering of the stockholder derivative suit as the procedural vehicle for obtaining judicial review of alleged mismanagement. Those suits, as well as the companion stockholder class action of more recent vintage, became the primary vehicles for obtaining judicial guidance on questions of corporate fiduciary law and statutory authority.[9]

The Delaware courts' increasing prestige in this area stemmed not only from the sheer volume of corporate cases brought before them, but also from the efficient manner in which those cases were handled and the sophistication and integrity evidenced in their decisions. A well-reasoned body of corporate precedent soon developed that the corporate bar viewed as superior to that of other jurisdictions both quantitatively and qualitatively, and that provided clear guidance on a multitude of corporate issues.[10] Those decisions benefited from the appointment of highly respected and capable persons to serve as Chancellors and Vice Chancellors. Notable among them was Chancellor Collins J. Seitz, who, as the sole Court of Chancery judge from the mid-1940s to the mid-1960s, almost singlehandedly developed a significant portion of Delaware's corporate jurisprudence.[11] Since the mid-1960s, that Court has benefited from having Chancellors of similar distinction, many of whom were practitioners from the corporate bar. Chancellor Seitz's successors to this day continue to perpetuate the high quality of that court's jurisprudence.[12]

The story of the evolution of the Court of Chancery would be incomplete, however, without addressing two additional extrinsic developments—one legal, the other economic, and both matters of historic accident—that occurred during the 1970s and 1980s.

---

8. Although many of the references in this article are to the Court of Chancery, they should be understood as also including the Delaware Supreme Court, which exercises direct appellate review over judgments of the Court of Chancery.

9. DREXLER, BLACK & SPARKS, *supra* note 2, at 1-6.

10. WOLFE & PITTENGER, *supra* note 5, § 1.03, at 1-5.

11. Chancellor Seitz was later appointed to the United States Court of Appeals for the Third Circuit, where he served as Circuit Judge and Chief Judge.

12. William T. Quillen & Michael Hanrahan, *A Short History of the Delaware Court of Chancery—1792-1992, in* COURT OF CHANCERY OF THE STATE OF DELAWARE—1792-1992 21, 49-55 (1993). *See also id.* at 65-93, for biographical sketches of members of the Court from 1792-1992.

The first development was the 1977 United States Supreme Court decision in *Santa Fe Industries, Inc. v. Green.*[13] That case became immensely significant because by the mid-1960s, the corporate litigation flow in most state courts, including the Court of Chancery, had begun to ebb. The reason was that corporate transactional lawsuits (particularly litigation attacking freeze-out mergers) were increasingly being brought in what the plaintiffs' bar regarded as a more hospitable forum—the federal courts, under the rubric of Section 10(b) of the Securities Exchange Act of 1934[14] and SEC Rule 10b-5.[15] That was possible because numerous federal courts had construed corporate management conduct that had traditionally been regarded as state-law breach-of-fiduciary-duty claims, to be actionable under Rule 10b-5, so long as a sale or exchange of securities was involved. By the mid-1960s it was widely believed that state corporate fiduciary and governance law would become "federalized" under Rule 10b-5, with the federal courts being the preferred forum for resolving those disputes, and the state courts being marginalized.[16] *Santa Fe v. Green* fatally dispelled that belief and led to the opposite result. There, the Supreme Court held that claims based solely on state-law fiduciary-duty breaches are not actionable under Rule 10b-5 absent material misrepresentations or omissions. A critical consequence of *Santa Fe* was the reallocation of (formerly Rule 10b-5) corporate fiduciary duty litigation to the state courts. That development increased significantly the volume of corporate litigation in the Delaware Court of Chancery, because much Rule 10b-5 litigation involved Delaware corporations.

Santa Fe and its aftermath set the stage for the second, and most dramatic, development in the evolution of the Delaware courts—the advent of hostile takeover litigation—which gave the Court of Chancery and the Delaware Supreme Court a unique, nationally profiled role. By the 1980s, several circumstances had combined to create that result. The first was economic: the capital markets were undervaluing many public corporations, making it cheaper to acquire a majority of a corporation's shares and replace its existing management than to acquire the company's assets in a negotiated transaction. The second circumstance was legal and regulatory: hostile takeovers through the capital markets were successfully accomplished by a new tool—the hostile tender offer. Although some of the early abuses of such offers were eliminated on the bidder side by the adoption of the federal Williams Act[17] in 1968, that legislation did not regulate the "flip side" of hostile takeovers—defensive measures adopted by incumbent boards that arguably served to entrench management in place by denying target corporation shareholders the opportunity to sell their shares into the hostile offer. Because Congress, the SEC and the state regulators did not express interest in regulating takeover defenses, and the federal courts rarely had subject matter jurisdiction in this area, by default that function was performed

---

13. 430 U.S. 462 (1977).
14. 15 U.S.C. § 78j(b).
15. 17 C.F.R. § 240.10b-5.
16. *See, e.g.*, Arthur Fleischer, Jr., *"Federal Corporation Law": An Assessment*, 78 Harv. L. Rev. 1146 (1965).
17. *See* 15 U.S.C. §§ 78m(d), 78n(d)-(f) (2006).

by the state courts.[18] The state tribunals that figured most prominently in developing takeover jurisprudence were the Delaware courts, since many highly publicized takeovers involved Delaware corporations and the application of Delaware law.

These combined developments, again the product of historical circumstance, made the 1980s and the 1990s the most significant period in the evolution of the Delaware courts. Hostile takeover litigation turned out to be so intensive and consuming of judicial resources that it became necessary to expand the Court of Chancery from three to five judges. Equally and perhaps more importantly, the then-existing fiduciary doctrine was outdated and inadequate to address the economic and legal subtleties of the technology underlying takeover defensive devices and strategy.[19] It therefore became necessary for the Delaware courts to develop an entirely new jurisprudence, through the common law method of case-by-case adjudication, to craft an appropriate legal framework for analyzing and resolving these complex issues. The result was the articulation of ground breaking, new standards for judicial review of takeover defenses adopted by target company boards. Those standards were announced in decisions so oft-cited that they are commonly referred to in shorthand form as (to cite but a few examples) *Unocal*,[20] *Revlon*,[21] *Moran*,[22] and *Blasius*.[23] These and later cases, which articulated and refined both takeover jurisprudence specifically and corporate governance principles generally, have continued to maintain the Delaware courts at the forefront of corporate law decision-making at the state level.

The story of how Delaware achieved primacy as a source of state corporate governance law would be incomplete without discussing a parallel development that occurred on the legislative front. By the mid-1960s, it had become apparent to the corporate law community that the DGCL had become outdated and insufficiently responsive to the needs of the American business community. That awareness prompted the creation of a committee of distinguished Delaware corporate practitioners, guided by Professor Ernest L. Folk, III of the University of Virginia, who served as reporter, to modernize the statute. The result was a complete statutory overhaul in 1967 that eliminated formalistic and anachronistic requirements and legal restrictions,[24] to provide a sound statutory format for governing and operating modern corporations. The process that resulted in the

---

18. William B. Chandler, III, *Hostile M&A and the Poison Pill in Japan: A Judicial Perspective*, 2004 Colum. Bus. L. Rev. 45, 49-50.

19. The reasons why the then-existing fiduciary review standards were inadequate in the hostile takeover setting are discussed in an article written by this author in 2006. *See* Jack B. Jacobs, *Implementing Japan's New Anti-Takeover Defense Guidelines, Part I: Some Lessons From Delaware's Experience in Crafting "Fair" Takeover Rules*, 2 N.Y.U. J.L. & Bus. 323, 328-30 (2006).

20. *Unocal Corp. v. Mesa Petroleum Co.*, 493 A.2d 946 (Del. 1985).

21. *Revlon, Inc. v. MacAndrews & Forbes*, 506 A.2d 173 (Del. 1985).

22. *Moran v. Household Int'l, Inc.*, 500 A.2d 1346 (Del. 1985).

23. *Blasius Indus. v. Atlas Corp.*, 564 A.2d 651 (Del. Ch. 1988).

24. By way of example, the 1967 revision permitted "greater freedom to pay dividends and make distributions; greater ease of charter amendment and lesser restrictions upon selling assets, mortgaging leasing and merging, due to the lower percentage of shareholder approval required and also by virtue of lesser rights of appraisal for dissenting minority shareholders; freedom from mandatory cumulative voting; permission to

1967 revision resulted in the formation of a more permanent group—the Corporation Law Section of the Delaware Bar Association. That body, which consists of highly experienced Delaware corporate practitioners, meets and deliberates continually and each year proposes amendments to the DGCL, which the Delaware General Assembly has never declined to adopt.[25] This institutional development has enabled the DGCL to be continually updated and modernized on a "real-time" basis.

****

How and why Delaware came to have primacy in the creation and application of state corporate and fiduciary law is a complex story with many moving parts. That story is one observer's best effort to capture as many of those moving parts within a short space.

> Jack B. Jacobs
> Justice
> Delaware Supreme Court

State law—and most prominently Delaware law, as so many companies are organized there—informs the requirements and procedures with which companies must comply in effecting mergers and acquisitions. We turn to these and other issues in this chapter in exploring this chapter's core sample agreement: an agreement to purchase a division of a public corporation.

In this book, we have considered the various ways in which commercial parties may work together in a variety of transactional settings to pursue complementary goals. The success of commercial transactions often depends in part upon the achievement of common interests through cooperation among the contracting parties.

Cooperation can take many forms, ranging from the transactions found in the services agreements in Chapter 3 and the purchase and supply agreement in Chapter 4 (with the appreciation that, in those chapters, master agreements spoke to an ongoing relationship and detailed the cooperative relationship at hand), to the more involved and integrated business relationships found in alliance agreements (on the topic of which we ask a few practitioners to opine in this chapter), to the ultimate in business-to-business cooperation and integration: agreements of merger and acquisition.

We begin our inquiry of these cooperative arrangements with an examination of letters of intent, then an overview of the basic types of M&A and cooperative transactions, before proceeding into an exploration of an asset purchase agreement.

---

have staggered boards of directors. . . . clearer rights of indemnification for directors and officer. . . ." Cary, *supra* note 1, at 27 (quoting Kaplan, *Foreign Corporations and Local Corporate Policy*, 21 Vand. L. Rev. 433, 436 (1968)).

25. Drexler, Black & Sparks, *supra* note 2 at 1-4, 1-5.

A. PRELIMINARY DOCUMENTS; LETTERS OF INTENT

The more complex the business transaction, perhaps the more involved the negotiations and the more complicated and lengthy the (potentially) resulting agreement. As we have seen in previous chapters, transactions can take on a certain sequence of events and documents. We saw in Chapter 1 that parties will often agree to a non-disclosure agreement (an "NDA") at the onset of negotiations for most any complex business transaction, certainly any negotiation that would involve the exposure of a party to another party's confidential information. Parties will generally wish to conduct significant "due diligence" before agreeing to a major transaction. For example, before acquiring another entity, the putative buyer (note that we use "buyer," "purchaser," and "acquiror" interchangeably throughout this chapter to refer to the acquiring party—we sometimes use "suitor" or "putative buyer" to refer to a party attempting to acquire—and "seller" and "target" to refer to the company being bought or acquired) will wish to investigate the company in order to understand what it would be purchasing. As due diligence is almost certain to involve the exposure of a party to the other's confidential information, the disclosing company generally will require the recipient party to execute an NDA before conducting its due diligence. In this context, NDAs help alleviate a potential "Catch-22" situation: Non-disclosure agreements help companies to flirt with transacting without compromising the confidentiality of the information necessary to flirt.

Due diligence can be complex and involve the review of extensive materials for a myriad of issues. To give you a "real world" sense for this, we asked two seasoned practitioners to explain some of the due diligence considerations pertaining to a specific concern: U.S. trade control compliance. (In reading through the following, you may wish to review the practitioner piece regarding U.S. export control laws in Chapter 4.)

A Practitioner Perspective: International M&A and U.S. Trade Control Due Diligence

U.S. trade control considerations have become increasingly important to the dynamic of corporate transactions in recent years. In part, this is due to the increasing complexity of the various U.S. trade control laws and regulations and the enhanced penalties associated with violating these rules. Perhaps more significantly, however, U.S. authorities have shown an increasing willingness to enforce theories of successor liability in this area and to hold parties accountable for a broader range of activity in corporate collaborations. As a result, for

---

instance, the surviving company in a merger or acquisition will generally be held accountable for prior trade compliance violations of the target, and the various U.S. trade control agencies will be prepared to pursue sometimes novel enforcement theories in an evaluation of a company's conduct in multi-party corporate collaborations or transactions.

Accordingly, companies have realized that trade control compliance issues must be carefully evaluated in the context of corporate due diligence for mergers, acquisitions, joint ventures and other collaborative structures. These issues must be afforded appropriate attention early in the planning process for any corporate transaction, and the parties must have a clear plan of action for identifying and resolving any concerns that emerge from a careful due diligence. Meaningful trade control compliance concerns can have a significant impact on the economics or viability of a planned corporate transaction, and it is important to identify any such concerns early in the process or to build into the negotiations appropriate financial protections against such discoveries.

Even where appropriate due diligence does not identify any meaningful cause for concern, the parties to a corporate transaction must take affirmative steps to ensure that these compliance challenges are appropriately addressed at the back end of any transaction—whether in an integrated compliance team following a merger or acquisition, in the operational phase of a joint venture, or in the post-delivery and start-up period of an infrastructure project. With the encouragement of the trade control enforcement agencies, companies are realizing that trade control compliance considerations warrant careful and ongoing attention from the earliest planning stages of any deal to the execution and integration phases.

A. Key Considerations for Due Diligence

Appropriate due diligence review of trade control compliance issues builds from the critical foundation of a thorough review of (1) the products, software, and technology mix of the target company; (2) the structure of target company's operations within and outside of the United States; and (3) the countries in which it operates and to which it supplies (or receives) products, technology, and services.

Following a thorough assessment of the target company's products, structure, and countries in which it operates, you should ensure that the due diligence review takes into account the following topics:

1. Review of Trade Control Compliance Organization

You should first try to assess the trade control compliance culture within the target company. While the focus of this checklist is on U.S. trade controls, it is also important to consider the compliance posture of the target company with respect to local or other trade controls.

- Review any corporate policies, statements, or compliance manuals used by the target company to satisfy its compliance obligations under U.S.

and any other trade control laws. This should include online resources (e.g., company intranets).

- More broadly, determine whether the target company has a structured and documented program for compliance with U.S. and any other trade control laws, whether it has a dedicated trade compliance officer or other export personnel, and the extent to which—if any—the target company has conducted trade control compliance training.

2. Commodity Classification Review

This step of the due diligence process concerns the U.S. export control status of any products (including software) or technology marketed or shipped cross-border by the target company. The focus is whether the target has taken adequate steps to classify its products and technology, whether it has adequate records of the export control status of its products, and whether there are red flags to indicate the target may not have correctly classified its products and technology.

- Determine whether the target company has obtained official commodity classification rulings from the Commerce Department's Bureau of Industry and Security ("BIS") for any of its products.
- Determine whether any of its products or technology are under the jurisdiction of another U.S. agency, such as the State Department's Directorate of Defense Trade Controls ("DDTC," defense articles), the Nuclear Regulatory Commission (equipment for nuclear power plants), the Department of Energy (nuclear technology), or the Drug Enforcement Administration (which controls certain sensitive drug precursors).

  - If the target company is registered with DDTC as a manufacturer or exporter of defense articles, careful scrutiny and advance planning will be needed. For instance, DDTC will need to be notified of the transaction (well in advance if the buyer is a non-U.S. entity), and the existing registration and any outstanding licenses will need to be amended and/or transferred.

- After reviewing any official commodity classifications, determine whether the target company has formally "self-classified" any of its items against the Commerce Control List ("CCL"). Ideally, there should be a reasoned scientific/engineering memorandum to support each self-classification. If there is not, review the technical specifications for at least a sample of the self-classified items against the Export Control Classification Numbers ("ECCN") descriptions on the CCL, and consider whether the ECCN classifications appear correct and/or what additional information is required to make a preliminary assessment regarding the accuracy of prior self-classification exercises.
- Identify in particular any products or technology that have been classified, or that apparently should be classified, under an ECCN *other than* "EAR99." As noted in Chapter 4, the designation EAR99 is the default

category assigned to non-sensitive products not specifically identified on the CCL. ECCNs other than EAR99 are consequently subject to tighter export restrictions, for some specific destinations, than EAR99 items.

- Inquire whether any products, technology, or services of the target company are subject to export controls administered by any non-U.S. government or other body (such as the European Union).

3. Export Compliance for Sensitive ECCNs

Each particular ECCN *other than* EAR99 may face different restrictions depending upon the export destination.

- Determine whether the target company has adequate procedures to ensure that non-EAR99 products and technology are not exported to prohibited/restricted destinations without a U.S. export license.
- Identify exports or reexports to or by the company over the past five years of items subject to the EAR and classified *other than* EAR99 that may have been made without proper licensing.

4. License Review

Review any export licenses issued in the past five years to the target company, particularly by BIS, DDTC, and/or the Treasury Department's Office of Foreign Assets Control ("OFAC"), and inquire about pending license applications.

- Inspect the underlying license applications and the target company's compliance with any recordkeeping or reporting requirements under such licenses.
- Inquire about and review any export licenses that the target company has received from a non-U.S. government or jurisdiction.

5. Countries Subject to U.S. Embargoes and Economic Sanctions

Carefully review whether the target company—and notably any of its non-U.S. affiliates—conducts any business involving countries that are subject to comprehensive U.S. economic sanctions (at present, Cuba, Iran, and Sudan) or comprehensive trade sanctions (at present, Syria and North Korea). This is a critical part of due diligence for non-U.S. targets, and should be conducted early in the process to identify any problems for post-acquisition integration. Targets not located in the United States or incorporated under U.S. law are largely outside the scope of U.S. embargo or economic sanction regulations, and could legitimately have extensive business ties with U.S.-sanctioned markets.

- In the case of Cuba, Iran, and Sudan, this review should include whether the target organization, through its foreign subsidiaries or otherwise, supplies products to these countries (directly or through distribution agreements); whether it has operations in any of these countries; whether it licenses any software or technology to these counties; and whether it engages in any financial transactions involving these countries.

- In the event a non-U.S. target or subsidiary conducts business with an embargoed country, review whether *any* transactional support has been provided by the U.S. company or by U.S. citizens or lawful permanent residents (i.e., "green card" holders) working abroad for the non-U.S. subsidiary or the foreign company target.

- For post-acquisition planning, bear in mind that, once a target company or subsidiary is part of a U.S.-based organization, it may be difficult or impossible for the target to continue trade with embargoed countries without prohibited approval or support from the parent company in the United States or other U.S. persons. In addition, you should be aware that even non-U.S. subsidiaries of U.S. companies are prohibited from transacting any unlicensed business with Cuba. Extricating the target from Cuba-related business may require very careful planning in advance of the acquisition, to avoid inconsistent obligations under U.S. law and laws outside the United States intended to blunt the U.S. embargo of Cuba.

- In the case of Syria and North Korea, this review should include whether the target organization, through its foreign subsidiaries or otherwise, supplies U.S.-regulated products to Syria or North Korea (directly or through distribution agreements); whether it licenses any software or technology to Syria or North Korea; and whether it engages in any financial transactions involving Syria or North Korea.

  - In the event the target company or one of its subsidiaries conducts business with Syria involving U.S.-regulated products or technology, promptly determine whether the required export licensing has been obtained for such business and the current status of any such transactions (which may need to be halted pending review).

- You should determine whether the target company is involved, or was at one time involved, in significant levels of exports to other "high-risk" countries. This would also include Burma (Myanmar), which currently is the target of an import ban, a prohibition on exports of financial services (broadly defined), and an investment embargo. If the target has any ongoing commercial ties to or with Burma or its government, these dealings should be carefully reviewed.

6. Restricted Parties Screening

Determine whether the target company has any dealings with parties with whom U.S. parties may not deal or who are ineligible to receive U.S.-regulated items.

- Assess whether the target company has been screening customers and vendors to ensure that it does not engage in trade or financial dealings with restricted parties, such as those designated on OFAC's List of Specially Designated Nationals and Blocked Persons. You should also consider whether the target company has a systematic process in place for compliance with "know your customer" guidelines, designed to uncover questionable circumstances or parties.

- Assess whether any of the target company's customers or vendors (including suppliers not only of goods but also of services, such as banks) are (i) located in or controlled by the governments of embargoed countries; (ii) parties designated on OFAC's List of Specially Designated Nationals and Blocked Persons (or majority-owned by such parties, even if not listed); (iii) parties designated on BIS's Entity List or Denied Persons List; or (iv), if the target company deals in defense articles and services, parties on DDTC's List of Debarred Persons.

7. Third-Party Relationships: Agents, Distributors, and Joint-Venture Partners

Third-party relationships—in the context of the target's distribution/supply chain and in the context of joint-venture arrangements or other collaborations—can create serious compliance risks that can quickly come to a head following an acquisition.

- Determine the extent to which the target company uses third parties, such as agents, sales representatives, and distributors. Determine whether relationships with third-party representatives are governed by written agreements. Examine whether those agreements contain provisions addressing export control and trade sanctions compliance. Consider the extent of any trade controls training that third parties receive. Consider whether they are required to make certifications of compliance with applicable trade controls and whether there are provisions in place to review the activities of the third parties.

- Similarly, determine whether the target company is involved in joint ventures outside the United States. Considerations for JV partners are similar to those listed above with regard to agents, sales representatives, and distributors. Consider how control of the JV is divided between the target and the JV partner and what understandings or policies have been adopted by the parties with respect to trade control compliance.

8. Administrative, Civil, or Criminal Actions

You should request information from the target about any prior or pending administrative, civil, or criminal actions, or possible violations, involving U.S. or other foreign trade controls.

- Review carefully any voluntary self-disclosures made by the target company to BIS or OFAC and any action resulting from such a disclosure.

Even in the absence of voluntary self-disclosures, you should inquire of the target about known violations in the past five years that have *not* been disclosed.

- Determine whether any potential or suspected violations have been reported under the company's internal compliance program or otherwise.
- Be aware that, after an acquisition, the acquiring company may have to consider whether any voluntary disclosure of potential violations that occurred before the acquisition should be made to U.S. authorities, either as a proactive measure or potentially to secure the required authorization to service or otherwise deal with items that are known to have been delivered in violation of applicable export control restrictions.

9. Recordkeeping

Various recordkeeping and export clearances requirements apply to any shipments from the United States or, to a lesser extent, involving items subject to the EAR. To the extent the target is involved in export transactions involving items subject to the EAR, you should review for completeness a selection of the target company's files relating to export transactions, including any transactions that may have taken place pursuant to an export license.

- Ensure that the target company has complied with all of the requisite export clearance procedures.
- Review any company procedures developed for the selection and management of freight forwarders as well as whether the target company has executed powers of attorney to authorize freight forwarders to prepare shipping documents on its behalf.

10. Deemed Exports and Computer Network Access Issues

As noted in Chapter 4, the disclosure of U.S.-regulated technology or software programming code to a national of a foreign country is treated as an export to the person's home country. This so-called "deemed export" rule applies to disclosures within the United States or abroad to individuals who are not citizens or lawful permanent residents of the United States.

- Determine whether the target company has a program for dealing with deemed exports and non-U.S. employees. As part of the review, investigate whether the target company stores any software or technology classified under an ECCN other than EAR99 on its computer system and whether adequate controls or safeguards have been put in place to restrict access to such software or technology by non-U.S. nationals (e.g., through password protection, firewalls, etc).
- Determine whether the target company's non-U.S. employees have had access to U.S.-origin or U.S.-content technologies or software source code classified under an ECCN other than EAR99. This includes both employees in the target's non-U.S. offices (if any) as well as non-U.S. employees in its U.S. offices.

- In planning post-acquisition integration of the target's business systems and computer networks with the acquiring company's systems and networks, it will also be necessary to develop appropriate controls to restrict access by certain foreign nationals to the acquiring company's networks and servers that contain controlled U.S.-origin/U.S.-content technologies that are restricted from export to that person's home country.

11. Compliance with U.S. Antiboycott Laws

U.S. Department of Commerce regulations generally prohibit U.S. companies and their foreign affiliates from complying with key provisions of international economic boycotts in which the United States does not participate. Separately, the U.S. Treasury Department imposes tax penalties as a result of boycott participation. Requests to participate in prohibited boycott activities must be reported quarterly to the Commerce Department and annually to the Internal Revenue Service ("IRS").

- Review any reports the target company has filed with the BIS Office of Antiboycott Compliance (made on form BIS 621-P for single requests or BIS 6051-P for multiple requests). Also review annual IRS reports concerning antiboycott activity (made on IRS Form 5713).
- If the target company or its non-U.S. subsidiaries have received boycott requests but have failed to make the legally required reports, that omission is itself a violation and needs to be considered as a potential liability that might be assumed by the acquiring company as part of the merger or acquisition.

B. Additional Priority Considerations for Corporate Transactions

In addition to the checklist of issues that have been identified above, you should more broadly consider the following points that also warrant careful consideration:

- Consider how the acquisition agreement itself addresses foreign trade control compliance issues and whether a clause more specific than, or in addition to, a general law-compliance clause is required. In this regard, consider whether it might be appropriate to secure from the target company a specific representation and warranty concerning past compliance with applicable U.S. trade controls.
- Consider how transactions in process at time of closing will be handled. For instance, promptly identify any transactions that are already underway and that may create compliance concerns once the transaction closes. Develop appropriate safeguards to ensure that the acquiring company does not mistakenly become entangled in a new violation upon closing.
- What happens if a violation of U.S. foreign trade controls is discovered after the merger or acquisition? How long will the buyer have to make such discoveries? Should an indemnity provision be included? You might consider in this regard having the seller place funds in escrow for a certain amount of time to satisfy any trade compliance violations that are

identified post-acquisition as well as fees in connection with preparing, filing,and settling any self-disclosures with the key agencies.

- Bear in mind that if the target company is ultimately acquired by a U.S. company, existing agency licenses and agreements (e.g., BIS, DDTC and OFAC) may have to be formally transferred to the new parent company. If required, a post-closing notification with DDTC might also trigger a required internal compliance review with associated agency reporting.
- Integration planning is as important in compliance as in the operational side of the business. Accordingly, consider early in the process whether modifications are needed to the acquiring company's existing compliance framework to take account of the acquisition. Develop and execute an appropriate integration plan post-closing to ensure consistency and uniformity in compliance efforts.
- As part of the integration process, prioritize a comprehensive compliance audit at the acquired company (building on the due diligence effort outlined above) and compliance training for the new operation.

Conclusion

A transactional lawyer who takes the time and effort to anticipate, assess, and remedy any issues relating to U.S. trade control measures can significantly affect a company's potential exposure to a damaging, costly government investigation. Due diligence specifically focused on these compliance risks is essential to any international deal.

Stephen P. Anthony
Partner
White Collar Defense and Investigations
Covington & Burling LLP

Peter L. Flanagan
Partner
International Trade and Finance
Member of the Management Committee
Covington & Burling LLP

As negotiations grow more serious and the parties reach a tentative accord on the basic terms of the deal, the parties may wish to set these terms out on paper. This helps to make sure that the parties are "on the same page" from the start. The parties may lay out these basic terms by drafting a "term sheet," "letter of intent" (or, "LOI"), "memorandum of understanding" (or, "MOU"), or "memorandum of intent" (or, "MOI"). These are all similar documents, each listing the basic deal terms and reflecting the contemplation of the parties that a final agreement is to follow, pending further negotiations and refinement of the remaining "nitty gritty."

Parties might intend these preliminary documents not to be binding, legally enforceable agreements. However, when a letter of intent does not clearly specify whether or not it is meant to establish a binding contract and a party later asserts the document is a binding contract, a court is left to try to discern the intent of the parties. On this issue, please consider the following perspective of a seasoned practitioner.

A Practitioner Perspective: An International Take on Binding Contracts

How important is the title of a legal document? As every lawyer knows, the answer is: "Not terribly, because it is the substance of the document that controls its legal effect." But Chinese law and one U.S. case teach us that the title of a document can be very important.

Under China's joint venture legislation, generally a "joint venture agreement" refers to a non-binding document concluded by the joint venture parties upon arrival at a unanimous opinion on certain main points and principles regarding the establishment of a joint venture, while a "joint venture contract" refers to a legally binding document concluded by the joint venture parties upon arrival at a unanimous opinion on the rights and obligations of a joint venture relationship. Because of this provision, in China the parties themselves, the government, and any third party can tell immediately whether the document is legally binding just from the title.

Consider *Pennzoil v. Texaco*, the largest civil verdict in U.S. history ($10.53 billion), in which Pennzoil sued Texaco for tortious interference because Texaco purchased at a higher price shares of Getty Oil that Pennzoil had agreed to purchase under a "Memorandum of Agreement" with the Getty Oil shareholders. The question of whether Pennzoil and the Getty shareholders had a binding contract or merely an unenforceable agreement in principle was put to a jury which found that the "Memorandum of Agreement" constituted a binding contract and Texaco had committed tortious interference with that contract. New York law requires knowledge by a tortfeasor of the existence of contractual rights as an element of tortious interference.

Has there been a repeat of *Pennzoil v. Texaco*? Not yet, but almost. Consider Citibank's bid for Wachovia during the week of September 29, 2008. Citibank signed a "letter agreement" with Wachovia that barred Wachovia from negotiating with anyone else an alternative deal for the sale of its shares, but Wells Fargo made a bid violating the letter agreement and was ultimately successful in acquiring Wachovia with the support of the FDIC. Citibank threatened to sue, but never did.

How could a repeat of *Pennzoil v. Texaco* be avoided? Perhaps Chinese law can give us some inspiration. If the parties intend the document to be elaborated on later, call it an "Initial Non-Binding Contract." As every lawyer knows, the best drafting advice would be to express in the body of a preliminary document whether it is intended to be binding.

Preston Torbert
Senior Counsel
Baker & McKenzie LLP
Lecturer in Law
The University of Chicago Law School

What language is sufficient to show that a letter of intent or other preliminary document is not intended to be binding? Consider the following preliminary document.

MEMORANDUM OF INTENT[26]

Memorandum of Intent for the Acquisition of 25% of the Stock of Arnold Palmer Golf Company in Exchange for Certain Assets of Fuqua Industries, Inc.

This memorandum will serve to confirm the general understanding which has been reached regarding the acquisition of 25% of the stock of Arnold Palmer Golf Company ("Palmer") by Fuqua Industries, Inc. ("Fuqua") in exchange for all of the outstanding stock of Fernquest and Johnson Golf Company, Inc. ("F & J"), a wholly-owned California subsidiary of Fuqua, and money in the amount of $700,000; and for the rendition of management services by Fuqua.

(1) *Form of the Combination.* Fuqua will transfer to Palmer all of the issued and outstanding stock of Fernquest & Johnson Golf Company and cash in the amount of $700,000 in exchange for an amount of common stock, $.50 par value, of Palmer ("Palmer Common Stock") equal to 25% of the total number of shares of Palmer Common Stock which will be outstanding, subject to option, or issuable upon conversion, after such issuance.

(2) *Conduct of Business.* The principal office of Palmer will be moved to Atlanta, Georgia, and the transfer of operations will occur as quickly as possible after Palmer has been qualified to do business in the state of Georgia. Fuqua will provide Palmer with management services including financial, marketing, legal, industrial engineering, insurance procurement, corporate planning, data processing, purchasing and general management services at Fuqua's cost. The general operating manager of Palmer, with the title of President and Chief Operating Officer, will be nominated by Fuqua but shall be subject to the approval of the Board of Directors of Palmer and shall serve at the pleasure of such Board. Arnold Palmer, individually, shall be Chairman of the Board of Palmer, and Mark McCormack will be Vice Chairman of the Board of Palmer.

(3) *License Rights to the Use of the Name "Arnold Palmer."* Palmer and/or a wholly-owned subsidiary shall possess an exclusive license or licenses in the form attached hereto for the use of the name "Arnold Palmer" in connection with the manufacture and sale of golf clubs, golf balls, golf bags and golf gloves in the United States and Canada. The licenses are for a period

---

26. This memorandum of intent is excerpted from the Appendix in *Arnold Palmer Golf Co. v. Fuqua Indus., Inc.*, 541 F.2d 584, 590-93 (6th Cir. 1976).

expiring in the year 1991 and are exclusive licenses. Certified copies of the licenses shall be attached as exhibits to the definitive agreement for the acquisition provided for in paragraph 10 below. Palmer shall represent and warrant as to the validity, exclusiveness and duration of such licenses.

(4) *Employment Contracts.* Palmer and/or its wholly-owned subsidiary will have employment contracts with Arnold Palmer and Mark McCormack expiring in the year of 1991 in the form attached hereto. Palmer will have no other written employment contracts except an acceptable contract with Robert Robinson.

(5) *Loans and Investments by Fuqua.* Fuqua agrees to advance to Palmer up to an aggregate of $700,000, payable 150 days after demand with interest payable from time to time at the rate then charged, giving effect to compensating balances, to Fuqua by The Chase Manhattan Bank, N.A. and successor lenders, plus one quarter of one per cent as an administrative charge, and secured by a pledge of the F & J common stock. From such funds Palmer shall cause F & J to repay to Fuqua up to the sum of $200,000 which Fuqua acknowledges will be the maximum amount owed by F & J to Fuqua. Additional funds may be advanced by Fuqua to Palmer upon such terms and conditions as the Board of Directors of Palmer and Fuqua may determine.

(6) *Investment Intent and Registration Rights.* The stock of Palmer issued to Fuqua shall be issued and received for investment and not with a view to the sale or other distribution thereof; Fuqua will execute an agreement evidencing the foregoing intent; and the certificates evidencing such shares shall be appropriately legended to express such investment intent. Fuqua will have "piggy-back" registration rights.

(7) *Palmer Qualified Stock Options.* Palmer has adopted a "Qualified Stock Option Plan" pursuant to the Internal Revenue Code of 1954, as amended. No options have been granted thereunder and all proposals to grant shares thereunder shall be canceled (EDK) (AJL). No other options will be granted prior to the Closing.

(8) *Financial Statements.* On or before the Closing, Palmer shall submit to Fuqua financial statements as of December 31, 1969, certified by Arthur Anderson and Company, independent public accountants, including (i) a balance sheet as of that date which shall not reflect any material adverse change in the condition of Palmer since the balance sheet audited by Arthur Anderson and Company as of December 31, 1968, a copy of which has been submitted to Fuqua, except for changes incurred as a result of the operating loss incurred in the calendar year 1969, and (ii) an income statement for the year then ended which shall reveal an operating loss of not in excess of $200,000. Fuqua has already delivered to Palmer a copy of the acquisition agreement pursuant to which Fuqua acquired F & J,

including financial statements attached thereto as exhibits, and shall represent and warrant that there has not been any material adverse change in the condition of F & J and its wholly-owned subsidiary as set forth in said acquisition agreement since the date thereof.

(9) *Representations, Warranties, Conditions and Covenants.* The definitive agreement provided for in paragraph 10 below for the combination of the businesses shall contain representations, warranties, conditions, and covenants in the general form used by Fuqua in connection with the acquisition of businesses by Fuqua. Fuqua has delivered to Palmer an example of such provisions.

In addition, such agreement will provide that the following shall be conditions to the obligations of Fuqua thereunder:

(a) Professional Golf Company ("Pro Golf") will advise Palmer in writing that its requirements contract with Palmer dated October 27, 1961, does not obligate Palmer to purchase future requirements from Pro Golf.

(b) There will be no obligation on the part of Palmer to continue under any lease from Pro Golf to Palmer.

(c) Termination of requirements contract with Windbreaker-Danville Company, dated January 20, 1962.

(d) The life insurance policies on the lives of Arnold Palmer and Mark McCormack will be assets of Palmer.

(e) There will be a warranty by Arnold Palmer that he has no present obligation to Wilson Sporting Goods Co.

(f) Palmer will have the written authority to disapprove any proposed future "premium sales" of golf clubs, golf balls, golf bags and golf gloves arranged by Arnold Palmer Enterprises, Inc. in the territories in which Palmer and/or its subsidiary are licensed to sell such products.

(g) Remlap Company shall be a wholly-owned subsidiary of Palmer.

(h) Palmer will warrant that there is no present obligation to pay royalties to Jack Harkins on the sale of golf balls and that there will not be in the future unless steel center golf balls are sold.

(10) *Preparation of Definitive Agreement.* Counsel for Palmer and counsel for Fuqua will proceed as promptly as possible to prepare an agreement acceptable to Palmer and Fuqua for the proposed combination of businesses. Such agreement will contain the representations, warranties, covenants and conditions, as generally outlined in the example submitted by Fuqua to Palmer and referred to in paragraph 9 hereof. In addition, the definitive agreement will provide for indemnification of Fuqua by the principal stockholders of Palmer (Arnold Palmer, Robert Caldwell, Mark McCormack and Hardwick Caldwell) (EDK) (AJL) for a period of three years after the closing in the event that Palmer shall have undisclosed liabilities in excess of $100,000, pursuant to which said principal stockholders will be obligated to indemnify Fuqua in an amount equal to only 25% of

so much, if any, of such undisclosed liabilities as are in excess of $100,000 and shall as a group in no event be obligated to make payments in excess of a total of $1,000,000 for all four stockholders combined (EDK) (AJL).

(11) *Conditions.* The obligations of Palmer and Fuqua shall be subject to fulfillment of the following conditions:

(i) preparation of the definitive agreement for the proposed combination in form and content satisfactory to both parties and their respective counsel;

(ii) approval of such definitive agreement by the Board of Directors of Fuqua;

(iii) approval of such definitive agreement by the Board of Directors of Palmer;

(iv) approval by the stockholders of Palmer of certain amendments to the Articles & Regulations of Palmer which are necessary in order to consummate said agreement;

(v) approval by the respective counsel of Palmer and Fuqua of all legal matters;

(vi) that between the date of the definitive agreement and the Closing, there shall have been no material adverse change in the business or financial condition of Palmer or F & J;

(vii) requisite approval by creditors of Palmer and Fuqua;

(viii) the Closing shall have occurred not later than March 31, 1970.

(12) *Publicity.* All announcements and publicity relating to the proposed combination shall be subject to the mutual approval of Palmer and Fuqua.

The foregoing correctly setting forth the general understanding and agreement of the respective parties, and parties hereby confirm their acceptance by signing and delivering copies of this memorandum, as of this day of December, 1969.

In determining whether the above document constituted a binding agreement, the Sixth Circuit, in *Arnold Palmer Golf Co. v. Fuqua Indus., Inc.*, explained:

> Upon first blush it may appear that the Memorandum of Intent is no more than preliminary negotiation between the parties. A cursory reading of the conditions contained in paragraph 11, by themselves, may suggest that the parties did not intend to be bound by the Memorandum of Intent.
>
> Nevertheless, the memorandum recited that a "general understanding (had) been reached." And . . . the entire document and relevant circumstances surrounding its adoption must be considered in making a determination of the parties' intention. In this case we find an extensive document that appears to reflect all essential terms concerning the transfer of Arnold Palmer stock to Fuqua in exchange for all outstanding stock in Fernquest and Johnson. The form of combination, the location of the principal office of Palmer, the license rights, employment contracts of Palmer personnel and the financial obligations of Fuqua are a few of the many areas covered in the Memorandum of Intent, and

they are all described in unqualified terms. The Memorandum states, for instance, that "Fuqua *will* transfer all of the . . . stock," that the "principal office of Palmer *will* be moved to Atlanta," that "Palmer . . . *shall* possess an exclusive license," and that "Fuqua *agrees* to advance to Palmer up to an aggregate of $700,000. . . ." (Emphasis added.)

Paragraph 10 of the Memorandum states, also in unqualified language, that counsel for the parties "will proceed as promptly as possible to prepare an agreement acceptable to (the parties). . . ." We believe that this paragraph may be read merely to impose an obligation upon the parties to memorialize their agreement. We do not mean to suggest that this is the correct interpretation. The provision is also susceptible to an interpretation that the parties did not intend to be bound.

As we have indicated above, it is permissible to refer to extrinsic evidence to determine whether the parties intended to be bound by the Memorandum of Intent. In this regard, we observe that Fuqua circulated a press release in January 1970 that would tend to sustain Palmer's claim that the two parties intended to be bound by the Memorandum of Intent. Fuqua's statement said that the two companies "have agreed to cooperate in an enterprise that will serve the golfing industry." . . .

We reject appellee's argument that summary judgment was appropriate because the obligations of the parties were subject to an express condition that was not met. We believe a question of fact is presented whether the parties intended the conditions in paragraph 11 to operate only if the definitive agreement was not in conformity with the general understanding contained in the Memorandum of Intent. The parties may well have intended that there should be no binding obligation until the definitive agreement was signed, but we regard this question as one for the fact finder to determine after a consideration of the relevant evidence.[27]

In determining whether a preliminary document creates a legally binding agreement, "the language of the agreement . . . is the most important."[28] As the Ninth Circuit has explained, "[T]he rights of private parties to enter into contracts also embraces their rights not to, and there is no contract where the objective manifestations of intent demonstrate that the parties chose not to bind themselves. . . ."[29] There, the court found that language in a letter of intent that "this letter of intent is of no binding effect" was sufficient to show that "[t]he one proposition to which they expressed their intention to agree was that they had not as yet agreed to the [deal]."[30] To express an intent that a document is not binding, the document itself should clearly, explicitly, and prominently

27. *Arnold Palmer Golf Co. v. Fuqua Indus., Inc.*, 541 F.2d 584, 589-90 (6th Cir. 1976).

28. *Adjustrite Sys., Inc. v. GAB Bus. Servs., Inc.*, 145 F.3d 543, 549-52 (2d Cir. 1998) (finding a two-page document not to create a binding contract, where "the document is entitled a 'proposal' and it merely states that [purchaser] 'desires' to purchase assets," the transaction "clearly was of the type that ordinarily would be committed not only to a writing but to a formal contract complete with representations and warranties and the other standard provisions usually found in sophisticated, formal contracts," and many important items were left open in the document.).

29. *Rennick v. O.P.T.I.O.N. Care, Inc.*, 77 F.3d 309, 316 (9th Cir. 1996) (California law).

30. *Id.*

state that the letter is not a binding, legally enforceable contract. For example, the mere inclusion of language in a letter of intent that the letter is "subject to" a later written agreement might not be sufficient to render the preliminary document non-binding.[31] In addition to the language of the preliminary document, courts generally will look to the following factors in determining whether a preliminary document is binding: (1) the context of the negotiations; (2) whether the parties have partially performed any of their putative obligations; (3) the existence of open terms in the preliminary documents; and (4) whether the transaction is of the kind customarily documented in a final written form.[32] If a preliminary document is found to constitute a binding contract, despite that it leaves certain items or issues open, then a court is likely either to impute commercially reasonable terms to fill the gaps or to instruct the parties to negotiate the remaining items in good faith.[33]

An important corollary is that sometimes parties will include specific provisions—for example, non-disclosure covenants and "no-shop" provisions (which we discuss later in this chapter)—that they wish to be binding *within* a letter of intent that they regard on the whole to be non-binding. In so doing, parties must be careful, as they run the risk of a court finding either (i) the specific provisions—those the parties wished to be binding—to be non-binding; or (ii) the whole document—including those provisions the parties wished to be non-binding—to be binding.[34] Prudent parties will expressly make clear which obligations they regard to be binding and which they do not. This can be accomplished in a variety of ways, including: (1) segregating the binding and non-binding provisions of the letter in separate sections so clearly marked; and (2) including a header at the beginning of the letter that states that the letter is not a binding agreement except for certain enumerated sections. This second method is demonstrated in the below excerpt from a letter of intent recently filed with the SEC:

> This Memorandum summarizes the principal terms of a series of proposed transactions involving the entities listed on Exhibit A ("Participating Entities"). This Memorandum of Terms is intended solely as a summary of the terms that are currently proposed by the parties and *shall not constitute a binding agreement except for the provisions under "Fees and Expenses", "Exclusive Negotiations", "Confidentiality," and "Access", which are intended and shall be the binding agreement of the parties.* It is understood that any party may, at any time prior to execution of a definitive agreement, propose different or additional terms as may be necessary to achieve

---

31. *Id.* at 316.
31. *See, e.g., Arcadian Phosphates, Inc. v. Arcadian Corp.*, 884 F.2d 69, 72 (2d Cir. 1989).
33. *See, e.g., Itek Corp. v. Chicago Aerial Indus., Inc.*, 248 A.2d 625, 629 (Del. 1968).
34. *See, e.g., Logan v. D.W. Sivers Co.*, 169 P.3d 1255, 1260 (Or. 2007) ("We conclude that, although the letter of intent was not, as a whole, a binding agreement for the sale and purchase of the property in question, it did contain certain promises that were binding, one of which was defendant's promise to neither solicit nor accept other offers on the property for a period of 60 days. The Court of Appeals thus was correct in holding that the trial court erred in granting a directed verdict to defendant on that ground.").

the overall plan as set out in the exhibits hereto. This Memorandum refers to entities that will be formed prior to or upon execution of a final agreement.[35]

A letter of intent will also sometimes include a purportedly binding obligation to consummate negotiations of the final agreement in good faith or in accordance with some other performance standard. These obligations do not require that the parties actually consummate a final deal—nor do they somehow make an LOI on the whole binding—but generally they do create a legally enforceable obligation to conduct negotiations toward a final deal in good faith (or however the LOI provides).[36]

B. THE BASIC TYPES OF M&A TRANSACTIONS AND THEIR ALTERNATIVES

There are three basic ways to acquire a corporation (i.e., a "target"): (1) acquire its assets; (2) acquire its stock; or (3) engage in some form of merger with it. A deal lawyer must appreciate the various benefits and drawbacks of each potential method in deciding the best way to structure a particular M&A transaction. On this topic, we asked two seasoned practitioners to share with us their experience, expertise, and perspective.

A Practitioner Perspective: Structuring Mergers and Acquisitions

An attorney often is asked to advise a client in connection with a possible acquisition of a business, and in that setting the client normally will ask the attorney for advice about how to structure the deal. A lawyer can provide valuable assistance in developing a recommendation about deal structure. However, deal structure is a matter that should be addressed with the collective input of the lawyer, an accountant, a tax advisor, and, especially in a deal involving a public company, an investment banker.

A complete discussion of all considerations that drive deal structure, including those relating to accounting and tax, involves complexity beyond the scope of this article. We address here the principal legal considerations and a few general

---

35. Pay By The Day Holdings Inc., Non-Binding Letter of Intent (Form 8-K), at Exhibit 10.1 (Mar. 12, 2010), *available at* http://www.sec.gov/Archives/edgar/data/1424455/000121390010000978/f8k031210 ex10i_ paybytheday.htm (emphasis added).

36. *See, e.g., In re Vylene Enters., Inc.,* 90 F.3d 1472, 1476 (9th Cir. 1996); *Howtek, Inc. v. Relisys,* 958 F. Supp. 46, 48 (D.N.H. 1997) ("The modern view, and the view endorsed by most scholars, is that agreements to negotiate in good faith, unlike mere 'agreements to agree,' are not unenforceable as a matter of law."). *But see, e.g., Ohio Calculating, Inc. v. CPT Corp.,* 846 F.2d 497, 501-02 (8th Cir. 1988) (agreements to negotiate are invalid under Minnesota law due to the impossibility of calculating damages); *Candid Prods., Inc. v. Int'l Skating Union,* 530 F. Supp. 1330, 1336-37 (S.D.N.Y. 1982) ("An agreement to negotiate in good faith is amorphous and nebulous, since it implicates so many factors that are themselves indefinite and uncertain that the intent of the parties can only be fathomed by conjecture and surmise."). Please see Chapter 4 for further discussion of "agreements to agree" and agreements to negotiate in good faith.

tax considerations that should inform the lawyer's input into the decision about deal structure.

The term "mergers and acquisitions" or "M&A" refers generally to a variety of different types of transactions involving the acquisition by one company of the business assets and related liabilities of another company or the acquisition of the outstanding capital stock of that other company. Some people think of an "acquisition" as any transaction in which one company acquires another, regardless of the legal mechanism used to complete the deal; likewise, some people think of a "merger" as any combination of two companies, regardless of the form of the deal, where there is no clear dominant "acquiring company." This article ignores those imprecise generalizations and focuses on the various technical legal structures for mergers and acquisitions, how those structures differ, and the circumstances under which various deal structures are most useful.

M&A transactions can involve corporations, limited liability companies, partnerships, business trusts, or any other form of legal entity. Most M&A transactions in the U.S. involve corporations, but the principles relevant to corporate deals are generally similar for deals involving other types of legal entities. As discussed below, there are several different ways to structure M&A transactions involving corporations.

Purchase of Assets

In its simplest form, an acquisition can be structured as a purchase of the business assets of another company and the assumption of that company's liabilities related to the business. The transaction might involve a purchase and assumption of all or substantially all of the assets and liabilities of another company or only a small portion of that company's assets and liabilities.

An asset purchase transaction normally would involve a purchase agreement that lists or describes the assets to be purchased and the liabilities to be assumed, the purchase price and how it will be paid, warranties about the seller's title to the assets and the character and condition of those assets and the nature and extent of the liabilities of the business, and indemnities or other remedies for breach of warranties.

In a deal structured as a purchase of assets, transfer of title to the purchased assets is completed through assignments and bills of sale, deeds for real estate, assignments of contracts, and other instruments of transfer of title for assets such as vehicles, patents, and trademarks, which must be recorded in appropriate offices. Assignments of the seller's contract rights included in the purchased assets often require the consent of other parties to the contracts. The need for separate instruments of transfer tends to make a purchase of assets cumbersome, and the need for third-party consents can make a purchase of assets impractical in some situations involving valuable contract rights, permits, or franchises. In these cases, a deal structured as a purchase of stock or a merger may avoid some of these potential problems associated with an asset purchase.

In a deal structured as an asset purchase, the buyer does not necessarily acquire all of the assets or assume all of the liabilities of the seller. When a buyer has a choice to structure a deal as a purchase of assets or a purchase of stock, the buyer will normally favor a purchase of assets because that transaction structure gives the buyer an opportunity to pick and choose what assets and liabilities will be transferred to the buyer as part of the deal. In that process, the buyer will naturally want to avoid the assumption of contingent and undisclosed liabilities such as litigation and potential environmental and tort claims.

In contrast, the prospective seller of the assets and the seller's shareholders normally prefer to structure the deal as a sale of stock of the company rather than a sale of the company's assets. The sale of stock avoids the risk that the company and its shareholders may be left to manage the liquidation of the residual assets and liabilities that the buyer did not agree to take over. Also, structuring the deal as a purchase of assets may present difficult issues regarding employees of the seller. Unless the buyer hires employees of the seller to continue the acquired business, the seller may be forced to terminate those employees, which may result in employment-related claims against the seller. In an asset purchase transaction, the buyer and seller typically negotiate strenuously over the liabilities to be assumed by the buyer and the liabilities to be retained by the seller and the consideration exchanged for the assumption of those liabilities.

Although structuring a deal as a purchase of assets gives the buyer an opportunity to "leave behind" unwanted liabilities of the seller, the buyer should be wary of the possibility of successor liability for claims that arise out of the seller's pre-closing conduct of the business or ownership of the assets. This is especially true for the seller's trade creditors who may not be paid, some environmental liabilities that follow ownership of real estate, and potential claims for personal injuries attributable to products of the acquired business.

Companies often have different businesses or product lines that are operated as distinct divisions but are not separately incorporated as subsidiaries of a holding company. The U.S. auto industry is a good example of this arrangement. A transaction involving an acquisition of a business that comprises only a portion of the assets and liabilities of a company normally needs to be structured as a purchase of assets. It can be difficult, however, to separate a division and its assets from other divisions sharing common or overlapping facilities, centralized functions, and management. A company preparing to divest the assets associated with an entire division sometimes will transfer the division assets into a subsidiary and seek a sale of stock of that new subsidiary rather than a sale of the division assets.

Sometimes the prospective seller of assets or a business division will divest other assets or businesses in order to prepare itself for a particular M&A transaction. These divestiture transactions can be accomplished through a sale of the unwanted assets to another buyer or the transfer of the assets to a new subsidiary followed by the distribution of the subsidiary shares as a non-taxable dividend to its parent company's shareholders in a transaction commonly referred to as a "spin-off."

An asset purchase transaction that results in the sale of substantially all of the assets of a corporation is likely to require approval of its shareholders under state corporation law. Depending on the state of incorporation and the company's charter, the required shareholder vote can range from a simple majority vote to a two-thirds vote or even a higher super-majority. The important point is that a sale of assets rarely requires unanimous approval of a company's shareholders, and minority shareholders who object to an asset sale have little recourse to block the transaction.

A purchase of assets of a corporation normally is a taxable transaction to the seller. As a result, the seller will recognize taxable gain or loss on the transaction, depending on the seller's tax status, tax basis in the assets, and other factors. If the seller is a corporation that will pay tax on gains recognized from the sale of its assets and the corporation intends to distribute the net after-tax proceeds to its shareholders, the prospective seller and its shareholders should be expected to seek a more tax-efficient deal structure to avoid the tax at the corporate level when the assets are sold and the additional tax that its shareholders will pay upon receipt of the distribution.

A buyer often prefers to structure a deal as an asset purchase because the acquired assets will have a tax basis in the hands of the buyer equal to the purchase price paid for those assets. That may result in a "stepped-up" tax basis in the assets, which will enable the buyer to deduct higher depreciation expense, reducing taxable income for the buyer over the depreciable lives of the purchased assets and improving cash flow due to lower taxes. However, it is also possible that the purchase price of the assets is less than the seller's tax basis in those assets, and a purchase of assets could result in a "step-down" in basis and lower depreciation deductions.

Purchase of Stock

A simple M&A deal also can be structured as a purchase of the capital stock of a company rather than a purchase of its assets. The stock may be held by a single shareholder or a small group of shareholders, or it may be held by hundreds or thousands of shareholders if a public company is involved.

A deal involving one or a relatively small number of selling shareholders normally involves a stock purchase agreement between the buyer and the shareholders. The stock purchase agreement typically includes a description of the stock to be acquired, the purchase price and how it will be paid, warranties from the selling shareholders about the condition of the business and assets of the company to be acquired and the company's liabilities, and remedies for breach of the sellers' warranties, including indemnity arrangements for breach of warranties.

In a purchase of stock, the buyer acquires the company with all of its assets, liabilities, and employees. For this reason, negotiations in stock purchase transactions often focus on warranties from the selling shareholders about all aspects of the company, in particular the liabilities of the company they are selling, and the buyer's remedies for breach of those warranties.

In a stock purchase transaction, there is no need for the purchase agreement to include a list or description of the assets of the company, and it is not necessary to obtain instruments of transfer of assets and liabilities of the target company because they remain with the company after the transfer of its stock to the buyer. However, debt instruments usually include acceleration provisions that are triggered by a change of control of the borrower, and contracts that prohibit assignment sometimes include termination provisions that are triggered upon a change of control through a sale of stock or similar transaction, so third-party consents may be required in connection with a stock purchase.

A purchase of stock is a sensible transaction structure when the buyer wants to acquire all of the assets of the target company and is willing to have all liabilities of the target company follow with the acquisition. This transaction structure is also useful if the target company has important assets, such as contract rights, permits, or franchises, that cannot be freely transferred in a sale of assets.

In contrast to a purchase of assets, a purchase of stock requires 100% participation by the target company's shareholders, unless the acquiring company is willing to allow minority shareholders to retain their shares. For this reason, a purchase of stock may not be a useful transaction structure if shareholders of the target company are not in unanimous agreement to sell the company.

A transaction structured as a sale of stock of a corporation normally is taxable to the selling shareholders, and no tax gain or loss is recognized by the acquired company. However, in some circumstances, a buyer can make an election under federal tax law to have the stock purchase transaction treated for federal income tax purposes as if the acquired company sold its assets to the buyer and recognized taxable gain from the sale. The resulting tax becomes the responsibility of the acquired company and its new parent company. The election generally allows the buyer to take a stepped-up tax basis in the assets of the acquired company.

Tender Offer

If the stock of the company to be acquired through a stock purchase is widely held, as will be the case, for example, if the target company is listed on a stock exchange, it is not practical to have the shareholders sign a stock purchase agreement in the form that normally would be used to acquire the stock of a company with just a few shareholders. In this case, the acquisition of the stock could be pursued through a transaction commonly referred to as a "tender offer."

In a tender offer, the acquiring company makes an offer directly to the shareholders of the target company. Shareholders may tender their shares for sale to the buyer, or they may retain their shares. The tender offer typically is subject to a number of conditions, so the buyer normally will purchase all tendered shares at one time if and when the conditions to the offer are satisfied.

Because shareholders of the target company have the option to tender their shares for sale to the buyer or retain their shares, a tender offer ordinarily includes a condition for receipt of tenders of a minimum number of shares that will enable the buyer to acquire a controlling interest in the target company.

In contrast to a simple stock purchase transaction, which usually is negotiated with the selling shareholders, in a tender offer there typically are no negotiations with the selling shareholders, and the selling shareholders give no warranties about the assets, liabilities or financial condition of the target company. The target company in a tender offer is usually a pubic company that is subject to disclosure requirements under federal securities laws. In lieu of relying on warranties, the buyer evaluates the assets, liabilities and financial condition of the target company through its required public disclosures, including its annual and quarterly financial statements. Since the buyer gets no warranties about the condition of the target company, it assumes the risk that the target company's assets, liabilities, and financial condition prove to be different from what the buyer expected when it made its decision to proceed with the tender offer.

A tender offer creates a contractual relationship between the buyer and each selling shareholder. In a tender offer, the buyer does not need to enter into an agreement with the target company prior to commencement of the offer. For this reason, a tender offer is a technique more commonly used in so-called "hostile" takeover proposals that are opposed by the target company.

Because shareholders have the option to tender their shares or retain them, a tender offer rarely results in the purchase of 100 percent of the target company's shares. For this reason, a successful tender offer normally is followed by a merger transaction structured to make the target company a wholly-owned subsidiary of the acquiring company, a transaction often referred to as a "clean-up" merger. In a hostile tender offer, the clean-up merger is proposed to the target company by the buyer after the buyer acquires a controlling interest in the target company through the tender offer.

A tender offer also can be used in a friendly transaction as a measure to get cash into the hands of the selling shareholders more quickly than could be accomplished through other deal structures. When a tender offer is used in a friendly acquisition, the buyer and the target company typically will enter into an agreement that sets forth the target company's consent to the tender offer and provides for the clean-up merger of the target company with the buyer or a subsidiary of the buyer following the buyer's completion of the purchase of a specified minimum number of target company shares.

The purchase price in a tender offer normally is paid in cash but could be paid in another form of consideration. In a cash tender offer, the tax consequences to the selling shareholders and the target company are generally the same as would be the case for a simple stock purchase transaction.

Exchange Offer

An exchange offer is a form of a tender offer in which the buyer offers to pay target company shareholders consideration other than cash, such as stock of the buyer, in exchange for their shares of stock in the target company. The form and structure of an exchange offer is otherwise very similar to a cash tender offer. However, it generally takes longer to complete an exchange offer because the buyer must register new securities with the SEC and send a lengthy prospectus to target company shareholders with information about the buyer, its financial history, and pro forma financial statements showing the expected financial condition of the buyer after giving effect to its acquisition of the target company.

Target company shareholders generally are less receptive to an exchange offer, compared to a cash offer, because they must make the more difficult decision to exchange their target company shares for the somewhat uncertain value of the buyer's securities.

There is another important difference between a cash tender offer and an exchange offer. If structured properly, an exchange offer can be tax-free to target company shareholders who exchange their target company stock for stock in the acquiring company. If the exchange offer qualifies as a tax-free transaction, former shareholders of the target company generally will not be taxed until they sell their shares of stock in the acquiring company.

Mergers

A merger is a particular form of business combination pursuant to the corporation laws of the states of incorporation of the merging companies. In a merger, if the requisite statutory procedures are followed, two companies can combine by operation of state statute to become a single company referred to as the "surviving" or "resulting" corporation, and the assets and liabilities of the two companies are combined to become the assets and liabilities of the single company resulting from the merger.

The principal procedural requisites for a merger of corporations under the laws of most states are: a merger agreement between the merging corporations, including a description of the cash, securities or other consideration that will be exchanged for shares of the merging companies; a statement of which of the merging companies will be the surviving corporation following the merger; and in most cases a vote of the directors and shareholders of one or both merging companies. Often the merger agreement includes warranties made by each company about its business, assets and liabilities, but these warranties usually serve only as closing conditions for the deal and provide no post-closing remedies for either merged company.

Assuming all requisite steps are taken and any required director and shareholder approvals are obtained, a merger is completed upon the filing of articles of merger (sometimes called a certificate of merger) with the secretary of state of each state in which the merged companies are organized or qualified to transact business as a foreign corporation. When the merger becomes effective under state law, the surviving corporation succeeds, by operation of state statute, to all assets and liabilities of the other corporation, without any requirement for instruments of assignment of assets and liabilities from one company to the other. In this respect, a merger bears similarities to both a purchase of assets and a purchase of stock: the surviving corporation acquires the equity of the acquired company and, at the same time, the assets and liabilities of the acquired company are transferred to the surviving corporation without any instruments of transfer.

A merger transaction can be structured several different ways. In its simplest form, a merger involves a merger of the target company "TC" with and into the acquiring company "AC," with "AC" as the surviving corporation. This is sometimes referred to as a "forward merger." Alternatively, a merger can be accomplished by merging "AC" with and into "TC," with "TC" as the surviving corporation. This is sometimes referred to as a "reverse merger." In another form, "TC" can be merged with and into a subsidiary of "AC," with that new subsidiary of "AC" as the surviving corporation. This is referred to as a "forward triangular merger." Alternatively, a merger can be structured as a merger of a subsidiary of "AC" with and into "TC," with "TC" as the surviving corporation and wholly-owned subsidiary of "AC." This is referred to as a "reverse triangular merger." The selection among these alternatives is primarily a matter of accounting and tax considerations but can also be driven by simple preferences around what company should be the surviving corporation and where and how the acquired company should fit into the post-merger corporate structure.

Mergers can also involve simultaneous combinations of more than two companies. Sometimes two or more companies will combine in a transaction referred to as a "consolidation," which is similar to a merger but generally involves the creation of a new company that becomes the resulting corporation. In a consolidation, the companies to be consolidated cease to exist as separate legal entities and a new corporation emerges as the surviving entity.

Sometimes a transaction is described as a "merger of equals." This label does not actually refer to a particular form of merger but refers, instead, to a desire for the parties to the transaction to avoid the appearance that one company is acquiring the other. Being identified as the acquired company can carry negative connotations that may generate opposition to a deal, and the buyer in a transaction involving a publicly held company is usually expected to pay a premium price for control of the target company. So parties to a transaction sometimes will describe the deal as a merger of equals to gain acceptance of the deal or justify a lower purchase price, even though, as a matter of deal structure, one company may actually be acquiring the other. In practice, a true merger of equals is rare. For example, Daimler-Benz and Chrysler announced their combination as a merger of equals. The companies structured the deal so each party to the merger ceased to exist, a new company called DaimlerChrysler was created, and each company's stockholders exchanged their old shares for stock in the new company. It did not take long for the former Daimler-Benz management to emerge as the dominant force in the new company.

A significant distinguishing feature of a merger is the compulsory effect of the shareholder vote. In a stock purchase or tender offer, shareholders of the target company have a choice to sell or retain their shares. In a merger, the merger agreement specifies what consideration the target company shareholders will receive for their stock, and if the requisite shareholder vote is obtained and other procedural requirements are followed, all shareholders of the target company must exchange their shares for the specified merger consideration (or an appraised fair value, as discussed below), including shareholders who voted against the merger or would refuse to sell in a tender offer or stock purchase transaction. This explains why a successful tender offer transaction typically is followed by a clean-up merger as a measure to acquire the target company shares that were not purchased through the tender offer. It also explains why a merger transaction is normally considered the most direct and simple way to complete any friendly acquisition of a public company.

A clean-up merger following a successful tender offer can be proposed by the buyer as soon as it acquires the requisite controlling interest in the target company. However, target company shareholders who do not tender their shares will be entitled to vote on that merger unless the buyer holds a sufficient number of target company shares to use a technique known as a "short form" merger. Under the corporation laws of many states, a company that holds at least 90 percent of all classes of stock of a subsidiary company can cause the subsidiary to merge with the parent company without a vote of directors or shareholders of the subsidiary company.

In some mergers, shareholders who do not vote in favor of the merger and who follow procedures specified by state corporation law will be entitled to file an action in state court seeking appraisal of their shares. The appraisal process will result in a court determination of the fair value of the shares, which the surviving corporation must pay to those shareholders in lieu of the consideration specified in the merger agreement. Shareholders who pursue this remedy of appraisal are referred to as "dissenting shareholders." The right for dissenting shareholders to seek appraisal under state law normally is a minor disadvantage of a merger transaction. However, if a significant number of shareholders exercise their appraisal rights, the acquiring company faces some degree of risk that a court will award the dissenting shareholders substantially greater consideration than specified in the merger agreement. Merger agreements often include provisions that give the buyer a right to back out of the deal if an excessive number of target company shareholders pursue their appraisal rights before the merger becomes effective.

The consideration in a merger can be cash, stock of the acquiring company, or other consideration or a combination of different forms of consideration. In some mergers, the merger agreement will give shareholders a right to elect to receive cash or stock of the surviving company.

Similar to an exchange offer, a merger can be structured so that it is a tax-free transaction for shareholders who exchange their target company shares for new shares in the company surviving the merger. However, shareholders who receive cash in addition to or in lieu of acquiring company stock in a tax-free merger transaction will recognize taxable gains to the extent of the cash received, similar to the tax treatment of a simple sale of stock for cash. If structured as a tax-free transaction, the merger will result in no gain or loss to the merged companies upon the transfer of the assets and liabilities from one company to the other.

Conclusion

Asset and stock purchase transactions are common forms of transactions involving privately held companies. An asset purchase is a useful deal structure in a transaction involving the purchase of a portion of the assets of a company or where the seller of the assets has liabilities that the buyer is unwilling to assume. A stock purchase is a simple and convenient way to purchase a company if the buyer intends to acquire the entire company with all of its assets and liabilities and all shareholders are willing to sell their shares.

A tender offer is practically the only way to purchase the stock of a widely held company and can be used in both hostile and friendly deals. However, it is unlikely to result in the acquisition of 100 percent of the stock of the target company. A merger is the typical choice in friendly acquisitions involving publicly held companies.

William A. Von Hoene, Jr.
Executive Vice President, Finance and Legal
Exelon Corporation

Bruce G. Wilson
Sr. Vice Pres. and Deputy General Counsel
Exelon Corporation

In addition to the classic types of "full-blown" M&A transactions, companies may consider engaging in highly cooperative relationships and agreements. We asked a few seasoned practitioners to offer their insight and perspective on the use of typical cooperative agreements in practice.

A Practitioner Perspective: Corporate "Partnership" Agreements

Companies frequently combine efforts to pursue common business goals. The nature of the combined effort is usually captured in a written agreement that describes the scope and duration of the relationship. Practice and custom have determined the commonly used names for these arrangements, in accordance with the scope and contemplated length of the cooperative relationship. Commonly, these cooperative arrangements may take the form of Alliance Agreements, Channel Partner Agreements, Teaming Agreements, and Joint-Venture Agreements.

Cooperative agreements, no matter the form, usually maintain as the basis a mutually beneficial relationship. A business with strong growth potential and innovative ideas may suddenly find new markets, greater capacity, and more technical resources while the partner business may benefit from the use and exploitation of innovative ideas. Often, business partnerships are formed where two independent companies have complementary expertise and intellectual property. It is not uncommon for software vendors to partner with consulting firms where the software company has a software product but is not an expert in the implementation of their software. By going to market together, the software company can advertise that its software is implemented by expert consultants, and the consulting firm can promote its consulting services together with the software product. Partnerships are particularly beneficial for international business where regional businesses can expand their presence globally without the capital investment necessary to establish itself in a foreign country. Additionally, legal complexities, such as the European Data Protection laws, may make it challenging for a US business to reach that market; however, with a partner physically located in Europe, the parties can structure a relationship where each entity benefits from the other's regional expertise while complying with local laws.

Partnering with another business can be complex, and it is fundamental that each party is clear as to its goals. All parties to the agreement should take time to understand each other's business and thoughtfully craft the aims and objectives of the partnership or alliance. The contract should clearly define what each party is contributing and what each party agrees to assume. Joining two companies in an endeavor is not unlike blending two families; it is important to identify and address cultural differences between the companies, in negotiating the relationship. If these differences are not understood and managed, the partnership may sour due to poor integration and cooperation.

The agreements that reflect these partnering arrangements can be relatively brief, or their pages can number in the hundreds and include multiple exhibits. Parties to these agreements will generally be careful to spell out the nature of the relationship between the parties. For instance, these agreements generally specify that, except as provided in writing in the document: (1) the parties are not agents of each other and cannot bind each other, (2) the agreement does not create a partnership between the parties, and (3) the agreement does not create a contractor/subcontractor relationship between the parties.

Common Types of Corporate "Partnership" Agreements

Alliance Agreements are used frequently by two independent firms seeking to announce to the market their cooperative efforts. Alliance agreements may designate a preferred provider or supplier for a larger effort that requires the skills of more than one of the participants in the alliance agreement. An alliance agreement would also be the title used for an arrangement where companies refer work to each other under specified circumstances. For example, a company may chose to ally itself with one in another country and refer to each other specified work on a non-exclusive basis. In recent years, airlines have formed alliances that involve complex reciprocity arrangements for client services.

Special Considerations for Alliance Agreements. While these capture a relatively loose arrangement between the partnering entities, the written document should specify:

- Jurisdiction(s) in which the alliance will operate
- Subject matter of the alliance
- How the alliance partners would refer to each other
- Public announcements; descriptions on company materials and other media
- Terms of use of each entity's intellectual property

An alliance agreement that permits entities to use each others' intellectual property, such as name and mark, could well require a separate license agreement for that property, in order to protect it from becoming "owned" by the using party. In addition, tax, antitrust, and international considerations would generally be addressed, in connection with forming the alliance.

Channel Partner Agreements are agreements by which one partner promotes the goods or services of another (such as a software vendor or an equipment manufacturer), in exchange for a share of the revenue associated with the sales it generates. The promoter may provide added value, such as training, service, and customization of the product or service to be sold, in exchange for consideration, such as product and marketing training, access to new products, discounts, or technical support.

Special Considerations for Channel Partner Agreements. They are best utilized when the promoter has demonstrated familiarity with the product or software, reliability, and success in presenting the product, and special expertise configuring the software in interaction with end users. The agreement should address:

- The parties' respective responsibility for responding to customer inquiries and concerns
- Territorial exclusivity for promoter
- Restrictive covenants, if promoter is to be precluded from representing other originators

Channel partner agreements are most successful when the parties have complementary products, skills, or services. As with other business partnering arrangements, consideration of the use of intellectual property is critical.

Teaming Agreements often are alliances among independent entities pursuing a particular business opportunity. Teaming agreements are frequently used by contractors who assemble themselves as a group to respond to a request for proposal from a government entity. The teaming agreement would specify the portions of the government contract that would be performed by each independent firm that is a member of the team, and the agreement would specify the obligations of the members in pursuing the opportunity. A teaming agreement could exist for the period of time in which the members of the team are bidding on a particular project or attempting to develop a prototype. Major defense contracts, for example, are pursued by numerous companies, who usually assemble themselves into teams, with each member of the team able to provide a specified area of expertise or products to respond to the request for proposal issued by the purchaser.

Special Considerations for Teaming Agreements. Unlike alliance agreements, which are commonly non-exclusive, teaming agreements generally specify the members of the team and do not permit substitutions of team members. The teaming agreement should specify:

- The proposal to which the team will be responding
- The obligations of the teaming parties during the bidding process, as to confidentiality, relations with members of other winning teams, and scope of work to be provided
- The obligations of the parties after the bid is awarded, in the case of a win or a non-win

- The obligations of the parties to each other with respect to confidentiality and future course of dealing

If the team in fact wins the project, the team does not usually enter into a contract with the client. Usually, the team designates a contractor who then subcontracts with the other members of the team. The structure could have a general contractor, with one or more subcontractors, some of which may have one or more subcontractors, depending on the products or services sold and the timing and complexity of the engagement.

Joint-Venture Agreements refer to a specific long-term endeavor of two or more independent companies. This endeavor usually includes the investment of capital, the dedication of specific company employees on a full-time basis for a relatively long period of time, and, possibly, the creation of a stand-alone entity owned by the joint-venture partners to accomplish a specified objective. Joint ventures are frequently used in oil and gas exploration, where two or more companies invest significant capital and dedicate personnel or jointly employ personnel for a period of time in a particular location. Joint ventures are also commonly used by extractive industries in countries that require a local partner.

Unlike an alliance agreement, which generally does not require significant investment of capital or exclusivity of relation, a joint-venture agreement specifies the percentage ownership interest of the partners and the value of the capital and other resources contributed. In joint ventures, the treatment of earnings or losses from the investment are carefully considered and documented. In many cases, the joint venture may be organized as a limited liability company, in order to limit liability to the joint-venture partners from risky activities and to permit the transfer of revenues from the joint-venture entity to the joint-venture partners on a tax-free basis. For example, joint ventures, usually organized as limited liability companies, have been created by oil companies and chemical companies to pursue the creation of new products for indefinite periods of time where the expertise of both companies is needed but where neither company wishes to assume the business risk of merging all of their operations. In some cases, joint ventures can generate revenues on par with Fortune 500 companies.

Special Considerations for Joint-Venture Agreements. As these usually involve the commitment of significant resources by two or more companies, a separate legal entity is usually created to house the venture activity, and the following terms should be considered:

- The terms of capital and other assets contributed by each business
- The governance of the joint-venture entity
- The mechanism for resolving dispute in the governance group
- The tax effect of the activity and how to allocate any benefits
- Applicable international or country of operation issues

Natalia Delgado
General Counsel and Corporate Secretary
Huron Consulting Group Inc.

Holli A. Simone
Senior Counsel
Huron Consulting Group Inc.

Beatriz M. Olivera
Assistant General
Counsel Huron Consulting Group Inc.

Now that we have established a baseline understanding of the various basic forms of M&A transactions and of cooperative relationships, you may be wondering what informs the decision to engage in one or the other. To address this question, we return to our seasoned M&A experts, who provide us with their perspective on the pros and cons of cooperative relationships and compare these with M&A transactions.

A Practitioner Perspective: Strategic Alliances and M&A

Although there may be compelling business reasons to seek growth through a merger or an acquisition of assets or stock of another company (M&A), M&A opportunities often do not materialize or proceed to a successful conclusion. The companies may not be able to agree on price, a potential acquiring company may not have access to the cash needed to complete a deal, and acquisitions involving the exchange of equity securities can stumble over disparity in the market's perceptions of the relative values of the companies' stocks. In addition, acquisitions often are challenged by differences in corporate cultures and social issues associated with combining the companies' offices and executive ranks. A deal also can be delayed or blocked altogether by requirements for regulatory approvals and antitrust clearance. For a variety of reasons, therefore, mergers and acquisitions normally are difficult and often impossible. Moreover, deals that are successfully completed often fail to achieve their intended purposes due to poor execution, inaccurate synergy estimates, weak business integration plans, departure of key personnel, or lack of understanding of the acquired business.

Mergers and acquisitions are pursued for a variety of different reasons. These include:

- Obtaining technology or specialized staff, knowledge or skills;
- Accessing resources needed for new development;
- Improving an under-performing business;
- Reducing risk through diversification;
- Accessing new markets;
- Diversification of products and services;
- Reducing cost and achieving economies of scale;
- Responding to competitive threats; and
- Accelerating organic growth.

A strategic alliance can achieve many of the same benefits of a merger or acquisition and may make sense in a circumstance where an acquisition is not possible. A strategic alliance may also avoid some of the common risks of an acquisition. In fact, a company that may not be an attractive acquisition candidate may be an ideal partner in a strategic alliance.

There is no universally accepted definition of a strategic alliance. A strategic alliance is a formal or informal arrangement between two or more companies to join forces and pool specified resources to engage in a particular project or undertaking or business activity for a specified or indefinite period in order to achieve a common objective.

There are many examples of strategic alliances—both in historical and modern times. For instance, Thomas Edison teamed with Corning Glass Works in 1879 to develop the incandescent light bulb. A group of construction companies established a corporation through which they pooled their resources to construct Hoover Dam, and the Dow Corning Corporation was originally established through a joint venture between Dow Chemical Company and Corning Incorporated. More recently, airlines have agreed to route-sharing and other alliances to reach more consumers, address competitive threats, improve flight operations, and create other efficiencies, and MSNBC was founded by Microsoft Corporation and General Electric's NBC unit (which is now NBC Universal).

Benefits of a Strategic Alliance

A strategic alliance may present a number of possible benefits, some of which are similar to the benefits of M&A transactions. These include:

Better access to markets: A strategic alliance may facilitate access to a larger customer base and geographic market, lowering the challenges of entry into new markets and allowing each party to expand its customer base more rapidly than it could do by itself. A strategic alliance may also open new marketing channels into existing markets and help build recognition and acceptance within a particular market. A strategic alliance may be particularly helpful when entering a foreign market, or even regional domestic or ethnic markets because of the need to adapt to cultural differences. A strategic alliance may also facilitate a quick defensive response to potential competitive threats as industry boundaries become blurred with changing technology and shifting consumer preferences. A merger or acquisition can produce similar benefits, but it can often take longer to conclude an M&A transaction than a simpler strategic alliance.

Build credibility: A company may have an excellent product or strategy but lack the reputation it needs to be successful in a particular market. A strategic alliance partner with broader recognition and a stronger reputation could raise the credibility of its strategic alliance partners and open doors for a new business venture. Joint ventures also can be a way to reduce political friction in some markets and improve local acceptability of a company or its products. A merger or acquisition would normally not be as successful in achieving these goals because the acquired company in an M&A transaction often loses its separate identity as it is absorbed into the acquiring company.

Access to technology or other assets or resources: Most businesses need technology and other assets to grow, but those assets can be expensive, and obtaining them and putting them to beneficial use can be risky and time-consuming. A strategic alliance may provide access to needed technology and other assets more quickly and with less risk through an arrangement with a company that already has the desired resources. A strategic alliance also can provide a party the benefits of the other party's access to raw materials, sources of supply, and other resources that would not otherwise be readily available. A merger or acquisition can achieve these benefits, often more effectively than a strategic alliance, because the M&A transaction will result in acquisition of control of the resources of the acquired company.

Sharing and limiting risks: New business ventures can be expensive and risky. Through a strategic alliance, companies can share access to business infrastructure already in place and share the cost of creation of new infrastructure and the risk of loss. In addition, a strategic alliance structured as a new entity can limit a company's exposure to risks of the new business venture by limiting the financial commitment and the exposure of other business assets to the new venture. Companies in a strategic alliance normally retain their individual properties and identities, which limits each company's exposure to risks of the new business. In contrast, in a merger or acquisition transaction, the parties often commit the entire company to the combination, although M&A deals can be structured to preserve the separate corporate existence of the acquired and acquiring companies in a parent-subsidiary or holding company structure.

Improve an under-performing business: The vision and way of thinking of the management of two companies is always different. A strategic alliance can provide access to new ideas about improved production and marketing techniques and strategies. A strategic alliance also can provide a mechanism for a company to test production and management techniques in unfamiliar markets. Strategic alliances may allow companies to pool capital or existing facilities to gain economies of scale or increase the use of facilities, thereby reducing manufacturing costs. A merger or acquisition can accomplish many of the same goals and may do so more effectively through synergies from the combination of two companies and elimination of redundant functions and facilities.

Step toward acquisition or divestiture: Some strategic alliances eventually result in an acquisition transaction between the parties. In a strategic alliance, one of the parties sometimes makes a minority equity investment in the other party. This practice has been common in the automotive industry. This can be a precursor to an eventual acquisition transaction or divestiture of a business segment. In contrast, a merger or acquisition often requires a larger investment at greater risk.

Platform for international expansion: A strategic alliance may be the only way that a company can participate in some international markets. Many countries restrict equity participation by foreign firms in local operations to less than 50 percent. Developing countries often give joint ventures preferential treatment because they present the desired mix of foreign technological and capital involvement and assure local management and control. Expansion through a merger or acquisition in these countries is normally not possible. In addition, international growth presents unique risks of exposure of long-term investment to potentially volatile economic and political conditions, which can be limited through a strategic alliance.

Potential Disadvantages

Dilution of profit potential: Much as a strategic alliance often provides for the sharing of risks and costs, it will just as often involve the sharing of profits and opportunities. In considering whether to enter into a strategic alliance, a company must weigh the dilution of profits and other opportunity costs against the benefits expected to be derived. In a merger or acquisition transaction, the acquiring company typically acquires 100 percent of the profit potential of the acquired company, but the purchase price for the deal will be set with reference to that profit potential.

Management gridlock: Managing a strategic alliance is an inherently difficult process. Strategic alliances are rarely established in a way that gives one party sole authority to make all decisions, and shared decision-making can often result in management gridlock. Each company typically wants a voice in management, which often leads to slower, more complex decision-making. In addition, the companies may have different, often conflicting goals for the alliance. The management process and decision-making are often further complicated by differences in the corporate cultures of the parties and ambiguities in the parties' respective roles. Some of these conflicts can also arise in M&A transactions, but the acquiring company typically obtains the control necessary to resolve differences quickly.

Loss of control: A strategic alliance normally requires each company to give up some degree of control over the business conducted by the venture and, possibly, some control over assets and other resources needed for success of the venture. In contrast, in a merger or acquisition, the acquiring company typically gains absolute control over the acquired business and the former owners of the acquired company normally lose their control of the acquired business.

Management time and attention: Partnering with another business can be challenging, and it takes time and effort to build the right relationship. Each party must be committed to the success of the strategic alliance and provide sufficient leadership and support in the early stages to build a good working relationship. In many cases, parties to the venture will need to make key personnel available to the venture for an extended period of time. Unless there is senior management endorsement and enthusiasm at the operating level, an alliance will struggle, particularly when tough issues arise. In these respects, a strategic alliance can require as much time and attention as necessary to make a merger or acquisition successful, although a merger or acquisition typically involves the acquisition of key personnel needed to continue to operate the acquired business.

Uncertain business objectives: Success in a strategic alliance depends on a careful definition of the objectives and agreement of the parties to pursue those objectives. If the parties have differing expectations and objectives for a strategic alliance or if the agreed objectives are not communicated clearly to everyone involved, the venture will be far less likely to succeed. In contrast, a merger or acquisition typically gives the acquiring company control over the business objectives but presents similar challenges in getting personnel of the acquired business to understand and align their actions with the objectives.

Shifting business objectives: Parties to a strategic alliance may develop incompatible objectives as they gain experience with the venture. For example, one party may develop a different attitude toward risk and may be prepared to accept short-term losses in order to build market share, to take on higher levels of debt, or to spend more on advertising or research and development. Similarly, the objectives of a participant may change if it sees an opportunity to gain direct access to the market served by the venture. By comparison, a merger or acquisition typically places one company in control of the acquired business, which reduces the potential for differences over the operation and strategy for the combined businesses.

Conflicting business cultures: Conflicting cultures and operational styles can result in poor integration and cooperation, which can detract from the effectiveness of a strategic alliance. A merger or acquisition involves similar challenges in combining the business cultures of two companies.

Choosing the wrong partner: If each company brings a unique and complementary strength to the strategic alliance, the parties are more likely to develop mutual trust and dependence that will contribute to the long-term success of the venture. Much as a strategic alliance can bolster the credibility of a party, the selection of the wrong strategic alliance partner can destroy trust, damage another party's reputation, and undermine credibility.

Unequal contributions: In strategic alliances, one party may get the stigma of the "weaker partner" because of a smaller investment or holding fewer voting rights or from lacking know-how, market access, or other resources to contribute to the success of the venture. An imbalance in levels of expertise, investment, or assets brought into the strategic alliance can create friction between the parties and may ultimately lead a party to withdraw from the alliance or reduce the resources it devotes to the alliance.

Financial and accounting concerns: A party to a strategic alliance will often find it difficult to integrate the alliance into a global strategy that involves substantial cross-border trading. In these circumstances, there can be difficulties with transfer pricing in transactions with affiliated companies. A party's desire for a centralized system of global cash management may lead to conflicts over controls on use of cash, management of foreign exchange, or the remittance of profits of the venture. A merger or acquisition does not create these same concerns when the acquired business is wholly owned by the acquiring company.

Conclusion

A strategic alliance can provide avenues for business development in circumstances where growth through M&A is not practical. Even if an acquisition is a

> viable option, a strategic alliance may provide some valuable advantages despite the disadvantages.
>
> William A. Von Hoene, Jr.
> Executive Vice President, Finance and Legal
> Exelon Corporation
>
> Bruce G. Wilson
> Sr. Vice Pres. and Deputy General Counsel
> Exelon Corporation

C. ASSET PURCHASE AGREEMENT

As discussed above, there are several ways to structure an M&A transaction, including three basic forms: (1) a merger; (2) an acquisition of stock; and (3) an acquisition of assets. An acquiror (or one of its subsidiaries) may merge with the target company in accordance with the statutory law of the companies' state(s) of incorporation. An acquiror may purchase all or a controlling amount of the stock of the target company directly from the company's current shareholders—thereby becoming the parent and owner of the target company. Or, as in the agreement below, an acquiror may purchase a single division of the seller—or the entire company—by purchasing the relevant assets of the seller.

Routinely, companies will issue press releases to announce to the public significant transactions the company has undertaken. In the M&A context, these may occur even at the non-binding-letter-of-intent stage.[37] In announcing the transaction memorialized by this chapter's sample agreement below, Piper Jaffray released the following statement.[38] Please review it both as a student of the deal, to get a preliminary sense of the basic terms and objectives of the agreement that follows, and, as a student of the deal process, of which communicating with the public may be a part.

---

37. *See, e.g.*, Datalink Corp., Datalink Enters into Non-Binding Letter of Intent to Purchase Incentra, LLC's Reseller Business (form 8-K), at Exhibit 99.1 (Oct. 21, 2009), *available at* http://www.sec.gov/Archives/edgar/data/1056923/000110465909059962/a09-32090_1ex99d1.htm.

38. The press release below is exerpted from Piper Jaffray Companies, Press Release (Form 8-K), at Exhibit 99.1 (Apr. 11, 2006), *available at* http://www.sec.gov/Archives/edgar/data/1230245/000095013406007046/c04209exv99w1.htm.

FOR IMMEDIATE RELEASE

Piper Jaffray Companies Announces Sale of Private Client Services Branch Network to UBS

MINNEAPOLIS—April 11, 2006—Piper Jaffray Companies (NYSE: PJC) today announced the signing of a definitive agreement to sell its Private Client Services branch network to UBS AG. The sale will include 100 percent of the Piper Jaffray Private Client Services branch network, which consists of more than 800 financial advisors and 550 branch support personnel in approximately 90 retail offices in 17 Midwest, Mountain and Western states.

The consideration includes $500 million in cash for the branch network plus the potential for additional cash consideration of up to $75 million after the sale closes, dependent on business performance. In addition, Piper Jaffray will be paid for the net assets of its branch network at the time of the close, which are expected to be valued at approximately $300 million.

The Private Client Services business offers financial planning and wealth management services for individuals. Piper Jaffray Companies will continue to operate its Capital Markets businesses, which include Corporate and Institutional Services and Public Finance Services.

"This sale will be the culmination of a thoughtful and comprehensive process, during which we concluded that this strategic direction will ensure that each of the business segments will have the necessary resources to achieve sustainable, competitive performance," said Andrew Duff, chairman and CEO of Piper Jaffray Companies. "This transaction will create the best overall result for our clients, employees and shareholders."

The sale will position the firm's heritage business in Private Client Services for future success. "We believe UBS will provide Private Client Services clients with some of the best wealth management services in the world, and will provide our transferred employees with a culture and strategy similar to the one we have at Piper Jaffray," said Duff.

The transaction will enable Piper Jaffray to focus all of its human and financial capital on one goal—becoming the leading middle-market investment bank. "This is an outstanding opportunity to build on the successful foundation we've established in the capital markets," said Duff.

Piper Jaffray will redeploy capital from the transaction to enhance existing businesses, expand into new businesses that support current strategies, pay down debt, and repurchase common stock.

"We will dedicate the appropriate resources to manage this transition smoothly for our clients as well as for the employees affected by this divestiture," said Duff. As part of this transaction, Piper Jaffray anticipates a reduction in staff of approximately 350 employees primarily in the Twin

Cities, and will provide enhanced severance packages and out-placement services for those affected.

The sale of the Piper Jaffray Private Client Services branch network will result in after-tax proceeds of approximately $510 million and an after-tax book gain of approximately $170 million, net of approximately $55-60 million in restructuring charges. Subject to customary regulatory approvals, the sale is expected to close early in the third quarter of 2006.

Investor Conference Call

Andrew S. Duff, chairman and chief executive officer, and Sandra G. Sponem, chief financial officer, will host a conference call to discuss the transaction on Tuesday, Apr. 11, 2006, at 11 A.M. ET (10 A.M. CT). The call can be accessed by dialing [omitted], or [omitted] international, and referring to conference ID 7868273 and the leader's name, [omitted].

Slides that accompany the call can be accessed at www.pjcinvestorinformation\analystsdeck.com. Callers should dial in at least 15 minutes early to receive instructions. A replay of the conference call will be available beginning at approximately 1 P.M. ET Apr. 11 by calling [omitted] or [omitted] international.

About Piper Jaffray Companies

Piper Jaffray Companies (NYSE: PJC) is a focused securities firm dedicated to delivering superior financial advice, investment products and transaction execution within selected sectors of the financial services marketplace. The company's Capital Markets business generates revenue through two groups, Corporate and Institutional Services and Public Finance Services. Through its chief operating subsidiary, Piper Jaffray & Co., the firm has served corporations, government and non-profit entities, institutional investors, and the financial advisory needs of private individuals since 1895. Piper Jaffray is headquartered in Minneapolis. For more information about Piper Jaffray, visit us online at www.piperjaffray.com.

Cautionary Note Regarding Forward-Looking Statements

Statements contained in this press release that are not historical or current facts, including statements about beliefs and expectations, are forward-looking statements. Forward-looking statements involve inherent risks and uncertainties, and important factors could cause actual results to differ materially from those anticipated, including the following: (1) the transaction announced in this press release may not be completed, or completed within the expected timeframe; (2) unforeseen difficulties associated with the transaction, including business disruption and loss of personnel, could delay completion of the transaction and/or cause it to be more expensive than anticipated and adversely affect our results of operations and financial condition; (3) the expected benefits of the transaction, including the growth of our Capital Markets business, increased profitability and shareholder returns, may take longer than anticipated to achieve and may not be achieved in their entirety or at all; (4) strategies with respect to the redeployment of transaction proceeds may take longer than anticipated to be realized or may not be achieved in their entirety or at all; (5) following consummation of the transaction we may be subject to increased competitive pressures and experience increased volatility in our financial results; and (6) other factors identified under "Risk Factors" in Part I, Item 1A of our Annual Report on Form 10-K for the year ended December 31, 2005, and updated in our subsequent reports filed with the SEC. These reports are available at our Web site at www.piperjaffray.com and at the SEC Web site at www.sec.gov. Forward-looking statements speak only as of the date they are made, and we undertake no obligation to update them in light of new information or future events.

Things to Consider . . .

As you read through the following agreement, please consider the following items. You will want to return to the agreement, as you study the substantive discussion that follows.

> **Provisional Interaction.** Pay attention to the interplay of many of the provisions in this asset purchase Agreement. Of note, certain definitions (e.g., Business, Assets, Excluded Assets, Assumed Liabilities, Excluded Liabilities) are very important as they weave throughout the operative provisions of the Agreement. Pay close attention to the relationships among representations, warranties, covenants, conditions to closing, indemnification, and termination.

> **Concerns and Remedies.** As you read through the agreement, ask yourself what each party is trying to achieve and obtain under this Agreement, and how each party has planned for the potential failure of these objectives. What provisions address these potential concerns, and how? What types of redress does the Agreement provide?

> **Obligations.** Consider what obligations this Agreement imposes upon the parties. What is the obligation of each party to consummate the asset purchase? If the closing occurs, what continuing affirmative and negative obligations do the parties have? What happens if the closing does not occur?

ASSET PURCHASE AGREEMENT[39]

among

PIPER JAFFRAY COMPANIES,

PIPER JAFFRAY & CO.,

and

UBS FINANCIAL SERVICES INC.

Dated as of April 10, 2006

Relating to the Purchase and Sale of the
Private Client Services Business

TABLE OF CONTENTS
[PAGE NUMBERS OMITTED]

---

39. Piper Jaffray Companies, Asset Purchase Agreement (Form 8-K), at Exhibit 2.1 (Apr. 11, 2006), *available at* http://www.sec.gov/Archives/edgar/data/1230245/000095013406007046/c04209exv2w1.htm.

19. Interpretation
20. Counterparts
21. Entire Agreement
22. Bulk Transfer Laws
23. Severability
24. Governing Law
25. Specific Performance
26. Disclosure Schedule
27. Knowledge
28. Parent
Exhibit A—Key Terms of Transition Services Agreements
Exhibit B—Sellers' Officers
Schedule 12.3—Form of FIRPTA Certificate

INDEX OF DEFINED TERMS

TERM	REFERENCE
Employees	Section 5.17(a)
Environmental Claim	Section 5.16(a)(i)
Environmental Laws	Section 5.16(a)(ii)
Environmental Permits	Section 5.16(a)(iii)
ERISA	Section 5.13(a)
Estimated Acquisition Consideration	Section 3.1(c)
Estimated Net Asset Adjustment	Section 3.1(b)
Estimated Unretained Revenue Adjustment	Section 3.1(b)
Exchange Act	Section 1.1(p)
Excluded Assets	Section 1.2
Excluded Liabilities	Section 2.2
Final Margin Loan Amount	Section 3.2(a)(i)
Final Net Asset Adjustment	Section 3.2(f)
Final Net Asset Amount	Section 3.2(a)(ii)
Final Unretained Revenue Adjustment	Section 3.2(h)
Financial Statements	Section 5.3(a)
FTC	Section 9.4(b)
GAAP	Section 3.2(a)
Governmental Entity	Section 2.2(i)
Hazardous Substance	Section 5.16(a)(iv)
HIPAA	Section 8.3
HSR Act	Section 5.2(b)
Indemnitee	Section 11.4
Indemnitor	Section 11.4
IRS	Section 3.5(c)
Key Employees	Section 5.17(b)
Knowledge	Section 27
Leased Real Estate	Section 1.1(a)
Lien	Section 5.5(a)
Material Adverse Effect	Section 4.2(c)

TERM	REFERENCE
Material Contracts	Section 5.10(b)
Maximum Adjustment Amount	Section 3.2(h)(i)
NASD	Section 2.2(i)
Net Asset Statement	Section 3.2(a)
Notice Period	Section 11.4(b)
NYSE	Section 2.2(i)
Ordinary Course of Business	Section 5.14
Parent	Preamble
Permits	Section 1.1(h)
Permitted Liens	Section 5.6
Personal Property Leases	Section 1.1(d)
Policies	Section 5.12
Preliminary Net Asset Statement	Section 5.3(a)
Pro Rata Portion	Section 3.5(b)
Real Estate Leases	Section 1.1(b)
Regulatory Agreement	Section 5.15(e)
Retained Revenue Percentage	Section 3.2(a)(iii)
SEC	Section 2.2(i)
Seller Indemnified Person	Section 11.2(a)
Sellers	Preamble
Sellers' Flex Plans	Section 10.7
Sellers' Plans	Section 5.13(a)
Sellers' Retirement Plans	Section 10.8
Sellers' Severance Practice	Section 10.3
Tangible Personal Property	Section 1.1(c)
Tax Records	Section 3.5(c)
Tax Return	Section 3.5(d)
Taxes	Section 3.5(r)
Taxing Authority	Section 3.5(f)
Third-Party Claim	Section 11.4(a)

TERM	REFERENCE
Third-Party Claim Notice	Section 11.4(a)
Transfer Taxes	Section 3.4(b)
Transferred Employees	Section 10.1(a)
Treasury Regulations	Section 3.5(g)
WARN Act	Section 5.17(f)

ASSET PURCHASE AGREEMENT, dated as of April 9, 2006 (this "**Agreement**"), is made among Piper Jaffray Companies ("**Parent**"), Piper Jaffray & Co. (the "**Company**"), and UBS Financial Services Inc. ("**Buyer**"). Parent and the Company are collectively referred to herein as "**Sellers**."

RECITALS

A. Parent. Parent is a Delaware corporation having its principal place of business in Minneapolis, Minnesota.

B. The Company. The Company is a Delaware corporation having its principal place of business in Minneapolis, Minnesota. The Company is a wholly owned subsidiary of Parent.

C. The Business. The Company, through its Private Client Services division, is engaged in the business of providing securities brokerage, advisory, and other related services to investors through its network of retail sales offices (the "**Business**").

D. Acquisition of Assets. Sellers desire to sell, and Buyer desires to purchase, certain assets of Parent and the Company used primarily in the Business on the terms and subject to the conditions of this Agreement in consideration of the payment by Buyer of the Acquisition Consideration (as defined below) and the assumption by Buyer of certain liabilities and obligations of the Business described in this Agreement.

NOW, THEREFORE, in consideration of the [promises], and of the mutual covenants, representations, warranties and agreements contained herein, the parties agree as follows:

1. Purchase and Sale of Assets.

1.1 Generally. On the terms and subject to the conditions of this Agreement and subject to Section 1.2, Sellers agree to sell, transfer, convey, and deliver to Buyer, and Buyer agrees to purchase, all of the Company's right, title, and interest as of the Closing Date (as defined in Section 3.3) in all property and assets, whether tangible or intangible, used primarily in the Business (the "**Assets**"), including:

(a) the leasehold and subleasehold interests of the Company in all real property used primarily in the Business, together with all interests of the Company in the buildings, structures, installations, fixtures, and other improvements situated thereon and all easements, rights of way, and other rights, interests, and appurtenances of the Company therein or thereunto pertaining (collectively, "**Leased Real Estate**");

(b) all lease and sublease agreements to which the Company is a party relating to the Leased Real Estate (collectively, "**Real Estate Leases**");

(c) all furniture, fixtures, equipment (including computer hardware and data processing equipment), machinery, and other tangible personal property either (i) primarily related to the Business or (ii) used in the Business and located on the Leased Real Estate (collectively, "**Tangible Personal Property**");

(d) all leases of Tangible Personal Property as to which the Company is the lessee (the "**Personal Property Leases**");

(e) all warranties or guarantees by any manufacturer, supplier, or other transferor to the extent primarily related to any of the Assets;

(f) all unpaid accounts, notes, and other receivables in favor of the Sellers or any of their respective subsidiaries with respect to the Business (including notes receivable from Transferred Employees, as defined in Section 10.1), together with all collateral security therefor;

(g) subject to Sections 1.3(a) and 9.7, all contracts, commitments, and other agreements to which the Sellers or any of their respective subsidiaries is a party that are primarily related to the Business, including contracts relating to customer accounts and all rights, receivables or releases in favor of the Sellers or any of their respective subsidiaries under any compensation, loan, severance, settlement or other agreement between the Sellers or any of their respective subsidiaries and any Transferred Employee ("**Contracts**");

(h) subject to Section 1.3(a), the franchises, approvals, permits, licenses, orders, registrations, certificates, variances, and similar rights obtained from governments and governmental agencies primarily related to the Business, to the extent assignable (the "**Permits**");

(i) subject to Section 9.7, all information regarding customers of the Business and their accounts in the possession of the Company, to the extent permitted by law; *provided, however*, that Sellers shall have the right to keep a copy of such customer information to the extent required by applicable law;

(j) all other books and records primarily related to the Business (collectively, "**Books and Records**"); *provided however*, that Sellers shall have the right to keep a copy of such Books and Records to the extent required by applicable law;

(k) all rights of the Company under any refunds, other than refunds with respect to Taxes (as defined in Section 3.5(e)), deposits, rights of set off, and rights of recoupment, in each case that are primarily related to the Business;

(l) all prepaid expenses (including prepaid rent under the Real Estate Leases) and goodwill to the extent related to the Business (other than prepaid Taxes described in Section 1.2(n));

(m) subject to Section 9.7, all margin and other customer debit balances of the Sellers or any of their respective subsidiaries to the extent related to the Business;

(n) to the extent transferable, all telephone numbers used primarily in the Business;

(o) the net aggregate amount of the balances (positive and negative) credited to all Transferred Employees under Sellers' Flex Plans (as defined in Section 10.7) as of the Closing Date; and

(p) subject to Section 9.7, all customer relationships, customer accounts and customer property related to the Business, including all assets and rights (including any funds, securities, commodity positions or other instruments) held for customers by or on behalf of the Company (including for distribution or payment or as collateral) under the possession-and-control provisions of Section 15(c)(3) of the Securities Exchange Act of 1934 (the "**Exchange Act**") and Rule 15c3-3 thereunder or otherwise.

1.2 Excluded Assets. Sellers are not selling, transferring or assigning, and Buyer is not purchasing, any property or assets other than as described in Section 1.1 (the "**Excluded Assets**"). Without limiting the generality of the foregoing, the following property and assets of Sellers constitute Excluded Assets, notwithstanding anything to the contrary provided in Section 1.1:

(a) cash, cash equivalents, securities (whether or not marketable), and investments (except to the extent provided in Sections 1.1(k), 1.1(l), 1.1(m) and 1.1(p));

(b) all rights of either Seller to any refunds for Taxes levied and imposed upon, or in connection with, the Assets or the conduct or operation of the Business on or before the Closing Date (provided, that no rights of either Seller for any such refund shall be included in the Preliminary Net Asset Statement (as defined in Section 5.3(a));

(c) either Seller's rights under the contracts, commitments, and other agreements that primarily relate to any business of either Seller other than the Business;

(d) either Seller's rights under any policies of insurance or any benefits, proceeds, or premium refunds payable or paid thereunder or with respect thereto;

(e) the corporate charter, qualifications to conduct business as a foreign corporation, arrangements with registered agents relating to foreign qualifications, taxpayer and other identification numbers, Tax Returns (as defined in Section 3.5(d)) and other Tax Records (as defined in Section 3.5(c)), seals, minute books, stock transfer books, and similar organizational documents of either Seller;

(f) the rights of either Seller under this Agreement or any other agreement between either Seller and Buyer executed in connection with the transactions contemplated hereby;

(g) all Sellers' e-mail addresses, URLs, websites and website content;

(h) all copyrights, trademarks, trade names, domain names, service marks, logos, and goodwill appurtenant thereto, corporate names, or comparable intellectual properties, or any registration or application for any of the foregoing, owned or licensed by either Seller (or any of its affiliates);

(i) except as provided to the contrary in Section 10, all assets held with respect to Sellers' Plans (as defined in Section 5.13(a));

(j) other than Books and Records, all assets related to any accounting, information technology or services, legal, compliance, human resources, training and development, payroll, treasury, insurance, Tax, marketing, or other general and administrative services supplied by either Seller or any of its affiliates;

(k) all intercompany accounts between either Seller and any of its affiliates, which accounts are subject to Section 9.5;

(l) rights of either Seller to indemnification from clients and other third parties with respect to any of the Excluded Liabilities (as defined in Section 2.2) for actions occurring prior to the Closing;

(m) rights of either Seller in Piper Jaffray & Co. v. Trophy Properties, L.L.C., Case No. CI 05 3647 (Dist. Ct. of Lancaster County, NE), to the extent such rights relate to the recovery of amounts actually paid in respect of tenant improvements prior to Closing (as defined in Section 3.3);

(n) all prepaid Taxes to the extent such Taxes relate to any taxable period, or portion thereof, ending on or before the Closing Date;

(o) all contracts, commitments, other agreements, information, margin and other debit balances of Sellers or any of their respective subsidiaries to the extent related to a customer relationship that Buyer elects not to assume pursuant to Section 9.7;

(p) subject to Section 1.3(b), the Contracts set forth in Section 5.10(a)(v) of the Disclosure Schedule; and

(q) the assets set forth in Section 1.2(q) of the Disclosure Schedule.

1.3 Procedures for Assets not Transferable; Unassumed Contracts.

(a) If any Asset is not assignable or transferable to Buyer without the consent of any Governmental Entity (as defined in Section 2.2(i)) or third person (other than Sellers), and such consent has not been obtained on or prior to the Closing Date, this Agreement shall not constitute an assignment or transfer thereof unless and until such consent is obtained. In such case, Sellers shall (a) use reasonable best efforts and cooperate with Buyer to obtain such consent as soon as practicable after the Closing Date; (b) use reasonable best efforts to provide Buyer the benefit of the Assets and (c) cooperate in any reasonable and lawful arrangement designed to provide such benefits to Buyer. Nothing in this Section 1.3

shall affect the ability of a party hereto to assert the failure of a Closing condition set forth in Section 4 below.

(b) In the event that, following the date hereof, Buyer determines that it would like to assume any of the Contracts set forth on Section 5.10(a)(v), Buyer and Sellers shall cooperate to enter into a reasonable arrangement with respect to the transfer of such Contract to Buyer, to the extent (i) such Contract is transferable and (ii) such Contract is solely related to the Assets or the Business. Following such transfer, such Contract shall constitute a transferred Asset.

2. Assumption of Liabilities.

2.1 Generally. On the terms and subject to the conditions of this Agreement, at the Closing, Buyer shall assume, and hereby agrees to pay, perform and discharge, and observe fully and timely, all liabilities and obligations, known or unknown, asserted or unasserted, absolute or contingent, of Sellers to the extent solely relating to or arising out of the Business or the Assets, whether arising before, on, or after the Closing Date (collectively, the "**Assumed Liabilities**"), other than liabilities or obligations constituting Excluded Liabilities. To the extent that either Seller pays an Assumed Liability following the Closing Date, Buyer shall reimburse that Seller for any amount so paid reasonably promptly following a request from Sellers, accompanied by reasonable documentation, for payment. Without limiting the generality of the foregoing, the following liabilities constitute, to the extent related to the Business, Assumed Liabilities:

(a) to the extent arising from or related to any period following the Closing, all liabilities and obligations of Sellers under or in respect of the Leased Real Estate, Real Estate Leases, Personal Property Leases, and Contracts;

(b) to the extent arising from or related to any period following the Closing, all unpaid accounts payable of Sellers to the extent solely related to the Business and all accrued expenses of Sellers to the extent solely related to the Business;

(c) all liabilities and obligations with respect to Sellers' Plans expressly assumed by Buyer pursuant to Section 10;

(d) all liabilities and obligations under any client service transition agreements listed on Section 2.1(d) of the Disclosure Schedule to which a Transferred Employee is a party;

(e) all liabilities and obligations arising from any litigation, arbitration, customer complaint, workers' compensation, or other claim brought by any person or entity, or proceeding pending or threatened against the Business or the Assets, including those identified in Section 5.11 of the Disclosure Schedule (as defined in

Section 5) as well as any claims or proceedings, known or unknown, asserted or unasserted, relating to the sale of products or services provided by the Business, or otherwise related to the operation of the Business, whether arising before, on, or after the Closing Date (including the responsibility to manage such matters), except to the extent provided to the contrary under Section 2.2;

(f) all liabilities and obligations relating to the ownership or condition of the tangible Assets on or after the Closing Date;

(g) any obligation or liability of Sellers to pay or perform any obligation or liability (i) pursuant to any guaranty or obligation or lien, security interest, or other encumbrance on, or in respect of, any collateral of any Seller (other than the Assets) to ensure performance given or made by any such Seller to the extent solely in connection with the Business, or (ii) that otherwise arises on or after the Closing Date as a matter of law or contract to the extent solely in connection with the Business;

(h) all Taxes attributable to the Assets (other than Taxes for which Sellers are liable), as set forth in Section 3.4;

(i) all customer cash and margin credits; and

(j) all deferred revenue related to annual customer account fees.

2.2 Excluded Liabilities. Notwithstanding anything to the contrary provided herein, Buyer does not assume and will not become responsible for any liability of Sellers except the Assumed Liabilities (the "**Excluded Liabilities**"). To the extent that Buyer pays an Excluded Liability following the Closing Date, Parent shall cause the Company to reimburse Buyer for any amount so paid reasonably promptly following a request from Sellers, accompanied by reasonable documentation, for payment. Without limiting the generality of the foregoing, and not withstanding anything to the contrary herein, the following liabilities constitute Excluded Liabilities and shall be the responsibility of the Sellers:

(a) any liability or obligation of Sellers or their respective subsidiaries for money borrowed;

(b) any liability or obligation of Sellers or their respective subsidiaries for Taxes as set forth in Section 3.4;

(c) any liability or obligation of Sellers or their respective subsidiaries for costs and expenses (other than Buyer's liability for Transfer Taxes, as defined in Section 3.4(b)) in connection with the negotiation and execution of this Agreement or the consummation of the transactions contemplated hereby;

(d) any liability or obligation of Sellers or their respective subsidiaries under this Agreement or under any other agreement between one or both Sellers and Buyer executed in connection with the transactions contemplated hereby;

(e) any liability or obligation relating to Sellers' Plans except as expressly provided to the contrary in Section 10;

(f) all payment obligations relating to compensation, cash commissions, transition payments, cash awards, incentive payments and bonuses that are payable with respect to services performed by Employees (as defined in Section 5.17(a)) on or before the Closing Date except as expressly provided to the contrary in Section 10;

(g) all liabilities and obligations under any client service transition agreements except as expressly provided in Section 2.1(d) hereof;

(h) all intercompany accounts between either Seller and any of its affiliates, which accounts are subject to Section 9.5;

(i) any liability or obligation of Sellers or their respective subsidiaries in connection with any regulatory proceeding, investigation, charge, or sanction relating to or arising from the conduct of the Business prior to the Closing Date by or before any government, state, territory or other political subdivision, any entity exercising executive, legislative, judicial, regulatory or administrative functions of or pertaining to government, including the United States Securities and Exchange Commission (the "SEC") or any other government authority, agency, department, board, commission or instrumentality of the United States, any state or territory of the United States or any political subdivision thereof, and any governmental or non-governmental self-regulatory organization, agency or authority (including the New York Stock Exchange (the "NYSE"), National Association of Securities Dealers (the "NASD") and the Commodity Futures Trading Commission) (each, a "Governmental Entity");

(j) the litigation and related matters described on Section 2.2(j) of the Disclosure Schedule;

(k) any liability or obligation of Sellers relating to compensation (including without limitation deferred compensation) forfeited or claimed to have been forfeited by any Employee in connection with the transactions contemplated hereby;

(l) to the extent arising from or related to any period prior to the Closing, any liability of the Business that has been or would be accounted for by the Business or the Sellers in connection with the Business as "checks and drafts payable," "payables to broker-dealers," "stock loans," "trading securities sold short," "employee compensation," "contingent reserves," or "accounts payable and accrued expenses;"

(m) to the extent arising from or related to any period prior to the Closing, all liabilities and obligations of Sellers under or in respect of the Leased Real Estate, Real Estate Leases, Personal Property Leases, and Contracts;

(n) to the extent arising from or related to any period prior to the Closing, all unpaid accounts payable of Sellers and all accrued expenses of Sellers; and

(o) liabilities and obligations to the extent related to any Excluded Asset (including, without limitation, customer relationships that Buyer elects not to assume pursuant to Section 9.7 and any litigation, arbitration, customer complaint or other claim or proceeding to the extent related to such customer relationship) or to any business of either Seller other than the Business.

2.3 Relationship to Indemnification. Nothing in this Section 2 shall limit the indemnification obligations of Sellers under Section 11.1(a)(i) or Buyer under Section 11.2(a)(i).

3. Acquisition Consideration; Closing; Taxes.

3.1 Acquisition Consideration.

(a) As consideration for the Assets, Buyer shall assume the Assumed Liabilities and shall pay to Sellers, in the manner described herein, an amount (such amount, the "**Acquisition Consideration**") equal to:

(i) $575,000,000 (the "**Base Acquisition Consideration**");

(ii) plus the Final Margin Loan Amount (as defined in Section 3.2(a)(i));

(iii) plus or minus, as applicable, the Final Net Asset Adjustment (as defined in Section 3.2(f));

(iv) minus the Final Unretained Revenue Adjustment (as defined in Section 3.2(h)).

(b) Not later than five business days prior to the scheduled Closing Date, the Company shall deliver to Buyer the Sellers' good faith estimates (together with reasonably detailed back-up data to support such estimates), which estimates shall be reasonably acceptable to Buyer, of (i) the Final Net Asset Adjustment (such estimate, the "**Estimated Net Asset Adjustment**") and (ii) the Final Unretained Revenue Adjustment (such estimate, the "**Estimated Unretained Revenue Adjustment**"). The Estimated Net Asset Adjustment and Estimated Unretained Revenue Adjustment shall each be prepared in accordance with the methodologies to be used in the determination of the Final Net Asset Adjustment and the Final Unretained Revenue Adjustment, in each case as described herein.

(c) At Closing, Buyer shall deliver to Sellers' an amount (such amount, the "**Estimated Acquisition Consideration**") equal to (i) the Base Acquisition Consideration, (ii) plus or minus, as applicable, the Estimated Net Asset Adjustment, (iii) minus the

Estimated Unretained Revenue Adjustment. Such payment shall be made at the Closing by wire transfer of immediately available U.S. funds to an account to be specified in a written notice delivered by Sellers to Buyer at least five business days prior to the Closing.

3.2 Closing Statement; Final Margin Loan Amount; Final Net Asset Adjustment; Final Unretained Revenue Adjustment.

(a) Within sixty days following the date upon which the operational and accounting systems of the Business are converted to Buyer's operational platform (such date, the "**Conversion Date**"), Buyer will prepare and deliver to Sellers an unaudited statement of the net assets of the Business acquired by Buyer as of the Closing Date (the "**Net Asset Statement**"), prepared by Buyer in accordance with U.S. generally accepted accounting principles ("**GAAP**") applied on a basis consistent with the Preliminary Net Asset Statement (as defined in Section 5.3(a)). Concurrent with the delivery of the Net Asset Statement, Buyer will deliver a statement (the "**Closing Statement**") to Sellers, setting forth:

(i) the net value of all margin loans (calculated as (A) the sum of customer cash debits and customer margin debits, minus (B) the sum of customer cash credits and customer margin credits) as of the Conversion Date (the "**Final Margin Loan Amount**");

(ii) the amount, which may be positive or negative, as of the Closing Date of (A) the assets set forth on the Net Asset Statement and actually acquired by Buyer less (B) the liabilities set forth on the Net Asset Statement and actually assumed by Buyer, in each case excluding any amounts included in the Final Margin Loan Amount (the "**Final Net Asset Amount**"); and

(iii) (A) the names of those financial advisors that either were employed in the Business as of thirty days following the Conversion Date (to be determined based on financial advisors converted to Buyer's operating platform) or were employed in the Business immediately following the Conversion Date but terminated by Buyer during such thirty-day period, (B) the "product revenue" (as such term is used in the Business) of the Business generated by each such financial advisor (expressed as a both a dollar amount and as a percentage of the total product revenue generated by all advisors employed by the Business at March 31, 2006), in each case for the twelve-month period ended March 31, 2006, and (C) the aggregate percentage of total product revenues of the Business generated by all such financial advisors for the twelve-month period ended March 31, 2006 (such aggregate percentage, the "**Retained Revenue Percentage**").

(b) The Company shall have a period of thirty days from the date of delivery by Buyer to review the Closing Statement. If the Company agrees with the Closing Statement or does not give written notice of any disagreement within such thirty-day period, then upon the Company advising Buyer that the Closing Statement is acceptable or the expiration of such thirty-day period, whichever is earlier, such Closing Statement shall be considered accepted and binding upon Sellers and Buyer.

(c) If the Company does not agree with any portion of the Closing Statement, then, within thirty days of the date the Closing Statement is given to the Company, it shall give notice thereof to Buyer and list the areas of disagreement. All amounts not disputed in the notice delivered from the Company to Buyer shall be considered accepted and binding on the Sellers and Buyer. The parties shall work in good faith to try to resolve these differences. If, within ten business days after the delivery of the Company's notice (if any) to Buyer, the Company and Buyer are unable to resolve any differences arising as a result of the Closing Statement, the parties shall submit, within twenty days following the expiration of such ten business day period, a statement of all unresolved differences together with copies of the Net Asset Statement and the Closing Statement to the national office of an independent, nationally recognized accounting firm to be mutually agreed upon by the parties (the "**Accountants**") for a binding and nonappealable determination, which the parties shall request be rendered within thirty days after such submission. All fees and expenses of the Accountants incurred in this capacity shall be billed to and shared by the Company and Buyer equally. In the event the Accountants are then unwilling or unable to serve as contemplated hereby, Buyer and the Company shall use their reasonable best efforts to select another mutually agreeable independent nationally-recognized certified public accounting firm to render a final determination.

(d) Each party hereto may file with the Accountants such briefs, affidavits and supporting documents as they deem appropriate; provided, that such materials shall be submitted not later than the expiration of the twenty-day period referred to in Section 3.2(c) above. The Accountants shall only be authorized on any one issue to decide in favor of and choose the position of either of the parties. The Accountants shall base their decision solely upon the express terms of this Agreement (including, without limitation, the requirement that the Net Asset Statement be prepared in accordance with GAAP) and the submissions of the parties and not upon an independent investigation. The parties shall request that the Accountants' decision be in writing, set forth the calculations made in reaching its decision and describe the manner in which such calculations were made.

(e) Upon final determination of the Final Margin Loan Amount, Buyer shall pay to the Company the Final Margin Loan Amount.

(f) The "**Final Net Asset Adjustment**" shall be an amount (which amount may be a positive or negative number) equal to the Final Net Asset Amount (as such amount may be finally determined in accordance with this Section 3.2) minus $23,520,000.

(g) Upon final determination of the Final Net Asset Adjustment, (i) if the Final Net Asset Adjustment Amount is greater than the Estimated Net Asset Adjustment, then Buyer shall pay to the Company the amount of such excess, and (ii) if the Final Net Asset Adjustment is less than the Estimated Net Asset Adjustment, then Sellers shall pay to Buyer the amount of such shortfall.

(h) The "**Final Unretained Revenue Adjustment**" shall be an amount determined as follows:

(i) if the Retained Revenue Percentage is less than 80%, the Final Unretained Revenue Adjustment shall be $75 million (the "**Maximum Adjustment Amount**");

(ii) if the Retained Revenue Percentage is 80% or greater but less than 90%, the Final Unretained Revenue Adjustment shall [be] the Maximum Adjustment Amount multiplied by the Adjustment Factor (as defined below); and

(iii) if the Retained Revenue Percentage is 90% or greater, than the Final Unretained Revenue Adjustment shall be zero.

(i) The "**Adjustment Factor**" shall equal (i) .90 minus the Retained Revenue Percentage (expressed as a decimal number), multiplied by (ii) 10.

(j) Upon final determination of the Final Unretained Revenue Adjustment, (i) if the Final Unretained Revenue Adjustment is greater than the Estimated Unretained Revenue Adjustment, then Sellers shall pay to Buyer the amount of such excess, and (ii) if the Final Unretained Revenue Adjustment is less than the Estimated Unretained Revenue Adjustment, then Buyer shall pay to the Company the amount of such shortfall.

(k) Any payments due pursuant to Sections 3.2(e), (g) or (j) shall be made by wire transfer of immediately available funds within two business days of the final determination of the amount in question.

(l) The parties hereto agree that judgment may be entered upon the determination of the Accountants in any court having jurisdiction over the party against which such determination is to be enforced.

3.3 Closing. The consummation of the transactions contemplated hereby (the "**Closing**") shall be held at such place as the parties shall agree at such time as they agree not later than the fifth business day to occur following the date on which all of the conditions to Closing set forth in Section 4 shall have been satisfied or waived (other than those to be satisfied or waived at the Closing, but subject to the satisfaction or waiver thereof at Closing), or at such other time and day as the parties may agree; *provided, however*, that in no event shall Closing occur prior to the 60th day following the date upon which the notices and consent requests are mailed to customers in accordance with Section 6.5. The date on which the Closing occurs is referred to as the "**Closing Date**." At the Closing:

(a) Buyer shall pay to the Company the Estimated Acquisition Consideration, and the Company shall deliver to Buyer a receipt in respect of such payment;

(b) the Company and Buyer shall deliver to each other a Bill of Sale, Assignment and Assumption Agreement, executed by the Company and Buyer in a mutually acceptable form, and any other endorsements, consents, resignations, appointments, assignments and instruments of conveyance and other documents that Buyer reasonably determines to be necessary or appropriate to transfer the Assets to Buyer;

(c) the Company and Buyer shall deliver to each other the transition services agreement referenced in Section 9.9, executed by the Company and Buyer, respectively;

(d) Sellers shall deliver to Buyer a complete and accurate list of all Employees terminated by the Sellers during the ninety days preceding the Closing Date and the dates of such Employees' terminations; and

(e) Sellers and Buyer shall deliver to each other the certificates referred to in Sections 4.2(f) and 4.3(c).

3.4 **Taxes.**

(a) **Property Taxes and Assessments.** In the case of real property Taxes, personal property Taxes, special assessments relating to the Assets and similar *ad valorem* obligations that are levied with respect to the Assets or the Business for assessment periods within which the Closing Date occurs, Sellers shall pay their Pro Rata Portion of such taxes and Buyer shall pay its Pro Rata Portion of such taxes. If Tax statements for any Assets or the Business are sent directly to any Seller by a Taxing Authority (as defined in Section 3.5(f)) after the date of this Agreement, then that Seller shall cause such statements to be forwarded promptly to Buyer.

(b) **Transfer Taxes.** All applicable sales, use, value-added, business, goods and services, transfer, documentary, conveyancing, or similar taxes or expenses and all recording fees that may be imposed as a result of the sale and transfer of the Business and the Assets to

Buyer under this Agreement, together with any and all fines, penalties, interest, and additions to Tax with respect thereto ("**Transfer Taxes**") shall be shared equally by Buyer and Sellers. Each party hereto hereby agrees to cooperate and timely make all filings, returns, reports, and forms with respect to Transfer Taxes. Buyer shall execute and deliver to Sellers at the Closing any appropriate exemption certificate relating to an occasional sale exemption or any other exemption from Transfer Taxes.

(c) **Taxes Generally.** Except as otherwise provided in this Agreement, as among the parties hereto, (i) Sellers shall be responsible for and pay all Taxes levied and imposed upon, or in connection, with the Assets on or before the Closing Date; (ii) Buyer shall be responsible for and pay all Taxes levied or imposed upon, or in connection with, the Assets after the Closing Date; and (iii) Sellers and Buyer will each be responsible for their own income and franchise taxes, if any, arising from the transactions contemplated by this Agreement.

(d) **Contest Provisions.** Buyer shall promptly notify Sellers in writing upon the receipt of notice of any pending or threatened audits or assessments with respect to Taxes for which Sellers (or their affiliates) may be liable hereunder. Sellers shall be entitled to participate at their expense in the defenses of any tax audit or administrative or court proceeding relating to Taxes for which Sellers may be liable, and, at their option, take control of the complete defense of, any tax audit or administrative or court proceeding relating to Taxes for which Sellers may solely be liable, and to employ counsel of their choice at their expense. Buyer may not agree to settle any claim for Taxes for which Sellers may be liable without prior written consent of the Sellers.

Sellers shall promptly notify Buyer in writing upon receipt of notice of any pending or threatened audits or assessments with respect to Taxes for which Buyer (or its affiliates) may be liable hereunder. Buyer shall be entitled to participate at its expense in the defenses of any tax audit or administrative or court proceeding relating to Taxes for which Buyer may be liable, and, at its option, to take control of the complete defense of, any tax audit or administrative or court proceeding relating to Taxes for which Buyer may solely be liable, and to employ counsel of its choice at its expense. Sellers may not agree to settle any claim for Taxes for which Buyer may be liable without prior written consent of Buyer.

3.5 **Definitions Relating to Taxes.**

(a) "**Code**" means the Internal Revenue Code of 1986, as amended.

(b) "**Pro Rata Portion**" means, with respect to Sellers, the number of days in any assessment period within which the Closing Date occurs falling on or before the Closing Date, and with respect to Buyer, the number of days in any such period falling after the Closing Date.

(c) "**Tax Records**" means copies of all records of any kind and in whatever format, including all documents, microfiche, microfilm and computer records (including magnetic tape, disc storage, card forms and printed copy) that relate to any withholding Tax imposed on or in connection with the Assets or the Business, or any information return required to be filed in connection with the Assets or the Business (including Internal Revenue Service ("**IRS**") Forms 1099, 1098, 1042, 1042-S, 945, W-2, W-4, I-9, W-8, W-9 and similar forms and IRS determination letters with respect thereto).

(d) "**Tax Return**" means any return, statement, report, or form, including in each case any amendments thereto, required to be filed with any Taxing Authority by or with respect to Taxes or any claim for refund.

(e) "**Tax**" or "**Taxes**" means all federal, state, local, or foreign income, profits, franchise, gross receipts, net receipts, capital, capital stock, net worth, sales, use, withholding, turnover, value added, *ad valorem*, registration, general business, employment, social security, disability, occupation, real property, personal property (tangible and intangible), recording, stamp, transfer, conveyance, severance, production, excise, and other taxes, withholdings, duties, levies, imposts, license and registration fees, and other similar charges and assessments, whether payable directly or by withholding and whether or not requiring the filing of a Tax Return (including all fines, penalties, and additions attributable to or otherwise imposed on or with respect to any such taxes, charges, fees, levies, or other assessments, and all interest thereon and any liability arising pursuant to the application of Treasury Regulation section 1.1502-6 or any similar provision of any applicable state, local or foreign Tax law) imposed by or on behalf of any Taxing Authority.

(f) "**Taxing Authority**" means any foreign, federal, state or local government, political subdivision or governmental or regulatory authority, agency, board, bureau, commission, instrumentality or court or quasi-governmental authority, body, or instrumentality exercising any authority to impose, regulate, or administer the imposition of Taxes.

(g) "**Treasury Regulations**" means the U.S. treasury regulations (including any successor regulations) promulgated pursuant to the Code.

3.6 Allocation of Acquisition Consideration. Buyer and Sellers agree to determine the amount of and allocate the Acquisition Consideration (and all other capitalizable costs) among the Assets for all tax purposes in a reasonable manner as calculated by Buyer (the "**Allocation**"). The Allocation shall be consistent with the provisions of Section 1060 of the Code and the Treasury Regulations thereunder and will be binding on the Buyer and Sellers for all Tax reporting purposes. Buyer shall deliver a draft of such Allocation prior to the Closing. If Sellers disagree with any items reflected on the draft Allocation so provided, Sellers shall notify Buyer of such disagreement and the reasons for so disagreeing, in which case Buyer and Sellers shall attempt in good faith to resolve the disagreement. If Buyer and Sellers cannot agree on a mutually acceptable Allocation after 30 days of good faith negotiations, each of Buyer and Sellers shall use its own allocation for all Tax purposes, and Buyer and Sellers shall not be bound by the provisions of this Section 3.6. Buyer and Sellers will each prepare an IRS Form 8594 in a timely fashion in a manner that conforms with the Allocation. Neither Buyer nor Sellers, nor any of their respective affiliates, shall take any position on any Tax Return or audit inconsistent with the Allocation unless required to do so by applicable law. To the extent the Acquisition Consideration is adjusted after the Closing Date, Buyer and Sellers will each revise their IRS Form 8594 in accordance with the above procedures. Each of the parties agrees to notify the other if the IRS or any other Taxing Authority proposes a reallocation of such amounts.

4. Conditions to Closing.

4.1 Conditions to Each Party's Obligation. The respective obligations of the parties to effect the Closing are subject to the fulfillment or written waiver of each of the following conditions:

(a) <u>No Injunction</u>. No Governmental Entity of competent jurisdiction shall have, after the date of this Agreement, enacted, issued, promulgated, enforced or entered any statute, rule, regulation, judgment, decree, injunction or other order (whether temporary, preliminary or permanent) which is in effect and prohibits consummation of the transactions contemplated by this Agreement.

(b) <u>Governmental Proceedings</u>. No proceeding initiated by a Governmental Entity that seeks to challenge or restrain the consummation of any of the transactions contemplated by this Agreement shall remain pending.

(c) <u>Governmental and Regulatory Consents</u>. All consents, approvals and authorizations of, filings and registrations with, and notifications to, all Governmental Entities required for the consummation of the transactions contemplated hereby shall have been obtained or made and shall be in full force and effect and all waiting periods required by law shall have expired.

4.2 Buyer's Obligation. The obligation of Buyer to effect the Closing is also subject to the fulfillment or written waiver by Buyer of each of the following conditions:

(a) <u>Representations and Warranties</u>. The representations and warranties of Sellers set forth in (i) Section 5.1 (Organization and Authority), 5.2 (Non-Contravention), 5.3 (Financial Statements) and 5.6 (Assets) shall be true and correct in all material respects and (ii) all other representation and warranties shall be true and correct except where the failure to be so true and correct would in the aggregate not have a Material Adverse Effect (as defined below), in each case as of the Closing Date as though made on and as of such date (except to the extent such representations and warranties speak only as of an earlier date, in which case such representation and warranty shall be true and correct in all material respects, or true and correct except where the failure to be so true and correct would in the aggregate not have a Material Adverse Effect, as applicable, as of such date). For purposes of this Section 4.2, except with respect to clause (a) of Section 5.14, such representations and warranties shall be read without giving effect to any qualification or limitation as to materiality or "Material Adverse Effect."

(b) <u>Performance of Obligations of Sellers</u>. Sellers shall have performed or complied with, in all material respects, all obligations and covenants required by this Agreement to be performed or complied with by Sellers by the Closing.

(c) <u>No Material Adverse Effect</u>. No Material Adverse Effect shall have occurred. As used in this Agreement, "**Material Adverse Effect**" means any event, change, effect, fact, circumstance or other occurrence that, individually or in the aggregate, is, or would reasonably be expected to be, materially adverse to (x) the operations, results of operations, properties, assets, or condition (financial or otherwise) of the Business as a whole, other than any such change or effect resulting from (i) any change, event, or occurrence generally affecting the industry in which the Business operates; (ii) general economic or securities market conditions in the United States; (iii) changes in laws, regulations, or accounting principles applicable to the Business; (iv) natural disasters or acts of terrorism or war (whether or not declared); (v) the public announcement of this Agreement; or (vi) the loss of any employees, brokers, financial advisors, consultants, customers or customer assets following the announcement of this Agreement or the transactions contemplated hereby, except in each case referred to in clauses (i), (ii), (iii) and (iv), to the extent disproportionately affecting the Business, or (y) the ability of Sellers to perform their obligations under this Agreement or to consummate the transactions contemplated hereby.

(d) <u>Third Party Consents</u>. All consents or approvals of all persons, other than Governmental Entities, required for or in connection with the execution, delivery and performance of this Agreement and the consummation of the transactions contemplated hereby, including (i) any consents or approvals required pursuant to the Real Estate Leases, (ii) any consents or approvals which are required in connection with the transfer of the Assets to Buyer and (iii) any consents or approvals which are required for the continued operation of the Business by Buyer as heretofore conducted by the Company shall have been obtained and shall be in full force and effect, unless the failure to obtain any such consent or approval would not be material to the operation of the Business.

(e) <u>No Burdensome Condition</u>. None of the consents, approvals and authorizations of, filings and registrations with, and notifications to, Governmental Entities required for the consummation of the transactions contemplated hereby shall have resulted in the imposition of any condition that would require any of the actions, or impose any of the limitations, referred to in Section 9.4(c).

(f) <u>Closing Certificates</u>. Sellers shall have delivered to Buyer a certificate dated the Closing Date and signed by an executive officer of each Seller confirming the satisfaction of the conditions set forth in Sections 4.2(a) and (b).

4.3 Sellers' Obligation. The obligation of Sellers to effect the Closing is also subject to the fulfillment or written waiver by Sellers of each of the following conditions:

(a) <u>Representations and Warranties</u>. The representations and warranties of Buyer set forth in this Agreement shall be true and correct in all material respects as of the Closing Date (except where the failure to be so true and correct would not have a material adverse effect on Buyer's ability to consummate the transactions contemplated herein).

(b) <u>Performance of Obligation by Buyer</u>. Buyer shall have performed or complied with, in all material respects, all obligations and covenants required by this Agreement to be performed or complied with by Buyer by the Closing.

(c) <u>Closing Certificates</u>. Buyer shall have delivered to Sellers a certificated dated the Closing Date and signed by an executive officer of Buyer confirming the satisfaction of the conditions set forth in Sections 4.3(a) and (b).

5. Representations and Warranties of Sellers. Except as set forth in a correspondingly numbered Section of the disclosure schedule delivered by

Sellers to Buyer concurrently with the execution of this Agreement, which shall be arranged in sections corresponding to the number and lettered sections contained in this Section 5 (the "**Disclosure Schedule**"); *provided, however*, that disclosure in any section of the Disclosure Schedule shall be deemed to have been set forth in all other applicable sections of the Disclosure Schedule where it is reasonably apparent on the face of the disclosure that such disclosure is applicable to such other sections notwithstanding the omission of any cross reference to such other section), Sellers hereby jointly and severally represent:

5.1 **Organization and Authority.** Each Seller is a corporation duly organized, validly existing, and in good standing under Delaware law. Each Seller and each of their respective subsidiaries engaged in the Business is duly qualified and in good standing to do business as a foreign corporation in each jurisdiction in which the Assets or the nature of the Business requires it to be qualified, except where the failure to be so qualified or in good standing does not have a Material Adverse Effect. Each Seller has all requisite corporate power and authority to enter into this Agreement and to consummate the transactions contemplated hereby. All corporate acts and proceedings required to be taken to authorize the execution, delivery, and performance by Sellers of this Agreement and the consummation by Sellers of the transactions contemplated hereby have been duly and properly taken. No vote of any security holders of the Sellers is required under applicable laws to consummate the transaction contemplated hereby. This Agreement has been duly executed and delivered by each Seller and, assuming due authorization, execution, and delivery of this Agreement by Buyer, constitutes a valid and binding obligation of each Seller, enforceable against each Seller in accordance with its terms, except as such enforceability may be limited by bankruptcy, insolvency, moratorium, and other similar laws affecting creditors' rights generally and by general principles of equity.

5.2 **Non-Contravention.**

(a) The execution, delivery, and performance by Sellers of this Agreement do not, and the consummation by Sellers of the transactions contemplated hereby will not, (i) conflict with, or result in any violation of, any provision of the certificate of incorporation or bylaws of either Seller or any of their respective subsidiaries engaged in the Business, or (ii) conflict with, result in any violation of, or constitute a default under, or create a lien (other than a Permitted Lien, as defined in Section 5.6) on any of the Assets under, or result in the acceleration or termination of, or result in an increase in payment obligations under, any instrument, contract, commitment, agreement, or arrangement to which either Seller or any of their respective subsidiaries engaged in the Business is a party or by which either Seller or any of their respective subsidiaries engaged in the Business or any of the Assets are bound, or any judgment, order, writ, injunction, or decree to which either Seller has been specifically identified as subject, or result in any violation of any statute, law, ordinance, rule, or regulation applicable to either Seller or the Assets (except for customer consents, which are governed by Section 6.5), and except, in the case of clause (ii), where such conflict, violation, default, lien acceleration, termination, or increased obligations would not be material to the Business.

(b) No consent, approval, license, permit, order or authorization of, or registration, declaration, or filing with, any Governmental Entity is required to be obtained or made by or with respect to Sellers in connection with the execution, delivery, and performance by Sellers of this Agreement or the consummation by Sellers of the transactions contemplated hereby other than compliance with and filings under the Hart-Scott-Rodino Antitrust Improvements Act of 1976 (the "**HSR Act**") and the approval of the NASD pursuant to NASD Rule 1017; *provided, however,* that no representation is made as to whether any governmental consents, approvals, licenses, permits, orders, authorizations, registrations, declarations, or filings will need to be obtained by Buyer by reason of the nature of its business or the laws to which it is subject.

(c) To the Knowledge of Sellers, except for customer consents (which are addressed in Section 6.5) and consents required for the transfer of Real Estate Leases, no consent, approval, license, permit, order, authorization, registration, declaration or filing that is material to the Business is required to be obtained by Seller from any person that is not a Governmental Entity in connection with the execution, delivery, and performance by Sellers of this Agreement or the consummation by Sellers of the transactions contemplated hereby.

5.3 Financial Statements.

(a) Section 5.3(a) of the Disclosure Schedule sets forth (a) an unaudited statement of net assets of the Business to the extent to be acquired by Buyer and unaudited statement of income of the Business to the extent to be acquired by Buyer each as of December 31, 2005 and (b) an unaudited statement of net assets of the Business to the extent to be acquired by Buyer as of March 31, 2006 and an unaudited statement of income of the Business to the extent to be acquired by Buyer for the three-month period ended March 31, 2006 (the statements listed in clauses (a) and (b) are referred to as the "**Financial Statements**" and the unaudited statement of net assets listed in clause (a) is referred to as the "**Preliminary Net Asset Statement**"). The Financial Statements fairly present, in all material respects, the assets, liabilities, and financial condition of the Business to the extent to be acquired by Buyer at their respective dates and the results of operations of the Business to the extent to be acquired by Buyer for the respective periods covered thereby. The Financial Statements have been prepared in accordance with GAAP on a basis consistent with the principles historically applied by Parent in the preparation of the financial statements for its Private Client Services segment included in Parent's filings with the SEC, except as expressly disclosed in the notes to the Financial Statements and except that Excluded Assets and Excluded Liabilities and profits and losses related thereto are excluded from the Financial Statements.

(b) Section 5.3(b) of the Disclosure Schedule sets forth a true, complete and correct schedule of all financial advisors that were employed in the Business as of the March 31, 2006, and the amount of product revenue and the percentage of the total product revenues generated by each such financial advisor, in each case for the twelve-month period ended March 31, 2006, and the aggregate assets or rights (including any funds or securities and any commodity positions) of customers of such financial advisors held by the Company under the possession-and-control provisions of the Exchange Act as of March 31, 2006.

(c) The financial information set forth on Section 5.3(c) of the Disclosure Schedule is true and correct in all material respects.

(d) Section 5.3(d) of the Disclosure Schedule set forth a true, complete and correct list of all intercompany accounts related to the Business between either Seller, on the one hand, and any of their respective affiliates, on the other, as of December 31, 2005 and March 31, 2006.

(e) Neither the Sellers nor any of their respective subsidiaries engaged in the Business have any liabilities of any nature, whether accrued, absolute, fixed, contingent, or otherwise, whether due or to become due and whether or not required to be recorded or reflected on a balance sheet under GAAP, other than such liabilities (i) reflected or reserved against in the Financial Statements, (ii) that are Excluded Liabilities or (iii) incurred in the ordinary course of business consistent with past practice after the date of the most recent Financial Statements and that are not material to the Business.

5.4 Nonforeign Certification. No Tax is required to be withheld pursuant to Section 1445 of the Code as a result of the transfers contemplated by this Agreement because neither Seller is a "foreign person" within the meaning of that section and the Treasury Regulations thereunder.

5.5 Taxes.

(a) All Tax Returns including, without limitation, consolidated federal income tax returns, withholding tax returns and declarations of estimated tax and tax reports, required to be filed on or prior to the Closing Date by Sellers (or their affiliates) with respect to any Tax that, if not paid, might result in a Lien upon any of the Assets, other than Permitted Liens, have been duly and timely filed and are true, correct and complete, and all Taxes due or claimed to be due pursuant thereto have been paid. For purposes of this Agreement, "Lien" means any lien, encumbrance, mortgage, deed of trust, security interest, easement, pledge, assessment, lease, adverse claim, levy, charge, transfer restriction, option or other restriction or third-party right.

(b) Each Seller represents that there are no outstanding written requests, agreements, consents or waivers to the extent the statutory period of limitations applicable to the assessment of any Taxes or deficiencies against either such Seller.

5.6 Assets. Sellers have, or will have immediately prior to Closing, and upon Closing will transfer to Buyer, good title to each of the Assets, in each case free and clear of all liens, security interests, and other encumbrances, except (a) mechanics', materialmen's, carriers', workmen's, warehousemen's, repairmen's, landlords', or other like liens on tangible Assets securing obligations that are not delinquent; and are not, individually, or in the aggregate, in excess of $15,000 (b) Liens for Taxes and other governmental charges that are not due and payable or the validity or amount of which is being contested in good faith through appropriate proceedings; (c) liens, security interests and other encumbrances evidenced by any security agreement, financing statement, purchase money agreement, conditional sales contract, capital lease, or operating leases set forth in Section 5.6 of the Disclosure Schedule; and (d) imperfections of title and encumbrances that do not, individually or in the aggregate, materially impair the value or the continued use and operation substantially in the current manner of the Assets to which they relate (the liens, security interests, and other encumbrances described in clauses (a) through (d) above being referred to collectively as "**Permitted Liens**"). Section 5.6 of the Disclosure Schedule sets forth a true, complete and correct list of all Tangible Personal Property as of March 31, 2006.

5.7 Real Property.

(a) Section 5.7(a) of the Disclosure Schedule sets forth a true, complete and correct list of all Leased Real Estate. Assuming good fee title vested in the landlord, the Company has valid leasehold or subleasehold interests in all Leased Real Estate, in each case free and clear of all mortgages, liens, security interests, easements, restrictive covenants, rights-of-way, encroachments, and other encumbrances, except (i) Permitted Liens; (ii) easements, restrictive covenants, rights-of-way, encroachments, purchase options, lease-termination options, rights of first refusal or first offer, and other encumbrances and matters that are included in or disclosed by the documents relating to each parcel of Leased Real Estate made available by Sellers to Buyer prior to the date hereof; (iii) mortgages, liens, security interests, or encumbrances that have been placed by any developer, landlord, or other third party on any Leased Real Estate; and (iv) (A) platting, subdivision, zoning, building, and other similar restrictions, and (B) easements, restricted covenants, rights-of-way, encroachments, and other similar encumbrances and any conditions not of record that may be shown by a current, accurate survey or physical inspection of the Leased Real Estate, none of which items set forth in this clause (iv) individually or in the aggregate materially interferes with the continued use and operation of the Leased Real Estate substantially in the manner in which the Leased Real Estate is currently used and operated.

(b) Sellers do not own or lease any real estate primarily related to the Business except for the Leased Real Estate.

5.8 Condition of Assets. The tangible Assets (a) have no material defects, (b) are in good operating condition and repair (giving due account to the age and length of use of same), ordinary wear and tear excepted, (c) are suitable for use in connection with the Business, and (d) in the case of real property Assets are structurally sound, except where failure of any of the representations in clauses (a) through (d) above would not have a Material Adverse Effect. The Assets constitute all of the property and assets (tangible and intangible) used in the Business in the manner conducted as of the date of this Agreement. EXCEPT AS SET FORTH EXPRESSLY IN THIS AGREEMENT, SELLERS DISCLAIM ANY EXPRESS OR IMPLIED WARRANTY WITH RESPECT TO THE ASSETS, TANGIBLE OR INTANGIBLE, INCLUDING IMPLIED WARRANTIES OF NONINFRINGEMENT, FITNESS, MERCHANTABILITY, OR FITNESS FOR A PARTICULAR PURPOSE.

5.9 Intellectual Property. To the Knowledge of Sellers, (a) no outstanding claims against either Seller have been made in writing since January 1, 2004 by any other person challenging or questioning either the right of the Sellers or their subsidiaries to use, or the validity of, any patent, trademark, trade name, service mark or copyright used solely in the Business in any jurisdiction, domestic or foreign (other than claims, challenges or questions by governmental intellectual property office examiners as part of the application process) and (b) no outstanding claims of patent, trademark, trade name, service mark or copyright infringement have been made in writing since

January 1, 2004 by any person against either Seller with respect to the right of Sellers or their subsidiaries to continue to sell any product or service of the Business without payment of a royalty, license fee, or similar fee to such person, except in the case of clauses (a) and (b) as does not have a Material Adverse Effect.

5.10 Contracts.

(a) Section 5.10 of the Disclosure Schedule sets forth a true and correct list of all of the following agreements, understandings or contracts, whether oral or written, in effect as of the date of this Agreement and related to the Business or the Assets:

(i) each agreement or form thereof providing confidentiality, non-solicitation or non-competition restrictions applicable to any Employee or any former employee of the Business (identifying the Employees and former employees who are subject to such agreements and, if applicable, which form applies to each such Employee or former employee);

(ii) each covenant not to compete or other obligation that restricts or purports to restrict the operation of the Business as presently conducted;

(iii) each material agreement or contract of the Company with any of its affiliates or any current officer or director of either Seller (other than contracts constituting Sellers' Plans));

(iv) each Personal Property Lease (except for any such lease calling for payments of less than $25,000 per year);

(v) any agreement for the purchase or provision of materials, supplies, goods, services, equipment or other assets that provides for either (i) annual payments of $25,000 or more, or (ii) aggregate payments of $50,000 or more;

(vi) each radio, television, or newspaper advertising agreement that provides for annual payments of $25,000 or more;

(vii) any indenture, mortgage, promissory note, loan agreement, guarantee or other borrowing of money or the deferred purchase price of property in excess of $25,000 (in either case, whether incurred, assured, guaranteed or secured by any asset);

(viii) each Real Estate Lease and each Personal Property Lease;

(ix) any agreement relating to the acquisition or disposition of any business or operations (whether by merger, sale of stock, sale of assets, out-sourcing or otherwise);

(x) any agreement that creates future payment obligations in excess of $50,000 in the aggregate and which by its terms does not terminate or is not terminable without penalty upon notice of 180 days or less;

(xi) any agreement involving consideration with a value in excess of $50,000;

(xii) any agreement pursuant to which any person is providing an indemnity, guarantee, letter of credit, bond or similar instrument in respect of the Business; and

(xiii) any agreements between the Sellers, their respective subsidiaries or any of their respective employees, on the one hand, and a customer of the Business, on the other hand, other than agreements entered into in the Ordinary Course of Business.

(b) Each agreement and contract required to be described in Section 5.10 of the Disclosure Schedule (collectively, the "**Material Contracts**") is a valid and binding agreement of the Company, and to the Knowledge of the Company, the counterparty or counterparties thereto, and in full force and effect, except as such enforceability may be limited by bankruptcy, insolvency, moratorium, and other similar laws affecting creditors' rights generally and by general principles of equity. Neither Seller is (with or without the lapse of time or the giving of notice, or both) in breach of or in default under any of the Material Contracts, and, to the Knowledge of Sellers, no other party to any of the Material Contracts is (with or without the lapse of time or the giving of notice, or both) in material breach of or in material default under any of the Material Contracts. A true and complete copy of each Material Contract has been made available to Buyer prior to the date hereof.

5.11 Litigation; Decrees. No actions, lawsuits, arbitrations, investigations, or proceedings, are pending or, to the Knowledge of Sellers, threatened, against either Seller with respect to the Business (other than routine challenges by governmental intellectual property office examiners as part of the application process) that, if decided adversely to such person, would have a Material Adverse Effect. Neither Seller is subject to any outstanding judgment, order, or decree of any Governmental Entity.

5.12 Insurance. Section 5.12 of the Disclosure Schedule sets forth a list of the policies of insurance currently maintained by either Seller (including any policies of insurance maintained for purposes of providing benefits such as workers' compensation and employers' liability coverage) (collectively, the "**Policies**"). All such Policies are with reputable insurers, and are in full force and effect and cover the assets and risks of the Business in a manner consistent with customary practices of companies engaged in businesses and operations similar to those of the Business. All premiums due on such Policies have been timely paid and no notice of cancellation or termination or intent to cancel has been received by Sellers with respect to such Policies.

5.13 Employee Benefits; ERISA.

(a) Section 5.13 of the Disclosure Schedule sets forth a complete and correct list of each plan, program, arrangement or agreement that is an employment, compensation, retention, consulting, employee pension, profit sharing, savings, retirement, incentive bonus or other bonus, stock bonus, stock option, stock purchase, stock appreciation rights, deferred compensation, medical, dental, vacation, insurance, sick pay, disability, severance, or other plan, fund, program, policy, agreement, contract, or arrangement (including any "employee benefit plan" as defined in Section 3(3) of the Employee Retirement Income Security Act of 1974, as amended ("**ERISA**")) providing employee benefits that is maintained or contributed to by either Seller in which any Employees or their beneficiaries, dependents or former dependents are participating, which is maintained for the benefit of the Employees or their beneficiaries, dependents or former dependents or under which any Employees or their beneficiaries, dependents or former dependents have accrued any benefits to which they remain entitled (collectively, "**Sellers' Plans**"). The Company has made available to Buyer prior to the date hereof true and complete copies or accurate summaries of all Sellers' Plans, including but not limited to all amendments thereto, any trust or other funding instruments and insurance contracts forming a part of any Sellers' Plan, all summary plan descriptions, and with respect to each Sellers' Plan the most recent required IRS Form 5500, the most recent actuarial report and all IRS determination letters.

(b) Each Sellers' Plan that is subject to ERISA or is intended to be qualified under the Code has been operated and administered in accordance with, and is in compliance with, ERISA and the Code in all material respects, and each Sellers' Plan has been operated and administered in accordance with, and is in compliance with, all other applicable laws in all material respects. Each Sellers' Plan which is an "employee pension benefit plan" within the meaning of Section 3(2) of ERISA and which is intended to be qualified under Section 401(a) of the Code has received a favorable determination letter from the IRS with respect to its qualified status under the current provisions of the Code, and to the Knowledge of either Seller there are no circumstances which could be reasonably likely to result in the revocation of such letter or the loss of such qualified status. Neither the Company nor any of its subsidiaries has engaged in any transactions with respect to any Sellers' Plan which could be reasonably likely to subject the Company or any of its subsidiaries, directly or indirectly, to a material tax, penalty or other liability imposed by Section 4975 of the Code or Section 409, 502(i) or 502(l) of ERISA.

(c) Neither the execution nor the effectiveness of this Agreement will, alone or in combination with any other event, (i) entitle any

Employee or any Employee's beneficiaries, dependents or former dependents to severance pay or other benefits or entitlements or to any increase in severance pay or other benefits or entitlements in connection with any termination of employment, (ii) accelerate the time of payment or vesting or result in any payment or funding of any compensation or benefits under, increase the amount payable under, or result in any other material obligation under any Sellers' Plan or otherwise in respect of any Employee, (iii) limit or restrict the right of the Company or any of its subsidiaries to merge, amend or terminate any of the Sellers' Plans or (iv) result in an "excess parachute payment" to any Employee, within the meaning of Section 280G of the Code.

(d) There is no material pending or, to the Knowledge of Sellers, threatened claim, litigation proceeding, action or audit relating to any of Sellers' Plans. Neither the Company nor any of its subsidiaries has any obligations for post-employment benefits under any Sellers' Plan.

(e) None of Sellers' Plans is (i) a "multiemployer plan" within the meaning of Section 3(37) or 4001(a)(3) of ERISA or (ii) a "multiple employer plan" within the meaning of Section 4063 of ERISA.

(f) Each Sellers' Plan that is a "nonqualified deferred compensation plan" within the meaning of Section 409A(d)(1) of the Code subject to Section 409A of the Code has been operated in compliance with Section 409A of the Code since January 1, 2005, based upon a good faith reasonable interpretation of (A) Section 409A of the Code and (B)(1) the Proposed Regulations issued thereunder or (2) Internal Revenue Service Notice 2005-1.

5.14 Absence of Changes or Events. Since December 31, 2005, (a) there has not occurred a Material Adverse Effect, (b) except to the extent required by the terms of this Agreement, the Business has been operated in the ordinary course of business consistent with past custom and practice ("**Ordinary Course of Business**") and (c) other than this Agreement, neither Sellers nor any of their respective subsidiaries have engaged in any material transaction with respect to the Business or entered into any material agreement with respect to the Business outside of the Ordinary Course of Business.

5.15 Compliance with Laws.

(a) Neither Seller nor any of their respective subsidiaries is or has been within the past three years in conflict with, in default with respect to or in violation of, (i) any laws applicable to the Business or by which any of the Assets is bound or affected, including but not limited to ERISA and the Code and the regulations promulgated thereunder or (ii) any note, bond, mortgage, indenture, contract, agreement, lease, license, permit, franchise or other instrument or obligation related to the Business or by which any of the Assets is bound or affected, except, in each case, where such default or violation would not be material to the Business.

(b) Section 5.15(b) of the Disclosure Schedule sets forth a true, complete and correct list of all Permits. Sellers and each of their respective subsidiaries (to the extent such subsidiaries conduct the Business) are in compliance with the terms of such Permits, except, in each case, where the failure to comply would not be material to the Business.

(c) Since December 31, 2002, no Seller has engaged in any act and has not permitted to exist any state of affairs which (i) has led to a request (whether or not the request has the force of law and whether or not it is pending or was subsequently withdrawn or reviewed) by any Governmental Entity in any jurisdiction in which it operates to materially modify or change the manner in which the Business is or was carried on or (ii) has resulted in any disciplinary or enforcement action being commenced or threatened against any Seller in respect of the conduct of the Business (other than any such actions that are not reasonably likely to materially affect the Business).

(d) Section 5.15(d) of the Disclosure Schedule sets forth a true, complete and correct list of each of the Sellers or any of their respective subsidiaries that conduct the Business and are registered as a broker-dealer, as well as the federal, state and foreign jurisdictions in which such entity is so registered. Each Seller and each of its employees and representatives involved in the Business who are required to be registered, licensed or qualified as a broker-dealer, investment adviser, a registered representative or other applicable regulatory category with the Federal Reserve, the Comptroller of the Currency, the NASD, the SEC, the securities commission of any state or foreign jurisdiction or any self-regulatory organization is duly registered, licensed and/or qualified as such and such registrations, licenses and/or qualifications are in full force and effect. None of the registered representatives is subject to a "statutory disqualification" as defined in Section 3(a)(39) of the Exchange Act, or is subject to a disqualification that would be a basis for censure, limitations on the activities, functions or operations of, or suspension or revocation of, the registration as a broker-dealer under Section 15 of the Exchange Act. To the Knowledge of Sellers, there is no current investigation, whether formal or informal, or whether preliminary or otherwise, that is reasonably likely to result in, any such censure, limitations, suspension or revocation.

(e) With respect to the Business, no Seller is, or since December 31, 2002, has been a party to any order, statutory disqualification, or any written agreement, consent agreement or memorandum of understanding with, or a party to any commitment letter or similar undertaking to, or is subject to any order or directive by, or has been ordered to pay any civil penalty by, or is a recipient of any supervisory letter from, or has adopted any board or member resolutions at the request or suggestion of, any Governmental Entity related to any Seller (each, a "**Regulatory Agreement**"), nor has any Seller been advised by any Governmental Entity that such Governmental Entity is considering such a Regulatory Agreement nor is there any pending or, to the Knowledge of Sellers threatened, non-routine regulatory investigation related to the Business.

(f) Since December 31, 2002, none of the Sellers has received any notice from a Governmental Entity alleging that in connection with the conduct of the Business, Sellers have failed to comply in a material respect with any applicable data or consumer protection laws, nor has any Seller received any material claim from any individual seeking compensation for breaches, actual or alleged, of applicable data and consumer protection laws in connection with the conduct of the Business.

(g) In connection with the Business, each Seller has adopted and implemented an anti-money laundering policy and a customer identification program, each of which complies in all material respects with the requirements of applicable laws. Each Seller has devised and maintained systems of internal controls with respect to the Business sufficient to be in material compliance with the requirements of the Exchange Act and the rules and regulations of each applicable self-regulatory organization. In connection with the Business, each Seller maintains "know your customer" policies and procedures and obtains information concerning customers sufficient to know the "essential facts" concerning its customers as required under the USA Patriot Act and the rules of each applicable self-regulatory organization.

5.16 Environmental Matters.

(a) As used in this Section 5.16:

(i) "**Environmental Claim**" means any written claim, investigation, notice, suit or administrative or regulatory action alleging potential liability on the part of the Business (including liability for investigatory costs, cleanup costs, personal injury, natural resource or property damage or governmental response costs) arising out of, based on, or resulting from (A) the presence, or release of any Hazardous Substance at, in, from or onto any Leased Real Estate, or (B) circumstances forming the basis of any violation, or alleged violation, of any Environmental Law by the Business;

(ii) "**Environmental Laws**" means all applicable federal, state, and local statutes, regulations, laws, or ordinances relating to (A) the protection, pollution, contamination, clean up or remediation of the environment; (B) exposure of employees or third parties to Hazardous Substances; (C) release, management, use, storage, or disposal of Hazardous Substances; or (D) the presence of Hazardous Substances in any building, fixture or physical structure

(iii) "**Environmental Permits**" means all permits, licenses, or authorizations required pursuant to any Environmental Law; and

(iv) "**Hazardous Substance**" means contaminants, hazardous, industrial or solid wastes, raw materials, mold, polychlorinated biphyenyls, asbestos-containing material, petroleum or any fraction thereof, and any other hazardous materials listed in, regulated under or giving rise to liability under any Environmental Law.

(b) The operation of the Business is and has been in material compliance with all applicable Environmental Laws and required Environmental Permits.

(c) There are no Environmental Claims pending or, to the Knowledge of Sellers, threatened within the last three years, with respect to the Business, except for such Environmental Claims that are not likely to give rise to any material liability.

(d) To the Knowledge of Sellers, no Hazardous Substances are present in, on, or under, the Leased Real Estate in material violation of any Environmental Law or in circumstances that would reasonably be expected to give rise to a material Environmental Claim.

Notwithstanding any other representation and warranty in Section 5, the representations and warranties contained in this Section 5.16 constitute the sole representations and warranties of Sellers relating to any Environmental Law, Environmental Permits or to any Hazardous Substance.

5.17 Employee and Labor Relations.

(a) Section 5.17(a) of the Disclosure Schedule sets forth a complete and accurate list of all employees who are employed primarily in the retail sales offices of the Business and the regional directors of the Business and whom Sellers expect to transfer with the Business ("**Employees**") together with the following information with respect to each Employee: (i) minimum guaranteed base wage, salary or draw for the current year and the three preceding calendar years; (ii) commissions earned during the twelve months preceding the date hereof; (iii) most recently awarded bonus; (iv) whether or not the Employee is an "exempt employee" for purposes of the Fair Labor Standards Act of 1938, as amended, and the regulations promulgated thereunder; (v) in the case of each Employee who is not an "exempt employee," the Employee's hourly wage as in effect in the current year and the three preceding calendar years; (vi) total compensation for the current year and the three preceding calendar years; (vii) title; (viii) primary work location; (ix) date of hire; (x) age; and (xi) whether the Employee is actively employed or is on medical, disability, family or other leave of absence as of the date hereof. In respect of clauses (i), (v) and (vi), such information for 2002 shall be provided by Sellers to Buyer within 10 business days of the date hereof. Section 5.17(a) of the Disclosure Schedule shall be updated from time to time by the Sellers in their sole discretion (but only after consultation with Buyer) during the period between the date hereof and the Closing Date.

(b) Section 5.17(b) of the Disclosure Schedule sets forth a list of all employees of the Business who are Key Employees ("**Key Employees**"), which Sellers shall update from time to time through the Closing Date.

(c) Neither Seller is a party to any collective bargaining agreement covering any Employee, and no union or association has been certified or recognized, or brought any proceeding or petition seeking certification, as the collective bargaining representative of any Employees or has attempted to engage in negotiations regarding terms and conditions of employment of any Employees.

(d) With respect to all Employees (i) no labor strikes, lockouts, or material labor disputes or work stoppages are pending or, to the Knowledge of Sellers, have been threatened from January 1, 2005 to the date of this Agreement against or affecting the Employees, and (ii) to the Knowledge of Sellers, no union organizational campaign has occurred from January 1, 2005 to the date of this Agreement with respect to the Employees. Neither the Company nor any of its subsidiaries is the subject of (nor, to the Knowledge of either Seller, is there threatened) any grievance or any charge, claim or complaint asserting that the Company or any of its subsidiaries has committed any unfair labor practice or employment discrimination with respect to any Employee under Applicable Law. The Company and all of its subsidiaries have paid all wages, commissions and other compensation to Employees when due.

(e) Neither the Company nor any of its subsidiaries has violated any statute, law, ordinance, rule or regulation, or any order, ruling, decree, judgment or arbitration award of any court, arbitrator or any government agency regarding (i) the terms and conditions of employment of Employees or of former or prospective employees of the Business, including any applicable law relating to minimum wages, deductions from compensation and/or overtime or (ii) other labor related matters, in each case including without limitation laws, rules, regulations, orders, rulings, decrees, judgments and awards relating to discrimination, fair labor standards and occupational health and safety, wrongful discharge or violation of the personal rights of Employees or of former or prospective employees of the Business.

(f) Since January 1, 2005, Sellers have not engaged in any plant closing, workforce reduction, or other action related to any Employee that has resulted or would result in liability under or has required issuance of notice pursuant to the Worker Adjustment and Retraining Notification Act of 1988 or under any successor federal law or comparable law or regulation of a state or a foreign jurisdiction (collectively, the "WARN Act").

(g) Neither the Company nor any of its subsidiaries is a federal contractor for purposes of Executive Order 11246, as amended or any other applicable law.

(h) Within ten business days of the date hereof and to the extent Sellers track such information, Sellers shall provide to Buyer, on Section 5.17(h) of the Disclosure Schedule, a list detailing the following information, if any, with respect to each Employee: (i) business expense deductions, (ii) overpayment deductions and (iii) charge backs of financial advisors in each case, taken for the current year and the four preceding calendar years.

5.18 Regulatory Matters. Since January 1, 2002, Sellers and, to Sellers' Knowledge, the Transferred Employees in their capacity as Employees, have complied with the Exchange Act; the Investment Advisers Act of 1940 and the rules and regulations promulgated thereunder; the rules and regulations of the state commissions regulating the business of securities broker-dealers in the states in which the Company is licensed to do business; the rules and regulations promulgated under ERISA and the Code, including Section 4975 thereof; the rules and regulations of any state commissions regulating the business of investment advisers in the states in which the Company has made a notice filing as an investment adviser; the NASD Rules; the rules and regulations of the NYSE; the rules and regulations of the Municipal Securities Rulemaking Board; and the rules and regulations of the Securities Investor Protection Corporation; in each case except for noncompliance that does not have in the aggregate a Material Adverse Effect.

5.19 Records. The Books and Records of the Business are true, accurate and complete in all material respects and contain all of the documents and information required by applicable law and the Sellers' current written procedures and policies except where the failure to contain such documents and information would not have a Material Adverse Effect. Such Books and Records reflect full and current reconciliation of all financial information for each customer of the Business. Sellers have prepared all customer account statements required by applicable law and the governing documents pertaining to such customer relationship, the financial information in such account statements, including any historical account performance information contained therein, is true, accurate (with respect to historical account performance information, by reference to guidelines of the Association for Investment Management and Research) and complete and such account statements have been sent to the relevant customers.

5.20 Referral Relationships, Etc. Section 5.20 of the Disclosure Schedule sets forth, as of the date hereof, each contract relating to the Business pursuant to which any Seller or any of its affiliates is obligated to pay any referral fees, finders' fees, retrocessions or similar fees or compensation with respect to any customer of the Business, each customer relationship with respect to which any such fees are or may be payable and the amount and payment schedule for fees payable pursuant to such contracts.

5.21 Custodial Assets. The Assets will include all of Sellers' rights in funds, investments, collateral assets or other property of any kind held or required to be held as custodial assets pursuant to or in connection with the terms of any instrument or agreement governing a customer relationship. All such custodial assets are maintained on a fully reconciled basis.

5.22 Customer Relationships.

(a) Each customer of the Business has been in all material respects originated and serviced (i) in conformity with the applicable policies of the Business, (ii) in accordance with the terms of any applicable instrument or agreement governing the relationship with such customer, (iii) in accordance with any instructions received from such customers, (iv) consistent with each customer's risk profile and (v) in compliance with all applicable laws and Sellers' constituent documents, including any policies and procedures adopted thereunder. Each instrument or agreement governing a relationship with a customer of the Business has been duly and validly executed and delivered by such Seller and, to the Knowledge of Sellers, the other contracting parties, each such instrument of agreement constitutes a valid and binding obligation of the parties thereto, except as such enforceability may be limited by bankruptcy, insolvency, moratorium, and other similar laws affecting creditors' rights generally and by general principles of equity, and the relevant Seller and the other parties thereto have duly performed in all material respects their obligations thereunder and the relevant

Seller and, to the Knowledge of Sellers, such other person is in compliance with each of the terms thereof.

(b) No instrument or agreement governing a relationship with a customer of the Business provides for any material reduction of fees charged (or in other compensation payable to any Seller thereunder) at any time subsequent to the date hereof.

(c) No Seller or any of their respective directors, officers, employees or affiliates (i) is the beneficial owner of any interest in any of the accounts maintained on behalf of any customers of the Business or (ii) is a party to any contract pursuant to which it is obligated to provide service to, or receive compensation or benefits from, any of the customers of the Business after the Closing.

(d) Each account opening document, margin account agreement, investment advisory agreement and customer disclosure statement conforms in all material respects to the forms provided to Buyer prior to the date hereof.

(e) The Books and Records include documented risk profiles signed by each customer.

5.23 Loans and Receivables.

(a) Section 5.23(a) of the Disclosure Schedule lists all of the customer loans with a face value of $1,000 or more outstanding as of March 31, 2006. Each such loan that is not secured by a mortgage has been issued in conformity with Sellers' applicable margin criteria and has been secured by valid liens on and security interests in invested assets having a value sufficient to cause such loan to conform to such margin criteria. Such liens and security interests have been perfected and have first priority, and such invested assets are (i) fully transferable and (ii) held in non-physical form. Each such loan that is secured by a mortgage has been issued in conformity with the credit standards of the Business and such mortgage is a valid and perfected first priority lien on residential real property having a value equal to or in excess of the principal amount outstanding under the applicable loan.

(b) All trade accounts, notes receivable and other receivables of the Business (including margin loans and customer cash debits) represent valid obligations arising in the ordinary course of business, and are collectible net of any reserve shown in the Preliminary Net Asset Statement.

5.24 Bundled Fee Accounts. No customer of the Business is charged a single fee for services relating to both (a) one or more services of the Business and (b) other services provided by Sellers or their affiliates unrelated to the Business.

5.25 No Brokers. No broker, finder or similar intermediary (other than Goldman, Sachs & Co. and Piper Jaffray & Co.) has acted for or on behalf of, or is entitled to any broker's, finder's or similar fee or other commission from, Sellers or any of their affiliates in connection with this Agreement or the transactions contemplated hereby. Sellers will be solely responsible for, and will pay when due, any fees and expenses payable to Goldman, Sachs & Co. or Piper Jaffray & Co. in connection with the transactions contemplated by this Agreement.

5.26 **Limitation of Representations and Warranties.** Except as may be expressly represented or warranted in this Agreement, neither Seller makes any representation or warranty whatsoever with regard to any asset being transferred to Buyer or any liability or obligation being assumed by Buyer or as to any other matter or thing.

6. Covenants of the Company. The Company covenants as follows:

6.1 **Access.** Subject to Buyer's obligations under the Confidentiality Agreement between Parent and Buyer (the "**Confidentiality Agreement**"), between the date of this Agreement and the Conversion Date, Sellers, subject to applicable law related to the exchange of information, will (i) give Buyer and its officers, employees, agents, and representatives reasonable access, during normal business hours and upon reasonable notice, to the personnel, properties, and Books and Records of the Business, (ii) furnish to Buyer such regularly prepared financial and operating data and other information relating to the Business as Buyer may reasonably request and (iii) instruct the employees and representatives of Sellers to cooperate with Buyer in its preparation to integrate the Business; *provided, however,* that such access shall not unreasonably disrupt the normal operations of Sellers or the Business; and *provided, further,* that Sellers acknowledge that the integration and communication plans provided by Buyer to Sellers are reasonable and necessary in order to prepare for the orderly conversion of the customers of the business to Buyer's operating platform and agree to cooperate with Buyer in the implementation of such plans.

6.2 **Ordinary Conduct.** Except as set forth in Section 6.2 of the Disclosure Schedule or as otherwise expressly required by this Agreement, from the date hereof through the Closing Date, the Company will cause the Business to be conducted in the Ordinary Course of Business in substantially the same manner as presently conducted and will maintain proper business and accounting records, and use reasonable best efforts consistent with past practices to preserve in all material respects the business organization of the Business and relationships of the Business with its material customers and suppliers, employees, and others with whom it has a material business relationship. In addition, except as set forth in Section 6.2 of the Disclosure Schedule or as otherwise expressly required by this Agreement, Sellers will not do any of the following with respect to the Business or the

Assets without the prior written consent of Buyer (which consent shall not be unreasonably withheld):

(a) other than retention agreements not extending past the Closing Date, enter into or amend or renew (other than by its terms) any employment, consulting, severance or similar Contracts with any officer, employee or consultant of the Business, or grant any salary or wage increase or increase any benefit (including incentive or bonus payments) to any such officer, employee or consultant *except* (i) for individual increases in compensation to employees in the Ordinary Course of Business, (ii) for any changes that are required by applicable law, (iii) to satisfy contractual obligations set forth in Section 6.2 of the Disclosure Schedule, (iv) for any incentive, commission or bonus payment in respect of any period prior to the Closing Date, whether or not payable prior to the Closing Date;

(b) enter into any labor or collective bargaining agreement or, through negotiation or otherwise, make any commitment or incur any liability to any labor organization with respect to the employees;

(c) terminate the employment of any employee who is a Key Employee identified in Section 5.17(b) of the Disclosure Schedule for reasons other than such Key Employee's misconduct or unsatisfactory performance or transfer any Key Employee outside of the Business, other than transfers in the Ordinary Course of Business. Section 5.17(b) of the Disclosure Schedule shall be updated from time to time by the Buyer through the Closing Date;

(d) grant any mortgage, pledge, lien, or encumbrance on, or agree to the imposition of any restriction or charge of any kind with respect to, any of the Assets;

(e) sell, transfer, lease, mortgage, encumber or otherwise dispose of any Assets (other than the sale of short-term investment assets in the Ordinary Course of Business);

(f) acquire all or any portion of the assets, business, deposits or properties of any other entity except in the Ordinary Course of Business;

(g) terminate any Material Contracts or amend or modify in any material respect any of its existing Material Contracts or enter into any contract that would be a Material Contract;

(h) make any change in accounting methods or principles applicable to the Business, except as required by changes in GAAP;

(i) create, incur or assume any borrowed money indebtedness in respect of the Business or otherwise related to the Assets other than in the Ordinary Course of Business;

(j) make any commitment for any capital expenditure to be made following the Closing Date in excess of $15,000 in the case of any single expenditure or $50,000 in the case of all capital expenditures, in each case in respect of the Business;

(k) pay, discharge, settle, compromise or satisfy or agree to pay, discharge, settle, compromise or satisfy, any material claim relating to the Business, other than claims involving solely money damages not in excess of $50,000;

(l) materially alter or vary its methods and policies of conducting the Business;

(m) transfer any Assets to Sellers' operations or branches that are not Leased Real Estate;

(n) except as required by law, make any material change in its bookkeeping or recordkeeping policies or procedures with respect to customers;

(o) take any action that would impose any penalties or fees on any customer in connection with the transfer of the Assets to Buyer;

(p) make any loan or advance to any customer of the Business other than loans made in the Ordinary Course of Business consistent with the credit standards of the Business;

(q) purchase, assume or accept any brokered deposits;

(r) knowingly disclose to any person other than Buyer and its representatives or any Governmental Entity any information relating to customers of the Business, including account statements, other than disclosures as required by applicable law;

(s) enter into any leases for real property or purchase any real property relating to the Business; and

(t) agree or commit, whether in writing or otherwise, to do any of the foregoing.

6.3 Confidentiality. Sellers will keep confidential and cause their affiliates to keep confidential all non-public information relating to the Business that does not also relate to any of the other businesses of Sellers or any of their affiliates from and after the date hereof and following the Closing, except for (a) disclosures required by law or administrative process (including disclosures required in Tax Returns or in other governmental filings) and disclosures in the defense of any third-party claim or the contest of any Tax claim; *provided, however,* that Sellers shall have provided Buyer with reasonable notice of any required disclosure, and cooperated with Buyer in any attempt to contest such disclosure and (b) information that becomes public other than as a result of a breach of this Section 6.3. Notwithstanding the foregoing provisions of this Section 6.3, nothing in this Agreement shall restrict the ability of Sellers to retain certain information as permitted under Sections 1.1(i) and (j). Sellers shall not use any information permitted to be retained by Sellers pursuant to Section 1.1(i) and (j) for any commercial purpose or in any manner that would result in a violation of Section 6.7.

6.4 Insurance. Sellers will maintain in effect through the Closing Date all Policies relating to the Business and maintained by Sellers on the date hereof or procure comparable replacement policies and maintain such replacement policies in effect through the Closing Date. As of the Closing, Sellers' insurance coverage shall cease, and from and after the Closing Date, Buyer shall be responsible for all insurance protection for the Leased Real Estate and the activities conducted thereon.

6.5 Customer Consents.

(a) As soon as reasonably practicable after the date hereof, the Company shall:

(i) send a written notice, the form to be mutually satisfactory to Sellers and Buyer as soon as reasonably practicable after the date hereof, informing each customer of the Business of the assignment of the customer's advisory and brokerage contracts to Buyer as a result of the transactions contemplated by this Agreement (which notice shall provide the customer a reasonable period of time in which to object to the assignment of the customer's contracts to Buyer) in order to effect a bulk transfer of customer accounts pursuant to negative-consent letters in a form and substance consistent with interpretations of NASD Rule 2110 and applicable law; and

(ii) with respect to customer contracts for which negative-consent letters may not be used under applicable law, use reasonable best efforts to obtain the consents of customers of the Business to assign all such contacts to Buyer as contemplated hereunder (provided, that and any documents used in connection therewith shall be mutually satisfactory to Sellers and Buyer).

(b) The Company shall promptly notify Buyer of the Company's receipt of any communication received from a customer of the Business with respect to such consent.

(c) Notwithstanding anything contained in this Agreement to the contrary, this Agreement shall not constitute an assignment of, or an agreement to assign, any customer contract if either the applicable customer objects to the assignment or if affirmative consent from the customer is required for the assignment and such consent is not obtained.

(d) Sellers shall have no liability to Buyer with respect to the non-assignability or non-transferability of any customer contract to the extent such non-assignability or non-transferability arises solely as a result of the applicable customer objecting to assignment or failing to give an affirmative consent to assignment; *provided, however*, that nothing in this Section 6.5(d) is intended to affect the acquisition consideration adjustments set forth in Section 3.2.

6.6 Non-Solicitation. Each Seller hereby agrees that such Seller will not, and will cause its affiliates not to, for a period of three years following the Closing Date, directly or indirectly solicit, hire or attempt to solicit or hire any employee of the Business for employment or in any other capacity (including, without limitation, as an independent contractor or consultant) with such Seller or any other person; *provided, however*, that nothing in this Section 6.6 shall prohibit any Seller from publishing or posting open positions in the course of normal hiring practices which are not specifically sent to, or do not specifically target, employees of the Business.

6.7 Non-Competition.

(a) Each of the Sellers agrees and covenants that, from and after the date hereof, each such Seller and its affiliates shall not, prior to the third anniversary of the Closing Date, without the prior written consent of Buyer, directly or indirectly (i) induce, solicit or encourage or attempt to induce, solicit or encourage (or induce, solicit or encourage any other person to induce, solicit or encourage or attempt to induce, solicit or encourage) any customers, clients or other persons who have relationships with the Business to terminate or otherwise adversely modify their relationship with, or to conduct business with any competitor of, the Business or (ii) whether or not for compensation, participate in or become associated with any person or entity, whether as a principal, partner, member, employee, consultant, shareholder or in any other capacity (other than as a holder of a passive investment not in excess of 5% of the outstanding voting shares of any publicly traded company), that, directly or indirectly, competes with the Business; *provided, however*, that the foregoing shall not prevent Sellers from (w) operating the Company's existing executive services desk, on a relative scale to the Company's corporate and institutional services business no greater than such relative scale on the date hereof, which desk is limited to providing trading and related investment services for directors and executives of the corporate clients of the Company (provided such trading and investment services relationship is originated in connection with a transaction in which the Company serves as underwriter or financial advisor (or in a similar capacity) to such corporate client) or (x) operating an asset management business that creates, manages and distributes only proprietary advised funds, proprietary managed funds, proprietary alternative asset investments and other similar proprietary products; *provided, however*, that (i) the assets under management of private clients will not exceed 35% of the aggregate assets under management of such asset management business, (ii) the Company will not seek to grow such private client component of such asset management business disproportionately to the overall growth of such asset management business, (iii) the Company will not hire additional marketing staff focused on such private client component of such asset management business prior to the Conversion Date, (iv) in the course of conducting such asset management business the Company will not solicit client accounts of the Business or customers of the Business to conduct business with such asset management business, or induce, solicit or encourage any such client accounts to terminate or otherwise modify their relationship with the Business (other than accounts of the Company's directors and officers and their family members provided that the Company shall endeavor to refer such directors, officers and family members to Buyer or its affiliates for brokerage services), and (v) such asset management business will not offer trust or estate planning services, and the Company will endeavor to recommend Buyer as a preferred provider for such trust or estate planning services. In the event Sellers or such asset management business determines to enter an arrangement with a third-party to provide trust or estate planning services to such asset management business, Sellers shall provide Buyer and its affiliates a bona fide and reasonable opportunity to bid for and negotiate to provide such services. It is understood and agreed that the restrictions contained in this Section 6.7 shall not be binding upon or apply to any person or entity that acquires (through merger or otherwise) all of the business and assets of the Sellers; provided that (A) the shareholders of Parent and its affiliates immediately before such transaction and Parent and its affiliates beneficially own, immediately following such transaction, no more than 50% in the aggregate of the outstanding equity interests of each of the acquiring persons and their affiliates and any other surviving entity in connection with such transaction, (B) the shareholders of Parent and its affiliates immediately before such transaction and Parent and its affiliates, in the aggregate, do not have the right to elect or appoint more than 50% of the Board of Directors or other similar governing body of each of the acquiring persons and their affiliates and any other surviving entity in connection with such transaction, and (C) such transaction is not undertaken primarily for the purpose of avoiding the restrictions set forth in this Section 6.7.

(b) Prior to the fifth anniversary of the Closing Date, Sellers shall not conduct any business, and shall not permit any person to conduct any business, (i) under or using the brand or trade name Piper Jaffray Private Client Services or (ii) that competes with the

Business under or using any brand or trade name that includes "Piper Jaffray."

6.8 Certain Acknowledgements.

(a) Each Seller understands and acknowledges that the restrictive covenants contained in Sections 6.3, 6.6 and 6.7 formed an essential part of the consideration for Buyer to enter into this Agreement. Each Seller hereby represents and warrants that such restrictive covenants do not pose any extreme hardship on such Seller and are reasonable under the circumstances (considering such Seller's exposure to the highest level of information due to such Seller's relationship with the Business) and that such restrictive covenants are necessary to protect the legitimate business interests of Buyer and the Business and have been reasonably tailored as to time and place and are not overly broad as to the activities proscribed.

(b) The covenants contained in Sections 6.3, 6.6. and 6.7 shall survive Closing (subject, if applicable, to any time period specified therein), and each Seller acknowledges that, without prejudice to other remedies available at law, Buyer shall be entitled to equitable relief in the event of a breach or threatened breach of Sections 6.3, 6.6 and 6.7.

6.9 No Solicitation of Alternative Transactions. From and after the date of this Agreement until the earlier of the Closing or the termination of this Agreement, none of the Sellers nor any of their respective affiliates or representatives shall, directly or indirectly, initiate, solicit or encourage (including by way of furnishing non-public information or assistance), or enter into negotiations of any type, directly or indirectly, or enter into a confidentiality agreement, letter of intent or purchase agreement, merger agreement or other similar agreement or understanding (whether binding or nonbinding or oral or written) with any person, firm or corporation other than Buyer with respect to a sale of all or any portion of the Assets or the Business. Sellers will notify Buyer (on or before the business day following receipt) of the identity of, and all relevant terms of any inquiry or proposal by, a third party to do any of the foregoing which the Sellers or their respective affiliates or representatives may receive relating to any of such matters and, if such proposal is in writing, the Sellers shall deliver to Buyer a copy of such inquiry or proposal together with such written notice.

7. Representations and Warranties of Buyer. Buyer hereby represents and warrants to Sellers as follows:

7.1 Organization and Authority of Buyer. Buyer is a corporation duly organized, validly existing, and in good standing under the laws of Delaware. Buyer is duly qualified to do business and is in good standing in the jurisdictions where its ownership or leasing of property or the conduct of its business requires it to be so qualified. Buyer has all requisite corporate power and authority to enter into this Agreement and to consummate the transactions contemplated hereby. All corporate acts and proceedings required to be taken to authorize the execution, delivery, and performance by Buyer of this Agreement and the consummation by Buyer of the transactions contemplated hereby have been duly and properly taken. This Agreement has been duly executed, and delivered by Buyer and, assuming due authorization, execution and delivery of this Agreement by Sellers, constitutes a valid and binding obligation of Buyer, enforceable against Buyer in accordance with its terms, except as such enforceability may be limited by bankruptcy, insolvency, moratorium, and other similar laws affecting creditors' rights generally and by general principles of equity.

7.2 Non-Contravention. The execution, delivery, and performance by Buyer of this Agreement do not, and the consummation by Buyer of the transactions contemplated hereby will not, (a) conflict with, or result in any violation of, any provision of the charter or bylaws of Buyer, or (b) conflict with, result in any violation of, or constitute a default under, any instrument, contract, commitment, agreement, or arrangement to which Buyer is a party or by which Buyer or the property or assets of Buyer is bound, or any judgment, order, writ, injunction, or decree to which Buyer has been specifically identified as subject, or result in any violation of any statute, law, ordinance, rule, or regulation applicable to Buyer or its property or assets (except where such conflict, violation, or default would not materially impair the ability of Buyer to consummate the transactions contemplated hereby). No material consent, approval, license, permit, order, or authorization of, or registration, declaration, or filing with, any Governmental Entity is required to be obtained or made by or with respect to Buyer in connection with the execution, delivery, and performance by Buyer of this Agreement or the consummation by Buyer of the transactions contemplated hereby other than compliance with and filings under the HSR Act and compliance with the applicable rules and regulations of the NASD and NYSE.

7.3 Litigation. There are no actions, lawsuits, proceedings, or investigations pending (with respect to which Buyer has been served or otherwise notified) or, to the Knowledge of Buyer, threatened against Buyer as of the date of this Agreement that, if decided adversely to Buyer, would materially impair the ability of Buyer to consummate the transactions contemplated hereby.

7.4 Availability of Funds. At Closing, Buyer shall have available cash and/or existing committed borrowing facilities that are sufficient to enable it to consummate the transactions contemplated by this Agreement.

7.5 No Brokers. Buyer has not employed any broker or finder, or incurred any brokers or finders commissions or fees, in connection with the transactions contemplated by this Agreement, other than such brokers or finders fees that will be the sole responsibility of Buyer.

8. Covenants of Buyer. Buyer covenants as follows:

8.1 No Representations or Warranties. Buyer acknowledges that neither the Company nor any other person has made any representation or warranty, express or implied, as to the accuracy or completeness of any information regarding Sellers, the Assets, or the Business not expressly included in this Agreement or in any certificate signed by any Seller and delivered pursuant hereto, and no Seller or any other person will have or be subject to any liability to Buyer or any other person resulting from the distribution to Buyer, or Buyer's use, of any such information.

8.2 Substitution of Collateral. Following the Closing Buyer shall cooperate with Sellers and use commercially reasonable efforts to secure the unconditional release and, as appropriate, return to Sellers, of those letters of credit and collateral given to the issuer thereof, escrowed funds, guarantees, bonds, and other collateral given by or on behalf of any Seller in respect of the Business as set forth in Section 8.2 of the Disclosure Schedule; *provided, however*, that in no event shall Buyer be required to provide any replacement letter of credit, funds, guarantee, bond or other collateral in an amount in excess of the letter of credit, funds, guarantee, bond or other collateral being replaced. Nothing in this Section 8.2 shall limit or otherwise affect the assumption by Buyer of all liabilities and obligations constituting Assumed Liabilities.

8.3 HIPAA. Buyer shall enter into such confidentiality agreements with respect to all Books and Records relating to the Transferred Employees as may be reasonably required under the Health Insurance Portability and Accountability Act of 1996 and the regulations promulgated thereunder ("**HIPAA**"). Sellers may withhold from Buyer any portions of such Books and Records that contain protected health information on Transferred Employees or their dependents to the extent Sellers reasonably determine that disclosure of such information to Buyer would violate HIPAA.

8.4 No-Solicitation. From the date hereof until the Closing Date, Buyer hereby agrees that it will not, and will cause its affiliates not to, hire or attempt to solicit or hire any employee of the Business for employment or in any other capacity (including, without limitation, as an independent contractor or consultant) with Buyer or any other person expect in connection with the transaction contemplated hereby without the prior written consent of Sellers; *provided, however*, that nothing in this Section 8.4 shall prohibit Buyer from publishing or posting open positions in the course of normal hiring practices which are not specifically sent to, or do not specifically target, employees of the Business.

9. **Mutual Covenants.** Sellers and Buyer covenant as follows:
   9.1 **Cooperation; Further Assurances.**

(a) From and after the Closing Date, Buyer and Sellers shall cooperate with each other and shall cause their respective affiliates and the officers, employees, agents, and representatives of themselves and their respective affiliates to cooperate with each other and use reasonable best efforts to ensure the orderly transition of the Business and the Assets from Sellers' to Buyer's ownership and to minimize any disruption to the respective businesses of Sellers or Buyer that might result from the transactions contemplated hereby (including for purposes of effecting the integration and communications plans provided by Buyer to Sellers. Following the Conversion Date, each party shall reimburse the other for reasonable out-of-pocket costs and expenses incurred in assisting the other pursuant to this Section 9.1. Neither party shall be required by this Section 9.1 to take any action that would unreasonably interfere with the conduct of its or its affiliates' businesses; *provided, however,* that Sellers acknowledge that the integration and communication plans provided by Buyer to Sellers are reasonable and necessary to prepare for the orderly conversion of the customers of the Business to Buyer's operational platform and agree to cooperate with Buyer in the implementation of such plans. Following the date hereof, Sellers shall cooperate with Buyer and shall use reasonable best efforts to enforce any contracts that contain confidentiality, non-compete or no solicitation of employees covenants, to the extent relating to the Business. Buyer shall reimburse Sellers for reasonable expenses incurred by Sellers in connection with enforcing such contracts following the Closing Date.

(b) Without limiting the provisions of any other Section hereof, after the Closing, upon reasonable written notice, Buyer and Sellers shall, subject to applicable law related to the exchange of information, furnish or cause to be furnished to each other and each other's officers, employees, agents, and representatives access, during normal business hours, such information relating to the Business and the Assets and such other assistance as is reasonably necessary for financial reporting and accounting and other reasonably appropriate purposes; *provided, however,* that such access or assistance shall not unreasonably disrupt the normal operations of Sellers or Buyer. Without limiting the generality of the foregoing, (i) Sellers and their representatives shall have the right to reasonable access to the Books and Records maintained by Buyer at reasonable times during normal working hours upon reasonable notice to Buyer for so long after the Closing as Buyer retains such Books and Records for the purpose of examining the Books and Records as is reasonably necessary for financial reporting and accounting and other reasonably appropriate purposes and (ii) Buyer and its representatives shall have the right to reasonable access to any books and records relating to the Company retained by Sellers at reasonable times during normal working hours upon reasonable notice to Sellers for so long after the Closing as Sellers retains such books and records for the purpose of examining the books and records as is reasonably necessary for financial reporting and accounting and other reasonably appropriate purposes. Buyer shall retain the Books and Records, and Sellers shall retain the books and records related to the Business and retained by Sellers, for at least seven years after the Closing.

(c) From time to time after the Closing, as and when requested by a party hereto, the other parties shall use reasonable best efforts to (i) execute and deliver, or cause to be executed and delivered, all such documents and instruments, and take, or cause to be taken, all such further or other actions, as such requesting party may reasonably deem necessary or desirable to give full effect to this Agreement, (ii) make the required person available to testify in any proceedings and do all other acts that may be necessary or desirable in the reasonable opinion of the other party to protect or effectuate any rights arising from this Agreement or to aid in the prosecution or defense of any rights arising from this Agreement or the operation of the Business or the ownership of the Assets by Sellers prior to the Closing, and (iii) make the required person available to testify, provide information and otherwise assist with any review, investigation, or other types of inquiry or proceeding by the SEC, NASD, NYSE, any state securities regulatory authority or any other Governmental Entity, all without further consideration other than reimbursement by the requesting party to the requested party of reasonable out-of-pocket expenses.

9.2 Publicity. Effective from the date of this Agreement, no public release or announcement concerning this Agreement or the transactions contemplated hereby shall be issued by either Sellers, on the one hand, or Buyer, on the other hand, on or prior to the Closing Date without the prior written consent of the other party (which consent shall not be unreasonably withheld). The parties will consult with each other as to the form and substance of any such public disclosures and seek to agree regarding the form and substance of such disclosures. Notwithstanding the foregoing, nothing contained herein will prohibit either party from making a public release or announcement as may be required by law or the rules or regulations of any United States or foreign securities exchange, in which case the party required to make the release or announcement shall, if practicable under the circumstances, allow the other party reasonable time to comment on such release or announcement in advance of such issuance.

9.3 Reasonable Efforts. Subject to the terms and conditions of this Agreement, each party will use its reasonable best efforts in good faith to take, or cause to be taken, all actions, and to do, or cause to be done, all things necessary, proper or desirable, or advisable under applicable law (i) to satisfy as promptly as practicable all conditions to Closing set forth in this Agreement that are within such party's control and (ii) to arrange for the orderly conversion of the operational and accounting systems of the Business to Buyer's operational platform, including the conversion of financial advisors and client accounts to Buyer's operating platform as promptly as practicable (taking into consideration the integration and communications plans provided by Buyer to Sellers) after the Closing Date, in each case so as to permit the consummation of the transactions contemplated hereby as promptly as practicable, and each party shall cooperate fully with each other to that end (including, without limitation, as contemplated by the integration and communication plans attached as Schedule 6.1). Each party shall pay their own costs and expenses associated with such preparation for Closing and conversion (including, without limitation, any costs and expenses incurred by Sellers in complying with such cooperation and integration plans and otherwise preparing for conversion, except as contemplated by the transition services agreement to be entered into by the parties pursuant to Section 9.9). Each of Sellers and Buyer will use its reasonable best efforts to obtain consents of all third parties necessary to the consummation of the transactions contemplated by this Agreement. Without limiting the generality of the foregoing, as promptly as practical following the date hereof, Seller shall seek any landlord consents required to transfer the Real Estate Leases.

9.4 Regulatory Applications.

(a) Buyer and Sellers shall each use their respective reasonable best efforts to prepare all documentation, to effect all filings and to obtain all permits, consents, approvals and authorizations of all third parties and Governmental Entities necessary to consummate the transactions contemplated by this Agreement. Buyer and Sellers agree that they will consult with each other, subject to applicable law, with respect to the obtaining of all material permits, consents, approvals and authorizations of all third parties and Governmental Entities necessary or reasonably advisable to consummate the transactions contemplated by this Agreement and each will keep the other party apprised of the status of material matters relating to completion of the transactions contemplated hereby.

(b) Without limiting the generality of the foregoing, each of Parent and Buyer (or its ultimate parent) will as promptly as practicable, but in no event later than ten days following the execution and delivery of this Agreement, file with the United States Federal Trade Commission (the "FTC") and the United States Department of Justice (the "DOJ") the notification and report form required for the transactions contemplated hereby and any supplemental information required in connection therewith pursuant to the HSR Act. Each party hereto represents and warrants that such notification and report form and all such supplemental information submitted by such party or its ultimate parent, and any additional supplemental information filed by such party or its ultimate parent after the date of the original filing, will be in substantial compliance with the requirements of the HSR Act. Buyer and Sellers shall each furnish to the other such necessary information and reasonable assistance as the other may request in connection with its preparation of any filing or submission that is necessary under the HSR Act. Sellers and Buyer shall keep each other apprised of the status of any communications with, and inquiries or requests for additional information from, the FTC or the DOJ, and shall use their reasonable best efforts to comply promptly with any such inquiry or request. Sellers and Buyer will each use its reasonable best efforts to cause the expiration or early termination of the waiting period required under the HSR Act as a condition to the purchase and sale of the Assets and shall use reasonable best efforts to defend against any action of the FTC or the DOJ to enjoin the sale of the Assets to Buyer.

(c) Nothing in this Agreement shall obligate Buyer or any of its affiliates to agree (i) to limit in any manner whatsoever, or not to exercise, any rights of ownership of any securities, or to divest, dispose of or hold separate any securities or all or a portion of their respective businesses, assets or properties or of the Business or (ii) to limit in any manner whatsoever the ability of such entities (A) to conduct their respective businesses or own such assets or properties or to conduct the Business or own the Assets or (B) to control their respective businesses or operations or the Business. In addition, without the prior written consent of Buyer, to be delivered in its sole and absolute discretion, neither Seller nor any of their respective affiliates shall take any action required or requested in connection with obtaining any clearance from any Governmental Entity relating to the transactions contemplated by this Agreement or to take any other action that would adversely affect the Business or any of the benefits expected to be derived by Buyer and its affiliates from the transactions contemplated by this Agreement.

9.5 Intercompany Accounts. All intercompany accounts between Sellers and their affiliates relating to the Business or the Assets shall be, at Sellers' election, either (a) paid in full on or prior to the Closing Date, (b) paid in full promptly, but in any event within 30 days, after the Closing Date, or (c) canceled without payment (provided, that any such cancellation shall be effected prior to Closing).

9.6 Notification of Certain Matters. Each party will give prompt notice to the other party of (a) the occurrence, or failure to occur, of any event or existence of any condition that has caused or could reasonably be expected to cause any of its representations or warranties contained in this Agreement to be untrue or inaccurate in any material respect at any time after the date of this Agreement, up to and including the Closing Date, (b) any failure on its part to comply with or satisfy, in any material respect, any covenant, condition or agreement to be complied with or satisfied by it under this Agreement, and (c) any material written notice or other material communication from any third party alleging that the consent of such third party is or may be required in connection with the transactions contemplated by this Agreement. But no such disclosure will be deemed to prevent or cure any such breach of or inaccuracy in, amend or supplement any Disclosure Schedule to, or otherwise disclose any exception to, any of the representations and warranties set forth in this Agreement.

9.7 Rejection of Certain Customer Relationships.

(a) Buyer shall have the right to elect not to assume any customer relationship and not take ownership of that Assets and liabilities with respect to such customer relationship for any of the following reasons:

(i) such customer's actual, alleged or apparent involvement in illegal activities (including violations of laws regulating insider trading, violations of Tax laws and fraudulent or deceptive activities or practices) or the existence of facts which form the basis for a reasonable belief that a transaction of the customer (A) involves funds derived from illegal activities or is intended to hide or disguise funds or assets derived from illegal activities, (B) is designed to evade any requirements of the Bank Secrecy Act or its implementing regulations or (C) has no apparent lawful purpose;

(ii) such customer being (i) deemed to be "politically sensitive", "high profile" or a "politically exposed person" in conformity with Buyer's applicable policies and procedures or (ii) a senior foreign political figure, or any of such political figure's immediate family members or close associates, as defined for purposes of Section 312 of the IMLAFA or for purposes of the USA Patriot Act.

(b) In the event that Buyer so elects not to assume any such customer relationships and the related Assets and liabilities, Buyer shall provide to Sellers, not less than five business days prior to the scheduled Closing Date, a statement containing a list of each of the customer relationships that are being rejected. Buyer and Sellers shall cooperate with respect to the termination of such accounts. For the avoidance of doubt, the rejection of certain customer relationships by Buyer in accordance with this Section 9.7 is not intended to have any affect on the acquisition consideration adjustment set forth in Section 3.2.

9.8 Distribution Arrangements. Sellers and Buyer agree to discuss the potential for entering into a distribution arrangement for certain of Sellers' underwritten equity and fixed income products; *provided, however,* that this Section 9.8 shall create no obligation on behalf of Sellers or Buyer to enter into any such arrangement.

9.9 Transition Services Agreement. Sellers and Buyer shall enter into a transition services agreement mutually satisfactory to the parties with respect to the operation of the Business between Closing and the conversion of the operational and accounting systems of the Business to Buyer's operational platform. The key terms of such transition services agreement are set forth on Exhibit A. Beneficial ownership of the Assets specified in Section 1.1(m) shall transfer to Buyer at Closing and shall be managed by Sellers on behalf of Buyer pursuant to such transition services agreement.

9.10 Performance by Parties. From the date of this Agreement to the Closing Date, neither Buyer nor Seller will not take any action that could reasonably be expected to cause any of their respective representations and warranties to be or become untrue in any material respect or cause any of the conditions to closing under this Agreement not be satisfied.

9.10 Limited License. To the extent that, as of the Closing Date, the Assets consist of supplies, packaging, or other materials or signage that incorporate or display any trademark or trade name that is an Excluded Asset, Sellers hereby grants to Buyer, effective as of the Closing Date, a non-exclusive, non-transferable, non-sublicensable license, until the earlier to occur of (i) the depletion of such supplies or (ii) December 31, 2006, to use such trademarks or trade names on such supplies or signage in the manner as such trademarks were used prior to the Closing Date. Buyer agrees not to alter, modify, edit or change such trademarks or trade names in any manner without the prior written consent of Sellers. All goodwill arising from the foregoing use of such trademarks shall inure solely to Seller.

9.11 Shared Properties. Sellers and Buyer shall use their reasonable best efforts to enter into a mutually satisfactory sublease or space sharing arrangements with respect to the any office space that hosts both operations of the Business and operations of business of the Sellers other than the Business.

10. Employees and Employee Benefits.
10.1 Offers of Employment.

(a) Buyer will offer employment effective immediately after the Closing to all Employees who are actively employed as of the Closing Date. The offered employment shall in each case be at a minimum guaranteed base wage, salary or draw equal or greater to such Employee's minimum guaranteed base wage, salary or draw in effect with Sellers at Closing, shall provide each Employee with the opportunity to earn commissions for which similarly situated employees of Buyer are eligible, and shall provide each Employee the Replacement Equity Awards set forth on Schedule 10.1(a) of the Disclosure Schedule. The Replacement Equity Award will be conditioned on the Employee releasing Buyer, Sellers and their respective representatives from all liabilities and obligations, and waiving all claims, rights and causes of action that the Employee had, has or may have in connection with his or her equity award. Other terms and conditions of employment offered by Buyer to Employees shall be no less favorable in the aggregate to the terms and conditions provided to similarly situated employees of Buyer. The Employees who accept such offers and become employees of Buyer are referred to in this Agreement as "**Transferred Employees.**" For purposes of clarification and notwithstanding anything in this Agreement to the contrary, Buyer shall not be obligated to provide Transferred Employees with any commission grid override to which such Transferred Employees may be entitled immediately prior to the Closing Date. Nothing in this Section 10.1 shall obligate Buyer to continue the employment or any terms of employment of any such Transferred Employee for any specific period following the Closing Date.

(b) Buyer shall be responsible for any liability under, or requirement of notice pursuant to, the WARN Act which arises out of or results from any termination of employment of Transferred Employees by Buyer or any of its affiliates after the Closing. Sellers shall promptly notify Buyer of any termination of any employee of either Seller or of any affiliate of either Seller that could be reasonably likely to affect Buyer's obligation to provide the notice referred to in the preceding sentence and that occurs prior to the Closing, and Sellers acknowledge that Buyer is relying on and will rely on this covenant for purposes of assessing its obligation to provide such notice. Sellers shall be responsible for any liability under or requirement of notice pursuant to the WARN Act which arises out of or results from any termination of employment of (i) any Employees prior to the Closing and (ii) any Employees who do not become Transferred Employees in connection with the transactions contemplated hereby.

10.2 Buyer's Employee Benefit Plans Generally. As of the Closing, Buyer shall provide Transferred Employees with employee benefits that are no less favorable in the aggregate to the benefits provided to similarly situated employees of Buyer ("**Buyer's Plans**"). After the Closing, the following shall apply:

(a) Except as otherwise provided in the following subsections of this Section 10, (i) Sellers shall be responsible for providing welfare benefits (including, without limitation, medical, hospital, dental, accidental death and dismemberment, life, disability and other similar benefits) to Transferred Employees for claims incurred and benefits earned at or prior to 12:01 a.m. on the Closing Date and (ii) Buyer shall be responsible for providing such benefits with respect to all claims incurred and benefits earned after 12:01 a.m. on the Closing Date to the Transferred Employees, provided that Buyer provides such benefits under Buyer's Plans to the applicable Transferred Employee and Buyer's Plans provide benefits to other similarly situated employees of Buyer under similar circumstances following the Closing. For purposes of this Section 10.2(a), any claim that relates to a continuous period of hospitalization shall be deemed to have been incurred at the commencement of such period of hospitalization and all other claims shall be deemed to be incurred on the date that services are rendered.

(b) Buyer shall give each Transferred Employee credit for purposes of eligibility, vesting and benefit accrual (other than accrual of benefits under Buyer's DC Plan (as defined in Section 10.8)) under Buyer's Plans or personnel policies that cover the Transferred Employee , including Buyer's vacation, sick leave, and severance policies, for the Transferred Employee's service with the Company and its affiliates prior to the Closing, shall allow such Transferred Employees to participate in each such Buyer's Plan without regard to preexisting-condition limitations, waiting periods, evidence of insurability, or other exclusions or limitations not imposed on the Transferred Employee by the corresponding Sellers' Plans immediately prior to the Closing Date, and shall credit the Transferred Employee with any expenses that were covered by Sellers' Plans for purposes of determining deductibles, co-pays, and other applicable limits under Buyer's Plans.

10.3 Severance Benefits. In the event Buyer does not offer employment to any Employee on the terms specified in Section 10.1(a) (other than as a result of an Employee's failure to pass Buyer's standard drug testing and criminal and credit background check policies), Buyer will be responsible for any severance benefits under Sellers' Severance Practices (as defined below) to which such Employee may become entitled as a result of Sellers' termination of such Employee's employment within ten business days following the Closing Date or, in the case of Employees retained by Sellers to assist with the Conversion, within ten business days following the Conversion Date; provided that, with respect to such Employees retained by Sellers to assist with the Conversion, Buyer's obligation to provide severance benefits shall be limited to those benefits to which such Employee would have been entitled had he or she been terminated by Sellers on the Closing Date. Following the Closing, Transferred Employees will be eligible for severance benefits under Buyer's Plans to the extent and in the circumstances that similarly situated employees of Buyer are so eligible. Notwithstanding the foregoing, if any Transferred Employee who is not classified as a financial advisor or commissioned employee is involuntarily terminated by Buyer within 12 months following the Closing Date under circumstances that would have qualified the Transferred Employee for severance benefits under any of Sellers' severance plans or practices listed in Section 5.13 of the Disclosure Schedule other than the Sellers' Supplemental Severance Plan ("**Sellers' Severance Practices**") if the Transferred Employee had been terminated involuntarily by Seller before the Closing Date, Buyer will provide to the Transferred Employee under Buyer's Plans benefits that are at least equal to the severance pay and other benefits provided under the applicable Sellers' Severance Practices.

10.4 Commissions. For purposes of determining commissions earned by any Transferred Employee, Buyer shall credit to such Transferred Employee historical production levels equal to the "trailing six months" production level such Transferred Employee was assigned by Sellers as of the Closing Date.

10.5 Disability Benefits and Leaves. Sellers' Plans shall retain the liability for all long-term and short-term disability benefits payable to any Employee under the terms of Sellers' long-term and/or short-term disability plans after the Closing with respect to any disability that occurred prior to the Closing (but not with respect to any reoccurrence of such a disability after the Closing). Buyer's Plans will govern the determination of what, if any, short-term and long-term disability benefits will be paid to any Transferred Employee whose disability occurs after the Closing (or that reoccurs after the Closing).

10.6 COBRA Coverage. Buyer will satisfy (or cause a Buyer's Plan to satisfy) all entitlements under Code Section 4980B, Part 6 of Title I of ERISA, or any similar state law (collectively, "**COBRA**"), with respect to any Transferred Employee or any dependent or former dependent of any Transferred Employee, whose qualifying event occurs following the Closing and Buyer shall have no other COBRA obligation or liability whatsoever with respect to any Employee.

10.7 Flexible Spending Accounts. Buyer will credit each Transferred Employee (and any "qualified beneficiary" of a Transferred Employee within the meaning of Section 4980B(g) of the Code who has COBRA rights described in Section 10.7 with respect to flexible spending accounts) under a health care and dependent care flexible spending account plan or plans maintained by Buyer ("**Buyer's Flex Plans**") with a balance (positive or negative) as of the Closing equal to the balance credited to the individual under the applicable health care and dependent care flexible spending account plans of Sellers listed in Section 5.13 of the Disclosure Schedule ("**Sellers' Flex Plans**") as of the Closing, and will reimburse each such individual under terms and conditions no less favorable than those that applied under the applicable Sellers' Flex Plan on the Closing Date for expenses incurred during the current plan year of such Sellers' Flex Plan (whether incurred before or after the Closing) that had not been reimbursed under such Sellers' Flex Plan prior to the Closing. Buyer and Sellers will treat the arrangement described in this Section 10.9 as a spin-off of the applicable portions of Sellers' Flex Plans and a merger of such portions into Buyer's Flex Plans.

10.8 Qualified Retirement and 401(k) Plans. Buyer will have no liability for benefits payable under the Parent Retirement Plan, the Parent Non-Qualified Retirement Plan, or the Parent Deferred Compensation Plan (1995 Restatement) (collectively, "**Sellers' Retirement Plans**"). Buyer either currently maintains, or will establish not later than 30 days after the Closing Date, one or more qualified defined contribution plans ("**Buyer's DC Plan**") that will contain all provisions necessary for the acceptance of direct rollovers of "eligible rollover distributions" as defined in the Code and applicable regulations that Transferred Employees are eligible to receive from Sellers' Retirement Plans without adversely affecting the qualified status of any Sellers' Retirement Plan. Buyer's DC Plan will contain provisions to permit any such direct rollover to include the promissory notes representing any Plan loans outstanding to the Transferred Employee under the Parent Retirement Plan on the date of the direct rollover, and Buyer will cooperate with Sellers to enable such direct rollovers to occur before such loans become defaulted.

10.9 Other Retained Sellers' Plans. Sellers will retain all liabilities and obligations with respect to compensation or benefits of any kind payable to or with respect to any Employee, including Transferred Employees, under Sellers' Plans except as specifically provided in Section 2.1(d), 2.1(e) (but only in respect of workers compensation claims) and 10. Notwithstanding anything to the contrary herein, Sellers shall (a) treat every Transferred Employee who is eligible as of the Closing Date for post-employment medical benefits or who would become eligible for such post-employment medical benefits within six months following the Closing Date, as if such Transferred Employee had retired from employment with Sellers as of the date on which his or her employment with Buyer terminates and shall provide each such Transferred Employee with all such post-employment medical benefits at the time and in the form provided under the applicable Sellers' Plans (to the extent Sellers continue to provide benefits under any post-employment medical plan to any employees or former employees of Sellers) and (b) with respect to the outstanding equity awards or cash awards held by Transferred Employees as of the Closing Date, treat every Transferred Employee who is eligible as of the Closing Date for "retirement" status under Sellers' equity and cash incentive plans as if such Transferred Employee had retired from employment with Sellers as of the Closing Date; *provided* that, Transferred Employees who are or become eligible for post-employment medical benefits in accordance with clause (a) of this sentence shall have the same rights with respect to the amendment and termination of Sellers' Plans providing such benefits as do similarly situated employees of Sellers; *provided* further that no interest will accrue upon post-employment medical benefit accounts of any Transferred Employee during the period between the Closing Date and the date, if any, on which such Transferred Employee elects to receive retiree medical benefits and interest will accrue thereafter, if at all, in accordance with the terms of the relevant plans. In connection with Transferred Employees' eligibility for post-employment medical benefits under Sellers' Plans, Buyer will use its reasonable best efforts to notify Sellers of the termination of any Transferred Employee's employment with Buyer.

10.10 No Third-Party Beneficiaries. Without limiting the generality of Section 14, this Section 10 shall not confer any rights or remedies upon any employee or former employee of any Seller or Buyer or any other person other than the parties and their respective successors and assigns. Nothing in this Agreement, including this Section 10, shall be deemed to constitute Sellers' "consent" for purposes of any Sellers' Plan or any other agreement or arrangement between either Seller or any of Sellers' affiliates and any Employee (including without limitation in connection with any vesting conditions contained in any restricted stock agreement or stock option agreement), to any Employee providing services to Buyer.

10.11 Retention Program.

(a) Buyer will provide Transferred Employees, as applicable, with the retention awards set forth on Section 10.11(a) of the Disclosure Schedule, subject to any terms or conditions of such retention awards as determined by Buyer in its sole discretion.

(b) Sellers will put in place a retention program, consistent with Section 10.11(b) of the Disclosure Schedule, with respect to the retention of certain employees of the Business from the date hereof through the Conversion Date for the purpose of facilitating the Closing and the conversion.

11. Indemnification.

11.1 Indemnification by Sellers.

(a) Subject to the limitations set forth in Section 11.1(b), following the Closing, Sellers, jointly and severally, shall indemnify Buyer and its employees, officers, directors, representatives and affiliates (each, a "**Buyer Indemnified Person**") against any loss, liability, claim, damage, or out-of-pocket expense (including reasonable legal fees and expenses) (collectively, "**Damages**") suffered or incurred by the Buyer Indemnified Persons as a result of, arising out of or relating to:

(i) to the extent not indemnified pursuant to Section 11.1(a)(iv) or (v) below, breach of any representation or warranty made by Sellers contained in this Agreement, the Disclosure Schedule, or the certificate delivered pursuant to Section 4.2(f); or

(ii) breach of any covenant of Sellers contained in this Agreement; or

(iii) any liability for Taxes arising out of or in connection with or related to any of the Assets or the Business other than the Assumed Liabilities as described in Section 2.1; or

(iv) to the extent not an Excluded Liability, (A) the matters set forth in Sections 5.11 (Litigation; Decrees), 5.15 (Compliance with Laws) and 5.18 (Regulatory Matters) of the Disclosure Schedule or (B) any breach of Section 5.11 (Litigation; Decrees); or

(v) Excluded Liabilities.

(b) Sellers will have no obligation to indemnify the Buyer Indemnified Persons (i) pursuant to Section 11.1(a)(i) in respect of Damages arising from the breach of, or inaccuracy in, any representation or warranty described therein unless the aggregate amount of all such Damages incurred or suffered by the Buyer Indemnified Persons exceeds $4 million (at which point Sellers will indemnify the Buyer Indemnified Persons for all such Damages in excess of $4 million) or (ii) pursuant to Section 11.1(a)(iv) unless the aggregate amount of all such Damages incurred or suffered by the Buyer Indemnified Persons exceeds $6 million (at which point the Sellers will indemnify the Buyer Indemnified Persons for all such Damages in excess of $6 million); *provided, however*, that Sellers' aggregate liability in respect of claims for indemnification pursuant to Section 11.1(a)(i) and 11.1(a)(iv) will not exceed 40% of the Base Acquisition Consideration; *provided, further*, that the foregoing limitations will not apply to (i) claims for indemnification pursuant to Section 11.1(a)(i) in respect of breaches of, or inaccuracies in, representations and warranties set forth in Section 5.1 (Organization and Authority), Section 5.2 (Non-Contravention), Section 5.4 (Nonforeign Certification), Section 5.6 (Assets) and Section 5.25 (No Brokers) or (ii) claims based upon fraud or intentional misrepresentation. Claims for indemnification pursuant to any other provision of Section 11.1(a) are not subject to the monetary limitations set forth in this Section 11.1(b).

(c) For purposes of this Section 11, the representations and warranties of Sellers shall be read without giving effect to any qualification or limitation as to materiality or "Material Adverse Effect."

(d) For the purposes of this Section 11.1, in computing such individual or aggregate amounts of claims, the amount of each claim shall be deemed to be an amount net of any insurance proceeds and any indemnity, contribution or other similar payment actually recovered and received by or for the benefit of the Buyer Indemnified Person from any third party with respect thereto. Notwithstanding the preceding sentence, to the extent the Buyer Indemnified Person (or any of its affiliates) actually recovers federal or state income taxes (whether in the form of a reduction in Taxes payable, or by the receipt of a refund of Taxes) (collectively, "Tax Recovery") as a result of a claim arising under this Section 11.1, the Buyer Indemnified Person shall, promptly following such Tax Recovery, refund the amount of such Tax Recovery to Sellers.

(e) Following the Closing, in the absence of fraud, Buyer's sole and exclusive remedy with respect to any claims relating to the subject matter of this Agreement or the transactions contemplated hereby (including claims for breaches of representations, warranties, covenants, and agreements contained in this Agreement) shall be pursuant to the indemnification provisions set forth in this Section 11.1.

11.2 Indemnification by Buyer.

(a) Subject to the limitations set forth in Section 11.2(b), following the Closing, Buyer shall indemnify Sellers and their respective employees, officers, directors, representatives and affiliates (each, a "**Seller Indemnified Person**") against any Damages suffered or incurred by the Seller Indemnified Persons as a result of, arising out of or relating to:

    (i) breach of any representation or warranty of Buyer contained in this Agreement or the certificate delivered pursuant to Section 4.3(c);

    (ii) material breach of any covenant of Buyer contained in this Agreement; or

    (iii) Assumed Liability.

(b) Buyer will have no obligation to indemnify the Seller Indemnified Persons pursuant to Section 11.2(a)(i) in respect of Damages arising from the breach of, or inaccuracy in, any representation or warranty described therein unless and until the aggregate amount of all such Damages incurred or suffered by the Seller Indemnified Persons exceeds $4 million (at which point Buyer will indemnify the Seller Indemnified Persons for all such Damages from the first dollar), and the Buyer's aggregate liability in respect of claims for indemnification pursuant to Section 11.2(a)(i) will not exceed 40% of the Base Acquisition Consideration; *provided*, *however*, that the foregoing limitations will not apply to (i) claims for indemnification pursuant to Section 11.2(a)(i) in respect of breaches of, or inaccuracies in, representations and warranties set forth in Section 7.1 (Organization and Authority) or Section 7.5 (No Brokers) or (ii) claims based upon fraud or intentional misrepresentation. Claims for indemnification pursuant to any other provision of Section 11.2 are not subject to the monetary limitations set forth in this Section 11.2(b).

(c) For the purposes of this Section 11.2, in computing such individual or aggregate amounts of claims, the amount of each claim shall be deemed to be an amount net of any insurance proceeds and any indemnity, contribution or other similar payment actually recovered by or for the benefit of the Seller Indemnified Person from any third party with respect thereto. Notwithstanding the preceding sentence, to the extent the Seller Indemnified Person (or any of its affiliates) actually receives a Tax Recovery as a result of a claim arising under this Section 11.2, the Seller Indemnified Person shall, promptly following such Tax Recovery, refund the amount of such Tax Recovery to Buyer.

(d) Buyer will not be liable under Section 11.2(a) with respect to any Damages to the extent arising from Sellers' failure to take, or cause to be taken, such action as Sellers in the prudent management of the Business would customarily pursue to protect its interests and the interests of Buyer and its affiliates or otherwise to mitigate the amount of such Damages.

11.3 Time for Claims.

(a) No claim may be made or suit instituted seeking indemnification pursuant to Section 11.1(a)(i) or Section 11.2(a)(i) for any breach of, or inaccuracy in, any representation or warranty unless a written notice pursuant to Section 11.4 is provided to the Indemnitor (as defined below):

(i) at any time, in the case of any breach of, or inaccuracy in, the representations and warranties set forth in Section 5.1 (Organization and Authority), Section 5.6 (Assets), Section 5.25 (No Brokers), Section 7.1 (Organization and Authority) or Section 7.5 (No Brokers);

(ii) at any time prior to the sixth anniversary of the Closing Date, in the case of a breach of, or inaccuracy in, the representations and warranties set forth in Section 5.16 (Environmental Matters);

(iii) at any time prior to the 60th day following the expiration of the applicable statute of limitations, in the case of a breach of, or inaccuracy in, the representations and warranties set forth in Section 5.5 (Taxes) and Section 5.13 (Employee Benefits; ERISA); or

(iv) at any time prior to the second anniversary of the Closing Date, in the case of any breach of, or inaccuracy in, any other representation and warranty in this Agreement.

(b) Claims for indemnification pursuant to any other provision of Section 11.1 and Section 11.2 are not subject to the limitations set forth in this Section 11.3.

11.4 Procedures Relating to Indemnification. All claims for indemnification by a party entitled to be indemnified under this Section 11 (an "**Indemnitee**") by another party (an "**Indemnitor**") shall be asserted and resolved as follows:

(a) If any claim or demand for which the Indemnitee may claim indemnity pursuant to Section 11.1 or Section 11.2, as the case may be, (other than claims for indemnity pursuant to Section 11.1(a)(iv) is asserted against or sought to be collected from the Indemnitee by a third party (a "**Third-Party Claim**"), then the Indemnitee shall give written notice to the Indemnitor as promptly as practicable following the receipt by the Indemnitee of the Third-Party Claim, but in no event later than 10 days after the service of summons or complaint, which notice must specify the nature of the Third-Party Claim and the amount or the estimated amount thereof to the extent then feasible (which estimate shall not be conclusive of the final amount of the Third-Party Claim) (the "**Third-Party Claim**

Notice"); *provided, however,* that the failure so to notify the Indemnitor will not relieve the Indemnitor from any liability it may have to the Indemnitee under this Section 11 except to the extent the failure so to notify results in the loss of rights or defenses.

(b) The Indemnitor shall have 30 days from the date on which the Third-Party Claim Notice is duly given (the "**Notice Period**") to notify the Indemnitee whether or not the Indemnitor desires, at its sole cost and expense, to defend the Indemnitee against the Third-Party Claim with counsel of its choice reasonably satisfactory to the Indemnitee.

(c) If the Indemnitor notifies the Indemnitee within the Notice Period that it desires to defend the Indemnitee against the Third-Party Claim, then (except as provided below) the Indemnitor shall defend, at its sole cost and expense, the Indemnitee by appropriate proceedings, shall use reasonable best efforts to settle or prosecute the proceedings to a final conclusion in such a manner as to avoid the Indemnitee becoming subject to any injunctive or other equitable order for relief, and shall control the conduct of such defense. The Indemnitor shall not be entitled to assume the defense of any Third-Party Claim if the Third-Party Claim seeks any relief other than money damages, including any type of injunctive or other equitable relief; *provided, however,* that if all claims for injunctive or other equitable relief in the Third-Party Claim are dismissed or otherwise disposed of with prejudice, then the Indemnitee shall so notify the Indemnitor, and the Indemnitor may assume the defense of the remainder of the Third-Party Claim. If the defendants named in any Third-Party Claim include both the Indemnitor and the Indemnitee, and the Indemnitee shall have reasonably concluded that there are legal defenses or rights available to the Indemnitee that are in conflict with those available to the Indemnitor, then the Indemnitee shall have the right to select one law firm to act at the Indemnitor's expense as separate counsel, on behalf of the Indemnitee. If the Indemnitee desires to participate in, but not control, any other defense or settlement, it may do so at its sole cost and expense and the Indemnitor shall cooperate with the Indemnitee in connection therewith. So long as the Indemnitor is defending in good faith any such Third-Party Claim, the Indemnitee shall not settle such Third-Party Claim without the consent of the Indemnitor, which consent shall not be unreasonably withheld or delayed. Notwithstanding the foregoing, to the extent Buyer itself defends any claim pursuant to Section 11.1(a)(iv), Buyer may not consent to the entry of any judgment or enter into any compromise or settlement with respect any such claim without the prior written consent of Sellers (which consent may not be unreasonably with-held or delayed).

(d) The Indemnitor will not consent to the entry of any judgment or enter into any compromise or settlement with respect to any Third-Party Claim without the prior written consent of the Indemnitee unless such judgment, compromise or settlement (i) provides for the payment by the Indemnitor of money as sole relief for the claimant, (ii) results in the full and general release of the Buyer Indemnified Persons or Seller Indemnified Persons, as applicable, from all liabilities arising or relating to, or in connection with, the Third-Party Claim and (iii) involves no finding or admission of any violation of applicable law or the rights of any person or entity and no effect on any other claims that may be made against the Indemnitee.

(e) If it is determined that a Third-Party Claim encompasses mat-ters for which the Indemnitee is entitled to indemnification from the Indemnitor as well as matters for which the Indemnitee is directly li-able to the third-party claimant and not entitled to indemnification from the Indemnitor, then the Indemnitor shall be responsible for those Damages for which the Indemnitee is entitled to indemnifica-tion hereunder and the Indemnitee shall be responsible for those Damages for which it is not entitled to indemnification hereunder.

(f) To the extent Buyer itself defends a Third-Party Claim, Buyer shall defend such claim in a reasonably prudent manner and in good faith.

11.5 Survival of Representation and Warranties. The representa-tions and warranties (i) contained in Section 5.1 (Organization and Authority), Section 5.6 (Assets), Section 5.25 (No Broker), Section 7.1 (Organization and Authority) and Section 7.5 (No Broker) shall survive the Closing indefinitely, (ii) contained in Section 5.16 (Environmental Matters) shall survive the Closing until the sixth anniversary thereof, (iii) contained in Section 5.5 (Taxes) and Section 5.13 (Employee Benefits; ERISA) shall survive the Closing until the 60th day following the expiration of the applicable statute of limitations and (iii) con-tained elsewhere in this Agreement shall survive the Closing until the second anniversary thereof; *provided, however*, that if any party hereto shall have made a claim for indemnification under Section 11.1(a)(i) or Section 11.2(a)(i) (as applicable) prior to such date with respect to the breach of a representation or warranty, then (notwithstanding the expiration of such period) the representation or warranty applicable to such claim shall survive until, but only for purposes of, the final resolution of such claim. Covenants contained herein shall survive until such time as they are performed or satisfied.

11.6 Certain Tax Matters. Sellers, on the one hand, and Buyer, on the other hand, agree that, for Tax purposes, all payments made by

Sellers, on the one hand, or Buyer, on the other, to or for the benefit of the other under any indemnity provision of this Agreement and for any misrepresentations or breaches of warranties or covenants, shall be treated as adjustments to the Acquisition Consideration and that such treatment shall govern for all purposes hereof except to the extent that the laws of a particular jurisdiction provide otherwise.

12. Tax Matters.

12.1 Cooperation. Buyer and Sellers shall, and shall cause their respective subsidiaries and other affiliates to, cooperate with respect to Tax matters. Buyer and Sellers shall provide one another with such information as is reasonably requested in order to enable the requesting party to complete and file all Tax Returns that they may be required to file with respect to the Business or the Assets or to respond to audits, inquiries or other proceedings by any Taxing Authority and otherwise to satisfy Tax requirements. Such cooperation shall further include (a) promptly forwarding copies of appropriate notices, forms, or other communications received from or sent to any Taxing Authority, and (b) promptly providing reasonably requested copies of all relevant Tax Returns together with accompanying schedules and related workpapers, documents relating to rulings, audits, or other determinations by any Taxing Authority and records concerning the ownership and tax basis of property, in each case only to the extent such materials relate to the Business or the Assets.

12.2 Filing Responsibility. Sellers shall prepare and timely file all Tax Returns (a) with respect to Taxes attributable to the Assets or the Business that are required to be filed (taking into account extensions therefor) on or prior to the Closing Date (taking into account an extension therefore). Buyer shall timely file or cause to be timely filed all Tax Returns (taking into account extensions therefor) attributable to the Assets or the Business after the Closing Date. Buyer and Sellers shall discharge all Tax liabilities shown on Tax Returns based on the assumption and allocation of Tax liabilities provided in this Agreement without regard to the party that has prepared the Tax Return, and the party responsible for payment of any amount of Taxes shown due on a Return shall pay such unpaid amount to the party filing the Tax Return no later than one business day prior to the filing of such Tax Return.

12.3 FIRPTA Certification. Each Seller agrees to provide to Buyer a certificate that, as of the Closing Date, such Seller is not a "foreign person" within the meaning of section 1445 of the Code and the Treasury Regulations thereunder, such certificate to be substantially in the form attached as Schedule 12.3 hereto. If each Seller does not deliver such certificate to Buyer, Buyer shall be entitled to withhold 10% of the Acquisition Consideration as required by section 1445 of the Code.

12.4 Other Tax Matters. Notwithstanding anything in this Agreement to the contrary, Sellers shall (i) maintain, solicit and collect from their clients any forms, certifications and other information required in connection with federal, state, local or foreign tax withholding, backup withholding or reporting requirements applicable to the Assets or the Business (including IRS Forms W-9 and W-8 for any taxable period (or portion thereof) ending on or before the Closing Date (collectively, "**Customer-Provided Information**")); (ii) prepare with respect to the 2005 calendar year and the portion of the 2006 calendar year ending on or prior to the Closing all forms, information and reports, and shall timely withhold, deposit and pay all amounts, required in connection with federal, state, local or foreign tax withholding, backup withholding or reporting requirements applicable to the Assets or the Business (including IRS Forms 1099, 1098, 1042, 1042-S and 945); and (iii) provide Buyer with reasonable opportunity on or prior to the Closing to review the systems used to effectuate the foregoing.

13. Assignment. This Agreement and the rights hereunder shall not be assignable or transferable by Buyer or Sellers without the prior written consent of the other party hereto, which consent may be withheld in a party's sole discretion; *provided, however*, that Buyer shall be permitted to assign its rights hereunder to any affiliate of Buyer; *provided, further*, that no such assignment shall relieve Buyer of its obligations hereunder.

14. No Third-Party Beneficiaries. This Agreement is for the sole benefit of the parties hereto and their successors and permitted assigns, and nothing herein expressed or implied shall give or be construed to give to any person, other than the parties hereto (or, as specified in Section 11 the Seller Indemnified Parties and the Buyer Indemnified Parties), and such successors and assigns, any legal or equitable rights hereunder.

15. Termination.
15.1 Generally. Anything contained herein to the contrary notwithstanding, this Agreement may be terminated and the transactions contemplated hereby abandoned at any time prior to the Closing as follows:
(a) by mutual written consent of Sellers and Buyer;
(b) by Sellers or Buyer, if either (i) a breach by the other party of any representation or warranty contained herein, which breach cannot reasonably be or has not been cured within 30 days after the giving of written notice to the breaching party of such breach; or (ii) a breach by the other party of any of the covenants or agreements contained herein, which breach cannot reasonably be or has not been cured within 30 days after the giving of written notice to

the breaching party of such breach and, in the case of either (i) or (ii), which breach, individually or in the aggregate with other such breaches, would cause the conditions set forth in Section 4.2(a) or (b), in the case of a breach by Sellers, or Section 4.3(a) or (b), in the case of a breach by Buyer, not to be satisfied;

(c) by Sellers or Buyer, if the approval of any Governmental Entity required for consummation of the transactions contemplated by this Agreement shall have been denied by such Governmental Entity, or such Governmental Entity shall have requested the withdrawal of any application therefor, or any such approval shall be made subject to any condition or restriction described in Section 4.2(e); or

(d) by Sellers or Buyer, if the Closing does not occur on or prior to September 30, 2006;

provided, *however*, that the failure to satisfy the conditions or consummate the transactions contemplated by this Agreement did not result from the breach in any material respect by the party seeking termination pursuant to clause (b), (c) or (d) of any of its representations, warranties, covenants, or agreements contained in this Agreement.

15.2 Effect of Termination. In the event of termination by Sellers or Buyer pursuant to this Section 15, written notice thereof shall forthwith be given to the other party and the transactions contemplated by this Agreement shall be terminated, without further action by any party. If the transactions contemplated by this Agreement are terminated as provided herein:

(a) Buyer shall return to Sellers all documents and other material received from or on behalf of Sellers relating to the transactions contemplated hereby, whether so obtained before or after the execution hereof; and

(b) all confidential information received by Buyer shall be treated in accordance with the Confidentiality Agreement, which shall remain in full force and effect in accordance with the terms thereof notwithstanding the termination of this Agreement.

15.3 Survival of Certain Provisions. If this Agreement is terminated and the transactions contemplated hereby are abandoned as described in this Section 15, this Agreement shall become void and of no further force and effect, except for the following provisions: (a) Section 6.1 relating to the obligation of Buyer to keep confidential certain information and data obtained by it from Sellers; (b) Section 16 relating to certain expenses, (c) Section 9.2 relating to publicity; (d) Sections 5.25 and 7.5 relating to finder's fees and broker's fees and commissions, and (e) Sections 15 and 24. Upon any termination pursuant to this Section 15, no party shall have any further liability or obligation hereunder other than for any pre-termination willful or intentional breach by such party of the terms and provisions of this Agreement or for pre-termination breach of any payment obligations under this Agreement.

16. Expenses. Whether or not the transactions contemplated hereby are consummated, and except as otherwise provided in this Agreement, all costs and expenses incurred in connection with this Agreement and the transactions contemplated hereby shall be paid by the party incurring such costs or expenses.

17. Amendments; Waiver. No amendment to this Agreement shall be effective unless it shall be in writing and signed by all parties hereto. No waiver will be effective unless memorialized in writing and signed by the party against whom such waiver is to be enforced; and no waiver of any breach of this Agreement will be implied from any forbearance or failure of a party to take action thereon.

18. Notices. All notices or other communications required or permitted to be given hereunder shall be in writing and shall be delivered by hand, or sent by telecopy, or sent, postage prepaid, by United States registered, certified, or express mail, or reputable overnight courier service, and shall be deemed given, if delivered by hand, when so delivered, or if sent by telecopy, when received, or if sent by mail, three business days after mailing (two business days in the case of express mail), or if sent by overnight courier service, one business day after delivery to such service, as follows:
[Notice Information Omitted.]
Any party hereto may change the address to which notices and other communications are to be delivered or sent by giving the other parties notice in the manner herein set forth.

19. Interpretation. In this Agreement, the Disclosure Schedule and any exhibits hereto:
(a) words denoting the singular include the plural and vice versa and words denoting any gender include all genders;
(b) "including" means "including without limitation";
(c) "affiliate" has the meaning set forth in Rule 12b-2 of the General Rules and Regulations under the Exchange Act;
(d) "business day" means any day other than a Saturday, Sunday, or a day that is a statutory holiday under the laws of the United States or the States of Minnesota or New York;
(e) "law" means all statutes, laws, ordinances, rules, orders, and regulations of any Governmental Entity applicable to the Business;

(f) "person" means an individual, partnership, joint venture, corporation, limited liability company, trust, unincorporated organization, government, governmental department, or agency or other entity;

(g) the use of headings is for convenience of reference only and shall not affect the meaning or interpretation of this Agreement, the Disclosure Schedule, or any exhibits annexed hereto;

(h) when calculating the period of time within which or following which any act is to be done or step taken, the date that is the reference day in calculating such period shall be excluded and, if the last day of such period is not a business day, the period shall end on the next day that is a business day;

(i) all dollar amounts are expressed in United States funds, and all amounts payable hereunder shall be paid in United States funds;

(j) money shall be tendered by wire transfer of immediately available federal funds to the account designated in writing by the party that is to receive such money;

(k) the words "hereof," "hereby," "herein," "hereunder" and similar terms in this Agreement refer to this Agreement as a whole and not only to a particular Section in which such words appear; and

(l) all references to [statutes] or regulations are deemed to refer to such statutes and regulations as amended from time to time or as superseded by comparable successor provisions.

20. **Counterparts.** This Agreement may be executed in counterparts, all of which shall be considered one and the same agreement, and shall become effective when counterparts have been signed by each of the parties and delivered to the other parties.

21. **Entire Agreement.** This Agreement (including the Disclosure Schedule and the exhibits hereto) and the Confidentiality Agreement contain the entire agreement and understanding between the parties hereto with respect to the subject matter hereof and supersede all prior agreements and understandings relating to such subject matter.

22. **Bulk Transfer Laws.** Subject to Sellers indemnification obligation pursuant to Section 11.1(a)(iii), Buyer acknowledges that Sellers and Buyer will not comply with the provisions of any bulk transfer laws or tax laws relating to bulk transfers of any jurisdiction in connection with the transactions contemplated by this Agreement, waives any requirement of compliance with such laws, and agrees that such non-compliance does not constitute a breach of any representation, warranty, or covenant of

Sellers contained in this Agreement notwithstanding anything stated in Section 5 or any other Section of this Agreement.

23. Severability. If any provision of this Agreement or the application of any such provision to any person or circumstance shall be held invalid, illegal, or unenforceable in any respect by a court of competent jurisdiction, such invalidity, illegality, or unenforceability shall not affect any other provision hereof.

24. Governing Law. This Agreement shall be governed by and construed in accordance with the laws of the State of New York applicable to agreements made and to be performed entirely within such state, without regard to the conflicts-of-law principles of such state.

25. Specific Performance. The parties agree that irreparable damage would occur if any provision of this Agreement were not performed in accordance with its terms and that prior to the Closing, the parties shall be entitled to an injunction to prevent breaches of this Agreement or to enforce specifically the performance of the terms hereof, in addition to any other remedy to which the parties are entitled. Notwithstanding anything herein to the contrary, no party shall be entitled to any indirect, special, incidental or consequential damages except in the case of bad faith, intentional breach, fraud or intentional misrepresentation.

26. Disclosure Schedule. Matters reflected in the Disclosure Schedule are not necessarily limited to matters required by this Agreement to be reflected in the Disclosure Schedule. Such additional matters are set forth for informational purposes and do not necessarily include other matters of a similar nature.

27. Knowledge. For all purposes of this Agreement, "Knowledge" of Sellers or a similar phrase means the actual knowledge of those officers of Sellers set forth on <u>Exhibit B</u>, based upon the reasonable diligence of such persons exercised in the ordinary course of carrying out their duties and responsibilities with respect to the Business.

28. Parent. Parent agrees to take all action necessary to cause the Company to perform all of its obligations under this Agreement.
[Signature Page Omitted]

1. Familiarity Breeds Fluency: A Review

At this juncture, our hope is that, while this *particular* document and the transaction to which it speaks may be unfamiliar to you, its structure and many of its provisions ring a bell.

- Section 3.3 of the Agreement explains the events that are to constitute and occur at the Closing, and, in § 4, we find conditions to Closing. What is a closing? How do conditions operate, generally? What concerns do these conditions address? Why are "conditions" used as opposed to other provisions (e.g., covenants) to address these concerns? (See Chapters 4 and 5.)

- Section 5.3 states a representation and a warranty with regard to Sellers' financial statements and refers to creatures like a "balance sheet" and "GAAP." What are financial statements? What information do they convey about parties that may be of interest to a potential lender or a potential acquiror? What is GAAP? (See Chapter 5.)

- Notice that the Agreement in several places draws upon an "ordinary course of business" concept. For examples, see §§ 5.3(e)(iii), 5.10(a)(xiii), 5.14, 5.23(b), and 6.2. What does it mean for something to occur in the "ordinary course of business"? How does the Agreement define this? (See Chapter 5.)

- Sections 5.13 and 10 speak to employment issues. What is ERISA generally? What is the purpose of the representation and warranty in § 5.13 (Employee Benefits; ERISA)? Do these provisions make "third-party beneficiaries" out of certain employees? (See Chapters 1 and 2.)

- Sections 6.3, 6.6, and 6.7, respectively, impose restrictive covenants not to disclose, not to solicit, and not to compete. What is the general test for enforceability of these types of provisions? (See Chapters 1 and 2.)

- Section 9.3, among other sections of the Agreement (e.g., §§ 1.3(a), 3.2(c), 6.2), provides that each party will use "reasonable best efforts" to perform certain acts. What is the meaning of this and similar "performance standard" provisions? (See Chapter 4.)

- Section 15.1(b) provides that certain breaches, if gone uncured, are grounds for termination. What does it mean to "cure" a breach or other failing? (See Chapter 5.)

- Notice how this Agreement adopts a hybrid approach to defining its terms: Terms are defined as used throughout the Agreement, and an

"Index of Defined Terms" precedes the Agreement for ease of reference. (See Chapter 3.)

- Also, notice that § 19 of the Agreement provides guidance as to how the Agreement should be interpreted (and certain terms, defined). For example, consistent with the general rule of interpretation regarding "including," § 19 explains that "including" means "including without limitation" and precedes a non-exhaustive, exemplary list. In addition, § 19 makes clear that "herein" refers to the entire Agreement and not any particular Section—an issue we encountered in a previous agreement. (See Chapter 3.)

2. Acquiring Which Assets

In an agreement for the purchase of assets, it is important—fundamental—to provide what the seller is and is not selling to the buyer. Asset purchase agreements may accomplish this task by describing in one section the assets to be included in the sale and separately in another section the assets to be excluded from the sale. There are a variety of potential approaches to describing included and excluded assets: An agreement may describe each generally, list each specifically, or do some combination thereof. You will notice the Agreement takes a hybrid approach.

Section 1 of the Agreement provides this information, stating generally that the Sellers agree to sell and that the Buyer agrees to buy all of the assets used *primarily* in the *Business*, which is defined in the recitals as the business of the Company's Private Client Services division. This language reflects a compromise between (i) giving the Buyer all of the assets used in any way in the Business (which could force the Seller to divest assets used in its other businesses) and (ii) giving the Buyer only the assets used solely in the Business (which could deprive the Buyer of assets that are important to the Business but that are used even marginally in the Seller's other businesses). In asset purchase agreements, the definition of "Business" is fundamental, as several terms of the agreement may be stated in terms of the "Business" in order to accomplish the ultimate acquisition of the Business.

To articulate further what this perhaps vague definition of Assets includes—and, so, what is being sold under the Agreement—§ 1.1 specifically enumerates certain categories of assets to be included among the assets sold. This is a common device of contracts and statutes alike, to state a general rule or proposition and then to provide specific enumerations or examples of that rule, which are exemplary but not exhaustive. In this way, one can be sure that whatever a general provision may capture, it certainly captures certain items. As § 1.1 explains what *is* included among the assets transferred under the Agreement, § 1.2 provides what is *not* and, in so doing, takes a similar tack to the structure and approach of § 1.1. Section 1.2 states generally that all assets not described in § 1.1 are not being sold under the Agreement (and, so, are Excluded Assets; in other words, under this Agreement, Excluded Assets are everything that are not Assets). This is an area that requires careful attention—an asset purchase agreement should be clear about whether the list of excluded assets "trumps" the list of included assets, or vice versa. This also demonstrates the importance of defining terms: Where assets are described with reference to defined terms, a prudent drafter must be sure only to include the intended assets.

Drafting Note: "Without Limiting the Generality" and "Notwithstanding the Contrary"

Note the potential confusion created, in § 1.2 of the Agreement, by the use of both "without limiting the generality of the foregoing" and "notwithstanding anything to the contrary provided in Section 1.1" as attached to the same statement (that "the following property and assets of Sellers constitute Excluded Assets"). Because the "foregoing" provides that Excluded Assets (assets not being sold under the Agreement) are those not described in § 1.1, what function can the "notwithstanding anything to the contrary provided in Section 1.1" clause serve *without* limiting the foregoing?

This seems to work as follows: The Assets sold under this Agreement are those provided by § 1.1 (as provided by the general statement and the enumerated examples there); any Assets not specified by § 1.1 are Excluded Assets as provided by the general statement in § 1.2; any Assets enumerated in § 1.2 are also Excluded Assets; and, if any of the *enumerated* Excluded Assets in § 1.2 are also (included) Assets under § 1.1, then they are Excluded Assets (this does not serve to limit the generality of the foregoing sentence in § 1.2 that provides that the Sellers are not selling and the Buyer is not buying anything not described in § 1.1). Accordingly, the list in § 1.2 serves to provide a non-exhaustive list of Excluded Assets (which does not limit the generality of the foregoing sentence in § 1.2), but, whereas the first sentence in § 1.2 is deferential to § 1.1 (it states that Excluded Assets are the scraps leftover after § 1.1 does its work), the enumerated list that follows in § 1.2 *trumps* § 1.1. So, while potentially highly confusing, the use of "notwithstanding the contrary" and "without limiting the generality" can be reconciled here: The dual use highlights that the enumerated list does not limit the general statement (i.e., they are not exhaustive) and that the enumerated items are absolutely examples of, in this case, Excluded Assets. That is, the list acts as a "safe harbor"—it is possible to be an Excluded Asset without being any of the enumerated items, but if something is one of the enumerated items, it certainly is an Excluded Asset.

A simpler way to accomplish the same task in this case would be to avoid the use of *both* "without limiting the generality of the foregoing" and "notwithstanding anything to the contrary" so as to avoid the dual application and interaction of both "rules." For example, the following accomplishes the same task while

> avoiding the potential confusion: "The following is a non-exhaustive list of Sellers' property and assets that constitute Excluded Assets, notwithstanding anything to the contrary in Section 1.1."

How does the enumerated list of Excluded Assets in § 1.2 work to ensure that the Sellers are only selling the Private Client Services division and nothing more? Please consider the specific items excluded in answering this question.

a. Anti-Assignment Provisions Revisited

As we discussed in Chapter 1 and revisited in the context of intellectual property rights in Chapter 4, assets (including rights under a contract) may or may not be assignable. In addition, some rights may provide by their own terms that they are not assignable; indeed, licensed patent and copyright rights are presumed non-assignable, under federal law, absent express language providing to the contrary.[40] Whether a merger constitutes an assignment or transfer of rights (potentially violative of an anti-assignment clause in a merger party's contract with a non-merger party) is not clear. Under Delaware General Corporation Law and the 2002 Model Business Corporation Act (the "MBCA"), the effect of a merger is to "vest" (neither statute mentions "transfer" or "assign") the rights, privileges, and assets of the constituent companies in the surviving company.[41] Courts vary in their conclusions as to whether a merger amounts to an assignment or transfer.[42] Some states have passed statutes that expressly provide that a merger does not amount to a transfer.[43] In addition, while there may be uncertainty as to whether a merger constitutes an assignment, a sale of

---

40. *See Cincom Sys., Inc. v. Novelis Corp.*, 581 F.3d 431, 436-37 (6th Cir. 2009).

41. *See* DEL. CODE ANN. tit. 8, § 259 (1967); MODEL BUSINESS CORPORATION ACT § 11.07(a)(3) (2002).

42. *Compare PPG Indus., Inc. v. Guardian Indus. Corp.*, 597 F.2d 1090, 1096 (6th Cir. 1979) ("A transfer is no less a transfer because it takes place by operation of law rather than by a particular act of the parties. The merger was effected by the parties and the transfer was a result of their act of merging."), *Cincom Sys.*, 581 F.3d at 438-39 (reaffirming *PPG* under Ohio's revised statute that removed language that all property shall be deemed "transferred to"), *Freeman Mgmt. Corp. v. Shurgard Storage Ctrs., Inc.*, No. 3:06cv0736, 2007 WL 1541877, at *4 (M.D. Tenn. May 23, 2007) ("In fact, the Tennessee Supreme Court appears to have concluded that property rights and other interests that 'vest' in a surviving corporation as a result of a merger actually transfer by operation of law."), *with TXO Prod. Co. v. M.D. Mark, Inc.*, 999 S.W.2d 137, 142 (Tex. App. 1999) ("Under the merger statutes it is clear that all of TXO's interests vested in Marathon immediately upon the merger. Further, under these provisions there is no transfer of the rights of the merging corporation; rather, the rights vest automatically and without further action."). There is also the question of whether the surviving company into which another company has merged (e.g., in a reverse merger) has effected an "assignment." *Compare Lewis*, 2003 WL 22461894, at *4 n. 18 ("If a reverse triangular structure is used, the rights and obligations of the target are not transferred, assumed or affected."), *with SQL Solutions, Inc. v. Oracle Corp.*, No. C-91-1079 MHP, 1991 WL 626458, at *3-4 (N.D. Cal. Dec. 18, 1991) (finding the target to have "transferred" its rights in a triangular merger where the target survived).

43. *See, e.g.*, TEX. BUS. ORGS. CODE ANN. § 10.008(a)(2)(C) (Vernon 2007) ("[A]ll rights, title, and interests to all real estate and other property owned by each organization that is a party to the merger is allocated to and vested, subject to any existing liens or other encumbrances on the property, in one or more of the surviving or new organizations as provided in the plan of merger without . . . any transfer or assignment having occurred."); COLO. REV. STAT. ANN. § 7-90-204(1)(a) ("A merger does not constitute a conveyance, transfer, or

stock does not.[44] Accordingly, as we saw in Chapter 1, a party may wish to include broad language in an anti-assignment provision to include mergers and other combinations and similar events among the activities that constitute prohibited assignment and, in addition, may wish to specify that the consequence of such prohibited assignment (so broadly defined) is to terminate the rights that are assigned.

On this topic, § 1.1 of the Agreement provides that certain assets are to be sold, but what if the Sellers do not have the power to sell an Asset to the Buyer? Section 1.3(a) creates a *post-Closing* obligation on the part of the Sellers to use "reasonable best efforts" and otherwise to cooperate with the Buyer to obtain any necessary consent to effect the transfer of the Asset. What is the obligation of the Buyer to obtain the ability to convey and to convey the Assets *prior* to Closing?

3. Assuming and Succeeding to Liability

In deals for the purchase of assets, the general rule is that the purchaser of the assets does not "succeed" to the liabilities of the seller.[45] That is, the liabilities of the seller remain those of only the seller, save for a few exceptions to this general rule. The first exception is straightforward: Where the purchaser agrees to assume certain liabilities, it will be found to have succeeded to those liabilities.[46] We see this first exception at work in the Agreement.

When companies acquire a division or a whole company by acquiring its assets, they may also expressly "assume" certain of its liabilities. A business—be it a division or a legally distinct company—is more than its assets. As we explored a bit in Chapter 5, from a balance sheet perspective, a business is comprised of assets and liabilities, with the difference amounting to stockholders' equity (also called "net assets"). Whether a buyer "purchases" certain liabilities along with certain assets is largely a business issue and a question of price and leverage. Presumably, a buyer is willing to pay more for a package of just assets than a package of those assets and some liabilities; so, what liabilities are and are not

---

assignment. Nothing in this section affects the validity of contract provisions or of reversions or other forms of title limitations that attach conditions or consequences specifically to mergers.").

44. *See, e.g., White v. Hitachi, Ltd.*, No. 3:04-CV-20, 2007 WL 2725888, at *5 (E.D. Tenn. Sept. 17, 2007) ("A sale of stock does not result in the violation of a contract provision prohibiting assignment absent express language prohibiting a change of control, because a license or other contract does not transfer from one corporation to another when the stock of the corporation is sold.").

45. *See, e.g., Berg Chilling Sys., Inc. v. Hull Corp.*, 435 F.3d 455, 464 (3d Cir. 2006) ("The ordinary rule of successor liability is rooted in corporate law, and it states that a firm that buys assets from another firm does not assume the liabilities of the seller merely by buying its assets."); *Debnam v. Crane Co.*, 976 A.2d 193, 197 (D.C. 2009).

46. *See Berg*, 435 F.3d at 464 ("The first exception covers situations where the buyer either expressly or implicitly agrees to assume some or all of the seller's liabilities. It is usually straightforward in application. Because this exception is based on interpreting the terms of the parties' agreement, it is characterized most strictly as contract law.").

assumed is likely to be reflected in the price of a deal. In addition, a buyer may ultimately be liable for certain liabilities anyway (as we see below in the discussion of the other "successor liability" exceptions); as the express assumption of liabilities may affect a negotiated price, it may behoove a buyer to include certain liabilities in the deal, inasmuch as the buyer assumes some risk of paying for these liabilities anyway.

Liabilities may come in many forms. A party may knowingly take on liabilities that are certain and absolute; for example, a party may borrow money from a bank or purchase goods on account or in exchange for a note payable. Or, a party may bear contingent liabilities, which turn on the occurrence of a future event, such as the owing of damages that depends on the outcome of litigation. Liabilities may be owed in the future to "involuntary creditors"—third parties, such as tort victims, who did not negotiate or wish to be owed an obligation at all.

Under § 2.1 of the Agreement, the Buyer assumes all liabilities—absolute or contingent—of the Sellers that *solely* relate to the Business or the Assets. Notice how Buyer has negotiated a narrow definition of Assumed Liabilities (i.e., those that relate "solely" to the Business) as compared to the definition of Assets (i.e., those used "primarily" in the Business). Why do you think this is?

As certain liabilities may not accrue until after the closing but still pertain to the Assets—for example, products liability claims—the Agreement makes clear that the Buyer is assuming these liabilities as well ("whether arising before, on, or after the Closing Date"). Section 2.1 explains that these Assumed Liabilities do not include any Excluded Liabilities. Note that § 2.1 further provides that the Buyer will indemnify the Sellers if the Sellers pay an Assumed Liability after Closing. This indemnification obligation may be important, as a third-party claimant does not lose its claim against a seller merely because the seller "sold" its liability to a buyer.[47] Mirroring § 1.1, which identifies the Assets to be purchased, § 2.1 enumerates examples of liabilities that constitute Assumed Liabilities. Predictably, § 2.2 specifies which liabilities are Excluded Liabilities—and, so, the continuing responsibility of the Sellers alone and not an Assumed Liability of the Buyer as part of this transaction. To continue the parallelism, as § 2.1 indemnifies the Sellers for paying an Assumed Liability, § 2.2 indemnifies the Buyer for paying an Excluded Liability. As we will soon see, this provides the Buyer with additional protection and comfort should it be

---

47. *See, e.g., Thermo Electron Corp. v. Waste Mgmt. Holdings, Inc.*, No. Civ.A. 01-3054, 2003 WL 354864, at *5 (Mass. Super. Feb. 12, 2003) (holding that a seller of assets and liabilities, which included guarantee obligations, did not discharge its contractual obligations under the guarantee by virtue of the sale); *see also Reserves Dev. LLC v. Crystal Props., LLC*, 986 A.2d 363, 370 (Del. 2009) ("Unless the obligee agrees otherwise, neither delegation of performance, nor a contract to assume the duty discharges any duty or liability of the delegator-obligor."). With regard to contractual obligations, this is an application of the discussion of "delegation" in Chapter 1. There, we discussed that A may generally delegate to C an obligation owed to B but that delegation—while creating an obligation on the part of the delegatee (C) to perform for the delegator (A) and for B, as a third-party beneficiary—does not relieve the delegator (A) of its original obligation to B.

liable in the end (under a "successor liability" theory) for a liability it did not wish to assume.

There are other exceptions to the general rule that a purchaser of assets does not come to be liable for the liabilities of the seller. In addition to the first exception—where the purchaser has agreed to assume liabilities—discussed above, there are three well-accepted exceptions.[48] First, where a buyer and seller enter into a transaction fraudulently for the purpose of escaping certain liabilities, a creditor of the seller may be able to reach the buyer.[49] Second, where a purchasing company is a "mere continuation" of the selling company, the purchasing company is subject to successor liability. And, third, successor liability is similarly available where the asset transaction between the purchasing company and the selling company is a "de facto" merger.[50] As many courts have explained, "In effect, the *de facto* merger and continuation exceptions are identical."[51] Generally, courts will engage in a multi-factor test to determine whether an asset purchase (or other non-merger transaction in form) amounts to a de facto merger and/or the mere continuation of the seller's operations. As the Third Circuit has explained, these factors generally include whether:

> (1) There is a continuation of the enterprise of the seller corporation, so that there is continuity of management, personnel, physical location, assets, and general business operations.
>
> (2) There is a continuity of shareholders which results from the purchasing corporation paying for the acquired assets with shares of its own stock, this stock ultimately coming to be held by the shareholders of the seller corporation so that they become a constituent part of the purchasing corporation.
>
> (3) The seller corporation ceases its ordinary business operations, liquidates, and dissolves as soon as legally and practically possible.

---

48. *See, e.g., Fish v. Amsted Indus., Inc.*, 376 N.W.2d 820, 823 (Wis. 1985) ("As a general rule, a corporation which purchases the assets of another corporation does not succeed to the liabilities of the selling corporation. There are four well recognized exceptions to this general rule: (1) when the purchasing corporation expressly or impliedly agreed to assume the selling corporation's liability; (2) when the transaction amounts to a consolidation or merger of the purchaser and seller corporations; (3) when the purchaser corporation is merely a continuation of the seller corporation; or (4) when the transaction is entered into fraudulently to escape liability for such obligations.") (internal citations and quotation marks omitted).

49. *See Berg*, 435 F.3d at 464 ("The second exception applies where a transaction is entered into fraudulently in order to evade liability.").

50. *See id.* at 464-65 ("The third and fourth exceptions, *de facto* merger and mere continuation, are generally treated identically, as both arise where there is continuity of identity between the buyer and seller. 'Mere continuation' analysis focuses on whether the new corporation is merely a restructured form of the old, while *de facto* merger analysis inquires whether a transaction—though structured as an asset purchase—factually amounts to a consolidation or merger.") (internal citations omitted).

51. *Ruiz v. Blentech Corp.*, 89 F.3d 320, 325 (7th Cir. 1996) (explaining that the test for both exceptions is the same under both Illinois and California law); *see also Berg*, 435 F.3d at 464 ("The third and fourth exceptions, *de facto* merger and mere continuation, are generally treated identically.") (citations omitted); *IDT Telecom, Inc. v. CVT Prepaid Solutions, Inc.*, No. 07-1076, 2009 WL 5205968, at *11 (D.N.J. Dec. 28, 2009) ("The second and third exceptions to the presumption against successor liability are often analyzed in tandem, and this Court will do the same.").

(4) The purchasing corporation assumes those obligations of the seller ordinarily necessary for the uninterrupted continuation of normal business operations of the seller corporation.[52]

Of interest, in *Berg*, the court found that the acquisition of a division—as opposed to an entire entity—could not constitute a "de facto" merger (or, presumably, a mere continuation) for the purposes of the successor-liability doctrine under Pennsylvania law.[53] However, the court further explained that under New Jersey law, "a corporation purchasing an entire division may meet the requirements of a 'mere continuation,' despite the fact that all other divisions of the selling corporation remain extant and viable."[54] Indeed, while these four exceptions (i.e., agreement, fraud, mere continuation, and de factor merger) have been widely regarded as the traditional exceptions to the general no-successor-liability rule, jurisdictions vary in their willingness to find a mere continuation or a de facto merger in particular situations. As an example, in addition to the above illustration, states disagree about whether there must be a "continuity of shareholders" in order to find either a de factor merger or mere continuation.[55]

An additional and controversial successor-liability exception is the "products-line" rule, first crafted in California,[56] and later adopted in a few other states.[57] Under the products-line exception, when the successor corporation continues essentially the same manufacturing operation as the predecessor operation, the successor may be held strictly liable in tort for the predecessor's defective products.[58] With products liability cases, injuries and claimants may arise in many different states. This hamstrings a successor company's ability to limit which liabilities it is assuming—or, more pointedly, which liabilities it is *not* assuming. For example, imagine a company enters into a bona fide

---

52. *Berg*, 435 F.3d at 468-69.

53. *Id.* at 470 ("In sum, the APA [Asset Purchase Agreement] resulted in a combination of like corporate *divisions,* but not of corporate *entities.* Thus, the *de facto* merger exception to the rule of successor non-liability will not render [the purchaser liable for the seller's breach of a third-party contract].") (emphasis in original); *see also Schumacher v. Richard Schear Co., Inc.,* 451 N.E.2d 195, 198 (N.Y. 1983) (the mere-continuation exception "refers to [a] corporate reorganization . . . where only one corporation survives the transaction; the predecessor corporation must be extinguished.").

54. *Berg*, 435 F.3d at 463 (citing *Koch Materials Co. v. Shore Slurry Seal, Inc.*, 205 F. Supp. 2d 324, 337 (D.N.J. 2002)).

55. *Compare Ruiz v. Blentech Corp.*, 89 F.3d 320, 325 (7th Cir. 1996) ("In either Illinois or California, a court will conclude that an asset sale merges two corporations or makes the buyer the continuation of the seller only if it finds an identity of ownership between the two."), *and Tracey v. Winchester Repeating Arms Co.*, 745 F. Supp. 1099, 1110 (E.D. Pa. 1990) (explaining that continuity of ownership is an "essential element" of the de facto merger exception), *with Marshak v. Treadwell*, 595 F.3d 478, 490 (3d Cir. 2009) (finding the successor company to be a mere continuation and subject to successor liability, despite that changes in ownership and management "weighed against" this finding).

56. *See Ray v. Alad Corp.*, 560 P.2d 3 (Cal. 1977).

57. *See, e.g., Dawejko v. Jorgensen Steel Co.*, 434 A.2d 106, 111 (Pa. Super. Ct. 1981); *Ramirez v. Amsted Indus., Inc.*, 431 A.2d 811, 824-25 (N.J. 1981).

58. *See Ray*, 560 P.2d at 11 ("[A] party which acquires a manufacturing business and continues the output of its line of products under the circumstances here presented assumes strict tort liability for defects in units of the same product line previously manufactured and distributed by the entity from which the business was acquired."); *Ramirez*, 431 A.2d at 819.

purchase—there has been no fraud and there is no overlap in management or ownership—of substantially all of the assets of another company that has sold goods used in all 50 states. The buyer may expect products liability actions—based on the goods sold prior to the buyer's purchase of the selling company's assets—to arise all over the country, including, say, California. Accordingly, the buyer may be, in effect, purchasing potential products liability actions, irrespective of what its contract with the seller has to say about assumed and excluded liabilities.

Your instinct might be that a choice-of-law provision in the asset purchase agreement (such as § 24 of the Agreement) should alleviate this concern.[59] However, as then-Judge Alito explained in *Berg*, "In general, while it makes sense to allow the parties to a contract to control which law applies to their agreement, it does not follow that the contract provisions should control an inquiry that, by its nature, looks beyond the contract."[60] In *Berg*, the Third Circuit went on to conclude, "Ultimately, in conducting choice of law analysis for this situation, we should look to the substance of the transaction, rather than to the form of the agreement; therefore, the [Asset Purchase Agreement's] choice of law provision does not control."[61] Accordingly, in determining in an asset deal whether to find a purchaser to be responsible for the seller's liabilities to third parties, a court is likely to defer to the asset purchase agreement's choice-of-law provision with respect to the question of whether the purchaser agreed to assume certain liabilities.[62] As to the other exceptions, a forum court may opt not to defer to a contractual choice-of-law provision in applying its choice-of-law principles to determine which state's law applies and, then, to apply this law to determine whether a successor-liability exception operates to allow a third party to reach a successor company for the predecessor company's liability.[63]

There are additional specific ways in which an acquiring company may be found liable for the liabilities of the target. The U.S. Foreign Corrupt Practices Act is one such example. On this topic, we asked two seasoned practitioners to provide an overview.

A Practitioner Perspective: The U.S. Foreign Corrupt Practices Act

It is increasingly important for corporate and transactional lawyers to understand the basic scope and applicability of the U.S. Foreign Corrupt Practices Act ("FCPA"), U.S. export control laws, and economic sanctions. These are complicated sets of rules and regulations that, on several levels, can have a significant impact on corporate transactions:

---

59. Please see Chapter 1 for more on "choice-of-law" provisions.
60. *Berg*, 435 F.3d at 466.
61. *Id.*
62. *See, e.g., id.* at 464 (citing *T.H.S. Northstar Assocs. v. W.R. Grace & Co.-Conn.*, 840 F. Supp. 676, 677-78 (D. Minn. 1993)).
63. *Id.*

With the encouragement of the enforcement agencies, companies are realizing that FCPA and trade control compliance considerations warrant careful and ongoing attention from the earliest planning stages of any deal, through due diligence, and to the execution and integration phases.

A. Overview of the U.S. Foreign Corrupt Practices Act

The U.S. Foreign Corrupt Practices Act ("FCPA") contains two sets of provisions: anti-bribery provisions and accounting provisions. The anti-bribery provisions impose civil and criminal penalties on covered persons and entities that bribe officials of foreign governments. The accounting provisions, which likewise are enforceable civilly and criminally, require covered companies to reflect payments in their books and records in an accurate manner and to have an adequate system of accounting controls. A transactional lawyer should have a general familiarity with both sets of provisions and should consider their implications for corporate transactions. While this discussion focuses on the U.S. FCPA, many other countries have adopted anti-bribery laws, and companies should be alert to the potential applicability of those countries' laws to their operations.

B. Why the FCPA Matters in Corporate Transactions

FCPA considerations are critically important in the context of corporate due diligence for mergers, acquisitions, joint ventures, and other collaborative structures. This is so for several reasons. First and foremost, an acquiring company may have successor liability imposed upon it if the target is found to have committed FCPA violations prior to the transaction. Stock acquisitions generally result in such successor liability. While the traditional position of transactional lawyers is that asset purchases should not result in successor liability, U.S. law enforcement authorities have often shown indifference to whether a deal is structured as a stock acquisition or an asset purchase. For example, successor liability may be imposed after an asset purchase where the purchasing entity is deemed to be a mere continuation of the selling corporation. A variation on this exception is the doctrine of "continuity of enterprise," which reflects a judgment that a successor that takes a benefit must assume the liability that ought, as a matter of equity, to go along with it. If the key assets acquired are long-term contracts and business relationships procured through bribery, the authorities will not likely be deterred by the fact that the transaction was an asset sale. Thus, even in the context of asset purchases, it is important for due diligence to confirm that there is no improper conduct related to any assets being purchased.

A second reason for the importance of due diligence is the fact that the acquiring company will be liable for all of the subsidiary's post-acquisition conduct, including any future improper payments as well as violations of the books and records and accounting controls provisions going forward. Thus, if the target company has a culture problem and an ongoing pattern of inappropriate payments, those problems can quickly become a source of exposure for the acquiring company.

A third, related reason for FCPA due diligence is to prevent the acquiring company from unknowingly overpaying for the target company. The acquiring company needs to know in advance whether the target's book of business will shrink once a robust anti-corruption program is put in place.

While there is no explicit statutory requirement to conduct pre-acquisition FCPA due diligence, the SEC and DOJ have emphasized that they expect companies to conduct adequate anti-corruption due diligence in transactions with an international component. DOJ has stated that it considers the nature and quality of pre-closing due diligence when it makes its charging decisions.

In practice, M&A due diligence has been a significant source of FCPA enforcement actions. Pre-acquisition due diligence has turned up evidence of improper payments that has led to significant investigations and settlements. In some instances, the merger has gone forward once the liability has been resolved. In other instances, deals have been slowed down or blown up entirely—including at least one multi-billion-dollar deal—when an FCPA issue has arisen and could not be resolved promptly.

C. Anti-Corruption Representations and Warranties

Any merger, acquisition, or joint venture involving a company with international operations or reach should be conditioned on the target company's executing representations and warranties attesting to its past compliance with the FCPA and any other applicable anti-corruption laws. If the target shows reluctance to enter into such provisions, that in itself presents a red flag regarding corruption risk.

D. Post-Acquisition Measures

Once the acquisition is done, the corporate or transactional lawyer may be tempted to turn to other deals, but the acquiring company still has work to do. It should roll out its own robust anti-corruption policy within the newly acquired operation as quickly as reasonably possible. It is advisable to conduct anti-corruption training soon after the deal closing, focusing first on those portions of the acquisition target that represent the greatest corruption risk. It may be advisable to conduct a post-acquisition risk assessment, now that the acquiring company has access to additional information that may not have been available during pre-acquisition due diligence. Once the acquiring company's anti-corruption policies and procedures have been rolled out within the target, the company should monitor compliance with them. Internal audit should devise means of auditing compliance with the company's FCPA and anti-corruption policies. Finally, any issues or allegations suggesting corruption risks that may arise post-closing should be quickly elevated to the company's legal department for an appropriate response. A slow or inadequate response could significantly increase the company's legal exposure.

> Stephen P. Anthony
> Partner
> White Collar Defense and Investigations
> Covington & Burling LLP
>
> Peter L. Flanagan
> Partner
> International Trade and Finance, and
>   Member of the Management Committee
> Covington & Burling LLP

Again, because a purchaser cannot completely insulate itself from successor liability in its contract with the seller, the purchaser may wish to price the risk of incurring certain liabilities into the deal. This may be attempted by adjusting the purchase price for this risk of liability without expressly assuming the liability, or by expressly assuming the liabilities and reducing the purchase price to compensate for this assumption. As discussed above and seen in this Agreement, another—perhaps "most effective"[64]—solution is for a buyer to obtain an indemnity from the seller—or certain other parties—for successor liability related to liabilities excluded under the contract.

With this discussion, we just touch upon the nuances involved in M&A transactions with multi-*state* dimensions—as successor-liability rules vary state to state. Ever more complex are M&A deals with multi-*national* dimensions. For a glimpse into this world, we turn to a seasoned practitioner.

A Practitioner Perspective: Special Considerations for Cross-Border M&A Transactions

While purely domestic M&A transactions present a range of challenging legal issues, cross-border deals involving multinational organizations add considerable layers of complexity, and require additional dexterity by the lawyers involved. This is the case even if both parties are U.S.-based corporations. The following are just a few examples of special considerations that may apply:

- *Shareholder Approvals.* Not every country replicates the straightforward approach of most U.S. jurisdictions providing for up-or-down votes on proposed business combinations. For example, the applicable rules in the United Kingdom in many cases require transactions to be done either through direct offers to shareholders or through court-approved "schemes of arrangement".

---

64. David I. Albin et al., *Special Issues in Asset Acquisitions, in* 1 Negotiating Business Acquisitions § H, at 19 (American Bar Association 2007).

- *Regulatory Approvals.* While the attitude of the U.S. Federal Trade Commission and Department of Justice towards antitrust (Hart-Scott-Rodino) approvals of proposed transactions can vary considerably depending on the Administration, competition law approvals in other jurisdictions can present increasingly high hurdles to getting deals done, and can be more difficult to achieve than in the U.S. One well-known example of foreign scrutiny killing a deal was the EU Competition Commission's rejection of a proposed merger of General Electric with Honeywell. And, in countries like India and China, the approval regime goes far beyond specific competition concerns; it simply is not possible to acquire voting control over many enterprises without prior official consent, if at all.

- *Employment Laws.* One of the biggest differences between the legal framework in the U.S. and those in place elsewhere is the wide chasm that often exists in the degree of protection applicable to workers whose jobs might normally be expected to be at risk in order for a proposed business combination to achieve the economic "synergies" that can be their principal rationale. While much of the non-unionized domestic labor force continue to be "employees at will" who can be separated on short notice and at relatively little expense, in countries like Germany and Russia, there is no general ability to separate at all (at any price) and others, including France, the Netherlands and Spain, impose costly severance formulae that can significantly drive up the cost of a deal. Moreover, permissible "mass layoffs" that might be allowed must often be performed within rigid confines; in Germany, for example, the most recently-hired tend to be the first that need to go, and social cost requirements also mandate that those with families to support receive preferential treatment. Non-competition agreements that most U.S.-trained lawyers (at least outside of California) view as standard are often unenforceable in other countries, and must be carefully reviewed on a by-jurisdiction basis. Finally, works councils and other representative bodies are common throughout Europe, and typically must be consulted with and won over in order for transactions to move forward.

- *Tax/Fiscal Issues.* Cross-border deals always need to be intensively scrutinized for their potential impact on the surviving entity's tax situation and position, both at the local country level and overall in the eyes of the IRS. For example, changes in control can destroy or impair the value of deferred tax assets such as net operating losses and dual consolidated losses on a by-jurisdiction basis, and some countries still apply stamp taxes on share-for-share exchanges. Moreover, even the basic accounting of overseas assets being acquired will likely need to be harmonized, as most countries utilize International Financial Reporting Standards, which are different in important ways from U.S. Generally Accepted Accounting Principles.

- *Trademarks.* Just about every international business combination requires the registration of existing (usually those of the acquiror) or entirely new (in so-called "mergers of equals") trademarks, service marks and other trade names. While this process is becoming less cumbersome in Europe with the increasing ability to file EU-wide applications that parallel the U.S. federal structure, it continues to be a tough, multi-country slog through Asia and Latin America, often consuming months or years post-closing with uncertain results.

- *Representations, Warranties and Indemnities.* While most U.S.-trained lawyers are used to being able to limit their clients' damages for indemnities relating to transaction-related issues such as breaches of representations and warranties, many of the world's most important economies (Germany is an example) are unfriendly to caps on damages. This of course makes choice-of-law and venue clauses in business combinations even more important for international transactions than for purely domestic ones, and even when the documents provide for acceptable law to govern it can remain unclear the extent to which local foreign courts may honor the parties' choice.

- *General Political Risk.* Finally, depending on the country, there can be a higher degree of pure political protectionism engaged in by local government officials, who often fret when "national champions" agree to be acquired by foreign interests. French politicians over the years have been notorious for this kind of behavior, but even countries assumed to more closely share U.S.-style business values can get into the act; one example that attracted a lot of recent attention was the concessions that British officials attempted to extract from Kraft during its negotiations to acquire Cadbury. Addressing these risks on behalf of clients often requires skills outside of most lawyers' toolkits, and can merit the retention of separate public affairs specialists and lobbyists in the relevant countries to help smooth a proposed transaction's way towards closing.

While the foregoing list is hardly exhaustive, it provides an overview of the kinds of issues—over and above the standard litany that most always apply to any transaction—that can arise in the context of international business combinations. American lawyers advising their clients on multinational deals will often retain local counsel in the countries where the target company does business to assist them in addressing these items, but need to be prepared to develop specific strategies that frequently involve risk profiles that can surprise U.S.-based clients, to inform the clients of the risks they'll be running, and to ensure that their team goes into the transaction with their eyes wide open.

Mark H. Berlind
Vice President and General Counsel
Booz & Co.

4. M&A Consideration

a. *Types of Consideration*

While cash is a common form of consideration that a buyer may pay in acquiring a company, it is only one type of consideration. The purchaser may alternatively or additionally pay in the form of stock (of the purchaser-company or of another company), notes payable, or virtually any other type of asset.[65] Even the purchaser's assumption of the seller's liabilities may be understood as a form of consideration paid by the purchaser to the seller.

Where stock is used as consideration, there may be valuation issues even where the stock is listed and priced on a national exchange, as the price of stock fluctuates day to day.[66] As follows, the parties may agree on certain price bounds, on which the closing of the deal is conditioned.[67] For example, the buyer may have to offer additional consideration if the stock falls below a certain price before the buyer can cause the seller to close the deal (and, if the buyer does not provide the additional consideration, the seller may have the right to terminate the agreement per its terms).[68] The buyer may also offer debt consideration, which can be attractive to the buyer for a few reasons, some of which include: (1) most obviously, paying with debt does not require the buyer to lay out as much cash immediately, which may be desirable; (2) if the seller turns out to be liable to the buyer under an indemnity obligation, then the buyer may be able to offset this indemnification right against its debt obligation, especially if the note provides as much; and (3) potential tax benefits.[69]

b. *Price and Adjustments*

Once the parties have figured out what exactly it is that the buyer is acquiring (and what the buyer is not) and what liabilities the buyer is assuming (and what the buyer is not), then they may settle on a price. However, the value of the company—partly based on the latest financial information at the time—may shift between execution of the agreement and the closing. While this period of time between signing and closing varies in length from deal to deal (as it may take time to obtain regulatory approval, third-party consents, security registration, among other things), it is often a few months.[70] The parties may settle on a fixed price as of execution, effectively putting the risk of increased value on the seller and the risk of decreased value on the buyer, or the parties may include

---

65. For more on alternative forms of consideration in M&A transactions, please see Leigh Walton & Kevin Kreb, *Purchase Price Adjustments, Earnouts and Other Purchase Price Provisions*, *in* Negotiating Business Acquisitions, *supra* note 64, at § F.

66. *Id.* § F, at 2-3.

67. *Id.*

68. *Id.*

69. *Id.* § F, at 6.

70. *Id.* § F, at 8.

adjustment formulae that attempt to account for any fluctuation in value that may occur before the closing.[71] As evidenced by § 3.1 of the Agreement, the parties to this Agreement chose the latter approach. Why might a buyer argue that a seller should assume the risk of value fluctuation between signing and closing?

c. Contingent Consideration: Earnout Provisions

As we saw above, parties may agree to a formula for adjusting the price from the time of the signing of the agreement to the date of closing; this makes sense when the parties agree on the value of the target business but want to shift the risk of a change in this valuation that occurs before closing. Quite differently, the parties may also agree to a mechanism by which the seller may receive additional consideration *after* the closing. Because the buyer and the seller may *disagree* about the future prospects and profitability of the business to be acquired, they may have a hard time coming to terms on price.[72] One potential means of reconciling the buyer's price position with the seller's is for the parties not to strike an agreement on price entirely as of signing but instead to leave a portion of the price contingent on the acquired business satisfying certain performance criteria over a period of time after closing. This type of device is called an "earnout."

For more on earnout provisions, we turn to a seasoned practitioner, Brian Hoffmann, who is co-chair of Clifford Chance's M&A practice in the Americas and whose deal experience has included advising Lenovo Group Ltd. on its $1.75 billion acquisition of IBM's Personal Computing Division and Terra Firma on its $5.2 billion acquisition of Pegasus Aviation Finance Company.

A Practitioner Perspective: Earnouts

An earnout is a contractual provision stating that the seller of a business is entitled to obtain additional future compensation *after* the date on which the seller has sold the business, based on the business achieving certain predefined future financial or other targets after the sale has been consummated. An earnout is a method of compensating a seller based on the future earnings of a business.

Earnout provisions are particularly useful if the parties' views of the value of the business or its prospects are widely divergent or if the business is presumed to be on the brink of significant financial improvement. The parties may disagree on the anticipated future value of the business because they have different opinions about the projected earnings. Often, the buyer relies on the seller's projections of future earnings in setting the price to be paid for the business. The

---

69. For more on purchase price adjustments, see *id.*

70. For a further discussion of this and earnout provisions more generally, please see *id.* § F, at 21.

buyer and seller may disagree on the business' ability to realize the projected results. In those situations, an earnout is effective in bridging the price gap. An earnout will allow the seller to prove the value of the business by actually delivering on those projections before getting paid full value for the projected earnings, while allowing the buyer to reduce the risk of overpaying for an underperforming business.

Earnouts require consideration of various factors: the type of contingent payment (cash or securities), the measurement of performance (EBITDA, operating income, cash flow, net income, revenues or other), the measurement period, the timing of payments and the tax treatment and structuring of the earnout.

An earnout can be measured based on earnings, EBITDA or a similar profit measure. Another alternative is measuring the earnout using a revenue-based test, or to simply entitle the seller to a percentage of the company's revenues for a period of time. Yet another alternative is to issue securities that become exercisable in the event certain performance, developmental or sales thresholds are achieved. An earnout typically lasts for a period of years after the closing, with the measurement being made annually, as well as the payments, if any. A typical earnout might provide that the seller will receive an additional payment in each of the first three years after the closing, provided that in each of those years the acquired business realizes operating income above a certain level. One issue to consider in the negotiation of such an earnout provision is shortfalls in any given year. If the earnings fall short of the target in the second year, resulting in no payment to the seller, but exceed the target in the third year, so that on a cumulative basis the seller would have received a payment with respect to the second year, should the seller's payments be recouped or are amounts not earned in any given year lost for good? In addition, the buyer may also consider whether there should be an obligation to refund an earnout payment made to the seller in the first year if the results in the second and third years are substandard.

In negotiating the measurement of performance to be used in calculating the earnout, there are a number of considerations the buyer and seller will need to consider. The buyer will want to be sure that any earnings come from continuing operations and not extraordinary or nonrecurring events. The seller may insist that the earnout provide that the business be operated separately from the buyer's other businesses, if any, and consistently with past practice, because if the buyer combines certain of the business' operations with its own or modifies them, such changes will be difficult to factor into the levels of earnings to be achieved in connection with the earnout.

In addition, the negotiation of an earnout requires the buyer to fully understand the seller's accounting principles and practices. Typically, an earnout provision specifies that the payment is to be calculated using accounting principles and policies consistent with those used by the business pre-closing. As a result, a complete understanding of matters like revenue recognition policies and allocation of overhead and similar items as well as the treatment of expenses and other items relating to the transaction becomes critical if post-closing misunderstandings involving the earnout are to be avoided.

Another basic issue that an earnout provision raises, is how to strike the right balance between protecting the seller's ongoing interest in the performance of the business post-closing and protecting the buyer's interest in maintaining control of the business during the earnout period. The seller is interested in ensuring that changes in the operation of the business post-closing do not affect the business' ability to attain the earnout targets. As a result, the seller will negotiate for covenants protecting it against the buyer's ability to take actions that will affect earnings without the seller's consent. The buyer will argue that these covenants will unreasonably restrict its ability to run the business post-closing. In addition, sellers may seek to impose an express contractual duty on the buyer to "use commercially reasonable efforts" or "to use good faith efforts" to achieve or maximize the earnout. Even more difficult issues may arise where the contract is silent on the buyer's rights and obligations with regard to achieve-ment of the earnout. For example, in *Sonoran Scanner v. PerkinElmer*, 585 F.3d 535 (1st Cir. 2009), a recent case before the United Stated Court of Appeals for the First Circuit, the earnout provision that was the subject of the dispute did not contain any sort of "reasonable efforts" language; however, the plaintiff seller argued that notwithstanding the lack of language to that effect in the contract that there should be an implied obligation on the part of the buyer to exert reasonable efforts in achieving an earnout, and the court agreed, stating that there is an implied obligation of reasonable efforts in an earnout provision. Therefore, as a result of this decision, as a practical matter when negotiating earnout provisions on behalf of a buyer, you should ensure that the earnout provision contains language to the effect that "except as explicitly provided herein, the buyer shall have no obligation to achieve or maximize the value of the earnout."

Earnout provisions also typically include dispute resolution mechanisms. Parties usually provide for issues relating to earnouts to be resolved in informal arbitration-like proceedings. Typically, one party's accountants will prepare the financial statements and the other party's accountants will have a certain amount of time to review the statements and present their objections in writing. If agreement cannot be reached, the parties will then typically pick an indepen-dent nationally recognized accounting firm to resolve the issues. Generally, the parties agree that the decision of that accountant is binding upon the parties.

No one earnout provision is appropriate for all contracts, and no matter how fully negotiated an earnout provision is there can be no assurances that disputes will not arise post-closing. Nevertheless, careful consideration by the parties of the issues that commonly arise in earnouts can help to reduce misunderstand-ings and the likelihood of disputes.

Brian Hoffmann
Partner and Co-Head of Americas M&A
Clifford Chance US LLP

For more on earnout provisions and the duties a successor company has to facilitate (or not to stymie) the satisfaction of an earnout provision, please see the discussion of the implied covenant of good faith and fair dealing in Chapter 4.

5. Representations and Warranties

In the Agreement, we see representations and warranties playing familiar roles. As we first discussed in Chapter 3, representations are factual assertions upon which the receiving party may rely and, if made falsely, bring suit for misrepresentation, and warranties are promises of fact upon which the receiving party may bring suit for breach of warranty if the warranty is untrue. These are the default powers and consequences of representations and warranties. (You may wish to revisit *CBS v. Ziff-Davis* and its discussion of representations and warranties in the context of an asset purchase transaction, in Chapter 3.) However, as we first touched upon in Chapter 3, representations and warranties may serve the same (or a very similar) function, as they may be used toward a variety of the same ends, in complex agreements.

For one, *because* representations and warranties provide the recipient with remedies in the event of inaccuracy, representations and warranties serve a "due diligence" function. While a prudent buyer may wish to conduct its own due diligence, representations and warranties place the onus on their maker to ensure their accuracy, lest the maker suffer liability for their falsity. Receiving representations and warranties may give a party comfort before signing a merger agreement—comfort that those asserted facts are true and, if they are not, that the party has recourse. This brings us to a second common feature of representations and warranties—one we have already seen and discussed in Chapter 5 in the context of lending agreements and which we discuss below in the context of closing and conditions. That is, the accuracy of representations and warranties in M&A agreements is typically a condition of closing, the failure of which may allow a party to terminate the agreement. Accordingly, not only may a recipient have potential claims for misrepresentation and breach of warranty, but a recipient may also avoid consummating a transaction in the event of an inaccurate representation or warranty, as provided for in the transaction's agreement. (Again, we see this concept in *Ziff-Davis* in Chapter 3, where CBS chose to close the deal despite its knowledge of the falsity of a warranty and proceeded to sue for breach of that warranty.) Furthermore, the parties may provide by contract that indemnification rights follow from the inaccuracy of a representation or warranty.

In a complex agreement, such as an asset purchase agreement, the distinction between representations and warranties may not be meaningful, as much of the importance of the representations and warranties, as used in the agreement, stems from the contractually created mechanisms of closing conditions and indemnification rights, which may treat representations and warranties as interchangeable.[73] In addition, as discussed in Chapter 3, while a representation and a warranty are different things in the legal abstract, a representation may be found in a warranty provision and a warranty may be found in a representation provision—that is, a warranty provision may be the source of a misrepresentation claim and a representation provision may be the source of a breach-of-warranty claim.[74] While some may consider it a "drafting nuisance" or contrivance to use the terms "representation" and "warranty" in contracts,[75] if a party wishes to create both representations and warranties (e.g., to lay the foundation for both misrepresentation and breach-of-warranty claims), the simplest way of doing so may be to signal the creation of both by expressly "representing and warranting."[76] This allays the concern that a judge might not find a representation in a "warranty," and vice versa. In sum, the distinction between a representation and a warranty might not be significant in the context of a contractual edifice (e.g., made up of closing conditions, termination provisions, and indemnities) built upon these devices because this contractual edifice might not draw any such distinction. However, inasmuch as a party may wish to use either device for its standard remedies (e.g., fraud, misrepresentation, breach of warranty), the distinctions between representations and warranties begin to matter and a contract may wish clearly to instruct a court that the parties intended to create both.

You will notice that § 5 (Representations and Warranties of Sellers) is much longer than § 7 (Representations and Warranties of Buyer). Is the Buyer more concerned about facts pertaining to the Sellers, or are the Sellers more concerned about facts pertaining to the Buyer? Why?

a. Representations and Warranties of Buyer

What does Buyer represent and warrant under this Agreement? As you see in § 7, Buyer makes variations of the fairly standard representations and warranties of organization, authority, and non-contravention. These types of representations and warranties are common to most any commercial agreement. To summarize, Buyer represents and warrants under § 7.1 (Organization and Authority of Buyer):

---

73. *See, e.g., Reliance Fin. Corp. v. Miller,* 557 F.2d 674, 682 (9th Cir. 1977).

74. *See, e.g.,* U.C.C. § 2-313(3) (2003) (providing that no "magic words" are required for the creation of an express warranty); *Edwin Bender & Sons v. Ericson Livestock Comm'n Co., Inc.,* 421 N.W.2d 766, 770 (Neb. 1988) ("A misrepresentation and a warranty are not necessarily mutually exclusive and may arise from the same representation on which a cause of action is based.").

75. *See, e.g.,* David I. Albin et al., *supra* note 64, at 68; Kenneth A. Adams, *A Lesson in Drafting Contracts: What's up with 'Representations and Warranties'?,* Bus. L. Today, Nov.-Dec. 2005, at 32-33.

76. *See, e.g.,* Tina Stark, *Nonbinding Opinion: Another View on Representations and Warranties,* Bus. L. Today, Jan.-Feb. 2006, at 8-9.

(i) Buyer is organized in its purported state of organization (i.e., Delaware) and qualified to do business where relevant;

(ii) Buyer has the power and authority to enter into this Agreement and to close;

(iii) any corporate procedures that need to occur for Buyer to agree to and perform the Agreement and close the transaction have occurred; and

(iv) the Agreement is a binding contract once signed by all parties.

Under § 7.2 (Non-Contravention), Buyer represents and warrants that Buyer's signing and performing the Agreement does not:

(i) violate Buyer's corporate governing documents (e.g., articles of incorporation, bylaws);

(ii) violate or constitute a default under any of Buyer's other contracts; or

(iii) violate any law or regulation applicable to Buyer or its property.

In § 7.3, Buyer further makes standard representations and warranties that Buyer has not received notice of any lawsuits and to its Knowledge (a defined term) there have been no lawsuits threatened against Buyer as of the Agreement. Notice that this representation is limited to only those pending or threatened lawsuits that would materially impair the Buyer's ability to consummate the transaction.

Similar, then, to § 7.3, § 7.4 provides a straightforward representation and warranty that Buyer will have sufficient cash available to it in order to consummate the transaction at Closing. Again, Sellers' primary concern with Buyer here appears to be that Buyer can actually buy the assets as contemplated by the Agreement.

Drafting Note: Defined Terms; Knowledge

Where does this Agreement define Knowledge? How is it defined? Does this definition make sense in the context of its use in § 7.3 with respect to Buyer's Knowledge? How might you draft this definition differently?

Knowledge may be defined to include only *actual* knowledge or also to include knowledge that one should have (e.g., "an individual has Knowledge if the individual actually knows or should know"). Note how "Knowledge" may be used to limit a representation and warranty: Rather than representing and warranting that something is the case, one may represent and warrant that something is the case, to one's Knowledge, or that one does not have Knowledge that something is not the case.

---

b. Representations and Warranties of Sellers

In contrast to Buyer, Sellers make a whole host of representations and warranties. Consider the respective obligations under this transaction. Sellers want Buyer to buy certain of the Company's assets and to assume certain of the

Company's liabilities—that is, Sellers want Buyer's money (note that, in other cases, other forms of consideration may be at issue, as we discuss above, which may complicate a buyer's obligations under an M&A agreement) and are primarily concerned that Buyer is able to pay up and acquire the assets as contemplated. On the other hand, Buyer is acquiring a business division—its assets and liabilities—to be Buyer's on an ongoing basis into the future. *Before* Buyer is obligated to pay a considerable sum for these operations (i.e., before Buyer must close), Buyer wants to make sure that what it is buying meets Buyer's desired "specifications" and that Buyer is not acquiring unexpected risk. We explore a sampling of these representations and warranties. The reader should return to § 5 of the Agreement to read and explore the balance (and, as always, should review the Agreement while studying the discussion below).

(1) Organization and Authority; Stockholder Approval

Section 5 starts out familiarly with § 5.1 on organization and authority. This is largely a mirror provision of § 7.1, except for a line in the middle of the paragraph that states, "No vote of any security holders of the Sellers is required under applicable laws to consummate the transaction contemplated hereby." In effect, Sellers are representing and warranting that *this* sale does not constitute a sale of "substantially all" of the Company's assets. Generally the holders of a majority of the voting shares of the seller must vote in favor of a sale before the corporation may sell "all or substantially all" of the corporation's assets.[77] A corporation's articles of incorporation may impose a more onerous supermajority voting requirement.[78] However, if a sale is for less than "substantially all" of a corporation's assets, then the seller need not obtain stockholder consent, unless the articles of incorporation provide otherwise.[79] The general rule, under state law, is that the buyer does not need approval of its stockholders, regardless of whether the purchase is for substantially all of the seller's assets.[80]

What constitutes "substantially all" is a good question. Delaware courts use a disjunctive qualitative-quantitative test, asking whether the assets to be sold are quantitatively vital to the company's operations or qualitatively substantial to its existence and purpose.[81] The 2002 MBCA speaks of a sale of "substantially all" a corporation's assets as leaving "the corporation without a significant

---

77. *See* Del. Code Ann. tit. 8, § 271(a) (2010); Model Business Corporation Act § 12.02(a) (2002).

78. *See* Del. Code Ann. tit. 8, § 102(b)(4) (2010); Model Business Corporation Act § 7.27(a) (2002).

79. *See* Model Business Corporation Act § 12.01 (2002); *In re Gen. Motors (Hughes) S'holder Litig.*, No. Civ. A. 20269, 2005 WL 1089021, at *20 (Del. Ch. 2005) ("Delaware law clearly provides that a corporation may dispose of property, amounting to less than all or substantially all its assets, without a shareholder vote.").

80. However, under the MBCA, if the purchasing corporation issues, as part of the transaction, shares that will comprise more than 20 percent of the voting power of the purchasing corporation, the purchasing corporation shareholders have voting rights. Model Business Corporation Act § 6.21(f)(1) (2002). Also, a buyer that is a public company may need shareholder approval before issuing a certain amount of stock in an acquisition, under stock exchange rules.

81. *See Hollinger Inc. v. Hollinger Int'l, Inc.*, 858 A.2d 342 (Del. Ch. 2004), *appeal refused*, 871 A.2d 1128 (Del. 2004); *Gimbel v. The Signal Cos., Inc.*, 316 A.2d 599 (Del. Ch. 1974).

continuing business activity."[82] The 2002 MBCA also provides a "safe harbor," where if the selling corporation retains a business activity that represented at least 25 percent of its total assets and 25 percent of either its income or revenue for the most recent year, then the sale will not be found to constitute a sale of "substantially all" the selling corporation's assets (or, in the MBCA's terms, then the sale will have left the seller-corporation with a "significant continuing business activity").[83] As with any safe harbor, satisfying the safe-harbor requirements is sufficient but not necessary: It is conceivable that a corporation could sell over 75 percent of its assets and still have retained a significant continuing business activity under the MBCA.

(2) Financial Statements and Disclosures

Please see Chapter 5 for a discussion of financial statements as well as representations and warranties of financial information. You will notice that § 5.3(a) contains a representation and warranty that the relevant financial statements (i) "fairly present" the financial condition of the business to be sold; and (ii) "have been prepared in accordance with GAAP." Furthermore, notice that § 5.3(a) limits the "fairly present" statement to "all material respects." In which party's interest is this "materiality" limitation? Also notice that § 5.3(a) provides not only that the Financial Statements have been prepared in accordance with GAAP but also "on a basis consistent with the principles historically applied," except as expressly disclosed. GAAP is not a set of rigid rules and may give a company considerable leeway. A buyer may want to be sure that a seller has not manipulated financial information, even within the confines of GAAP, and, in § 5.3(a), we see one way of addressing this.

Notice that this is a representation and warranty given by Sellers but not by Buyer. This, again, reflects the asymmetry of an asset-purchase transaction—Buyer may be concerned with the financial information pertaining to the Business it is acquiring, whereas Sellers may be less concerned about financial information as related to Buyer, except inasmuch as this information informs Buyer's ability to pay.

(3) Potential Encumbrances and Limitations on Assets

Sections 5.6-5.11 of the Agreement speak to Buyer's concern that it will be free to operate the Business, namely that Buyer will have sufficient (and sufficiently unencumbered) rights in the assets it is to acquire under the Agreement.

Section 5.6 provides that each of the Assets is free of liens, except for disclosed, immaterial, and other Permitted Liens, and that Sellers have or will transfer to Buyer good title in each of the Assets by the time of Closing.[84]

---

82. Model Business Corporation Act § 12.02(a) (2002).
83. Id.
84. Please see Chapter 4 for a discussion of title.

In § 5.8, Sellers provide representations and warranties regarding the condition of the tangible Assets, *but only to the extent* that a failure of any of these assertions would constitute a Material Adverse Effect. Importantly, § 5.8 further confirms that the Assets (remember, defined to include all of the assets to be acquired) constitute all those used in the operation of the Business. Lastly, § 5.8 contains a disclaimer of express and implied warranties. As you may recall from Chapters 3 and 4, express warranties ordinarily cannot be effectively disclaimed, and implied warranties ordinarily must be disclaimed "conspicuously" to be disclaimed effectively. Is this disclaimer of implied warranties conspicuous and effective?

Section 5.9 contains a limited warranty and representation of non-infringement, specifically that, *to Sellers' Knowledge*, no claims have been made against either Seller *in writing* either challenging the right of Sellers to use certain intellectual property used *solely* in the Business or asserting intellectual property infringement involving the right of Sellers to sell products or services of the Business without paying a fee. This representation and warranty is limited to those claims that have a Material Adverse Effect. Note the several ways this provision is cabined to limit Sellers' liability exposure.

Section 5.10(a) draws upon the statements made in a separate disclosure pertaining to certain contracts to which the Company is a party, as the Sellers represent and warrant that the disclosure presents a "true and correct list" of all of the contracts enumerated in § 5.10. This is important as § 5.26 limits Sellers' representations and warranties to only those representations and warranties expressly made in the Agreement. Section 5.10(b) reflects Buyer's concern that the Material Contracts it is acquiring are legally enforceable, specifically that Buyer will step in to have legally enforceable rights under them. Consider the use of "material breach" in § 5.10 in light of the discussion of material breach in Chapter 2 and that one party's material breach of a contract may release the other from its obligations under the contract.

(4) Absence of Changes or Events; No Material Adverse Effect

Section 5.14 of the Agreement actually serves two separate functions, containing two separate provisions. First, it contains a representation and warranty that there has been no Material Adverse Effect since December 31, 2005.[85] This date is significant because it is the date of the Business's most recent financial statements, which are set forth in a separate disclosure schedule, as we learn from § 5.3 (Financial Statements). An M&A agreement may contain an MAE provision as a representation and warranty and/or as a condition to closing. Even absent a separate no-material-adverse-effect condition to closing, the non-occurrence of a material adverse effect will generally still be made a condition to

---

85. An M&A agreement may contain this representation/warranty under separate cover in a section entitled, "No Material Adverse Effect."

closing via a "bring-down" provision in the conditions section of an M&A agreement. This type of bring-down provision states that the accuracy of certain representations and warranties is a condition of closing. We take up the concept of material adverse effect and bring-down provisions again and in greater depth in the context of closing conditions below.

In addition, § 5.14 contains assurances that Sellers have not done anything out of the ordinary with the Business since December 31, 2005, again the date of its most recent financial statements. It uses the concept of "ordinary course of business," which we explored in Chapter 5 and, there, in the context of *Medigroup v. Schildknecht*. The concern here is straightforward: Buyer's decision to acquire the Business for certain consideration is premised on the Business's financial condition, as evidenced by its financial statements. Buyer wants Sellers to continue to operate the Business as an ongoing concern but not to alter the Business in a meaningful way from the Business reflected in its most recent financial statements. To this end, a buyer may attempt to draft this provision to include specific acts that a seller must represent and warrant it has not done. These concerns can be additionally addressed in a seller's covenant, as we see in § 6.2 of the Agreement.

(5) Excluding Representations and Warranties

Section 5.26 is an example of a provision we discussed earlier in this book (in Chapter 3). To attempt to avoid claims (e.g., misrepresentation, fraud) based on representations allegedly made outside the four corners of an agreement, parties may include in their contract an express provision that the parties have made no other representations other than those expressly made in the agreement. For this reason, a prudent party that wishes to exclude extra-contractual representations will be sure specifically to provide as much, as the Agreement does in § 5.26. However, as noted in Chapter 3, a "standard" integration clause that does not specifically mention representations might not do the trick.[86]

Warranties are a bit trickier. We have seen in Chapters 3 and 4 that parties may disclaim implied warranties but generally may not disclaim or exclude express warranties. Accordingly, at least one court has found that, *if* an agreement is not *completely* integrated, oral or written terms that precede the agreement may be introduced as express warranty terms of the contract, even despite a provision that purports to exclude any warranties made outside the four corners of the agreement.[87] Importantly, inasmuch as an agreement is found to

---

86. *See, e.g., ABRY Partners V, L.P. v. F & W Acquisition LLC*, 891 A.2d 1032, 1058-59 (Del. Ch. 2006) ("Because of that policy concern, we have not given effect to so-called merger or integration clauses that do not clearly state that the parties disclaim reliance upon extra-contractual statements. Instead, we have held . . . that murky integration clauses, or standard integration clauses without explicit anti-reliance representations, will not relieve a party of its oral and extra-contractual fraudulent representations.") (internal citations omitted).

87. *See L.S. Heath & Son, Inc. v AT & T Info. Sys., Inc.*, 9 F.3d 561, 569-70 (7th Cir. 1991) (explaining that where an agreement is not fully integrated and express warranties may have been created outside of the

be completely integrated, it should also be found to be the exclusive source of the contract's express terms, including express warranties, as of the effective date of the agreement (remember, integration does not speak to the inclusion of terms allegedly created *after* the agreement and, depending on applicable law, a contract might not always prevent or control the modification or addition of terms, including warranties).[88] Note that integration has no bearing on a contract's *implied* warranties, as implied warranties are inherently a part of all contracts to which they apply—for example, contracts for the sale of goods under Article 2—that do not properly disclaim them.[89]

Also, note § 8.1, which is oddly placed among the "covenants of Buyer" in § 8 of the Agreement and is an acknowledgment that no representation or warranty has been made, as to the accuracy or completeness of certain information, outside of the Agreement and Sellers' authenticated certificates.

(6) Survival of Representations and Warranties (and Other Provisions)

When are the representations and warranties made in this Agreement "in effect"? This question contains a few landmines, starting with that representations and warranties may have several effects, as we have seen. For one, representations and warranties may allow a party to walk away from closing. In this respect, those representations and warranties, upon which closing hinges, are "in effect" as of the closing. Indeed, § 4.2(a) states that Buyer's obligation to close turns in part on certain representations and warranties of Sellers' being true and correct (subject to materiality limitations) "as of the Closing Date as though made on and as of such date."

On top of this, we know that the inaccuracy of a representation and warranty may provide tort-based and contract-based remedies. And, in addition, a contract may specify what remedies result from an inaccuracy of its representations and warranties, such as § 11 (Indemnification) of the Agreement. In these respects, the representations and warranties in the Agreement are "in effect" from the execution of the Agreement and continue to be operative at least until either the Closing or the Agreement's termination as provided in §§ 11.5 (Survival of Representation and Warranties) and 15.3 (Survival of Certain Provisions). Note that while a representation and warranty may be "operative" in the sense that the provision has not terminated, the content of the representation

---

agreement, a disclaimer within the agreement of any express warranties not provided by the agreement is not operable). An argument could be made that, if an agreement is *partially* integrated and includes a term that states the exclusion of all express warranties not included in the agreement, express-warranty terms outside of the contract that contradict the exclusion term should be excluded under the parol evidence rule. However, this was not how the court in *Heath v. AT & T* saw it, finding that if an agreement is not completely integrated, then any express-warranty terms may come in, even if there is a provision purporting to exclude any express warranty terms. *Id.*

88. *See, e.g., id.* at 569.

89. *Id.*

and warranty provision may speak as of a point of time or for a certain period of time, depending on the language of the provision.[90] Sections 11.5 and 15.3 further provide that, even after the Closing or the Agreement's termination, certain representations and warranties (and other provisions) will continue to be of effect—they will "survive." Why do you suppose these particular provisions are selected for survival?

In M&A agreements, parties will generally specify whether a representation and warranty is to "survive" closing or termination, should the closing not occur or the agreement terminate for another reason as provided by contract. As we first discussed in Chapter 1, survival generally refers to whether a contractual provision is still an operative contractual term after a certain point in time. That is, if a contract term is not to survive closing and the closing occurs, then the contract term no longer imposes rights or obligations on any of the parties to the contract. However, if a party breached a contractual provision while it was in effect (e.g., before closing), then a party may still be able to *bring a claim* for breach of that provision after the provision is no longer in effect.[91] In other words, a provision that merely states that a certain term does not "survive" closing does *not* mean that a claim—based on a breach of the term when it was in effect—may not be brought after closing. Stated yet another way, "survival" itself does not operate to impose a contractual "statute of limitations," and courts have found survival provisions not to have this effect without clearly and specifically saying as much.[92] As we discussed in Chapter 3, parties are generally free to agree contractually to temporal limitations on actions to be brought, as long as the contractual time period is reasonable. Because a contractual "statute of limitations" provision may be strictly construed against the party seeking to enforce

---

90. Generally, we think of a representation (at least of the sort that may form the basis of a misrepresentation claim) as an assertion of fact made to induce reliance, and a warranty as a promise that a statement is and/or will be true, depending on the language and nature of the warranty. Please see Chapter 3. While a "representation" of future fact generally may not form the basis of a misrepresentation claim, *see, e.g., Siemens Fin. Servs., Inc. v. Robert J. Combs Ins. Agency, Inc.*, 166 F. App'x 612, 617 (3d Cir. 2006), reliance might not be necessary to bring a contractual action for indemnification, depending on the language of a contract. Recall the earlier conversation of the usage of these terms and devices in practice in the context of complex agreements, which may involve the use of a "representation" provision to do more than support a claim for misrepresentation.

91. *See infra* note 92.

92. *See, e.g., W. Filter Corp. v. Argan, Inc.*, 540 F.3d 947, 952 (9th Cir. 2008); *Herring v. Teradyne, Inc.*, 242 F. App'x 469, 471 (9th Cir. 2007) ("Parties may contractually reduce the statute of limitations, but any reduction is construed with strictness against the party seeking to enforce it. Here, we find no clear and unequivocal language in the survival clauses that permits the conclusion that the parties have unambiguously expressed a desire to reduce the statute of limitations.") (internal citations omitted); *Hurlbut v. Christiano*, 405 N.Y.S.2d 871 (N.Y. App. Div. 1978) ("The clause in controversy here provides, in pertinent part, as follows: 'The parties hereto further agree that the representations and warranties set forth in Sections 4.01(d) and 4.03(g) of the Purchase Agreement between them dated February 29, 1972 shall survive the closing for a period of three (3) years.' The language of the agreement is clear and unambiguous and suggests nothing from which a shortened period of limitations can be inferred.").

it,[93] the provision should be clear and unequivocal. How does the Agreement address this issue squarely in § 11.3 (Time for Claims) and in the last sentence of § 15.3?

As a slight aside, notice that the proviso in § 11.5 is a bit nonsensical, if defensibly cautious: A representation or warranty need not "survive" for a claim to be brought, much less to be brought to final resolution, inasmuch as the claim is based on a breach of the representation or warranty that occurred when the provision was in effect. (Certainly, as discussed above and as evident in the Agreement, a contract may provide otherwise or may specifically provide when a claim can and cannot be brought.)

In addition to representations and warranties, notice that the Agreement provides, in the last sentence of § 11.5, that all covenants survive until they are performed or satisfied—presumably this means the covenants survive *Closing*, but § 11.5 does not make this explicit. Section 15.3 tells us that all of the Agreement's provisions become void and of no effect if the Agreement is terminated, save for certain covenants (and other provisions) that survive termination. Section 6.8(b) tells us that the Agreement's restrictive covenants (discussed below) found in §§ 6.3, 6.6, and 6.7 survive Closing (however, the restrictive covenants in §§ 6.6 and 6.7 are only effective for a certain number of years following Closing according to the terms of the covenant itself; again, survival means that a provision is legally operative but does not speak to the content of the provision).

6. Covenants of the Seller

a. Access

A buyer will generally want to be able to access certain files and information of the seller. While quite likely a buyer will have conducted due diligence investigations prior to signing an acquisition agreement and will have received certain representations and warranties in the acquisition agreement to supplement this due diligence, the buyer may want to be able to continue to investigate the business it is to acquire. For instance, the buyer may want to confirm the veracity of the seller's representations and warranties. In addition, the buyer may want to apprise itself of any changes or occurrences that affect the business or the buyer's rights and obligations under the agreement. For example, the buyer may want to have the ability to ascertain whether a material adverse effect has occurred that would obviate the buyer's obligation to close. Is § 6.1 reasonable to suit the interests of both parties? Why or why not?

---

93. *See supra* note 92.

b. Ordinary Conduct

Piggybacking on Sellers' representations and warranties in §§ 5.14(b) and (c), § 6.2 sets out to restrict the Company to conduct the Business in the Ordinary Course of Business. This covenant differs from the representations and warranties in a few respects. For one, the relevant time period in §§ 5.14(b) and (c) begins with the Business's latest financial statement—December 31, 2005—whereas § 6.2 imposes an obligation that begins with the execution of the Agreement—April 9, 2006. Note that, while the covenants in § 6.2 impose ongoing obligations from execution to Closing, the representations and warranties found in § 5.14 are stated as of the Agreement, and the language of § 5.14, at least, does not expressly suggest that § 5.14 warrants anything into the future. That is, § 5.14 ostensibly states that certain things are true and accurate as of the effective date of the Agreement. The representations and warranties found in § 5.14, however, must be accurate, as if stated on the Closing Date, before Buyer has an obligation to close. Both a breach of the § 6.2 covenants and an inaccuracy in the §§ 5.14(b)-and-(c) representations and warranties are potential grounds for: (i) Buyer's walking away from the deal as conditions to closing in §§ 4.2(a) and (b); and (ii) Buyer's indemnification rights as against Sellers under §§ 11.1(a)(i) and (ii). In addition to stating generally that the Company is to operate the Business as usual and to use "reasonable best efforts" to maintain its relationships, § 6.2 enumerates a list of acts that Sellers are not to do. Recall that § 5.14 does not contain any such exemplary list of prohibited behaviors. Another distinction is that § 5.14 contains representations and warranties made by Sellers (both the Parent and the Company), whereas § 6.2 imposes its covenants on the Company alone.

c. Restrictive Covenants Revisited: Sale-of-Business Context

In Chapters 1 and 2, we discussed restrictive covenants at length. In Chapter 1, we discussed non-disclosure agreements in both the employment and the commercial context, and, in this chapter, we have further touched upon how non-disclosure agreements may be used, specifically in the M&A context. In Chapter 2, we explored covenants not to compete as well as covenants not to solicit (both generally considered "restraints of trade") in the employment context. In this Agreement, we see how these same devices may be put to use in connection with M&A transactions.

A buyer of a business may be acutely concerned that the seller will turn around after the transaction and start anew in competition with the buyer and its newly acquired business. The ease with which a seller may do this—i.e., the risk of competition to the buyer—depends on the situation. Some (or almost all) of the real "assets" and value of a company might be its customer relations, its employees, and perhaps the know-how and savvy of its managers. These things are hard to "sell" and, absent a covenant not to, a seller may attempt to retain or reacquire them and/or otherwise to compete after selling its business. A buyer may obtain customer information as part of an M&A agreement and may hire certain employees along with its acquisition of the business, including executives and the owners of the sold business. But what is to keep, for example, a seller (or non-hired owners) from making use of this customer information to compete with the buyer, or any hired employees from going back to their old company, if it still exists? To answer the first question, a seller's non-compete covenant may prevent the seller from using customer information (or anything else) to compete with the buyer. To answer the second, the buyer might not agree to an M&A agreement unless, or might provide as a condition of closing that, certain employees agree to work for the acquired business. Then, as part of these employment arrangements, the buyer may have these new employees themselves agree to various restrictive covenants (which, in the employment context, are subjects of Chapters 1 and 2) so as to prevent their disclosing of the buyer's confidential information and their competition with the buyer's business. In addition, the buyer may present an individual seller with incentives to stay on with the company (e.g., to benefit under an "earnout" provision, as discussed above in the context of merger consideration).

In § 6.3 of the Agreement, we find a non-disclosure covenant; in § 6.6, a non-solicitation covenant; and, in § 6.7, a non-competition covenant. We know from § 6.1 that the parties have also executed a separate non-disclosure agreement (the Confidentiality Agreement). Separately including a confidentiality covenant within this Agreement has the effect of conditioning closing on material compliance with the covenant, given the setup of § 4.2(b).

Section 6.6 (Non-Solicitation) of the Agreement contains a covenant not to solicit employees. This covenant restricts each Seller from soliciting or attempting to hire any employee of the Business to be acquired. With regard to the meaning of "hire," the provision is careful not to trip over employment status (which we discuss in Chapter 2)—attempting to hire a Business employee as an employee, an independent contractor, or in any other capacity counts to breach the covenant. (However, the provision speaks of soliciting or attempting to hire only Business *employees*.) You will notice that this covenant is limited in time to three years after the Closing Date. Sellers have also negotiated a "safe-harbor" proviso in this restriction: Sellers may advertise open positions if they are not specifically sent to or not targeted at employees of the Business.

Drafting Note: "And" vs. "Or"

The proviso in § 6.6 reads (emphasis added):

provided, however, that nothing in this Section 6.6 shall prohibit any Seller from publishing or posting open positions in the course of normal hiring practices which <u>are not specifically sent to</u>, <u>or do not specifically target</u>, employees of the Business.

Is the intended meaning of this provision that Sellers may post open positions with impunity so long as they *either* do not specifically send the posting to the employees *or* do not specifically target the employees? Or, is the intended meaning that Seller may post with impunity so long as they *both* do not specifically send to *and* do not specifically target the employees? Would an employment posting specifically targeted at an employee (e.g., addressing the employee by first and last name) that is published in a newspaper and is in the course of normal hiring practices qualify a Seller for the proviso to the § 6.6 restriction on solicitation?

Regardless of which meaning was intended, either could be more clearly effected. If the parties meant that each of (i) Seller's posting without specifically targeting and (ii) Seller's posting without specifically sending is independently allowable under § 6.6, then they could have said:

> *provided, however*, that nothing in this Section 6.6 shall prohibit any Seller from publishing or posting open positions in the course of normal hiring practices, <u>if the open positions are either (i)</u> not specifically sent to, or <u>(ii)</u> not specifically target<u>ed at</u>, employees of the Business.

The original proviso on its face—with its use of "or" and distribution of "not" to each item—states that each of "not specifically sending" and "not specifically targeting" is independently sufficient to satisfy this component of the proviso.[94] Part of the confusion, however, lies in the floating "which" that is separated from the phrase to which it relates (i.e., "open positions")—the words in between make the sentence difficult to parse intuitively.[95] This problem is avoided by using an "if" clause to restate that phrase ("open positions") directly before the clause that modifies it. Adding "either" makes this disjunctive use of "or" explicit and clear, as do the romanettes, which signify that the "or" clause is meant formally and not as a mere restatement of the preceding clause.

---

94. Note that it is dangerous to use "not" prior to a series of items. Is it intended that the "not" simply be read as if placed before each of the items, or does the "not" apply to the whole? The distinction is meaningful—indeed, it is the same distinction as that between "and" and "or." In formal logic: Not (A or B) = Not A and Not B; Not (A and B) = Not A or Not B. This may not be intuitive at first, but think about it. If the statement "A or B" is false [i.e., "Not (A or B)"], then neither A nor B can be true because if either A or B were true, then the statement "A or B" would be true. If the statement "A and B" is false, then A is false, B is false, or they both are. Because both A *and* B must be true for "A and B" to be true, any false component of "A and B" (i.e., A, B, or both) is enough to render "A and B" false. How can you make English out of this? That is the question precisely. If you draft a sentence with a dangling "not" in front of a series of items, it may be unclear whether the "not" is intended to be read in front of each item in the series without flipping the "and" to an "or" (or vice versa) or whether the "not" is intended to apply to the whole series and distribute to each item in the series logically. In drafting, it is probably safer to do the work and distribute the "not" to each item—rather than state it once upfront—and use "and" or "or," depending on the desired meaning; this makes for more intuitive reading and takes the guesswork out of interpretation. This way a reader need not speculate as to how logically precise and savvy the drafters were in their language.

95. Note that if the original syntax were kept, "which" should be switched to "that." Removing the words that interfere reveals this most clearly (e.g., "nothing shall prohibit Seller from posting open positions that are not specifically targeted"). "That" is restrictive; it qualifies and limits the word or phrase it modifies, whereas "which" describes that to which it relates. For example: "I like pizza, which was invented in Italy. I like pizza that has pepperoni on it." The "which" clause teaches us about pizza, whereas the "that" clause restricts its reference to pizza to a subcategory: pizza with pepperoni on it.

We also did a bit of housekeeping by making both prongs "parallel," making both phrases work with "are." This also makes a bit more sense, as would-be employers—not "open positions"—"target" employees (in other words, "open positions" is not the appropriate subject to take the verb "target").

If the parties meant that Seller's posting is only allowable under § 6.6 when it is both without "specifically targeting" and without "specifically sending," then they could have said:

> *provided, however*, that nothing in this Section 6.6 shall prohibit any Seller from publishing or posting open positions in the course of normal hiring practices, <u>if the open positions are both (i)</u> not specifically sent to, <u>and (ii)</u> not specifically targeted <u>at</u>, employees of the Business.

In addition to the techniques used to remedy clarity issues just above, here we use "both" and "and" to communicate that each prong is necessary to satisfy the proviso. In addition, note that we needed the "are" to come before "both," lest the sentence read, "if the open positions both are. . . ." This would create the potential, unintended, at-least-initial confusion as to whether "both" modifies "open positions."

Section 6.7 (Non-Competition), in subsection (a)(i), contains a covenant not to encourage or solicit customers of (or others with a relationship with) the Business either to terminate their relationship with the Business or to do business with a competitor of the Business. This is not precisely a non-compete covenant in the traditional sense but rather a covenant not to solicit customers and otherwise not to interfere with the Business's relationships—it is sort of a contractual analog to tortious interference, with the benefit that a breach of this contractual provision may be easier to prove than a tortious interference claim.[96] Subsection 6.7(a)(ii) is a covenant not to compete, specifically proscribing Sellers from having any involvement with any person or entity (presumably, including a Seller itself, but this could be more clearly stated) that competes with the Business. This essentially gets at the idea that a Seller may compete in many ways—by competing with the Business itself, by investing in a company that competes with the Business, or by working for a company that competes with the Business. This non-compete covenant is not intended to prevent a Seller from investing in the stock market as a passive investor, which explains the exception that allows an investment of five percent or less in the outstanding voting shares of a competitor that is a publicly traded company. In addition, notice that Sellers have further negotiated several specific exceptions—activities, in which Sellers may engage, that do not constitute violations of § 6.7. Striking

---

96. Generally, tortious interference requires a showing that the interference was intentional and "wrongful" or "improper." *See, e.g.*, RESTATEMENT (SECOND) OF TORTS §§ 766 & 767 (1979). In contrast, a failure to perform a contractual term is a breach of contract, without inquiry as to intent or morality. *See, e.g.*, RESTATEMENT (SECOND) OF CONTRACTS § 235(2) (1981). Please see Chapter 1 for more on tortious interference.

this balance regarding what post-closing activities will constitute prohibited competition can be a highly contentious issue that may require intricate drafting to reach an accord. Like the non-solicitation covenant in § 6.6, the non-solicitation and non-compete covenants in § 6.7 are limited in time to three years after the Closing Date.

Recall from Chapters 1 and 2 that a big question with restrictive covenants is enforceability. With non-disclosure, non-solicitation, and non-compete covenants alike, the question is whether or not the restriction is "reasonable." We looked at the judicial tests for reasonableness in Chapters 1 and 2. To review, the test is usually some version of the following two prongs: (1) the restrictive covenant is no more restrictive than needed to serve a legitimate interest of the promisee; and (2) the restrictive covenant is not unduly harmful to the promisor or the public.[97] We also learned that courts are more suspicious of and stricter in testing for reasonableness with regard to those restrictive covenants that are "restraints of trade" (e.g., non-compete and non-solicitation covenants) than they are with those that are not (e.g., non-disclosure covenants generally). Where courts find a restrictive covenant to be unreasonable, they vary in their responses. Some are willing to modify the provision to be reasonable, some are willing to "blue pencil" the provision (which is a form of modifying that involves striking out portions of the provision if doing so leaves a sense-making, reasonable provision), and some are not willing to do anything, allowing the provision to fail entirely. We also learned that restraints of trade must be ancillary to another legitimate transaction or agreement (e.g., employment agreement, asset purchase agreement) to be enforceable. You may wish to turn back to Chapters 1 and 2 to review these concepts in more depth.

In the sale-of-business context, the test for reasonableness is generally the same.[98] However, courts are often self-consciously less wary of restrictive covenants employed as part of M&A transactions.[99] In this context, courts generally are more lenient in applying the reasonableness test to restrictive covenants.[100] As an extreme example, California, which does not enforce non-compete covenants at all in the employment context, will enforce reasonable non-compete

---

97. *See* RESTATEMENT (SECOND) OF CONTRACTS § 188(1) (1981).

98. *See id.* § 188(2) (providing that the reasonableness test described in part (1) applies to "a restraint that is ancillary to an otherwise valid transaction," where a valid transaction includes "a promise by the seller of a business not to compete with the buyer in such a way as to injure the value of the business sold").

99. *See, e.g., Palmer & Cay, Inc. v. Marsh & McLennan Cos., Inc.*, 404 F.3d 1297, 1303 (11th Cir. 2005) ("Georgia courts apply a low level of scrutiny to agreements ancillary to the sale of a business. . . ."); *Zimmer Melia & Assocs., Inc. v. Stallings*, No. 3:08-0663, 2008 WL 3887664, at *5 (M.D. Tenn. Aug. 21, 2008) ("In contrast, non-competes ancillary to the sale of a business are subjected to less intensive scrutiny. Courts have generally recognized that restrictive covenants are often necessary to secure value in the purchase of a business, particularly where substantial consideration is given for the business's good will.") (internal citation omitted); *Centorr-Vacuum Indus., Inc. v. Lavoie*, 609 A.2d 1213, 1215 (N.H. 1992) ("Because our caselaw looks upon contracts in restraint of trade with disfavor, courts normally construe noncompetition covenants narrowly. However, where, as in this case, the noncompetition covenant was ancillary to the sale of a business, it may be interpreted more liberally.") (internal citations omitted).

100. *See supra* note 99.

agreements that are ancillary to the sale of an entity or division.[101] Courts are also generally more *forgiving* of unreasonable restrictive covenants in the M&A arena. For example, while Georgia is a state that refuses to judicially tailor a restrictive covenant at all in the employment context, courts there *will* "blue pencil" restrictive covenant provisions that are ancillary to a sale of business.[102] As discussed in Chapters 1 and 2, it may be wise to include a "savings clause" that reminds a judge to modify a provision so as to make it enforceable if need be; however, such a clause is unlikely to make a court that is hostile to such measures change its mind.

Section 6.8(a) of the Agreement contains a representation and a warranty by Sellers that the Agreement's restrictive covenants are reasonable, tracking the standard elements of the reasonableness inquiry: that the covenants are necessary to protect Buyer's legitimate interests and do not impose undue hardships on the Sellers. This recitation neatly fits with the basic requirements of reasonableness and enforceability but is unlikely to dispose of the issue: An otherwise unreasonable restrictive covenant is not made reasonable by the parties' mere characterization.[103] While contractual recitations of reasonableness may be given some weight, a court is still likely to inquire into the actual facts and perform the same analysis regarding the reasonableness of a restrictive covenant.[104] However, as a practical matter, provisions like § 6.8 may help sway a court, frame a covenant as a bargained-for exchange between sophisticated commercial players, and demonstrate a legitimate interest by painting the picture of the intimate level of knowledge and exposure Sellers have with the Business.[105]

---

101. CAL. BUS. & PROF. CODE § 16601 (West 2008) ("Any person who sells the goodwill of a business, or any owner of a business entity selling or otherwise disposing of all of his or her ownership interest in the business entity, or any owner of a business entity that sells (a) all or substantially all of its operating assets together with the goodwill of the business entity, (b) all or substantially all of the operating assets of a division or a subsidiary of the business entity together with the goodwill of that division or subsidiary, or (c) all of the ownership interest of any subsidiary, may agree with the buyer to refrain from carrying on a similar business within a specified geographic area in which the business so sold, or that of the business entity, division, or subsidiary has been carried on, so long as the buyer, or any person deriving title to the goodwill or ownership interest from the buyer, carries on a like business therein.").

102. *See, e.g., Palmer*, 404 F.3d at 1303 (explaining that, in the sale-of-business context, Georgia courts "can reform, or 'blue-pencil,' any objectionable portions to bring them in conformance with Georgia law") (citation omitted).

103. *See, e.g., Jackson Hewitt Inc. v. Childress*, No. 06-CV-0909, 2008 WL 834386, at *10 (D.N.J. Mar. 27, 2008) (considering promisor's contractual acknowledgements along with other facts in performing reasonableness analysis); *Poole v. U.S. Money Reserve, Inc.*, No. 09-08-137CV, 2008 WL 4735602, at *8 (Tex. App. Oct. 30, 2008) ("[W]e conclude that the language of the agreement at issue here is but one consideration in our analysis to be viewed in conjunction with the record in its entirety.").

104. *See supra* note 103.

105. *See, e.g., Int'l Bus. Machs. Corp. v. Papermaster*, No. 08-CV-9078, 2008 WL 4974508, at *12 (S.D.N.Y. 2008) ("In particular, IBM persuasively argues that Mr. Papermaster's knowledge of the IBM 'Power' architecture is 'unique' and 'irreplaceable,' a fact that Mr. Papermaster himself acknowledged in his Noncompetition Agreement.").

d. Deal Protection Devices

Section 6.9 (No Solicitation of Alternative Transactions) of the Agreement is a version of a so-called "no-shop" provision, imposing a covenant on Sellers, in this case, not even to encourage the negotiation of any preliminary document (e.g., an LOI), much less final agreement, regarding the sale of the Assets or Business with anyone besides the Buyer. This covenant runs from the date of the Agreement until the Closing or the termination of the Agreement, whichever comes first.

It is often said that no would-be buyer wants to be a "stalking horse." In other words, a buyer does not want to have engaged in negotiations and to have seemingly settled on a price only to have the seller use these negotiated terms as a benchmark to shop the deal to other suitors, field additional bids, and drive up the price. In order to avoid this situation, "no-shop" covenants may be included as binding provisions within another preliminary document, such as a letter of intent (as seen earlier in this chapter), or within the M&A agreement itself (as seen in the Agreement), so as to prevent the seller from shopping the deal between execution and closing.

There are many devices used to attempt to "lock up" a deal, of which the "no-shop" provision is just one example, including (i) avoidance-of-third-party measures, such as "no-talk" provisions, which limit the target company from providing certain information to third parties and "no-shop" provisions (as we have seen), which limit the target company from negotiating alternative deals with third parties (sometimes a distinction is made between "no-shop" and "window-shop" provisions, the latter of which typically allows a seller to respond to unsolicited offers); (ii) affirmative obligations, such as "best efforts" provisions that require a target board to use its best efforts to consummate the deal and voting agreements that obligate certain shareholders to vote in favor of the merger; and (iii) failure-to-close back-up plans, such as breakup fees owed to the suitor by the target if the deal does not ultimately close as well as stock and/or asset purchase options, which give the suitor the right to purchase stock and/or certain assets of the target corporation if the deal does not close.[106] Note that even if the target company's board agrees to certain lock-up covenants, presuming their enforceability, this might not fully address the buyer's concern: A second suitor may go straight to the target's shareholders and offer a cash tender offer to purchase their shares directly or, if the transaction requires shareholder approval for consummation, may publicize a competing, better offer to encourage a "no" vote by the shareholders.[107]

---

106. *See generally* David A. Katz, *Takeover Law and Practice 2007*, *in* 2 Negotiating Business Acquisitions § N, at 54-62 (American Bar Association 2007). It is also possible for an agreement to include "reverse breakup fees," owed to the target (i.e., seller) by the suitor (i.e., buyer), as Mr. Gelston discusses in a practitioner comment later in this chapter.

107. *See* Diane Holt Frankle, *Fiduciary Duties in Considering Deal Lockups: What's a Board To Do?*, *in* Negotiating Business Acquisitions, *supra* note 64, at § K.

As you may learn about in much greater depth in a business organizations or an M&A course, the board of directors of a corporation owes fiduciary duties of care and loyalty to the corporation and its shareholders. The board of directors of a corporation cannot contract with a third party in contravention of these duties, and any such provision will likely be unenforceable.[108] Accordingly, in some deal protection covenants, parties may include a so-called "fiduciary-out" provision. A fiduciary-out provides that a seller's obligations under a deal protection covenant, for example, not to talk or negotiate with third-party suitors, are subject to the seller's fiduciary duties. In other words, a fiduciary-out provision allows the seller's board of directors to negotiate with third parties or to take other actions if its fiduciary duties require it to do so. In this way, a fiduciary-out provision is tantamount to a "savings clause" that serves to avoid the invalidity of the provision for being incongruous with a board's fiduciary duties.[109]

You may have noticed that § 6.9 of the Agreement does not contain a fiduciary-out provision. However, this is not problematic. Why? The Agreement is for the sale of a division of the Company, which appears not to constitute substantially all of its assets; thus, the Company's shareholders need not approve the transaction for the Company's board to bind the Company. That is, just as the Company may enter, for example, a services agreement—or an agreement for any other non-fundamental transaction—without shareholder approval and may contractually bind the Company to consummate such a transaction, so too may a Company sell some of its assets.[110] As with any other decision or activity, the board of directors owes duties of loyalty and care to the corporation and its shareholders. And, with everyday transactions, the decisions and activities of the board of directors is granted general deference and protection under the "business-judgment rule," "a presumption that in making a business decision the directors of a corporation acted on an informed basis, in good faith and in the honest belief that the action taken was in the best interests of the company."[111]

---

108. *See, e.g.*, Restatement (Second) of Contracts § 193 (1981) ("[A] promise by a fiduciary to violate his fiduciary duty or a promise that tends to induce such a violation is unenforceable on ground of public policy."); *Ace Ltd. v. Capital Re Corp.*, 747 A.2d 95, 104-05 (Del. Ch. 1999).

109. Please see Chapters 1 and 2 for a discussion regarding savings and severability clauses.

110. *See Omnicare, Inc. v. NCS Heathcare, Inc.*, 818 A.2d 914, 939 n.88 (Del. 2003) ("Merger agreements involve an ownership decision and, therefore, cannot become final without stockholder approval. Other contracts do not require a fiduciary out clause because they involve business judgments that are within the *exclusive* province of the board of directors' power to manage the affairs of the corporation.") (emphasis in original); *Grimes v. Donald*, 673 A.2d 1207, 1214-15 (Del. 1996) ("Likewise, business decisions are not an abdication of directorial authority merely because they limit a board's freedom of future action. A board which has decided to manufacture bricks has less freedom to decide to make bottles. In a world of scarcity, a decision to do one thing will commit a board to a certain course of action and make it costly and difficult (indeed, sometimes impossible) to change course and do another. This is an inevitable fact of life and is not an abdication of directorial duty.").

111. *Aronson v. Lewis*, 473 A.2d 805, 812 (Del. 1984), *rev'd on other grounds, Brehm v. Eisner*, 746 A.2d 244 (Del. 2000).

For further discussion of deal protection covenants in practice, we turn to a seasoned practitioner.

A Practitioner Perspective: Deal Protection Covenants

In public company acquisition agreements, deal protection covenants are often among the most heavily negotiated provisions. Deal protection covenants are designed to protect the buyer's negotiated deal by discouraging competing offers from other potential acquirors and, in some instances, to provide compensation to the party that is harmed if the acquisition agreement is terminated. Sellers often agree to deal protection covenants because they increase deal certainty and are often traded for other terms desired by sellers, such as an increase in the purchase price. Generally, deal protection covenants can be categorized into three broad categories: voting protection mechanisms, exclusivity provisions and compensation measures.

Voting protection mechanisms are designed to enable a seller to guarantee a certain percentage of its shareholders' votes in connection with a transaction. In situations where there is a majority shareholder or an easily ascertainable group of majority shareholders, a seller would ordinarily go to its majority shareholder(s) and facilitate an agreement pursuant to which its majority shareholder(s) agree(s) to deposit or tender shares in a take-over bid, or, if shareholders' consent is required, agree(s) to vote in favor of the acquisition before the actual shareholder vote is held. In transactions where ownership of a company is diverse, sellers can offer less voting protection to the buyer. While of questionable enforceability as the result of a much criticized Delaware Supreme Court case, combining a majority shareholder voting agreement with a seller agreeing to put an acquisition to a vote of shareholders can give an acquiror theoretical certainty.

Almost all buyers require the inclusion of exclusivity provisions in an acquisition agreement, often called "no-shop/no talk" provisions (however, where a deal is not subject to a pre-signing market check, the agreement may sometimes contain a "go-shop" provision, where the target is permitted to solicit interest). Such exclusivity provisions often (i) restrict the target company from (a) directly or indirectly soliciting or encouraging any other competing offers from a third-party acquiror, (b) providing confidential information to any such third-party acquiror and (c) discussing or negotiating with such third-party acquirors and (ii) requires the target company to disclose to the buyer the terms of any such proposal and the identity of the third-party acquiror. However, in the acquisition of a public company, a "fiduciary-out" provision is a common carve-out to the no-shop/no-talk provisions. Essentially, this carve-out provision acknowledges the target board of director's fiduciary obligations to the company's shareholders and permits the board to consider and possibly accept a superior proposal from a third-party acquiror. Numerous conditions are often imposed on what constitutes a superior offer and the circumstances under which the target company may accept a superior offer. For example, often it is a condition that the offer be deemed superior by the target's legal and financial advisors and that there is sufficient certainty that the superior transaction will actually be consummated.

Compensation measures are designed to reimburse the buyer for having spent significant time and expense involved in the transaction if it is ultimately unsuccessful. The most common compensation measure is a termination fee, which is simply a cash payment by the seller made to the originally intended buyer, typically in connection with the exercise of a fiduciary out. Other compensation measures include a stock lock-up, which is an option granted to the originally intended buyer to buy shares of the seller's stock upon a triggering event (for example, the acceptance by the target of a superior proposal), and an asset lock-up, which is an option granted to the originally intended buyer to buy an asset of the target upon a triggering event (and often the asset includes the most attractive asset of the target, otherwise known as its "crown jewel"). It should be noted that compensation measures also act as deterrents to bids from third-party acquirors because such acquirors will need to include the cost and effect of the compensation measures into its bid for the target.

In private company deals, deal protection covenants are often less germane because (i) private companies are often wholly-owned, (ii) when they have more than one shareholder, they often have contractual arrangements in place (such as a shareholders' agreement) in which the shareholders have agreed to the exit procedures that will govern upon a sale of the company or its assets and (iii) the alignment of shareholders' interests often reduce the risk of fiduciary challenges made to the decisions of the board of directors. In the public deal context, where the target's shareholder base is diverse and almost always lack contractual arrangements governing exit procedures, the board of directors of the target must be cognizant of its fiduciary duties. A target's board of directors in a public deal context needs the protections of deal protection covenants and fiduciary outs in order to provide deal certainty to its shareholders and to comply with its fiduciary obligations.

Brian Hoffmann
Partner and Co-Head of Americas M&A
Clifford Chance US LLP

As with other covenants, a breach of a deal protection covenant may allow a party to avoid closing (see § 4.2(b) of the Agreement), may allow a party to terminate the agreement (see § 15.1(b) of the Agreement), and may give rise to claims for damages and/or indemnification (see § 11.1(a)(ii) of the Agreement). In addition, as discussed by Mr. Hoffmann, parties may sometimes include "breakup fees," which are usually triggered by termination. In Delaware, breakup fees are not per se invalid, but, to be enforceable, a breakup fee must not amount to a preclusive or coercive defensive device (or otherwise cause a board to breach its fiduciary duties), in combination with other defensive measures.[112] Delaware courts have found breakup fees in the 2-4 percent range of the deal

---

112. *See, e.g., McMillan v. Intercargo Corp.*, 768 A.2d 492, 505 (Del. Ch. 2000).

value to be reasonable in certain cases.[113] In addition, a court might analyze breakup fees as liquidated-damages provisions, and breakup fees will not be enforced if they amount to penalties.[114] The Delaware Supreme Court has subjected a breakup fee to this analysis, where the agreement specifically referenced the provision as "liquidated damages."[115]

To shed light on the "real-world" relevance of these issues, we asked a seasoned practitioner, Philip A. Gelston, to offer his perspective on what he has found some of the contentious issues to be in his M&A practice. His response, which follows, highlights deal protection and material adverse change, the latter of which we discuss further in the section following Mr. Gelston's commentary.

A Practitioner Perspective: Contentious Issues in M&A Agreements

Merger agreements can be thick, complicated documents. Much of the bulk comes from the need to set forth the legal engineering that makes the transaction actually happen or consists of provisions, such as routine representations, warranties and covenants, that are important and need to be prepared carefully, but do not generate much heated controversy during meetings among lawyers. In most negotiations, however, much attention will be paid to two matters, the importance of which became more apparent in the aftermath of the recent credit and stock market meltdowns.

The first is allocation of the risk that something goes wrong between signing and closing. This could be, for example, an unwelcome change in the acquired company's business, and the provision covering that risk is the "material adverse change" clause—often called the "MAC". Years ago, MACs were relatively short and straightforward. Now they are heavily negotiated bespoke provisions with so many exceptions, exceptions to the exceptions and qualifiers to the exceptions to the exceptions that reading one can be challenging even to experienced lawyers. Despite the effort put into carefully crafting these clauses, when a purchaser actually tries to terminate a deal relying on a MAC, courts tend to interpret the complicated provisions as being substantively similar to the old-fashioned simple ones and to permit cancelation of the deal only if there has been a truly important change with long lasting significance that would not have been reasonably foreseeable by the buyer. Another risk is that regulatory clearance cannot be obtained without material changes to the combined business, including divestitures. The amount of change an acquiror will accept is usually expressed through a combination of the closing condition for regulatory approvals and the scope of the acquiror's obligation to cooperate with regulatory authorities. Negotiation of the latter obligation can result in extensive discussion about

---

113. *See, e.g., id.* (finding a breakup fee of 3.5 percent, while "at the high end of what our courts have approved," to be within the range of reasonableness); *In re The Topps Co. S'holders Litig.*, 926 A.2d 58, 86 (Del. Ch. 2007) ("Likewise, the termination fee and expense reimbursement he was to receive if Topps terminated and accepted another . . . was around 4.3% of the total deal value. Although this is a bit high in percentage terms, it includes Eisner's expenses, and therefore can be explained by the relatively small size of the deal.").

114. Please see Chapter 1 for further discussion of liquidated damages.

115. *See, e.g., Brazen v. Bell Atl. Corp.*, 695 A.2d 43, 47-48 (Del. 1997).

the difference between similar sounding terms like "best efforts," "reasonable best efforts," "commercially reasonable efforts" and "reasonable efforts."

The second is the strength of the commitment to close. Deal protection is one side of this set of issues. Deal protection provisions are designed to discourage third parties from making competing bids or to make stockholder approval of the original bid more likely even if there is competition (and to provide some compensation to a bidder who ultimately loses the deal for the service of setting a floor on subsequent offers). Negotiation of these provisions involves an unseen party—the judiciary, particularly of Delaware. The scope of deal protection must reflect both what the acquiror and the acquired company want and what the law will allow. The case law governing deal protection is voluminous, complicated and still evolving, but it reflects a basic principle that in all but the most extraordinary circumstances, deal protection should not be so extensive that stockholders are deprived of the opportunity to consider and accept the best deal someone will offer. This means that the lawyers frequently will advise a target board not to agree to overly strong deal protection even if the directors actually would like to do so. Of course, an acquired company may also insist on a conservative interpretation of what is "legal" because its board as a business matter would welcome competing bids but would prefer not to say so explicitly.

The consequences to the acquiror if it simply refuses to close are the other side of this set of issues. When stock prices were soaring, no one worried much about this. But when they tumbled a number of buyers, particularly but not exclusively private equity buyers, simply changed their minds. At that point, target companies began to focus on the real consequences of a reverse breakup fee provision. Reverse breakup fees began as a concession by private equity buyers to provide some penalty if they did not obtain financing—in the earlier form of private equity deals, the buyer either had a financing condition or was a judgment-proof shell entity. This concept evolved relatively quickly into a fixed fee that provided compensation for any breach by the buyer. In many deals, it was the exclusive remedy for any breach including a blatant refusal to close, ruling out greater damages or even specific performance. This proved to be an advantageous structure for buyers when the drop in stock values exceeded by many multiples the amount of the fee. Deals are still being done with the reverse breakup fee structure, even with strategic buyers, but sellers presumably are more conscious of the risks they are taking. More risk-averse sellers will seek some greater protection against buyer's remorse. At a minimum, the seller would want the right to seek specific performance. Even better from the seller's perspective is the right to seek damages, because when specific performance is the only remedy a purchaser wishing to get out of a deal has little disincentive to avoid an expansive reading of closing conditions, particularly the MAC; the only consequence of being wrong is an order to close which puts the purchaser in no worse position than it would have been if it had not asserted a condition. If the seller succeeds in negotiating the possibility of a damage claim (or more accurately, resists the buyer's effort to limit or eliminate damages), it should consider making clear that the calculation of damages will include the lost benefit of the bargain to stockholders. In some jurisdictions, it is not clear this is the case unless specified in the contract. Once rare, these provisions are increasingly common for sellers with bargaining power. In addition, when the buyer is a shell entity, the right to damages must be supported by an obligation by the funding parent to provide money for a successful damages claim.

> Philip A. Gelston
> Partner
> Chairman of Mergers and Acquisitions Practice
> Cravath, Swaine & Moore LLP

7. Closing and Conditions; Material Adverse Effect

Much of the discussion in this chapter, from structuring transactions to representations and warranties to covenants, has been a prelude to closing and the obligation to consummate the core transaction at issue in an agreement for merger or acquisition. Section 3.3 of the Agreement sets out when the Closing is to occur and what is to occur at the Closing. The Agreement leaves it up to the parties to later agree on the exact time and place of the Closing, except that it must occur by the fifth business day after all of the Closing conditions (not including those that are to be satisfied at the Closing) are satisfied. Note that § 3.3 itself contains a "condition"[116] to closing, providing that 60 days must pass from when certain notices and consent requests (as required by § 6.5) are sent before Closing may occur. This proviso limits the otherwise wide discretion given to the parties to decide when and where to close. While they did not opt to do so in this Agreement, the parties could have chosen to set a fixed date for closing.

At the Closing, Buyer and Sellers must deliver certain things to effectuate the acquisition. The Buyer must pay the merger consideration to the Company (and the Company must give Buyer a receipt). The parties are to exchange whatever documents are necessary to effectively transfer ownership of the Assets to Buyer.

---

116. Note that technically some courts and the *Restatement* suggest that "the passage of time" does not constitute a "condition." *See, e.g., Seaford Assocs. Ltd. P'ship v. Subway Real Estate Corp.*, No. Civ. A. 2248, 2003 WL 21254847, at *5 n. 30 (Del. Ch. 2003) ("A 'condition precedent' is defined as: 'An act or event, other than a lapse of time, that must exist or occur before a duty to perform something promised arises.'") (citing BLACK's LAW DICTIONARY 289 (7th ed. 1999)); RESTATEMENT (SECOND) OF CONTRACTS § 224 cmt. b (1981) ("Therefore, the mere passage of time, as to which there is no uncertainty, is not a condition and a duty is unconditional if nothing but the passage of time is necessary to give rise to a duty of performance."). However, the distinction may not be terribly relevant, as comment b to the *Restatement* further explains, "Performance under a contract becomes due when all necessary events, including any conditions and the passage of any required time, have occurred so that a failure of performance will be a breach." *See also* 8-30 CORBIN ON CONTRACTS § 30.5 ("If A has delivered the goods in exchange for B's promise to pay $100 in thirty days, we say that A has a 'right' and that B is indebted, even though no societal remedy will be available until after the passage of thirty days time. This is a right to future performance, not a right to immediate performance. It is not usually called a 'conditional' right, for the reason that the passage of time is regarded as a matter of such certainty that it is disregarded in description.").

Notice that Buyer is given some discretion here, as tempered by reasonableness, to determine what documents are necessary. Also, at the Closing, the Company and Buyer are to execute a transition services agreement. As § 9.9 explains, there will be a gap in time between Closing and when the operational and accounting systems of the Business are converted to Buyer's platform. Accordingly, while Buyer is to own the Assets as of Closing, Sellers will manage the Assets for Buyer according to the terms of this transition services agreement. Additionally, at the Closing, Buyer wants a list of all Employees that Sellers have terminated during a certain window before the Closing. And lastly, Sellers and Buyer must deliver to each other certain closing certificates, the delivery of which is a condition precedent to Closing obligations (see §§ 4.2(f), 4.3(c)). The closing certificates under the Agreement are signed statements by an executive officer of each Seller and Buyer confirming the satisfaction of certain of their respective conditions to Closing, namely those conditions pertaining to representations, warranties, and covenants.

These are the events that are to occur at the Closing under this Agreement, but we have to get there first. Before each party may bind the other to perform its obligations at Closing, certain conditions must first be satisfied. Please note that while the failure to satisfy a condition is not generally a "breach" of any obligation, the parties to this Agreement have agreed in § 9.3 (Reasonable Efforts) to use their "reasonable efforts" to satisfy all conditions to Closing within the party's control.[117]

a. Reciprocal Conditions to Closing

Under § 4.1 of the Agreement, before either party may obligate the other to close, certain governmental and regulatory conditions must be satisfied, including that: (a) no judgment or injunction prohibits the transaction; (b) no Governmental Entity (as defined) has initiated proceedings to challenge or restrain the transaction; and (c) all Governmental Entity authorizations, filings, and registrations required for the transaction have been obtained and any waiting periods (such as required by the Hart-Scott-Rodino Act) have elapsed. Obtaining antitrust clearance and agreeing on which party controls the process of dealing with the government can be extremely important issues in M&A transactions. The Agreement specifically lays out conditions that precede the Buyer's obligation to close in § 4.2 and those that precede Sellers' obligation in § 4.3.

---

117. Please see Chapter 4 for more on performance standards and conditions.

b. Conditions to Buyer's Obligation to Close

(1) The "Bring-Down" Provision: Representations and Warranties

In § 4.2(a), we find a so-called "bring-down" provision, which grafts a conditional effect onto the representations and warranties stated in the Agreement. Note that § 4.2 asks not whether a representation or warranty was false when made or untrue prior to Closing but rather whether or not the representation or warranty was true and correct "as though made on and as of" the Closing. Section 4.2(a)(i) provides that certain representations and warranties (§§ 5.1, 5.2, 5.3, and 5.6) must be correct "in all material respects" before Buyer is obligated to close. Separately, before Buyer must close, § 4.2(a)(ii) provides that all other representations and warranties must be true, "except where the failure to be so true and correct would in the aggregate not have a Material Adverse Effect." Restated, the failure of these other representations and warranties only gives Buyer a right to walk away where the failure, in conjunction with any other such failure, constitutes a Material Adverse Effect. By specifying "in the aggregate," § 4.2(a)(ii) addresses a situation where several individual failures of representations and warranties may not constitute a Material Adverse Effect on their own but *may* constitute an MAE when taken together. As § 4.2(c) already gives Buyer a "walk" right for the occurrence of a Material Adverse Effect, does this § 4.2(a)(ii) actually give Buyer anything it does not already have under § 4.2(c)?

The last sentence of § 4.2(a) speaks to a concern about "double materiality." The thought is that a representation or warranty itself may be cast in terms of materiality and that the "bring-down" provision then may add another layer of materiality to the mix. Does this mean that a representation and warranty that, say, a party must not fail to be in good standing in a way that causes a Material Adverse Effect, operates as a condition to closing that a party must not fail to be in good standing in a way that causes a Material Adverse Effect, in all material respects? And, if so, what does *this* mean? To avoid the head-spinning confusion or potentially unintended construction of the various interplays of materiality qualifications, parties will sometimes draft provisions, like that found in § 4.2(a), that wash away the original layer of materiality in favor of the bring-down provision's materiality qualifications. While there is some debate about whether "double materiality" is indeed a real problem or just a figment of the imagination of the overly cautious lawyer,[118] most cautious lawyers will attempt to draft with clarity and avoid the interaction of several materiality qualifications, which might at the very least introduce confusion.

You will note that this "double materiality" provision in § 4.2(a) excepts § 5.14 from its coverage. Why? Section 5.14(a) states a representation and

---

118. *See, e.g.*, Kenneth A. Adams, *A Legal-Usage Analysis of "Material Adverse Change" Provisions*, 10 FORDHAM J. CORP. & FIN. L. 9, 15 (2004) ("In any event, the absence of any case law discussing double materiality makes it difficult to assess whether it is a real issue or a theoretical construct.").

warranty that there has been no Material Adverse Effect since December 31, 2005. In the context of the bring-down provision in § 4.2(a)(ii), § 5.14(a) would be meaningless if we took out "Material Adverse Effect" and applied the condition that the representation and warranty shall be correct except where the failure to be correct constitutes a Material Adverse Effect—*what* shall be correct? Absent its own "Material Adverse Effect" language, § 5.14(a) says literally nothing. As to "double materiality," if § 5.14(a) were to fail because a Material Adverse Effect occurred since December 31, 2005, then, the failure of § 5.14(a) *could* be found also to constitute an MAE for § 4.2(a)(ii) purposes.[119]

(2) "Bringing Down" Covenants and Other Obligations

Section 4.2(b) "brings down" the covenants and other obligations imposed by the Agreement on Sellers. The failure of Sellers materially to perform or comply with those covenants and obligations that Sellers must perform or comply with by the Closing Date gives Buyer the right not to close. Notice that Buyer did not obtain a provision here parallel to the provision in § 4.2(a) to address "double materiality" in the covenants context. Why might "double materiality" be a Buyer concern in this context?

(3) Material Adverse Effect or Change

Throughout Chapters 5 and 6, we have seen a wide variety of ways "Material Adverse Effect" language can be put to use—from qualifying a representation and warranty (e.g., Party Z represents and warrants that A is true, except where the failure to be true does not constitute a Material Adverse Effect) to stating a representation and warranty (e.g., Party Z represents and warrants that no Material Adverse Effect has occurred since December 31, 20XX) to stating a condition to closing (e.g., Party Z's obligation to close is conditioned on a Material Adverse Effect not having occurred since the Effective Date of this Agreement).

Section 4.2(c) does two things. First, it provides a condition to Closing—that no MAE "shall have occurred" before Buyer is obligated to consummate the Closing. Second, it defines MAE, which under the Agreement is any event that by itself or in combination with other events is or *would reasonably be expected to be*

---

119. However, the Agreement is not clear as to when the relevant "starting date" is for measuring a MAE for the purposes of § 4.2(a)(ii). Inasmuch as the relevant measuring date for an MAE under § 4.2(a)(ii) is different from that of § 5.14(a) (e.g., the date of execution of the Agreement, the Closing Date), then it may be meaningful that the MAE limitation in § 4.2(a)(ii) would seem to require that any MAE since December 31, 2005 under § 5.14(a) must also constitute an MAE under § 4.2(a)(ii)—i.e., an MAE since the unspecified start date—for the condition in § 4.2(a)(ii) to fail and for Buyer to be allowed to walk for this reason. That is, even if an MAE since December 31, 2005, has occurred, Buyer cannot walk under § 4.2(a)(ii) unless this also constitutes an MAE under § 4.2(a)(ii), which theoretically could involve a different MAE inquiry, given the lack of clarity. Accordingly, for the sake of clarity, § 4.2(a)(ii) (and § 4.3) may wish to specify "since when" for their MAE conditions. However, it seems strange to think a court would find an MAE to have occurred since the Closing, if the court did not find an MAE to have occurred since a date earlier than the Closing.

materially adverse to (x) the operations, property, financial condition, or other condition of the Business as a whole, or (y) Sellers' ability to perform their obligations under the Agreement or to sell the Assets to Buyer. These get at different concerns: Clause (x) is a way for Buyer to walk if the Business changes in certain undesirable ways, whereas clause (y) excuses Buyer's performance of the transaction if Sellers' ability to perform the Agreement or the transaction has been compromised.

Sellers obtained several carve-outs from what constitutes a "type-x" MAE, including any changes or effects that result from an event that affected the Business's entire industry, U.S. markets, changes in laws, regulations, or accounting principles applicable to the Business, natural disasters, terrorism, or war, the public announcement of the Agreement, or the loss of employees or customers following the announcement of this Agreement or the sale of the Assets. Notice that even these carve-outs contain an exception: According to § 4.2(c), where changes due to the industry, the market, laws, natural disasters, terrorism, or war disproportionately affect the Business, this disproportionate effect may still be considered an MAE. A good question is "disproportionate vis-à-vis what?" For instance, the change in U.S. laws might disproportionately affect a business vis-à-vis all world businesses and a business vis-à-vis all U.S. businesses but perhaps not a business vis-à-vis all U.S. businesses in that business's industry. For the term "disproportionately" to have meaning, there must be a basis for comparison. These carve-outs and the disproportionality exception to the carve-outs all apply only to the first prong of what may constitute an MAE under the Agreement. Separately, something may be an MAE if it is or would be reasonably expected to be materially adverse to Sellers' ability to perform their obligations or to consummate the sale. That is, if a change in law occurs (a carve-out from "type-x" MAE) that does not disproportionately affect the Business (not an exception to the carve-out), this may still be an MAE, according to the language of § 4.2(c) if the change in law is materially adverse to Sellers' ability to perform its obligations under the Agreement.

What constitutes an "MAE" has been the subject of considerable litigation. As the occurrence of an MAE allows a buyer to walk away from a deal, a buyer may make a calculated decision to litigate the matter rather than to close on a deal and acquire a business that has gone sour. In thinking about what might constitute an MAE and trigger "walk rights," please consider the following case.

In re IBP, Inc. Shareholders Litigation
Court of Chancery of Delaware, 2001.
789 A.2d 14.

STRINE, Vice Chancellor.

This post-trial opinion addresses a demand for specific performance of a "Merger Agreement" by IBP, Inc., the nation's number one beef and number two pork distributor. By this action, IBP seeks to compel the "Merger" between itself and Tyson Foods, Inc., the nation's leading chicken distributor, in a transaction in which IBP stockholders will receive their choice of $30 a share in cash or Tyson stock, or a combination of the two.

The IBP-Tyson Merger Agreement resulted from a vigorous auction process that pitted Tyson against the nation's number one pork producer, Smithfield Foods. To say that Tyson was eager to win the auction is to slight its ardent desire to possess IBP. During the bidding process, Tyson was anxious to ensure that it would acquire IBP, and to make sure Smithfield did not. By succeeding, Tyson hoped to create the world's preeminent meat products company-a company that would dominate the meat cases of supermarkets in the United States and eventually throughout the globe.

During the auction process, Tyson was given a great deal of information that suggested that IBP was heading into a trough in the beef business. Even more, Tyson was alerted to serious problems at an IBP subsidiary, DFG, which had been victimized by accounting fraud to the tune of over $30 million in charges to earnings and which was the active subject of an asset impairment study. Not only that, Tyson knew that IBP was projected to fall seriously short of the fiscal year 2000 earnings predicted in projections prepared by IBP's Chief Financial Officer in August, 2000.

By the end of the auction process, Tyson had come to have great doubts about IBP's ability to project its future earnings, the credibility of IBP's management, and thought that the important business unit in which DFG was located—Foodbrands—was broken.

Yet, Tyson's ardor for IBP was such that Tyson raised its bid by a total of $4.00 a share after learning of these problems. Tyson also signed the Merger Agreement, which permitted IBP to recognize unlimited additional liabilities on account of the accounting improprieties at DFG. It did so without demanding any representation that IBP meet its projections for future earnings, or any escrow tied to those projections.

After the Merger Agreement was signed on January 1, 2001, Tyson trumpeted the value of the merger to its stockholders and the financial community, and indicated that it was fully aware of the risks that attended the cyclical nature of IBP's business. In early January, Tyson's stockholders ratified the merger agreement and authorized its management to take whatever action was needed to effectuate it.

During the winter and spring of 2001, Tyson's own business performance was dismal. Meanwhile, IBP was struggling through a poor first quarter. Both companies' problems were due in large measure to a severe winter, which adversely affected livestock supplies and vitality. As these struggles deepened, Tyson's desire to buy IBP weakened.

This cooling of affections first resulted in a slow-down by Tyson in the process of consummating a transaction, a slow-down that was attributed to IBP's on-going efforts to resolve issues that had been raised about its financial statements by the Securities and Exchange Commission ("SEC"). The most important of these issues was how to report the problems at DFG, which Tyson had been aware of at the time it signed the Merger Agreement. Indeed, all the key issues that the SEC raised with IBP were known by Tyson at the time it signed the Merger Agreement. The SEC first raised these issues in a faxed letter on December 29, 2000 to IBP's outside counsel. Neither IBP management nor Tyson learned of the letter until the second week of January, 2001. After learning of the letter, Tyson management put the Merger Agreement to a successful board and stockholder vote.

But the most important reason that Tyson slowed down the Merger process was different: it was having buyer's regret. Tyson wished it had paid less especially in view of its own compromised 2001 performance and IBP's slow 2001 results.

By March, Tyson's founder and controlling stockholder, Don Tyson, no longer wanted to go through with the Merger Agreement. He made the decision to abandon the Merger. His son, John Tyson, Tyson's Chief Executive Officer, and the other Tyson managers followed his instructions. Don Tyson abandoned the Merger because of IBP's and Tyson's poor results in 2001, and not because of DFG or the SEC issues IBP was dealing with. Indeed, Don Tyson told IBP management that he would blow DFG up if he were them.

After the business decision was made to terminate, Tyson's legal team swung into action. They fired off a letter terminating the Agreement at the same time as they filed suit accusing IBP of fraudulently inducing the Merger that Tyson had once so desperately desired. . . .

. . . Primarily implicated in this case are the following representations and warranties:

> . . . Section 5.10. *Absence of Certain Changes.* Except as set forth in *Schedule 5.10* hereto, the Company 10-K or the Company 10-Qs, since the Balance Sheet Date, the Company and the Subsidiaries have conducted their business in the ordinary course consistent with past practice and there has not been:
> (a) any event, occurrence or development of a state of circumstances or facts which has had or reasonably could be expected to have a Material Adverse Effect. . . .

D. Was Tyson's Termination Justified Because IBP Has Suffered A Material Adverse Effect?

Tyson argues that it was also permitted to terminate because IBP had breached § 5.10 of the Agreement, which is a representation and warranty that IBP had not suffered a material adverse effect since the "Balance Sheet Date" of December 25, 1999, except as set forth in the Warranted Financials or Schedule 5.10 of the Agreement. Under the contract, a material adverse effect (or "MAE") is defined as "any event, occurrence or development of a state of circumstances or facts which has had or reasonably could be expected to have a Material

Adverse Effect" . . . "on the condition (financial or otherwise), business, assets, liabilities or results of operations of [IBP] and [its] Subsidiaries taken as whole. . . ."

Tyson asserts that the decline in IBP's performance in the last quarter of 2000 and the first quarter of 2001 evidences the existence of a Material Adverse Effect. It also contends that the DFG Impairment Charge constitutes a Material Adverse Effect. And taken together, Tyson claims that it is virtually indisputable that the combination of these factors amounts to a Material Adverse Effect.

In addressing these arguments, it is useful to be mindful that Tyson's publicly expressed reasons for terminating the Merger did not include an assertion that IBP had suffered a Material Adverse Effect. The post-hoc nature of Tyson's arguments bear on what it felt the contract meant when contracting, and suggests that a short-term drop in IBP's performance would not be sufficient to cause a MAE. To the extent the facts matter, it is also relevant that Tyson gave no weight to DFG in contracting.

The resolution of Tyson's Material Adverse Effect argument requires the court to engage in an exercise that is quite imprecise. The simplicity of § 5.10's words is deceptive, because the application of those words is dauntingly complex. On its face, § 5.10 is a capacious clause that puts IBP at risk for a variety of uncontrollable factors that might materially affect its overall business or results of operation as a whole. Although many merger contracts contain specific exclusions from MAE clauses that cover declines in the overall economy or the relevant industry sector, or adverse weather or market conditions, § 5.10 is unqualified by such express exclusions.

IBP argues, however, that statements in the Warranted Financials that emphasize the risks IBP faces from swings in livestock supply act as an implicit carve-out, because a Material Adverse Effect under that section cannot include an Effect that is set forth in the Warranted Financials. I agree with Tyson, however, that these disclaimers were far too general to preclude industry-wide or general factors from constituting a Material Adverse Effect. Had IBP wished such an exclusion from the broad language of § 5.10, IBP should have bargained for it. At the same time, the notion that § 5.10 gave Tyson a right to walk away simply because of a downturn in cattle supply is equally untenable. Instead, Tyson would have to show that the event had the required materiality of effect.

The difficulty of addressing that question is considerable, however, because § 5.10 is fraught with temporal ambiguity. By its own terms, it refers to any Material Adverse Effect that has occurred to IBP since December 25, 1999 unless that Effect is covered by the Warranted Financials or Schedule 5.10. Moreover, Tyson's right to refuse to close because a Material Adverse Effect has occurred is also qualified by the other express disclosures in the Schedule, by virtue of (i) the language of the Annexes that permits Tyson to refuse to close for breach of a warranty unless that breach results from "actions specifically permitted" by the Agreement; and (ii) the language of the Agreement that makes all disclosure schedules apply to Schedule 5.10 where that is the reasonably apparent intent of the drafters. Taken together, these provisions can be read to require the court to examine whether a MAE has occurred against the December 25, 1999 condition of IBP as adjusted by the specific disclosures of the Warranted Financials and the Agreement itself. This approach makes commercial sense because it establishes a baseline that roughly reflects the status of IBP as Tyson indisputably knew it at the time of signing the Merger Agreement.

But describing this basic contractual approach is somewhat easier than applying it. For example, the original IBP 10-K for FY 1999 revealed . . . a company that is consistently profitable, but subject to strong swings in annual EBIT and net earnings. The averages that emerge from this data are of EBIT of approximately $386 million per year and net earnings of $2.38 per share. If this average is seen as weighting the past too much, a three-year average generates EBIT of $376 million and net earnings of $2.29 per share.

The original Warranted Financials in FY 2000 also emphasize that swings in IBP's performance were a part of its business reality. For example, the trailing last twelve month's earnings from operations as of the end of third quarter of FY 2000 were $462 million, as compared to $528 million for full year 1999, as originally reported. In addition, the third quarter 10-Q showed that IBP's earnings from operations for the first 39 weeks of 2000 were lagging earnings from operations for the comparable period in 1999 by $40 million, after adjusting for the CFBA Charges.

The financial statements also indicate that Foodbrands was hardly a stable source of earnings, and was still much smaller in importance than IBP's fresh meat operations. Not only that, FY 2000 Foodbrands performance was lagging 1999, even accounting for the unusual, disclosed items.

The Rawhide Projections add another dimension to the meaning of § 5.10. These Projections indicated that IBP would not reach the same level of profitability as originally reported *until FY 2004*. In FY 2001, IBP was expected to have earnings from operations of $446 and net profits of $1.93 a share, down from what was expected in FY 2000. This diminishment in expectations resulted from concern over an anticipated trough in the cattle cycle that would occur during years 2001 to 2003. Moreover, the performance projected for FY 2001 was a drop even from the reduced FY 2000 earnings that Tyson expected as of the time it signed the Merger Agreement.

These negotiating realities bear on the interpretation of § 5.10 and suggest that the contractual language must be read in the larger context in which the parties were transacting. To a short-term speculator, the failure of a company to meet analysts' projected earnings for a quarter could be highly material. Such a failure is less important to an acquiror who seeks to purchase the company as part of a long-term strategy. To such an acquiror, the important thing is whether the company has suffered a Material Adverse Effect in its business or results of operations that is consequential to the company's earnings power over a commercially reasonable period, which one would think would be measured in years rather than months. It is odd to think that a strategic buyer would view a short-term blip in earnings as material, so long as the target's earnings-generating potential is not materially affected by that blip or the blip's cause.

In large measure, the resolution of the parties' arguments turns on a difficult policy question. In what direction does the burden of this sort of uncertainty fall: on an acquiror or on the seller? What little New York authority exists is not particularly helpful, and cuts in both directions. One New York case held a buyer to its bargain even when the seller suffered a very severe shock from an extraordinary event, reasoning that the seller realized that it was buying the stock of a sound company that was, however, susceptible to market swings. Another case held that a Material Adverse Effect was evidenced by a short-term drop in sales, but in a commercial context where such a drop was arguably quite critical.[154] The non-New York authorities cited by the parties provide no firmer guidance. . . .

Practical reasons lead me to conclude that a New York court would incline toward the view that a buyer ought to have to make a strong showing to invoke a Material Adverse Effect exception to its obligation to close. Merger contracts are heavily negotiated and cover a large number of specific risks explicitly. As a result, even where a Material Adverse Effect condition is as broadly written as the one in the Merger Agreement, that provision is best read as a backstop protecting the acquiror from the occurrence of unknown events that substantially threaten the overall earnings potential of the target in a durationally-significant manner.[155] A short-term hiccup in earnings should not suffice; rather the Material Adverse Effect should be material when viewed from the longer-term perspective of a reasonable acquiror. In this regard, it is worth noting that IBP never provided Tyson with *quarterly* projections.

When examined from this seller-friendly perspective, the question of whether IBP has suffered a Material Adverse Effect remains a close one. IBP had a very sub-par first quarter. The earnings per share of $.19 it reported exaggerate IBP's success, because part of those earnings were generated from a windfall generated by accounting for its stock option plan, a type of gain that is not likely to recur. On a normalized basis, IBP's first quarter of 2001 earnings from operations ran 64% behind the comparable period in 2000. If IBP had continued to perform on a straight-line basis using its first quarter 2001 performance, it would generate earnings from operations of around $200 million. This sort of

---

154. In *Pan Am Corp. v. Delta Air Lines*, 175 B.R. 438, 492-93 (S.D.N.Y. 1994), Pan Am airlines suffered sharp decline in bookings over a three-month period that was shocking to its management. The court held that a MAC had occurred. It did so, however, in a context where the party relying on the MAC clause was providing funding in a work-out situation, making any further deterioration of Pan Am's already compromised condition quite important.

155. A contrary rule will encourage the negotiation of extremely detailed "MAC" clauses with numerous carve-outs or qualifiers. An approach that reads broad clauses as addressing fundamental events that would materially affect the value of a target to a reasonable acquiror eliminates the need for drafting of that sort.

annual performance would be consequential to a reasonable acquiror and would deviate materially from the range in which IBP had performed during the recent past.

Tyson says that this impact must also be coupled with the DFG Impairment Charge of $60.4 million. That Charge represents an indication that DFG is likely to generate far less cash flow than IBP had previously anticipated. At the very least, the Charge is worth between $.50 and $.60 cents per IBP share, which is not trivial. It is worth even more, says Tyson, if one realizes that the Rawhide Projections portrayed Foodbrands as the driver of increased profitability in an era of flat fresh meats profits. This deficiency must be considered in view of the overall poor performance of Foodbrands so far in FY 2001. The Rawhide Projections had targeted Foodbrands to earn $137 million in 2001. In a January 30, 2001 presentation to Tyson, Bond had presented an operating plan that hoped to achieve $145 million from Foodbrands. As of the end of the first quarter, Foodbrands had earned only $2 million, and thus needed another $135 million in the succeeding three quarters to reach its Rawhide Projection. IBP's overall trailing last twelve month's earnings had declined from $488 million as of the end of the third quarter of 2000 to $330 million.

As a result of these problems, analysts following IBP issued sharply reduced earnings estimates for FY 2001. Originally, analysts were predicting that IBP would exceed the Rawhide Projections in 2001 by a wide margin. After IBP's poor first quarter, some analysts had reduced their estimate from $2.38 per share to $1.44 a share. *Even accounting for Tyson's attempts to manipulate the analyst community's perception of IBP,* this was a sharp drop.

Tyson contends that the logical inference to be drawn from the record evidence that is available is that IBP will likely have its worst year since 1997, a year which will be well below the company's average performance for all relevant periods. As important, the company's principal driver of growth is performing at markedly diminished levels, thus compromising the company's future results as it enters what is expected to be a tough few years in the fresh meats business.

IBP has several responses to Tyson's evidence. IBP initially notes that Tyson's arguments are unaccompanied by expert evidence that identifies the diminution in IBP's value or earnings potential as a result of its first quarter performance. The absence of such proof is significant. Even after Hankins generated extremely pessimistic projections for IBP in order to justify a lower deal price, Merrill Lynch still concluded that a purchase of IBP at $30 per share was still within the range of fairness and a great long-term value for Tyson. The Merrill Lynch analysis casts great doubt on Tyson's assertion that IBP has suffered a Material Adverse Effect.[161]

---

161. Tyson's only expert on this subject testified that a MAE would have occurred in his view even if IBP met the Rawhide Projections, because those Projections were more bearish than the analysts. This academic theory is of somewhat dubious practical utility, as it leaves the enforceability of contracts dependent on whether predictions by third-parties come true.

IBP also emphasizes the cyclical nature of its businesses. It attributes its poor first quarter to an unexpectedly severe winter. This led ranchers to hold livestock back from market, causing a sharp increase in prices that hurt both the fresh meats business and Foodbrands. Once April was concluded, IBP began to perform more in line with its recent year results, because supplies were increasing and Foodbrands was able to begin to make up its winter margins. Bond testified at trial that he expects IBP to meet or exceed the Rawhide Projection of $1.93 a share in 2001, and the company has publicly indicated that it expects earnings of $1.80 to $2.20 a share. Peterson expressed the same view.

IBP also notes that any cyclical fall is subject to cure by the Agreement's termination date, which was May 15, 2001. By May 15, IBP had two weeks of strong earnings that signaled a strong quarter ahead. Moreover, by that time, cattle that had been held back from market were being sold, leading to plentiful supplies that were expected to last for most of the year.

Not only that, IBP notes that not all analyst reporting services had been as pessimistic as Tyson portrays. In March, Morningstar was reporting a mean analyst prediction of $1.70 per share for IBP in 2001. By May, this had grown to a mean of $1.74 a share. Throughout the same period, Morningstar's consensus prediction was an FY 2002 performance of $2.33 range in March, and $2.38 in May. Therefore, according to Morningstar, the analyst community was predicting that IBP would return to historically healthy earnings next year, and that earnings for this year would fall short of the Rawhide Projections by less than $.20 per share.

IBP also argues that the Impairment Charge does not approach materiality as a big picture item. That Charge is a one-time, non-cash charge, and IBP has taken large charges of that kind as recently as 1999. While IBP does not deny that its decision to buy DFG turned out disastrously, it reminds me that DFG is but a tiny fraction of IBP's overall business and that a total shut-down of DFG would likely have little effect on the future results of a combined Tyson/IBP. And as a narrow asset issue, the charge is insignificant to IBP as a whole.

I am confessedly torn about the correct outcome. As Tyson points out, IBP has only pointed to two weeks of truly healthy results in 2001 before the contract termination date of May 15. Even these results are suspect, Tyson contends, due to the fact that IBP expected markedly better results for the second week just days before the actual results come out. In view of IBP's demonstrated incapacity to accurately predict near-term results, Tyson says with some justification that I should be hesitant to give much weight to IBP's assurances that it will perform well for the rest of the year.

In the end, however, Tyson has not persuaded me that IBP has suffered a Material Adverse Effect. By its own arguments, Tyson has evinced more confidence in stock market analysts than I personally harbor. But its embrace of the analysts is illustrative of why I conclude that Tyson has not met its burden.

As of May 2001, analysts were predicting that IBP would earn between $1.50 to around $1.74 per share in 2001. The analysts were also predicting that IBP would earn between $2.33 and $2.42 per share in 2002. These members are based on reported "mean" or "consensus" analyst numbers. Even at the low end of this *consensus* range, IBP's earnings for the next two years would not be out of line with its historical performance during troughs in the beef cycle. As recently as years 1996-1998, IBP went through a period with a three year average earnings of $1.85 per share. At the high end of the analysts' consensus range, IBP's results would exceed this figure by $.21 per year.

This predicted range of performance from the source that Tyson vouches for suggests that no Material Adverse Effect has occurred.[170] Rather, the analyst views support the conclusion that IBP remains what the baseline evidence suggests it was-a consistently but erratically profitable company struggling to implement a strategy that will reduce the cyclicality of its earnings. Although IBP may not be performing as well as it and Tyson had hoped, IBP's business appears to be in sound enough shape to deliver results of operations in line with the company's recent historical performance. Tyson's own investment banker still believes IBP is fairly priced at $30 per share. The fact that Foodbrands is not yet delivering on the promise of even better performance for IBP during beef troughs is unavailing to Tyson, since § 5.10 focuses on IBP as a whole and IBP's performance as an entire company is in keeping with its baseline condition.

Therefore, I conclude that Tyson has not demonstrated a breach of § 5.10. I admit to reaching this conclusion with less than the optimal amount of confidence.[171] The record evidence is not of the type that permits certainty.[172] . . .

. . . Tyson is in breach of the Merger Agreement because it improperly terminated in late March, 2001. That is, it is in breach of its obligation to close the Cash Election Merger on or before May 15, 2001.[200] . . .

---

170. Again, I emphasize that my conclusion is heavily influenced by my temporal perspective, which recognizes that even good businesses do not invariably perform at consistent levels of profitability. If a different policy decision is the correct one, a contrary conclusion could be reached. That different, more short-term approach will, I fear, make merger agreements more difficult to negotiate and lead to Material Adverse Effect clauses of great prolixity.

171. Tyson has tried to suggest that other factors exist that contribute to the conclusion that IBP has suffered a Material Adverse Effect. These include unsubstantiated charges that other Foodbrands units suffer the same type of serious accounting problems as DFG and that other IBP assets are impaired, as well as the effects of DFG-related lawsuits that Tyson admits were covered by Schedule 5.11. I find none of Tyson's other Material Adverse Effect arguments meritorious.

172. If I am incorrect and IBP bore the burden to prove the absence of a Material Adverse Effect by clear and convincing evidence in order to obtain an order of specific performance, it would not have met that burden. It would prevail under a preponderance standard, regardless of whether it bore the burden of persuasion.

200. Throughout the course of this case, IBP has urged upon me another proposition that it believes compels a ruling in its favor. IBP asserts that under New York law, a party cannot refuse to close on a contract in reliance upon a breached contractual representation if that party knew that the representation was false at the time of contracting. Put directly, IBP says it can win this case even if there was a breach of a representation in the Merger Agreement so long as it can prove that it informed Tyson of facts that demonstrate that the representation was untrue and thus that Tyson did not in fact rely upon the representation in deciding to sign the Merger Agreement. IBP's arguments find some support in some cases applying New York law. *See, e.g.,* *Rogath v. Siebenmann*, 129 F.3d 261, 264-65 (2d Cir.1997) ("Where the seller discloses up front the inaccuracy of certain of his warranties, it cannot be said that the buyer-absent the express preservation of his rights—believed

IV. IBP Is Entitled to an Award of Specific Performance

Having determined that the Merger Agreement is a valid and enforceable contract that Tyson had no right to terminate, I now turn to the question of whether the Merger Agreement should be enforced by an order of specific performance. Although Tyson's voluminous post-trial briefs argue the merits fully, its briefs fail to argue that a remedy of specific performance is unwarranted in the event that its position on the merits is rejected.

This gap in the briefing is troubling. A compulsory order will require a merger of two public companies with thousands of employees working at facilities that are important to the communities in which they operate. The impact of a forced merger on constituencies beyond the stockholders and top managers of IBP and Tyson weighs heavily on my mind. The prosperity of IBP and Tyson means a great deal to these constituencies. I therefore approach this remedial issue quite cautiously and mindful of the interests of those who will be affected by my decision.

I start with a fundamental question: is this is a truly unique opportunity that cannot be adequately monetized? If the tables were turned and Tyson was seeking to enforce the contract, a great deal of precedent would indicate that the contract should be specifically enforced. In the more typical situation, an acquiror argues that it cannot be made whole unless it can specifically enforce the acquisition agreement, because the target company is unique and will yield value of an unquantifiable nature, once combined with the acquiring company. In this case, the sell-side of the transaction is able to make the same argument, because the Merger Agreement provides the IBP stockholders with a choice of cash or Tyson stock, or a combination of both. Through this choice, the IBP stockholders were offered a chance to share in the upside of what was touted by Tyson as a unique, synergistic combination. This court has not found, and Tyson has not advanced, any compelling reason why sellers in mergers and acquisitions transactions should have less of a right to demand specific performance than buyers, and none has independently come to my mind.

In addition, the determination of a cash damages award will be very difficult in this case. And the amount of any award could be staggeringly large. No doubt the parties would haggle over huge valuation questions, which (Tyson no doubt would argue) must take into account the possibility of a further auction for IBP

---

he was purchasing the seller's promise as to the truth of the warranties."). There is, however, no definitive authority from the New York Court of Appeals to this effect, and the leading case can be read as being at odds with IBP's position. *See CBS v. Ziff-Davis Publishing Co.,* 75 N.Y.2d 496, 554 N.Y.S.2d 449, 553 N.E.2d 997, 1000-01 (1990). Most of IBP's cases also deal with a distinct context, namely situations where a buyer signed the contract on day one, learned that a representation is false from the seller on day three, closed the contract on day five, and sued for damages for breach of warranty on day 10. The public policy reasons for denying relief to the buyer in those circumstances are arguably much different than are implicated by a decision whether to permit a buyer simply to walk away before closing in reliance on a specific contractual representation that it had reason to suspect was untrue as of the time of signing. In any event, my more traditional contract analysis applies settled principles of New York contract law and eliminates any need to delve into these novel issues of another state's law.

or other business developments. A damages award can, of course, be shaped; it simply will lack any pretense to precision. An award of specific performance will, I anticipate, entirely eliminate the need for a speculative determination of damages.

Finally, there is no doubt that a remedy of specific performance is practicable. Tyson itself admits that the combination still makes strategic sense. At trial, John Tyson was asked by his own counsel to testify about whether it was fair that Tyson should enter any later auction for IBP hampered by its payment of the Rawhide Termination Fee. This testimony indicates that Tyson Foods is still interested in purchasing IBP, but wants to get its original purchase price back and then buy IBP off the day-old goods table. I consider John Tyson's testimony an admission of the feasibility of specific performance.[204]

Probably the concern that weighs heaviest on my mind is whether specific performance is the right remedy in view of the harsh words that have been said in the course of this litigation. Can these management teams work together? The answer is that I do not know. Peterson and Bond say they can. I am not convinced, although Tyson's top executives continue to respect the managerial acumen of Peterson and Bond, if not that of their financial subordinates.

What persuades me that specific performance is a workable remedy is that Tyson will have the power to decide all the key management questions itself. It can therefore hand-pick its own management team. While this may be unpleasant for the top level IBP managers who might be replaced, it was a possible risk of the Merger from the get-go and a reality of today's M & A market.

The impact on other constituencies of this ruling also seems tolerable. Tyson's own investment banker thinks the transaction makes sense for Tyson, and is still fairly priced at $30 per share. One would think the Tyson constituencies would be better served on the whole by a specific performance remedy, rather than a large damages award that did nothing but cost Tyson a large amount of money.

In view of these factors, I am persuaded that an award of specific performance is appropriate, regardless of what level of showing was required by IBP. That is, there is clear and convincing evidence to support this award. Such an award is decisively preferable to a vague and imprecise damages remedy that cannot adequately remedy the injury to IBP's stockholders.

V. Conclusion

For all the foregoing reasons, IBP's claim for specific performance is granted. Tyson's claims for relief are dismissed. The parties shall collaborate and present a conforming partial final order no later than June 27. In addition, the parties shall schedule an office conference with the court to occur later that same week.

---

204. It may also be Tyson's preference, if it has to suffer an adverse judgment. Any damages award will be huge and will result in no value to Tyson.

Comments

Vice Chancellor Strine decided *IBP* under New York law. Subsequent Delaware cases have followed *IBP* to decide material-adverse-effect issues under Delaware law. For instance, in *Frontier Oil Corp. v. Holly Corp.*, Vice Chancellor Noble explained:

> The notion of an MAE is imprecise and varies both with the context of the transaction and its parties and with the words chosen by the parties. The drafters of the Merger Agreement had the benefit of the analysis in *In re IBP, Inc. Shareholders Litigation* ("*IBP*") which considered whether the acquiring party in a merger transaction could successfully invoke an MAE provision to escape the agreed-upon combination. . . . Although *IBP* involved application of New York law, I see no reason why the law of Delaware should prescribe a different perspective.[120]

In *Frontier v. Holly*, Holly argued that certain threatened litigation constituted an MAE under its agreement with Frontier. Piggybacking on the long-term focus adopted in *IBP*, the court explained:

> The question of whether a particular "problem" would have an MAE has both quantitative and qualitative aspects. In any given year, particularly in light of the cyclical nature of Frontier's business, the burden of paying defense costs, such as those projected here, could be difficult. Holly, however, has not shown that Frontier could not pay them or that their payment would have had a significant effect if viewed over a longer term. The forward-looking basis for evaluating an MAE as chosen by Holly and Frontier does not allow the Court to look at just one year (assuming, as one may here, that the short-term consequences would not significantly interfere with the carrying on of the business). Instead, given Frontier's enterprise value, it is reasonable to conclude that Frontier could absorb the projected defense costs without experiencing an MAE. More importantly, Holly has not proved that the defense costs would have, or would reasonably be expected to have, a Frontier MAE.[121]

For more on how contractual parties and courts use and understand MAC clauses, we asked Professor Todd Henderson for further explanation.

The Use and Effect of "Material Adverse Change" Clauses

An increasingly common contractual term in business combination transactions is the "material adverse change" clause (MAC), also known as a "material

---

120. No. Civ. A. 20502, 2005 WL 1039027, at *34 (Del. Ch. Apr. 29, 2005).
121. *Id.* at *37.

adverse effect" clause (MAE). These clauses generate a large amount of litigation and are often the most contentious and important contractual provisions in negotiating merger agreements. Although these clauses take many forms and much depends on the specific language of them, the general idea is simple—the seller agrees to allow the buyer a low-cost way out of its obligation under the contract if there is a change that materially reduces the value of the seller before the closing. MACs are commonly accompanied by reverse break-up fees, which put a dollar figure on the buyer's decision to withdrawal from the deal.[1]

MAC clauses simply allocate the risk of a change in value of the seller from the time the deal is signed until the time the deal is closed. This time may be quite long: deals seldom close within 90 days, and regulatory delays (e.g., antitrust review) may extend the time between signing and closing for up to one year. During this time, buyers of companies face a significant risk that the company they have agreed to buy will not be the one they eventually do buy. There are three primary reasons for this.

First, sellers have superior information about the value of the business during the selling phase, and have incentives to make the company appear more valuable than it really is. This incentive to puff is known euphemistically as "putting lipstick on the pig." Although buyers conduct due diligence, the seller will retain an informational advantage, in part because there are diminishing marginal returns to investments in diligence and because the seller controls the flow of information. The true value of the company may be revealed, as additional information is uncovered during the initial stages of integration prior to the deal closing. A buyer may be surprised at what they learn during this pre-closing period. (Sellers typically use no-reliance clauses in diligence proceedings to reduce their liability and risk.)

Second, there may be changes in the state of the world beyond the buyer and seller that negatively impact the value of the seller in ways unexpected by the parties' bargain. An external shock, like 9/11 or Hurricane Katrina or the stock market crash of Black Monday, October 19, 1987,[2] are examples of events that may change the value of a business, without regard to anything particular about the business. If an event like this occurs after the deal is signed but before it closes, the price the parties agreed to may not represent the value of the business on the date of the close. Excusing buyers from the risk of such an exogenous shock would be akin to a force majeure clause found in most commercial contracts. (Most MAC clauses exclude such "acts of God," and when they do not, courts will imply that they do.)

Third, and most importantly, there may be a change in the affairs of the seller that is unique to it. For instance, the seller may lose a key employee or customer, suffer a loss of market share to a competitor, or suffer an unexpected legal or

---

1. For instance, Cerberus recently backed out of its deal to buy United Rentals, and paid $100 million for the privilege. *See United Rentals, Inc. v. Ram Holdings, Inc.*, 937 A.2d 810 (Del. Ch. 2007).

2. Courts generally do not find MACs from such events. *See, e.g., Bear Stearns Co. v. Jardine Strategic Holdings*, No. 31371187, slip. op. (N.Y. Sup. June 17, 1988), *aff'd mem.*, 143 A.D. 2d 1073, 533 N.Y.S. 2d 167 (App. Div. 1988) (noting MAC very unlikely for short-term drop in seller's stock price as a result of Black Monday).

regulatory setback.[3] The problem is exacerbated by the fact that the nature of the selling process may make these events more likely. Controlling these risks is likely under the control of the seller, and once the parties have agreed on a price, the seller's incentive to spend firm resources to mitigate them is reduced. The money and time spent to do so might otherwise be available to the managers, and will do nothing to increase the value of the money the managers or shareholders of the seller will receive in the deal. Thus managers, whether acting selfishly or to enhance shareholder value, will not rationally spend money to preserve or increase the value of the seller after the deal is struck.

Faced with these risks, one can see how MAC clauses are important to allocate the risk between the parties. In general, by letting buyers walk away under certain conditions, MAC clauses reduce the risk of the transaction for the buyer. This should make acquisitions more likely in general. But these clauses increase the risk for the seller, since some transactions may be unwound, either legitimately or erroneously, thus defeating the expectations of the seller. Therefore would-be sellers may *prefer* aggressive MAC clauses, as they make a deal more likely to occur; whereas, once a deal has been struck, sellers may prefer a more narrow interpretation. This is especially true because the costs of adjudicating the scope of the clause may give buyers room to act opportunistically when they have a case of buyer's remorse. There is thus a tradeoff between encouraging efficient investments during the time the deal is being done or avoiding combinations that turn out to be less valuable than keeping the firms separate, and giving the buyer too much wiggle room to walk away when they strike a bad deal. A poorly designed MAC can thus turn a deal into a simple and low-cost option for the buyer; something the seller may not want to do, especially in a competitive bidding process.

So how do parties allocate these risks in practice? A MAC clause has two parts: first, an operative part that describes the conditions under which the buyer will be excused; and second, a list of exceptions delineating the identifiable situations that will not be covered by the clause. According to some recent data, about 80 percent of MAC clauses include numerous exceptions, while the remaining 20 percent are broader and more general.[4]

An example of a typical operative part is:

> Any event, occurrence or development of a state of circumstances or facts which has had or reasonably could be expected to have a Material Adverse Change on the condition, financial or otherwise, of the business, assets, liabilities, or results of operations of the Seller and its subsidiaries taken as a whole.

---

3. So far, legal-change claims have been losers. For example, in *Frontier Oil v. Holly*, No. Civ. A. 20502, 2005 WL 1039027 (Del. Ch. Apr. 29, 2005), the court held that the losses from or costs of a significant environmental contamination class action were not likely to impact the seller's stock price over the "longer term." *See also S.C. Johnson & Son, Inc. v. DowBrands, Inc.*, 167 F. Supp. 2d 657, 672-73 (D. Del. 2001) (holding patent infringement suit did not constitute a MAC unless it made a significant asset of the business worthless).

4. Nixon Peabody Surveys, Sixth Annual MAC Survey 9 (2007), http://www.nixonpeabody.com/linked_media/publications/MAC_survey_2007.pdf.

The exceptions carve out circumstances the parties do not intend to be covered by the MAC. For instance, a MAC may exclude changes in the value of the seller due to: (1) the announcement of the deal; (2) changes in general economic or political conditions; (3) changes in law; (4) hostilities or war; or (5) shocks to the industry of the seller. In most cases, the parties exclude from these exceptions events enumerated that impact the seller disproportionately. So if the seller sees a big drop in its earnings, it may be a MAC allowing the buyer to back out. But if the drop is due to the recent financial crisis or a cataclysmic terrorist attack, then it may not be a MAC under the second or fourth exception above. However, if the drop is much bigger for the seller than for other firms in their industry, then it may be a MAC after all.

The scope of the MAC will therefore be primarily determined by negotiation between the parties. Courts generally do not intervene in these cases if the parties have clearly described their obligations. At base then, courts will respect the bargain of the parties about risk allocation, as they should. In the negotiation over MAC clauses, the number and scope of the exceptions is where rubber meets the road: the more the exceptions and the broader, the more risk the buyer will bear, and vice versa.

The experience to date with MACs suggests some lessons for transaction planners. Most importantly, where a MAC is ambiguous, courts will aggressively fill in the gaps to determine the contours of the MAC coverage. Crudely, the court will try to determine whether the buyer is acting opportunistically to undo a deal that turns out to be a bad one for the buyer, or whether the seller has acted opportunistically by forgoing efficient investments in the combined company. In addition, courts may consider whether the deal, which presumably was a socially good one under one set of facts about the world, turns out to be a bad one from a social welfare perspective based on changed circumstances. For instance, a deal that will bankrupt the buyer, force the buyer and seller to complete a deal against their will, or result in an unexpected windfall for the seller, may be undone under an ambiguous MAC. Courts are also reluctant to impose specific performance and force the parties to consummate the acquisition, especially for cases in which the parties are truly hostile towards each other.

A series of cases provides a glimpse at the developing common law default rules. The leading case is the Delaware Chancery Court's opinion in *IBP Inc. v. Tyson Foods, Inc.*[5] In that case, the court defined a MAC as a "backstop protecting the acquiror from the occurrence of *unknown* events that substantially threaten the overall earnings potential of the target in durationally-significant manner."[6] There are two components of this. First, the court distinguished between "undisclosed problems" of the seller, which may be a MAC, and "unknown consequences of a disclosed problem," which would likely not be a MAC. In addition,

---

5. 789 A.2d 14 (Del. Ch. 2001).
6. *Id.* at 68 (emphasis added).

the court interpreted the contractual language from the perspective of a long-term, strategic buyer. Thus short-term changes in the earning power of the seller, even if dramatic, would likely not rise to the level of a MAC. The court held that the locus of inquiry should be one that is "consequential to the company's earning power over a commercially reasonable period, which one would think would be measured in years rather than months."[7] The court showed its suspicion that the buyer, who was complaining about a drop in quarterly earnings of the seller, was acting opportunistically: "It is odd to think that a strategic investor would view a short-term blip in earnings as material, so long as the target's earnings-generating potential is not materially affected by that blip or the blip's cause."[8]

A more recent case from Tennessee follows the *Tyson* approach to gauging the seriousness of a change in the fortunes of the buyer by focusing on the product of the size of the change and the duration of the change. In *Genesco, Inc. v. The Finish Line*, Inc., the court took a three-step approach.[9] First, it estimated the magnitude of the change in the fortunes of the seller. Second, it asked whether "the change relates to an essential purpose or purposes the parties sought to achieve by entering the merger."[10] And, third, it estimated the duration of the change to determine the significance to a reasonable strategic buyer. Applying this test to the facts, the court found a MAC had occurred, but nevertheless ruled in favor of the seller, because the seller's business was part of a secular industry decline, which was an exception to the MAC clause.[11]

One way to avoid the uncertainty and cost of litigation is to be clear with the contractual language. But this has a cost too, since it may result in an otherwise profitable deal not getting done based on a contingency that is very unlikely to arise. This means MAC clauses will likely continue to be somewhat ambiguous on the margin, and therefore generate litigation about their scope. Based on the cases to date, courts will be very reluctant to invoke a MAC (no court in Delaware has yet as of this writing), and the buyer will bear a heavy burden in showing that its desire to back out is the efficient rather than the opportunistic one.

Professor M. Todd Henderson
The University of Chicago Law School

c. Conditions to Sellers' Obligation to Close

As § 4.2 lists the conditions that precede *Buyer's* obligation to close, § 4.3 lists the conditions that precede *Sellers'* obligation to close. Section 4.3(a) is thinner than § 4.2(a) and states that Buyer's representations and warranties must be

---

7. *Id.* at 67.
8. *Id.*
9. No. 07-2137-II(III), 2007 WL 4698244 (Tenn. Ch. Dec. 27, 2007)
10. *Id.* at 34.
11. *Id.* at 33.

true in all material respects as of the Closing Date, except where the failure to be true would not have a material adverse effect on Buyer's ability to consummate the transactions. The most important clause in this provision may be wrapped in parentheses. The crux of this provision is the "material adverse effect" language because the failure of a Buyer representation or a warranty *only* gives Sellers a right to walk away *if* the failure has a material adverse effect on Buyer's ability to consummate the transaction (i.e., pay). Absent this material adverse effect, it is irrelevant to this condition whether a representation or warranty is true at all. Notice that the parties did not capitalize "material adverse effect." Do you think this evidences purpose or neglect? If purpose, would you have accomplished this purpose by the same means? Also, notice this provision does not address "double materiality" concerns. Does this strike you as problematic? If at all, for whom?

The remaining provisions of § 4.3 mirror § 4.2. Sections 4.3(b) and (c) are verbatim the same as §§ 4.2(b) and (f), respectively, save for the party references. Before Sellers are obligated to close the deal, Buyer must have performed, in all material respects, its covenants under the Agreement that are to be performed by Closing, and Buyer must have delivered closing certificates. Unlike § 4.2(c), there is no independent MAE condition to closing in § 4.3. This is because the MAE provision in § 4.2(c) is chiefly concerned with the degradation of the Business that Buyer is acquiring. However, one could argue that the concerns of the "type-y" MAE in § 4.2(c) apply equally to both parties. If you represented Sellers, what arguments would you make in favor of the inclusion of such a provision? What arguments would you anticipate from Buyer's counsel in response, and how would you address these?

8. Indemnification

a. *Indemnification Obligations of Each Party*

Section 11 of the Agreement specifies the various indemnification obligations each party owes to the other, *following the Closing*. Sections 11.1(a)(i) and 11.2(a)(i) provide the obligations of the Buyer, on the one hand, and the Sellers, on the other, to indemnify each other (as well as employees, officers, directors, representatives, and affiliates) for any Damages (as defined) suffered relating to a breach of a representation or warranty made in the Agreement, closing certificates, or (in the case of indemnification by Sellers) the Disclosure Schedule. Similarly, §§ 11.1(a)(ii) and 11.2(a)(ii) provide reciprocal indemnities for a breach of any covenant in the Agreement. However, note that Buyer's obligation to indemnify Sellers is only for Buyer's *material* breach of a covenant, whereas Sellers' obligation to indemnify Buyer is for any breach of a covenant (unqualified).

Sections 11.1(a)(v) and 11.2(a)(iii) are also reciprocal in the sense that Sellers must indemnify Buyers for any Damages related to Excluded Liabilities (i.e., those liabilities that Buyer is not "acquiring"), and Buyer must indemnify Sellers for any Damages related to Assumed Liabilities (i.e., those liabilities that Buyer *is* "acquiring"). This maps onto the language in §§ 2.1 and 2.2 that provides that to the extent one party pays the other's liabilities (e.g., "To the extent that either Seller pays an Assumed Liability following the Closing Date"), the other is to reimburse the paying party.

Section 11.1(a) imposes a few additional indemnification obligations on Sellers, having to do with Taxes regarding the Assets or the Business (where the Buyer has not assumed the liability for the Taxes), certain matters described in the separate Disclosure Schedule, and any breach of § 5.11 (Litigation; Decrees) of the Agreement. Is there any utility to including § 11.1(a)(iv) (or any part thereof) as an item separate from § 11.1(a)(i), which addresses indemnification for breach of any representation or warranty, including those made in the Disclosure Schedule and those made in the Agreement? (See the discussion in section (b) below.)

Notice that § 11.1(c) provides that "materiality" or "Material Adverse Effect" language found in representations or warranties of Sellers is to be ignored for the purposes of indemnification and § 11. That is, Sellers must indemnify Buyer for a breach of a representation or warranty that would occur if the representation or warranty did not contain any materiality language. If we ignore those materiality qualifications found in representations and warranties for indemnification and we ignore them for closing conditions, is there any purpose to including them in the first place? Note that Buyer must indemnify Sellers for an actual breach of a representation or warranty, according to the language of that representation or warranty, including any materiality qualifications. Also, materiality qualifications of covenants are not disregarded for indemnification purposes for Buyer and Sellers alike.

You will notice that for a party to assert its right to indemnification under the Agreement, it must follow the procedures laid out in § 11.4. One advantage of adopting an indemnification approach to claims, similar to the dispute-resolution procedures that we discussed in the context of employment agreements in Chapter 2, is that the parties may agree on notice and other procedural requirements before an indemnitor is liable. These provisions may also govern the rights of an indemnitee and an indemnitor to defend and settle claims with regard to third parties. A significant feature is that an indemnitor may have the right to take over the defense against certain third-party claims, as an indemnitor may prefer to have control over this liability exposure (including the expense of litigation as well as any potential adverse judgment) than to write a blank check (subject to whatever monetary limitations may qualify the obligation to indemnify) when all is said and done. Please review § 11.4 for the specific procedural mechanisms that govern indemnification between the parties to this particular Agreement.

b. "Caps" and "Baskets"

In M&A agreements, it is common for indemnification obligations to be limited by a so-called "basket" and by a so-called "cap." We have already encountered a "cap" with limitation-of-liability provisions in Chapter 3. There, we addressed the interaction of limitation-of-liability and indemnification provisions in some depth, and you may wish to return to that discussion to review. Of interest, a "cap" in M&A agreements is often applicable to indemnification obligations, whereas limitation-of-liability provisions in other agreements (as we saw with services agreements in Chapter 3) may apply to all liability under or related to a contract *except* for indemnification obligations. Why do you suppose this is? In some agreements (e.g., M&A agreements), indemnification provisions are often a chief or sole means of redress for liability related to the contract, which means that contractual parties wishing to limit this liability must apply such a limitation provision to the contract's indemnification provisions. In other agreements (e.g., services agreements), indemnification provisions sometimes apply only to third-party claims (e.g., IP infringement), and the contractual parties may agree not to limit the liability for these specific indemnifications, despite that they may agree to limit liability more generally under the agreement.

A "basket," on the other hand, is concerned with the opposite side of the spectrum. A basket essentially is a condition precedent to a party's obligation to indemnify, providing that the putative indemnitor does not have an obligation to indemnify until the amount that would be due reaches a certain dollar threshold. One of the underlying concerns of a basket provision is that an indemnitor may not want to deal with trifles. Indeed, materiality language is often ignored at the indemnification level, as we saw in § 11.1(c) of this Agreement, where a basket establishes what is "material" by setting a dollar-amount threshold.

Baskets may come in assorted varieties. The indemnitor may push for a "deductible-style" basket, where the indemnitor's obligation, once triggered, is only for every dollar *above* the threshold amount. With this type, if the basket is $500,000, and the indemnification amount is $750,000, the indemnitor owes $250,000. In contrast, the indemnitee may push for a non-deductible (i.e., "from-the-first-dollar") basket, where the indemnitor's obligation, once triggered, is for the entire amount of the liability starting from dollar one. With this type, if the basket is $500,000, and the indemnification amount is $750,000, the indemnitor owes $750,000. Another concern with indemnification baskets (and caps) is what counts and how: Does the basket apply to each individual "claim" for indemnification or to all claims, in the aggregate, over time? With both caps and baskets, parties may craft provisions to apply to different liabilities differently, perhaps setting different threshold baskets and different maximum caps for different types of liabilities. In this vein, as we saw with limitation-of-liability provisions, parties may carve out certain liabilities from the coverage of a cap, a basket, or both.

Turning to the Agreement, we see all of these concerns at play. Sections 11.1(b) and 11.2(b) impose "cap" and "basket" restrictions on the indemnification rights and obligations provided by §§ 11.1(a) and 11.2(a), respectively. Both §§ 11.1(b) and 11.2(b) impose a basket of $4 million on the aggregate dollar amount of indemnification obligations pertaining to the inaccuracy or breach of any representation or warranty described in § 11.1(a)(i) and § 11.2(a)(i), respectively. However, note an important difference between the two provisions. Section 11.1(b) imposes a deductible basket on Buyer's indemnification rights under § 11.1(a)(i), where Sellers will indemnify Buyer Indemnified Persons (as defined to include Buyer and other related parties) for such Damages only above the $4 million mark. In contrast, § 11.2(b) imposes a non-deductible basket on Sellers' indemnification rights under § 11.2(a)(i), where Buyer will indemnify Seller Indemnified Persons (again, as defined) for such Damages, including the amount below the $4 million trigger. In both cases, once the threshold amount is tripped, the indemnification obligation is triggered going forward; that is, all such Damages *in the aggregate* count against the basket. With respect to these same indemnification claims (i.e., based on representations and warranties), both §§ 11.1(b) and 11.2(b) provide a cap of 40 percent of the Base Acquisition Consideration (defined in § 3.1(a)(i) as $575,000,000). Again, notice that this is in the aggregate.

Notice that § 11.1(b) provides a separate basket for Sellers' indemnification obligations under § 11.1(a)(iv) (which we discussed, and about which we inquired, above) of $6 million. As with the other basket for Sellers' indemnification obligations pertaining to representations and warranties, this basket operates as a deductible, and Sellers only owe an obligation for the amount in excess of the $6 million. In addition, as a separate basket and because § 11.1(a)(i) is carefully drafted to exclude § 11.1(a)(iv), Damages incurred by the Buyer Indemnified Parties that go toward the $4 million basket (with regard to § 11.1(a)(i)) do not go toward the $6 million basket (with regard to § 11.1(a)(iv)). While the baskets operate independently, notice that the cap in § 11.1(b) treats indemnification claims under §§ 11.1(a)(i) and 11.1(a)(iv) the same: "Sellers' aggregate liability in respect of claims for indemnification pursuant to Section 11.1(a)(i) and 11.1(a)(iv) will not exceed 40% of the Base Acquisition Consideration." Sellers' total indemnification obligation for both types of indemnification is not to exceed the cap.

Each basket-and-cap provision also includes certain carve-outs. Both §§ 11.1(b) and 11.2(b) remove inaccuracies and breaches of the representations and warranties pertaining to "organization and authority" (§§ 5.1, 7.1) and to "no brokers" (§§ 5.25, 7.5), as well as claims based on fraud or intentional misrepresentation, from basket-and-cap coverage. Additionally, § 11.1(b) also carves out inaccuracies and breaches of certain other representations and warranties by Sellers—"non-contravention" (§ 5.2), "nonforeign certification" (§ 5.4), and "assets" (§ 5.6)—from the basket and cap. Accordingly, Sellers' obligation to indemnify for inaccuracies or breaches of these representations and warranties is unlimited. How do you account for this disparate treatment of Buyer's and Sellers' indemnification obligations?

Sections 11.1(b) and 11.2(b) each end with clarifying statements that the other indemnification obligations under §§ 11.1(a) and 11.2(a), respectively, are not limited by the basket-and-cap limitations found within each section.

Notice that § 11.1(e) provides that, following the Closing, indemnification under § 11.1 is Buyer's exclusive remedy with respect to any claims (except where fraud is involved) relating to the subject matter of the Agreement. Section 11.2 does not include a parallel exclusive-remedy provision with regard to Sellers' post-Closing claims against Buyer. If you were called upon to decide, would you conclude that Sellers' exclusive remedy for post-Closing claims against Buyer is pursuant to the indemnification mechanism in the Agreement? For more on exclusive remedies, please see Chapters 3 and 5.

9. Termination

Section 15 of the Agreement provides for how the Agreement may be terminated. As we have seen, the obligation of each party to sell is conditioned on several factors. Until those conditions are satisfied, there is no obligation to close, but conditions to closing, by themselves, do not give a party the right to end its obligations under an agreement altogether in the event of a condition's failure. Under this Agreement, § 4 imposes conditions that stand in between a party and its obligation to close (or, on the flipside, its right to obligate the other party to close), and once these conditions are satisfied, then the obligation to close accrues. Accordingly, § 4 does not operate to cut off the possibility of future satisfaction of the conditions and the obligation to close later accruing (although, depending on their language, certain conditions may not be able to be satisfied once they have failed). Section 15 does this work, allowing the parties to terminate the agreement altogether in certain instances.

Section 15 starts off by stating the obvious, that all the parties to an agreement can agree to terminate the agreement. Even absent such a provision, this is generally the case.[122] The real work begins with § 15.1(b), which provides that a party has a right to terminate, if: (1) the other party "breaches" a representation, warranty, covenant, or other agreement contained in the Agreement that cannot be cured or has not been cured within 30 days of written notice;[123] *and* (2) the

---

122. *See* RESTATEMENT (SECOND) OF CONTRACTS §§ 283 & 273 (1981).

123. Please see Chapter 5 for a discussion of what it means to "cure." Also, note how § 15.1(b) is careful to specify "any representation or warranty *contained herein.*" This way, even if a court were somehow to count

breach would cause, either by itself or in combination with other breaches, a condition to closing found in §§ 4.2(a) or (b) (if the breach is by Sellers) or §§ 4.3(a) or (b) (if the breach is by Buyer) to fail. Sections 4.2(a) and (b) and 4.3(a) and (b) are the conditions to closing that provide in essence that a party's representations and warranties must be true as of the Closing Date and that a party must have performed and complied with its obligations and covenants.

Section 15.1(c) allows either party to terminate the Agreement if a Governmental Entity approval, required to consummate the sale, is denied. Section 15.1(d) sets a date, by which the Closing must occur, or else Sellers and Buyer will have the unilateral *right* (but not the obligation) to terminate the Agreement. Notice that this date is *not* the Closing Date (which is defined earlier in the Agreement in § 3.3), but a so-called "drop-dead" date allowing the parties to avoid the deal. This helps avoid an awkward scenario, where the Closing has not occurred and will not occur but the Agreement remains in force.

Very importantly, under the Agreement, all of these rights to terminate (except for mutual termination under § 15.1(a)) are subject to a proviso—that the party seeking to terminate the Agreement did not cause the transaction not to be consummated or a closing condition not to be satisfied by breaching any provision of the Agreement in any material respect. This avoids a situation where a party breached the Agreement in a way that causes the Closing not to occur and, yet, wants to terminate the Agreement. For example, suppose a party materially breached the Agreement in a way that causes the Closing not to occur by September 30, 2006 (the drop-dead date in § 15.1(d)); that breaching party will not have the right under § 15.1(d) to terminate the Agreement, and the non-breaching party may still have the ability to close the deal. Under this Agreement, termination is especially important given its preclusive effect on claims, as discussed below.

As we discussed earlier in this chapter, termination means generally that the Agreement and its provisions are of no effect as of the termination date. Section 15.3 provides as much, but preserves certain provisions, by providing that they "survive." Which provisions survive termination? Why do you think the parties selected each of these provisions to survive?

We discussed earlier that survival generally refers to whether a particular provision is still of effect—not whether a claim may be brought based on the breach of a provision. Of course, a provision cannot be breached if it is of no effect, and in this way "survival" may affect whether a claim may be brought. Parties can additionally contract about when claims may be brought and can otherwise limit liability under a contract. In § 15.3, we see the parties chose to provide that after termination, no party will be liable to the other. This includes

---

representations or warranties from outside the Agreement, the right to terminate provided by § 15.1(b) is only triggered by a breach of those representations or warranties within the Agreement's four corners.

breaches that occur *prior* to termination, with an exception for willful or intentional breaches and any obligation to pay that was breached prior to termination. Note the severity of this provision—for example, if a party unintentionally breaches a non-payment obligation of the Agreement in a way that gives the other a right to terminate, the non-breaching party cannot terminate the Agreement without granting the breaching party immunity for the breach, according to the terms of § 15.3.

· INDEX ·